SAP® Activate Project Management Certificat

SAP PRESS is a joint initiative of SAP and Rheinwerk Publishing. The know-how offered by SAP specialists combined with the expertise of Rheinwerk Publishing offers the reader expert books in the field. SAP PRESS features first-hand information and expert advice, and provides useful skills for professional decision-making.

SAP PRESS offers a variety of books on technical and business-related topics for the SAP user. For further information, please visit our website: *www.sap-press.com*.

Aditya Lal

SAP® Activate Project Management Certification Guide

Certified Associate Exam

Editor Megan Fuerst
Acquisitions Editor Emily Nicholls
Copyeditor Julia McNamee
Cover Design Graham Geary
Photo Credit iStockphoto.com: 1180602990/© Dimitris66
Layout Design Vera Brauner
Production Graham Geary
Typesetting SatzPro, Krefeld (Germany)
Printed and bound in the United States of America, on paper from sustainable sources

ISBN 978-1-4932-2029-8

1st edition 2021

Library of Congress Cataloging-in-Publication Data
Names: Lal, Aditya, author.
Title: SAP activate project management certification guide : certified associate exam / Aditya Lal.
Description: 1st edition. | Boston : Rheinwerk Publishing, [2020] | Includes index.
Identifiers: LCCN 2020043759 (print) | LCCN 2020043760 (ebook) | ISBN 9781493220298 (paperback) | ISBN 9781493220304 (ebook)
Subjects: LCSH: Project management--Examinations--Study guides. | SAP HANA (Electronic resource)--Examinations--Study guides.
Classification: LCC HD69.P75 L345 2020 (print) | LCC HD69.P75 (ebook) | DDC 658.4/040285536--dc23
LC record available at https://lccn.loc.gov/2020043759
LC ebook record available at https://lccn.loc.gov/2020043760

I dedicate this book to Swapnil Lal, my son and best friend.

Contents at a Glance

Dear Reader,

I'd be lost without my GPS.

Having recently relocated several neighborhoods away from my old Boston apartment, my sense of direction has taken a hit. Whether I'm running errands or getting carryout (the only reasons I leave my apartment, like so many of us in 2020), I rely on my phone's GPS app to take me there. Sometimes, I'm brave enough to trust my memory, but this choice usually results in confusion, stress, and at least ten minutes tacked on to the trip. Turns out Boston has a lot of one-way streets!

SAP Activate is effectively your project management GPS when it comes to SAP S/4HANA implementations. However, instead of roads and lanes to worry about, you have workstreams and deliverables, plus a whole lot more. When it comes time to get your SAP Certified Associate – SAP Activate Project Manager badge, however, your challenge is to commit this map to memory (a feat I'm still working on when it comes to my new neighborhood).

To help you prove your mastery on exam day, SAP Activate expert Aditya Lal has created the guidebook you need to prepare for, practice for, and eventually ace, your exam. Avoid wrong turns, U-turns, and bumps in the road!

What did you think about *SAP Activate Project Management Certification Guide: Certified Associate Exam*? Your comments and suggestions are the most useful tools to help us make our books the best they can be. Please feel free to contact me and share any praise or criticism you may have.

Thank you for purchasing a book from SAP PRESS!

Megan Fuerst
Editor, SAP PRESS

meganf@rheinwerk-publishing.com
www.sap-press.com
Rheinwerk Publishing · Boston, MA

Contents

Appendices 481

Preface

Welcome to this guide to the SAP Certified Associate – SAP Activate Project Manager certification! Since SAP announced the launch of the SAP Activate methodology—a universal project management approach for the SAP S/4HANA implementation—in 2015, more than 3,000 clients have implemented SAP S/4HANA, as of the writing of this book. Many professionals, with or without an SAP background, have used the SAP Activate methodology, and there is a need and constant demand for the certification knowledgebase. This book will fill that void, help professionals gain considerable knowledge regarding the SAP Activate methodology, and further their interests to be certified.

The focus of this book is SAP certification, but many professionals will find it useful as their first read about the SAP Activate methodology. In this book, we've detailed all the topic areas including the basics of the methodology, the agile and the Scrum framework, the eleven workstreams, and the three transition paths—new implementation, system conversion, and selective data transition. To enhance the readability and sync with the certification exam, each chapter represents a certification topic.

Who This Book Is For

This book is for anyone interested in learning about or preparing to take the SAP Activate certification exam (C_ACTIVATE12). Program and project managers, customers, implementation partners, business leaders, process owners, and end users will find this book a starting point to gain industry-standard knowledge on SAP Activate. In fact, many project management professionals, practicing either the agile or waterfall methodology from non-SAP backgrounds will find this book a useful resource to gain a deep understanding of the SAP Activate methodology and make a career switch to SAP technology.

Each chapter in this book starts with high-level capabilities and drills down to the detail level, providing you with a sound understanding of the topic for the purposes of the exam. However, this book doesn't cover any specific templates or accelerators as they aren't part of the exam, which you can always find on the Roadmap Viewer. Additionally, several products and tools, such as SAP Solution Manager or SAP's application lifecycle management (ALM) tool, are used throughout the book without going into the details of their setup to keep the book focused on the SAP Activate certification. Nevertheless, this book will help you build a great foundation on SAP Activate in your efforts to gain a competitive advantage.

How This Book Is Organized

We've organized this book solely on the certification topics that you'll find for the C_ACTIVATE12 exam (*http://s-prs.co/v519400*). Each certification topic represents a chapter in this book, which are in order of increasing complexity. We start the book by providing some basic concepts of the SAP Activate methodology, delving into the details of the agile and Scrum frameworks, and then deep diving into the three transition paths, segregating them based on cloud or on-premise implementations.

To get the maximum benefits, we recommend reading the book sequentially, especially if you don't have considerable SAP or SAP S/4HANA experience. However, if you have substantial SAP S/4HANA experience or you're a seasoned project management professional looking for some specific topics, you can go directly to any chapter. Now let's review, at a high-level, what is covered in each chapter of this book:

- **Introduction: The Path to Certification**
  This chapter explains the certification program and provides some useful tips, courses, resources, and test-taking tips. We'll review the certification exam format, types of questions, topics covered and their weightage, and SAP courses relevant to the SAP Activate certification. We'll conclude this chapter by providing some useful tips to follow before and during the exam.
- **Chapter 1: SAP Activate Overview**
  In this chapter, we'll provide you a high-level view of the SAP Activate methodology starting with the three pillars it's based on. We'll also give you a glimpse of fit-to-standard analysis, which will form the basis of the product backlog. This foundation chapter covers the characteristics and structure—phases, workstreams, deliverables, and tasks—of the SAP Activate methodology. We'll conclude this chapter by outlining the governance, roles, and responsibilities of the team members, as well as the differences between SAP Activate and the other SAP methodologies.
- **Chapter 2: SAP Activate Elements**
  We'll study the elements of the SAP Activate methodology and build upon the knowledge you've gained so far by reviewing the content, tools, and methodology. In the content element, we'll review the business processes, project library, and the migration and integration content. The tools section of the chapter focuses on the self-service configuration, expert configuration, SAP solution builder tool, and SAP Solution Manager.

- **Chapter 3: Agile Project Planning**
  In this chapter, we'll switch gears and introduce the concept of the agile framework and Scrum framework. We'll start the discussion with the Agile Manifesto, a key document that outlines the four values and twelve principles of the agile framework, and delve into the Scrum framework, which is based on the agile methodology. You'll also learn some of the key terminologies used throughout the book. We'll look into the Scrum team, the four Scrum ceremonies, and the Scrum artifacts. This chapter will also establish the relationship between the Scrum and SAP Activate methodologies. We'll then review the responsibilities of some key roles, including the product owner and Scrum master, through the lens of the SAP Activate methodology. The chapter concludes with a review of agile project organization in SAP S/4HANA implementations, and a discussion of the product backlog and its relevance to the explore phase.
- **Chapter 4: Agile Delivery Approach**
  We'll continue our agile and Scrum learning path in this chapter by reviewing the delivery approach that goes beyond the product backlog. We'll start the chapter by discussing release planning, which is based on the product backlog. This section of the chapter also covers backlog prioritization, technical interdependency, and backlog estimation. We'll firm up your understanding by looking into a real-life example of release planning and the sprint cycle. In the final section, we'll assess the testing activities and review the cutover planning. We'll conclude this chapter by reviewing scaled agile.
- **Chapter 5: Workstreams Overview**
  This chapter focuses on the eleven workstreams of the SAP Activate methodology, starting with the project management workstream, continuing through the rest of the workstreams, and concluding with the operations and support workstream. For each workstream, we've provided the high-level concepts necessary to understand the workstream itself, identified the roles and the corresponding responsibilities relevant to that workstream, and listed the commonly used tools and accelerators in the given workstream. This chapter will give you a fair idea of the vastness of the SAP Activate methodology, yet the confined processes within each workstream will help you appreciate the thought given to build the product.
- **Chapter 6: New Implementation SAP S/4HANA Transition Path**
  This chapter reviews the three transition paths and describes the workstreams, deliverables, and activities for each phase of the new implementation of SAP S/4HANA. We'll start with the discover phase and review the strategic planning, creating the point of view document, and creating several other deliverables to ensure and build a common understanding of SAP S/4HANA vis-à-vis customer requirements. In the prepare phase of the on-premise implementation, we'll focus on the detail-oriented project planning, strong organizational change management processes, and planning other activities, including data migration, testing, training, infrastructure, extensibility, and other aspects of the SAP implementation. During the explore phase, we'll revisit the fit-gap analysis and

tailor the process to fit the on-premise implementation. You'll also understand the activities and deliverables of the realize and deploy phases of the project that are specific to the on-premise implementation. The chapter concludes by quickly looking into the deliverables of the run phase of the on-premise implementation.

- **Chapter 7: New Implementation SAP S/4HANA Cloud, Essentials Edition Transition Path**
  The structure of Chapter 7 is similar to that of Chapter 6 but with a focus on the multitenant edition of cloud deployment with SAP S/4HANA Cloud, essentials edition. At the beginning of this chapter, you'll learn about the multitenant and the single-tenant cloud architecture in the context of SAP S/4HANA deployments and the differences between the two. The chapter follows the same learning path and starts with the discover phase of the project where the prospective customer, in partnership with SAP, establishes and ensures the fitment of the cloud deployment option vis-à-vis their requirements and builds the strategy and the implementation roadmap. You'll further learn the planning and preparation activities carried out by the project team during the prepare phase of the project. The chapter will continue to discuss the deliverables and the activities during the subsequent phases of the cloud implementation.
- **Chapter 8: New Implementation SAP S/4HANA Cloud, Extended Edition Transition Path**
  The focus of Chapter 8 is the deployment of SAP S/4HANA Cloud, extended edition, although the structure of this chapter is similar to that of the previous two chapters. The chapter starts by defining the characteristics of SAP S/4HANA Cloud, extended edition (previously known as the single-tenant edition); describing the landscape overview; discussing the five golden rules in detail; and listing the benefits of the extended edition. The chapter then focuses on the deliverables and activities from the discover to the run phase of the project, emphasizing key deliverables, such as fit-to-standard and product backlog during the explore phase of the project, extensibility, and integration—a much-needed aspect of the SAP S/4HANA Cloud, extended edition implementation—throughout the project. The chapter concludes by defining the deliverables of the run phase of the project.
- **Chapter 9: System Conversion Transition Path**
  The system conversion transition path is the second transition path and defines the transition approach of the current SAP implementation to SAP S/4HANA. This chapter discusses the considerations that will help you decide whether to go for the system conversion or the new implementation. You'll learn the landscape details and the benefits of the system conversion approach. Once again, the chapter follows a similar path from here on, focusing on the deliverables and the activities during each phase of the project, starting from the discover phase until the run phase. The specific deliverables include prototyping, transition planning, and transition preparation in the prepare phase; fit-to-standard for the system conversion approach, release planning and configuration in the

realize phase; and cutover planning in the deployment phase for the system conversion approach.

- **Chapter 10: Selective Data Transition Path**
  This is the final chapter of your certification journey, where you'll learn about the transition path that focuses on the transition of specific data from the legacy environment to the SAP S/4HANA environment. Once again, this chapter is very similar in structure to Chapters 6–9, which starts with discussing the deliverables and activities during the discover phase and concludes with identifying the deliverables and activities during the run phase.

This book concludes with two practice tests in Appendix A and Appendix B. In Appendix C, you can find the answers to both practice tests.

Throughout the book, we've also provided text boxes that will help you access useful information, as shown here:

Note
Notes will provide other resources to explore or special tools or services from SAP that will help you with the topic under discussion.

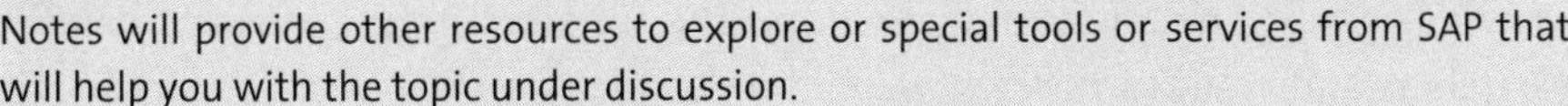

Tip
Tips call out useful information about related ideas and provide practical suggestions for how to use a particular function.

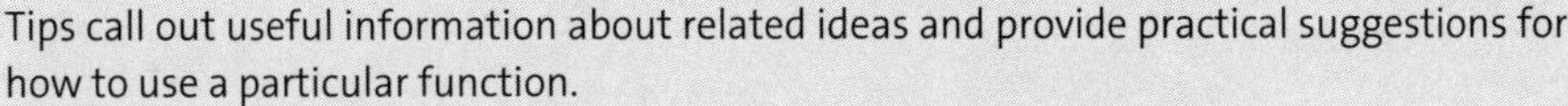

Example
Examples provide practical scenarios and explain, in detail, how particular functions can be applied.

Acknowledgments

As a project management professional, I'm sure you appreciate teamwork and that no one can complete a project single-handedly, especially a book of this nature.

When no one believed in me, Emily Nicholls, the senior acquisitions editor at Rheinwerk Publishing, stepped up and gave me an opportunity to share my idea of the book. I truly and sincerely believe that this book would not exist without her mammoth initial support. After the idea took shape, we started executing the project, and Megan Fuerst, an associate development editor at Rheinwerk Publishing, stepped in, guided me throughout the writing of this book, and helped me achieve the timeline and maintain the quality of the work. I am sure I couldn't have completed this book without her tireless help and diligent updates.

Bob Byrne, a senior product manager at SAP, and Lisa Kouch, a senior product manager at SAP, helped me through the final few chapters of the book by providing much-needed support by answering my questions and resolving challenges related to SAP Activate and the Roadmap Viewer. Without their help, I wouldn't have completed the book accurately within the given time frame.

For me, this book was an unprecedented opportunity, and everyone in my family stepped up. I have my day job as a project management practitioner of a major business transformation initiative that took most of my day and evening time. My wife, Sonali Chakraborty, and my son, Swapnil Lal, supported me throughout the writing of this book, and I'm extremely thankful to them. They are the inspiration behind this book.

Apart from the aforementioned people, there are several other professionals without whose help a book can't be published. These professionals include editors, proofreaders, typesetters, reviewers, and many other unsung heroes whom I am thankful to for their extraordinary work and support.

This is an unprecedented time. The world is going through the COVID-19 pandemic, and I strongly believe that no acknowledgement would be complete without mentioning the legends of the era and those on the frontline who are fighting to save us. These include the doctors and the nurses who are keeping us alive, researchers and volunteers working on the vaccination, the postal person delivering the mail daily, the grocery workers and deliverers packing and delivering food, the farmers growing our food, and the countless others we'll never see or meet but who play a vital role in our livelihood and help us live.

Conclusion

Reading this book will provide you with a comprehensive overview of the SAP Activate methodology and will not only empower you to engage confidently in any SAP S/4HANA implementation but also provide you with a competitive advantage. This book will serve as your foundational source of knowledge for the SAP Activate methodology, will build on your knowledge, and will help you on your journey to get the much-coveted SAP certification. We wish you the very best on your certification journey. Let's start now by introducing the certification.

Introduction: The Path to Certification

Techniques You'll Master

- Understand the relevant certification offerings for the SAP Activate methodology
- Find the courses required for the certification
- Learn techniques for taking the certification exam
- Identify further relevant SAP Training and Adoption offerings for SAP Activate
- Explore additional resources for SAP Activate on the Roadmap Viewer

In this chapter, we'll focus on seemingly minor topics that play a critical role in the success of your certification journey. Although you've heard it's best to work smart, not hard, both are equally important in this context. As a part of working smart, we'll show you the certification path, provide some test-taking advice that is applicable for before and during the test, and show you how to complement your knowledge by getting the right information from the right source. In the rest of the book, you'll have the opportunity to work hard to ensure that you're successful in the first certification attempt.

In 2015, SAP announced the launch of SAP S/4HANA and the SAP Activate methodology, which is the project management approach for the SAP S/4HANA implementation. All three implementations—on-premise SAP S/4HANA, SAP S/4HANA Cloud, essentials edition (previous referred to as the multitenant cloud edition), and SAP S/4HANA Cloud, extended edition (previously referred to as the single-tenant edition)—will require knowledge of the SAP Activate methodology. Although SAP hasn't shut down the ASAP methodology, it's no longer being updated and will be sunset in upcoming years, which shows the significance of the SAP Activate methodology.

Regardless of your role in the SAP implementation, whether you're a sales executive, customer project manager, implementation lead, data migration or testing lead, functional or technical consultant, power user, or a user, it's imperative that you understand the SAP Activate methodology to a certain degree. It's equally important to understand the big picture and know the nooks and corners of the SAP world to find the right information at the right time.

If you've read this book so far, you already understand the importance of the SAP Activate certification. However, in this chapter, we'll review the details of the certification and give you some tips that will help you go through the certification process. We've also included a sample planner that will help you plan your certification journey tirelessly but relentlessly. Finally, we'll look at some useful additional resources to complement what you'll learn from this book to prepare for the certification exam and eventually work with SAP S/4HANA implementations.

Target Audience

This book focuses on the topics as outlined by SAP that are necessary to master to achieve the C_ACTIVATE12 certification. This is written especially for those who are preparing for the SAP Certified Associate – SAP Activate Project Manager (C_ACTIVATE12) exam.

However, as we mentioned previously, SAP Activate is the go-to methodology for SAP S/4HANA implementations. For example, as a technical lead, you need to understand when and under which transition path to order the trial system provisioning; as a client deployment lead, you must know the activities to carry out during the other phases of the implementation and not just the deploy phase; as a functional consultant, you should be aware of the fit-to-standard processes; and, as a system integration project manager, you must know release planning and other aspects of the product backlog.

Without doubt, this book is for all the project managers who are leading the SAP S/4HANA implementation projects. If you're a senior team member and want to move into SAP project management, this book is indeed for you. Furthermore, this book will also help you if you're a project manager from a non-SAP background but would like to move into SAP projects.

How about the functional consultants or the technical leads? A functional consultant needs to carry out fit-to-standard processes, help build the product backlog, estimate the effort, and understand the nuances of the different project management aspects and phases of the project. On the other hand, a technical lead must understand when to deliver infrastructure sizing, whether to transport from a sandbox environment, or even the activities during the prepare phase of the project. Nonetheless, this book will satisfy your thirst for knowledge about the SAP Activate methodology. Developers who want to specialize in project management or to gain a good understanding of the common business processes with SAP S/4HANA can also find value in this book by understanding the details of fit-to-standard processes.

As a client who will consume the SAP S/4HANA and the upcoming innovations, this book will help you understand the usages of the trial system, your role during the fit-to-standard processes, and other aspects of the implementation. This book is also helpful for power users and end users, to some extent. Those working as users or power users should use this book to expand beyond that role and to get a deeper and broader understanding of the implementation to support consultant roles and improve the overall organizational readiness.

This book covers a broad and deep scope of the SAP Activate methodology and the three transition paths for the SAP S/4HANA implementation. This book serves as a refresher course for experienced professionals. Often, as you gain more experience, you become specialized in a specific part such as the deploy phase, run phase, or fit-to-standard during the explore phase. This book will help you look again at the complete picture of SAP Activate and at the same time get upskilled to the specifics of SAP S/4HANA.

This book will also help you gain considerable knowledge if you're just getting introduced to the SAP Activate methodology, for example, if you recently joined an SAP implementation partner or a client who is embarking on their transformation journey using the intelligent enterprise resource planning (ERP)—SAP S/4HANA.

Succinctly, this book is for anyone who is a part of the SAP S/4HANA implementation. Additionally, irrespective of your role and current knowledge level, you should start with Chapter 1.

SAP Activate Certification: C_ACTIVATE12

The SAP Certified Associate – SAP Activate Project Manager certification verifies the candidate's competency in managing an SAP S/4HANA implementation project. It ensures that the successful candidates have the sound knowledge, expertise, and experience in applying the methodology, tools, and techniques to implement SAP S/4HANA projects, as well as an advanced level of business skills. This certification also verifies that the successful candidate possesses advanced communication and presentation skills, internal and external stakeholders management skills, basic knowledge of change management processes, and ability to communicate these processes to others. Furthermore, the exam also tests the candidate's ability to manage the end-to-end transition of the project from sales to realization, to develop roadmaps for project execution, and to understand testing and quality management. In particular, for SAP-related projects, the exam verifies that the project manager can apply the SAP Activate methodology. The format of the certification exam is as follows:

- Length of exam: 180 minutes (up to three hours).
- Exam questions: 80 questions, either multiple choice or multiple selection.
- Exam location: Online through the Certification Hub or certification center.

The Certification Hub is a subscription-based system that delivers SAP certifications. You subscribe annually and can take six certification attempts within the given period, meaning if you successfully pass on the first attempt, then you can get up to six different certifications in the area of your interest. Additionally, to ensure the worthiness of the certification and its processes, you get a maximum of three tries for a given certification.

Note

You can find more information at *https://training.sap.com/shop/course/cer006*.

Based upon your location, either you can appear for the certification exam from the comfort of your home (certain restrictions apply), or you can visit a certified certification partner to take the certification in a moderated classroom. For more information, visit *https://training.sap.com*, or call your local training contact (you can get the contact number from the training shop site).

The 80 certification questions are of the following types:

- Multiple choice, for which you must select one correct answer out of the four available options
- Multiple select (type 1), for which you must select the two correct answers out of the four available options
- Multiple select (type 2), for which you must select the three correct answers out of the five available options

There are no other question types than these. You must get all answers correct for each question for the question to be considered correctly answered. To pass the certification, you must answer 61% of the questions correctly. This means you must answer 49 out of 80 questions completely correctly. It's also important to note that there is no negative marking, meaning if you made a mistake, your marks won't be deducted.

After you complete the test, the system will show you the percentage of marks obtained on each of the 10 topic areas. The web page will also show the outcome of the test—pass or fail. After you clear the certification exam, you'll receive a digital badge that you can proudly display on social media, such as LinkedIn, as shown in Figure 1.

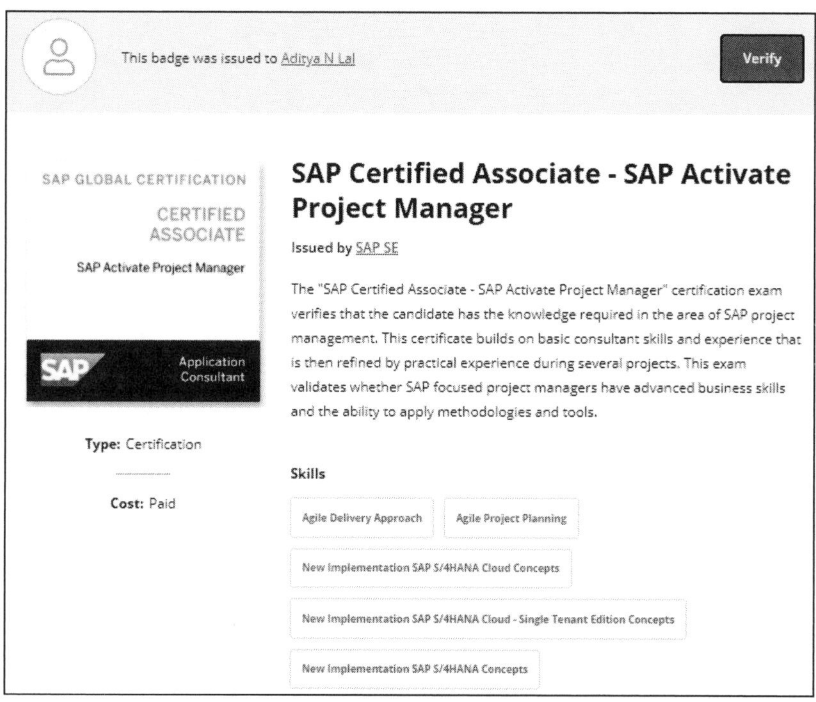

Congratulations, you have successfully cleared the exam ...

Topic
Agile Delivery Approach
Workstreams Overview
Agile Project Planning
Transition Path "New Implementation SAP S/4HANA Cloud"
SAP Activate Elements
SAP Activate Overview
Transition Path "New Implementation SAP S/4HANA Cloud, Single Tenant Edition"
Transition Path "System Conversion"
Transition Path "Selective Data Transition"
Transition Path "New Implementation SAP S/4HANA"

Figure 1 Digital Badge

The structure of the book closely resembles the topic areas of the certification, as shown in Figure 2.

Topic Areas

Please see below the list of topics that may be covered within this certification and the courses that cover them. Its accuracy does not constitute a legitimate claim; SAP reserves the right to update the exam content (topics, items, weighting) at any time.

Agile Delivery Approach	> 12%	›
Workstreams Overview	> 12%	›
Agile Project Planning	8% - 12%	›
Transition Path "New Implementation SAP S/4HANA Cloud"	8% - 12%	›
SAP Activate Elements	8% - 12%	›
SAP Activate Overview	8% - 12%	›
Transition Path "New Implementation SAP S/4HANA Cloud, Single Tenant Edition"	< 8%	›
Transition Path "System Conversion"	< 8%	›
Transition Path "Selective Data Transition"	< 8%	›
Transition Path "New Implementation SAP S/4HANA"	< 8%	›

Figure 2 Topic Areas

Table 1 shows the approximate weightage and number of questions that you can expect per area.

Topic	Percentage (%)	Approx. Number of Questions	Book Chapter
SAP Activate Overview	8–12	6–10	1
SAP Activate Elements	8–12	6–10	2
Agile Project Planning	8–12	6–10	3
Agile Delivery Approach	> 12	10	4
Workstreams Overview	> 12	10	5
Transition Path “New Implementation SAP S/4HANA”	< 8	6	6
Transition Path “New Implementation SAP S/4HANA Cloud”	8–12	6–10	7

Table 1 Topic Weightage

Topic	Percentage (%)	Approx. Number of Questions	Book Chapter
Transition Path "New Implementation SAP S/4HANA Cloud, Single-Tenant Edition"	< 8	6	8
Transition Path "System Conversion"	< 8	6	9
Transition Path "Selective Data Transition"	< 8	6	10

Table 1 Topic Weightage (Cont.)

Ways to Learn

Figure 3 shows the learning path for the certification exam and some of the skills that the candidates should have. You can access this learning path at *http://s-prs.co/v519401*.

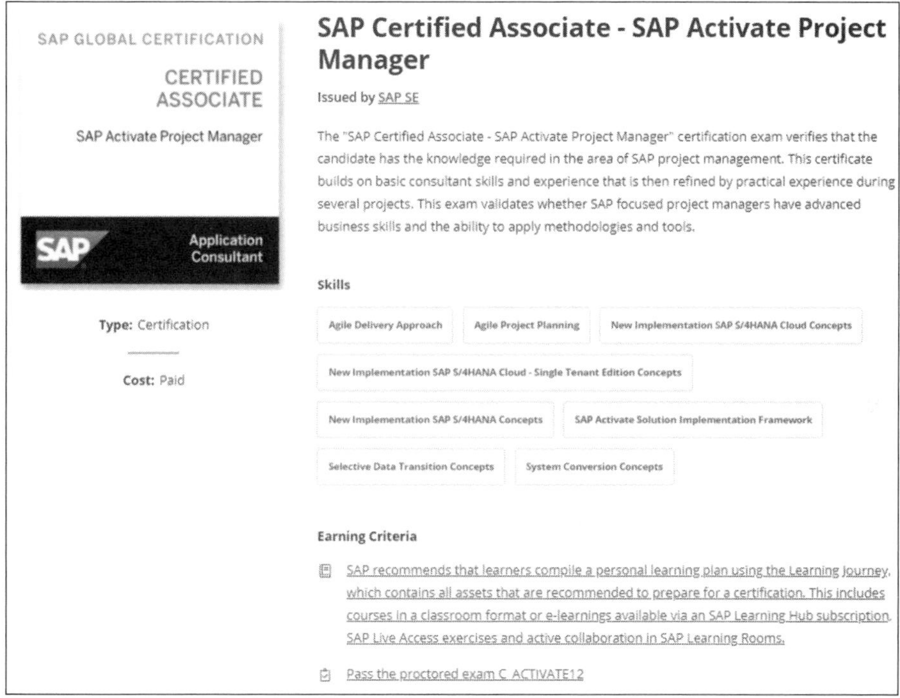

Figure 3 C_ACTIVATE12 Learning Path

In addition, it's highly advisable to take the courses outlined in Figure 4. The two courses are ACT100, which focuses on the SAP Activate methodology, and ACT200, which focuses on agile project delivery.

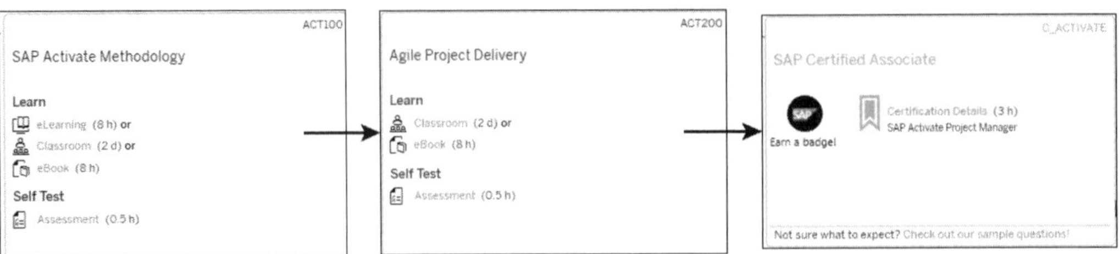

Figure 4 Courses for the SAP Activate Certification

You can choose to learn and consume the standard SAP Training and Adoption courses in a variety of ways:

- **Virtual classes**
  A virtual classroom is the best option if you don't get distracted with your daily activities or regular phone calls from your supervisor or clients. The virtual classroom provides all the options that you have in the classroom training. You can chat with other participants, draw to explain something, ask questions, and even exchange your contact details with other participants, if necessary. From a learning and understanding perspective, virtual classes are the best option; however, the virtual training sessions won't give you the same feel as classroom training when it comes to networking.
- **Classroom training**
  Classroom training is still a very common way to learn, especially when you're new to the subject. It offers an environment to provide immediate feedback, and gives you an opportunity to network with other participants and the trainer, ask questions during the break, and understand each other's body language that is almost impossible in a virtual classroom session. In addition, you can avoid your daily work and can focus on your learning goals away from your supervisor.
- **eAcademy training**
  SAP Training and Adoption provides training as another option to meet your learning goals. You'll receive the following:
  - SAP's live training system for hands-on sessions that will reinforce your learning and test scenarios on your own
  - Presentation slides with audio commentary, recorded system demonstrations, and practice simulations
  - Manuals in the PDF or other electronic format
  - Help desk support that guarantees an answer to all your queries within 24 hours during working days
  - Technical support for the system via online web conferencing and scheduled expert instructor sessions, as well as the Ask the Expert feature
- **SAP Learning Hub**
  SAP Learning Hub (*https://training.sap.com/shop/learninghub*) is SAP's latest tool in the line of learning and development. It's a cloud-based offering with an

annual subscription. This tool offers a multitude of courses and knowledge materials that will help you ace the certification exam and enhance your knowledge base.

Tips for Taking the Certification Exam

Let's turn our attention to a few tips that will help you better prepare for the exam. It's imperative to study the book, assess your understanding by answering all the chapter-end questions, review the answers and explanations, and relate the knowledge you've gained with your practical experience. In addition, ensure that you practice the sample tests at the end of the book. These sample questions test your knowledge, and the only way to enhance your knowledge is to look at the wrong answers. We've often noticed that candidates look at the correct answers and don't reevaluate or review the wrong answer topics. Don't make that mistake. Even if you have only one wrong answer, review the topic to make sure that you understand it correctly. That's the sole key to success; however, certain tips will help you prepare for the exam in a better way, as we'll discuss next.

Realign Your Perspective

After you know and decide that SAP Activate certification is the right certification for you, don't procrastinate! As a professional, you're already engaged with many work-related activities, whether you're talking to clients to understand their requirements or preparing for go-live. It's imperative that you spend at least 30 minutes, preferably an hour, daily to meet your personal goals, whether it's the SAP Activate certification or the New York City marathon.

The sole objective of this book is to help you prepare and pass the certification exam for the SAP Activate methodology. As mentioned earlier, your experience and the knowledge gained through this book will go hand-in-hand, but when you run across conflicting scenarios, you should go with what is suggested in this book. For the certification, knowledge and an understanding of the material and scope of the courses is most important.

Remember that the certification exam isn't about memorizing the content but rather to understand the concept thoroughly, relate that with your experience, and realign your experience, if needed.

Before the Exam

Depending upon whether you choose to appear for the online certification exam or at the certification center, you'll need to follow one of two paths.

Online certification means you don't have to leave your home to take the exam, but it comes with certain nuances. You must visit the Certification Hub to understand the technical requirements. Go to *http://s-prs.co/v519402* to visit the page shown in Figure 5. You must upgrade the browser by clicking on the **Install / Detect Questionmark Secure** button and test the bandwidth by clicking on **Test Communication and Bandwidth**. If you read the content carefully, you'll notice the following requirements:

- Two forms of unexpired ID with your photograph and name must be provided.
- Your name should match exactly what you provided to the Certification Hub.
- At least one form of ID should be a government-issued photo ID
- The room should be quiet.
- No one, including pets, can visit you during the test.
- You can't step away from your chair.
- You must have your webcam on throughout the duration of the test.
- Your desk must be clean; the proctor may ask you to turn the webcam to show your desk and surroundings.
- No phone calls, text messages, or any sort of communication with anyone is allowed.

We also recommend the following:

- For your own benefit, review the technical requirements, go through the FAQ, and be ready at least 15 minutes before the exam.
- Wear comfortable business casual attire, even though you're appearing for the exam from the comfort of your home. It's helpful to set a professional mind-set before taking the exam.
- You're not allowed to leave during the exam, so take care of any needs beforehand.

Alternatively, if you're going for the in-person certification exam, we recommend the following:

- ID requirements remain the same, but double-check with the Certification Hub and the test center.
- You should visit the test center at least one week prior around the same time as that of your appointment to understand the driving time. Don't just rely on your GPS with traffic on.
- Follow the instructions that you may receive through email about reaching the test center and carrying cell phones or any study materials. Generally, cell phones, study materials, and any pieces of paper aren't allowed inside the test center. They will ask you either to keep those in your car, or they may provide a locker if they have one. Some test centers may not have lockers at all, so be prepared.

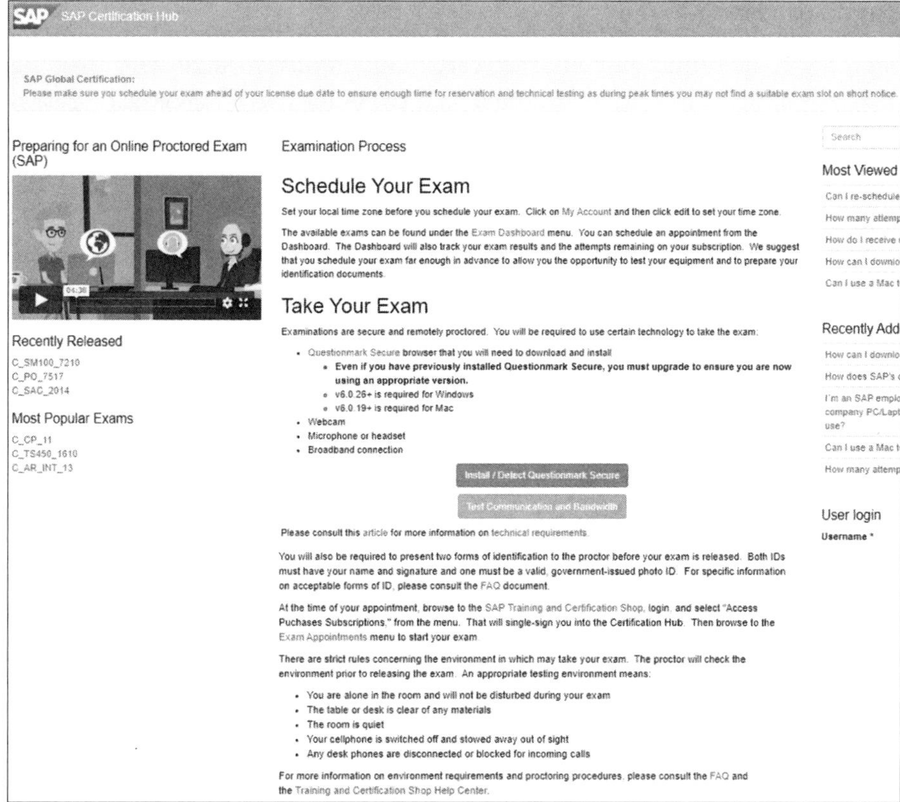

Figure 5 Before the Exam

Regardless of the option you choose, there's another point to consider before taking your exam. Let's do a small experiment. You just need a timer and your favorite book. Take the items, find a comfortable place where no one will disturb you, and read the book. No cheating; you can't watch the movie version of your favorite novel! You'll likely enjoy the reading, but it's also likely that you'll find three straight hours of continuous focus on this task to be a bit of a challenge (especially with how many distractions we encounter nowadays). The question is, if this is a difficult task with a book you enjoy, how will you sit for three continuous hours for an admittedly far less exciting certification exam? The only two options are practice and more practice.

The two sample tests at the end of this book (Appendix A and Appendix B) are for your sitting practice. They not only test your knowledge but also ensure that you sit for the exam continuously for three hours. You cannot answer 20 questions in the morning, 20 in the afternoon, and the remaining 40 after dinner while watching your favorite web series. You must complete each test as if you're appearing for the real certification exam with the difference that you're using pen and notebook in the practice test. Furthermore, make sure you don't mark your answers on the book if you want to revisit the test again.

During the Exam

There are 80 questions for you to answer in 180 minutes, meaning slightly more than two minutes to read, understand, and chose the correct choice(s) for each question. All the questions will be either multiple choice or multiple section questions. The three types of questions that you'll see during the exam are as follows:

- **Multiple-choice questions**
  The multiple-choice questions are straightforward with only one correct answer. Figure 6 shows one such example.

This is a multiple choice question. This is the most frequently asked question and there is only one correct answer. The system will NOT allow you to choose more than one answer. Choose the correct answer:

O A. This is a wrong choice.
O B. This is also wrong.
✓ C. This is a correct choice.
O D. This choice may be wrong.

Figure 6 Multiple-Choice Questions with One Correct Answer

- **Multiple selection – two out of four choices**
  In these questions, two out of four choices are correct. Figure 7 shows a sample multiple-selection question in which you must select two options as correct out of the four. To answer such questions, read the question carefully, and, if needed, read it twice; read all the options; and select the choices that best fit the scenario.

This is another type of question that you may see during the exam. At least 15-20% of the questions belong to this category. The question will clearly state that there are two correct answers. Choose the correct answers. (There are two correct answers.)

❑ A. This is a wrong choice.
❑ B. This is also wrong.
✓ C. This is a correct choice.
✓ D. Oh! This is correct.

Figure 7 Multiple-Selection Question with Two Correct Answers Out of Four Choices

In the multiple-selection question, you need to select both correct answer options to have the answer marked correct. SAP doesn't give points for half a correct answer because it doesn't deduct points for a wrong answer.

Tip
There are several lengthy, wordy, and trick questions in this book to help test your mastery of the topics. However, it's important to note that in the actual exam, you won't get wordy, lengthy, or trick questions. The longest question that I encountered had four sentences with important details. You must pay attention to those details, though.

Don't try to memorize the book; rather, seek to understand the main concepts and try to relate the concepts with your experience. This is true for tools and accelerators as well. There is no need to memorize the tools and accelerators listed in this book. Just review them a couple of times, and when you see the options in the exam, the right choice should click automatically as long as you read and understand the concepts.

- **Multiple-selection – three out of five choices**
  Next in difficulty is the multiple-choice question with three correct options out of five, as shown in Figure 8. It enhances the complexity of the question and increases the time it takes to read the questions and options. Just keep your cool; you can easily eliminate one of the five choices leaving you with three correct options out of four. Now, it's easier to find the three correct choices or one wrong choice by process of elimination.

This is the third type of question that is less frequent. Only 5-10% of the questions will belong to this category. Choose the correct answers. (There are three correct answers.)

✓ A. Bingo! This is a correct choice.
❑ B. This choice is wrong.
✓ C. This is a correct choice.
✓ D. Oh! This is correct.
❑ E. One additional wrong choice.

Figure 8 Multiple-Selection Question with Three Correct Answers Out of Five Choices

The process of elimination works best in such questions. If you know the answers correctly, just go for them. However, if not, use the process of elimination by removing the obviously wrong answer. In such questions, you'll definitely get one choice that you can eliminate easily. After that, you'll be left with four choices and three correct answers. From there on, you'll need to rely on your knowledge and experience.

Relax is the mantra during the exam. You'll see certain questions and think you haven't studied that topic at all. Don't lose you cool. If you lose your focus, you tend to make more mistakes in the subsequent questions. Mark all such questions and revisit them at the end of the certification exam before submitting the exam. The system keeps track of unanswered questions. Before submitting the exam as final, always answer all questions to the best of your ability. There is no penalty for wrong answers, so submitting no answer is a wasted chance at an educated guess. From a time-tracking perspective, if you've answered 45 or more questions by the end of 90 minutes, then you're working at the right pace.

For a given certification exam, you can take it a maximum of three times. However, don't expect the same questions and options as these are randomized.

Sample Plan

Planning is the key to success. Table 2 depicts a detailed plan specific to the SAP Activate project manager certification. It's best to always start with the sample test that is available on the SAP certification exam, and this plan is no exception. This is a 50-day plan where you spend up to 60 minutes every day to learn the concepts of the SAP Activate methodology.

Day	Topic	Status
Day 1	Sample test.	Note your score.
Day 2	Introduction: The Path to Certification.	
Day 3	Review the certification website and additional resources. If not procured, purchase the SAP Global Certification.	
Day 4	Chapter 1: SAP Activate Overview. Complete the chapter-end questions, and review the wrong answer topics.	
Day 5	Chapter 2: SAP Activate Elements. Complete the chapter-end questions and review the wrong answer topics.	
Day 6	Review Chapters 1–2.	
Day 7	Take a day to rest.	
Day 8	Chapter 3: Agile Project Planning.	
Day 9	Chapter 3: Agile Project Planning. Complete the chapter-end questions, and review the wrong answer topics.	
Day 10	Review Chapters 1–3.	
Day 11	Chapter 4: Agile Delivery Approach.	
Day 12	Chapter 4: Agile Delivery Approach. Complete the chapter-end questions, and review the wrong answer topics.	
Day 13	Take the day off to rest.	
Day 14	Chapter 5: Workstreams Overview.	
Day 15	Chapter 5: Workstreams Overview.	
Day 16	Chapter 5: Workstreams Overview. Complete the chapter-end questions, and review the wrong answer topics.	
Day 17	Review Chapters 4–5.	
Day 18	Review Chapters 1–5.	
Day 19	Review Chapters 1–5.	
Day 20	Chapter 6: New Implementation SAP S/4HANA Transition Path.	

Table 2 50-Day Plan

Day	Topic	Status
Day 21	Take the day off to rest.	
Day 22	Chapter 6: New Implementation SAP S/4HANA Transition Path. Complete the chapter-end questions, and review the wrong answer topics.	
Day 23	Chapter 7: New Implementation SAP S/4HANA Cloud, Essentials Edition Transition Path.	
Day 24	Chapter 7: New Implementation SAP S/4HANA Cloud, Essentials Edition Transition Path. Complete the chapter-end questions, and review the wrong answer topics.	
Day 25	Review Chapters 6–7.	
Day 26	Chapter 8: New Implementation SAP S/4HANA Cloud, Extended Edition Transition Path.	
Day 27	Chapter 8: New Implementation SAP S/4HANA Cloud, Extended Edition Transition Path. Complete the chapter-end questions, and review the wrong answer topics.	
Day 28	Take the day off to rest.	
Day 29	Chapter 9: System Conversion Transition Path.	
Day 30	Chapter 9: System Conversion Transition Path. Complete the chapter-end questions, and review the wrong answer topics.	
Day 31	Review Chapters 8–9.	
Day 32	Chapter 10: Selective Data Transition Path. Complete the chapter-end questions, and review the wrong answer topics.	
Day 33	Review Chapters 6–10.	
Day 34	Review Chapters 6–10.	
Day 35	Take the day off to rest.	
Day 36	Review Chapters 1–5.	
Day 37	Review Chapters 1–5.	
Day 38	Review Chapters 1–10.	
Day 39	Review Chapters 1–10.	
Day 40	Review Chapters 1–10.	
Day 41	Review Chapters 1–10.	
Day 42	Take the day off to rest.	
Day 43	Take sample test 1.	Note your score.
Day 44	Review all the questions and answers from sample test 1.	

Table 2 50-Day Plan (Cont.)

Day	Topic	Status
Day 45	Review the wrong answer topics.	
Day 46	Take sample test 2.	Note your score.
Day 47	Review all the questions and answers from sample test 2.	
Day 48	Review the wrong answer topics.	
Day 49	Take the day off to rest.	
Day 50	Appear for the certification exam.	

Table 2 50-Day Plan (Cont.)

Tips and Tricks

The following are some useful tips to use when preparing for the exam:

- Create a plan best suited for you, and follow that plan.
- Attempt all the questions presented at the end of each chapter.
- Always relate concepts with your experience; it will help you remember them.
- A good night's sleep before the exam is very helpful; you want to be 100% attentive during the exam.

The following are some useful tips to follow during the exam:

- There is *no* penalty for wrong answers, so make sure you answer all questions.
- Experience has shown that your initial selection is usually better than a revised one. Be cautious of going back over questions and answering too many times.
- It's a good idea to keep track of the time, but don't worry too much about it. Prepare a scale, for example, 20 minutes or less for each 10 questions or 40 minutes for 20 questions, which is 25% of the exam. In most cases, you'll get enough time to review the questions and your answers at least twice.
- Keep your cool when you see unfamiliar questions. It may affect the next question that you might actually know, but it's highly likely you'll make a mistake if you lose your focus.
- Read and reread the question, review the choices twice, make sure that you understand the question, and now answer the question.
- Process of elimination always works best; eliminate the obvious wrong answer, as you'll always get one. It will make your life easier.

Additional Learning Resources

This book focuses on the SAP Activate certification C_ACTIVATE12 and is sufficient to clear the exam successfully. However, it's worthwhile to understand that tons of additional information is available that will help you understand the big picture. These additional educational materials will complement the knowledge that you'll gain from this book.

Nevertheless, the continuous innovation and regular updates of SAP Activate require you to understand those innovations and changes for the successful implementations. Therefore, it's of paramount importance for you to keep your knowledge up to date; in the following subsections, we share a few useful resources for you.

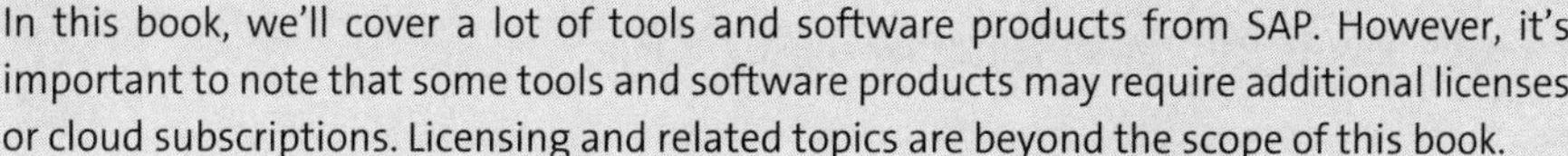

Note

In this book, we'll cover a lot of tools and software products from SAP. However, it's important to note that some tools and software products may require additional licenses or cloud subscriptions. Licensing and related topics are beyond the scope of this book.

Roadmap Viewer

You can access the Roadmap Viewer at *https://go.support.sap.com/roadmapviewer/*. The Roadmap Viewer, a cloud-based repository and a part of the SAP Activate innovation adoption framework, contains the procedures, methods, deliverables, tasks, and accelerators that can help customers and professionals in their SAP S/4HANA implementation journey. Start the Roadmap Viewer by clicking **What does Roadmap Viewer offer?** Select the **Getting started with SAP Activate in Roadmap Viewer** and **How to start your project in SAP Solution Manager** documents available on the Roadmap Viewer. Figure 9 shows the two general roadmaps. You can select **Solution Specific** for specific roadmaps.

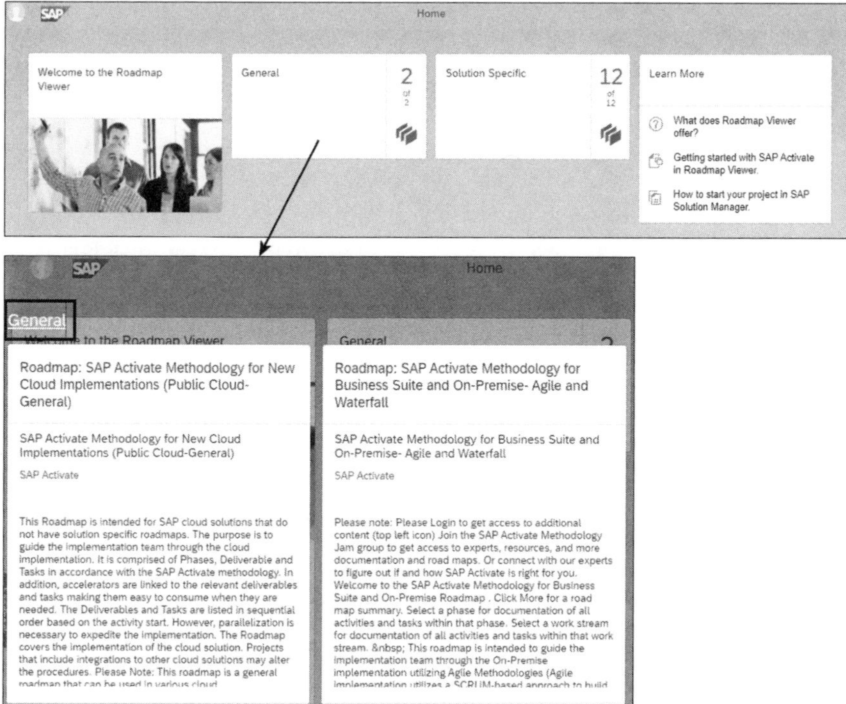

Figure 9 Roadmap Viewer

SAP Jam

SAP Jam is a cloud-based enterprise collaboration tool, inspired by social media platforms, focusing on the SAP products, tools, and the latest innovations. You can access SAP Jam via *https://jam4.sapjam.com/home*. It provides a great learning platform about almost every topic related to the SAP products. On the top-left corner, you'll see the **Groups** of which you're a member. You can also search for any specific document from the search box located on the top-middle portion of the web page. Figure 10 shows the home page of SAP Jam.

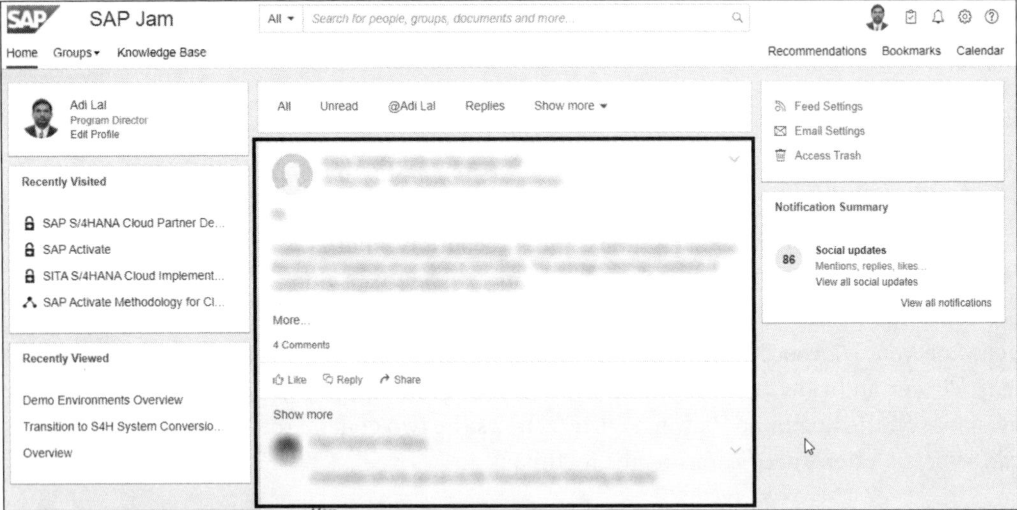

Figure 10 SAP Jam

SAP Blogs and Articles

SAP blogs and articles are more great ways to keep yourself up to speed on the changes. You can log in to the blog web page at *https://blogs.sap.com/*. You can search for any specific topic, any author, or any keyword of your interest. Figure 11 shows the SAP blog's home and a sample search based on the name of the author.

SAP Training and Adoption Materials

SAP Training and Adoption, in partnership with the development departments, which build the solutions, creates the education materials that will help you stay current. These materials are released and are made available on the SAP Learning Hub, which requires a valid license, for every SAP Activate release.

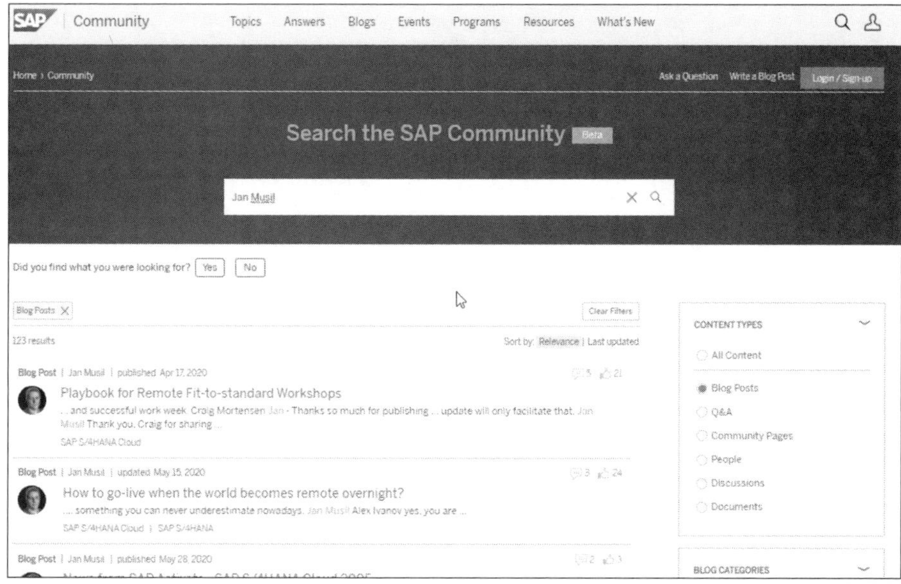

Figure 11 SAP Blogs

SAP Best Practices Explorer

As an SAP Activate practitioner, you're aware that SAP S/4HANA implementation starts with an SAP Best Practices package. SAP Best Practices, also known as SAP Rapid Deployment solutions, make up a repository of ready-to-run business processes built by SAP based on its multitude of years of combined experience. Based on the customer's requirements, you may either adapt the best practice with some minor change, use a recommended option, or customize the process to fulfill the requirements and gaps, if any. You can access the SAP Best Practices via *https://rapid.sap.com/bp/*. It has detailed definitions of the best practice solution scopes, business process diagrams, and several accelerators such as test scripts outlining the steps to perform various business processes. Figure 12 shows the SAP Best Practices Explorer home page and the best practice solution scope and accelerators.

SAP Help Portal

You can access SAP Help Portal via *https://help.sap.com/viewer/index*. It's a go-to place for any SAP products. You can view the learning path or search for any other help that you may need. With every release of SAP S/4HANA, SAP shares the what's new documentation, feature scope description, simplification list, and several guides such as the installation guide, upgrade guide, conversion guide, and several other documents. Figure 13 shows the home page of the SAP Help Portal.

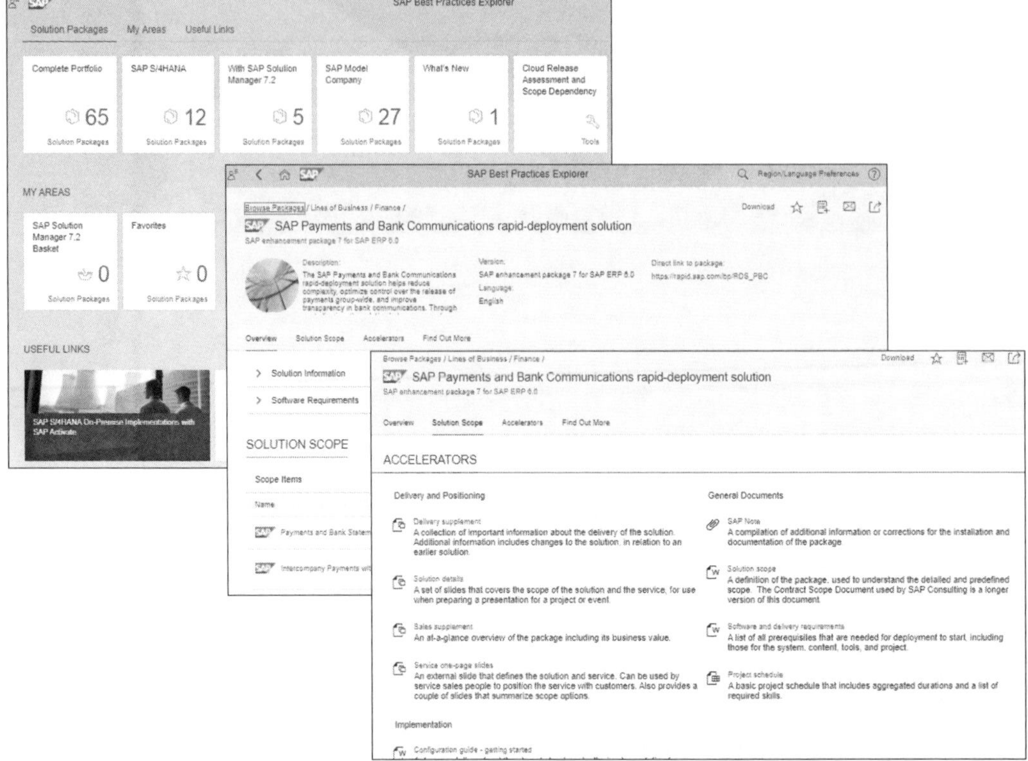

Figure 12 SAP Best Practices Explorer

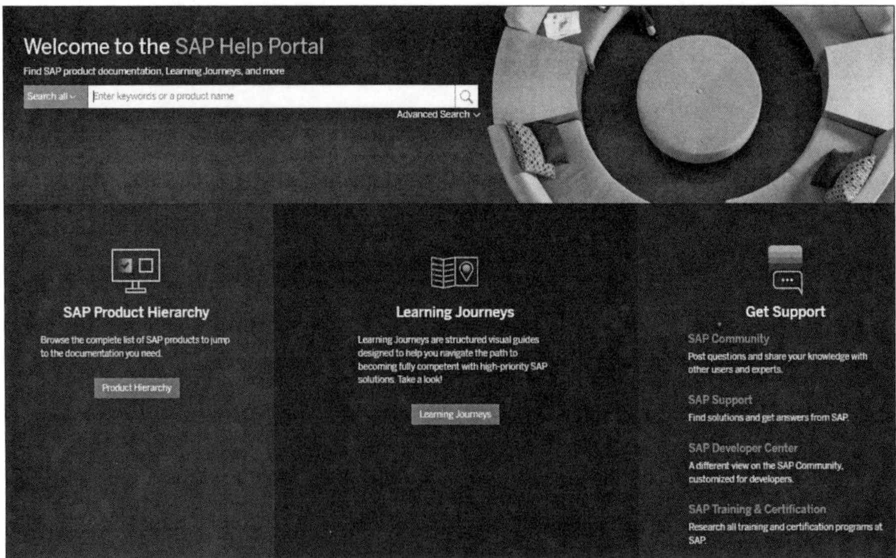

Figure 13 SAP Help Portal

Figure 14 shows the simplification list for the SAP S/4HANA 1909 initial shipment pack with a glimpse of the detailed information.

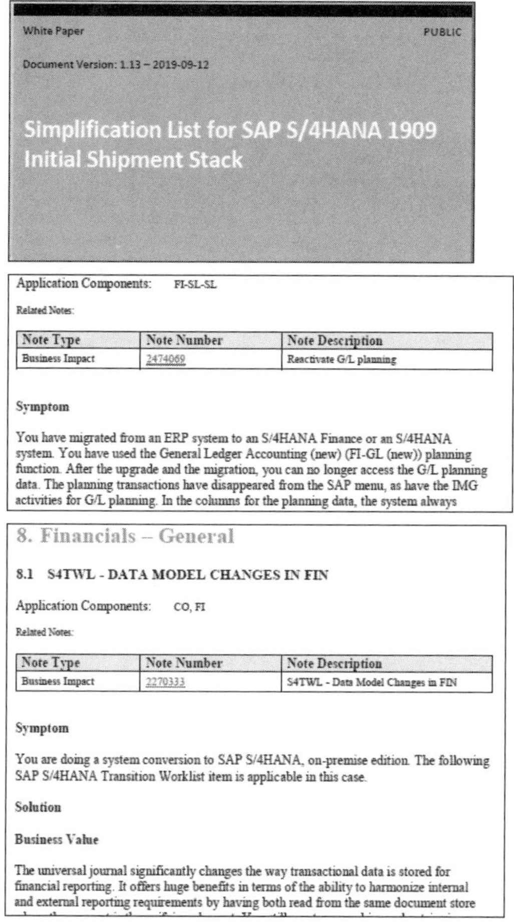

White Paper PUBLIC

Document Version: 1.13 – 2019-09-12

Simplification List for SAP S/4HANA 1909 Initial Shipment Stack

Application Components: FI-SL-SL

Related Notes:

Note Type	Note Number	Note Description
Business Impact	2474069	Reactivate G/L planning

Symptom

You have migrated from an ERP system to an S/4HANA Finance or an S/4HANA system. You have used the General Ledger Accounting (new) (FI-GL (new)) planning function. After the upgrade and the migration, you can no longer access the G/L planning data. The planning transactions have disappeared from the SAP menu, as have the IMG activities for G/L planning. In the columns for the planning data, the system always

8. Financials – General

8.1 S4TWL - DATA MODEL CHANGES IN FIN

Application Components: CO, FI

Related Notes:

Note Type	Note Number	Note Description
Business Impact	2270333	S4TWL - Data Model Changes in FIN

Symptom

You are doing a system conversion to SAP S/4HANA, on-premise edition. The following SAP S/4HANA Transition Worklist item is applicable in this case.

Solution

Business Value

The universal journal significantly changes the way transactional data is stored for financial reporting. It offers huge benefits in terms of the ability to harmonize internal and external reporting requirements by having both read from the same document store

Simplification List for SAP S/4HANA 1909 Initial Shipment Stack

8. **Financials – General** 166
   8.1 S4TWL - DATA MODEL CHANGES IN FIN 166
   8.2 S4TWL - REPLACED TRANSACTION CODES AND PROGRAMS IN FIN 173
   8.3 S4TWL - Plan data is not migrated to SAP S/4HANA 175
9. **Financials - Accounts Payable/Accounts Receivable** 180
   9.1 S4TWL - Integration with FSCM Biller Direct (FI-AR) 180
   9.2 S4TWL - Integration with FSCM Biller Direct (FI-AP) 181
10. **Financials - Asset Accounting** 182
   10.1 S4TWL - DATA STRUCTURE CHANGES IN ASSET ACCOUNTING 182
   10.2 S4TWL - ASSET ACCOUNTING 184
   10.3 S4TWL - INTEGRATION TO LEASE ACCOUNTING ENGINE (LAE) 201
   10.4 S4TWL - JOINT VENTURE ACCOUNTING (JVA) 202
   10.5 S4TWL - SELECTED BUSINESS FUNCTIONS IN FINANCIAL ACCOUNTING (FI-GL AND FI-AA) 203
11. **Financials - Cash Management** 207
   11.1 S4TWL - CASH MANAGEMENT - GENERAL 207
12. **Financials – Controlling** 221
   12.1 S4TWL - Reference and Simulation Costing 221
   12.2 S4TWL - Summarization Hierarchies in Controlling 222
   12.3 S4TWL - Technical Changes in Material Ledger with Actual Costing 224
   12.4 S4TWL - TECHNICAL CHANGES IN CONTROLLING 231
   12.5 S4TWL - PROFIT AND LOSS PLANNING AND PROFIT CENTER PLANNING 234
   12.6 S4TWL - ACTIVITY-BASED COSTING 238
   12.7 S4TWL - GENERAL COST OBJECTS AND COST OBJECT HIERARCHIES 241

Figure 14 SAP Simplification List

SAP S/4HANA Cloud Customer Community

You can access the cloud community via *https://s4hanacloud.community.sap/home*. In this community, you'll be connected to your peers and SAP experts. Here you can search for answers or exchange information about the products, including the SAP Activate methodology. Figure 15 shows the **SAP S/4HANA Cloud Customer Community** page. In addition, at the bottom, you can see the available links.

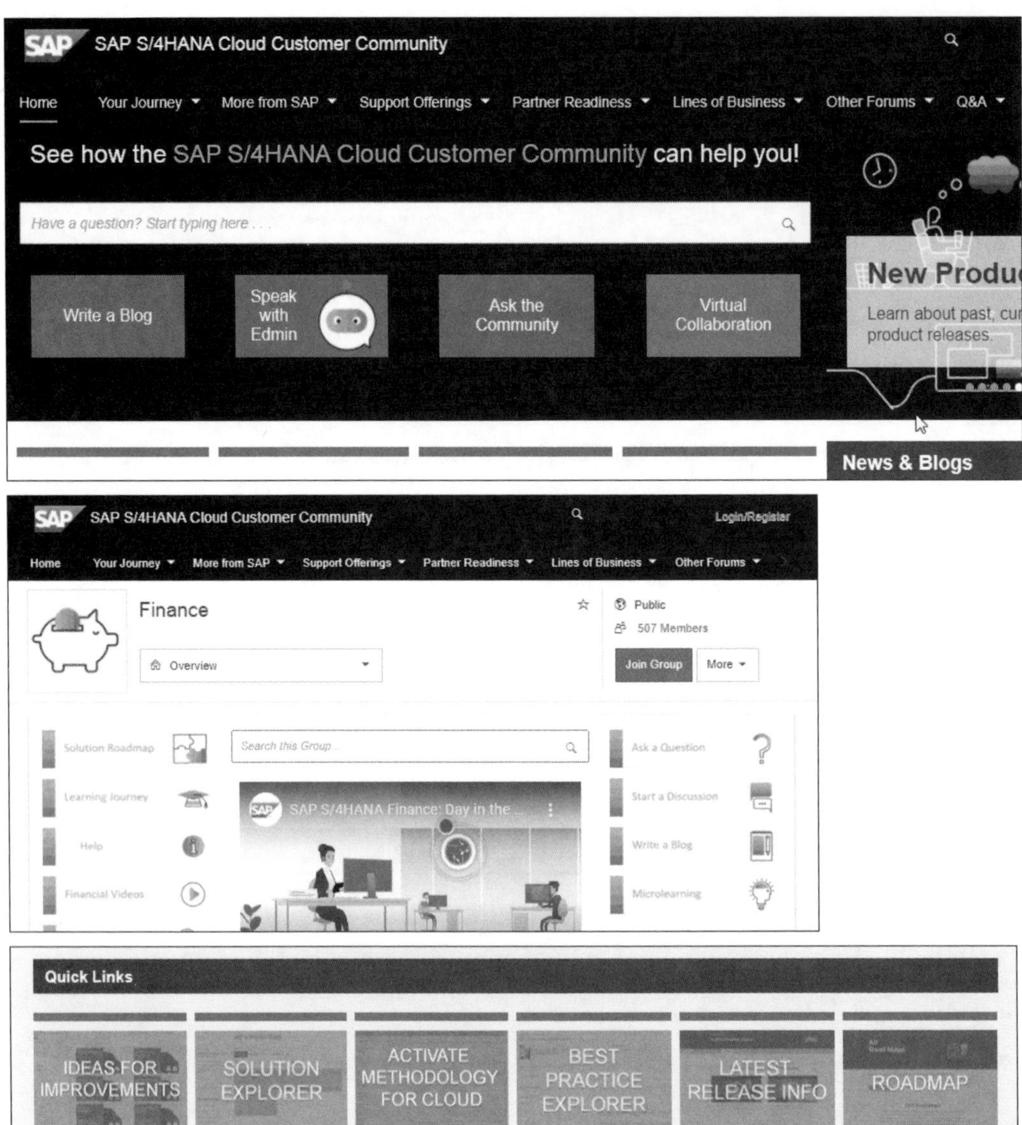

Figure 15 SAP S/4HANA Cloud Customer Community

SAP Fiori Apps Reference Library

The SAP Fiori apps reference library is another resource for you, which you can access via *https://S/4HANAcloud.community.sap/*. You'll find all the apps available for SAP Fiori, as shown in Figure 16.

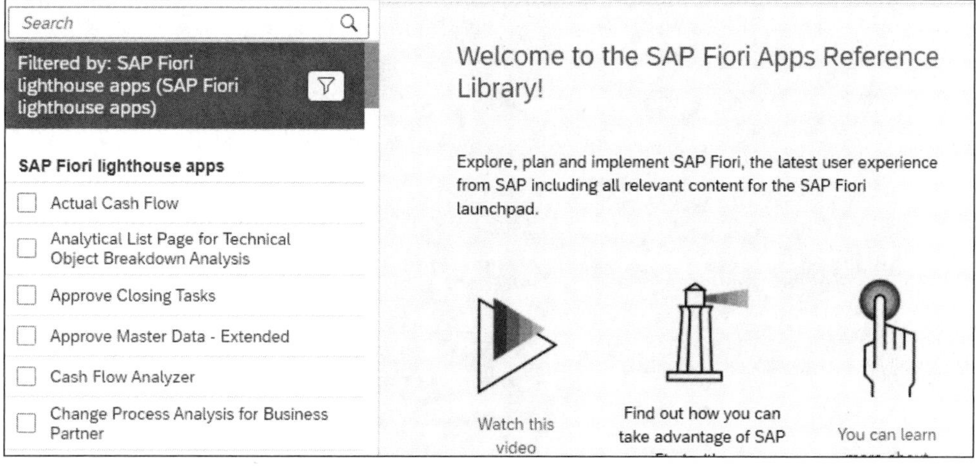

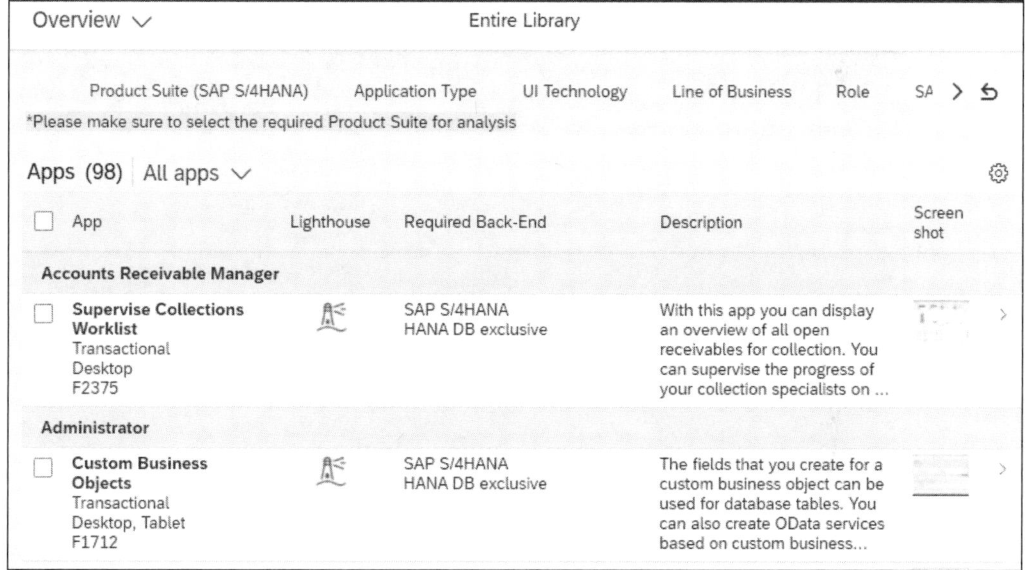

Figure 16 SAP Fiori Apps Reference Library

openSAP

openSAP is SAP's free massive open online course (MOOC) enterprise offering that you can access via *https://open.sap.com/*. It has many ongoing courses and several self-paced courses where anyone can enroll and learn that topic. These courses have topic end questions and answers that will help you self-assess. It's a wonderful resource to keep up with all the latest innovations and trends without requiring prior knowledge of the topics. Figure 17 shows the openSAP home page and the available courses at the time of writing this book. This list is updated continuously based on the additional courses.

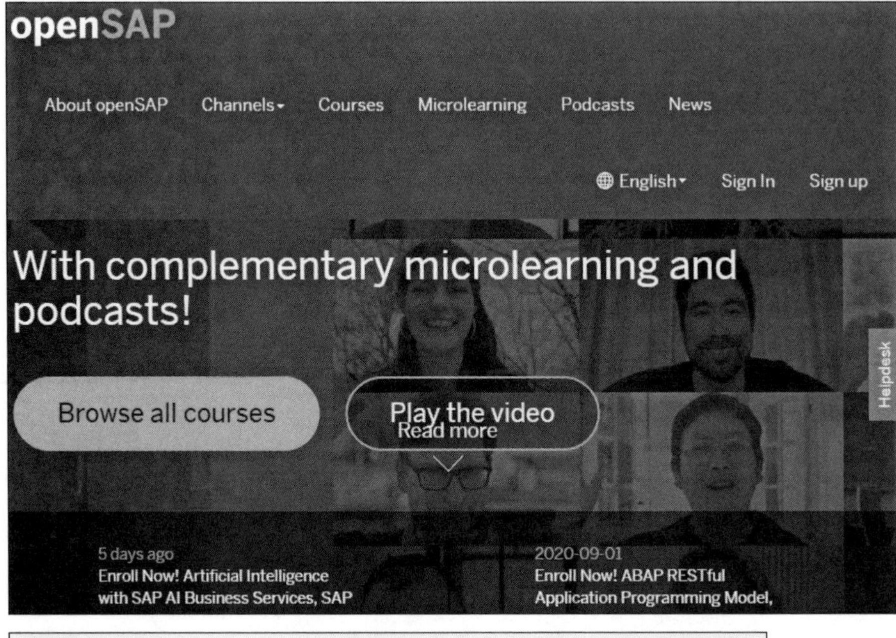

Figure 17 OpenSAP

SAP Cloud Appliance Library

SAP Cloud Appliance Library is the online library of preconfigured, ready-to-use business solutions. You can deploy these solutions quickly using your own cloud accounts to kick-start your SAP S/4HANA implementation. You can access SAP Cloud Appliance Library via *https://cal.sap.com/*. Before you dive deeper into the SAP Cloud Appliance Library, watch the **What is SAP Cloud Appliance Library** video posted at the bottom of the page. Figure 18 shows the **SAP Cloud Appliance Library** home page with a list of available solutions and configuration options.

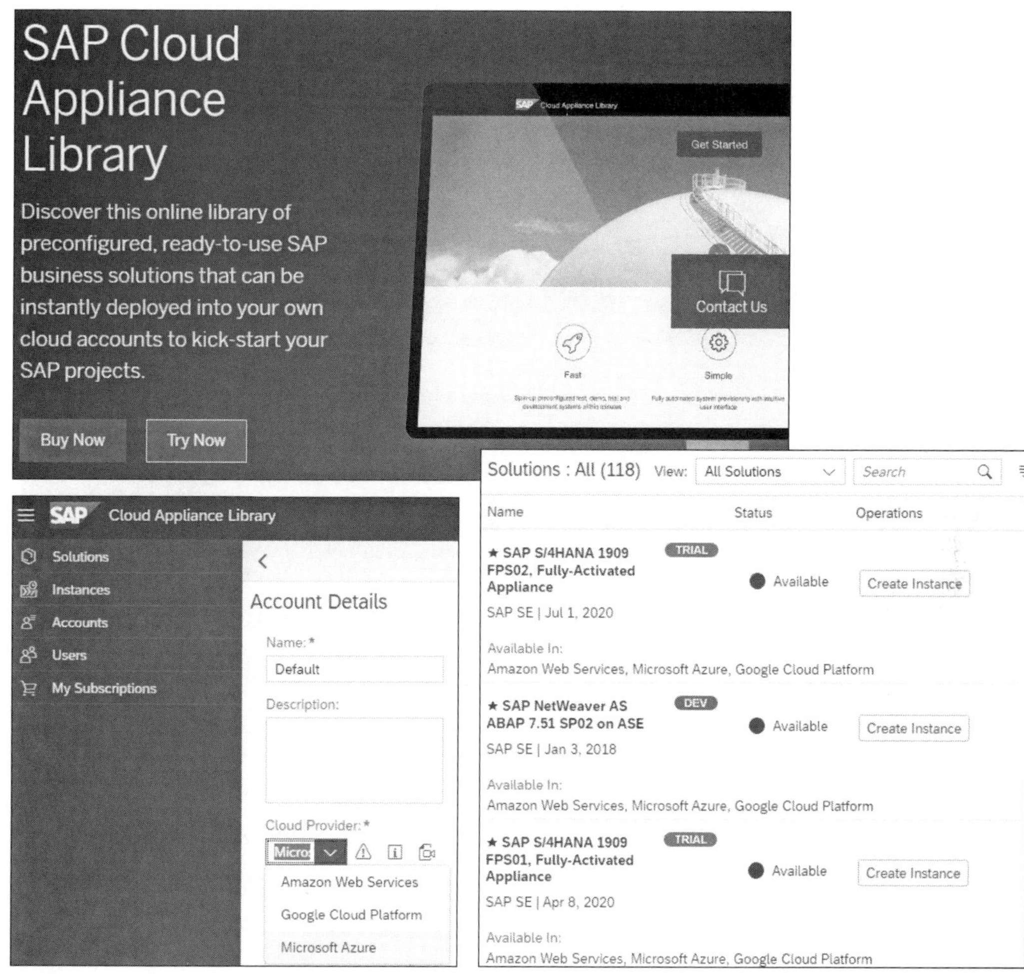

Figure 18 SAP Cloud Appliance Library

SAP Sample Questions

Although there are only eight sample questions on the certification website, they will give you a good idea of the types of questions that you'll get in the actual exam. It's important that you take this test, preferably before continuing your journey. Figure 19 shows how to access sample questions.

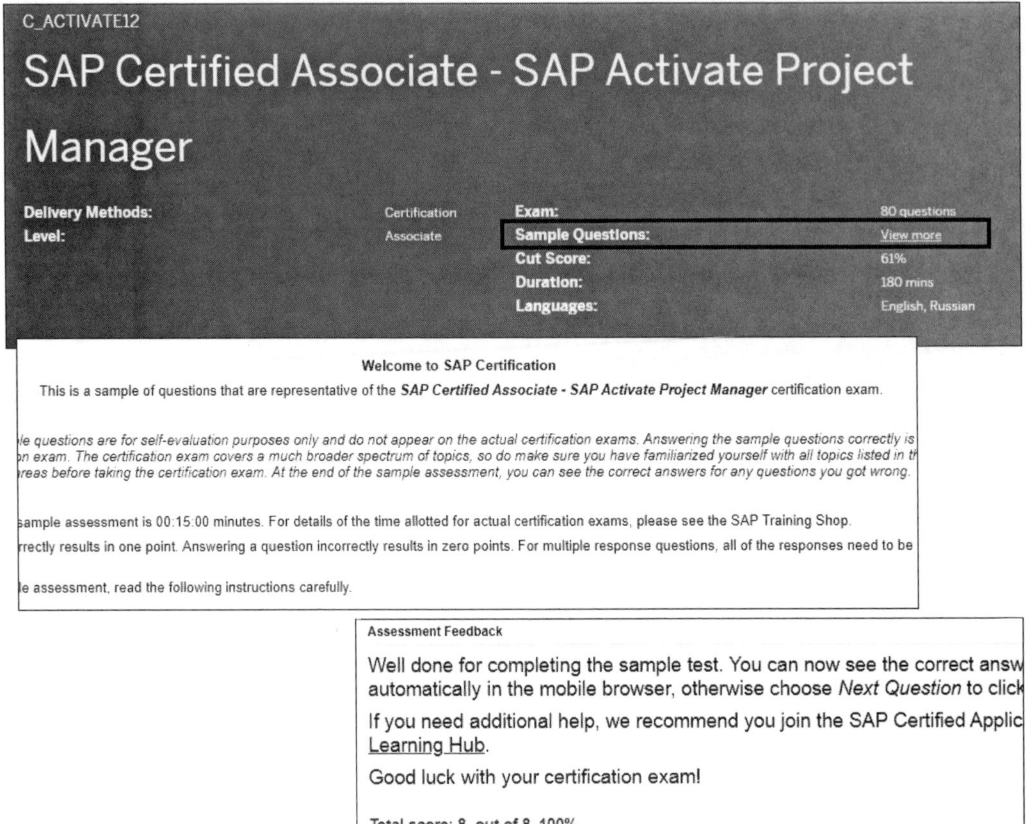

Figure 19 Sample Questions

Summary

In this chapter, we examined the various options for SAP Activate certification and how to prepare. We reviewed the topics, exam structure, and the required passing score for C_ACTIVATE12. We also reviewed the question types that you'll encounter on the exam, and finally looked into tips for before and during the exam.

In the next chapter, we'll dive into the basics of the SAP Activate methodology and look into its three pillars, as well as discuss fit-gap analysis, key characteristics, and the structure of the SAP Activate methodology.

Chapter 1
SAP Activate Overview

Techniques You'll Master

- Understand the basics of SAP Activate
- Explain the transition roadmap
- Walk through the three pillars of SAP Activate
- Understand fit-to-standard analysis and fit-gap analysis
- Review the key characteristics of SAP Activate
- Explain the structure of SAP Activate
- Describe the governance model in SAP Activate
- Understand roles and responsibilities in the SAP Activate methodology

SAP Activate, a project management framework to implement SAP S/4HANA, is an intelligent innovation as a service, which is pioneered on three pillars: *SAP Best Practices*, *guided configuration*, and *one methodology*. This chapter will introduce the SAP Activate methodology, including the three pillars; fit-to-standard analysis; key characteristics; structure, including the different phases of the methodology; and the roles and responsibilities of the project team. The main differences between SAP Activate and the ASAP methodology—the prior version of project management methodology to implement SAP ERP—will be summarized in this chapter followed by some important terms and questions and answers to test your understanding.

Real-World Scenario

After you completed your graduation in retail management three years ago, you joined a major chain of clothing store as a subject matter expert (SME). You've also worked as a software developer in a regional retail organization for two years prior to starting your graduation.

You learned that the company has decided to implement a major enterprise resource planning (ERP) system called SAP S/4HANA. As a student, you were always fascinated to work on the SAP platform, and this is your big chance. You approached your supervisor to speak about this opportunity.

During your conversation, your boss briefs you about this transformation initiative. Although your boss admits to not being an SAP expert, his understanding is that the project is to implement various modules of SAP, including finance and accounting, human resources, core retail, warehouse management, supply chain, and many more. They are also planning to migrate legacy system data to the new environment. You learn that the project is starting in the next few weeks, and offer your assistance and experience in pricing, option planning, stock transfer, and retail analytics—your core area of expertise.

Your boss appreciates your interest, and brings up the methodology that the business will follow to make this transition: SAP Activate. Your boss asks you to start looking into it and conduct knowledge-sharing sessions with all team members, eventually leading the fit-to-standard sessions on certain processes.

So, you have a new task at hand! What is SAP Activate, and how should you get started?

Objectives of This Portion of the Test

The certification examination will test your knowledge about the following topics:

- Basic understanding of SAP Activate
- Principles behind SAP Activate (the three pillars)
- Fit-to-standard analysis and its usage to build the product backlog
- Structure of SAP Activate—phases, deliverables, workstreams, and tasks
- Governance model in SAP Activate
- Roles and responsibilities of different teams and team members.

In the subsequent sections, you'll learn about and understand these key concepts followed by some questions and answers.

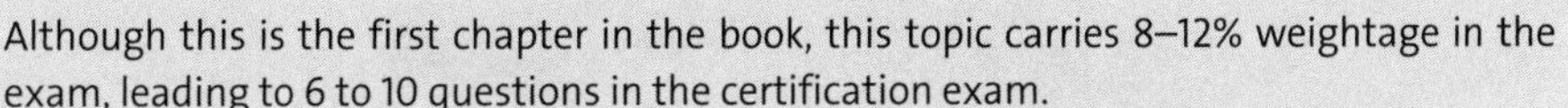

Note

Although this is the first chapter in the book, this topic carries 8–12% weightage in the exam, leading to 6 to 10 questions in the certification exam.

Key Concepts Refresher

This section will help you understand the latest from SAP by introducing SAP Activate and taking you deeper into the topic. This chapter is the foundation for all the SAP Activate-related tasks. As mentioned in the Introduction, it's important to understand this chapter irrespective of your role in the project.

What Is SAP Activate?

SAP Activate is a project management methodology used to implement SAP S/4HANA. It's adopted from Scrum, which is capable of quick adaptation and makes it easy to adopt quarterly innovations from SAP and expand the solution footprint. One of the key challenges in the traditional implementation approach was a "big-bang," large, and complex implementation of business functionalities led by IT. SAP Activate, on the other hand, to overcome the challenge, enables a business-driven, self-service approach with frequent innovations.

Before SAP Activate, the two implementation methodologies were *ASAP 8.0*, which was used for on-premise implementations, and *SAP Launch*, which was used for cloud implementations. The ASAP implementation methodology, driven by the waterfall approach, has six implementation phases, namely project preparation, blueprinting, realization, final preparation, go-live support, and run. SAP Launch, based on agile, has four implementation phases: prepare, realize, verify, and launch.

SAP Activate replaces both of these methodologies, as shown in Figure 1.1, and is a hybrid approach that provides the framework, tools, accelerators, questionnaires, checklists, and playbooks throughout the SAP S/4HANA implementations, on-premise or cloud. We'll look into more detail about the phases in the SAP Activate methodology later, but, for now, just understand that there are six phases in the SAP Activate methodology.

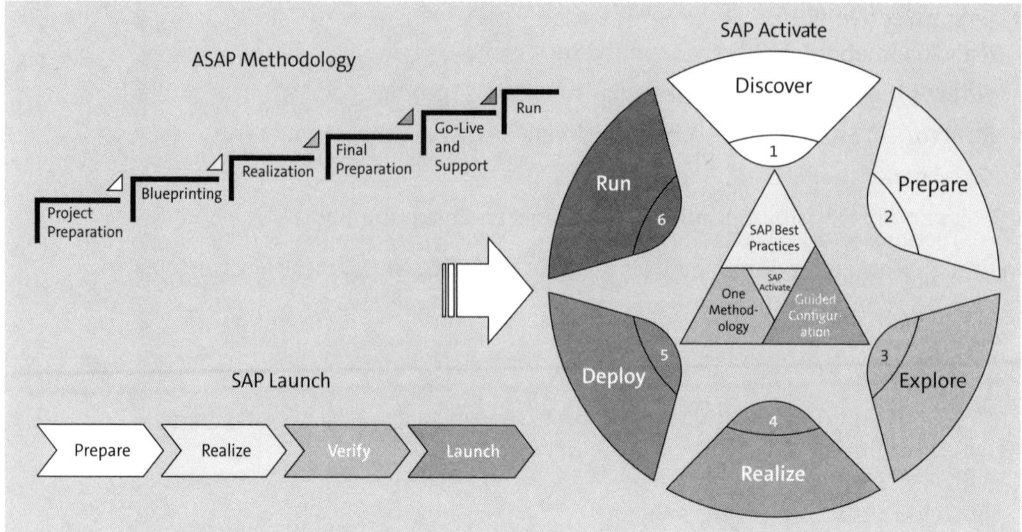

Figure 1.1 SAP Activate

SAP S/4HANA has three transition roadmaps, as shown in Figure 1.2.

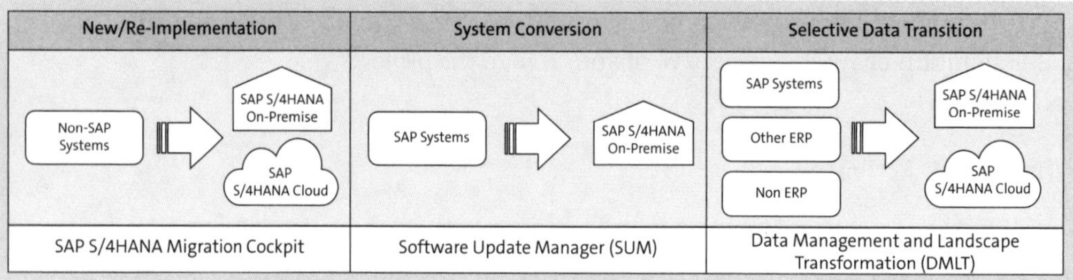

Figure 1.2 Transition Roadmaps

Let's walk through each roadmap:

- **New implementations**
  These are greenfield implementations in which the client isn't on SAP and wants to implement SAP S/4HANA. Data migration from non-SAP systems to the industry-leading, intelligent, simplified, and ready-to-run business processes on SAP S/4HANA may be a key component of greenfield implementations. A new implementation is also applicable if the customer wants to reengineer their current processes based on the current innovations. New implementations have the following characteristics:
  - Reengineering of existing processes
  - Adoption of simplifications based on the latest innovations
  - Utilization of innovative business processes with preconfigured processes
  - Initial data load

- **System conversions**
  This roadmap will provide the path, tools, accelerators, and other artifacts when a client is on an SAP system such as SAP ERP 6.0 on SAP HANA or on another database (from this point referred to as *anyDB*) and wants to move their ERP system to SAP S/4HANA. These are also known as brownfield implementations. System conversions have the following characteristics:
  - Technical conversion followed by adoption of business innovations
  - Ability to adopt innovations at your own pace
  - Quick to go live on the new platform
  - Lower implementation cost
- **Selective data transition (formerly known as landscape transformations)**
  The most complex scenario is when a client wants to consolidate their existing ERP systems, including functionality transformation, consolidation of global business units, or simply retiring an outdated ERP system into a new SAP S/4HANA instance. This transition approach balances the need for innovations and the historical data migration. Selective data transitions have the following characteristics:
  - Balance between reengineering and reuse
  - Option to merge/split instances
  - Migration of selective data (time slice, client, organizational units, etc.)
  - De-risk implementation

New implementations on all three platforms, system conversions, and selective data transition will be covered in detail from Chapter 6 to Chapter 10.

Note
Notice that in system conversion, you can't move the existing SAP system to SAP S/4HANA Cloud because of the customization in the current implementation. In an ideal scenario of zero customization, you can convert the existing system to the cloud, but we all know that an "ideal" system doesn't exist.

The one question that remains unanswered is the need for another implementation methodology when you have ASAP 8.0 and SAP Launch. Over a period of time, you might have noticed the changing business expectation to continuously reduce the implementation cost. Yet, the continuous change in business functionalities leads to longer delivery time, which increases the cost. This reality led to placing Scrum—an agile framework to implement software faster—at the center of the implementation methodology and revolutionize the approach from big bang to incremental. It reduces the overall risks as well as enhances the business value by faster and repeated delivery of the business functionalities. Finally, the enhanced usages of cloud and mobile technology led to a demand in diversity for solution deployments, such as cloud, on-premise, and hybrid, or quick and easy information access through handheld devices. The need for another implementation methodology is summarized in Figure 1.3.

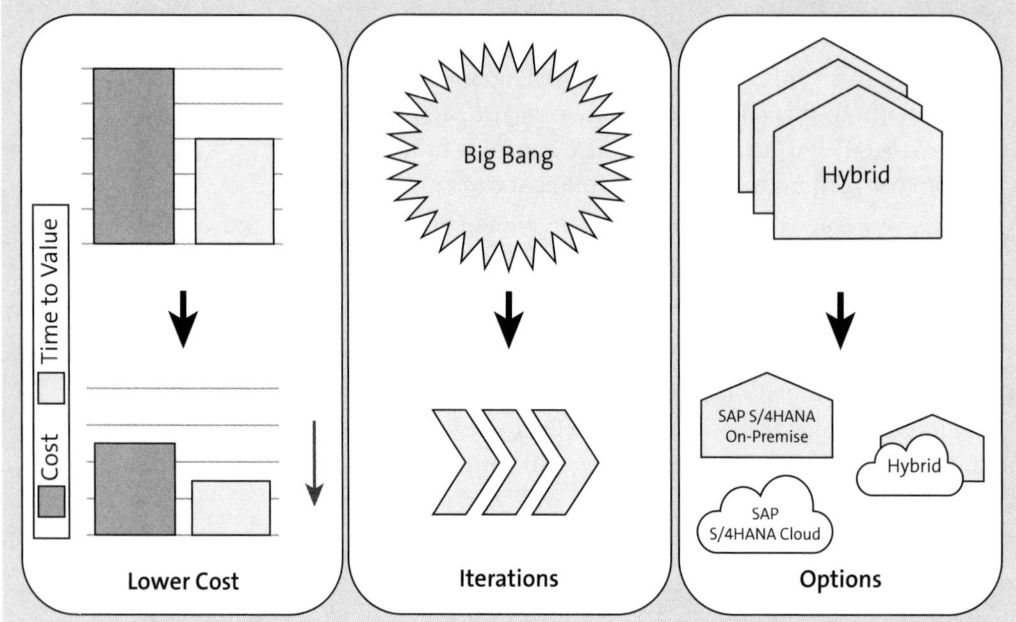

Figure 1.3 Need for SAP Activate

Three Pillars of SAP Activate

SAP Activate is based on three pillars: SAP Best Practices, guided configuration, and one methodology for any SAP S/4HANA implementation, as shown in Figure 1.4.

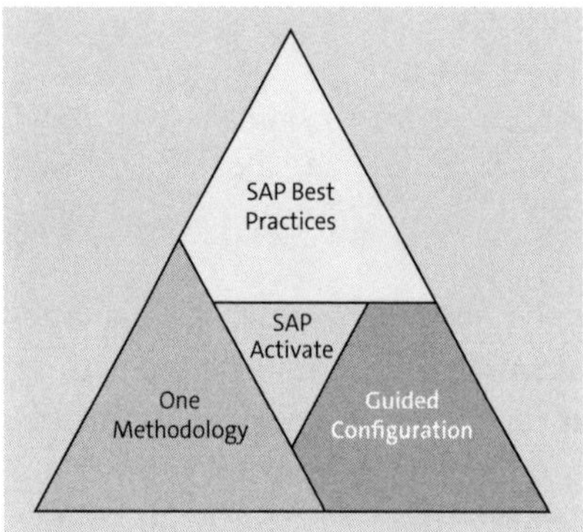

Figure 1.4 Three Pillars of SAP Activate

We'll look into the three pillars of SAP Activate in this section.

SAP Best Practices

The first of the three pillars is SAP Best Practices. Implementation of any ERP requires sound functional knowledge and a strong understanding of the business requirements. The first pillar of SAP Activate is meant to provide a standard, consistent, and preconfigured ready-to-run business process optimized for SAP S/4HANA. SAP Best Practices support the new implementations as well as the migration and integration of system conversion. For selective data transitions (or landscape transformations), SAP Best Practices, apart from the use cases, migration, and integration, includes extensibility of the existing business processes with the customer's own process.

SAP Best Practices help the project team in the following:

- **Faster time to value**
  The ready-to-run, preconfigured processes, along with other assets, will help jump-start the implementation. If followed, it drastically reduces the implementation time, and customers can reap the benefits quickly.
- **Predictable results**
  The variety of business scenarios across the industry provides repeatable and predictable results. SAP Best Practices along with some localization generally forms the implementation baseline.
- **Quick and simple onboarding to the cloud**
  The easy deployment to the cloud provides flexibility for clients.

You can access SAP Best Practices from *https://rapid.sap.com/bp*. If you know the URL of a specific best practice, then you can access it directly. For instance, the URL for SAP Best Practices for SAP S/4HANA is *https://rapid.sap.com/bp/BP_OP_ENTPR*.

Figure 1.5 shows the SAP Best Practices Explorer home page, best practices for SAP S/4HANA for the US version 1909, and the tutorials that you access from the home page. We strongly recommend going through the tutorial videos.

Figure 1.5 SAP Best Practices

Each SAP Best Practices page has the following sections:

- **Overview**
  You'll find the details about the solution and the software requirements here, as shown in Figure 1.6.

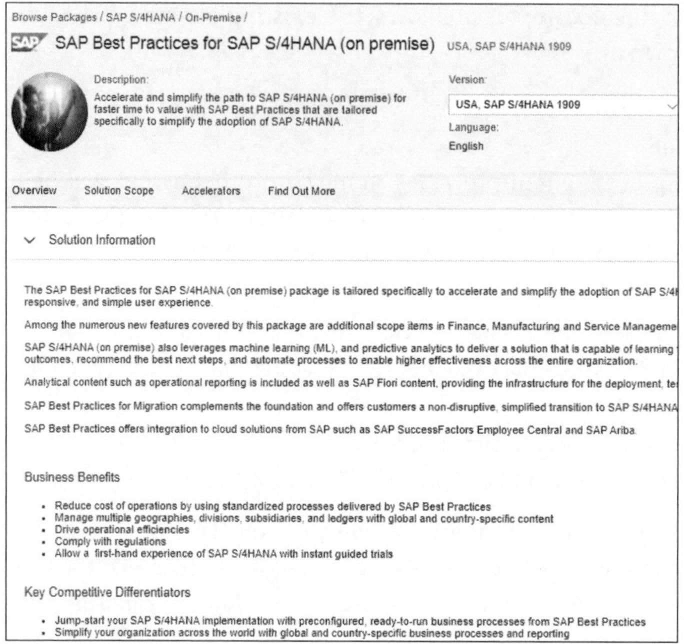

Figure 1.6 Overview

- **Solution Scope**
  This section covers scope item groups, which can be expanded to go to the specific scope item that you want, as shown in Figure 1.7.

Browse Packages / SAP S/4HANA / On-Premise /
SAP Best Practices for SAP S/4HANA (on premise) USA, SAP S/4HANA 1909
Overview Solution Scope Accelerators Find Out More
SOLUTION SCOPE
Scope Item Groups

Name	Description
Finance	Achieve excellenc at any time, from a
Accounting and Financial Close	Reduce cost and e valuation approac
Accounting and Financial Close (J58)	This scope item pr
Accounting and Financial Close - Group Ledger IFRS (1GA)	This scope item pr period-end closing
Accounting for Incoming Sales Orders (2FD)	This scope item pr entries along with
Actual Costing (33Q)	This scope item er countries (such as

Figure 1.7 Solution Scope

- **Accelerators**
  Several tools and techniques here will help you deliver the solution faster, as shown in Figure 1.8.

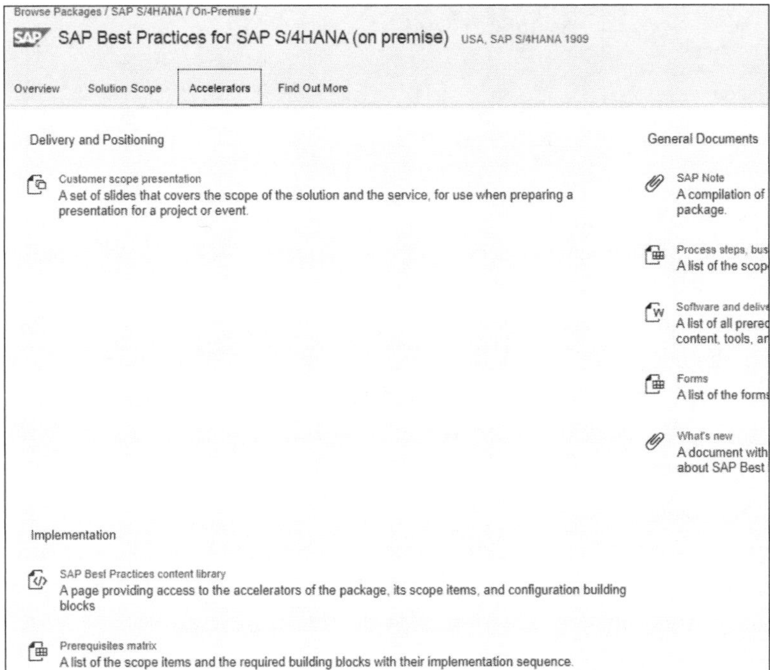

Figure 1.8 Accelerators

- **Find Out More**
  Any other related topics, blogs, or solutions are found here.

Succinctly, SAP Best Practices will give you ready-to-run, preconfigured business processes. However, you need to configure the system to move from the current landscape to a desired landscape to meet the client's business objectives. To do so, SAP Activate provides you a set of tools wrapped under guided configuration.

Guided Configuration

Guided configuration, the second pillar of SAP Activate, supports SAP S/4HANA implementations by providing a framework, accelerators, playbooks, checklists, tools, and many other assets. Because SAP Activate is a common methodology to implement on-cloud or on-premise, the tools for guided configuration vary based on the chosen landscape—cloud or on premise. In simple terms, guided configuration is your personal assistant that will help you configure the system. For SAP S/4HANA Cloud, it also helps in managing the lifecycle of the preconfigured business process. However, guided configuration behaves differently for on-premise SAP S/4HANA and SAP S/4HANA Cloud versions, as shown in Figure 1.9.

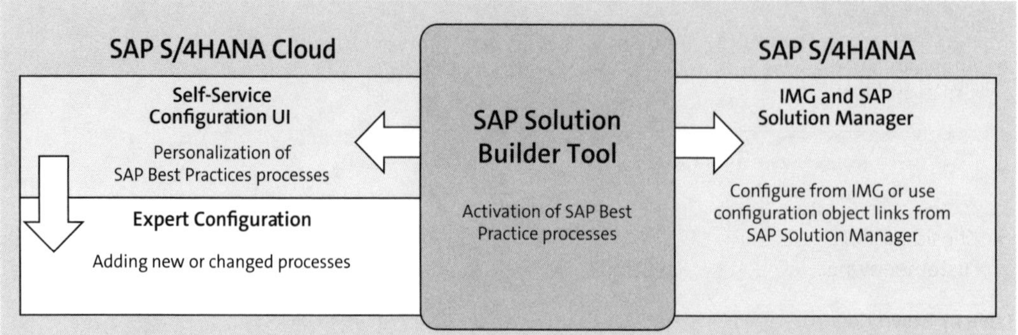

Figure 1.9 Guided Configuration

The SAP solution builder tool is the first step of guided configuration, which allows you to activate the best practices. Within the SAP solution builder tool, processes are modeled as scope items. You can develop and structure configuration content based on the industry model. Let's explore the guided configuration for cloud and on-premise implementations:

- **SAP S/4HANA Cloud**
  In the activated environment, a customer or a partner can use self-service configuration via the Self-Service Configuration User Interface (SSCUI) to adjust and personalize the solution. SSCUI contains the following features:
  - Personalized processes
  - Ability to adjust settings based on client's needs
  - Easy-to-use SAP Fiori apps

  The expert configuration capabilities, on the other hand, are available only to SAP's service center team, which works closely with the customer and/or partner to implement the desired configuration settings in the system. Expert configuration capabilities include the following:
  - Deeper configuration changes
  - Ability to add new processes or adjust preconfigured processes

  Expert configurations are implemented in the quality system by the SAP service center team. Table 1.1 shows what is allowed and what is restricted by the expert configuration.
- **SAP S/4HANA (on-premise)**
  The implementation team starts with the activated SAP Best Practices in the sandbox environment. After the fit-gap analysis, covered later in the chapter, the implementation team uses the standard implementation guide (IMG) for the configuration. Furthermore, the team uses SAP Solution Manager to capture and store the project documentations in one location.

Allows	Restricts
▪ Adaptation of editable fields within SAP Best Practices ▪ Creation of new processes in the customer-owned area (Z scope items and Z building blocks) ▪ Consideration of namespaces for customer-owned processes	▪ Deletion of SAP Best Practices contents ▪ Change in noneditable fields in SAP Best Practices content

Table 1.1 Expert Configuration

You can access the guided configuration using the Manage Your Solution SAP Fiori app to gain the following benefits:

- Evaluations of activated business processes
- Initial configuration of the activated solution and updates for continuous innovations
- A process-driven approach to test your configured business process
- A migration engine for simple data migration and end-user training

One Methodology

The third pillar of SAP Activate, which is the successor of the ASAP and SAP Launch methodologies, is the methodology itself—one modular, simpler, and agile methodology. Some of the salient features of the SAP Activate methodology are shown in Figure 1.10. SAP Activate methodology is wide ranging and supports the initial implementations as well as the continuous innovations on one spectrum, while on the other spectrum, it also covers the implementations of broad SAP solutions such as SAP S/4HANA, SAP cloud solutions, and SAP Business Suite. And, on yet another spectrum, it enables co-innovations with partners and customers.

The SAP Activate methodology not only provides a structured and cohesive approach to implement the solution, but it also provides the solution, contents, and accelerators for the three transition paths. The Roadmap Viewer is the tool where you can find the methodology, contents, and accelerators, whereas SAP Best Practices will provide you the business solution and related accelerators. The methodology, by default, uses the agile delivery approach and provides ready-to-use, preconfigured solutions and the corresponding documentation in SAP Best Practices. Furthermore, the methodology provides fit-to-standard analysis, conducted during the explore phase of the project, to identify the gaps and adjust the baseline solutions to fit the customer's needs.

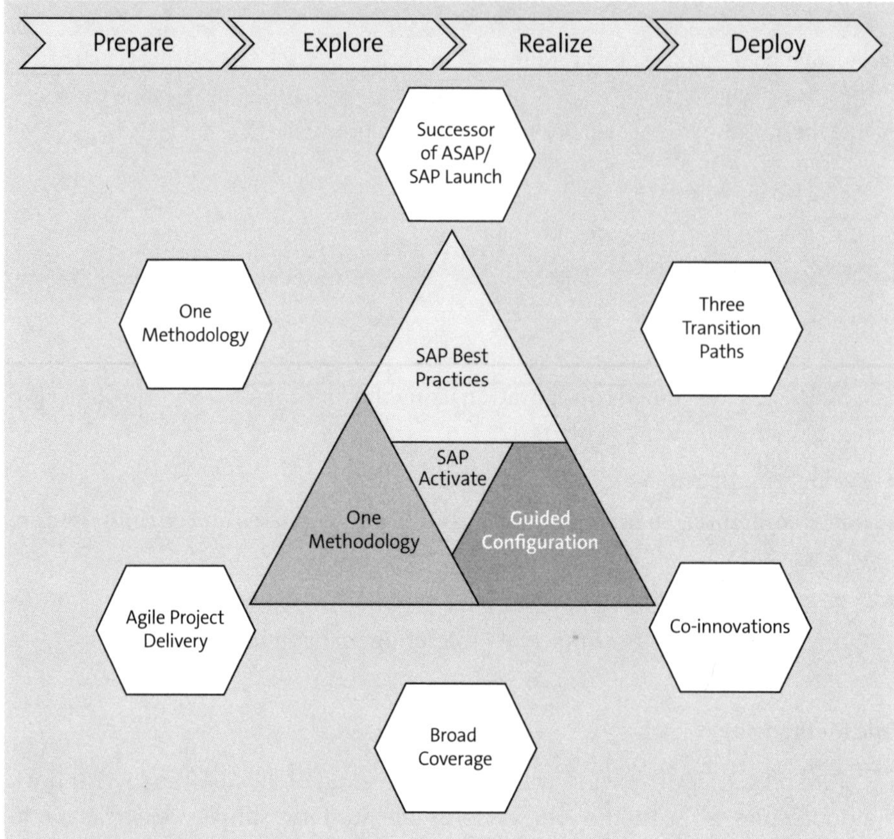

Figure 1.10 SAP Activate: One Methodology

Key Characteristics

Figure 1.11 shows the six key characteristics of the SAP Activate methodology. You start working on a system with preselected scope items based on SAP Best Practices ❶. You can leverage the cloud environment to set up the system, which is easy and quick to deploy ❷. It also provides you with additional flexibility and the speed to deploy the solution. Subsequently, the team performs the fit-gap analysis as a part of the solution validation to build the product backlog, establishes the delta requirements, and identifies any perceived gaps ❸.

SAP Innovation Control Center, SAP Mission Control Center, and SAP Operations Control Center, premium engagement services from SAP, play a key role during and after the implementation ❹. During the implementation, for example, you can engage them to review the perceived gaps (known as gap validation service) to ensure that these are product gaps and can be implemented in the product. Another such example is the use of SAP ActiveEmbedded to ensure high performance and high scalability, address risk and issues related to the performance, and handle technical integrity and stability.

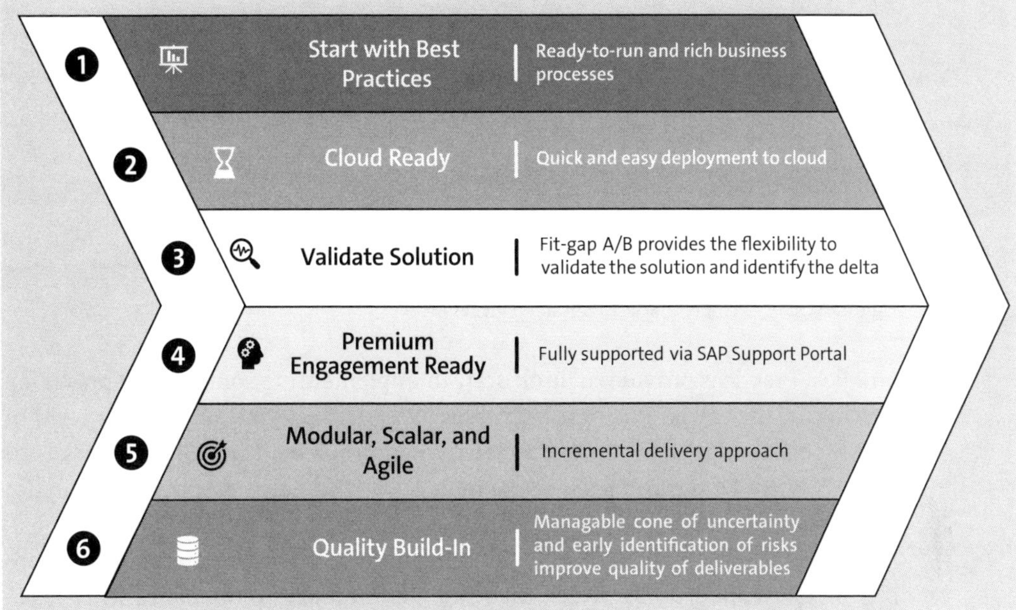

Figure 1.11 Key Characteristics of SAP Activate Methodology

Using the same versatile SAP Activate methodology, you can implement a six-week project of SAP S/4HANA Finance on the cloud or a 60-week complex and global implementation project of SAP S/4HANA. These projects are of different sizes and complexity, yet you can pick and choose the deliverables and tasks from the same basic framework. Additionally, the framework scales up or down depending on the project and solution requirements. The iterative approach and incremental build from the agile framework are woven into SAP Activate to improve the quality of deliverables and the solution by conducting frequent validations ❺.

Quality, a continuous focus of all SAP methodologies, is built into the SAP Activate methodology, including structured quality management plans, quality gates at different stages of the project, the agile iterative approach, continuous and frequent validations, focus on testing and integration, and a business-driven solution approach ❻.

We'll walk through these six characteristics in more detail in subsequent sections.

Start with SAP Best Practices

Figure 1.12 shows the SAP Best Practices Explorer screen, displaying the prepackaged solutions arranged in different tiles such as **SAP Model Company** or **SAP S/4HANA – Solution Packages**.

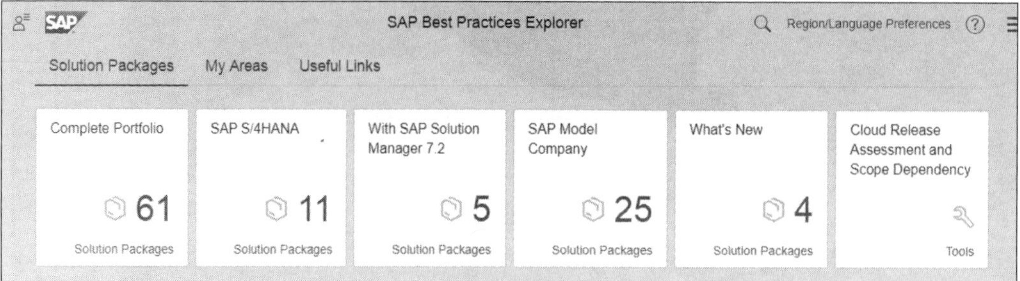

Figure 1.12 SAP Activate Characteristics: SAP Best Practices

SAP Best Practices provides a jump-start in implementing solutions by providing rich and ready-to-run business processes along with sample data in the form of SAP Model Company. As an example, if you're implementing HR analytics with SAP Analytics Cloud, you'll get scope item 41E – HR Analytics with SAP Analytics Cloud preconfigured as a part of SAP Best Practices. This scope item provides business users in the HR and finance lines of business with four comprehensive dashboards for **Workforce Overview, Diversity, Performance**, and **Finance** in easy-to-consume analytics.

SAP Model Company offers preconfigured packages that can be easily deployed on the client's environment to start the fit-to-standard process. For example, SAP Model Company for Automotive offers a comprehensive reference solution to support the processes of an automotive company, as shown in Figure 1.13. It's delivered with preconfigured automotive-specific scenarios, relevant business content, accelerators, and enablement services.

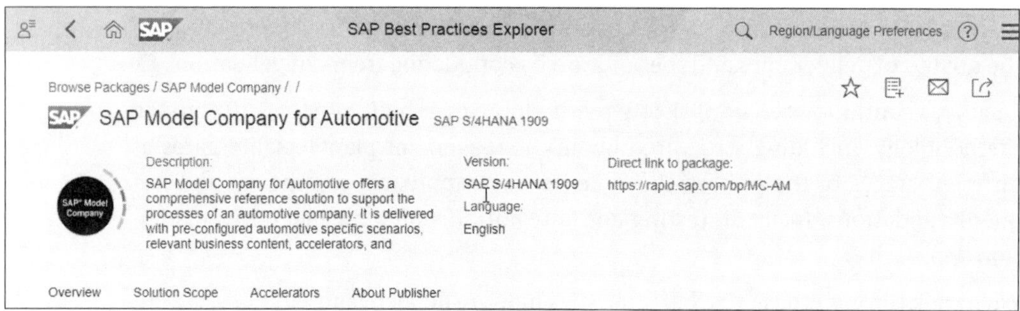

Figure 1.13 SAP Model Company for Automotive

Apart from these core best practices, SAP Best Practices also includes integration and migration best practices, as shown in Figure 1.14.

SAP Best Practices for SAP S/4HANA Cloud and SAP S/4HANA are similar except that the on-premise version has additional scope items. Because the content of SAP Best Practices is changing continuously, we won't list it here. However, you can find the SAP Best Practices for SAP S/4HANA Cloud and SAP S/4HANA at *https://rapid.sap.com/bp/#/BP_CLD_ENTPR* and *https://rapid.sap.com/bp/BP_OP_ENTPR*, respectively.

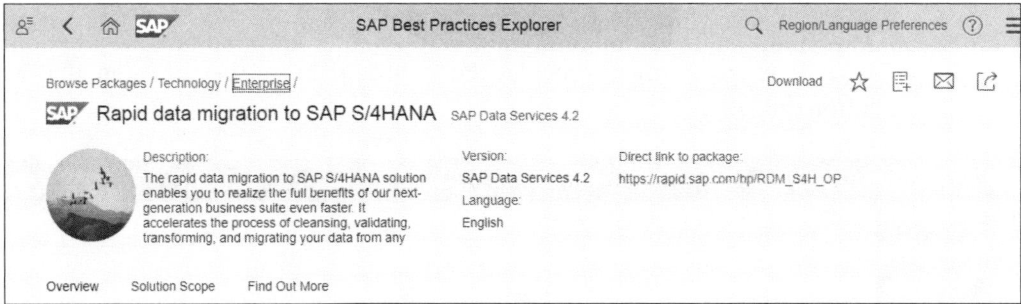

Figure 1.14 Data Migration Best Practices

SAP Best Practices contains details such as the project library, documentation, ready-to-run solutions, cloud deployment accelerators, and so on. Let's walk through the available ready-to-use content:

- **Simple cloud onboarding**
  You can move from SAP S/4HANA to SAP S/4HANA Cloud, extended edition to start your cloud journey. You can also use onboarding accelerators for faster deployment.
- **Predictable results**
  Project management tools, documentation, and accelerators are provided.
- **Faster time to value**
  Preconfigured solutions, ready-to-run system configurations, base solution documentation, and the key performance indicator (KPI) catalog are provided.

Note

In the home screen of SAP Best Practices Explorer, you'll notice a tile for **Cloud Release Assessment and Scope Dependency**. It's a personalized and critical tool to identify the impact of changes within your scope items with every innovation. In Figure 1.5, shown earlier, it's highlighted with a box.

Cloud Ready

The "cloud ready" characteristics go well with the "start with the best practices" advice by providing ready-to-run and ready-to-deploy processes in the cloud for the initial work while determining the final infrastructure—on-premise or cloud.

Tip

Pay attention to the benefits of SAP Best Practices. You'll most likely get a question from this topic. The question can be framed to identify the benefits of SAP Best Practices such as "predictable results," "faster time to value," or "cloud ready."

In the SAP S/4HANA journey, the project team can set up the sandbox environment using SAP S/4HANA software appliances, which are available in SAP Cloud Appliance Library, as shown in Figure 1.15. You can also set up the sandbox environment using the Blu-ray media shipped by SAP.

The sandbox environment provides the starting point of the next step, that is, solution validation.

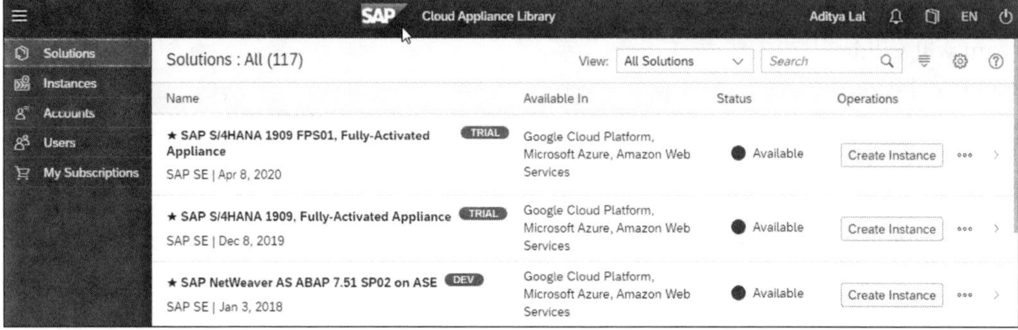

Figure 1.15 SAP Cloud Appliance Library

Note

This characteristic is applicable for on-premise implementations, despite the name. The project team can use the cloud environment to set up their landscape and use that for the fit-gap analysis.

Table 1.2 shows the options for the cloud deployments and the SAP Cloud Appliance Library features.

Cloud Deployment Options	SAP Cloud Appliance Library
▪ SAP S/4HANA Cloud, essentials edition ▪ SAP S/4HANA Cloud, extended edition ▪ SAP HANA Enterprise Cloud	▪ Preconfigured solutions ▪ Model companies ▪ Trials ▪ Fully activated appliances

Table 1.2 Cloud Deployment Options

Validate Solution

At this stage, the sandbox system is ready, and the project team is all set to start the fit-to-standard or fit-gap analysis. This step is performed during the explore phase of the SAP Activate methodology. For the cloud implementation, it's called fit-to-standard, and for the on-premise implementation, it's called fit-gap. Let's review both processes.

Fit-to-Standard

The main objective of this workshop for SAP S/4HANA Cloud implementations is to establish that the best practices provided by the SAP Activate methodology fit either as is or with some additional but minor configuration requirements (through self-service configuration, expert configuration, or extensibility) with the client's functional requirements. The project team will have a series of workshops to demonstrate SAP Best Practices to the client's business owner, SMEs, project manager, and other key stakeholders. The SME and the other members of the team will validate the SAP Best Practices and either conform to the standard or identify the gaps. These gaps can be filled in by some minor configurations that can be performed either by the project team through SSCUI, expert configuration through the SAP Support Portal, or through extensibility.

It's an iterative process and isn't a learning exercise for the implementation partner and the client. SAP warns about the preparedness that is required to conduct a fit-to-standard workshop; the experience required to conduct such a workshop includes sound functional knowledge; strong understanding of the SAP Best Practices content; familiarization with sample data and test scripts, documentation, and process flow; some strong soft skills; and several internal dry runs. You must be able to differentiate the "must have" requirements from others such as "should have" or "could have" requirements. These "must have" requirements are mostly covered in SAP Best Practices. The prioritization technique to identify "must have," "should have," "could have," and "won't have" is discussed in Chapter 3.

The fit-to-standard process contains the following steps, as shown in Figure 1.16:

❶ **Review SAP Best Practices**
The implementation team will explain the process flow to the client using SAP Best Practices.

❷ **Demonstrate business scenarios**
Plug in the data provided by the client and perform basic configuration. Demo the system's best practices, highlighting areas that may require configuration.

❸ **Fit SAP Best Practices with client's requirements**
Discuss and decide with the client whether SAP Best Practices fit well with the client's requirements.

❹ **Identify gaps**
Identify the gaps, and update the product backlog.

❺ **Identify required configurations**
Identify the configuration requirements, and raise a formal request to the customer for their value lists.

❻ **Enable customers**
Provide access to customers, and guide them to execute scenarios of their own.

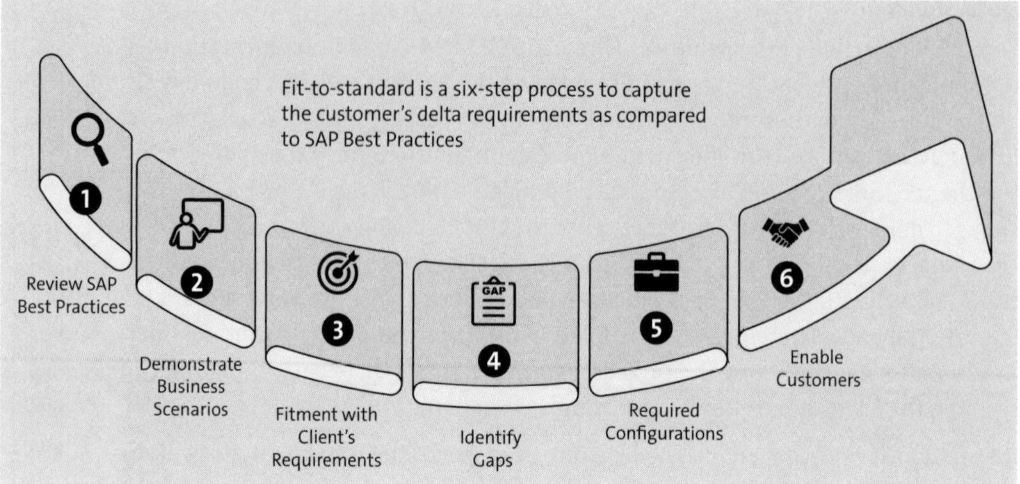

Figure 1.16 Fit-to-Standard

Fit-Gap Analysis

Fit-gap analysis is an explore phase process for on-premise SAP S/4HANA implementations that is conducted through two workshops: workshop A, which is also called a *solution validation workshop*, and workshop B, otherwise known as a *delta solution design workshop*. Similar to fit-to-standard analysis, these workshops are also iterative and conducted multiple times. In simpler words, the project team defines and agrees upon a "problem statement" during workshop A and identifies the possible solution during workshop B. The team will implement the agreed-upon resolution during the realize phase of the project.

The prime objective of the fit-gap analysis is to identify the gaps and capture the delta requirements. During these workshops, the project implementation team discusses the solution design and then identifies and prioritizes the delta requirements and gaps to ensure that the customer's business objectives are met. A strong fit-gap analysis process will reduce the probability of rework during the later phases of the project. Let's look at the two workshops conducted during the fit-gap analysis:

- **Workshop A (solution validation)**
  In this workshop, the project implementation team ensures that the changes to SAP Best Practices are real requirements or are affecting more than one business value. The output of workshop A is in the form of delta requirements and gaps. The business team will prioritize the requirements to facilitate the right sequence of implemented features. In addition, based on numerous factors, they may remove some of the requirements as well. However, the team must be careful of "must have" requirements that should not be removed, as shown in Figure 1.17.

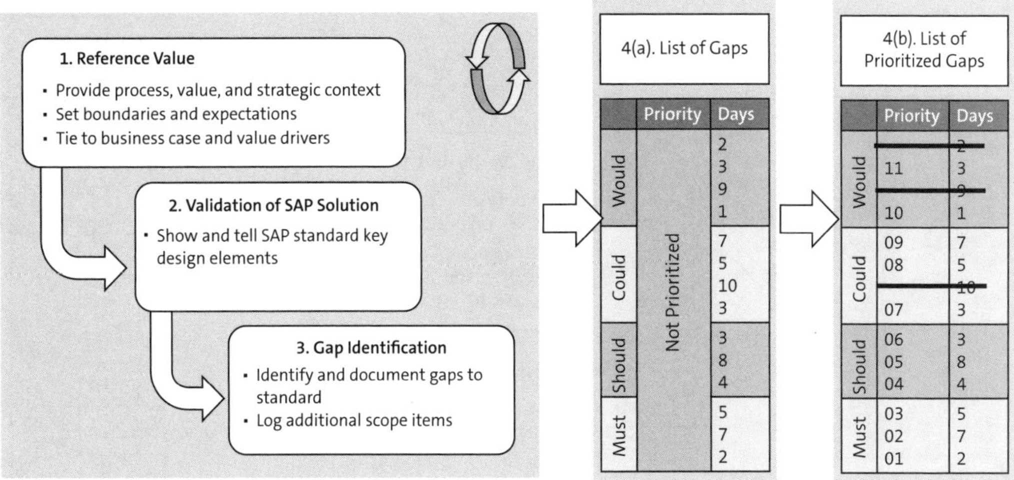

Figure 1.17 Workshop A: Solution Validation

Note

For premium engagement projects, SAP Innovation Control Center enables the project team to validate integration projects and prepare for smooth operations, enabling agile and continuous deployment of changes to the customer system. Project teams can submit gaps to SAP Mission Control Center for validation using Transaction SMFG. Figure 1.20, later in this section, shows the premium engagement model.

- **Workshop B (delta design)**
  The list of prioritized gaps will feed into workshop B. Based on the delta requirements and the priority, the project team will update the reference system, including real business data and scenarios to visualize it correctly. It will help the team understand the far-reaching effect of the change, if any. The project team will invite the client's SMEs and other stakeholders for the verification of the build and drive acceptance, as shown Figure 1.18.

Note

Fit-to-standard and fit-gap analysis are very similar processes with subtle changes. Fit-to-standard is for the cloud implementations, and fit-gap analysis is for the on-premise implementations.

Figure 1.19 summarizes the fit-gap analysis, the input required at each step, and the output produced, namely the product backlog, which is an input to the realize phase of the project.

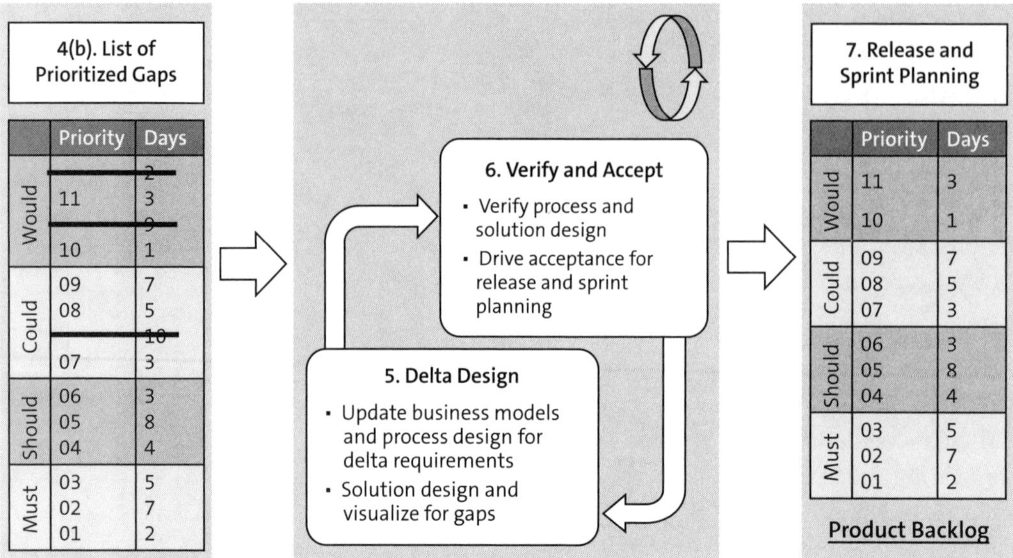

Figure 1.18 Workshop B: Delta Design

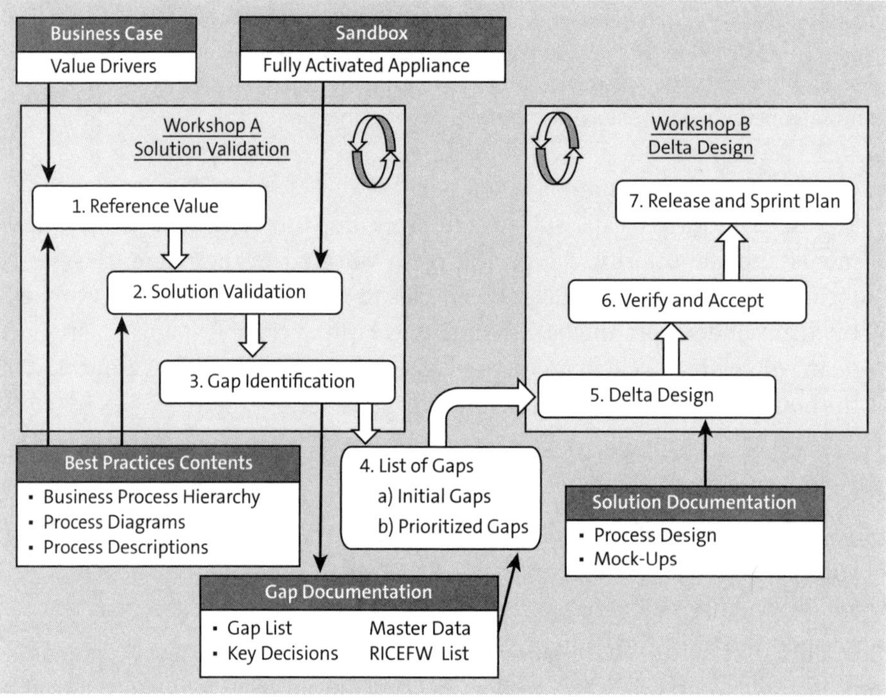

Figure 1.19 Summary of Fit-Gap Analysis

Premium Engagement Ready

SAP provides two types of premium engagement models:

- **SAP MaxAttention**
  This premium-level engagement provides professional services to help deliver the expected outcome.
- **SAP ActiveAttention**
  This premium-level engagement with SAP helps customers safeguard their landscape, implementation, and operation.

Both premium engagement models ensure that the client gets all the necessary support and attention, ensuring 100% service delivery and business continuity. Figure 1.20 shows the different engagement types at the various core phases of the SAP Activate methodology. Each phase is well connected via SAP support to keep innovating and at the same time making sure that operations aren't affected. Premium engagement ensures that we build SAP like a factory and run SAP like a factory.

SAP Innovation Control Center supports the "*build* SAP like a factory" directive. SAP Innovation Control Center, a huge repository of prototypes, new business models, and processes, supports the new business and co-innovations within the budget. It also supports building the prototypes and pilots with the line of business (LoB). The prime focus of SAP Innovation Control Center is to drive the innovations and provide support to customers during implementations. SAP Innovation Control Center includes the following advantages:

- Accelerated time-to-value
- Reduced implementation cost
- Smooth transition to operations
- Co-innovation
- Support for new business models
- Ability to build prototypes
- Assistance in adopting industry best practices

SAP Operations Control Center, on the other hand, supports the "*run* SAP like a factory" directive. It focuses on streamlining and optimizing the operations, both business and system, and running the solutions at their peak performance level. It facilitates the user efficiency, simplifies the system landscape, and ensures the connected and integrated enterprise. SAP Operations Control Center includes the following advantages:

- Higher degree of automation
- Better business performance
- Enhanced business continuity
- Reduced operational cost
- Enhanced user efficiency

- Simplified system landscape
- Always-connected model

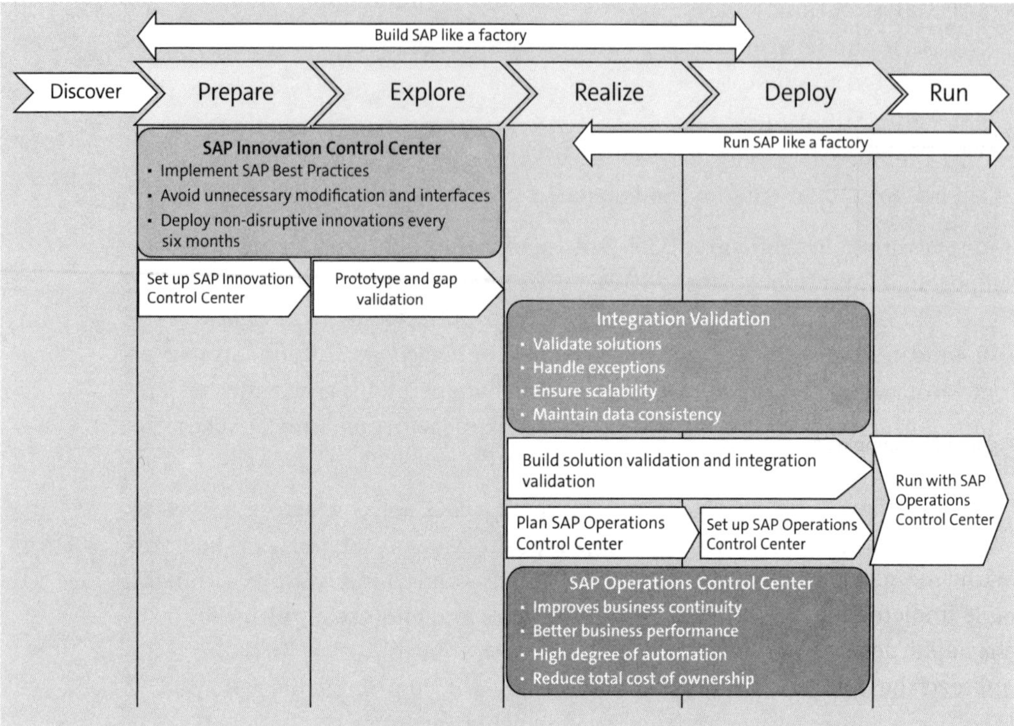

Figure 1.20 Premium Engagement Model

SAP Mission Control Center is the binding force between the SAP Development Center and SAP business units. It supports both SAP Innovation Control Center and SAP Operations Control Center by providing professionals with the right skillset, information to the customer or partner, and so on. SAP Mission Control Center includes the following advantages:

- Entire knowledge and experience of the SAP system
- Integration with SAP Development Center
- Ensured implementation for optimized operations
- Risk mitigation during the project
- Alignment with the value advisory center

Figure 1.21 displays an example of the activities performed by the various control centers during the four project phases. You may notice that the SAP Innovation Control Center services include gap validation and support for integration validation. They also support the project team in content usages such as for SAP Best Practices. SAP Operations Control Center, on the other hand, focuses on the operation setup, zero downtime for upgrades, and continuous improvement of business processes.

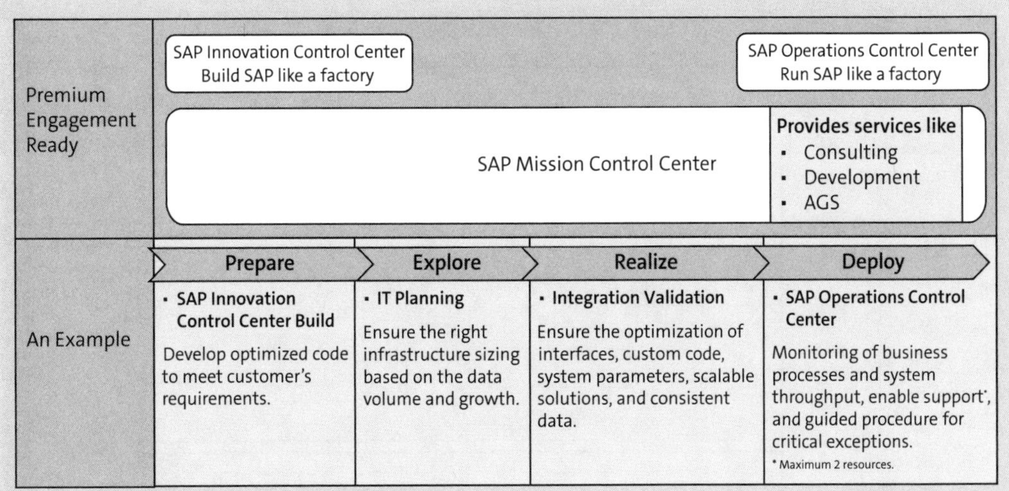

Figure 1.21 Example of Premium Engagement Ready

Modular, Scalable, and Agile

With SAP Activate, the projects are structured to deliver solutions directly. It's an agile implementation methodology that will help the customer adapt quickly to the rapid development cycle. To facilitate customer co-innovation, the whole approach has been modularized, with full support for initial deployment and continuous business innovation. The methodology is highly scalable and supports projects with vivid scope and varied complexity. Its flexible framework allows you to provide prescriptive guidance for any SAP project.

Figure 1.22 shows the agile-driven framework for the build, that is, the realize phase of the project. The upper portion of Figure 1.22 shows the four mandatory ceremonies of a sprint iteration while the lower portion shows the Scrum methodology to build the product of the project. We'll review the concept of agile and Scrum, their ceremonies, and the nuances of SAP Activate and Scrum in Chapter 3 and Chapter 4.

At a high level, the team will complete the release planning to decide upon the sprint details, and the product backlog is the input to the release planning. At the start of each sprint, the team completes the sprint planning that will start the build work. The development team builds the product and conducts daily Scrums to manage the progress. At the end of the sprint, the product owner accepts (or rejects) the product during the sprint review meeting. Finally, the team conducts the sprint retrospective meeting to understand and implement any improvement areas. Each sprint follows the same cycle. Based on many factors, the product owner may decide to release the product after sprint 4.

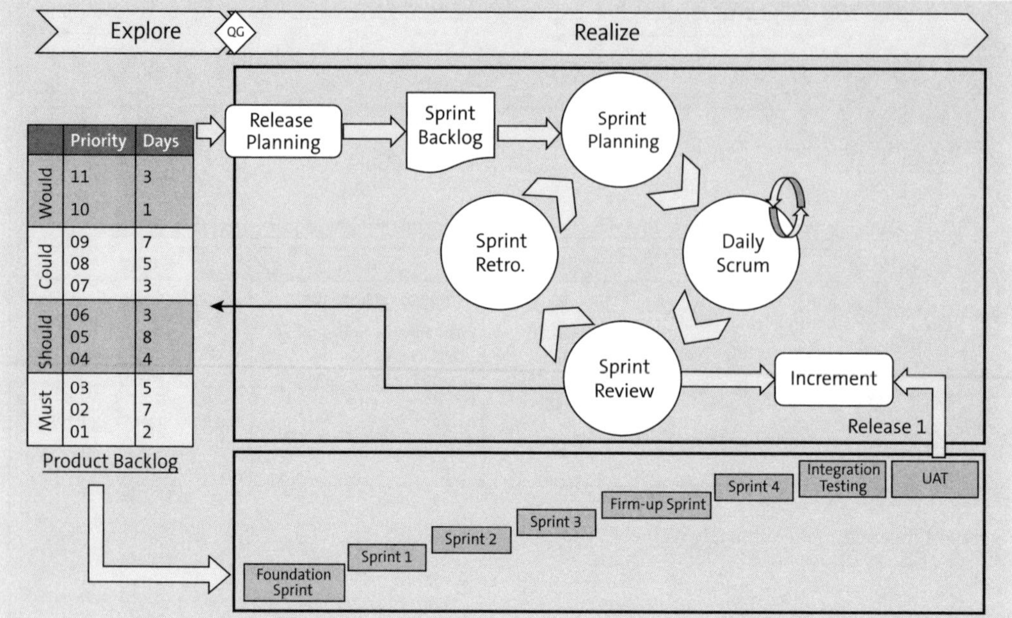

Figure 1.22 Scrum-Based Approach

Quality Built-In

You can identify risk early with the total quality approach provided by SAP Activate. Although ASAP and SAP Launch had concepts of quality gates, with SAP Activate, formal risk and quality management with a structured quality management plan and predefined quality gates are built into the project from the start. SAP recommends to follow these quality steps:

1. Before starting the SAP implementation project:
   - Explore and follow dos and don'ts as recommended by SAP.
   - Explore and understand SAP Quality Awards criteria and categories.
   - Add SAP Quality Awards participation to KPIs.
2. During the project:
   - Define the quality management plan along with the project management plan.
   - Define and rigorously follow quality gates.
   - Define quality gate exit criteria.
   - Embed the 10 SAP quality principles.
   - Prepare a quality checklist based on the template provided by SAP.
3. After the project implementation:
   - Participate in the SAP Quality Awards.

The 10 quality principles promoted by SAP to ensure successful implementation are as follows:

1. Anchor business value in the project.
2. Start scoping early.
3. Cooperate with stakeholders, and use a proper governance model.
4. Ensure timely delivery and effective tracking.
5. Staff the project with sufficient, competent, and motivated people.
6. Apply an appropriate methodology and plan for quality.
7. Identify and manage risks and issues throughout the project.
8. Exploit standard functionality and deliver best practices.
9. Achieve production readiness.
10. Use organizational change management (OCM) to transform your business.

Structure

Figure 1.23 shows the structure of the SAP Activate methodology, which has a total of six phases (including four project or core phases), eleven workstreams, and several tasks and deliverables. In this section, we'll look into the phases of the project, understand the workstreams, and identify the high-level tasks/activities that the project team will perform under each phase/workstream and the corresponding deliverables. SAP mandates the four quality gates after the prepare, explore, realize, and deploy phases.

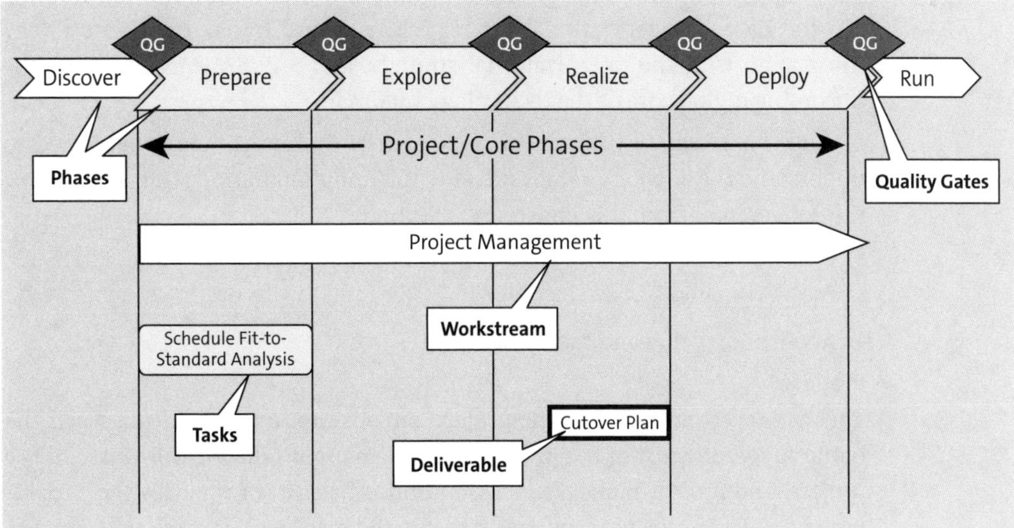

Figure 1.23 SAP Activate Structure

Phases

A *phase* of the project is a group of activities or tasks grouped together logically within a specific stage of the project. There are several activities that can and will expand into multiple phases. However, the project and the project team can't move forward to the next stage (i.e., phase) without completing and without getting approval during the mandatory quality gate checkpoint process—an important feature taken from the waterfall methodology.

There are four mandatory quality gates to move from the prepare, explore, realize, and deploy phases to the next phase. The SAP Activate methodology provides a template with a questionnaire that helps the team execute each quality gate. At the beginning of the phase, the team performs the readiness quality gate, which verifies that the team is well prepared to start the new phase. At the end of the phase, the team performs the acceptance quality gate, which verifies whether the team meets the acceptance criteria. It's recommended that the team combines the acceptance quality gate of the current phase with the readiness quality gate of the next phase. The acceptance quality gate in the deploy phase is the last quality gate, and is for the project closure.

Each phase of the project delivers a specific, predetermined value that helps in achieving the business objective of the project. Let's review the six phases of the SAP Activate methodology and understand the value (or deliverables) that it delivers:

- **Discover**
  This is the most strategic phase from the organizational change perspective whereby the executive team builds the digital transformation strategy leveraging the overall organizational strategy. The digital transformation strategy must align with the organizational strategy, and SAP S/4HANA may be the upcoming digital core of the technology roadmap.

  During this phase of the project, a cloud trial system can be provisioned to understand the business value and build the implementation strategy. Some of the deliverables from this phase are as follows:
  - Cloud trial
  - Discover assessment
  - Application value and assessment
- **Prepare**
  This is the second phase of the project, but it's the first project phase. As the name suggests, most of the project planning happens during this phase of the project. The project manager kicks off and officially commences the project. Based on the approved resource planning, the resources are assigned, and the starter system—initial technical environment—is provisioned (set up) during the prepare phase of the project. Some of the deliverables from this phase are as follows:

  - Project plan and its components, including the risk management plan, communication plan, scope management plan, project schedule and its management plan, budget management plan, quality management plan, and a few others
  - OCM roadmap
  - Fit-to-standard analysis preparation
  - End-user learning strategy
  - Phase closure and sign-off phase deliverables
- **Explore**
  The project team conducts the fit-gap (or fit-to-standard) analysis to ensure the alignment, understand the gaps (if any), and finalize an acceptable solution to bridge the gaps. This is the most complicated phase of the project where the team has to perform a fine balancing act. Some of the deliverables from this phase are as follows:
  - Project execution and monitoring
  - Fit-to-standard analysis
  - Customer execution of standard process
  - Solution definition
  - Product backlog
  - Phase closure and sign-off phase deliverables

Note

One of the key outputs of the explore phase is the product backlog, which we'll discuss further in Chapter 3. However, it's important to understand that the product backlog is a living document and will change continually during the realize phase of the project. It's *not* signed off to freeze the requirement, unlike in the ASAP methodology.

- **Realize**
  The project team uses the Scrum approach to build and test the business solution based on the product backlog that was built during the fit-gap (or fit-to-standard) analysis in the explore phase of the project. During this phase, the project team further plans the operation and cutover activities. They will also migrate the legacy data and carry out some additional planning work. Like any other phase, the project team must clear the quality gate to move to the next phase of the project. Some of the deliverables of the realize phase are as follows:
  - Project execution and monitoring
  - Solution build
  - Data migration
  - Operation planning
- **Deploy**
  This is the phase with the most apprehension when the go-live happens. The team sets up the production environment, completes the customer readiness

check, conducts the end-user training, and carries out the other production cutover activities. The team ensures the seamless go-live, carries out hypercare activities, documents the lessons learned, and transitions the project to the operations. Some of the deliverables of the deploy phase are as follows:

  - Project execution and monitoring
  - Go-live system

- **Run**
  In this final phase, the operation is carried out based on the operation strategy and planning, including other activities such as benefit realization, enhancements, bug fixes, and optimization. Some of the deliverables of the run phase are as follows:
  - Continuous improvements
  - Continuous consumption of innovations

Figure 1.24 shows the high-level activities carried out in each phase of the project.

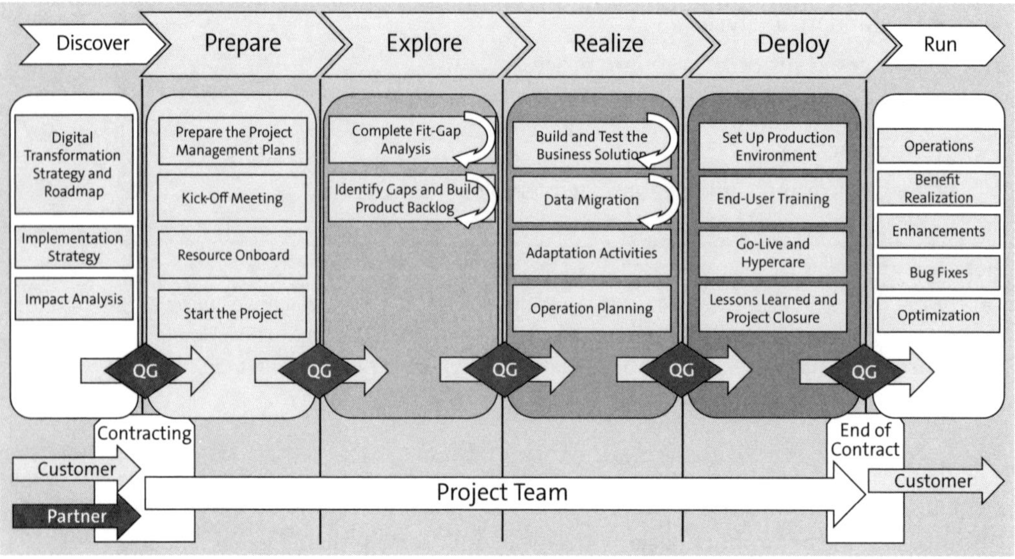

Figure 1.24 SAP Activate Phases and Corresponding Activities

Workstreams

Workstreams are collections of related deliverables that span the phases. They are attributes assigned to a deliverable and the related tasks. A deliverable must be a part of a workstream that is delivered at a predefined phase of the project. For example, fit-gap analysis is a part of the application design and configuration workstream, which should be delivered during the explore phase of the project. Table 1.3 shows the different workstreams and what they consist of.

Workstream	Description
Project management	Covers all aspects of the initiation, planning, executing, monitoring and controlling, and project closure
Application: Design and configuration*	Covers all aspects within the scope of work, starting from scope validation, fit-gap analysis (solution validation and delta design), configuration, unit testing (except custom development), and customer reviews at the end of each sprint
Application: Testing*	Covers all aspects of testing the solution, including test cases, test strategy, test planning, and different types of testing based on the need (e.g., regression testing, performance testing, penetration testing, user acceptance testing, etc.)
Application: Integration*	Covers all aspects of integration, including integration requirements, related documentation, approach, planning, and setting up the middleware between the solution and the third-party system
Application: Solution adoption*	Key workstream for user's adaptability of the solution across the organization and includes OCM, training management, and value management
Application: Customer team enablement*	Focuses on the project team and ensures the project team readiness to prepare the product backlog effectively
Analytics	Covers the analytics portion of the SAP S/4HANA implementation
Extensibility	Covers the design, development, testing, deployment, and integration of custom code
Data management	Covers all tasks/activities related to the data migration, such as discovery, planning, mapping, cleansing, and migration of the legacy data, as well as cutover planning/execution and hypercare support
Technical architecture and infrastructure	Covers the solution landscape, technical architectural requirements, organization policies, and conformance related to security and its setup, operations, standardization, and processes
Operations and support	Covers all aspects of transitioning the project to operation, including helpdesk processes, change management process, service-level agreement (SLA) management, incident management, problem management, and user-related operations and processes
*These workstreams are a set of application workstreams. They cover the core of the work done in building the complete business solution.	

Table 1.3 Workstreams and Their Descriptions

There are four workstream states: planning, preparation, execution, and operations preparation.

Deliverables, Tasks, and Artifacts

Here's a final note on a few key terms at work within the SAP Activate methodology:

- **Deliverables**
  A deliverable is an outcome that is delivered during the course of the project. Several deliverables are included within a workstream.
- **Tasks**
  A task is work to be performed. The outcome of a set of related tasks is a deliverable.
- **Artifacts**
  An artifact is the information or the document created during the process of implementation or conversion; examples are project plan, status report, internal estimation sheet, and so on. Figure 1.25 shows how an artifact is created by completing the deliverable or carrying out the given activity.

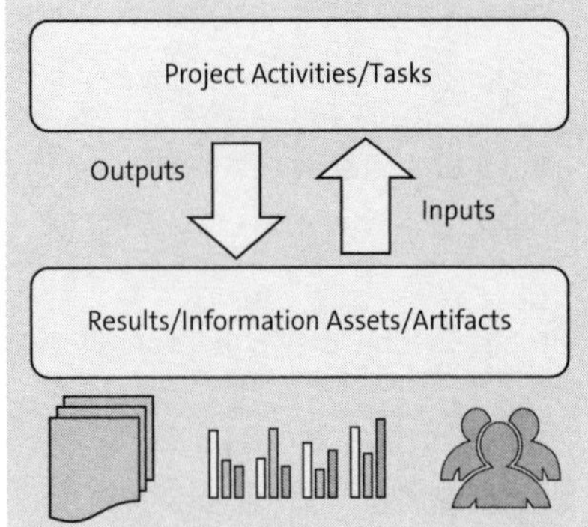

Figure 1.25 Artifacts

These key components can be summarized as shown in Figure 1.26.

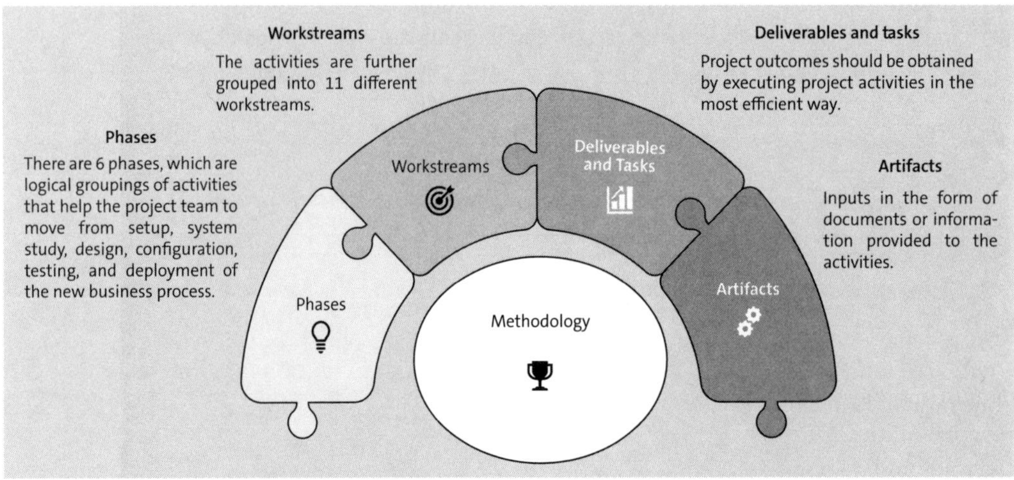

Figure 1.26 Summary of the Four Components

Governance, Roles, and Responsibilities

Many studies have found that stakeholder-oriented governance of projects correlates positively with project success. SAP S/4HANA's SAP Activate framework defines the roles and responsibilities of key stakeholders as a guideline to ensure that project oversight is maintained and the objective of the project is met within the defined metrics and KPIs. In this section, we'll look into an example governance model.

The project governance will do the following:

- Provide project oversight.
- Outline the stakeholder's relationships.
- Manage communication between the stakeholders.
- Equip the team with efficient and effective tools.
- Protect from organizational politics and provide the right direction.

Figure 1.27 shows two governance models for an on-premise implementation project of similar size and scope. In the top half of Figure 1.27, the project management office (PMO) is matured, while in the bottom half of Figure 1.27, the PMO is of a supporting type. In an organization with a matured PMO, the PMO owns the projects and makes all necessary decisions in consultation with the executive board. In addition, at times, the responsibilities among the PMO, steering committee, and executive board overlap.

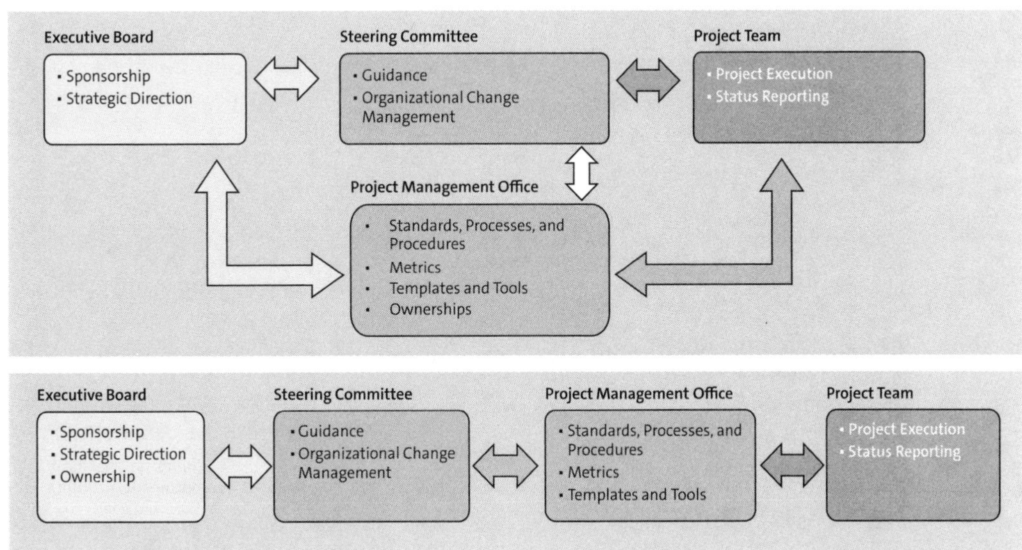

Figure 1.27 Governance Model

One of the key aspects of any governance model is to establish clear roles and responsibilities for the project team and its members. We'll take a closer look at the roles and responsibilities in Chapter 3.

SAP Activate versus ASAP

ASAP and SAP Launch are the predecessors of the SAP Activate methodology for on-premise and cloud deployments, respectively. Let's review the salient improvements of SAP Activate:

- Flavor of agile/Scrum delivery
- Supported by rich, ready-to-use, and ready-to-deploy SAP Best Practices
- Supported by a long list of accelerators, process maps, many assets, and guided configurations
- Fit-gap analysis with the explore phase replacing the blueprinting phase
- Reduced project lifecycle with only four core phases
- Combines ASAP with SAP Launch into one methodology
- 10 or less key deliverables for each phase

Table 1.4 shows the different variants of SAP implementation methodologies.

Variant	Old Methodology	New Methodology
New Implementations		
▪ SAP S/4HANA (on-premise) ▪ SAP Business Suite (SAP ERP, SAP Customer Relationship Management [SAP CRM], SAP Supplier Relationship Management [SAP SRM], etc.)	ASAP	SAP Activate methodology for on-premise edition
▪ SAP S/4HANA Cloud – enterprise, marketing, project services ▪ SAP SuccessFactors, SAP Sales Cloud/SAP Service Cloud, and SAP Ariba	SAP Launch	SAP Activate methodology for cloud edition
System Conversions		
▪ SAP S/4HANA (on-premise)	N/A	SAP Activate methodology for system conversion
Selective Data Transitions (Landscape Transformations)		
▪ SAP S/4HANA ▪ SAP S/4HANA Cloud – enterprise, marketing, project services	N/A	SAP Activate methodology for selective data transition

Table 1.4 SAP Activate Variants

Important Terminology

For this exam objective, you're expected to understand the following terms:

- **Fit-gap analysis**
  This analysis is performed to understand the fit of SAP Best Practices with the client's requirements for SAP S/4HANA implementations, find the gaps, finalize the delta design, and build the product backlog.
- **Fit-to-standard analysis**
  This variant of fit-gap analysis is performed to understand the fit of SAP Best Practices with the client's requirements for SAP S/4HANA Cloud.
- **Guided configuration**
  The second pillar of the SAP Activate methodology provides accelerators, tools, techniques, playbooks, and many other assets to help the project team bridge the gap between SAP Best Practices and the client's requirements.
- **One methodology**
  The SAP Activate methodology is applicable both for cloud deployments and on-premise implementations.
- **SAP Innovation** Control **Center**
  This support center facilitates customer and partner innovations to enhance time-to-value and avoid modifications post deployment.
- **SAP Mission** Control **Center**
  This support center provides consultation, custom development, and support throughout the project lifecycle.
- **SAP Operations** Control **Center**
  This support center focuses on the operation of the solution by enhancing the business value and reducing the total operational cost.
- **Workshop A (solution validation)**
  This is the first part of fit-gap analysis where the project team will work closely with the client's SME to validate the solution build using SAP Best Practices.
- **Workshop B (delta design)**
  This is the second part of the fit-gap analysis where the project team and the client discuss and finalize the design to bridge the gaps identified in workshop A.

 Practice Questions

These practice questions will help you evaluate your understanding of the topics covered in this chapter. The questions shown are similar in nature to those found on the certification examination. Although none of these questions will be found on the exam itself, they will allow you to review your knowledge of the subject. Select the correct answers, and then check the completeness of your answers in the "Practice Question Answers and Explanations" section. Remember that on the exam, you must select all correct answers and only correct answers to receive credit for the question.

1. What are the phases and correct order of the SAP Activate methodology?

- ☐ **A.** Prepare, explore, realize, deploy, run
- ☐ **B.** Prepare, explore, realize, deploy
- ☐ **C.** Discover, prepare, explore, realize, deploy, run
- ☐ **D.** Prepare, explore, realize, deploy

2. Which of the following are pillars of the SAP Activate methodology? (There are two correct answers.)

- ☐ **A.** SAP Best Practices
- ☐ **B.** Supervisory configuration
- ☐ **C.** Global methodology
- ☐ **D.** Self-service configuration
- ☐ **E.** One methodology
- ☐ **F.** IT best practices

3. You're a seasoned project manager and have sound knowledge of the SAP Activate methodology. Your organization just hired an exceptional FICO resource who wants to transition into SAP project management. Although this resource has full support from your supervisor, at times, they annoy you by asking questions when you're in the middle of some critical work. You're meeting with a client project manager to explain the cloud trial deployment. The FICO resource, in front of the client project manager, asked you to explain the resource assignment. How would you handle the situation?

- ☐ **A.** You explain to them that the two of you can talk later in the evening.
- ☐ **B.** You ignore them.
- ☐ **C.** You explain that you can assign the resources in the current phase because the contract is already signed.
- ☐ **D.** You explain that currently you're in the discover phase and can assign resources only in the prepare phase.
- ☐ **E.** You explain that you've completed the prepare phase and all the resources are already assigned.

4. What are the two reasons to use the SAP Activate methodology as compared to the ASAP methodology for on-premise implementations? (There are two correct answers.)

- ☐ **A.** The ASAP methodology is no longer available to use.
- ☐ **B.** The SAP Activate methodology will jump-start the project by providing SAP Best Practices.

☐ **C.** The SAP Activate methodology is cloud ready and will provide ready-to-run and ready-to-deploy best practices.

☐ **D.** SAP Launch should be used for the on-premise deployment; the ASAP methodology is used only for SAP ERP 6.0 deployments.

5. Validate solution is one of the key characteristics of the SAP Activate framework. Which statements are correct? (There are two correct answers.)

☐ **A.** The project is using the SAP Launch methodology.

☐ **B.** The project is in the explore phase.

☐ **C.** The project team will use fit-gap analysis as a part of solution validation.

☐ **D.** The project is in the prepare phase.

☐ **E.** The project team has completed the fit-gap analysis, and the solution is validated by the client.

6. Match Column A (Taxonomy) with Column B (Example) in Table 1.5.

Column A (Taxonomy)	Column B (Example)
Deliverable	Run
Phase	Cutover plan
Task	Analytics
Workstream	Schedule delta design session

Table 1.5 Question 6

7. Which of the following are correct about SAP Activate phases? (There are two correct answers.)

☐ **A.** Project management is an example of an SAP Activate workstream.

☐ **B.** A phase can have multiple workstream attributes.

☐ **C.** The project team must clear the quality gates to move to the next phase of the project.

☐ **D.** A deliverable can span multiple phases.

☐ **E.** Run isn't an example of an SAP Activate phase.

8. Your old friend and longtime colleague is new to the SAP Activate methodology, although he has sound project management expertise. He is confident that managing an SAP project using SAP Activate would be easy and doesn't require any training or learning exercises. You understand the challenge and wanted to tell him the importance of learning and how different SAP Activate is from ASAP and SAP Launch. If you ask your friend to identify the correct

statement about the workstreams, which two options will he pick to demonstrate sound SAP Activate knowledge? (There are two correct answers.)

☐ **A.** Workstream is an attribute assigned to the deliverables and tasks.

☐ **B.** There are five types of application-specific workstreams.

☐ **C.** Each workstream will deliver exactly one deliverable.

☐ **D.** Each workstream is applicable to all the project phases.

☐ **E.** The project management workstream isn't applicable during the run phase of the project.

9. Which of the following is delivered as SAP Best Practices within the SAP Activate framework?

☐ **A.** Only the core processes

☐ **B.** Core process and some migration processes

☐ **C.** Core, migration, and integration processes

☐ **D.** Accelerators, SSCUI, expert configuration

☐ **E.** None of the above

10. A pizza delivery company has 100+ franchise and owned business locations across the continental United States. Last year, the company incurred huge losses because their billing and interactive voice recognition systems (IVRS) failed. They were unable to receive any orders online or by phone for three days, which also affected their brand reputation adversely. Although they were able to receive in-person orders, the reconciliation of inventory and accounts receivables was a nightmare. They are still recovering from the losses and have a limited budget. Furthermore, they want to complete the implementation before the start of the holiday season, which will be in four months. Which of the following landscapes will you choose based on these requirements?

☐ **A.** SAP S/4HANA Cloud seems to be a good fit because of their extensive and disbursed locations across the continental United States.

☐ **B.** SAP S/4HANA Cloud doesn't seem to be a good fit because of their extensive and disbursed locations across the continental United States. They should go with an on-premise SAP S/4HANA deployment instead.

☐ **C.** Assuming they will agree to SAP Best Practices, the SAP S/4HANA Cloud option is best because it not only caters to their outage issue but also addresses their low budget and tight implementation timeline.

☐ **D.** Assuming they will agree to SAP Best Practices, the on-premise SAP S/4HANA option is best because it not only caters to their outage issue but also addresses their low budget and tight implementation timeline.

☐ **E.** None of the above.

11. You're a seasoned project manager for SAP S/4HANA Cloud. One of the interns asked you about the possibility of using the SAP S/4HANA Cloud version. Which of the following options is correct?

☐ **A.** You use the SAP Activate methodology for the SAP S/4HANA Cloud deployment also. It's the same as that of SAP Launch.

☐ **B.** You can't use system conversion to move the current SAP ERP 6.0 setup to SAP S/4HANA Cloud because of numerous customizations.

☐ **C.** You suggest that the SAP Activate methodology for the on-premise version is much more robust yet flexible to accommodate a client's requirements as compared to the SAP Activate methodology for the cloud deployments.

☐ **D.** You appreciate the SAP vision to launch the SAP Activate methodology, which will resolve all the issues related to the ASAP 8.0 methodology.

☐ **E.** None of the above.

12. Which of the following are correct about fit-gap analysis? (There are three correct answers.)

☐ **A.** Fit-gap analysis requires good preparation, strong functional knowledge, and sound understanding of SAP Best Practices.

☐ **B.** There is no need to include a client's SME as you must have someone within the implementation team who has sound business knowledge about the scope items.

☐ **C.** Appropriately performed fit-gap analysis will reduce the probability of rework during the realize phase of the project.

☐ **D.** Fit-gap analyses are generally performed during the explore phase of the project. However, in extraordinary scenarios, you can also perform fit-gap analysis during the start of the realize phase.

☐ **E.** Fit-gap analysis is an iterative process to understand the gaps and build the delta design that is best suited for the client's business needs.

13. Which of the following is incorrect about a deliverable?

☐ **A.** A deliverable is a result of coordinated tasks.

☐ **B.** Work for a deliverable can start in one phase and complete in the next phase.

☐ **C.** Work for a deliverable can start in one workstream and complete in another workstream.

☐ **D.** Both A and B.

☐ **E.** None of the above.

14. Which activity are you performing based on the following scenario?
    You just completed a marathon meeting with a client that was attended by several participants from both sides. However, Roger, who is the SME for the procure-to-pay process, was unable to attend due to personal reasons. The client project manager insisted on continuing with the meeting and suggested that he has some preliminary knowledge of the procure-to-pay process, but he is also doubling as the budgeting specialist. The group must complete the analysis of at least one process today.

☐ **A.** You're performing fit-gap analysis for the procure-to-pay process.

☐ **B.** You're performing fit-gap analysis for the budgeting process.

☐ **C.** The meeting was originally scheduled to complete the fit-gap analysis for the budgeting process, and the team continued with the process.

☐ **D.** The meeting was originally scheduled to complete the fit-gap analysis for the budgeting process, but the team decided to complete the fit-gap analysis for the procure-to-pay process.

☐ **E.** It was a general status update meeting.

15. What is wrong with the following defined setup?
    You work as a project manager for an SAP S/4HANA Cloud implementation for a retail outlet. The contract is already signed, and all the preparation work is completed. You've submitted all planning documents to the client, which they agreed upon. The gaps between SAP Best Practices and the client's requirements are identified. You have your functional specialists working closely with the client's SME of the related processes to build the delta design. The client is very appreciative of the work performed by the team, but you could feel the tension in the air when you met with the steering committee yesterday.

☐ **A.** There is no cloud option for the SAP S/4HANA retail industry solution.

☐ **B.** There is no need for a dedicated project manager for such a small project.

☐ **C.** The client must return the duly signed and formally accepted planning documents.

☐ **D.** For the cloud deployments, the team should not complete delta design.

16. Match Column A (Key Characteristics) with Column B (Attributes) in Table 1.6.

Column A (Key Characteristics)	Column B (Attributes)
Start with the best practices	May carry delta design workshops
Cloud ready	Modular, scalable, and agile
Validate solution	May increase the implementation costs

Table 1.6 Question 16

Column A (Key Characteristics)	Column B (Attributes)
Premium engagement ready	Provides rich and ready-to-run business processes
Modular, scalable, and agile	Quality built-in
Quality built-in	For the on-premise version also, helps the project team set up a sandbox environment

Table 1.6 Question 16 (Cont.)

17. Which of the following statements is correct about workstreams?

☐ **A.** There is no workstream to set up operations.

☐ **B.** There is no workstream for knowledge transition to the client's team.

☐ **C.** The analytics workstream will give you the project analytics and is useful for project reporting.

☐ **D.** The organizational change management (OCM) and the end-user training–related workstream is active throughout the core phases of the SAP Activate methodology.

☐ **E.** The integration workstream will integrate the cloud-based functionalities with the on-premise version for the selective data transition project.

18. Which of the following is true about SAP S/4HANA guided configuration?

☐ **A.** It's an equivalent of IMG for the SAP Activate methodology.

☐ **B.** The project team can complete the solution configuration.

☐ **C.** This help tool is available for functional consultants and can be downloaded from the SAP website after procuring the SAP S/4HANA licenses.

☐ **D.** A and C.

☐ **E.** B and C.

☐ **F.** None of the above.

19. When will you execute the cutover plan? (There are two correct answers.)

☐ **A.** In the deploy phase of SAP Activate for the cloud deployment

☐ **B.** In the go-live phase of SAP Activate for the cloud deployment

☐ **C.** As a part of the system and data migration workstream

☐ **D.** As a part of the technical architecture and infrastructure workstream

☐ **E.** After proper discussion with the client and their approval toward the end of the realize phase of the project

☐ **F.** None of the above

20. What is the purpose of SAP Model Company delivered with the SAP Activate methodology?

☐ **A.** It's an alternative approach to data migration.

☐ **B.** It helps the project team complete the project documentation.

☐ **C.** It's a preconfigured, ready-to-use, end-to-end solution for a specific industry or line of business (LoB).

☐ **D.** None of the above.

Practice Question Answers and Explanations

1. Correct answer: **C**

   There are six phases of SAP Activate methodology: discover, prepare, explore, realize, deploy, and run. Out of these, four phases are the core (or project) phase: prepare, explore, realize, and deploy. Most of the sales activity happens during the discover phase, and support activities are carried out during the run phase of the project.

2. Correct answers: **A, E**

   The three pillars of SAP Activate methodology are SAP Best Practices, guided configuration, and one methodology. Self-service configuration is a part of guided configuration, and there is nothing named supervisory configuration or global methodology.

3. Correct answer: **D**

   This lengthy question is loaded with so much information to distract the candidate. What it's simply asking is the phase in which the resource assignment will happen. The resources are assigned during the prepare phase of the project. In addition, because you're working with the client's project manager on a cloud trial deployment means you're in the discover phase of the project.

4. Correct answers: **B, C**

   Option A is misleading. The ASAP methodology is still available, but it's not being updated anymore, whereas option D is wrong. SAP Launch was for the cloud deployment and ASAP was for the on-premise installations. SAP Activate provides the ready-to-start and ready-to-deploy best practices that jump-start the project.

5. Correct answers: **B, C**

   The question is asking you to choose the correct answer in context with "validate solution", which is one of six key characteristics. If you're validating the solution with the client, it means you're using fit-gap analysis, and the project is in the explore phase.

6. Correct answers: See Table 1.7.

Column A (Taxonomy)	Column B (Example)	Explanation
Deliverable	Cutover plan	The cutover plan deliverable is completed during the realize phase and executed during the deploy phase of the project.
Phase	Run	The six phases of SAP Activate are discover, prepare, explore, realize, deploy, and run.
Task	Schedule delta design session	As a part of fit-gap analysis, the project team completes the delta design workshop, also known as workshop B.
Workstream	Analytics	Analytics is a workstream specific for SAP S/4HANA analytics.

Table 1.7 Answers for Question 6

7. Correct answers: **B, C**
   The question is asking specifically about SAP Activate phases and not workstreams. Although project management is one of the eleven workstreams of SAP Activate, option A, though correct, isn't the right choice for the given question. Option B is correct because a phase can have activities related to multiple workstreams, for example, during the realize phase, the workstreams may include activities related to project management, technical architecture and infrastructure, data migration, and more. Option C states that the project team must clear the quality gates to move to the next phase of the project, referring to a methodology with quality built-in, which is the sixth characteristics of SAP Activate. Options D and E are incorrect.
8. Correct answers: **A, B**
   Option A is correct because a workstream is defined as an attribute to deliverables and tasks. Options C and D are incorrect as there can be multiple deliverables in a workstream, and not all workstreams can span all the phases of the project, for example, operations and support starts during the explore phase of the project. Option E is also wrong. While option B is correct, the five application-specific workstreams are application design and configuration, testing, integration, solution adoption, and customer team enablement.
9. Correct answer: **C**
   SAP Best Practices delivers the rich and ready-to-deploy processes for the core processes, along with migration and integration processes. Accelerators, self-service configuration, expert configuration, and so on are the part of guided configuration.

10. Correct answer: **C**

    On-premise isn't the right option because of the budget and timeline constraints. Although option A correctly chooses the SAP S/4HANA Cloud deployment, the stated reason is incorrect. Option C is the correct choice with proper assumption related to SAP Best Practices.

11. Correct answer: **B**

    This question gives you limited information about the SAP S/4HANA Cloud deployment, so you have to pay close attention to each of the options. Option A is incorrect because SAP Activate is different from SAP Launch. Option C is also incorrect because SAP Activate is one methodology for both the cloud and on-premise deployments. However, option D is twisted by stating that SAP Activate will resolve all the issues related to ASAP methodology.

Tip

Look out for extreme words such as "all," "never," "forever," and so on, as these choices are often incorrect.

12. Correct answers: **A, C, E**

    Options B and D are incorrect because fit-gap analysis is only performed during the explore phase of the project in the presence of the client's SME whose absence will never allow you to fulfill the objective of the fit-gap analysis.

13. Correct answer: **C**

    A deliverable is produced only by a set of coordinated tasks that can span multiple phases. One such example is the project plan, which will start in the discover phase and complete in the prepare phase of the project. However, there are no deliverables in SAP Activate that will start in one workstream and complete in another workstream. The project team may create a deliverable in one workstream, such as the cutover plan in the project management workstream, while its execution will be done in another workstream, which is data management.

14. Correct answer: **B**

    This scenario can be from any meeting, but all the options except option E talk about the fit-gap analysis. This isn't a regular status meeting because the client project manager stresses the need to complete at least one process.

    From the fit-gap perspective, the process SME from the client side must be present during the workshop. Roger, who is the procure-to-pay specialist from the client side, is absent, so the team can't complete the fit-gap analysis for the procure-to-pay process. However, the client project manager, who is also the budgeting specialist, is available, so the team can complete the fit-gap analysis for the budgeting process.

15. Correct answer: **D**

    Look for the keywords in the questions. The planning document is already completed, and they have accepted it, meaning the project has moved from the prepare phase to the explore phase. Options A and B are incorrect statements in general while option C is wrong in this context. Option E is unethical and hence not the correct choice. In a cloud deployment, workshop A is conducted to identify the gaps, but no delta design is conducted.

16. Correct answer: See Table 1.8.

Column A (Key Characteristics)	Column B (Attributes)	Explanation
Start with the best practices	Provides rich and ready-to-run business processes	SAP Best Practices provides rich and ready-to-run business processes.
Cloud ready	For the on-premise version also, helps the project team set up a sandbox environment	Cloud ready is applicable for the on-premise installation as well.
Validate solution	May carry delta design workshops	It's a fit-gap analysis.
Premium engagement ready	May increase the implementation costs	SAP charges extra for these services and hence increased cost.
Modular, scalable, and agile	Modular, scalable, and agile	One methodology is used.
Quality built-in	Quality built-in	Quality is built-in.

Table 1.8 Answers for Question 16

17. Correct answer: **D**
    Operations and support is the workstream to set up operation, and knowledge transition is carried out during the customer team enablement workstream. The analytics workstream is for SAP S/4HANA analytics, and the integration workstream is for third-party application integration. The OCM and end-user training are part of solution adoption, which is carried throughout the SAP Activate core phases.

18. Correct answer: **B**
    Options A and C are wrong. Guided configuration is neither equivalent to the IMG nor is it a downloadable tool for functional consultants. It's s built-in feature of the SAP Activate methodology that helps the project team complete the solution configuration.

19. Correct answers: **A, C**
    There is no go-live phase in the SAP Activate methodology, so option B is incorrect. The cutover planning happens during the realize phase and the cutover plan is executed during the deploy phase. The cutover execution activities are part of the data management workstream.

20. Correct answer: **C**

    SAP Model Company for the specific industry or LoB in conjunction with SAP Best Practices jump-starts the project and also supports the project team in testing the solution. It's not an alternative approach to data migration nor does it help the team in completing the documentation.

Takeaway

This chapter introduced you to the latest project management methodology, presented by SAP originally in 2015 with regular updates since then (at the time of writing, the latest update was in October 2020 for the SAP S/4HANA and SAP S/4HANA Cloud deployments). We started with the three pillars—SAP Best Practices, guided configuration, and one methodology—of the SAP Activate methodology and discussed the importance of each.

You learned more about the methodology by looking into the six key characteristics— start with best practices; cloud-ready; validate solution; premium engagement ready; modular, scalable, and agile; and quality built-in—of the SAP Activate methodology. We looked at how best practices and being cloud ready complement each other to jump-start the project. We explored the validate solution concept by understanding the complete fit-gap analysis process and how the other three characteristics help the project team in fulfilling the client's business objective. We'll study the agile approach of SAP S/4HANA implementation project delivery in Chapter 3 and Chapter 4.

Finally, we studied the taxonomy of SAP Activate and understood the concept of project phases, workstreams, deliverables, and tasks. We reviewed the high-level governance model and the roles and responsibilities of the project team, which we'll look deeper into in Chapter 3. We closed this chapter by explaining the difference between the new SAP Activate methodology and its older peers: ASAP and SAP Launch.

Summary

From this chapter, you now understand the basics of the SAP Activate methodology and its principles. This is a foundation chapter in which you learned about SAP Activate's three pillars, key characteristics, and taxonomy. We dived deep into the fit-gap analysis and understood its usages across the multiple transition roadmaps.

In the next chapter, you'll build on the basic knowledge gained in this chapter and learn more about the three pillars, including accessing SAP Best Practices, tools for the project team, and the methodology itself.

Chapter 2
SAP Activate Elements

Techniques You'll Master

- Understand SAP Activate content
- Review the available SAP Activate tools
- Explain the SAP Activate methodology

In the previous chapter, we discussed the basics of the SAP Activate methodology. Now, let's move on to the three elements of SAP Activate: contents, tools, and methodology. First, we'll look into the four types of content that are available. Next, we'll cover the four tools: self-service configuration, expert configuration, SAP solution builder, and SAP Solution Manager. Finally, we'll study the four different components of the methodology.

Real-World Scenario

You're new to SAP. Although you have sound experience in portal development using Java technologies, you've always wanted to make your career in SAP as a FICO process consultant and utilize your education and prior experience in the subject area. You spoke with your friend, who is an SAP sales executive in an IT consulting organization, a number of times in the past but to no avail.

Last night, she told you about a big deal that she got from a New York-based global bank to implement SAP S/4HANA. She was excited, and, knowing your interest, your knowledge on banking processes, your educational background as a certified public accountant, and your current enrollment as an MBA student in an elite business school, she promised to speak with HR and the project manager on your behalf.

A few days later, she called and confirmed that the team is ready to interview you. She provided some background of the project without divulging material and confidential information about the project or client. She stressed, however, that prior knowledge of SAP isn't required as the team is looking for subject matter experts (SMEs) with banking knowledge, although some basic understanding of the SAP Activate methodology will help you score some additional brownie points.

A quick Google search for SAP Activate methodology left you with a lot of information, but more questions than answers. More importantly, you're uncertain of where to start your learning journey for SAP Activate. A strong foundation in the basic elements is needed to leave a good impression!

Objectives of This Portion of the Test

The certification examination will test your knowledge about the following topics:

- Content element of SAP Activate, including business processes, project libraries, migration content, and integration content
- Tool element of SAP Activate, including self-service configuration, expert configuration, the SAP solution builder tool, and SAP Solution Manager

- Methodology element of SAP Activate, including phases, workstreams, deliverables, and artifacts

In the subsequent sections, you'll learn and understand these key concepts followed by some questions and answers.

Note

This chapter on the elements of SAP Activate is important in your overall understanding of the methodology. This topic carries 8–12% weightage in the certification examination, meaning you'll get anywhere from 6 to 10 questions from the topics in this chapter.

Key Concepts Refresher

This section will help you understand the content, tools, and methodology elements of the SAP Activate methodology and will advance your knowledge on how these elements make the SAP Activate methodology a robust framework to implement SAP S/4HANA. These concepts are critical for you to pass the exam.

Contents

The following four components of the content element of the SAP Activate methodology are shown in Figure 2.1:

- Business process content
- Project library
- Migration content
- Integration content

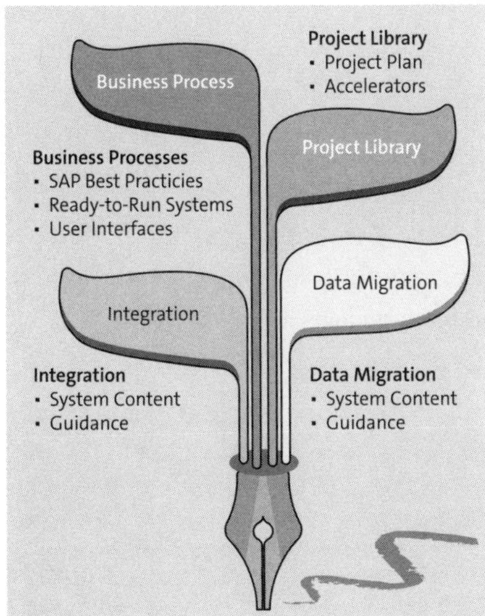

Figure 2.1 Contents

We'll discuss each component in the following sections.

Business Process Content

A business process is a set of specific tasks or activities performed in a given order that provides the desired outcome. Let's take an example of the legal control (1W8) process for SAP S/4HANA Cloud that supports global trade compliance with checks of relevant documents for adherence to the defined trade regulations. Figure 2.2 shows the business process flow of how the software works as standard for legal control (1W8).

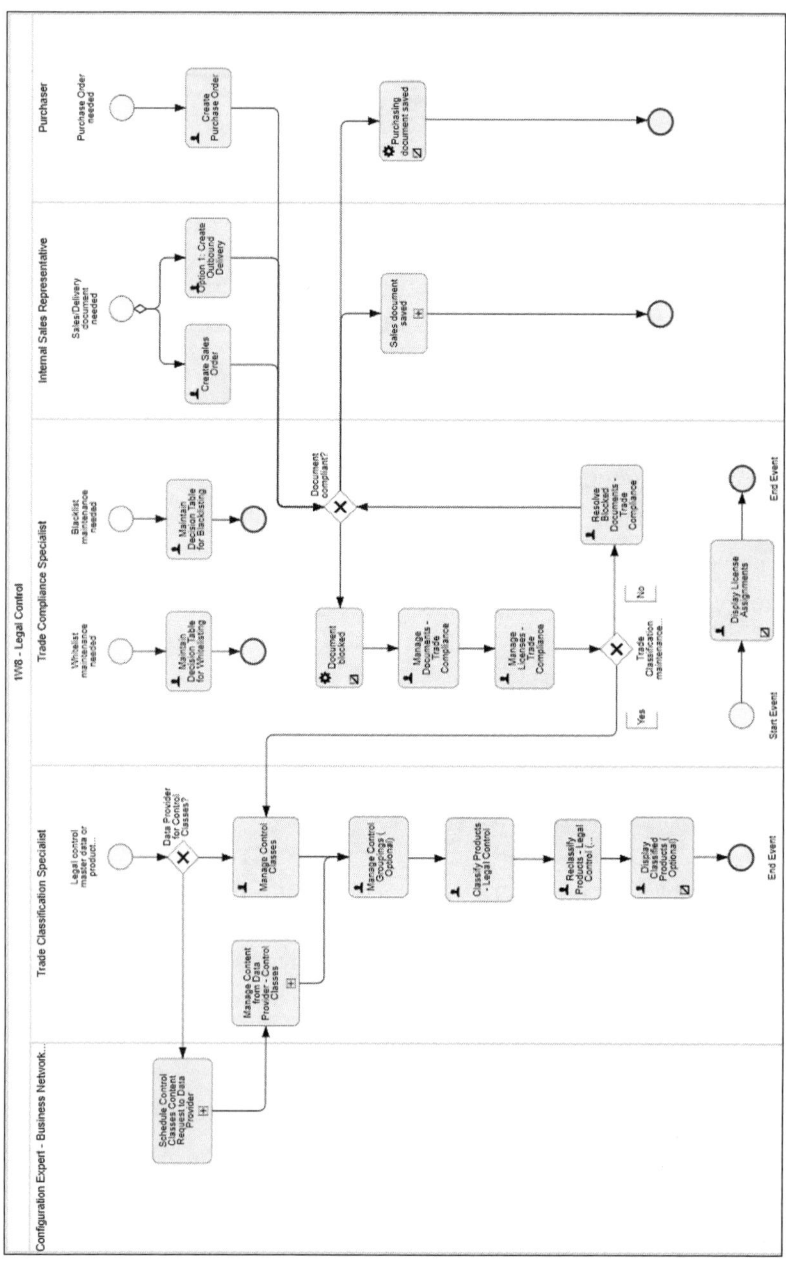

Figure 2.2 Business Process Flow Example

The three components of the business process are shown in Figure 2.3 and will be covered in the following sections.

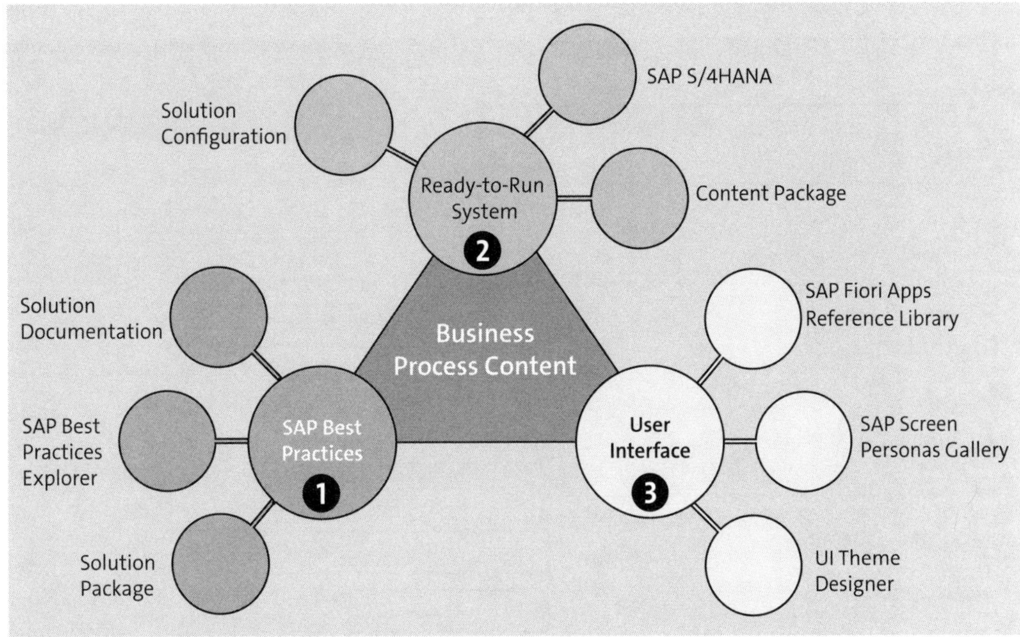

Figure 2.3 Business Process Content: The Three Components

SAP Best Practices

SAP Best Practices provides the solution documentation, as shown in Figure 2.4. It shows the SAP Best Practices Explorer view that provides the solution documentation, including process flows, setup instructions, test scripts, and other accelerators for a given process, in the legal control example.

SAP Best Practices should be the starting point for any SAP implementations, irrespective of the platform; it supports the implementation team by providing well-structured content, and is recommended by SAP to document your solution and business processes. In Chapter 1, we discussed how to access the best practices and touched upon the three sections of the best practices. Let's consider how these sections can help you in your implementations. Apart from the general information, you'll find the following content in the library after you use your S-user ID to log in:

- **Description**
  Describes the scope items (predefined processes) at the top of the screen.
- **Business Benefits**
  Explains the benefits to implement the scope item.
- **Key Process Flows**
  Lists the key process flows within the scope item.

- **Details**
  Includes a lot of information, such as process flows, configuration instructions, test scripts, and so on.

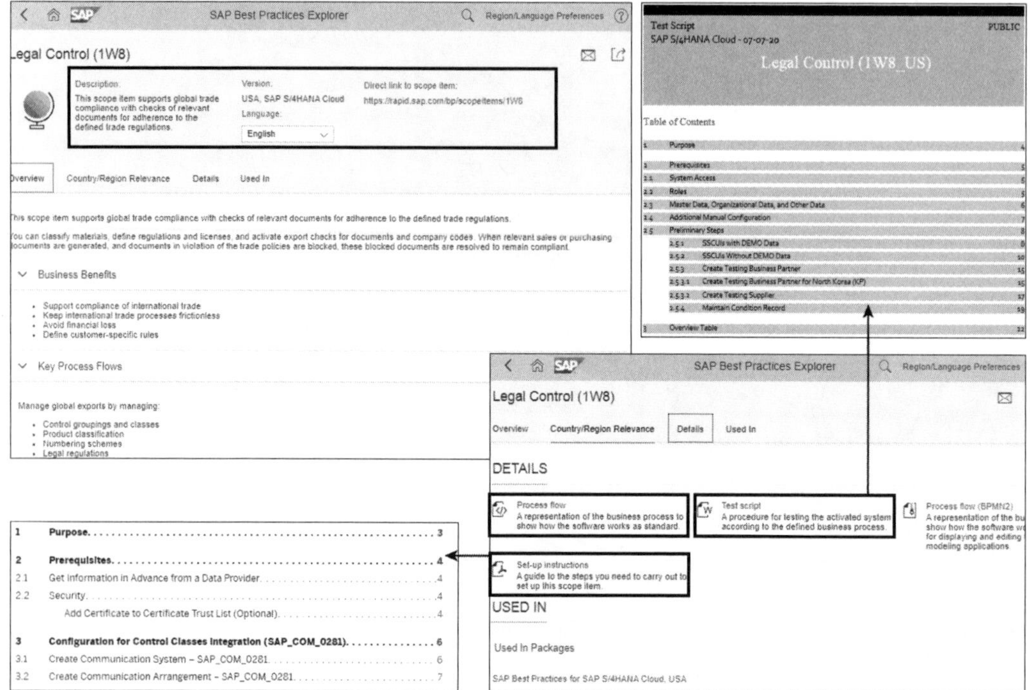

Figure 2.4 Business Process: Solution Documentation (Legal Control)

The configuration guide and test scripts are also shown via the arrows in Figure 2.4. Figure 2.2, shown previously, illustrates the corresponding flow in the Business Process Model and Notation (BPMN) format.

Note

BPMN is the de facto way to specify business processes. For more information, refer to *www.bpmn.org*.

Figure 2.5 shows some basic but powerful controls:

❶ You can download the best practice from the SAP Software Download Center.

❷ You can save the best practice as your favorite.

❸ You can add the best practice to SAP Solution Manager 7.2 basket.

❹ You can add the package to the customized solution.

❺ You can report an issue with the best practice by sending your feedback.

❻ You can share the content.

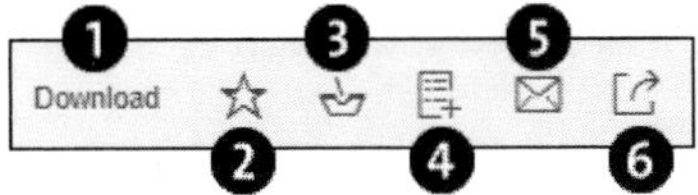

Figure 2.5 SAP Best Practices Controls

There are also accelerators available that will kick-start your project. Figure 2.6 shows a partial list of the accelerators that are available to you for SAP Best Practices for SAP S/4HANA Cloud (USA).

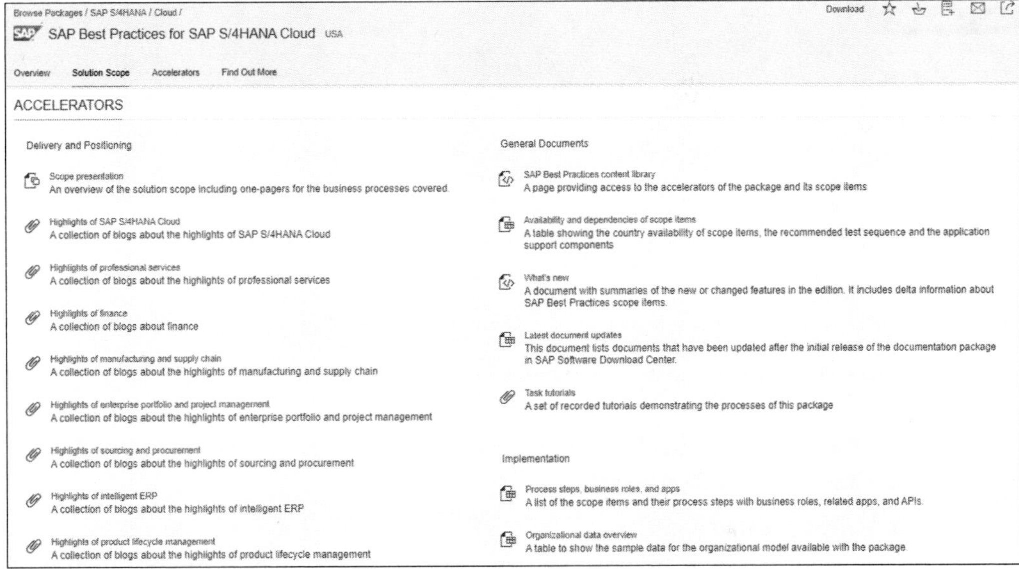

Figure 2.6 SAP Best Practices: Accelerators

Ready-to-Run System

The SAP S/4HANA ready-to-run system enables you to configure the system using various tools. Solution configuration is a function of the ready-to-run SAP S/4HANA system. This system contains the specific objects needed for the configuration and execution of the given process. These objects are deployed with the activation of the solution package. We'll look into the configuration tools in the "Tools" section later in this chapter. The solution configuration version should match the solution documentation version. Figure 2.7 shows a ready-to-run system on the cloud.

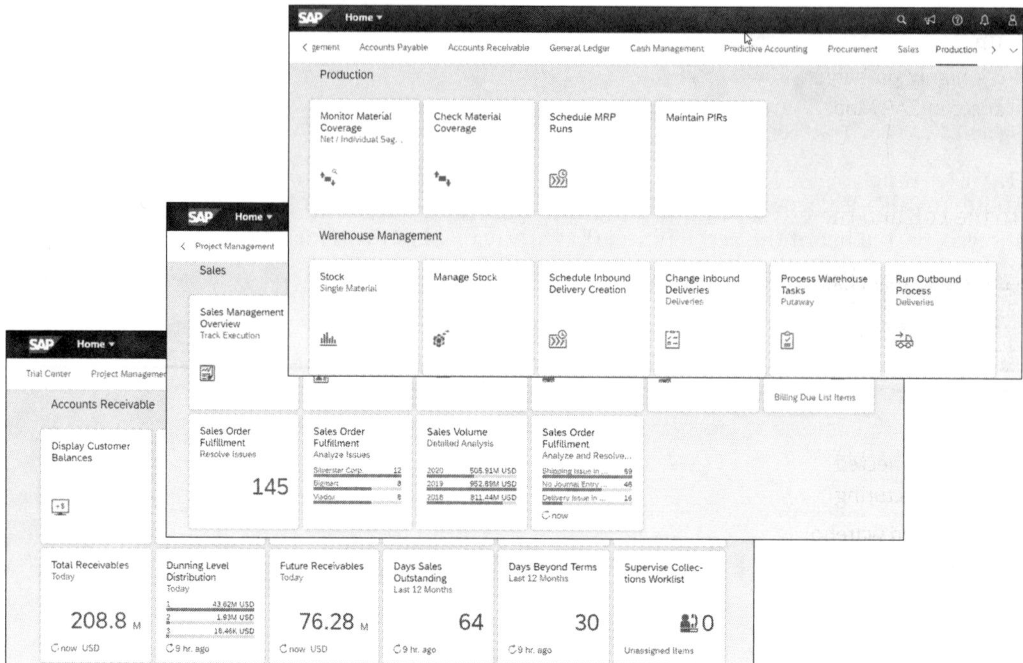

Figure 2.7 Ready-to-Run System: SAP S/4HANA Cloud Trial Version

For the on-premise deployment, customers can decide between either of the following two ready-to-run systems:

- **Fully activated appliance**
  An appliance is a compressed system image that an administrator can extract quickly to create a regular system instance. A fully activated appliance is a prepackaged software bundle based on the customer's requirement that contains preconfigured SAP Best Practices and demo scenarios. SAP can ship it to a specific location on Blu-ray media for your own on-premise infrastructure. Alternatively, the customer can access it on the cloud through SAP Cloud Appliance Library.

- **SAP Model Company**
  SAP Model Company offers a comprehensive, preconfigured, ready-to-run reference solution with business content for multiple industries and lines of business (LoBs). Based on the experience and real-life transformation projects, SAP has built the solution that fits the needs of a specific LoB or an industry. These needs are fulfilled by the state-of-the-art applications and well-established best practices.

  The delivered reference solution contains the configuration specific to the scope of the reference solution, covering end-to-end scenarios, baseline configurations, and SAP Best Practices. SAP Model Company enhances quality, accelerates adoption, and reduces costs while decreasing risk during the discover, explore, and realize phases of a project.

Tip

It's highly probable that you'll encounter a question about either fully activated appliances or SAP Model Company.

Table 2.1 and Table 2.2 shows the planned portfolio of SAP Model Company specific to the LoB and the industry for 2020, respectively.

Digital Supply Chain	Customer Experience	Financial Services	Human Capital Management (HCM) with SAP SuccessFactors
▪ SAP Connected Assets ▪ SAP Connected Manufacturing ▪ Extended warehouse management (EWM) ▪ Logistics execution ▪ R&D/engineering and sustainability ▪ Supply chain planning	▪ SAP Customer Experience ▪ SAP Marketing Cloud ▪ Shared services ▪ SAP Billing and Revenue Innovation Management	▪ Finance	▪ Manage workforce ▪ Attract and acquire ▪ Identify and grow ▪ Pay for performance ▪ Educate and develop ▪ Time off

Table 2.1 Portfolio of SAP Model Company (LoB)

Consumer	Discrete	Public Service	Energy and Natural Resources	Service Industry
▪ Agribusiness ▪ Consumer products ▪ Wholesale distribution ▪ Core retail ▪ Fashion and vertical business ▪ Trade management for consumer products ▪ Pharmaceutical	▪ Automotive ▪ High-tech ▪ Industrial machinery and components	▪ Defense logistics ▪ Public sector	▪ Chemicals ▪ Mill products ▪ Mining production execution ▪ Oil & gas ▪ Integrated utilities	▪ Airline back offices ▪ Telecommunications

Table 2.2 Portfolio of SAP Model Company (Industry)

> **Note**
>
> The list is continuously changing, and SAP is adding LoBs and industries regularly. For the latest offerings, go to *http://s-prs.co/v519403*. From an exam perspective, you don't need to remember the list; we presented the table here for your reference purpose only.

Figure 2.8 shows a partial list of SAP Model Company solutions that are available on the SAP Best Practices Explorer screen.

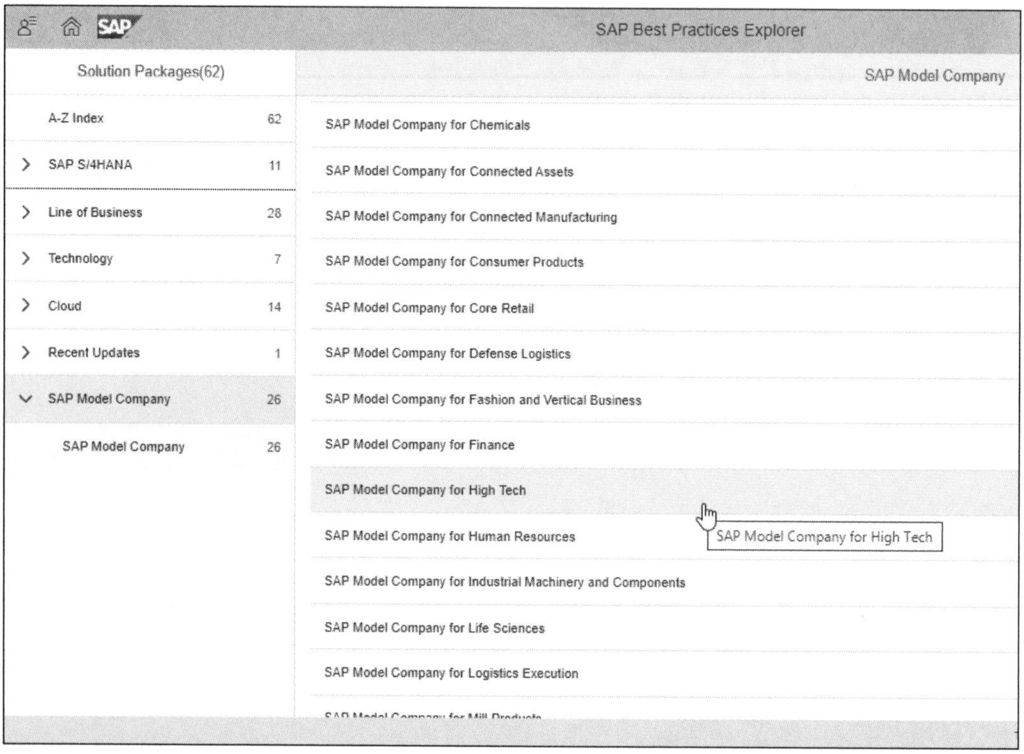

Figure 2.8 Ready-to-Run Solutions: SAP Model Company

User Interface

The third component of SAP business process content is the user interface (UI) by which users can access the configured system. SAP provides several content-provisioning tools that can access ready-to-use apps based on SAP Fiori and SAP Screen Personas. SAP also provides a wide variety of tools for custom development to meet business requirements, such as showing the search output on the same screen rather than on a new screen.

Project Library

The project library hosted on the Roadmap Viewer, which is a cloud extension of SAP Solution Manager and an integral part of the SAP Activate methodology, provides a rich and varied set of documents. These documents include project plan templates, accelerators, templates, standards, strategies, decision-making processes, and several other artifacts to help in the overall execution of the project management workstream and the underlying processes. Figure 2.9 shows a sample set of documents.

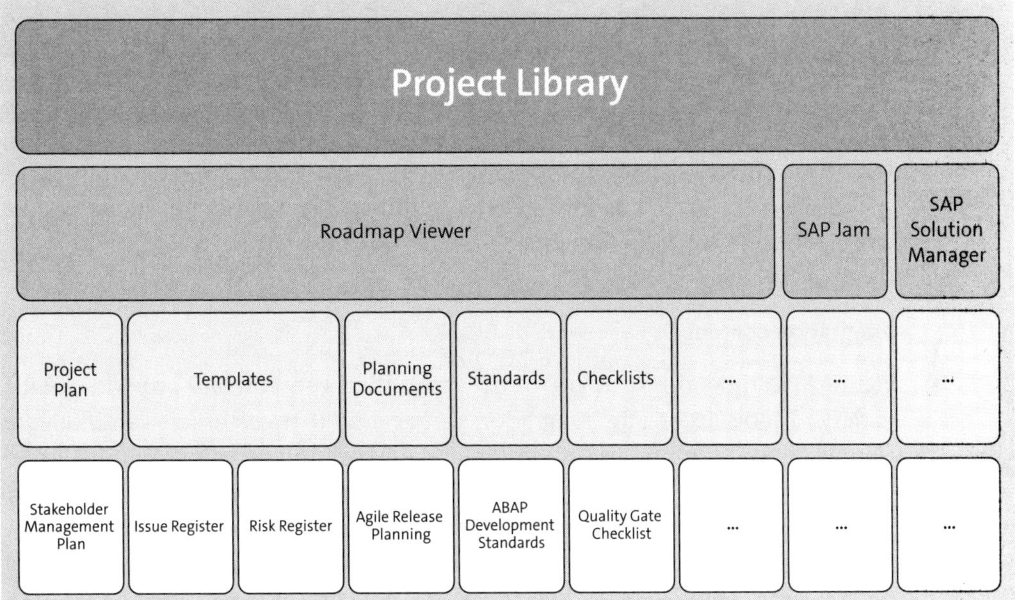

Figure 2.9 Project Library

Migration Content

In Chapter 1, you learned about the three transition roadmaps for SAP S/4HANA: new implementations, system conversions, and selective data transition (formerly known as landscape transformation). The project team employs different tools to migrate data in each of the three scenarios. Table 2.3 shows a partial list of data migration tools.

Source System	Target System	
	SAP S/4HANA	**SAP S/4HANA Cloud**
SAP R/3 SAP ERP Non-SAP	▪ SAP Data Services ▪ SAP Information Steward ▪ Rapid data migration content ▪ SAP S/4HANA migration cockpit with the migration object modeler	▪ SAP S/4HANA migration cockpit

Table 2.3 Data Migration Tools

The structure of data migration content is available in multiple places:

- **Data migration templates**
These templates are available within the SAP S/4HANA and SAP S/4HANA Cloud migration cockpits.
- **SAP Software Downloads Center**
SAP Software Downloads Center provides rapid data migration content, including SAP Data Services 4.2 content, as well as alternative files containing the definition of data stores, migration projects and jobs, web reports, migration services, and so on. SAP Support Launchpad includes an SAP Note on installing content from SAP Software Downloads Center.
- **SAP Best Practices Explorer**
SAP Best Practices Explorer includes solution documentation for rapid data migration to SAP S/4HANA.

Integration Content

Figure 2.10 shows the structure of the integration content. SAP provides a wide variety of tools and ready integration packages so that customers can integrate cloud solutions, on-premise solutions, and any third-party solutions. You'll find the integration solution and scope items on integration in SAP Best Practices, whereas SAP API Business Hub provides ready-to-use integration application programming interfaces (APIs), source code, and best practices. For example, you'll find ready-to-use integration APIs to integrate the SAP S/4HANA implementation with SAP SuccessFactors. The Cloud Integration Automation service provides a guided workflow while the SAP Help Portal will provide detailed integration instructions.

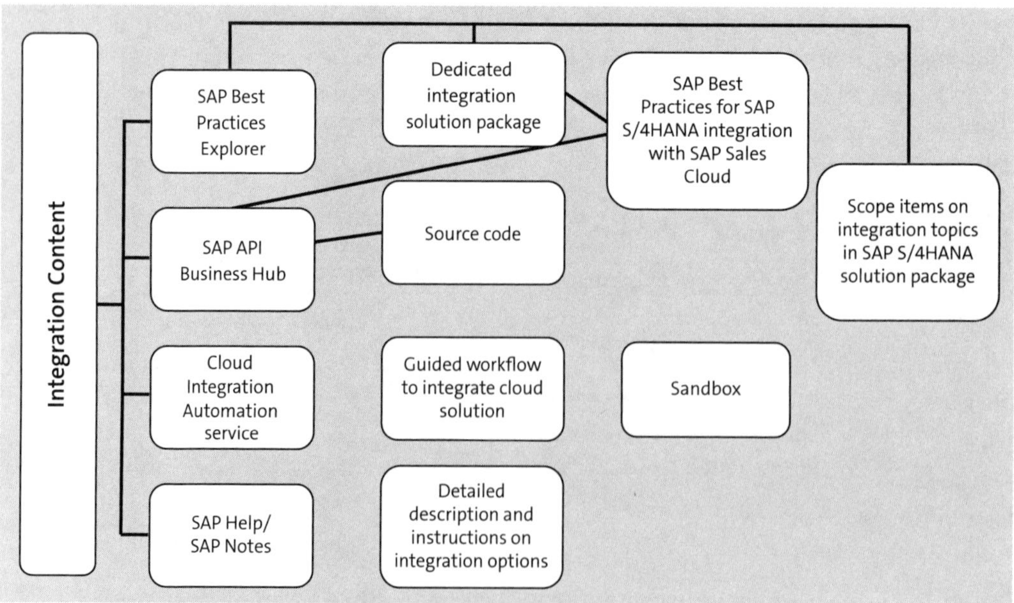

Figure 2.10 Integration Content Structure

Tools

SAP has made available several tools to configure SAP S/4HANA and SAP S/4HANA Cloud. In this section, we'll drill down into the details of these tools and their usages.

Self-Service Configuration

The Self-Service Configuration User Interface (SSCUI) is a cloud-based tool that facilitates the required configuration to run the business processes and conduct the fit-to-standard workshops. It leverages the SAP Fiori UI. The only constraint is that it restricts changes to the business process flow, such as procure-to-pay and plan-to-manufacture. Figure 2.11 shows the task details on the Roadmap Viewer.

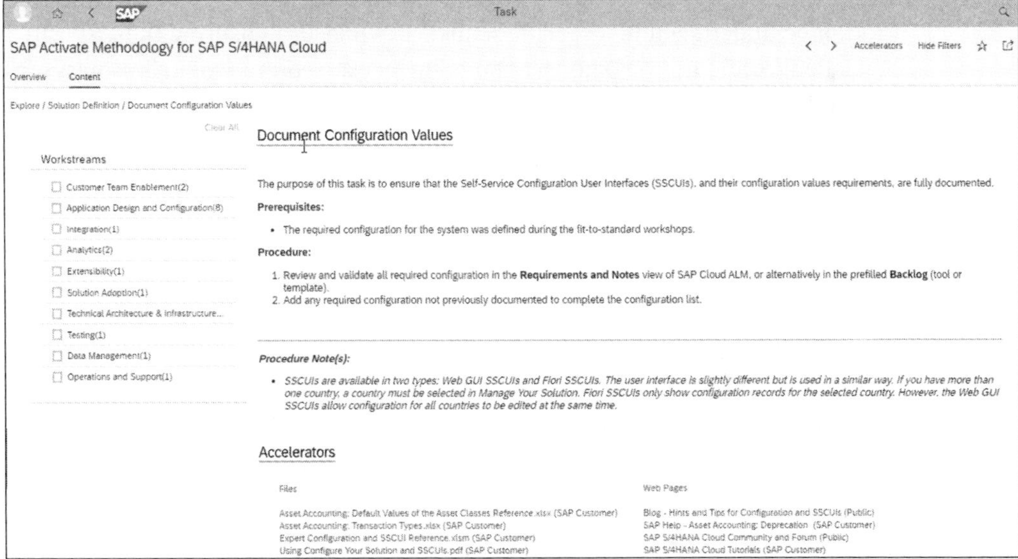

Figure 2.11 Accessing Self-Service Configuration Values Using the Roadmap Viewer

Expert Configuration

The expert configuration tool, used for SAP S/4HANA Cloud, enables SAP consultants to not only make changes to the standard available configurations of existing business processes and SAP Best Practices but also to build business processes that are specific to a company's business needs. For example, configuring a business process to enable multiple people to purchase expensive assets, known as a release strategy, is possible only with this tool. Similarly, this tool enables end-to-end configuration of new order types to specific production processes in the textile industry, such as spinning, weaving, bleaching, or dyeing.

Table 2.4 shows the differences between the two.

SSCUI	Expert Configuration
Adapt activated SAP Best Practices processes	Adapt activated SAP Best Practices processes and add complementary processes
Done by the implementation team	Done by the SAP service center
Examples: production area, plant address, logos	Example: release strategy

Table 2.4 SSCUI versus Expert Configuration

SAP Solution Builder Tool

The SAP solution builder tool enables the logical and sequential import and implementation of business-relevant SAP Best Practices provided for SAP Activate for SAP S/4HANA. As SAP is a highly integrated system, it requires that system configuration be undertaken in a specific sequence, while also ensuring the associated dependent configuration (known as building blocks) required to run business processes are also in place. Further, it helps ensure that the correct master data is in place, which is required to simulate and test business processes in SAP S/4HANA.

SAP Solution Manager

SAP Solution Manager 7.2, which supports the SAP Activate implementation approach, can be used as a project management tool. It consists of templates, checklists, and testing tools required during SAP S/4HANA implementation. It's also possible to make changes to SAP Best Practices and to document them in SAP Solution Manager using BPMN. In other words, SAP Solution Manager consolidates all the project management activities and process modeling into a single system.

From the exam perspective and from the real-world work perspective, SAP Solution Manager is one of the most critical tools for success. It's assumed that you've worked with SAP Solution Manager 7.2, but let's look into some of the key aspects of SAP Solution Manager in this section. Throughout the book, we discuss SAP Solution Manager where specific to a particular topic, and the intention of this section is to familiarize you with SAP Solution Manager as a whole.

Note

For detailed reading, refer to *SAP Solution Manager for SAP S/4HANA* written by Marc O. Schäfer and Matthias Melich (SAP PRESS, 2016; *www.sap-press.com/4162*).

Tip

You may see at least two questions about SAP Solution Manager 7.2 on the exam.

Project Management Capabilities

Let's first review the SAP project management structure defined in Table 2.5.

Element	Definition
Project definition	Defines the project with some basic elements such as objective of the work and tentative duration of the project that applies to the complete project
Phase	Signifies the specific set of activities that the team should perform for the given time period
Task	Action item that produces results, deliverables, documents, and so on carried out by the human resources assigned to the project
Milestone	A specific task, deliverable, or objective that is significant and generally used to measure the progress of the project
Project role	A position within the project organization that is assigned to a resource
Resource	A specific person, group of persons, or any other facility (internal or external to the project), such as infrastructure used within the project

Table 2.5 SAP Project Management Structure

SAP Solution Manager has multiple options available to clients and consultants. These options range from third-party integration tools (e.g., preconfigured add-ons) to end-user experience monitoring as a feature available to SAP Enterprise Support customers. Figure 2.12 shows the options that are available in SAP Solution Manager.

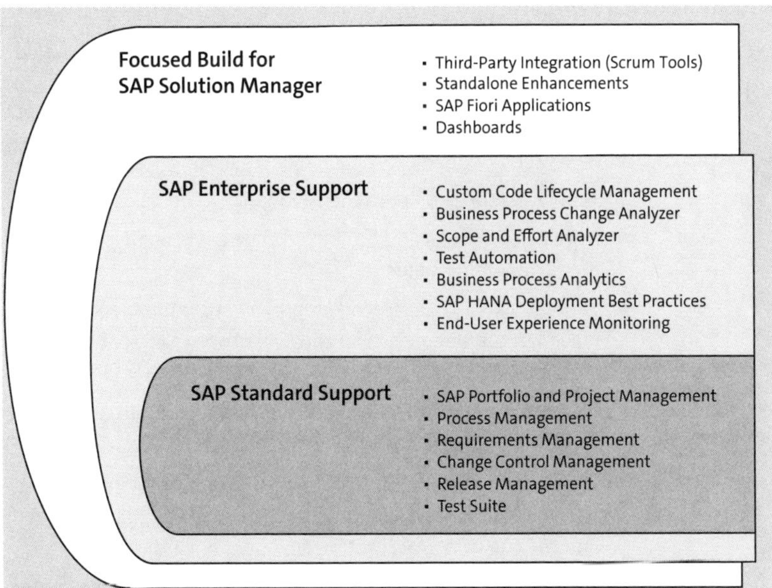

Figure 2.12 SAP Solution Manager Options

The processes listed for SAP Standard Support in Figure 2.12 are strongly integrated. The integrated process and information flow are shown in Figure 2.13.

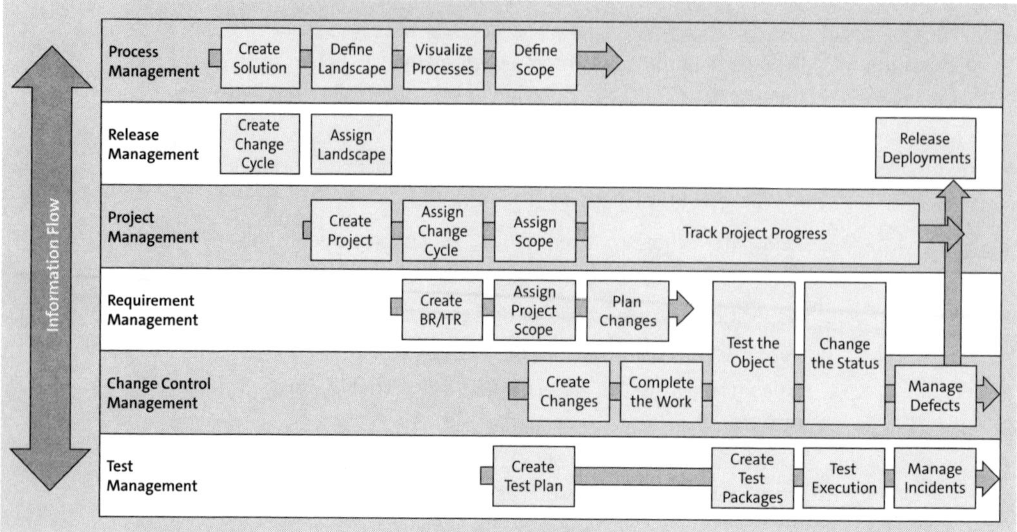

Figure 2.13 Integrated Process Flow: SAP Solution Manager

A minor change in the project scope within the change control block can impact the project created in the project management block. That requirement for the change should be managed within the project management block, tested in the test management block, and the status of the work should flow back to the requirement management and project management blocks. Integration provides easy flow of information, as shown by the arrow in Figure 2.13, but it should be managed responsibly due to the huge impact.

Now let's move on to what you can do in SAP Solution Manager at a higher level, as shown in Table 2.6.

What Can You Do?	Description
Project view summary	You can view the project in the following: ■ Detail view: Tasks and project structure will be displayed in detail, including fields. ■ Tabular view: Tasks and other project structures will be displayed in tabular view. You can drill down to look at the specific task. ■ Graphical view: Project structure and other details are represented in a Gantt chart.
Import project plan	You can import the project plan into SAP Solution Manager. You can download the project plan from the Roadmap Viewer and upload the file into SAP Solution Manager, including phases, tasks, and deliverables that will fast-track the project setup.

Table 2.6 What You Can Do in SAP Solution Manager

What Can You Do?	Description
Resource management	You can create, assign, and monitor the resources throughout the project and resource lifecycle. You can allocate efforts to a resource based on demand and availability, and you can monitor its cost and duration. Some of these activities are based on the role authorization.
Release planning	SAP Solution Manager provides the capability to plan the detail activities related to the release. We'll discuss the release terminologies in the next subsection.
Status reporting	You can generate the detail status report in a PDF in either the standard or customized format.
Dashboard and analytics	SAP Solution Manager has several embedded analytics on the project and portfolio level, such as scope changes, cost or schedule overrun, and number of projects.

Table 2.6 What You Can Do in SAP Solution Manager (Cont.)

Release Terminologies

A project can have one or more releases, which can be used by several parallel projects within the organization. A release is a result of planned work, work packages, and customer reviews and feedback throughout the end of sprints, waves, and phases. The following key terms are important when performing a software release:

- **Work item**
  The project team executes these tasks, which are realized during the sprint execution.
- **Work packages**
  These groups of related work items are intended to deliver a specific outcome. These are the lowest unit of work that a project can be broken down into to create a work breakdown structure (WBS).
- **Sprint**
  A sprint is a time boxed, generally two to four weeks, period during which the project team works on a list of prioritized requirements specific to that sprint. It ends with a demo session to the business.
- **Waves**
  A wave is a well-defined function scope that the business will review at the end of the wave. It has to go through a quality-gate process at the end of the wave. The typical duration of wave is 8 to 12 weeks.
- **Phase**
  A phase is a logical grouping of deliverables and activities that ends with the quality gate. A project phase can have multiple waves.
- **Release**
  A project release synchronizes go-live, and a project can have multiple incremental releases.

Project Management Institute Knowledge Areas

SAP Solution Manager supports all 10 Project Management Institute (PMI) knowledge areas. Three knowledge areas, cost management, HR management, and procurement, are supported through the project and portfolio management functionality of SAP Solution Manager that integrates with SAP S/4HANA. The supported knowledge areas are as follows:

- Project integration management
- Project scope management
- Project time management
- Project risk management
- Project quality management
- Project communication management
- Project stakeholder management
- Project cost management
- Project HR management
- Project procurement management

Value Chain

SAP Solution Manager provides four value chains with corresponding artifacts, as shown in Figure 2.14.

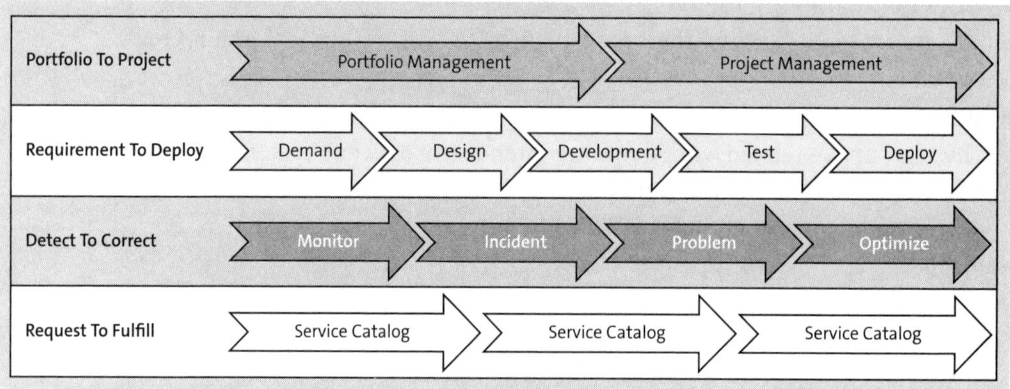

Figure 2.14 Value Chain

Let's walk through each:

- **Portfolio to project (P2P)**
  Portfolio to project provides a unified viewpoint across the project management organization, enterprise architecture, and service portfolio. It also provides the strategy to balance the portfolio.
- **Requirement to deploy (R2D)**
  Requirement to deploy starts with the business demand per their time frame

and dictates their desired outcome; the demand goes through the process of design to develop, test, and then deploy.

- **Detect to correct (D2C)**
  Detect to correct anticipates the production problem and helps the team resolve it via continuous monitoring, incident identification, problem management, and business solution optimization.
- **Request to fulfill (R2F)**
  Request to fulfill manages the requests and fulfills the catalog. It presents a single catalog from multiple suppliers and then manages and measures fulfillment across them.

Tip

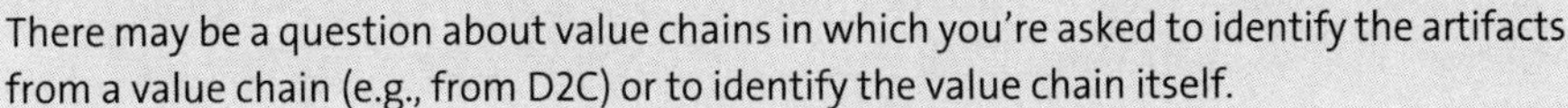

There may be a question about value chains in which you're asked to identify the artifacts from a value chain (e.g., from D2C) or to identify the value chain itself.

Implementation Portal for SAP S/4HANA Cloud

The implementation portal for SAP S/4HANA Cloud supports a fast, self-guided, and content-driven implementation of SAP S/4HANA Cloud based on the SAP Activate methodology. SAP Best Practices Explorer and implementation tasks are embedded in SAP Cloud ALM. Some of the features of the implementation portal are as follows:

- Preconfigured and content-driven implementation
- Fast onboarding of the project team
- Instantaneously available—no configuration or setup needed—with the following steps:
  - Receive an email to get instantaneous access.
  - Define the implementation scope.
  - Onboard your team, and assign roles and responsibilities.
  - Monitor the progress.
- Management and monitoring of implementation tasks
- Convenient and powerful visualization of business models
- Support for fit-to-standard workshop
- Progress monitoring

Tip

There may be one question about the implementation portal for SAP S/4HANA Cloud. Remember that it's used for the cloud implementations and *not* for on-premise implementations.

Methodology

To review, the four components of SAP Activate methodology are as follows:

- **Phases**
  The six phases of the SAP Activate methodology are discover, prepare, explore, realize, deploy, and run. Out of these six, prepare, explore, realize, and deploy are the core phases, which are also known as project phases. The purpose is to break the project activities into logical group of goal-oriented activities leading to a milestone and quality gate. The project moves to the next phase after clearing the quality gate and achieving the milestone.
- **Workstreams**
  There are eleven workstreams. These workstreams are also logical groups of activities, which transcend project phases. However, there are no quality gates between the workstreams. We'll study workstreams in detail in Chapter 5.
- **Deliverables and tasks**
  Project teams carry out the activities to achieve the milestones and create several deliverables.
- **Artifacts**
  These activities require certain inputs in the form of documents or information to produce the outputs. Artifacts are these inputs.

We've discussed the four components of the Activate methodology in detail in Chapter 1.

Important Terminology

For this exam objective, you're expected to understand the following terms:

- **Artifacts**
  This document or information will feed into the process or is the output of the process.
- **Expert configuration**
  SAP support central performs this configuration on the behalf of the implementation team.
- **Fully activated appliance**
  This prepackaged software bundle is based on the customer's requirements.
- **Implementation portal for SAP S/4HANA Cloud**
  This portal supports fast and guided implementation for SAP S/4HANA Cloud.
- **Ready-to-run system**
  A ready-to-run system can be configured using various tools.
- **SAP Model Company**
  This is a comprehensive, preconfigured, ready-to-run solution for several industries and LoBs.

- **SAP Solution Manager value chain**
  There are four value chains in SAP Solution Manager: P2P, R2D, D2C, and R2F.
- **Self-service configuration**
  This tool is used in the business configuration for cloud deployments.
- **Sprints**
  This is a time-boxed period, generally two to four weeks, to complete the project activities.

 Practice Questions

These practice questions will help you evaluate your understanding of the topics covered in this chapter. The questions shown are similar in nature to those found on the certification examination. Although none of these questions will be found on the exam itself, they will allow you to review your knowledge of the subject. Select the correct answers, and then check the completeness of your answers in the "Practice Question Answers and Explanations" section. Remember that on the exam, you must select all correct answers and only correct answers to receive credit for the question.

1. What are the elements of the SAP Activate methodology?

☐ **A.** Methodology, documentation, and self-service configuration

☐ **B.** SAP Best Practices, tools, and methodology

☐ **C.** SAP Best Practices, methodology, and guided configuration

☐ **D.** Content, methodology, and tools

2. You're working as a project manager deploying the SAP S/4HANA Cloud solution for a global bank. You're doing the fit-to-standard workshop for a process when one of the key stakeholders asked you to explain the activities during the realize phase of the project. How would you respond?

☐ **A.** It's not the right time to discuss the realize phase. We'll discuss it during the quality gate of the current phase, which is prepare.

☐ **B.** During the realize phase, the implementation team will follow the Scrum approach and build the release incrementally based on the product backlog that we'll create during the explore phase.

☐ **C.** In the realize phase, we'll fine-tune and prioritize the product backlog, complete the data migration process, and initiate the customer enablement workstream.

☐ **D.** It's too early to dive into the realize phase and discuss its activities. However, you can review the Roadmap Viewer for SAP S/4HANA Cloud for a better understanding and a fruitful discussion at a later stage.

☐ **E.** Both **B** and **C**.

3. What are the components of the business process content?

☐ **A.** Three components are SAP Best Practices, ready-to-run systems, and the UI.

☐ **B.** Four components are SAP Best Practices, solution documentation, ready-to-run systems, and the UI.

☐ **C.** Three components are the Roadmap Viewer, ready-to-run systems, and the UI.

☐ **D.** Four components are SAP Best Practices, self-service configuration, the Roadmap Viewer, and the UI.

4. Where can you find the accelerators to help set up the project library?

☐ **A.** SAP Best Practices.

☐ **B.** Roadmap Viewer.

☐ **C.** Both **A** and **B**.

☐ **D.** SAP provides the detailed project plan, and you can build the library from your previous repository.

☐ **E.** None of the above.

5. Data migration templates are available within the migration cockpit for SAP S/4HANA and SAP S/4HANA Cloud. True or false?

☐ **A.** True

☐ **B.** False

6. Where can you locate the SAP Best Practices for SAP S/4HANA integration with SAP S/4HANA Cloud?

☐ **A.** SAP Best Practices

☐ **B.** SAP API Business Hub

☐ **C.** SAP Help Portal/SAP Notes

☐ **D.** Both **A** and **B**

☐ **E.** Both **A** and **C**

☐ **E.** Both **B** and **C**

7. Identify the correct statements. (There are two correct answers.)

☐ **A.** SAP Activate has six different project phases.

☐ **B.** SAP Activate has six phases.

☐ **C.** SAP Activate has 13 workstreams.

- ☐ **D.** Project management is a dedicated phase in the SAP Activate methodology that emphasizes the effective management of an SAP implementation project.
- ☐ **E.** Analytics is a workstream in the SAP Activate methodology.

8. Fill in the blanks. Any _____ or documents as an input to a process or _____ from a process are termed artifacts.

- ☐ **A.** Information, deliverables
- ☐ **B.** Information, outputs
- ☐ **C.** Project plan updates, outputs
- ☐ **D.** Project plan updates, deliverables

9. Which of the following are artifacts? (There are three correct answers.)

- ☐ **A.** Contract undergoing legal review
- ☐ **B.** Project team meeting
- ☐ **C.** Agile review
- ☐ **D.** Scrum documents
- ☐ **E.** Spreadsheet shared by the project manager outlining the milestones

10. What is the purpose of the solution adoption workstream?

- ☐ **A.** To demonstrate the adoptability of the SAP S/4HANA solution across multiple industries and business processes
- ☐ **B.** To provide the processes and procedures that help people and organizations adopt the new business system effectively
- ☐ **C.** To provide change management, user training, and hypercare support
- ☐ **D.** To help test the integrated solution

11. The project team completed the fit-gap analysis for all the scope items. The team had built and prioritized the requirements coming from the delta design workshops, and they are working on the user stories from those delta requirements. Identify the project phase and the probable workstream from the preceding scenario.

- ☐ **A.** Explore phase, integration workstream
- ☐ **B.** Realize phase, customer team enablement workstream
- ☐ **C.** Realize phase, extensibility workstream
- ☐ **D.** Explore phase, extensibility workstream
- ☐ **E.** Discover phase, extensibility workstream

12. What is the purpose of the run phase of the project?

☐ **A.** During this phase, the project team establishes a safe, efficient, and continuous operation of the newly created system.

☐ **B.** During this phase, the project team can terminate the contract and leave the client in the hands of their IT team.

☐ **C.** The project performs the system go-live.

☐ **D.** The project plans the transition methodology to the run team.

13. You've completed all the sprints as identified in the project plan. It's a greenfield implementation, and the client wants to migrate only the master data. All the master data is ready in the format as requested by the implementation partner, and the data load is complete. All the planning related to the adaptation and operation is complete. You just came out of a marathon quality-gate meeting where the client has provided a number of cosmetic changes but agreed to move forward. In the given scenario, what will you do next? (There are two correct answers.)

☐ **A.** Create a plan to incorporate all the cosmetic changes, discuss with your team, and get your supervisor's approval.

☐ **B.** Create a plan to incorporate all the cosmetic changes, discuss with your team, and schedule another quality-gate meeting with the key stakeholders.

☐ **C.** Focus on the organization readiness check, go-live activities, and hypercare support. In parallel, you'll work with the client's project manager to incorporate the suggested changes.

☐ **D.** Because these are cosmetic changes only, let your team member work with the respective process owners to include them in the solution while you prepare the team for the final integration sprint.

☐ **E.** Ask your team member and the product owner in the sprint planning meeting to review these changes and insist to incorporate them in the testing sprint.

14. What are the four components of the SAP Activate methodology?

☐ **A.** Phases, workstreams, deliverables and tasks, and artifacts

☐ **B.** Phases, workstreams, deliverables and tasks, and SAP Best Practices

☐ **C.** Phases, workstreams, SAP Best Practices, and artifacts

☐ **D.** Phases, SAP Best Practices, deliverables and tasks, and artifacts.

☐ **E.** SAP Best Practices, workstreams, deliverables and tasks, and artifacts

15. What is the purpose of the discover phase of the project?

☐ **A.** The implementation partner works closely with the client in their journey to implement SAP S/4HANA and helps them complete the requirement documents.

☐ **B.** The prospective client organization discovers the business benefits that they may achieve by implementing the SAP S/4HANA solution.

☐ **C.** The client organization works directly with the SAP team. The implementation organization provides system administrators to work with the SAP team.

☐ **D.** None of the above.

16. Which tool will you *not* use for configuring business processes in a cloud-based deployment?

☐ **A.** IMG

☐ **B.** SSCUI

☐ **C.** Guided configuration

☐ **D.** Expert configuration

17. Which one of these can you use as a project management tool?

☐ **A.** Project Systems

☐ **B.** Roadmap Viewer

☐ **C.** SAP Solution Manager

☐ **D.** SAP Best Practices Explorer

18. Which tool will you use to import and implement SAP Best Practices?

☐ **A.** SAP Solution Manager

☐ **B.** SSCUI

☐ **C.** SAP solution builder tool

☐ **D.** SAP Activate methodology

19. Using expert configuration for SAP S/4HANA Cloud, essentials edition, SAP can make changes to the available configurations of the business process and build a business process specific to the organizational need. True or false?

☐ **A.** True.

☐ **B.** False.

20. You've completed the configuration of most of the master data, such as chart of accounts, general ledgers, product groups, and other data necessary for setting up a procure-to-pay process on the cloud. You also wanted to implement a release strategy for the purchase order, and you've contacted SAP support central for the configuration. Furthermore, you noticed that your project manager is accessing and storing many project-related documents on a web-based tool. In the current scenario, which tool or tools would you use?

☐ **A.** You used SSCUI, SAP will use expert configuration, and your project manager was accessing the Roadmap Viewer.

☐ **B.** You used expert configuration, SAP will use SSCUI, and your project manager was accessing the SAP solution builder tool.

☐ **C.** You used SSCUI, SAP will use expert configuration, and your project manager was accessing SAP Solution Manager.

☐ **D.** You used expert configuration, SAP will use SSCUI, and your project manager was accessing SAP Solution Manager.

☐ **E.** You used expert configuration, SAP will use SSCUI, and your project manager was accessing SAP Solution Manager.

Practice Question Answers and Explanations

1. Correct answer: **B**

   Option A is incorrect because documentation isn't an element of SAP Activate. Option C is also incorrect because the guided configuration is one of the tools from the tools element of SAP Activate. Content is a part of SAP Best Practices. The three components are SAP Best Practices, tools, and methodology.

2. Correct answer: **B**

   Option A is incorrect because the project team just completed the fit-to-standard process, which means the project is in the explore phase and not in the prepare phase. Furthermore, option C is incorrect because the product owner will prioritize the product backlog in the explore phase. Options D and E are provided to confuse you. During the realize phase, the project team will follow the Scrum approach to build the product based on the prioritized product backlog.

3. Correct answer: **A**

   The three components of the business process contents are SAP Best Practices, ready-to-run systems, and the UI. Options B and D are incorrect because they mentioned four components. The Roadmap Viewer in option C is one of the ways to explore business contents, so it's incorrect.

4. Correct answer: **B**

   Option A is incorrect because SAP Best Practices have accelerators related to business processes. To build the project library, you'll need accelerators related to project management. You can get those only in the Roadmap Viewer. SAP doesn't provide the detailed project plan, but one of the accelerators is the project plan template, which you can get in the Roadmap Viewer. Option C is meant to confuse you.

5. Correct answer: **A**

   True. Data migration templates are available within the migration cockpit for SAP S/4HANA and SAP S/4HANA Cloud.

6. Correct answer: **D**

   You can find the SAP Best Practices for SAP S/4HANA integration in SAP API Business Hub as well as SAP Best Practices. Because options A and B are true, that makes option **D** the correct answer.

7. Correct answers: **B, E**

   Be extra careful when reading the choices. There is a subtle difference between project phases and the phases in the SAP Activate methodology. *Project phases* refer to the core phases of prepare, explore, realize, and deploy, whereas *phases* implies all six phases. Option A is incorrect, but option B is correct. There are eleven workstreams, and project management is one of them, so both options C and D are incorrect. Analytics, indeed, is a workstream in the SAP Activate methodology.

8. Correct answer: **B**

   An artifact is a document or piece of information feeding into the process or is an output of the process. Do note that a deliverable is a subset of the output. For example, the minutes of an internal status meeting is an output of the process, but you don't deliver these minutes to the client. Therefore, options A and D are incorrect. A project plan update is just one of the many outputs of the several processes, making C an incorrect option.

9. Correct answers: **A, D, E**

   An artifact is a document or piece of information that feeds into (input) the process or is an output of the process. Options B and C are processes and therefore incorrect. Contract with review comments, Scrum documents, and the milestone schedule are documents and therefore artifacts.

10. Correct answer: **B**

    The solution adoption workstream has all the processes and procedures to help people and the organization adapt to the new business system using SAP S/4HANA. It includes change management processes and excludes user training and readiness, which is a customer team enablement process. Hypercare isn't part of the solution adoption workstream. Option A is incorrect, and option D refers to the testing workstream.

11. Correct answer: **C**

    The "team is working on the user stories" portion indicates clearly that the project is in the realize phase. Therefore, options A, D, and E are incorrect. Customer team enablement ensures that the customer team has all necessary skills and knowledge, while the extensibility workstream focuses on developing system extensions. Based on the given scenario, it's clear that the development team is developing user stories that may be part of the system extension.

12. Correct answer: **A**

    The run phase represents key steps in the continuous running and improving the operations of the environment. It includes proficient end-user support, efficient system monitoring, and other activities such as continuous improvements to the solution. Option B is incorrect as the termination of the contract is independent of the project phase.

13. Correct answer: **C**

    The activities such as "sprints are completed" and "data load is complete" indicate that the project is in the realize phase. The quality-gate meeting is to progress from the realize phase to the deploy phase, which the client has approved with certain cosmetic changes as indicated in the last statement "agreed to move forward." In this case, the team should focus on the deployment activities without losing sight of the feedback received. Therefore, options A and B are incorrect. Options D and E are incorrect and are included to create confusion. There are no sprints such as integration or testing sprint.

14. Correct answer: **A**

    Phases, workstreams, deliverables and tasks, and artifacts are the four components of the methodology. SAP Best Practices isn't a component of the methodology. Option A is the correct answer.

15. Correct answer: **B**

    During the discover phase of the project, the organization will discover the business benefits that it will achieve by implementing the project. Options A and C do not include the discover process and so are incorrect. Option B is the correct choice.

16. Correct answer: **A**

    SSCUI, guided configuration, and expert configuration are for the cloud deployments, while IMG is the traditional tool for the SAP on-premise deployment.

17. Correct answer: **C**

    Project Systems is an SAP module to track project implementation, so it's not a correct option. The Roadmap Viewer and SAP Best Practices Explorer support the implementation by providing accelerators and other documentation and tools, but you can't use them as a repository. SAP Solution Manager is the correct choice.

18. Correct answer: **C**

    The SAP solution builder tool is the only listed option that supports this functionality.

19. Correct answer: **A**

    Ture. Expert configuration will allow changing the available configuration and building a business process specific to the requirement.

20. Correct answer: **C**

    Only SAP can use expert configuration, so options B, D, and E are incorrect. SAP Solution Manager is the project management tool, making option B incorrect. The only correct choice is C.

Takeaway

In this chapter, you learned about the three elements of the SAP Activate methodology: content, tools, and methodology. In the first section, we explored the solution documentation and solution configuration aspects of the content. We reviewed the project library and touched upon the migration and integration content.

We then reviewed and discussed the usages of the four tools: SSCUI, expert configuration, the SAP solution builder tool, and SAP Solution Manager. You also saw the primary differences between self-service configuration and expert configuration. We closed the section by reviewing SAP Solution Manager and its capabilities as a project management tool.

Finally, we quickly relooked at the four components of the SAP Activate methodology. It's important that you clearly understand the components; if you don't; we highly recommend reading the related content from Chapter 1.

Summary

In this chapter, you learned about the three elements of SAP Activate. We looked into the content needed to build a system, the tools required to configure the system, and the processes to follow to build a productive system that meets the business objectives. In the next chapter, we'll start our journey to understand the agile framework.

Chapter 3
Agile Project Planning

Techniques You'll Master

- Understand agile and Scrum
- Learn about the Agile Manifesto
- Explain the differences between agile and Scrum
- Know key Scrum terminologies
- Understand Scrum ceremonies and artifacts
- Understand the use of Scrum in SAP Activate
- Explain the team structure, roles, and responsibilities
- Understand the product backlog

Continuous planning without any action is procrastination, but any action without a suitable plan can be catastrophic. Projects executed in the agile framework require a certain degree of planning. In this chapter, we'll start looking into the agile framework by understanding the basic concepts behind it and going through some agile terminologies. We'll further look into applicability of the agile framework through the SAP Activate methodology in SAP S/4HANA projects. Creating a realistic plan and successfully executing the plan is crucial to understanding the roles and responsibilities of the project team and its members. We'll cover this topic in detail.

The *product backlog*, one of the key agile artifacts, lists the product requirements, functional as well as technical. We'll go through this artifact thoroughly to appreciate its importance in the agile framework. In addition, you'll learn how to move items or requirements from the product backlog to an actionable list of items known as *sprint backlogs*.

Real-World Scenario

For the past 10 years, you worked as an SAP project manager in an IT consulting organization and mastered the art of project management using the ASAP methodology. During the latter part of your career, you also implemented SAP on the cloud using the SAP Launch methodology.

In 2016, your organization realized the need to build an SAP S/4HANA-based center of excellence that would cater to the future and the changing business and IT requirements. However, you were very busy during that period and ignored all the necessary training and knowledge-sharing sessions. Yet, you're a star performer in your organization and continue to excel in ASAP and SAP Launch methodologies. Now you're worried, however, that almost all the upcoming projects are utilizing the SAP Activate methodology.

In the recent past, your supervisor surprised you by asking you to lead a major SAP S/4HANA implementation project at a pharmaceutical manufacturing company. She is fully aware of the pros and cons of your assignment to this global, highly visible, multimillion-dollar program. She supported your assignment by citing your past performance, learning curve, ability to build relationships, and success stories. However, her only concern was your lack of experience with the SAP Activate methodology.

You're very excited for the upcoming project but have very little to no idea about the Scrum framework. In the past, you've also dodged several uncomfortable questions from your team members about your expertise level in agile, Scrum, and SAP Activate. Additionally, you fully understand the future of SAP and the importance of the SAP Activate methodology and want to continue to work as an SAP project and program manager. You feel the need to enhance your knowledge and understanding of agile, Scrum, and SAP Activate methodology. You're fully aware that SAP Activate leverages the Scrum framework and decided to deep dive into it.

Objectives of This Portion of the Test

The certification examination will test your knowledge about the following topics:

- The Agile Manifesto, its origination, and the history
- Key differentiators between agile and Scrum
- The lean approach and the importance of Scrum artifacts
- Scrum ceremonies (or meetings)
- How SAP Activate leverages the Scrum framework in managing the projects
- Organizing the project team structure in the Scrum framework and understanding the roles and responsibilities of the team and its individual members
- Key activities and tasks in the prepare phase of an agile project
- The differences between the sprint backlog and product backlog, and how to create a sprint backlog from a product backlog
- Enhancing the quality of the deliverables by understanding the definition of ready and the definition of done

In subsequent sections, you'll learn about these key concepts followed by some questions and answers.

Note

This chapter lays the foundation for your understanding of the agile framework, and the topic carries 8–12% weightage in the certification examination. You'll certainly get anywhere from 6 to 10 questions from the topics of this chapter.

Key Concepts Refresher

This section will help you understand the agile framework and will advance your knowledge on how it supports the SAP Activate methodology. These concepts are critical for you to pass the exam.

Agile and Scrum

We use agile and Scrum interchangeably, very often, without understanding the implication of the differences between them. Agile and the Scrum aren't the same. In this section, you'll learn about the agile methodology, the Scrum framework, and the key differences between them.

What Is Agile?

Agile is a methodology that promotes the continuous iteration of the software development lifecycle (SDLC) processes. It compresses the SDLC processes into a smaller and more manageable timeline that periodically yields an enhanced product build that generally satisfies the agreed-upon requirements. This methodology provides a flexible yet robust and simpler approach to building a product that may have undergone major changes through its development lifecycle.

The agile "software development" manifesto (aka Agile Manifesto) was published in 2001 when 17 software development practitioners who felt the need for an alternative approach of document-driven, heavyweight software development processes met in Utah to talk and find common ground. The manifesto is composed of four values and 12 principles. The four values of the Agile Manifesto are as follows:

1. *Individuals and interactions* over processes and tools
2. *Working software* over comprehensive documentation
3. *Customer collaboration* over contract negotiations
4. *Responding to change* over following a plan

According to the Agile Manifesto, while there's value in the items on the right-hand side of these statements, the items on the left-hand side are valued more. This is the core of the Agile Manifesto.

Tip

Take a moment to visit *www.agilemanifesto.org* to understand the history and concept behind the agile manifesto. It's critical to understand the four values and 12 principles to master the agile methodology.

What Is Scrum?

Per the Agile Manifesto, Scrum was invented in the early 1990s, much before the formation of Agile Manifesto, by Jeff Sutherland, one of the 17 participants in the February 2001 meeting in Utah. Mike Beedle and Ken Schwaber, who are early adopters of Scrum, coauthored the book *Agile Software Development with Scrum* (Prentice Hall, 2001).

Scrum is an iterative framework to develop complex products with continuous delivery. The framework is widely used on complex product development in multiple sectors. Per the *Scrum Guide*, written jointly by Ken Schwaber and Jeff Sutherland (*http://s-prs.co/v519404*):

> *Scrum has been used to develop software, hardware, embedded software, networks of interacting function, autonomous vehicles, schools, government, marketing, managing the operation of organizations and almost everything we use in our daily lives, as individuals and societies.*

To put it simply, Scrum is the following:

- Lightweight
- Simple to understand
- Difficult to master

Scrum, like several other methodologies such as Kanban, Extreme Programming (XP), Feature-Driven Development (FDD), and so on, is a type of agile methodology, as shown in Figure 3.1.

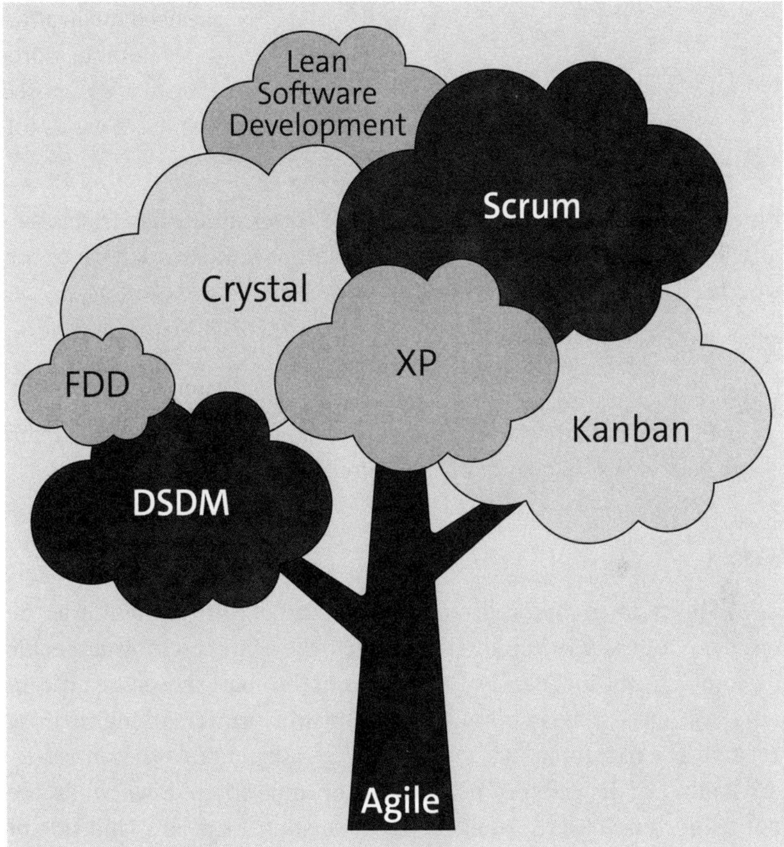

Figure 3.1 Agile versus Scrum

Now that you know a bit about agile and Scrum, it's important to understand the differences between them, as shown in Table 3.1.

Agile	Scrum
Agile is a methodology based on iterative processes.	Scrum is one of the approaches under the agile umbrella that follows an incremental build and regular delivery.
A less flexible approach is used.	A highly flexible framework is used.

Table 3.1 Agile versus Scrum

Agile	Scrum
Leadership plays a critical role.	The approach is self-organizing with cross-functional teams.
Strong and continual monitoring of the project phases occurs during the lifecycle.	No such monitoring mechanism is used except at the end of the sprint for regular feedback from business owners and end users.
Project lead takes care of most of the agile activities.	There is no team leader. The scrum master is also a regular member of the development team.

Table 3.1 Agile versus Scrum (Cont.)

Scrum Terminologies

So far, in this chapter, we've used certain Scrum-specific terminologies. In this section, we'll discuss all the jargon used in the Scrum framework. In addition to the expertise, you need the vocabulary.

Sprint

A sprint is a time-boxed period between two and four weeks when the Scrum team resolves the business problem by providing a working software.

Burn-Down Chart

The purpose of a burn-down chart is to show the amount of work remaining as the development team moves forward into the project. The chart can show a specific sprint or the complete product backlog. The x-axis of the chart shows the time, in days or weeks, while the y-axis shows the amount of work remaining in story points—a relative unit to estimate a user story—or in task hours. As the name suggests, the remaining hours or story points will continue to go down while the development team completes the assigned functionalities. The left-hand side of Figure 3.2 shows a sample burn-down chart.

If you show the work completed instead of the remaining work on the y-axis as shown in the right-hand side of Figure 3.2, then the chart becomes a burn-up chart where the graph is gradually moving upward, indicating the progress in the project as it shows the cumulative work done.

The burn-down chart shown in Figure 3.2 is for four-week (20 working days) sprints with 300 user stories. Note that the velocity of the sprint is more or less constant. This chart was drawn at the end of the sprint. On the other hand, the burn-up chart in Figure 3.2 is for a different product with an initial product backlog of 400 user stories that was drawn on the 11th month of the project; the first sprint was on February 2016 with 25 story points. In addition, note that the velocity of the sprints was slow at the beginning of the project, which improved after the fourth month of the project, predicting the final release month of June 2020.

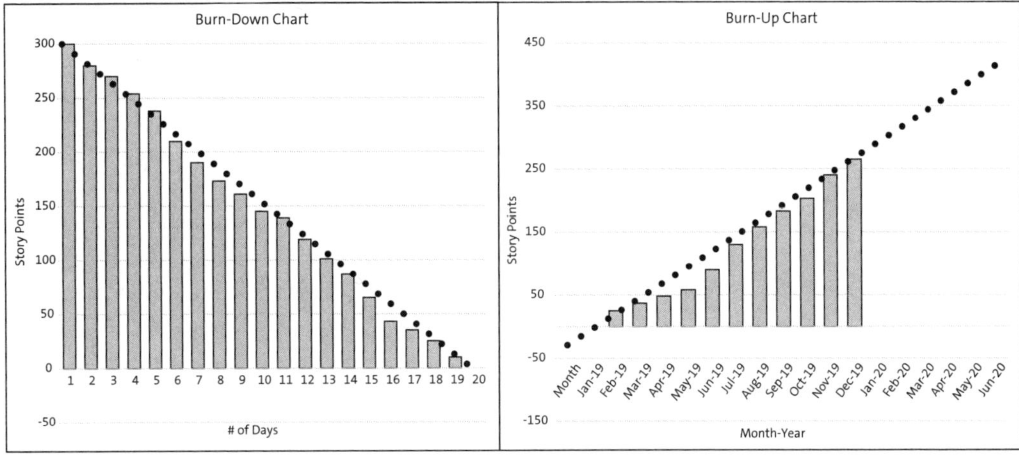

Figure 3.2 Burn-Down Chart and Burn-Up Chart

Epic

An epic is a large user story that spans multiple sprints. Epics can also span multiple Scrum teams. An epic is a high-level requirement either coming from the client or arising due to system requirements. In Figure 3.3, master data, requisition, sourcing, receipt, and payment are epics while the other items mentioned under each block are user stories, which we'll discuss next. The epic master data may not be the client's requirements, but you can't fulfill the client's requirements, for example, for purchase requisition, without completing the master data. An epic, for example, invoicing, will span multiple sprints and different development teams. However, a user story such as a vendor master must be completed in a sprint. If the estimate for a user story is more than the time-box for a sprint, then the story must be broken down into several stories so that the development team can complete each part in a sprint.

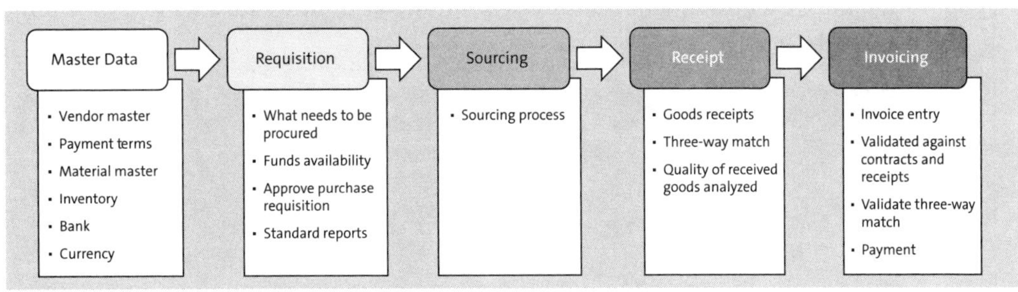

Figure 3.3 Epic

User Story

A user story is a high-level requirement with sufficient information that the development team can use to estimate the work product. Per Scrum, the user story has three components: a role, a feature, and a benefit. However, in SAP, we use a slightly different version of the user story, as shown in Table 3.2.

Scrum	SAP Project
As a <role>, I want <feature> so that <project value>.	▪ Capture the "headline" and a "short description" of the work product. ▪ In addition, prepare the traditional requirement document. ▪ Streamlined templates are available with SAP Activate.

Table 3.2 User Story

Example

As an approval authority, I need to have an automated process to approve the purchase requisition without logging into the SAP system, which will save a lot of time and speed up the approval process.

Background: I have to approve several purchase requisitions. The value of these requisitions varies from $1,000 to $5,000. However, I don't log in to the SAP system regularly and, very often, miss approving the requisitions, delaying the procurement process. An automated email notification with complete details of the purchase requisition and a link to the approval and rejection process will help me decide about the requisition without logging in to the system. Therefore, it will reduce the procurement time, improving the efficiency of the complete production line.

Product Backlog

A product backlog is a list of requirements, also known as user stories, arranged in a specific order to enhance the value of the delivered product that needs to work upon to create or maintain the product. The product backlog should be managed by the product owner. There can be only one product backlog for a product. Table 3.3 shows the partial product backlog from an SAP S/4HANA implementation project in the utility sector.

Priority	Item Description	Estimate (Story Points)
1	As a service member, I want to schedule the meter reading processes.	27
2	As a service member, I want a process to validate the meter reading.	12
3	As a service member, I want installation, repair, and replacement processes.	24

Table 3.3 A Sample Product Backlog

Priority	Item Description	Estimate (Story Points)
4	As a service manager, I want device inspection and certification processes.	5
5	As a service manager, I want device lifecycle management.	23
6	...	...

Table 3.3 A Sample Product Backlog (Cont.)

Sprint Backlog

A sprint backlog consists of the product backlog items for the given sprint along with a plan detailing the delivery of the increment—a functional software product—and the realization of the sprint goal. It's an output of the sprint planning meeting, which we'll look at in the "Scrum Ceremonies" section later in this chapter. The process to create the sprint backlog requires close coordination between the development team and the product owner.

Story Mapping

Story mapping is a key step in identifying the complete requirements or gaps in user stories. The map captures the activities and tasks that a user performs during a specific process. Let's take a deeper look into the story mapping by analyzing Figure 3.4.

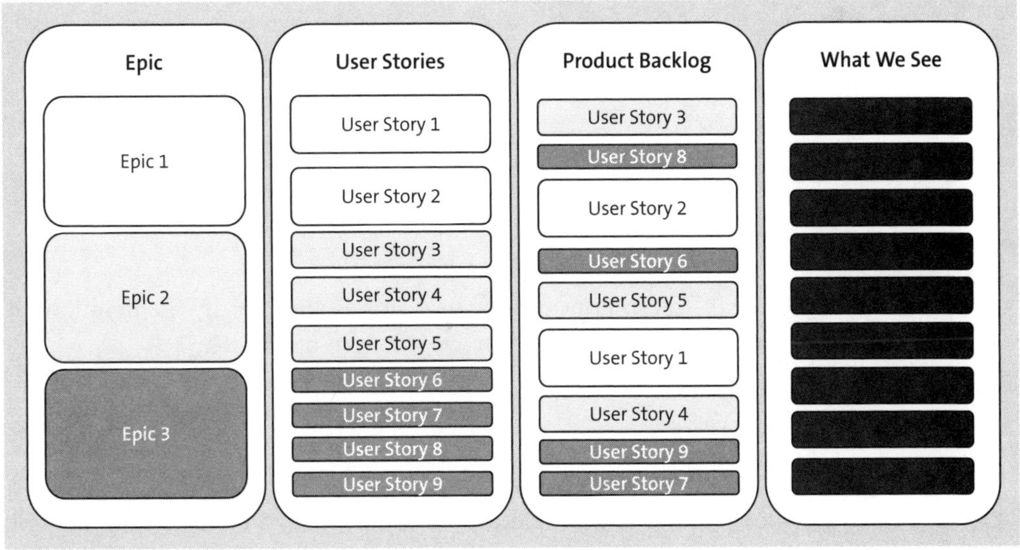

Figure 3.4 Story Mapping

Each epic is broken down into user stories and then moved to the product backlog. The product owner prioritizes these user stories based on the value that they will add to the product. However, the challenge is that most of the Scrum team, except the product owner, may not able to tie these stories back to the original epic or relate them to each other. For example, two consecutive user stories in a product backlog may be related to the user role and privilege, as well as the posting of an invoice; remember that the user stories are ordered based on the value. It becomes very difficult to identify any business gaps, and the Scrum team loses the business context of the user story.

There are several ways to mitigate this issue, but the most common way is to use a subject matter expert (SME) who will tell the complete process as a story, identifying each activity and task. The development team, as they hear the keywords such as task or activity, note down those tasks on a post-it. At the end, the team arranges those tasks in a horizontal way in left to right order. More than one option of a task arranged in a column identifies parallel or optional activities. The best way to identify any gaps is to "reverse role play" where someone from the development team will explain the tasks to the SME as captured in the story map. Figure 3.5 shows a sample story map with a business gap in it.

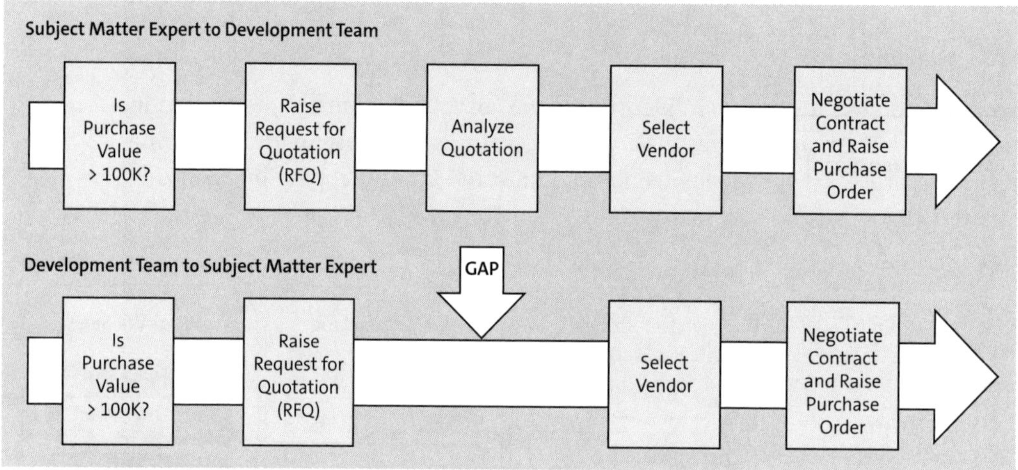

Figure 3.5 Story Mapping: Gap Identification

Once done, the team can prioritize the user stories and identify the iterations. It isn't a one-time exercise, and the team has to keep it up to date.

Velocity

Velocity is a key metric that gives you the amount of work a team is doing or can do in a single sprint. As you complete more sprints, you can calculate the velocity by summing all the work done divided by the number of sprints. If you look at the burn-up chart in Figure 3.2, shown earlier, note that the team completed 25 story points in February, 12 in March, 11 in April, and 10 in May. The formula to calculate the velocity is:

Velocity = (25 + 12 + 11 + 10) / 4 = 14.5 Story points

However, for the complete project, the velocity was 23.5. story points.

Scrum Board

How will you know about the status of each user stories while in a sprint? The Scrum board, as shown in Figure 3.6, is a tool that helps the team track the progress of each user story. The team updates the board on a regular basis and shows all the items that are required to be completed in the sprint.

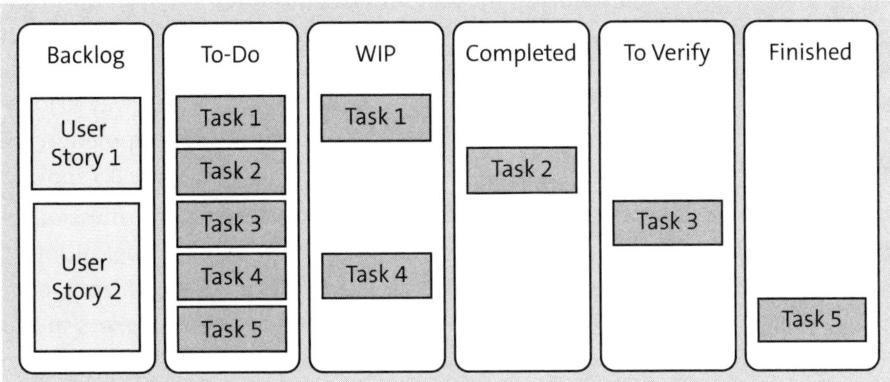

Figure 3.6 Scrum Board

Scrum Team

The Scrum team consists of a product owner, a Scrum master, and the development team. The Scrum teams are self-organizing and cross-functional. In a Scrum team, there is no hierarchy. There can be multiple Scrum teams and a Scrum of Scrums in one SAP S/4HANA implementation. We'll review this concept later in this chapter; however, let's first discuss the role of the different components of a Scrum team.

Scrum Master

The Scrum master isn't the master (or the manager) of the team but rather a servant leader who promotes and supports Scrum as defined in the *Scrum Guide*. For the internal members of the team, the Scrum master ensures that they all understand the Scrum theory, practices, rules, and values. Additionally, the Scrum master helps the members of the organization who aren't part of the Scrum team by guiding their interactions with the Scrum team. It's the responsibility of the Scrum master to maximize the value created by the Scrum team and help everyone understand this change process.

Note

Scrum is defined completely in the *Scrum Guide*, created by Ken Schwaber and Jeff Sutherland. The *Scrum Guide* is maintained independently of any company or vendor at *www.scrumguides.org*. It's important to go through the *Scrum Guide* for further clarity.

Product Owner

The product owner role is accountable for maximizing the value of the product. The product owner can take the input from various stakeholders to build the product backlog but is the sole owner of the backlog. No one else can change the product backlog. However, the owner, occasionally, can delegate this responsibility to the development team.

Development Team

The development team is a cross-functional team that consists of professionals who work on the user stories to deliver a releasable increment per the definition of "done" at the end of the sprint. The development team is a self-organizing team who manages their own work, enhancing the efficiency and effectiveness of the team.

Per the *Scrum Guide*, the ideal team size is between three and nine. Less than three members in a team decreases interactions and increases skill constraints, therefore affecting the overall team synergy and productivity gain. On the other hand, more than nine members in a team can cause chaos, demanding a huge coordination effort that also reduces the productivity and increases risks.

Table 3.4 compares the characteristics of a product owner, Scrum master, and the development team.

Scrum Master	Product Owner	Development Team
▪ Servant leader ▪ Ensures a fully functional team ▪ Removes impediments ▪ Ensures Scrum processes are followed ▪ Conducts Scrum ceremonies	▪ Manages product backlog ▪ Interacts with other stakeholders to get requirements ▪ Accepts/rejects product work	▪ Self-organizing ▪ Cross-functional ▪ Members have no titles ▪ Works with product owner to create sprint backlog ▪ Selects sprint goal and specifies work results

Table 3.4 Scrum Team

Scrum Ceremonies

Mandatory meetings in Scrum are called "ceremonies." There are four mandatory meetings that should happen at the specified time, as shown in Figure 3.7:

- **Sprint planning**
  - Who: Product owner, Scrum master, development team
  - When: Day 1
  - Input: Ordered product backlog
  - Output: Sprint backlog and goal
  - Objective: Define the work for the sprint
- **Daily Scrum, also known as standup meeting**
  - Who: Scrum master, development team
  - When: Daily for 15 minutes
  - Output: Work package, challenges, solutions
  - Objective: To gain quick understanding of what's going on
- **Sprint review or iteration review**
  - Who: Product owner, Scrum master, development team, stakeholders (optional)
  - When: End of sprint
  - Output: Approved/rejected increments
  - Objective: To review the work
- **Sprint retrospective**
  - Who: Product owner, Scrum master, development team
  - When: End of sprint
  - Output: Improvement
  - Objective: Foster continuous improvement

There are other meetings also, such as product backlog refinement, which we'll explore in this section. Additionally, you can also schedule other meetings as needed, such as for issue resolution or risk assessment.

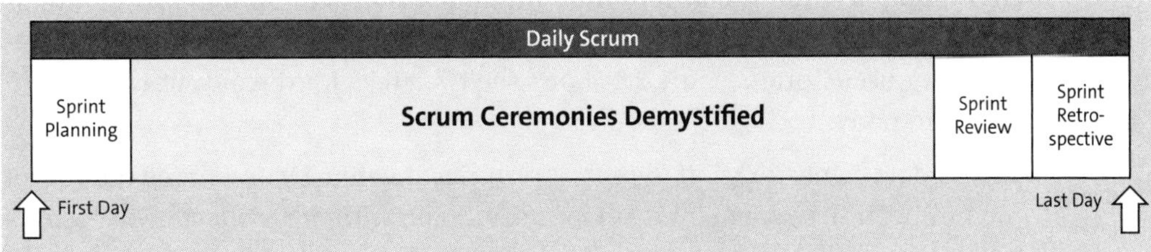

Figure 3.7 Scrum Ceremonies

Daily Scrum

This daily meeting must happen at the same time and same place to reduce the complexity. Ideally, it should not be conducted in a conference room where participants can sit down and relax. It should not exceed 15 minutes and should be conducted standing up, hence the name "standup." In this meeting, each member of the team answers the following three questions:

- What work did I complete yesterday?
- What items will I work on today?
- What impediments am I facing?

All these questions should be answered in front of all the team members. The Scrum master will note down the impediments and help resolve them; remember, the development team is self-organizing, and the Scrum master is part of the development team.

Daily Scrum is an internal meeting for the development team where no other members are allowed, including the product owner, other key stakeholders, or any member of the management team.

Tip

The "three questions" and conducting daily Scrum "standing up" is just a guideline. You can devise your own questions, but during this meeting, you can't go deeper into the status such as "why" or "why not," and so on. In addition, the *Scrum Guide* directs you to complete this meeting in 15 minutes.

There will likely be at least one question regarding Scrum ceremonies on the exam. You should answer based on the three standard questions.

Sprint Planning

The sprint planning meeting is the first step of the official start of the sprint. There are two logical parts of this meeting; in the first part of the meeting, the team decides "what" to build while during the second part of the meeting, the team discuss "how" to build. The goal of the sprint planning meeting is to identify items from the product backlog so that the team can work on those features, requirements, or user stories. Figure 3.8 shows the two steps for the output of the planning ceremony.

The product owner kicks off the sprint planning meeting by describing the goal of the sprint. The development team in consultation with the product owner selects the features from the product backlog based on their value, priority, "definition of ready," and its alignment with the sprint goal. At times, some of the high-priority items may not be aligned with the sprint goals, such as some technical enhancements, security features, or integration-related user stories.

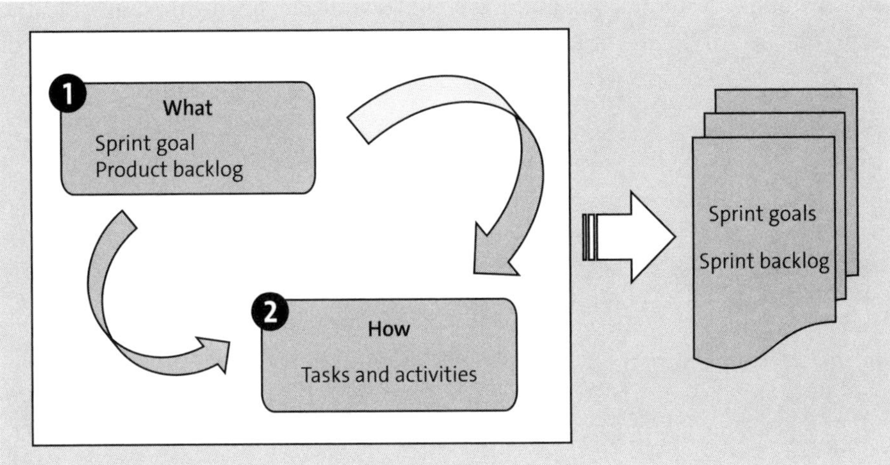

Figure 3.8 Sprint Planning

After the "what" is defined, the team moves on to discuss the details of each user story, identifying the ground-level tasks and activities. It helps facilitate better understanding of the requirement, technical and/or functional dependencies, required security features, integration functionalities, and a better estimate. Ideally, these dependencies should be a part of the product backlog refinement process and discussions. It's also important to understand that these dependencies are part of the product backlog, but it's always the best idea to discuss these during the sprint planning meeting for any missed dependencies. There is no guideline on whether to break all the user stories into smaller and more manageable tasks and activities or only the first few. Most of the Scrum team will break at least some of the user stories. It's important to remember that things can and will change during the sprint.

For a sprint of four weeks, the sprint planning meeting should not exceed eight hours. For shorter sprints, the time-box should reduce proportionately. The guideline provided here is for the maximum number of hours. The sprint planning meeting can be of seven hours for a four-week sprint, but it can't exceed six hours for a three-week sprint.

Sprint Review

The sprint review meeting, as shown in Figure 3.9, is an inspection meeting where the product owner inspects the product of the sprint or increment to ensure that the increment has correct, desired, and complete features per the sprint backlog.

The development team will provide the detailed demos of all the features in the system. The product owner and sometimes other key stakeholders and business heads/users will also participate in the demo session to review the increment. At the end of this meeting, the team notes the accepted and rejected features along with any bug or potential bug in the system. In addition, during this meeting, the team will check if the increment is complete in accordance with the "definition of done."

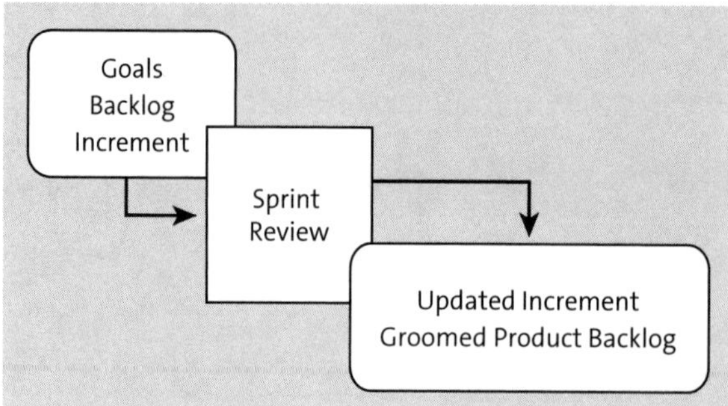

Figure 3.9 Sprint Review

The sprint review meeting is time-boxed to four hours for a four-week sprint. Once again, it's the maximum allowable duration and can be less.

Sprint Retrospective

The sprint retrospective meeting requires a lot of groundwork and preparation—it isn't your normal meeting. As a member of the team, you always go through certain highlights and lowlights during the sprint process. It's important to capture those moments with sufficient data and insights before one can attend and provide value to the sprint retrospective meeting.

The purpose of this meeting is to understand what went well, what went wrong, and what you've learned, as well as to ensure that the agreed-upon corrective action should be part of the sprint backlog in the next sprint. Figure 3.10 shows the three inputs that the team must convert into actionable items.

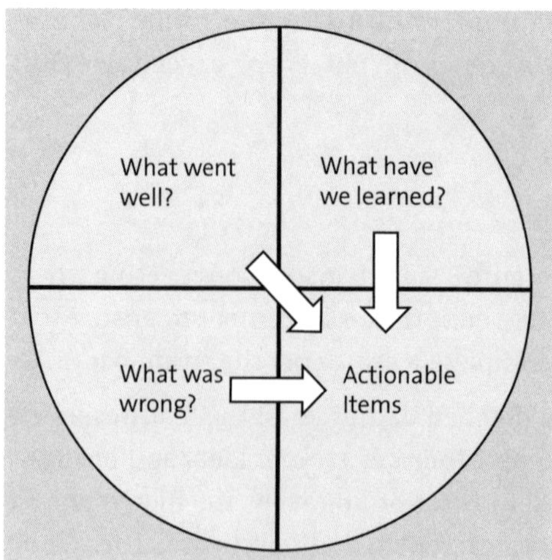

Figure 3.10 Sprint Retrospective

You can correlate this meeting with the lessons learned meeting from the waterfall methodology with the following exceptions:

- It's a time-boxed meeting. For a four-week sprint, it's boxed for three hours.
- Unlike the lessons learned meeting, which happens at the end of the project, the retrospective meeting happens at the end of each sprint.

Keep in mind that the sprint retrospective meeting is different from the sprint review meeting.

Product Backlog Refinement

Product backlog refinement, also known as product backlog grooming, as shown in Figure 3.11, generally happens toward the end of a sprint, preferably two to three days before the end of the sprint, to add enhanced details to the product backlog items. Product backlog refinement is attended by the product owner, Scrum master, and development team. This process ensures that the product backlog is ready with all the granular information for the upcoming sprint planning meeting.

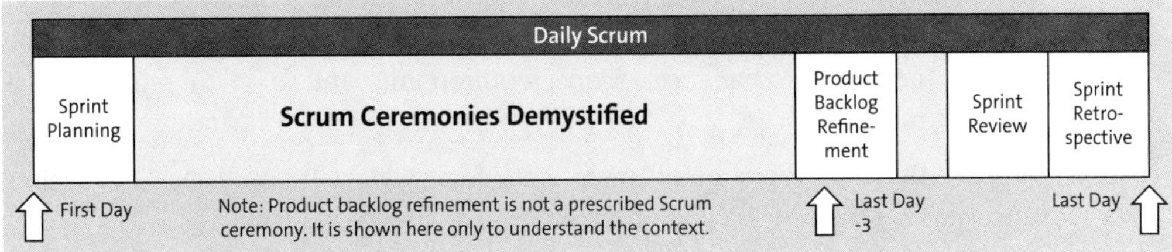

Figure 3.11 Product Backlog Refinement

Scrum Artifacts

Scrum's artifacts provide transparency across the project team and opportunities for inspection, adaptation, and improvements. One of the three pillars of Scrum is transparency, and these artifacts provide maximum transparency of key information so that everyone has the same understanding of the artifacts. Product backlog, sprint backlog, and increment are three artifacts of Scrum.

SAP Activate and Scrum

One of the first decisions that you face in implementing a project is the implementation methodology, that is, whether to go with a waterfall approach or to use the Scrum framework. Based on the methodology, the sponsor (or a project manager) will form a team and implement the project governance. In this section, we'll review the fit of the Scrum methodology to implement SAP projects.

There are four key aspects to consider the fitment of a project to the Scrum framework:

- **Project fit**
  Is the project more suitable for the Scrum framework or the traditional waterfall approach?
- **Organizational fit**
  How suitable is the client's organization for the Scrum approach? Are they ready? To what extent? Do they have the courage to make such a huge organizational-level change?
- **Project manager fit**
  Is the project manager chosen for this implementation a good fit for the Scrum framework?
- **Project team and stakeholder fit**
  Are the project team and other stakeholders a good fit for Scrum?

Let's understand the cone of uncertainty and see how it differs for Scrum as compared to the waterfall approach. In software development, the uncertainty is higher at the beginning when you know a little about the project and the product of the project. However, as you progress, you'll know more and more about the project, risks, issues, challenges, scope, requirements, and so on, therefore, reducing the uncertainty.

Figure 3.12 shows the cone of uncertainty for a waterfall approach. The level of uncertainty is high when you provide the effort and cost estimates.

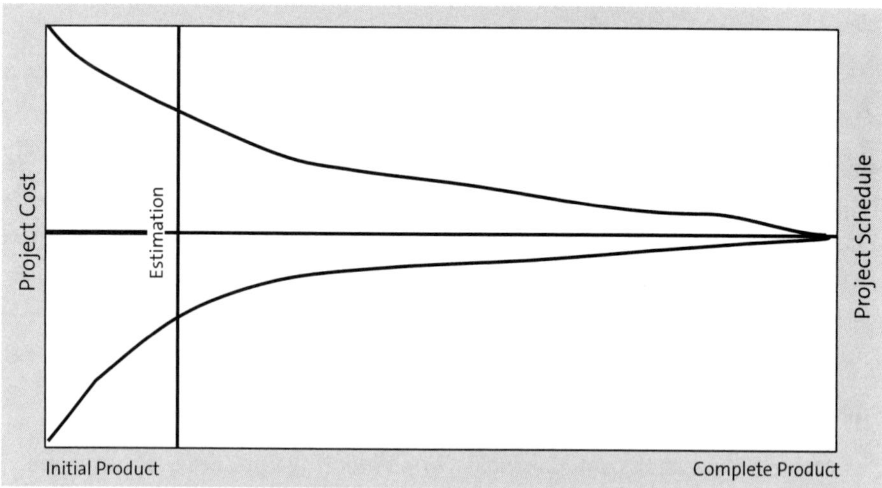

Figure 3.12 Cone of Uncertainty: Waterfall

However, in a Scrum framework, the cone of uncertainty reduces and limits it to the size of the sprint, as shown in Figure 3.13. For Scrum, you estimate only for the given sprint and have a better understanding of the limited features that you implement, so the team can provide better estimates.

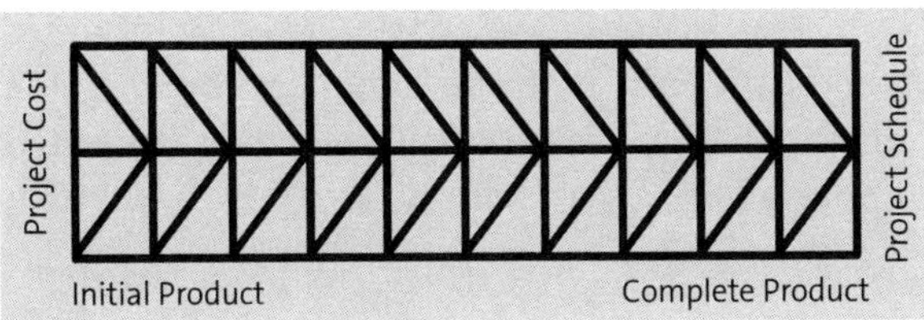

Figure 3.13 Cone of Uncertainty: Agile

Some of the key benefits of the Scrum framework are as follows:

- Robust requirement
- Rapid releases to the end users—repeat response mechanism
- Change compatible—the Scrum framework accepts changes
- Enhanced customer satisfaction
- Lower cost with enhanced efficiency

Roles and Responsibilities

For the successful execution of SAP implementation projects using the SAP Activate methodology, as a project manager, you must have a sound understanding of who is doing what. There are three roles in the Scrum framework as discussed briefly earlier in the "Scrum Team" section. In this section, we'll broaden the view to understand how those roles fit into the SAP S/4HANA implementation. We'll further compare the differences between the Scrum master and the traditional project manager.

Scrum Master

The Scrum master is the servant leader of the team who is different from the project manager. The key responsibilities of a Scrum master in the SAP S/4HANA project implementation is to facilitate, guide, motivate, and enhance the Scrum usage in the organization. The Scrum master is the one who is responsible for arranging and facilitating the Scrum ceremonies, creating necessary documentation and helping resolve any impediments. The Scrum master is a thought leader who has a thorough understanding of the concerned business process. Some of the key tasks and activities performed by the Scrum master are shown in Figure 3.14:

- **Product backlog refinement**
  The Scrum master must ensure that the ordered product backlog is available, and the high-priority items are detailed and can be estimated. They must also ensure the team concurrence before the sprint starts.
- **Project preparation**
  The Scrum master must complete and correct the project setup and make sure the product backlog is available, the technical environment/architecture is in place, and the key stakeholders are identified.

- **Sprint planning**
  The Scrum master must ensure the presence of the development team and the product owner. They must make sure that the ceremony agenda is circulated and followed with the following sequence:
  - Product background
  - Backlog item details
  - Estimation
  - Capacity

  They must establish the sprint goal and commitment.
- **Sprint in-progress**
  The Scrum master must conduct daily Scrum. They must also remove impediments and update the Scrum board, burn-down charts and burn-up charts, and other metrics. They must also conduct other Scrum ceremonies and timely clarification meetings with the product owner.
- **Sprint review**
  The Scrum master must ensure timely and effective reviews and document the findings. They must also ensure product feedback, and that feedback is incorporated into the subsequent sprint.
- **Sprint retrospective**
  The Scrum master must identify highlights and lowlights. They must also build a consensus to incorporate one lesson into the next sprint.

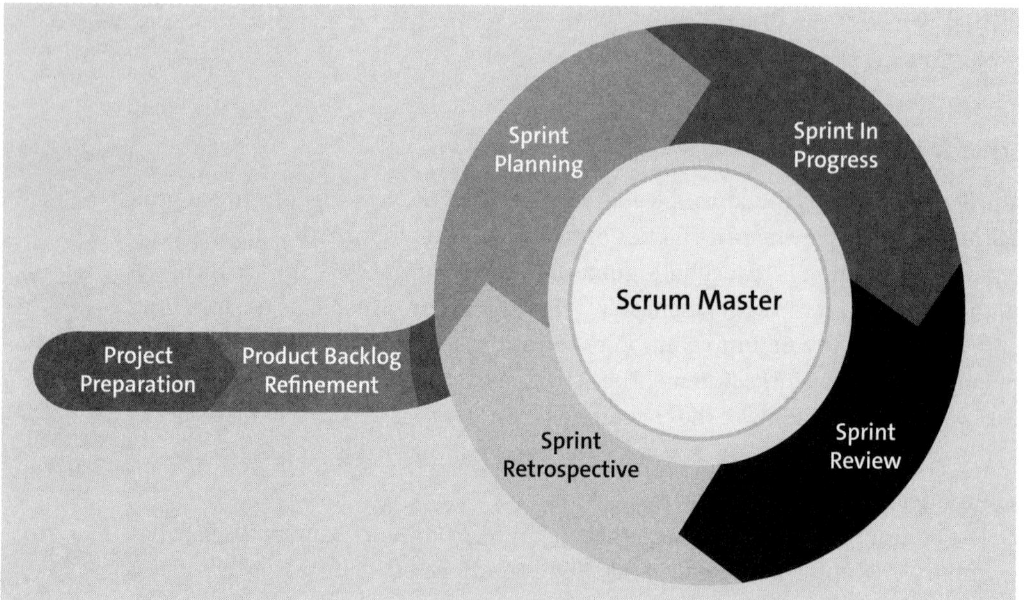

Figure 3.14 Scrum Master

Project Manager

A project manager in an SAP S/4HANA implementation project will oversee all the façades of the project management. The project manager will have traditional project management activities to fulfill the prime responsibility of meeting the business objective of the project within the defined triple constraints. The list of project management activities is as follows:

- Create the project charter.
- Create and conduct the project kick-off meeting.
- Create all the management plans, including the communication plan, stakeholder management plan, scope management, resource management, risk management, and others.
- Create the project management plan.
- Build a consensus across the project organization on the management plans.
- Ensure the approval of the management plans.
- Monitor and report the project triple constraints.
- Record other agreed-upon metrics.
- Track issues and risks.
- Perform other activities as needed to fulfill the project objectives.

A successful SAP S/4HANA project needs an excellent project manager.

Product Owner

In a traditional SAP implementation project, the business owners or process owners provide the requirements. The single point of contact (SPOC) facilitates the requirement-gathering meeting (or blueprinting). In the SAP S/4HANA implementation project, the product owner in consultation with the business/process owners provides the requirement in terms of user stories during the sprint planning meeting. The user story is further clarified, if the need arises, by the product owner with the necessary support from the business/process owner. The SPOC and process owner aren't the same, however.

By definition, a product owner represents the business and defines the product features, sorts them in a specific order, and decides the product (or implementation) release date. The success of the SAP S/4HANA implementation lies on the product owner, who can make all the relevant decisions related to the product features or business requirements. The product owner is the only role in the SAP Activate methodology who can accept or reject an increment or cancel the sprint.

The responsibilities and the success factors of a product owner are listed in Table 3.5.

Responsibilities	Success Factors
▪ Provides product vision and roadmap ▪ Works closely with the key stakeholders, process owners, and business owners ▪ Works closely with the development team to ensure the successful sprint ▪ Provides a complete user story and the necessary details for a good estimation ▪ Provides timely clarifications to the development team ▪ Promotes the SAP project within the organization	▪ Has sound business process knowledge ▪ Has expert-level knowledge of the Scrum framework and a good understanding of SAP ▪ Understands the organizational hierarchy and can navigate through the political hierarchy within the organization ▪ Dedicated to the success of the project/product ▪ Has strong management support

Table 3.5 Product Owner: Responsibilities and Success Factors

For the successful implementation of the SAP S/4HANA project, a sound product owner is required.

Development Team

The third pillar of the Scrum framework is the development team. In the SAP Activate methodology, the development team size lies between 4 and 10. The responsibilities of a development team are as follows:

- Seek clarifications from the product owner, and provide the estimation.
- Implement the user stories.
- Meet sprint goals and objectives.
- Inform the Scrum master of any impediments.
- Attend daily Scrums and all other Scrum ceremonies.
- Update the Scrum board on a regular basis.
- Ensure the self-organization and cross-functional nature of the development team.
- Support each other throughout the process.
- Demonstrate the increment during the sprint review.
- Provide the necessary feedback (highlights and improvement areas) during the sprint retrospective.
- Utilize SAP accelerators, wherever available.
- Proactively provide suggestions and recommendations to improve business processes.

Agile Project Organization

SAP S/4HANA implementation projects are generally large, spanning multiple geographies, including several functionalities from multiple business units. Although the Scrum framework warrants one product owner for a product, implementing a global, large, complex SAP S/4HANA project requires product owners to have multidisciplinary knowledge. In this section, we'll discuss the project organizational structure in an agile implementation.

Conway's Law

Melvin Conway in 1967 introduced an idea that "any organization that designs a system (defined broadly) will produce a design whose structure is a copy of the organization's communication structure."

Most organizations today identify the software development requirements based on their business goals, expecting to achieve an organization-wide business transformation. They fail to meet the transformation expectations, however, mainly because they overlooked Conway's law.

Let's take an example of an SAP implementation with finance and procurement. In this implementation, the finance team will bring in their expertise in the current processes related to bank master, vendor management (assuming the finance team is the owner for the vendor master), and accounts payable and receivable processes. While the procurement process owners will bring their expertise in all procurement processes, including purchase requisition, purchase order, related approval process, notifications, goods inspection, and receipts. Per Conway's law, these processes and systems will integrate in a way that reflects the way these departments communicate within the organization.

On the other hand, one organizational leader who favors a multidisciplinary approach will form a series of cross-functional teams driven by the business capabilities. In this scenario, the resulting product produced by the team will have more distributed capabilities and an architecture that delivers greater business goals and achieves the transformation objectives. The cross-functional, self-organizing Scrum teams are based on this concept.

Scrum Teams and Scaling Agile

SAP implementations and conversions are complex, often involving multiple locations and business units. For the complex projects, the project team is advised to use scaling techniques such as Nexus, Scaled Agile Framework (SAFe), or Large-Scale Scrum (LeSS). In Chapter 4, we'll review SAFe in more detail, but for this chapter, understand that you can scale your team based on the complexity of the project and still retain the agility of the product and processes.

In a simple SAP S/4HANA implementation, for example, the implementation of SAP S/4HANA Finance for a midsized pizza delivery company, as shown in Figure 3.15, the Scrum team will have a different structure as compared to a global SAP S/4HANA implementation of a drug manufacturing company. Figure 3.16 shows a typical team in the global implementation to implement, for example, SAP S/4HANA Finance, revenue recognition, warehouse management, production planning, procurement, sales and distribution, quality management, SAP Business Warehouse (SAP BW), SAP SuccessFactors, and SAP Concur.

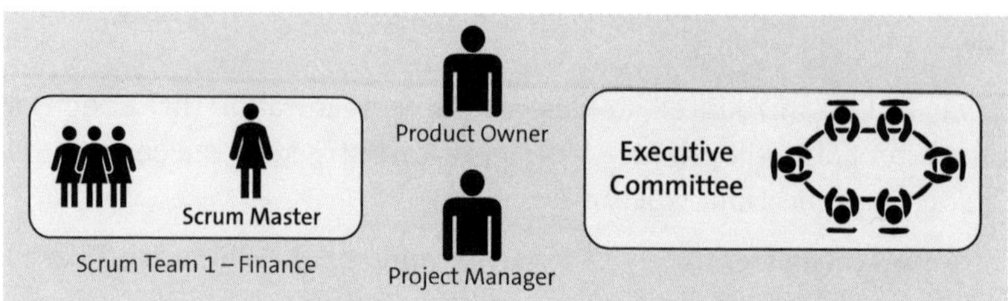

Figure 3.15 Simple Scrum Team

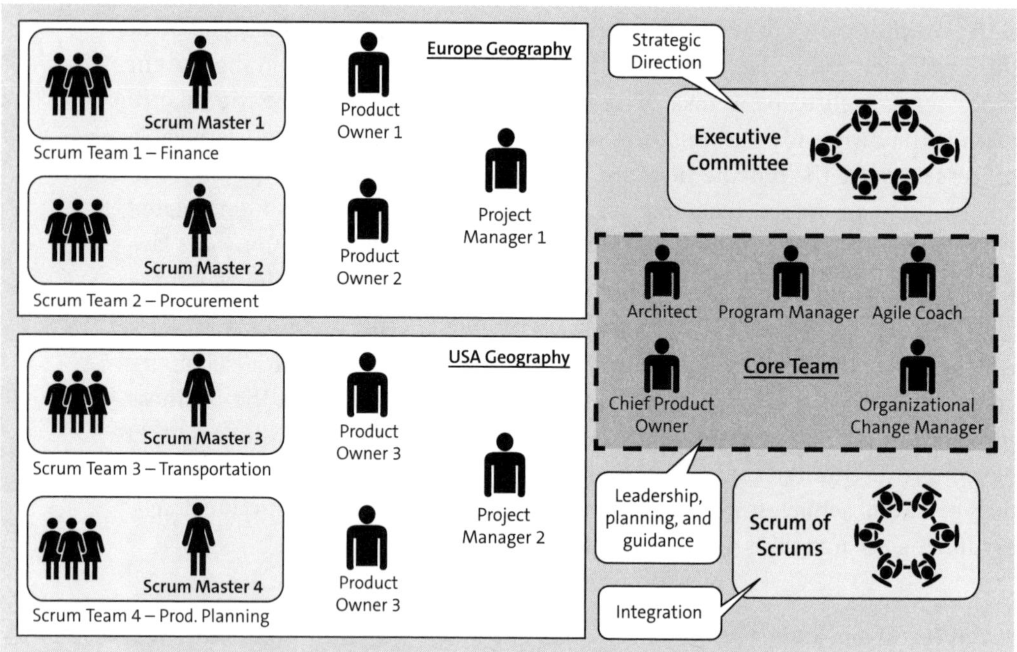

Figure 3.16 A Typical SAP Implementation Team

However, the Scrum teams in the global implementation team will be completely different, and there's a need to have multiple teams, product owners, project managers, and program managers.

Figure 3.16 shows one way of arranging the project team where each Scrum team focuses on an individual module, and the Scrum of Scrums as shown in Figure 3.17 will focus on integrating these modules. The Scrum of Scrums will consist of product owners, Scrum masters, project managers, and lead consultants from the individual Scrum teams. This team will focus on building a cohesive solution that fits the individual processes needs as well as the integrated requirements. They will work with the chief product owner, who is part of the core team, to build the product backlog for the development teams. Scrum of Scrums meetings have the following characteristics:

- Teams are allowed to discuss their work, focusing on overlaps and integration.
- Participants can be product owners, Scrum masters, project managers, and lead consultants.
- Optional participants include program managers, change managers, and others based on the needs of the project.

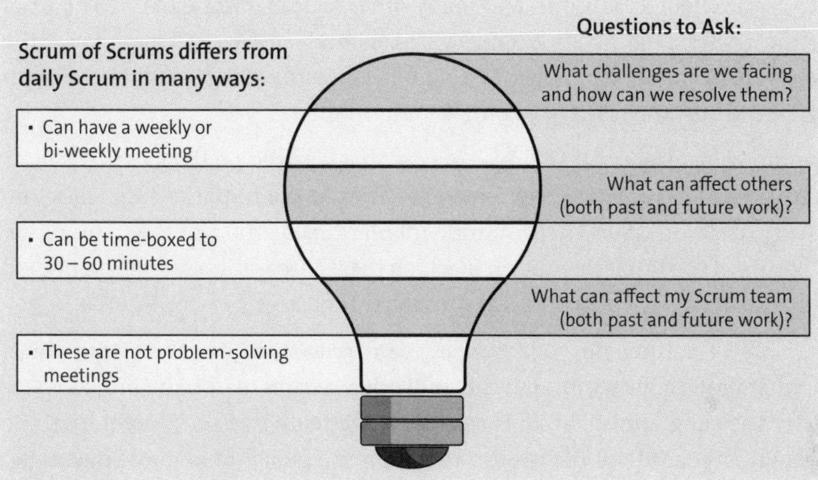

Figure 3.17 Scrum of Scrums

Tip

You'll most likely see at least one question about Scrum of Scrums on the exam. Remember that Scrum of Scrums may or may not be a daily meeting, is mostly used in large team setups, is an integration meeting, and is time-boxed not necessarily to 15 minutes (recommended for 30 or 60 minutes). In addition, it's *not* a problem-solving meeting.

In our example, the core team will consist of a program manager, chief product owner, chief architect, organizational change manager, and agile coach. An agile coach isn't required for a simpler team structure where the Scrum master will promote the agile concepts; however, it's required for a complex project setup like this. The core team will focus on the planning, continuous improvement, and risk management at the program level and provide leadership and guidance based on Conway's law, business objectives, and organization policies. Figure 3.16, shown previously, illustrated a typical SAP implementation team, with the various Scrum teams with their own product owner for different lines of business (LoBs) depicted on the left-hand side.

Based on various factors, you can have project managers; in Figure 3.16, project managers are set up based on different geography. The core team depicted on the right, along with the key meetings they hold, supports the implementations with key decisions and directions.

The executive committee will provide the strategic oversight and direction to the program.

Agile Project Setup

Agile project setup in an SAP S/4HANA implementation project may vary based on a number of factors, including the size and scope of the implementation, project budget, resource availability, geographical presence of the business users, political scenario at the client's locations, and many other factors. Although it isn't part of the certification exam, it's important to understand, at least at a high level, the project setup. What we've shown is a simple implementation and one way of implementing SAP S/4HANA in a complex environment.

A minimum value product (MVP) is a concept that is based on the fact that clients may want to include only the must-have features in the initial release. This concept is very useful in SAP S/4HANA implementations because of the tightly integrated nature of the implementation in which these integration requirements will become must-have in the second and subsequent releases.

Another way of setting up your project team is to consider the geographical spread, where each country can have its individual Scrum teams and project manager. After the geographical build is complete, the team can start integrating the multi-geography façade of the project based on the global roadmap. You should consider several factors for this approach, such as the local requirements, solution feasibility at the local level, and the global rollout roadmap.

A third approach could be functionality driven where clients want to complete the customer invoicing first, followed by accounts receivable, and then vendor invoicing followed by accounts payable, irrespective of geographical footprint.

Another approach specifically for the greenfield implementations follows the path of sunsetting the client's existing infrastructure and/or legacy enterprise resource planning (ERP) systems. If a certain legacy ERP system is retiring where the client has hosted their financial system, then you can target that system first.

Agile Project Prepare Phase

In this section, we'll look into the list of activities performed by the Scrum team during the prepare phase of the SAP Activate methodology. In this phase, the sponsor and the key stakeholders prepare for the successful implementation of the SAP S/4HANA project. At this time, the product owner, Scrum master, and the rest of the members of the Scrum team may or may not be assigned.

You've already seen the different phases of the SAP Activate methodology in Chapter 1. However, this section will provide the Scrum spin and enhance your knowledge by appending the agile-related activities performed by the organization. The activities are as follows:

- Define project goals and objectives while remembering the specific, measurable, achievable, relevant, time-bound (SMART) criteria.
- Assign the team, including identification of the product owner and Scrum master.
- Identify and onboard the other members of the development team. Remember that the development team is cross-functional and self-organizing.
- Finalize and socialize the roles and responsibilities of the project team members.
- Establish project standards, governance, and metrics that include the tracking and reporting mechanism.
- Promote agile to the organization, sponsor, key stakeholders, and members of the steering committee.
- Recommend the necessary agile-related training and coaching. Attend them and ensure that others also attend it.
- Get the initial system ready.
- Define the documentation standard.
- Prepare for vision and validation workshops.
- Ensure the necessary infrastructure, tools, and techniques for the Scrum teams.

You may be wondering about the documentation standard and its need when Scrum suggests lean documentation. Per the *Scrum Guide*, the only two required documents are the product backlog and sprint backlog. However, the SAP Activate methodology, which is an optimal mix of the waterfall approach and the agile framework, also requires you to create all other necessary documentation that is aligned with the organizational perspective, that can provide value, and that can be maintained. These documents, known as *information assets*, can be stored in SAP Solution Manager.

Creating Product Backlogs

Creating product backlogs is the first step in producing the business requirements. You perform this activity during the explore phase of the SAP Activate methodology. After you have the product backlog, the product owner, in partnership with stakeholders and business owners, prioritizes the user requirements. It's critical to understand that the product backlog contains only the high-level requirements, starting with epics. These epics are broken down into user stories, and the development team will estimate the work for each user story. Based on the "definition of ready," the prioritized user stories will move from the product backlog to the sprint backlog. The development team will follow the sprint backlog and carry out the activities to build the releasable increment by the end of the sprint based on the "definition of done."

Tip

There will likely be at least two questions about product backlog and related topics on the exam.

Let's walk through these activities in the following sections.

Explore Phase

In this phase of the project, the end users will explore the SAP standard business processes. You'll conduct the business process workshops that will help to evaluate the match between the SAP standard processes and the company business processes. The team will note down the matches and gaps during these workshops, which will become the initial backlog. Subsequently, during the backlog build, the team will enhance the initial backlog and fill the gaps through the configurable items. It's an iterative process, which will generate the process and solution documents. These documents will form the basis of the solution validation workshop.

Subsequent sections will detail the three steps in the requirements-gathering process. We'll also look into the prioritization of those requirements, which will lead to the product backlog.

Requirements Gathering

The three steps of the requirement-gathering process are as follows:

1. **Business process workshop**
   The first step in the explore phase is to build the business requirements. You'll demonstrate the SAP standard processes to the sponsor, key stakeholders, and end users. The success of this process relies on several factors, including the groundwork that you might have performed to educate the users and stakeholders. During the workshop, you build consensus on the SAP standards and SAP Best Practices. Any difference in business process, opinion, dissatisfaction, or deviation should be noted with follow-up action items to verify the gaps. These workshops will verify the processes and the overall scope of the work.

   The three substeps are as follows:
   - Demo SAP standards and SAP Best Practices.
   - Build consensus, and identify deviations, if any, and follow-up items.
   - Verify processes and scope of the work.

   Figure 3.18 shows the input and output for this process.

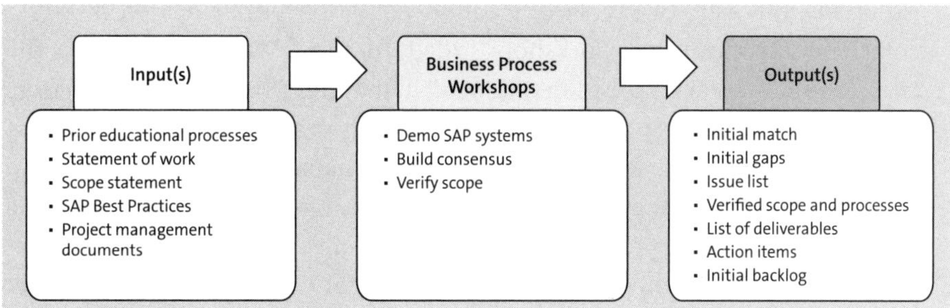

Figure 3.18 Business Process Workshop

2. **Baseline build**

   With the initial backlog items, gaps, and follow-up action items, you'll build the baseline solution in an iterative process. The baseline should be built using the client's data and the structure. You'll show the solution demo to the process owners, who will enhance the product backlog with further requirements for the solution. As a guideline, you should have these demo sessions every one to three weeks, preferably every two weeks. These intermittent reviews will help you demonstrate the continuous progress to process owners. Figure 3.19 shows input and output for this process.

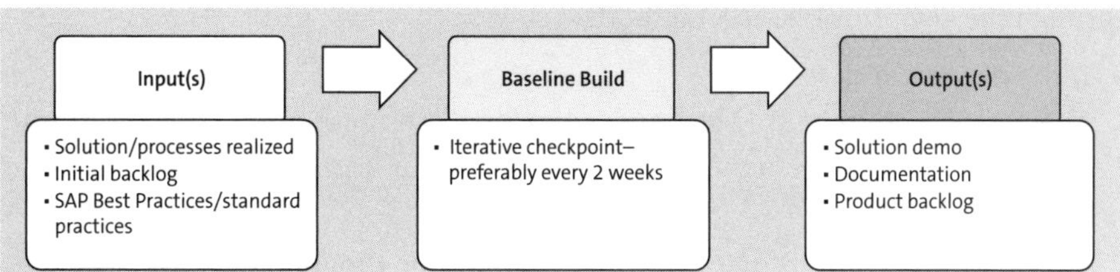

Figure 3.19 Baseline Build

3. **Solution validation workshops**

   Now that the baseline solution is built, it's time to identify any further gaps and delta requirements for the backlog. Furthermore, you'll also validate the baseline build with the business and end users. Figure 3.20 shows the inputs and outputs of this process.

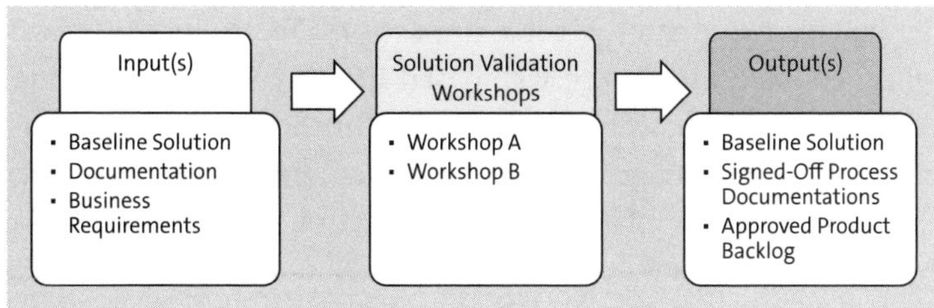

Figure 3.20 Solution Validation Workshop

Essentially, there are two types of solution validation workshops: workshop A (solution validation) and workshop B (delta design). We've looked into the details about these workshops in Chapter 1, in the "Key Characteristics" section. You may recall that the prime objective of workshop A is to identify the degree of fit and the gaps, while workshop B helps you visualize the solution design and architecture for the functional gaps and looks at the delta design to provide information on how to realize the solution and meet the prioritized requirements. However, it's important to understand that you prioritize the product backlog items before the delta design workshops to consider the higher priority items in the design first. We'll look into prioritization in the next section. For this section, let's assume that the backlog items are prioritized.

In Chapter 4, we'll review the different types of sprints in the explore phase and activities between the solution validation and baseline build.

Prioritization

There are several methods to prioritize the product backlog items. For the purpose of this certification, generally, there won't be any questions specific to the prioritization method; however, it's important to understand some of the prioritization techniques that you can use for the SAP S/4HANA implementations. Let's walk through the key prioritization methods:

- **MoSCoW method**
  The most commonly used method is the MoSCoW method, as shown in Figure 3.21, where the requirements or user stories are put into multiple buckets:
  - **Must-have**
    Without this requirement, you can't deliver the product, it may be illegal to use, or it may be unsafe. For a web-based banking software system, you must provide the second level of user authentication by sending a code to their phone number. If, for any reason, the system can meet the requirement with a workaround, then it can't be a must-have. These requirements should move to the should-have or could-have buckets.
  - **Should-have**
    These are critical requirements but not absolute musts. These requirements are important features but can be left out, in which case the system will function normally but have a greater adverse impact on the product's usages, market viability, and success. In the web-based banking software, linking multiple credit cards into one web-based account for the same Social Security Number is an example of a should-have requirement, which, if left out, most of the customers will complain, and the system usage will be drastically low.

- **Could-have**
  These are nice-to-have requirements that are less important than should-have items. Uploading the user's profile picture in a web-based banking solution is a requirement that many customers will love, but if left out, not many customers would notice or complaint about it.
- **Won't-have**
  If all the stakeholders agree to exclude a certain requirement from a given sprint, then that user story will go into this bucket.

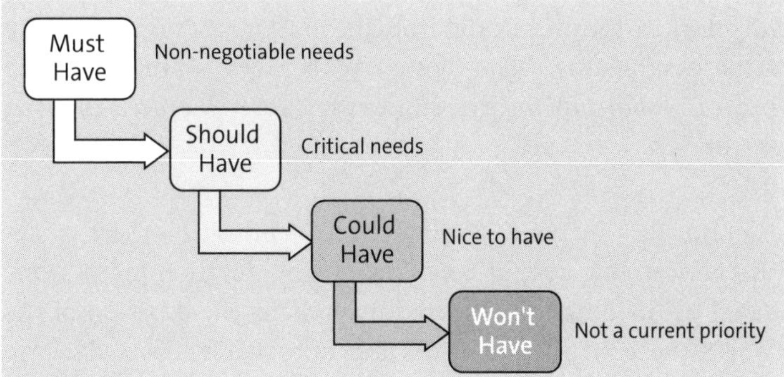

Figure 3.21 MoSCoW

Note
In another variant of MoSCoW, the fourth bucket may be "would-haves" instead of "won't-haves".

- **Kano model**
  The Kano model is similar (although not the same) to the MoSCoW model in which the user stories are categories based on the customer's needs and expectations. These categories are as follows:
  - **Must-be**
    A feature is termed must-be when the end customer expects that feature in the product.
  - **Attractive**
    These are nice-to-have requirements that don't make the product unattractive if they are absent.
  - **One-dimensional**
    These requirements make the users happy when the feature is included but will make the users unhappy if the feature is unavailable. For example, for a web-based banking application, the online wire transfer feature is a one-dimensional feature, which makes the customer happy. However, excluding that feature will make many customers unhappy.

  - **Indifferent**
    The features that have absolutely no impact, adverse or favorable, on the customer satisfaction or happiness will fall under this category.
  - **Reverse**
    The addition of any such features will make the customer unhappy, and the removal of such features will make them happy. For example, a second level of authentication on the name of improved security for any transaction greater than $100 will annoy customers.
- **Stack ranking**
  This method will prioritize the user stories from the most important, called "top of the stack," to the least ranking, called "bottom of the stack." At the end of the prioritization process, you'll rank the user stories from 1 to *n* where *n* is the total number of user stories.
- **Cost of delay**
  This is a complex prioritization method where the team prioritizes the user stories based on the descending cost of delay divided by duration (CD3) score, which is calculated by dividing the expected revenue by the duration of the work. In other words, the team will pick up the user story that is expected to provide the highest comparative revenue.

Although SAP doesn't recommend any prioritization method, it's important to understand the different approaches of prioritization.

Note

There may not be any questions related to the prioritization technique, but we cover this topic to ensure you understand the widely used prioritization techniques in SAP implementations.

Definition of Ready

Two important Scrum concepts that you must understand in the context of requirements and product backlogs are the definition of ready and definition of done. Let's discuss the definition of ready first.

In Scrum, there is nothing called "almost ready." Either the requirement is fully ready to work upon or it isn't ready—it's simply binary. The definition of ready as shown in Figure 3.22 describes the necessary components that the development team is looking for in the user stories from the product owner.

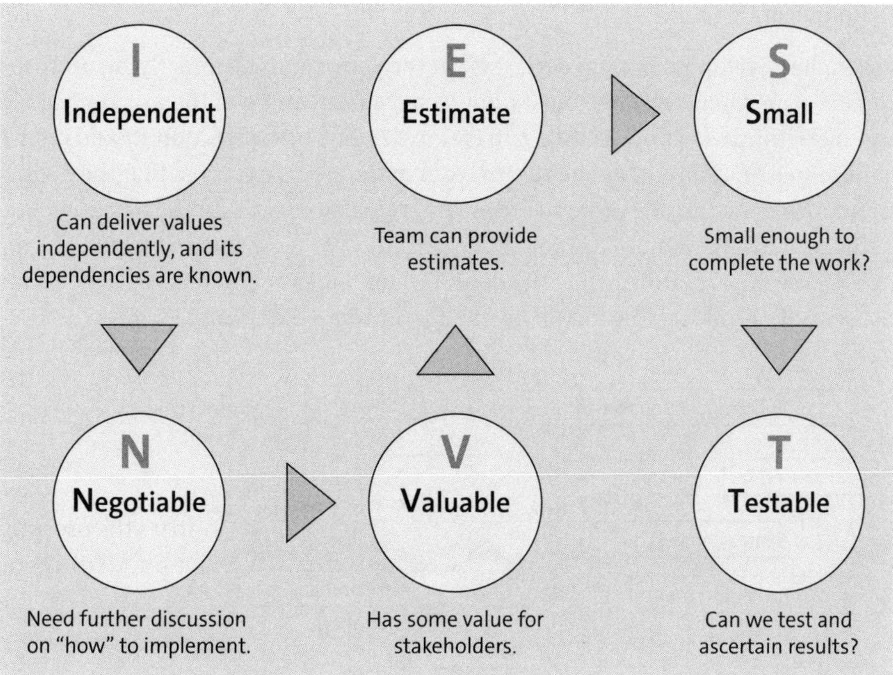

Figure 3.22 Definition of Ready

These components will enhance the clarity of the requirement and should have enough information such that the development team can provide a good and workable estimate that makes the requirement clear, concise, and actionable. Product backlog refinement is the process where the development team reviews the user stories and ensures that the requirements are meeting the definition of ready. The definition of ready tests the INVEST framework as follows:

- Independent
- Negotiable
- Valuable
- Estimates possible
- Small
- Testable

This definition provides a common understanding of the readiness of a user story. It provides the product owner with a tool to ensure that the user requirements are meeting the INVEST framework as described previously. For the development team, it's a key to the successful delivery of a sprint. However, it's important to note that the definition of ready may (or will) vary significantly per Scrum team.

Definition of Done

When the development team declares that the sprint and the underlying user stories are done, then everyone must understand the meaning of the word "done." A sample definition of done is shown in Figure 3.23. The interpretation should not be conditional or different. As the Scrum team matures, it's expected that the definition of done will include more stringent and valuable criteria for the better quality of the product. For a mobile product, the definition of done should include testing in iOS as well as Android, while the definition of done for a web-based agile product should include testing in Microsoft Edge, Chrome, Safari, and Firefox.

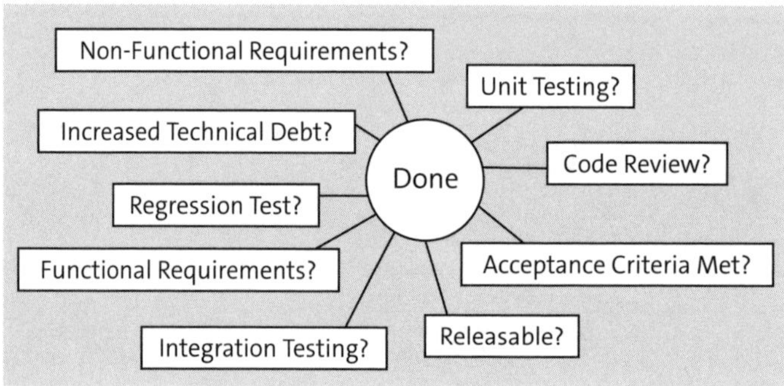

Figure 3.23 Definition of Done

Important Terminology

For this exam objective, you're expected to understand the following terms:

- **Baseline build**
  Baseline build is the software build based on the initial backlog items.
- **Burn-down chart**
  Burn-down charts show the amount of work remaining as the development team progresses in the project.
- **Business process workshop**
  This workshop is conducted at the beginning of the explore phase to build the business requirement.
- **Cone of uncertainty**
  The uncertainty in the software development estimates is higher during the requirement-gathering phase but diminishes to zero at the end of the project development where the risks are transferred to the support team.
- **Conway's law**
  Any organization that designs a system (defined broadly) will produce a design whose structure is a copy of the organization's communication structure.
- **Daily Scrum**
  The daily Scrum is a 15-minute time-boxed meeting with the development team to gather the status of the tasks. It isn't a problem-solving meeting.

- **Definition of done**
  The definition of done is a common understanding that eliminates the guesswork when the team completes and declares the completion of an activity or sprint.
- **Definition of ready**
  The definition of ready defines the set of information that should be included in the user stories for the development team to provide an estimate and move the feature item from the product backlog to sprint backlog.
- **Epic**
  An epic is a large user story that spans multiple sprints.
- **MoSCoW method**
  This is the most widely used prioritization method for SAP S/4HANA implementation projects. In this method, the features are moved to four different buckets: must-have, should-have, could-have, and won't-have.
- **Product backlog**
  A product backlog is a list of user stories arranged in descending order of business value. One product backlog exists for each product.
- **Product owner**
  The product owner provides the user stories in partnership with business owners and ensures that the list is arranged in descending order of business value.
- **Product refinement meeting**
  Although not a scrum ceremony, it helps to facilitate the sprint planning meeting at the start of the next sprint.
- **Scaling agile**
  The Scaled Agile Framework (SAFe) is used to guide the enterprise in scaling lean and agile practices. For more information, visit *www.scaledagileframework.com*.
- **Scrum artifacts**
  In Scrum, artifacts are the work of value that brings transparency; it's also one of the three pillars of Scrum.
- **Scrum board**
  Scrum board is a tool, promptly displayed, to track the progress of the project.
- **Scrum ceremonies**
  The Scrum framework mandate these different meetings, which have a special purpose and are time-boxed.
- **Scrum master**
  A Scrum master is a servant leader who promotes Scrum within the organization and facilitates the different Scrum ceremonies.
- **Scrum of Scrums**
  This is an integration meeting with a representative from all Scrums to discuss the integration aspect. It isn't a daily meeting.

- **Solution validation workshops**
  Solution validation workshops are the combination of solution validation and delta design during the explore phase of the project.
- **Sprint backlog**
  A sprint backlog is also a list of user stories arranged in descending order of business value with the difference that these user stories are planned to deliver in the given sprint.
- **Sprint planning**
  Sprint planning is a ceremony to decide the scope of work in the given sprint; the output of this meeting is the sprint backlog.
- **Sprint retrospective**
  The sprint retrospective meeting is to discuss the lessons learned during the sprint and finalize the improvement areas.
- **Sprint review**
  The sprint review is a meeting with the product owner (and possibly with other business stakeholders) where the team shows the work done during the sprint with an intention to get feedback from the product owner.
- **Story mapping**
  Story mapping is the process to identify any gaps in the complete requirement.
- **User story**
  A user story is a requirement stated from the end-user perspective.
- **Velocity**
  Velocity gives the amount of work done by the team in a sprint.

Practice Questions

These practice questions will help you evaluate your understanding of the topics covered in this chapter. The questions shown are similar in nature to those found on the certification examination. Although none of these questions will be found on the exam itself, they will allow you to review your knowledge of the subject. Select the correct answers, and then check the completeness of your answers in the "Practice Question Answers and Explanations" section. Remember that on the exam, you must select all correct answers and only correct answers to receive credit for the question.

1. What is the difference between the agile approach and Scrum framework?

☐ **A.** No difference

☐ **B.** Agile promotes Scrum framework

☐ **C.** Scrum framework is a form of agile approach

☐ **D.** Both B and C

2. What is the purpose of story mapping?

☐ **A.** To bridge the gap between regular features and integration features

☐ **B.** To help the team understand the requirements in detail

☐ **C.** To help bridge the knowledge gap between the geographically disbursed teams

☐ **D.** To help identify any gaps in the requirements

3. Which is the correct statement (see Figure 3.24)?

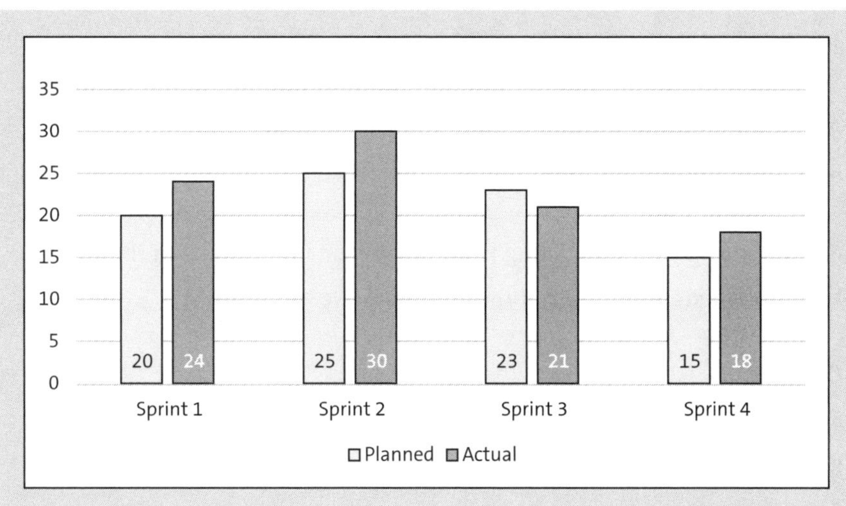

Figure 3.24 Velocity

☐ **A.** Planned velocity (after third sprint) = (20 + 25 + 23) / 3 = 22.67.

☐ **B.** Planned velocity (after third sprint) = (24 + 30 + 21) / 3 = 25.00.

☐ **C.** There are some planning errors leading to higher actual velocity as compared to the planned velocity.

☐ **D.** Actual velocity can't be higher than the planned velocity.

4. As per the *Scrum Guide*, which of the following are the core values of Scrum?

☐ **A.** Promise, courage, focus, openness, and respect

☐ **B.** Commitment, courage, focus, openness, and respect

☐ **C.** Promise, courage, attention, openness, and respect

☐ **D.** Commitment, courage, attention, openness, and admiration

5. What can be five buckets in the Scrum board?

☐ **A.** Product backlog, sprint backlog, work in progress, stuck, and complete

☐ **B.** Sprint backlog, work in progress, stuck, to-verify, and complete

☐ **C.** Product backlog, work in progress, stuck, to-verify, and complete

☐ **D.** Sprint backlog, to-do, work in progress, stuck, and complete

6. Which of the following is an agile ceremony?

☐ **A.** Lessons learned meeting

☐ **B.** Scrum retrospective

☐ **C.** Scrum of Scrums

☐ **D.** Product backlog refinement

7. You're a Scrum master and need to schedule a meeting for Scrum planning. Which two options will you choose? (There are two correct answers.)

☐ **A.** You'll schedule a seven-hour meeting for a four-week sprint.

☐ **B.** You'll schedule a six-hour meeting for a three-week sprint on the third day of the sprint.

☐ **C.** The sprint planning meeting must happen on the first day of the sprint.

☐ **D.** You'll schedule a four-hour meeting for a two-week sprint.

8. Which two of these aren't sprint artifacts?

☐ **A.** Increment

☐ **B.** Transparency

☐ **C.** Product refinement

☐ **D.** Sprint backlog

9. What are the benefits of the agile framework? (There are two correct answers.)

☐ **A.** Higher revenue for the implementation organization

☐ **B.** Cost savings for the client

☐ **C.** Stretches resources beyond their comfort zone to produce faster results

☐ **D.** Better understanding of the requirement

10. Which option describes a product owner?

☐ **A.** Leads the sprint planning meeting

☐ **B.** A tester in the organization who understands product features

☐ **C.** Orders the product backlog at times

☐ **D.** The only person in the organization who owns the product backlog

11. In a complex product development, there are four Scrum teams. However, the challenge is that there are only three Scrum masters. How will you, as a project manager, handle the situation?

- ☐ **A.** I'll ask the client to provide one more Scrum master. Each Scrum team must have at least one Scrum master.
- ☐ **B.** I'll propose that the client add one more Scrum master from my organization; it will boost our revenue.
- ☐ **C.** It doesn't matter; based on the workload, I'll propose to share three Scrum masters between the four Scrum teams.
- ☐ **D.** As a project manager, I can play the Scrum master role for the fourth team.

12. You're the project manager of an SAP S/4HANA implementation, which is implementing SAP S/4HANA Finance for a major power plant in the United States. Your company sees a lucrative opportunity, which is dependent on the success of the SAP S/4HANA Finance implementation. The product owner from the client side is demanding. After the sprint planning meeting, he asks you to reduce the sprint duration from three weeks to two weeks without changing the sprint backlog. What would you do?

- ☐ **A.** You complete the impact analysis and find that you can complete the sprint backlog in 11 working days. You ask your team member to work over the weekend and agree with the product owner, earning some brownie points for the future business.
- ☐ **B.** You inform the product owner that it isn't possible by quoting *Scrum.org* and providing a detailed analysis.
- ☐ **C.** Because you're an expert in Scrum, and you know that the development team is self-organizing, you agree with the product owner and informed the team about the change. You let them decide how to deliver the sprint backlog within 10 business days.
- ☐ **D.** You complain to the sponsor of the program, and ask her to remove the product owner.

13. Where would you keep the requirements for 128-bit encryption, peer review process, and approval from the quality assurance team?

- ☐ **A.** Definition of done
- ☐ **B.** Sprint backlog
- ☐ **C.** Definition of ready
- ☐ **D.** Product backlog

14. As the maturity of the sprint team increases, the definition of done does what?

☐ **A.** It expands.

☐ **B.** It changes—it can expand or contract depending upon the quality of the resource.

☐ **C.** It contracts.

☐ **D.** It should not be changed during the project lifecycle.

15. Which of the following are time-boxed events in Scrum? (There are two correct answers.)

☐ **A.** Product backlog refinement

☐ **B.** Release sprint

☐ **C.** Initial sprint (sprint 0)

☐ **D.** Daily Scrum

☐ **E.** Sprint retrospective

☐ **F.** Integration sprint

16. Burn-down charts can be used to visualize progress toward reaching a goal. What do the burn-up charts track?

☐ **A.** Productivity over time

☐ **B.** The amount of work completed over time

☐ **C.** The amount of work remaining over time

☐ **D.** Cost across time

☐ **E.** The capacity of the development team

17. Which of the following activities are performed by the development team? (There are two correct answers.)

☐ **A.** Estimating user stories

☐ **B.** Selecting the product owner

☐ **C.** Identifying technical dependencies

☐ **D.** Facilitating Scrum events

18. How can the Scrum master improve the productivity of the development team?

☐ **A.** By removing impediments

☐ **B.** By ordering user stories in the product backlog

☐ **C.** By doing the work for the development team

☐ **D.** By increasing the number of sprint retrospective meetings

19. Who owns the sprint backlog?

☐ **A.** Scrum master

☐ **B.** Product owner and development team

☐ **C.** Development team

☐ **D.** Product owner

☐ **E.** Scrum team

20. In an SAP S/4HANA implementation project, how will you handle the requirements related to technical dependencies?

☐ **A.** Work with the product owner, and add nonfunctional requirements to the product backlog.

☐ **B.** The development team can work on technical requirements without adding them to the sprint backlog.

☐ **C.** These are technical requirements and should not be part of either backlog. The development team should incorporate these nonfunctional requirements during the last sprint.

☐ **D.** Add these requirements to the definition of done.

☐ **E.** Work on these technical requirements during the gap between sprints.

Practice Question Answers and Explanations

1. Correct answer: **C**

   There are several agile approaches such as XP, Kanban, Scrum, and others. As mentioned in the "Agile and Scrum" section, Scrum was invented in the early 1990s, while the Agile Manifesto was signed in 2001. However, agile, an iterative approach of software development, was practiced much before the advent of Scrum. Clearly, option A is wrong, while option B is misleading. Option C is the right answer as Scrum is an approach based on the agile principles.

2. Correct answer: **D**

   During the story mapping process, the subject matter expert (SME) tells the whole process as a story, and the members of the development team note down all of their actions and activities and then arrange those tasks on the x-axis representing time. It will help the development team identify any missing tasks and activities, that is, the gaps in the requirement.

3. Correct answer: **A**

   The velocity is calculated by the sum of the story points divided by the number of sprints. Option B is calculating the actual velocity and not the planned velocity. Options C and D are irrelevant, as Scrum doesn't provide any guidelines for planned versus actual velocity.

4. Correct answer: **B**
   Promise, attention, and admiration aren't Scrum values. The five Scrum values are courage, focus, commitment, respect, and openness.
5. Correct answer: **D**
   The Scrum board can't have both the product backlog and sprint backlog. Additionally, the Scrum board must have a to-do list, without which, nothing will make sense.
6. Correct answer: **B**
   In the Scrum framework, there is no ceremony named "lessons learned." The Scrum of Scrums and the product backlog refinement aren't Scrum ceremonies.
7. Correct answers: **C, D**
   For a four-week sprint, the sprint planning meeting is time-boxed to eight hours, and for a three-week sprint, it should be six hours. The meeting may complete early, but you can't estimate that at the beginning of the meeting. In addition, you must conduct the sprint planning meeting on the first day of the sprint.
8. Correct answers: **B, C**
   The three artifacts are product backlog, sprint backlog, and increment. Product refinement isn't a valid term in Scrum, and transparency is one of the core values of Scrum.
9. Correct answers: **C, D**
   The agile frameworks provide an iterative approach to building a product, so it gives you a better opportunity to understand the requirement. Another key benefit is potential savings for the client. Scrum is silent about the higher revenue for the implementing entity and guides against stretching resources beyond a certain point.
10. Correct answer: **D**
    There is only one product owner for each product. At times, the product owner delegates responsibility to the development team to order the items, but the product owner is the only person who owns that backlog.
11. Correct answer: **C**
    Scrum proposes to have a Scrum master for each Scrum team, but it doesn't mandate to have one full-time equivalent (FTE). You can always share a Scrum master between multiple teams as long as the workload permits. As a project manager, you can't play the role of Scrum master for the fourth team.
12. Correct answer: **B**
    A product owner can cancel the sprint but can't change the sprint duration after the start of the sprint. The only correct answer is B. Both options A and C go against the principles of Scrum while option D is wrong.

13. Correct answer: **A**

    These requirements related to security and quality must go into the definition of done. As the Scrum team matures, the definition of done will become stringent and will continue to add security and quality-related activities in the definition of done.

14. Correct answer: **A**

    The definition of done increases with the maturity of the Scrum team. In that way, it facilitates greater stringent criteria for higher quality as the team develops.

15. Correct answers: **D, E**

    From the available options, only the sprint retrospective and daily Scrum are Scrum events. The product backlog refinement isn't a Scrum event. The rest of the options aren't described in the *Scrum Guide* nor are part of Scrum.

16. Correct answer: **B**

    While the burn-down charts measure the amount of work remaining, the burn-up charts measure the amount of work done.

17. Correct answers: **A, C**

    The development team estimates the user stories and identifies technical dependencies. The sponsor selects the product owner and the Scrum master facilitates the Scrum events.

18. Correct answer: **A**

    Make sure that you understand the roles and responsibilities of the Scrum master, product owner, and the development team. Within these options, the Scrum master can improve productivity by removing impediments. They cannot increase the number of sprint ceremonies or do the work for the development team. It's the responsibility of the product owner to order the product backlog.

19. Correct answer: **C**

    Make sure you understand that the product backlog and sprint backlog are two different artifacts. The product owner owns the product backlog, while the development team owns the sprint backlog. The sprint backlog is prepared from the product backlog with the help of the development team, product backlog, and Scrum master.

20. Correct answers: **A, D**

    The first step is understanding the question. There are no gaps between sprints, and the development team will only work on requirements that are in the sprint backlog. Therefore, options B, C, and E are incorrect. The team includes the technical requirements either in the product backlog, sprint backlog during the sprint planning, or in the definition of done.

Takeaway

In this chapter, you learned about the agile approach and one other approach that follows agile, that is, the Scrum framework. Our focus throughout this chapter was Scrum simply because SAP Activate leverages the Scrum framework. We looked into the Agile Manifesto because it's critical from a certification perspective and helps you understand the Scrum framework. You learned many terminologies such as burn-down chart, burn-up chart, epics, and more. In this chapter, you also learned about the three roles in Scrum: Scrum master, product owner, and the development team. Apart from the four Scrum ceremonies—daily Scrum, sprint planning, sprint review, and sprint retrospective—you also learned about the product backlog refinement meeting, although it isn't a Scrum ceremony.

One of the most important things you learned from this chapter is the product backlog and the process to build it during the explore phase of the SAP Activate methodology. Finally, two definitions, definition of ready and definition of done, are critical concepts that bring the same understanding across the team about building the sprint backlog and completing the sprint.

Summary

In this chapter, we discussed the agile and Scrum concepts. We also looked into SAP Activate to understand the Scrum concepts within the framework of an SAP S/4HANA implementation. With the foundation stone of Scrum and SAP Activate, we'll now look into the delivery approach in SAP Activate and the Scrum framework in the next chapter.

Chapter 4
Agile Delivery Approach

4

Techniques You'll Master

- Understand release planning
- Walk through sprint planning and the sprint cycle
- Explain the sprint structure
- Understand testing and deployment activities
- Know the sprint cutover tasks

In the previous chapters, you've learned the agile concepts vis-à-vis the SAP Activate methodology. We also reviewed the prepare phase of the project and went through the tasks and deliverables. Furthermore, we explored the explore phase of the project and covered the fit-to-standard/fit-gap analyses—the key set of tasks that build the product backlog. This chapter will build on what we studied earlier, further your knowledge on the sprint cycles during the realize phase of the project, and enhance your understanding of the testing activities that are carried out during this phase. In addition, you'll also understand the cutover activities that the team will complete using sprints during the deploy phase of the deployment.

Real-World Scenario

You're an SAP project manager with several years of experience who has a deep understanding of the ASAP methodology. You always wondered about the agile approach but struggled to learn the Scrum framework. However, you're the kind of person who always wants to fall forward and is ready to step up.

You stepped up your game, put your heart and soul in this learning exercise, progressed well, and voila!—an opportunity came knocking at your office door in the form of your supervisor. Aware of your charming personality, your abilities to build long-lasting relationships, your ethical behavior, and your recent successful consulting work on an SAP ERP 6.0 deployment at a global adhesive manufacturing company, your supervisor wants to introduce you to a prospective client, Ms. Martha J. Smith, executive vice president (IT) of a chemical manufacturing company.

You talked with Ms. Smith at length about a business transformation project that she is thinking about; you provided much input based on your recent experience and shared some best practices. However, she is well versed in SAP S/4HANA and the SAP Activate methodology where you struggled, specifically in the discussions targeting the latter part of the implementation.

Still, she was delighted with the discussion and invited you to visit their plant in New Jersey, three weeks from now, but you felt uncomfortable about those questions related to the multiple sprint planning, operations, realization, and so on. After she left, you informed your supervisor about the same, and he agreed to support you in this whole process. It was critical for your organization to get this business, but for you, it's a life-changing event as you fully comprehend that the successful implementation of yet another global business transformation project in the chemical industry will make you an expert in the area.

The next morning, your supervisor hands over this book and asks you to read this chapter, twice.

Objectives of This Portion of the Test

The certification examination will test your knowledge about the following topics:

- Release planning based on the prioritized product backlog
- Estimation methodologies—planning poker in SAP
- Multiple release planning
- Executing the realize phase in iterations
- User stories and the measure of completion
- Roles and responsibilities of the team members
- Test activities in Scrum
- Sprint cutover activities

In the following sections, you'll learn about these key concepts followed by some questions and answers.

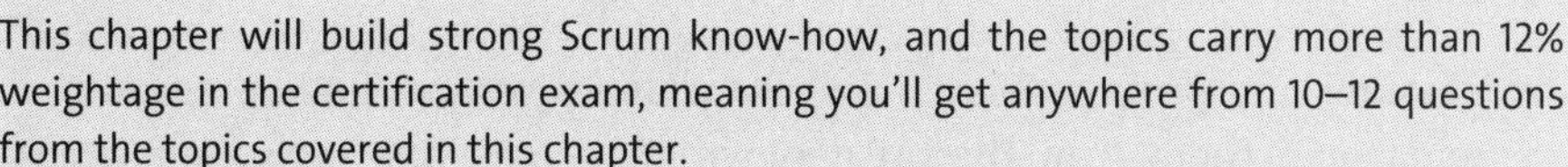

Note

This chapter will build strong Scrum know-how, and the topics carry more than 12% weightage in the certification exam, meaning you'll get anywhere from 10–12 questions from the topics covered in this chapter.

Key Concepts Refresher

This section will help you understand the release planning in the Scrum framework and will advance your knowledge on how to plan iterative releases, testing during the realize phase of the project, and production cutover activities during the deployment phase. These concepts are critical for you to pass the exam.

Release Planning

Release planning is a six-step process involving multiple stakeholders from business as well as client IT, apart from your own team and stakeholders from the implementation organization. Figure 4.1 shows the six steps, which will be explained further in this section.

During this process, the business owners, through the product owners, define the product backlog and prioritize the user stories based on its business value. However, the Scrum team must identify any other technical dependencies to complete the sprint. These dependencies, after discussions with the product owners, will also become part of the product backlog. After the team identifies the dependencies, they will estimate the work and complete the work. After completion of the work, the product owner, in partnership with the business owners, will review the work, provide feedback, and either approve or reject the sprint. The Scrum team, finally, will create the working software release.

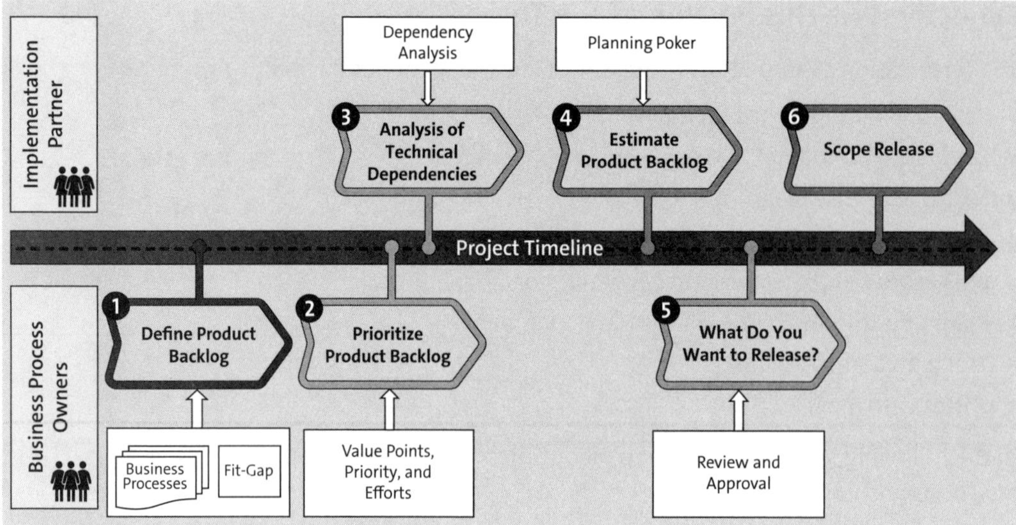

Figure 4.1 Release Planning

Organizations and projects have their own cadence to plan for the product features and release them; from the SAP deployment perspective, we've seen releases after every sprint, especially in cloud deployments, as well as releases after a group of sprints—mostly in on-premise deployments—depending on the business value that the release is adding. At the beginning of this process, the team reviews the three release constraints—scope, budget, and dates—and updates them, if necessary. The team's velocity, which is an estimated value for a new team and the historical value for an existing team, along with the product backlog and the detailed roadmap, serve as an input to the release planning.

The three constraints will dictate the release plan and will vary based on the team's level of flexibility. In almost all cases, the initial release plan happens based on the fixed scope during the proposal phase, and the team comes up with the high-level dates and budget. In the explore phase of the project, after the delta design workshops, the product backlog is ready with prioritized user stories, and constraints are known. The team completes the release planning and creates a list of product backlog items, known as a sprint map (see Table 4.1), that are tentatively mapped with appropriate detail, including estimates and prioritization.

	Release 1		Release 2			Release 3			Release 4
	Sprint 1	Sprint 2	Sprint 3	Sprint 4	Sprint 5	Sprint 6	Sprint 7	Sprint 8	Sprint 9
Functionality A			User story			User story			
Functionality B			User story			User story	User story		

Table 4.1 Sprint Map

	Release 1		Release 2			Release 3			Release 4
Functionality C		User story	User story			User story			
Functionality D	User story			User story	User story				
Functionality E		User story				User story	User story		
Functionality F			User story	User story			User story		
Functionality G	User story	User story			User story		User story	User story	User story
Functionality H				User story		User story	User story	User story	User story
Functionality I		User story		User story	User story		User story	User story	User story
Functionality J				User story			User story	User story	User story
Functionality K		User story		User story			User story	User story	User story
Functionality L	User story		User story	User story	User story	User story			
Functionality M			User story			User story		User story	User story
Functionality N	User story		User story	User story	User story	User story		User story	User story

Table 4.1 Sprint Map (Cont.)

At the end of each sprint, the release planning process repeats with greater details and fewer unknowns, as shown in Figure 4.2.

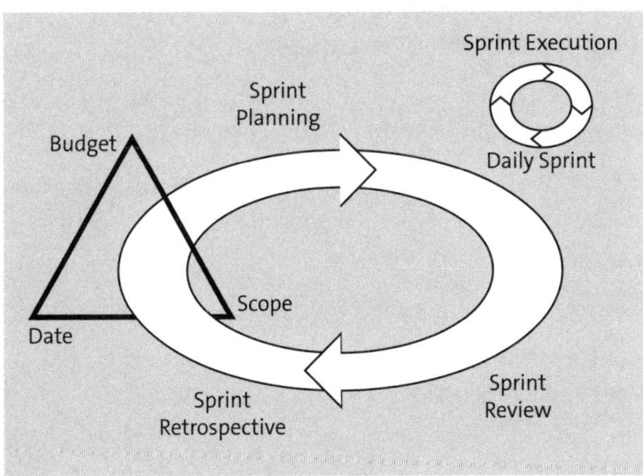

Figure 4.2 Overview of Release Planning

Now, with some understanding of the release planning, let's look at the six steps as mentioned earlier.

Step 1: Define Product Backlog

In Chapter 1, we studied the fit-to-standard process—solution validation, also known as workshop A, and delta design, also known as workshop B—in the explore phase of the project. The team will identify the required business capabilities in the solution; during the delta design workshops, the team will also identify the need for any additional configuration, extension, or integration. All these requirements will go into the initial backlog through which they will make it to the final product backlog, as shown in Figure 4.3.

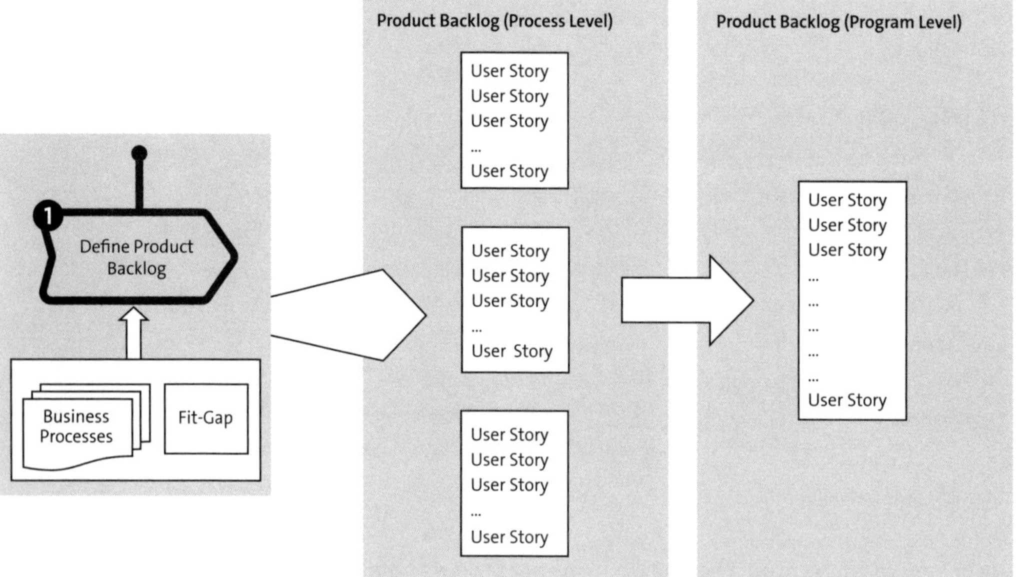

Figure 4.3 Define the Product Backlog

Some of the key features of the product backlog are as follows:

- The product backlog is a live document and will continuously change during the process, which is one of the four values of the Agile Manifesto.
- The product backlog represents the requirements that should go into the solution.
- The product owner owns the backlog.
- The product owner, in consultation with business owners, assigns the business value for each user story.
- The product owner prioritizes the user stories.

Step 2: Prioritize Product Backlog

The product owner prioritizes the program-level product backlog based on the business value. In Chapter 3, you saw several prioritization techniques, including the most common one—the MoSCoW method—where the requirements are categorized into the must-have, should-have, could-have, and won't-have buckets. When you have all the requirements in different buckets, the product owner must rank them within the group (cautiously, so that no items have the same ranking).

Step 3: Analysis of Technical Dependencies

Now, you have all the business requirements identified and prioritized. From a business perspective, let's say the business stakeholder assigned a higher value to the purchase order as compared to the purchase requisition. In another example of an approval workflow (e.g., purchase order approval), the team identifies the requirements for ABAP code and email notifications. In yet another example, the development team identifies the user stories for creating users and assigning roles based on the approved segregation of duties (SoD).

In the latter two examples, it's clear that the development team must identify the technical dependencies to ensure that the user story is ready per the definition of ready; they can then estimate the user story and deliver per the definition of done. In the first example also, the team must clarify the dependency with the business owner.

It's also important to understand the concept of technical debt. Technical debt is the implied cost of additional rework that the team must pay to choose the better or right solution instead of an easy "Band-Aid" solution. While completing the technical dependency analysis, the team must minimize the technical debt.

Step 4: Estimate Product Backlog

The Scrum team must provide the effort required to complete the user stories. Based on the team velocity, an input to the release planning process, the Scrum team will pick up the user stories that can be done within the sprint duration per the agreed-upon definition of done. Traditionally, you would estimate the effort of an activity in in-person days or hours, but in Scrum, you utilize story points—an abstract measure that determines the difficulty level of the Scrum, which relates to the risk, complexity, or simply effort—for effort estimation.

Story Points versus Hours

A story point is an abstract measure for estimating a user story. The Scrum team assigns the story point for each activity, and the summation of all the story points in a given sprint is the effort required to implement the sprint. The ratio between two story points is important rather than the actual numbers. For example, if the story point of activity A is five and that of activity B is 10, then activity B is twice as much of a story as compared to activity A. Assigning 500 and 1,000 for activity A and activity B, respectively, is absolutely fine. Another common approach for the story point estimation is the use of Fibonacci series, a sequence of numbers where each number is the sum of the two preceding numbers and can start with 0 or 1 (however, for estimation purposes, we start with 1).

Story points must include all the factors that affect effort:

- **Volume of work**
  The volume of work to configure chart of accounts is much less than configuring the material requirements planning (MRP).
- **Associated risk**
  Consider the associated risk while configuring a process where the business process owner has signed off on the requirements to that of a process where the clerk has provided the detailed requirements, but the business process owner is asking for many changes.
- **Complexity of work**
  Configuring MRP is, of course, much more complex than configuring chart of accounts.

Table 4.2 shows the salient features of story points compared to the other measure of effort, in-person days.

Story Points	In-Person Days
▪ Measure of complexity. ▪ Across many stories, the variability averages out. ▪ Each organization (sometimes projects within the organization) has a different scale to rate complexity.	▪ Productive time of the developer is measured. ▪ This measure varies with the technology.

Table 4.2 Two Units of Effort Estimation

Planning Poker

Let's play some poker. The best part is, no one will lose and there is no winner. It's a teamwork process where you build consensus and decide on the required effort to complete a user story. Figure 4.4 shows the process of planning poker:

1. **Read the story**
   The product owner or the customer reads the user story for the estimation.
2. **Team estimates**
   After initial discussion and clarification questions, each member privately selects a card representing that member's estimate.

3. **Reveal cards**
   All members (nonexperts) show their cards at the same time. Experts will show their cards after all the nonexpert members.
4. **Team discuss**
   If estimates are the same, then it becomes the estimate of that user story. If not, a discussion takes place that focuses on outliers. The process is then repeated until a consensus is reached.

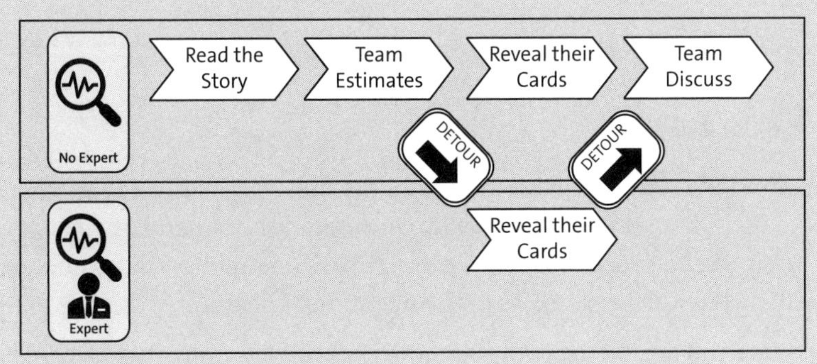

Figure 4.4 Planning Poker

You can play the planning poker with or without an expert; an expert, however, may help you and other members of the team with real-life examples, scenarios, and challenges that will lead to the more accurate estimation. The team composition may vary, and you can have all the members either with the same background or from different backgrounds. The end objective is to build the consensus.

Tip

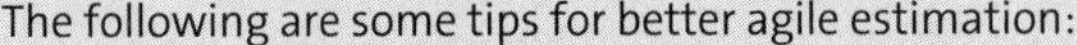

The following are some tips for better agile estimation:

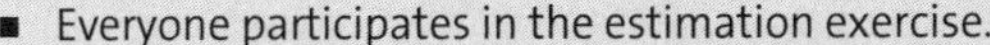

- Everyone participates in the estimation exercise.
- Everyone must be aware of the definition of done and the concept of velocity.
- During the estimation process, most of the communication is verbal.
- Experts from similar projects and functional areas will help improve the results.
- With multiple experts, the team must build the consensus.
- Ask clarifying questions, if needed.
- Use the same measure of estimation for the entire project.
- Build consensus for all user stories. If, for some reason, consensus isn't built, then try breaking down the story into smaller tasks. If it still doesn't work, then defer the estimate for the given story to a later time.
- Use a free "get out of poker room" card to take a break.

The game of planning poker has its own advantages and challenges, as shown in Table 4.3.

Advantages	Disadvantages
▪ Everyone in the team participates. ▪ No lengthy and complex written communication is used. ▪ Each member contributes to the estimate, leading to no (or less) conflict at a later stage. ▪ The process can help in team building.	▪ It takes longer to build consensus, especially with a new team member or with multiple experts. ▪ The process doesn't necessarily produce truly relative story points.

Table 4.3 Advantages and Disadvantages of Planning Poker

Step 5: What's in the Release?

At this stage, you have the complete requirements documented in the product backlog, a list of user stories prioritized by the business value, and team velocity, which is an input to the process. However, the three constraints—date, budget, and scope—will dictate the user stories in the upcoming release.

The product owner will decide the content of the release; remember that Scrum is about a value-driven mind-set where date and budget are fixed (e.g., time-boxed sprint). One of the values of the Agile Manifesto is "responding to change over following a plan."

Step 6: Complete Release Planning

This is the final step of the release planning. Table 4.4 shows the first release comprising two sprints similar to Table 4.1.

	Release 1 (Story Points)	Start	Sprint 1	Sprint 2
Planned	Work remaining at the start of sprint		274	247
	Velocity		35	27
	Additional requirements		5	5
	Work remaining at the end of sprint		244	225
Actual	Work remaining at the start of sprint		274	247
	Velocity		27	37
	Additional requirements		0	5
	Work remaining at the end of sprint	274	247	215

Table 4.4 Release 1: Complete Release Planning

In Scrum, you should always anticipate additional requirements during the sprint.

Multiple Releases

Table 4.5 shows a project of nine sprints across four releases. Table 4.5 shows the story map with the corresponding estimation and Table 4.6 expands on the release planning shown in Table 4.4 for the four releases.

Features	Release 1		Release 2			Release 3			Release 4	Total Story Points (Increasing Complexity)
	Sprint 1	Sprint 2	Sprint 3	Sprint 4	Sprint 5	Sprint 6	Sprint 7	Sprint 8	Sprint 9	
Functionality A			2			2				4
Functionality B			1			3	1			5
Functionality C		2	1			5				8
Functionality D	3			8	1					12
Functionality E		5				3	5			13
Functionality F			13	2			2			17
Functionality G	6	8			2		1	1	1	19
Functionality H				5		1	5	5	3	19
Functionality I		13		2	2		2	1	1	21
Functionality J				1			2	13	8	24
Functionality K		1		8			13	1	2	25
Functionality L	8		3	1	13	5				30
Functionality M			5			8		8	13	34
Functionality N	13		3	3	13	5		1	5	43
Total story points	30	29	28	30	31	32	31	30	33	274

Table 4.5 Story Points

Release		Release 1		Release 2			Release 3			Release 4
Sprint		Sprint 1	Sprint 2	Sprint 3	Sprint 4	Sprint 5	Sprint 6	Sprint 7	Sprint 8	Sprint 9
Planned	Work remaining at the start of the sprint	274	247	215	187	150	117	88	56	23
	Velocity	35	27	32	33	34	34	34	34	28
	Additional requirements	5	5	5	5	5	5	5	5	5
	Work remaining at the end of the sprint	274	247	188	159	122	88	59	27	0
Actual	Work remaining at the start of the sprint	274	247	215	187	150	117	88	56	23
	Velocity	27	37	34	36	37	35	34	34	33
	Additional requirements	0	5	6	-1	4	6	2	1	10
	Work remaining at the end of the sprint	247	215	187	150	117	88	56	23	0

Table 4.6 Multiple Releases

Sprint Cycle

It's important to run the realize phase of the project in iterations. Figure 4.5 shows the iterations from a real-life project, which you saw earlier in this chapter. There were four releases across nine sprints.

Chapter 3, Figure 3.7, shows the four Scrum ceremonies that are necessary during the sprint lifecycle. It's strongly recommended that you review the Scrum board, sprint ceremonies, and the product backlog refinement. It's important to understand that the sprints use the sprint backlog, which is defined by the product owner. The development team commits to deliver the sprint backlog at the end of each sprint. The Scrum team, however, estimates the sprint backlog.

Focused Build for SAP Solution Manager provides a digital Scrum board. You can access the demo version of Focused Build for SAP Solution Manager at *http://s-prs.co/v519405*.

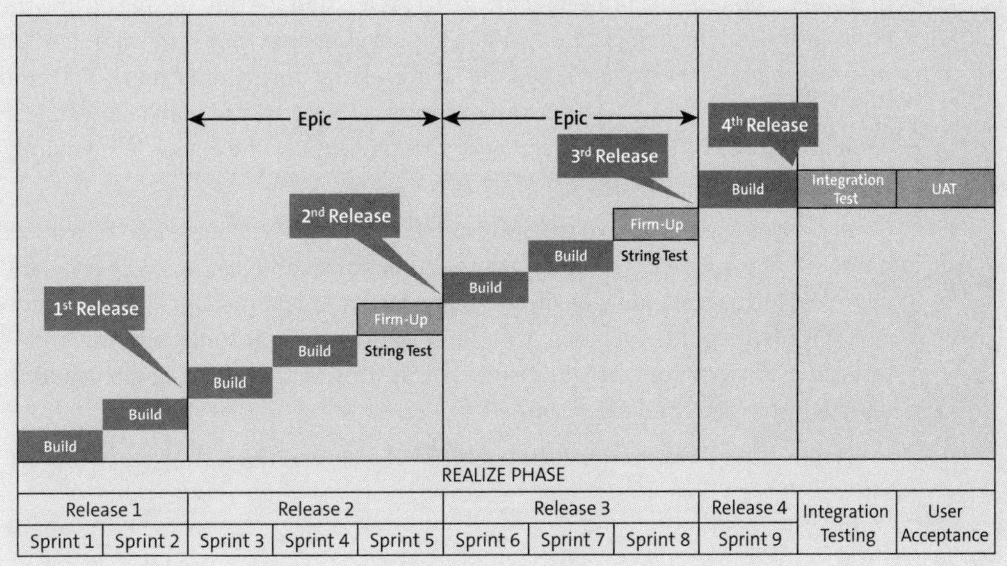

Figure 4.5 Sprint Cycle

Testing and Deployment

In this section, we'll review the different test activities involved in an agile project that the project team performs in different system environments. We'll also understand cutover activities using sprints.

Testing Activities

Figure 4.6 shows different testing activities and the environments where these activities are performed.

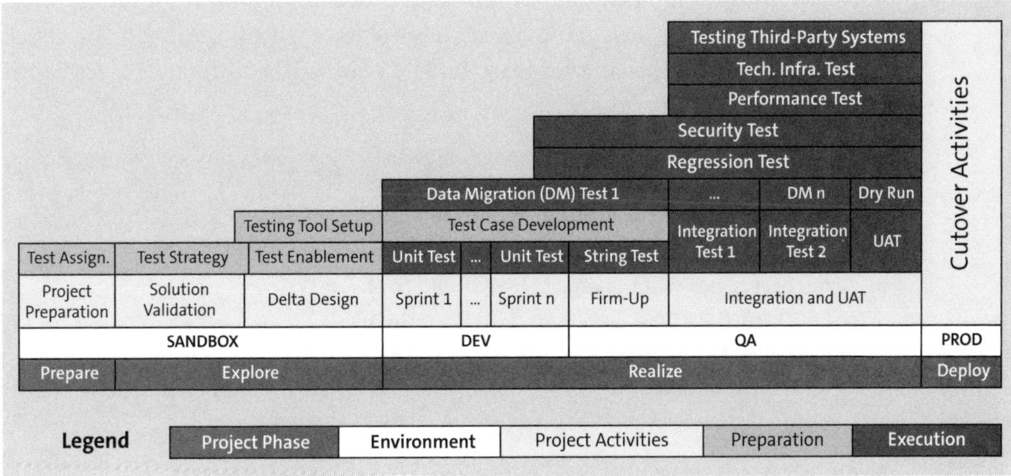

Figure 4.6 Overview of Testing Activities

In the realize phase, the project team, in this project, did the unit testing during the build sprint and the integration sprint in the development (DEV) environment. On the other hand, the team executed the string testing during the firm-up sprint in the quality assurance (QA) system environment. The team also did the integration testing followed by the user acceptance testing (UAT) in the QA system environment.

Every project differs and so does the test strategy, which is delivered in the explore phase of the project, reviewed by the functional and technical teams, and approved by the test manager, project manager, and client manager. The test strategy will identify the data migration and performance testing requirements—including the environment and how the testing data will be created and/or updated—the data, and the systems.

In Chapter 5, we'll review the different types of tests and the testing workstream.

Tip

At the end of each sprint, the team demos the solution to the business and end users to get their buy-in. During the UAT, after string and integration testing, the team again demos the solution to the business and end users. You may get a question in the exam asking about the user checkpoints in an agile delivery approach.

Cutover Plan

By now, the new system is ready with all the required business functionalities on the latest and greatest technology available today. However, the cutover plan—prepared during the prepare phase and fine-tuned during the realize phase—may make or break the new system. Therefore, it's important that you understand the cutover planning in detail.

A cutover plan is a list of detailed tasks in a specific sequence to migrate the data, build the production (PROD) environment, and decommission the legacy system. Every project has its own cutover requirements such as the need for mock cutovers to validate the cutover plan. Table 4.7 shows the different objectives of the mock and final cutovers.

Mock Cutover	Final Cutover
▪ To practice cutover to test the effectiveness of the cutover plan ▪ To discover issues that the project team will resolve before final cutover ▪ To give a good estimate of data quality and data load timing	▪ To follow the cutover plan and complete the cutover to the PROD environment ▪ To ensure the successful transition to the run team ▪ To have strong involvement of organizational change management (OCM) processes and team

Table 4.7 Objectives of Mock and Final Cutovers

For the previously mentioned project, there were two mock cutovers followed by the final cutover, as shown in Table 4.8.

Mock Cutover – 1	▪ Used on the production-like QA environment ▪ Applied manual configurations, performed partial data load, and executed cutover plan ▪ As a result, identified several data quality issues, performance issues during data load, and incomplete checklists and documentations
Mock Cutover – 2	▪ Used on the PROD environment ▪ Built PROD environment and created checklist ▪ Applied manual configurations, performed full data load, and executed cutover plan ▪ Improved data quality and completeness, resolved data load performance issues, and meticulously created documents and checklist ▪ Replicated and tested the disaster recovery environment ▪ Performed backup and restore operations ▪ No major issues identified
Final Cutover	▪ Rebuilt PROD environment by following the checklist ▪ Applied manual configurations, performed full data load, and executed cutover plan ▪ Voila!

Table 4.8 Mock Run of Large and Complex On-Premise Deployment

Figure 4.7 shows the different components of cutover planning and activities:

- **Site readiness**
  This checklist is used to ensure preparedness for the go-live. Although the cutover planning will identify all the activities, this checklist will ensure the execution of these activities.
- **Production build**
  This component will ensure that the PROD environment is ready and has the necessary configuration as identified during the planning.
- **Manual configuration**
  This component lists the manual configurations that can't be transported.
- **Historical data**
  This includes both master and transaction data that should be migrated, along with several other components, as outlined in the data migration plan.
- **Interfaces**
  This lists all the interfaces to run.

- **Go/no-go decision**
  This is a continuous process, and often these decisions are conditional. It should be properly documented and followed through.

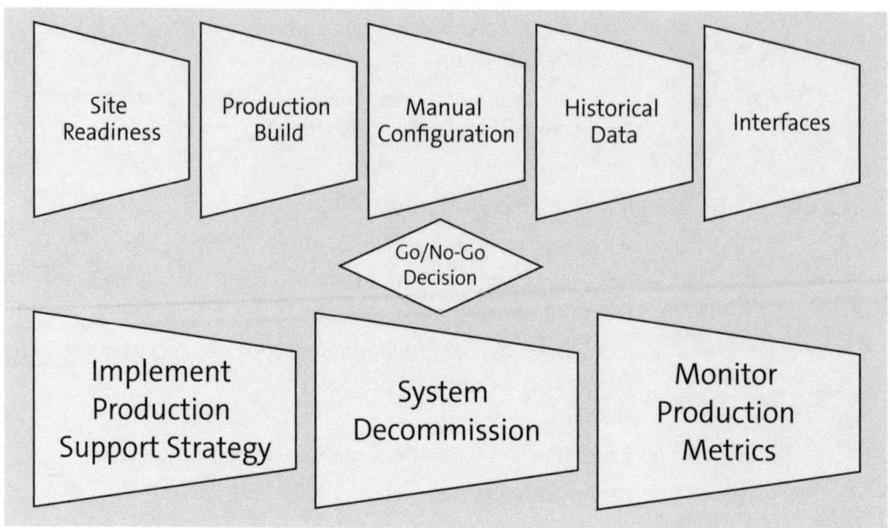

Figure 4.7 Cutover Components

After the system is live, the team must hand over the live system to the run organization along with certain processes:

- **Production support strategy**
  This should be created during the realize phase of the project and implemented during the run phase.
- **Legacy system decommissioned**
  Ensure that the legacy system is decommissioned. Many times, the user's access to the legacy system is revoked, keeping the system alive for any unforeseen circumstances.
- **Monitor production metrics**
  It's important to monitor service-level agreements (SLAs) and fine-tune them as the system matures.

Figure 4.8 and Figure 4.9 shows the create cutover plan step and production cutover step, respectively. In Figure 4.8, you can click the **MS Project Cutover Schedule Sample (SAP Customer)** accelerator to create the cutover plan via the Roadmap Viewer. In Figure 4.9, you must first complete the **Execute Production Set-up** task, and then the **Execute Cutover Plan** task. The latest information is available on the Roadmap Viewer.

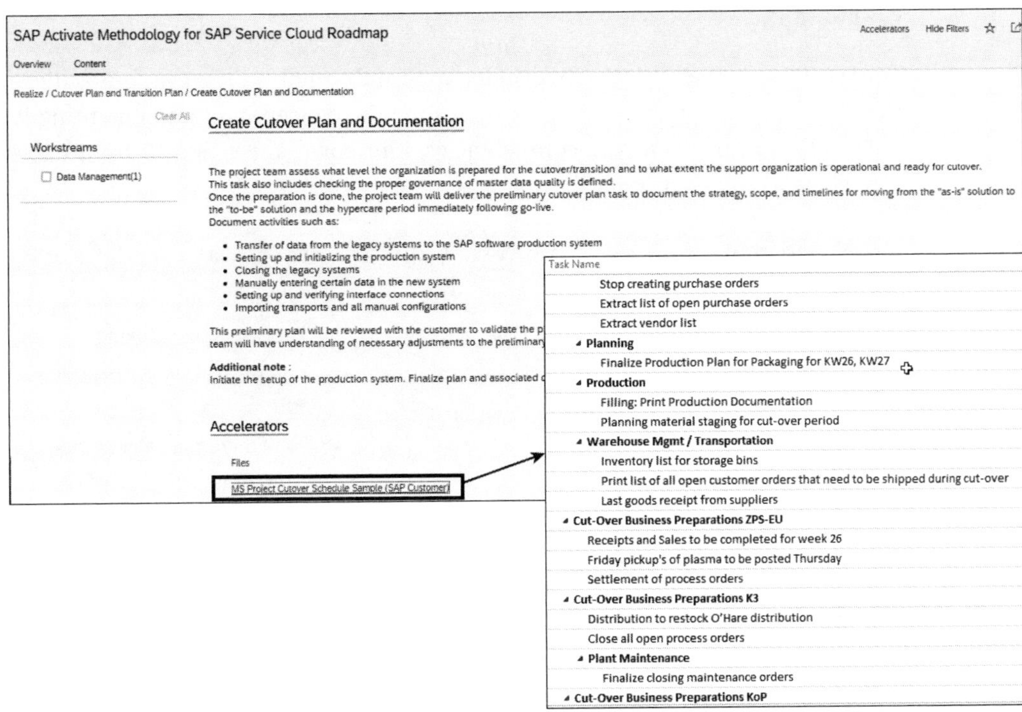

Figure 4.8 Create Cutover Plan

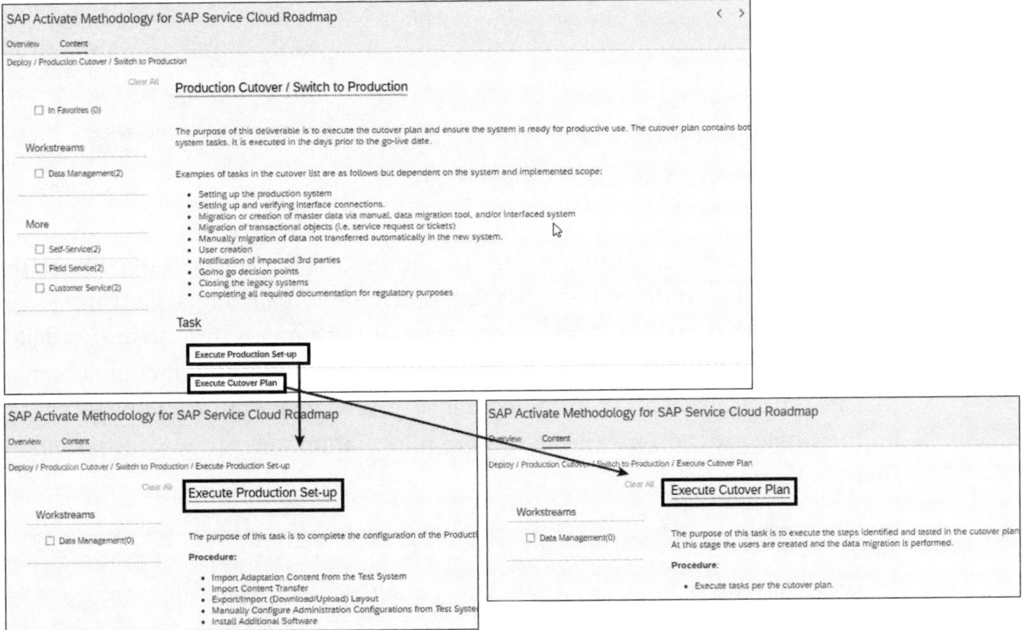

Figure 4.9 Production Cutover

Scaling Agile

The Scaled Agile Framework (SAFe) helps large and complex organizations achieve the benefits of the agile framework by scaling the concept and implementing it. SAFe is based on seven core competencies, four core values, and 10 immutable principles, as shown in Table 4.9.

Core Competencies	Core Values	Immutable Principles
▪ Team and technical agility ▪ Agile product delivery ▪ Enterprise solution delivery ▪ Lean portfolio management ▪ Organizational agility ▪ Continuous learning culture ▪ Lean-agile leadership	▪ Alignment ▪ Built-in quality ▪ Transparency ▪ Program execution	▪ Take an economic view ▪ Apply system thinking ▪ Assume variability; preserve options ▪ Build incrementally with fast, integrated learning cycles ▪ Base milestones on objective evaluation of working system ▪ Visualize and limit work in progress (WIP), reduce batch sizes, and manage queue length ▪ Apply cadence, synchronize with cross-domain planning ▪ Unlock the intrinsic motivation of knowledge workers ▪ Decentralize decision-making ▪ Organize around value

Table 4.9 Competencies, Values, and Principles of SAFe

Establishing team and technical agility—the first of the seven core competencies—teaches you to form the cross-functional, self-organizing agile team. SAFe also ensures that quality is an integral part of the process and organizes agile release trains (ARTs) around the flow of value. ARTs are cross-functional teams that are synchronized on a common cadence to deliver program increments based on the single program backlog. For more information, refer to *www.scaledagileframework.com/*.

Note

No questions will be asked about SAFe in the exam. However, the team, especially the project leadership team, must understand the concept of scalability, cross-functional team formation and aligning them to deliver regularly in a set cadence. Although it seems simple, in practical situations, the processes of formation and governance rapidly become complex and pose risks for communication gaps.

Important Terminology

For this exam objective, you're expected to understand the following terms:

- **Planning poker**
  This planning game is used to estimate a task by building consensus.
- **Release planning**
  This planning process divides the product backlog into multiple sprints and releases per the business needs.
- **Sprint cycle**
  In this part of the release planning process, the team works on iterations and delivers working software at the end of each sprint.
- **Sprint map**
  The sprint map provides you with the user stories planned across different sprints throughout the release cycle.
- **Story points**
  These are relative measures of effort.
- **Technical debt**
  This is a debt that the project team carries because of choosing an easy solution rather than the correct solution.

Practice Questions

These practice questions will help you evaluate your understanding of the topics covered in this chapter. The questions shown are similar in nature to those found on the certification examination. Although none of these questions will be found on the exam itself, they will allow you to review your knowledge of the subject. Select the correct answers, and then check the completeness of your answers in the "Practice Question Answers and Explanations" section. Remember that on the exam, you must select all correct answers and only correct answers to receive credit for the question.

1. What are the six steps of release planning in order?

☐ **A.** Define product backlog, prioritize product backlog, analysis of technical dependencies, estimate product backlog, what do you want to release, and scope release

☐ **B.** Define product backlog, prioritize product backlog, estimate product backlog, analysis of technical dependencies, what do you want to release, and scope release

☐ **C.** Define product backlog, prioritize product backlog, analysis of technical dependencies, what do you want to release, estimate product backlog, and scope release

☐ **D.** Prioritize product backlog, define product backlog, estimate product backlog, analysis of technical dependencies, what do you want to release, and scope release

2. What are the responsibilities of the business owner in release planning? (There are three correct answers.)

☐ **A.** Define product backlog

☐ **B.** Release the scope

☐ **C.** Prioritize product backlog

☐ **D.** Analysis of technical dependencies

☐ **E.** What do you want to release

☐ **F.** Estimate product backlog

3. What are the activities performed by the implementation partner during the release planning? (There are two correct answers.)

☐ **A.** Prioritize product backlog

☐ **B.** Release the scope

☐ **C.** Analyze technical dependencies

☐ **D.** Define product backlog

4. Which of these options are correct about the sprint map?

☐ **A.** The sprint map tentatively maps user stories with effort estimates only.

☐ **B.** The sprint map only includes the confirmed user stories with all relevant details.

☐ **C.** User stories are optional for the sprint map, but it must include release dates for all the upcoming releases.

☐ **D.** The sprint map will include user stories with tentative mapping with details such as effort estimates and prioritization.

☐ **E.** The sprint map will include the user stories with tentative mapping with details such as cost estimates and prioritization.

5. The project team prepares the product backlog during which time?

☐ **A.** Prepare phase

☐ **B.** Explore phase

☐ **C.** The project team will start preparing the product backlog during the explore phase and complete it in the prepare phase.

☐ **D.** Realize phase.

6. Which are the correct statements about the product backlog prioritization? (There are two correct answers.)

☐ **A.** The product owner prioritizes the product backlog.

☐ **B.** The product owner, in consultation with the Scrum master, prioritizes the product backlog.

☐ **C.** The items in the product backlog are in decreasing order of business value.

☐ **D.** The items in the product backlog are in increasing order of business value.

☐ **E.** The items in the product backlog are in decreasing order of complexity.

☐ **F.** The items in the product backlog are in increasing order of complexity.

7. Why does the implementation team perform the technical dependency analysis on the product backlog? (There are three correct answers.)

☐ **A.** Dependency analysis is an optional step to find out any irrelevant business items that might have been included in the product backlog.

☐ **B.** Dependency analysis is a critical step that helps identify any dependencies that may have been excluded in the product backlog.

☐ **C.** Dependency analysis helps to segregate technical requirements from business requirements.

☐ **D.** Dependency analysis determines the order of user stories.

☐ **E.** Dependency analysis can identify both technical and business dependencies.

☐ **F.** Dependency analysis can *only* identify technical dependencies and that's why the implementation partner performs this activity.

8. What are possible outputs of estimating the product backlog?

☐ **A.** Effort estimates

☐ **B.** Cost estimates

☐ **C.** Duration estimates

☐ **D.** A and B

☐ **E.** B and C

☐ **F.** A, B, and C

9. What is the purpose of planning poker?

☐ **A.** It's a fun game that we play during the long realization phase.

☐ **B.** It's a way to estimate user stories.

☐ **C.** It's a trick game to identify over- or under-estimations, if any.

☐ **D.** It's a team building exercise.

☐ **E.** B and C.

10. Which are correct statements about planning poker? (There are two correct answers.)

- ☐ **A.** It's a consensus-building game.
- ☐ **B.** Only senior team members can participate in this game.
- ☐ **C.** It's played during the deploy phase of the project to identify the scope creep.
- ☐ **D.** Everyone should participate in this game of effort estimation.

11. Story points measure what?

- ☐ **A.** Effort estimates
- ☐ **B.** Complexity of a user story
- ☐ **C.** Volume of work in a user story
- ☐ **D.** Associated risks in a user story
- ☐ **E.** All of the above

12. You're working as a FICO consultant on an on-premise implementation of SAP S/4HANA. Your coworkers aren't very cooperative, and you continue to have a bitter experience working with this team. You decided to take a three-week break from the project in hopes that things would get better after you return. On the first day back, to your surprise, the team invited you for a card game. Everyone has a set of cards, including the FICO team lead. The project manager read a story, everyone asked clarification questions, picked a card from the deck, and finally all except the FICO lead showed their card. What kind game were you in?

- ☐ **A.** The team realized your importance during your absence, thought to build a better team, and decided to play this game as a team-building exercise.
- ☐ **B.** It's a type of planning poker where the expert won't show his card until the consensus is built.
- ☐ **C.** You were playing house of cards.
- ☐ **D.** It's a type of planning poker where the expert will show his card after all other members of the game and help build consensus.

13. What are the benefits of planning poker? (There are three correct answers.)

- ☐ **A.** It is well documented.
- ☐ **B.** Each member can contribute to the estimates.
- ☐ **C.** Only experts can contribute to the estimates, leading to the near-perfect effort estimation technique.
- ☐ **D.** There's no need for long and boring documents.
- ☐ **E.** Everyone can participate in this game.
- ☐ **F.** The results have a high degree of accuracy.

14. What are two challenges with planning poker? (There are two correct answers.)

☐ **A.** The game lacks the documentary proof of estimation.

☐ **B.** At times, it takes longer to complete the estimation because of the consensus that needs to be built.

☐ **C.** Many times, it doesn't necessarily produce true story points.

☐ **D.** Due to expert participation, many new members are hesitant to reveal their cards and may not actively participate in discussion.

15. In Table 4.10, the average velocity after the completion of sprint 3 is _____, and the average velocity of release 2 is _______.

Release	Release 1		Release 2		
Particulars	Sprint 1	Sprint 2	Sprint 3	Sprint 4	Sprint 5
Number of user stories	25	27	26	34	33
Number of team members	5	5	5	5	5
Sprint duration	3 Weeks	3 Weeks	3 Weeks	3 Weeks	3 Weeks
Sprint velocity	25	27	26	34	33
Average velocity after each sprint	25	26	_____	28	29
Average release velocity	26		_____		

Table 4.10 Question 15

☐ **A.** 27, 31

☐ **B.** 26, 31

☐ **C.** 31, 26

☐ **D.** 26, 29

☐ **E.** 26, insufficient data to calculate the velocity of release 2

16. You're working as a project manager of an SAP S/4HANA on-premise deployment for a pharmaceutical manufacturing company. As project manager, you've just completed two projects with a similar size, scope, and geographical location. In the past, you've also successfully implemented similar projects on SAP S/4HANA Cloud deployment for UK-based pharmaceutical manufacturing companies. Your prospective client asked you to provide a ballpark estimate for the project with 200 user stories. You have the information available in Table 4.11. Based on this, what is the estimate that you'll provide? Assume that the sprint duration was three weeks for all four projects, user stories are of a similar nature, and your organization support allows you to leverage prior data to calculate ballpark estimates.

Project Details	Velocity
Project A – Last project of similar scope, size, and geography	20
Project B – Last project of similar scope, size, and geography	16
Project C – UK-based SAP S/4HANA Cloud deployment	28
Project D – UK-based SAP S/4HANA Cloud deployment	32

Table 4.11 Question 16

☐ **A.** You can't provide a ballpark estimate, as it may set the wrong expectation.

☐ **B.** Around 11–13 sprints each of a three-week duration.

☐ **C.** Around 6–8 sprints each of a three-week duration.

☐ **D.** Around 8–10 sprints each of a three-week duration.

17. In which of the following phases do you develop the test cases?

☐ **A.** Prepare phase

☐ **B.** Realize phase

☐ **C.** Explore phase

☐ **D.** Deploy phase

☐ **E.** Run Phase

18. In which of the following phases do you develop the test strategy?

☐ **A.** Prepare phase

☐ **B.** Realize phase

☐ **C.** Explore phase

☐ **D.** Deploy phase

☐ **E.** Run phase

19. What activities do you carry out during the run phase of the project? (There are three correct answers.)

☐ **A.** Implement the cutover plan.

☐ **B.** Monitor SLAs.

☐ **C.** Decommission the legacy system.

☐ **D.** Implement the production support strategy.

☐ **E.** Showcase value-adds to extend the contract.

20. What is fixed in a lean or agile approach of project management? (There are two correct answers.)

☐ **A.** Resource

☐ **B.** Risk

☐ **C.** Date

☐ **D.** Developers

21. The project team performs mock cutover activities to ensure that the cutover plan is effective and working to meet the project needs. True or false?

☐ **A.** True

☐ **B.** False

22. Who can decide the contents of a sprint backlog?

☐ **A.** Scrum master

☐ **B.** Project manager

☐ **C.** Product owner

☐ **D.** Scrum team

23. Who estimates the sprint backlog?

☐ **A.** Scrum master

☐ **B.** Project manager

☐ **C.** Product owner

☐ **D.** Scrum team

24. Which of these statements correctly describes the product owner?

☐ **A.** The product owner promotes Scrum within the organization and is responsible to ensure that everyone within the team follows the Scrum framework.

☐ **B.** The product owner is the customer who defines the business requirements and prioritizes them, at times with many stakeholders.

☐ **C.** The product owner is the sponsor of the project and ensures that all the meeting timings are adhered to in order to reduce the total cost of operations.

☐ **D.** The product owner can terminate any sprint without any explanation, as they are the sponsor of the product.

25. The product backlog is the requirement that hasn't been built in to the baseline build, but the team has to deliver the requirements. The team must capture all the requirements before prioritizing the requirements. True or false?

☐ **A.** True

☐ **B.** False

26. How does the project team achieve frequent checkpoints with the business in the agile delivery approach? (There are two correct answers.)

☐ **A.** Solution demo for sprints

☐ **B.** Sprint planning

☐ **C.** Quality gates

☐ **D.** User acceptance test

Practice Question Answers and Explanations

1. Correct answer: **A**
   Option A is the correct answer. Per option B, the team estimates the user stories without identifying technical dependencies, which will affect the accuracy of the estimate.

2. Correct answers: **A, C, E**
   The business owner defines the product backlog, that is, features of the product; prioritizes them in the order of decreasing business value; and decides what can or can't be released. Refer to the "Release Planning" section.

3. Correct answers: **B, C**
   The implementation partner estimates the user stories (not an option provided here), analyzes technical dependencies (option C), and releases the scope (option B). Refer to the "Release Planning" section.

4. Correct answer: **D**
   Refer to Table 4.1 for an understanding of sprint mapping. It tentatively maps the user stories with each sprint. The sprint map also includes the effort estimate and not the cost estimate, priority of the user story, and some other information. In sprints, there is no terminology called "confirmed user stories," which rules out options A and B. Option C is incorrect as it says the user stories are optional. Per option E, the cost estimate is included in the sprint map, which is incorrect.

5. Correct answer: **B**
   The project team will build the product backlog during the explore phase of the project during fit-to-standard. During the release planning in the realize phase, there might be certain additions of a few user stories, but the product backlog must be created in the explore phase.

6. Correct answers: **A, C**

   The product owner prioritizes the product backlog. It contains the items in descending order of business value. The product owner wants to implement the features first that gives maximum business value. Option B is confusing. It's true that a lot of prioritization happens in consultation with the Scrum team but *not* with the Scrum master. Option A is more appropriate than option B.

7. Correct answers: **B, D, E**

   Dependency analysis identifies the tasks that are dependent on other tasks. Although referred to as "technical," the analysis will identify both business and technical tasks. This is a critical step that the team must follow during the release planning.

8. Correct answer: **A**

   Estimate product backlog only provides effort estimates. Refer to the "Step 4: Estimate Product Backlog" section.

9. Correct answer: **B**

   Planning poker is a consensus-building game used to estimate the user stories in the Scrum framework. Refer to the "Planning Poker" section.

10. Correct answers: **A, D**

    Planning poker is a consensus-building game used to estimate the user stories in the Scrum framework. Refer to the "Planning Poker" section. In this game, everyone can participate, and everyone will contribute. It's mostly played during the realize phase of the project while release planning. In reality, it's a fun game with a lot of learning experience and team building.

11. Correct answer: **E**

    Story points measure effort estimates for the user stories in the agile framework. It includes the complexity of work, duration of work, and associated risks. A user story with 10 story points is doubly complex, will take twice as much time, and will have double risk as compared to a user story with 5 story points.

    Generally, we don't go beyond 13 story points. The team needs to break the user story into multiple smaller stories so that the story point doesn't exceed 13.

12. Correct answer: **D**

    Be aware of these situational questions as they provide a lot of information that you may not need to answer the question. The question is simply asking about a card game with an expert, which is planning poker. Options A and C are incorrect. Option B is incorrect because the expert will show his estimate after all the members to build the consensus and *not* after the consensus is built.

13. Correct answers: **B, D, E**

    In planning poker, which doesn't require any sort of documentation, everyone can participate and contribute. To certain extent, it doesn't provide a high degree of accuracy as mentioned in option F.

14. Correct answers: **B, C**

    Even planning poker with experts, although slightly more accurate than planning poker without experts, doesn't produce accurate story points. Many times, with multiple iterations, it takes a lot of time to build consensus for a complex user story. Option A is technically correct but it's not a challenge, while option D may also be true for a new team but is not appropriate here.

15. Correct answer: **B**

    At the end of sprint 3, the average velocity is calculated as

    Average velocity = Sum of the number of user stories / Number of sprints

    In this case, average velocity = (25 + 27 + 26) / 3 = 78 / 3 = 26

    On the same basis, the average velocity of release 2 is

    Sum of the number of user stories in release 2 / number of sprints in release 2

    In this case, average velocity = (26 + 34 + 33) / 3 = 93 / 3 = 31

16. Correct answer: **B**

    The question is testing your ability to identify correlated information. Projects C and D are for UK geography; moreover, these deployments are cloud based. On the contrary, the client is asking for a US-based, on-premise implementation. It means that you can only consider project A and project B to get the historical data and extrapolate.

    The average velocity of project A and B is 18; for 200 user stories, the number of sprints = 200/18 = 11.11. Therefore, the closest match is option B, 11–13 sprints.

17. Correct answer: **B**

    The project team develops the test cases in the realize phase of the project. The prepare and explore phases are too early to develop test cases as the team is working on the requirement, while deploy and run are too late because the testing is complete by the deploy phase, and the solution went live before the run phase.

18. Correct answer: **C**

    The project team develops the test strategy in the explore phase of the project. They work in tandem to produce the product backlog and the test strategy, along with many other documents.

19. Correct answers: **B, C, D**

    Implementing the product support strategy, decommissioning the legacy system, and monitoring the production metrics (or SLAs) are the three key tasks of the run phase of the project. Refer to the "Cutover Plan" section.

20. Correct answers: **A, C**

    In the agile project delivery approach, only resources (or budgets) and dates are fixed. Risks are always unknown, and developers aren't fixed and can vary depending upon the requirements.

21. Correct answer: **A**

    True. The prime purpose for the mock cutover is to test the cutover plan and ensure that it's working and producing the desired results.

22. Correct answer: **C**

    The product owner decides the content of the product backlog and sprint backlog. The product owner prioritizes them as well. The project manager and Scrum master have no role in deciding the product backlog. Although the Scrum team may identify certain technical dependencies, the decision regarding the content of the sprint backlog lies solely with the product owner.

23. Correct answer: **D**

    The Scrum team estimates the sprint backlog in partnership with the product owner. The Scrum master facilitates the estimation discussion.

24. Correct answer: **B**

    The product owner defines the business requirements and prioritizes them. Option A is incorrect because the Scrum master promotes the agile concepts in the organization and ensures that everyone follows the Scrum framework. Options C and D are simply incorrect statements.

25. Correct answer: **B**

    False. The prioritization of product backlog items can start as long as the team has a doable list. Agile promotes "change," so the product backlog is a living document.

26. Correct answers: **A, D**

    The solution demo at the end of each sprint and UAT are the two checkpoints. Sprint planning is a ceremony that happens at the beginning of the sprint to plan for the sprint, while quality gates are required to move from one phase to the next.

Takeaway

This chapter provided a detailed discussion of the sprint cycle and its ceremonies specific to the SAP implementations. We enhanced your knowledge on the ceremonies from the previous chapters, and you learned about release planning and multiple releases. We covered planning poker to help you understand estimation techniques and explored the concept of story points.

Toward the latter part of the chapter, we delved into the deploy and run phases of the project and understood the different testing activities. In the final run, we explored the cutover activities and the operation optimization techniques.

Summary

In this chapter, you learned about the concepts of sprint cycle, release planning, and multiple releases. We discussed the concept of story points and played planning poker. Lastly, we explored the deploy and run phases of the project. In the next chapter, you'll learn about the workstreams and the activities involved.

Chapter 5
Workstreams Overview

Techniques You'll Master

- Know the eleven workstreams
- Explain different tasks in each workstream
- Understand the deliverables in different workstreams
- Understand workstreams in different scenarios
- Understand tools and accelerators relevant to the workstreams

So far, we've studied the SAP Activate methodology, its three pillars and characteristics, taxonomy, transition paths, elements, and several other aspects of the latest project management methodology for SAP S/4HANA implementations. In the previous two chapters, we reviewed the agile and Scrum concepts, some key terminologies, and the usages of Scrum in SAP Activate. This chapter will build on the preliminary concepts of the eleven workstreams, introduced in the previous chapters, by diving deeper into each workstream, starting with the project management workstream. This chapter will explain the activities performed by the team in each workstream, inputs required to complete the activity, outputs or deliverables from the given process, role of the different project team members, and a few other concepts.

Real-World Scenario

You have several years of experience working as a Scrum master. Recently, you've also worked on scaled agile projects and have sound experience in managing Scrum ceremonies and Scrum of Scrums.

Your organization decided to implement SAP S/4HANA, and your supervisor wants you to promote agile, share your Scrum and scaled agile knowledge, and manage the implementation in collaboration with the implementation program manager from the partner organization.

This is the first time you'll be working on an SAP engagement, although you took a course on the SAP Activate methodology organized by your organization. You know you need to have a good understanding of the workstreams in SAP S/4HANA.

Objectives of This Portion of the Test

The certification examination will test your knowledge about the following topics:

- The eleven workstreams and the underlying core concepts
- A sound understanding of relevant tools and accelerators, including how they are used across the workstreams
- Activities and deliverables across the workstreams

In the following sections, you'll learn these key concepts followed by some questions and answers.

Note

This important chapter will lay the foundation about SAP workstreams, activities across the SAP projects, and deliverables during different workstreams. It carries more than 12% weightage, so you'll get at least 10 questions on the topics from this chapter.

Key Concepts Refresher

This section will help you understand the eleven workstreams and will advance your knowledge on the tools, accelerators, and deliverables across the workstreams. These concepts are critical for you to pass the exam.

Project Management

Project management, the first workstream, covers all the aspects of managing an SAP S/4HANA implementation, including new implementations, system conversions, and selective data transition. These include initiation, planning, execution, monitoring and controlling, governance, and project closing. The project management activities start from the prepare phase of the project and complete in the run phase. You've already completed the discover phase where you sign up and access the trial version of SAP S/4HANA and discover your solution.

In the following sections, we'll explore key concepts, roles, tools, and accelerators involved in the project management workstream, starting from sprint and release planning.

Concepts

In this section, you'll review some of the basic concepts of agile and the Scrum approach and usages in the SAP Activate methodology.

Sprints and Release Planning

Let's start by reviewing some of the basic concepts, especially those related to Scrum and agile. In Chapter 3 and Chapter 4, you learned about sprints and user stories. From an SAP Activate perspective, these are called *build sprints*. Additionally, in SAP Activate, there are *foundation sprints* and *firm-up sprints*. The differences between the three sprints are summarized in Table 5.1.

Foundation Sprint	Build Sprint	Firm-Up Sprint
▪ General settings, organizational structure ▪ Function/technical specifications, development, and analytics configuration ▪ Unit test, functional test, string test plan ▪ Role mapping, security test scenarios, roles in quality assurance (QA) system	▪ Core configurations, detailed design ▪ Function/technical specifications, development, and analytics configuration ▪ Unit test, functional test, string test plan ▪ Role mapping, security test scenarios, roles in QA system	▪ Adjusted core configurations ▪ Bug fixing, no technical debt ▪ String test, integration test protocol and plan ▪ Application security test protocol

Table 5.1 Differences among Foundation, Build, and Firm-Up Sprints

In Chapter 3, you learned that an epic is a large feature that a project team can't deliver in a sprint. For example, epic 1 in Figure 5.1 can be delivered after the third sprint and a firm-up sprint. The team needs a firm-up sprint before delivering an epic to fix any bugs, complete string testing, and fine-tune the core configurations. Additionally, epic 2 includes two sprints (S4 and S5) and one firm-up sprint.

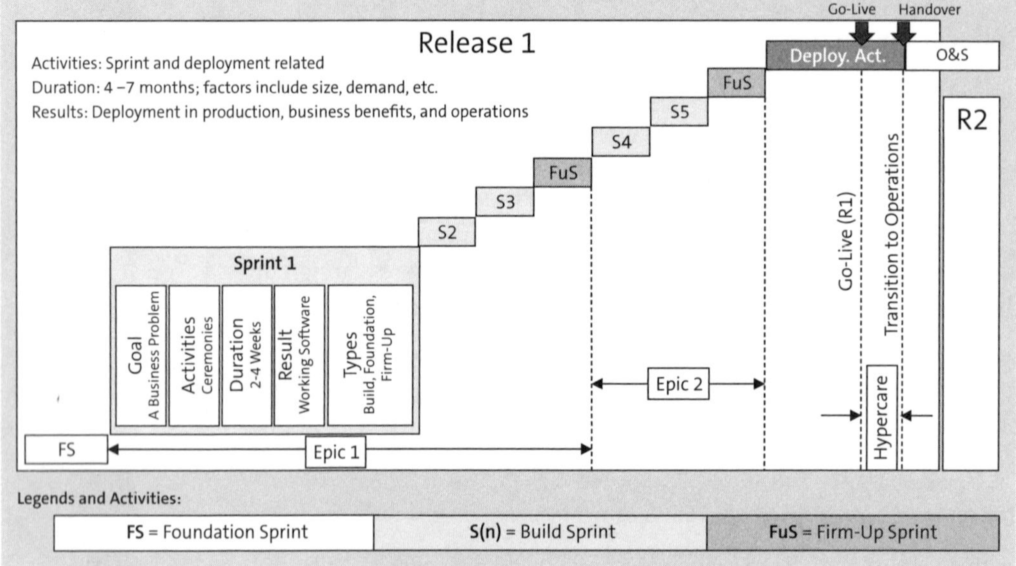

Figure 5.1 Basic Sprint Concepts

Note that the team will *deliver* a workable solution after every sprint, but the team may not *deploy* the solution after every sprint, as the product owner makes such decisions. In Figure 5.1, release 1 comprises two epics—epic 1 and epic 2—and the deployment activities lasting anywhere between four and seven months. The release duration will depend on many factors, including the scope of work, team size, customer requirements, and a few others.

If the product owner decides to deploy the workable solution to the production (PROD) system, the project team will conduct the deployment activities, including cutover, data migration, and go-live activities. This isn't a spontaneous decision, and the team must identify such releases through extensive planning during the release and sprint plan process in the explore phase of the project. Furthermore, any such production release will go through the hypercare period and then transition to the run phase of the project where the operation team will manage the solution and its benefit realization. Figure 5.2 shows a number of options that the project team can use while planning the release.

The first release, R1, starts with foundational sprint, followed by three build sprints, and one firm-up sprint when the epic one completes. The fourth and fifth sprints follow the epic one, which in turn is followed by another firm-up sprint and the deployment activities, including the cutover, go-live, and transition to the run organization.

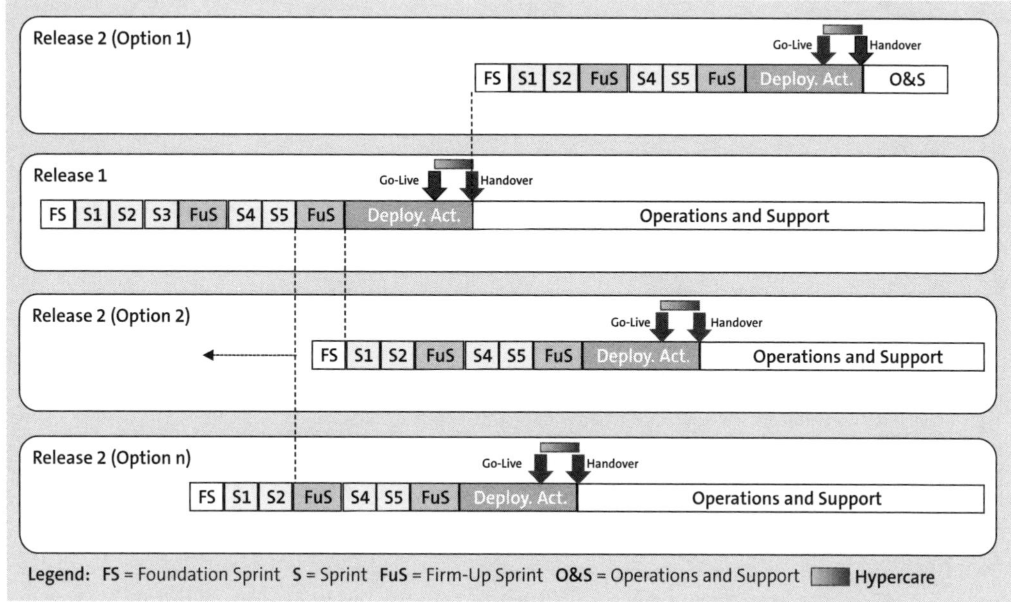

Figure 5.2 Release and Go-Live Planning

The project team has multiple options for release 2, which will be based on the resource availability, customer's needs, requirements and dependencies, and several other factors. The concept of the Scaled Agile Framework (SAFe) suggests to align the sprints in a specific cadence and organize agile release trains (ARTs) around the flow of value. We reviewed the SAFe concepts at a high level in Chapter 4.

Scrum in SAP Activate

SAP Activate supports both Scrum, which we introduced in Chapter 3, and the waterfall methodology. In addition, it also supports a hybrid approach. Figure 5.3 shows three different approaches that you can use with the SAP Activate methodology while implementing SAP S/4HANA projects.

In the agile approach, as we discussed in Chapter 3 and Chapter 4, the project team goes through the fit-to-standard process through multiple sprints and builds the delta design that finally leads to an updated and prioritized product backlog, which becomes the basis of the realize phase of the project. We'll review this concept in detail in the next section. During the realize phase, the team will continue to construct using the product backlog and will release working software at the end of each sprint.

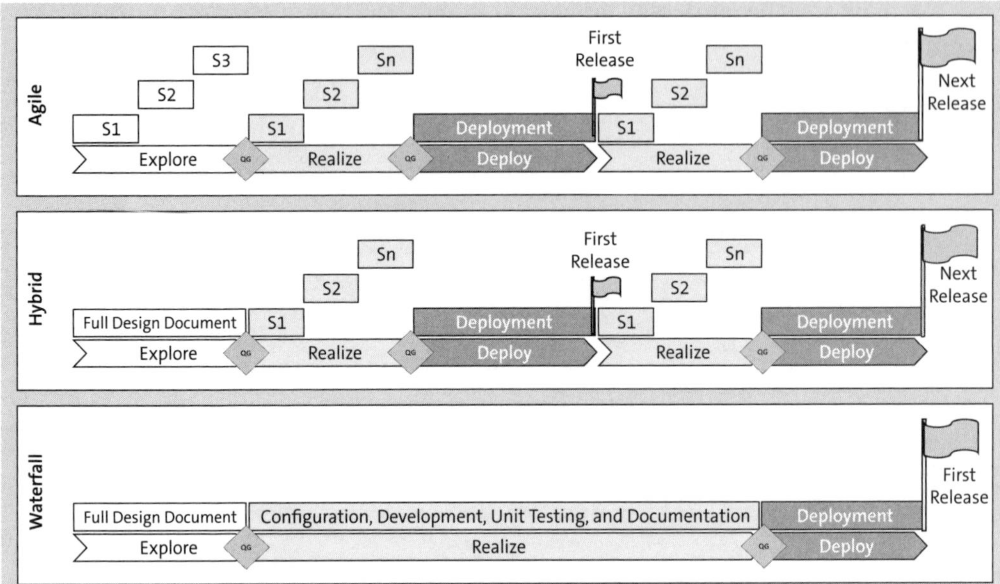

Figure 5.3 Scrum in SAP

However, based on the Scrum concepts, the team may deploy every release to production, and the product owner will make such a decision. In this example, the team decided to deploy after the end of the third and sixth sprint identified by the flag. The size of the flag denotes the size of the release, meaning the second release would encompass the first release and the additional sprints.

The hybrid approach is a little different as the team is creating complete design documents during the explore phase of the project, which will become the basis of further construction. From that point on, the approach is similar to the agile approach.

In the waterfall approach, the project team will complete the design in the explore phase of the project and then they will construct. Activities include the configuration, development, unit testing, functional testing, documentation, and so on of the software in the realize phase of the project. In this approach, the team will deploy only once at the end of the realize phase.

Scrum in the Explore Phase

In Chapter 3, we reviewed the explore phase and discussed the business process workshop, baseline build, and solution validation workshops. We went on to review the prioritization techniques and the definition of ready and definition of done. You also learned that the key activity in the explore phase is the fit-to-standard or fit-gap analysis, depending on the implementation platform. This activity has two main workshops: solution validation (aka workshop A) and delta design (aka workshop B), as we discussed in Chapter 1. We'll now discuss sprint planning in the explore phase.

Let's assume that the project team decided to follow the agile approach in the explore phase, in which case the team has initialized Scrum, including training, guidelines, tools, roles and responsibilities, and information radiators, that is, any material such as a handwritten post-it note or electronic display showing any relevant information (e.g., velocity or task status). Figure 5.4 shows a sample of information radiators.

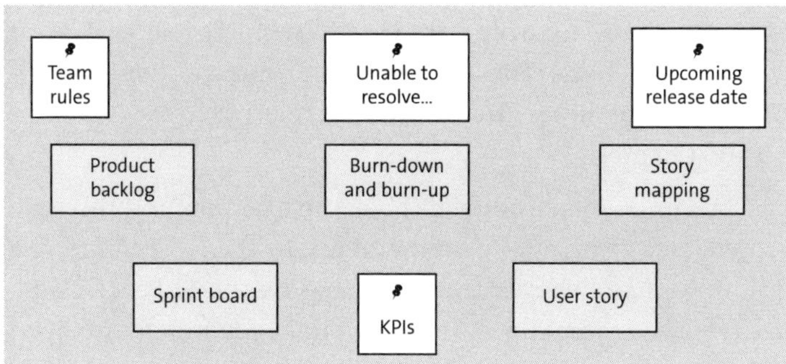

Figure 5.4 Information Radiators

We covered the fit-to-standard/fit-gap analysis process in Chapter 1 where we studied that the team will start conducting the solution validation workshops. After they complete the solution validation, the team will have a prioritized list of user stories as the initial backlog. The left portion of Figure 5.5 shows the flow in workshop A and its output (i.e., initial backlog) that is feeding into the delta design (workshop B).

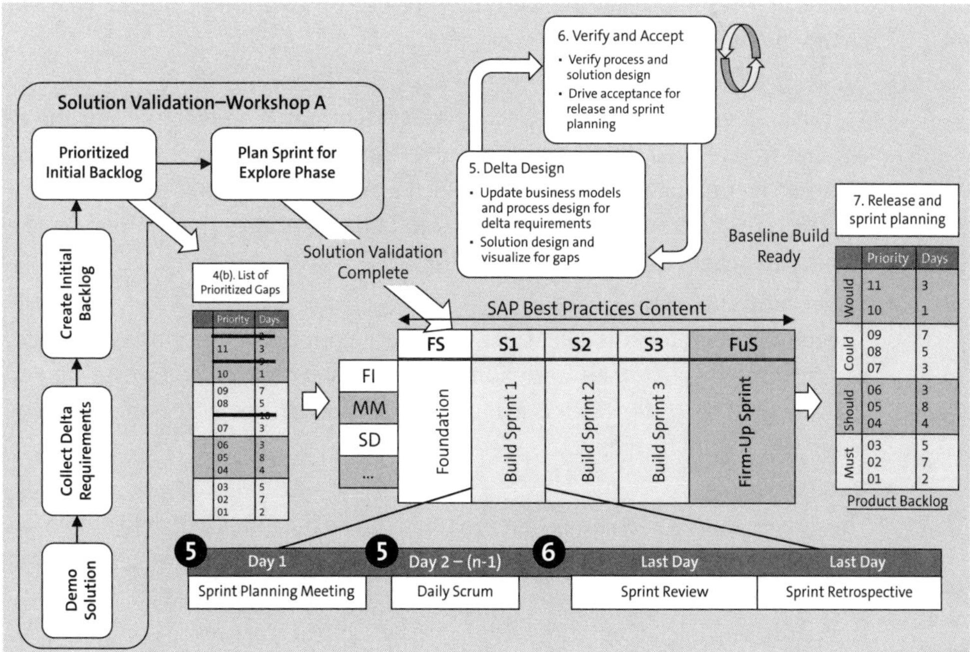

Figure 5.5 Scrum in the Explore Phase

In the agile approach, the team, during the sprint planning, splits the delta design into sprints, starting from foundation sprints, build sprints, and firm-up sprints. In the explore phase, because there are no deployment activities, the team can repeat the build and firm-up sprints per the requirement. The idea here is that the team will start with SAP Best Practices and incrementally build the baseline while in constant communication with the customer, which is a major benefit of the agile approach, and the prioritized product backlog. Sprint planning and daily Scrum—part of sprint execution—are delta design activities, whereas the sprint review is the verify and accept activity. The last part, sprint retrospective, is a self-assessment activity. We reviewed these activities, mostly referred to as Scrum ceremonies, in Chapter 3 and Chapter 4.

It's a known fact that SAP implementation can be complex, spanning multiple geographies and business areas with 50+ team members. In such a scenario, the project team is advised to use scaling techniques such as Nexus, SAFe, or Large-Scale Scrum (LeSS). We reviewed these concepts and program governance in Chapter 3 and Chapter 4.

Roles

The following list provides the roles and responsibilities of the project management workstream:

- **Project sponsor**
  The sponsor of a project champions the project objectives, provides strategy and direction, assigns the project manager, approves the project charter, and makes decisions for all aspects of the project. The customer's project sponsor chairs the steering committee.
- **Project manager**
  This person elaborates the project objectives, communicates to the stakeholders, and ensures that the team understands the objectives with complete clarity. The manager manages the different aspects of the projects and steers the project through different process groups and knowledge areas as defined by the Project Management Institute (PMI).
- **Project administrator**
  The requirement for this role is mainly in large projects to support the project managers in collecting and providing the status, collecting and ensuring key performance indicator (KPI) calculations, and taking care of logistics requirements and/or challenges.
- **Quality manager**
  The quality manager ensures that the team meets the quality of deliverables in accordance with the defined criteria and the team completes the quality gate procedures. In addition, the customer's quality manager also sets up the quality standards, ensures acceptance criteria are developed, ensures the definition of

ready and definition of done are defined, and supports the customer project manager during the quality gate processes.

- **IT manager**
  The IT manager, IT head, or IT director from the customer side ensures that the project objectives are aligned with the organizational objectives.

Some roles involving a group of people are as follows:

- **Executive committee**
  This committee sets the business goals, approves the project vision, allocates funds to the project, and delegates some of its responsibilities to the steering committee.
- **Steering committee**
  This committee approves the projects goals, results, and necessary changes. It delegates some of its authorities and responsibilities to the operating committee and escalates the challenges to the executive committee.
- **Operating committee**
  The prime responsibility of this committee is to monitor and coordinate the activities across the workstreams. For any unresolved challenges, it escalates to the steering committee and delegates some its responsibilities to the integration committee.
- **Integration committee**
  This committee operates in parallel with the operating committee with the responsibility to manage the integration, master data, and release strategy across the project.

We discussed the Scrum-related roles, such as Scrum master, product owner, Scrum team, and so on, in Chapter 3.

> **Tip**
> It's highly probable that you'll get a question related to the roles and responsibilities or be required to identify the entity (customer business, aka business, customer IT, or implementation partner) that fulfills the given role.

Tools

You'll use several tools throughout the project management workstream. Some of these tools are discussed throughout the book and not discussed specifically in this section:

- SAP Solution Manager
- SAP Cloud Appliance Library
- Roadmap Viewer
- SAP Best Practices Explorer

However, some of the additional tools used in the project management workstream are as follows:

- **SAP Cloud ALM**
  SAP Cloud ALM is an application lifecycle management (ALM) solution for customers who use the cloud solution from SAP. They use SAP Cloud ALM to avoid using the on-premise solution for ALM.
- **Implementation portal for SAP S/4HANA Cloud**
  The implementation portal for SAP S/4HANA Cloud is a self-guided and content-driven implementation of SAP S/4HANA Cloud based on SAP Activate. Some of the benefits are fast onboarding, instantaneous availability, support for the fit-to-standard process, implementation tasks management, and progress monitoring. It's the preferred ALM solution for SAP S/4HANA Cloud, extended edition (previously known as SAP S/4HANA, single-tenant edition).
- **SAP Jam**
  You can access SAP Jam via *https://jam4.sapjam.com/auth/login*. You need to register with the website, and SAP approves the registration generally in 24 hours. SAP Jam is a cloud-based social media platform that allows users to collaborate, share documents and ideas, and learn from each other. It is essentially Facebook for SAP S/4HANA. For more information on SAP Jam, refer to the Introduction of this book.
- **SAP Portfolio and Project Management**
  SAP Portfolio Management is about strategy alignment, innovation, idea generation, visibility, and the ability to make decisions. It provides you with complete visibility of all the projects and is centered around *doing the right things*. SAP Project Management is about the timeline, scope, communication, project execution, resource management, and project costing and is centered around *doing things right*.

Accelerators

The major accelerators in the project management workstream are shown in Table 5.2.

Note
It's important to know the list of accelerators available for the project management workstream. From an exam perspective, it's not required for you to know every detail of these accelerators, but to review the list and make sure you know the accelerators. For further information on these accelerators (SAP is continuously adding more), go to the Roadmap Viewer.

Discover	Prepare	Explore/Realize and Deploy
▪ Project plan ▪ Overview of transition to SAP S/4HANA	▪ Agile project implementation methodologies ▪ Agile roles and responsibilities ▪ Definition of ready and definition of done ▪ Project charter and business case template ▪ Project kick-off template ▪ Quality gate concept and checklist	▪ Backlog template ▪ Issue list ▪ Project status report template ▪ Change request log template ▪ Phase sign-off template and project closure report ▪ Lessons learned guide and template ▪ Agile Scrum meeting guideline ▪ Agile sprint breakdown and taskboard ▪ Agile sprint retrospective template ▪ Cutover strategy ▪ Cutover plan

Table 5.2 Project Management Accelerators

Solution Adoption

Imagine a system that is full of functionalities, useful user interfaces (UIs), efficient and expensive technologies, and sophisticated solutions but isn't shared or is shared only with limited users within the organization. One of the success criteria for a solution built to cater to business needs is its adoption and usages within the organization.

In the following sections, we'll explore the key concepts, roles, tools, and accelerators involved in the solution adoption workstream.

Concepts

The solution adoption workstream ensures that the application system is used across the organization as intended by implementing the organizational change management (OCM) processes, value management (VM), and end-user training. Table 5.3 shows the three substreams of the solution adoption.

Substream	Short Description
OCM	▪ Stakeholder identification ▪ Stakeholder involvement throughout the project lifecycle ▪ Stakeholder accepts changes

Table 5.3 Solution Adoption Substreams

Substream	Short Description
VM	■ Business value-based decisions ■ Achieve stakeholder's expected business value
End-user training	■ End-user readiness

Table 5.3 Solution Adoption Substreams (Cont.)

Roles

In this section, we'll list the roles and responsibilities of the solution adoption workstream.

The following OCM-related roles are relevant in the solution adoption workstream:

- **Change manager**
  This leadership position, generally without any supervisory responsibilities, is filled by the customer organization. The prime responsibilities include the fulfillment of change objectives by increasing the new system adoption and its usage across the user base within the given timeline, budget, and constraints. This person will provide guidance to the implementation partner, assimilate the artifacts, and disseminate the information based on the communication strategy while working closely with the change consultant.
- **Change consultant**
  This role, generally filled by the implementation partner, assists the change manager in developing the strategy and its execution plan. The consultant further helps the change manager by completing several assessments, including the change impact assessment, readiness assessment, current system usage assessment, and others. In consultation with the change manager, the change consultant builds the communication strategy that includes the design, development, timeline, and communication management.
- **End user**
  End users are the users within the business organization who execute the business processes in the new system after training. Some of these end users have deep involvement during the project lifecycle, including providing input during the explore phase and reviewing and approving the new system.

The following VM-related role is relevant in the solution adoption workstream:

- **Value expert**
  The implementation partner generally fills this position with someone who has sound knowledge and expertise in the related domain and understands the business objectives of the project. This person creates the value dashboard, performs the benchmarking analysis by comparing the derived value with the desired objectives, and recommends VM actions to the steering committee.

Finally, the following end-user training-related roles are relevant in the solution adoption workstream:

- **Training consultant**
  The implementation partner generally fills this position who, in consultation with the change manager/consultant, training coordinator, and other key stakeholders, builds and maintains the detailed training strategy. This strategy includes the type of training, user groupings, user authority, user knowledge and interest assessment, course curricula and topics, training-related communications, system accesses, and several others aspects.
- **Training coordinator**
  The training coordinator, generally from the customer organization, helps in scheduling the training and makes sure to capture the user experience and feedback to further improve the training. This person works closely with the end users to ensure their availability, resolve scheduling conflicts, ensure optimal participation, and manage other logistics such as training room availability.
- **Training material developer**
  This technical writer position is fulfilled generally by the implementation partner. For a global implementation, the person should either be bilingual or take the support from a certified technical translator to create the training materials based on the business solution and the other documentation.
- **Trainer**
  In the train-the-trainer approach, this position is generally fulfilled by the customer organization; the implementation partner, however, may fill this position otherwise. This person should have sound business knowledge, procedural changes, and SAP S/4HANA navigational skills. As the trainer, this person not only explains the implemented business functionality in detail to ensure that the implemented process flow is well understood by the end users but also navigates the implemented process to show the end-to-end process flow and reports. Sound knowledge of the local language, in the global implementation, and effective communication are key considerations for this position.

Tools

Some of the tools used in the solution adoption workstream are as follows:

- **SAP Enable Now**
  This tool enables the end user of the customer organization by providing a blend of learning that is highly engaging. It includes instructor-led training, self-placed 24/7 learning, interactions with several business-specific simulations, quizzes to test their process knowledge, and online need-based support. SAP Enable Now is a collaborative authoring, content management platform suitable for both SAP and non-SAP systems.

It improves the software adoption by fulfilling just-in-time training needs of the end user, increasing the productivity of the user base by streamlining the process adoption, and maximizing the value of the human resources.

- **SAP SuccessFactors Learning**
  This is an SAP software product that includes a learning management system, which allows the customer organization to provide a training environment to their end users. It includes course management, course schedules, qualifications, quizzes, examinations, and certifications.
- **KPI catalog**
  This cloud service for SAP Solution Manager contains the definition, technical documentation, and comprehensive descriptions of the KPIs and the associated metrics.

  You can access the KPI catalog by going to *http://s-prs.co/v519406*. Figure 5.6 shows some filter criteria and search criteria to find a specific KPI or a set of KPIs.

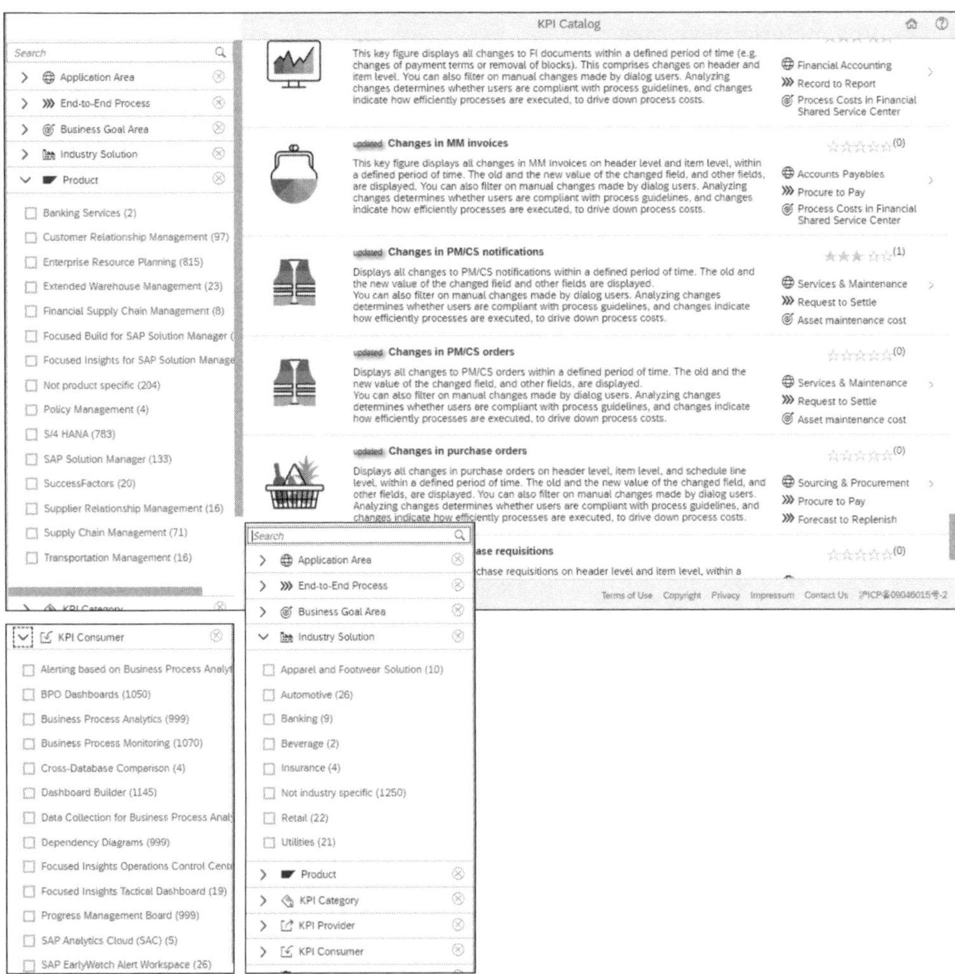

Figure 5.6 KPI Catalog

> **Note**
>
> It's highly recommended to open the KPI catalog and filter the key figures on application area, end-to-end process, and several other filters provided. As of writing this book, there are 1,344 KPIs in the catalog, and that is changing and improving with every release.

- **SAP Value Lifecycle Manager**
  Transformation to SAP requires investment and a business case to get through the organizational approval process. SAP Value Lifecycle Manager helps businesses estimate business improvements based on selected business priorities. The graphical outputs are for executive leaders and decision makers to highlight the potential benefits to the organization, division, or business area. Figure 5.7 shows the values that SAP transformation can bring to a sample bank.

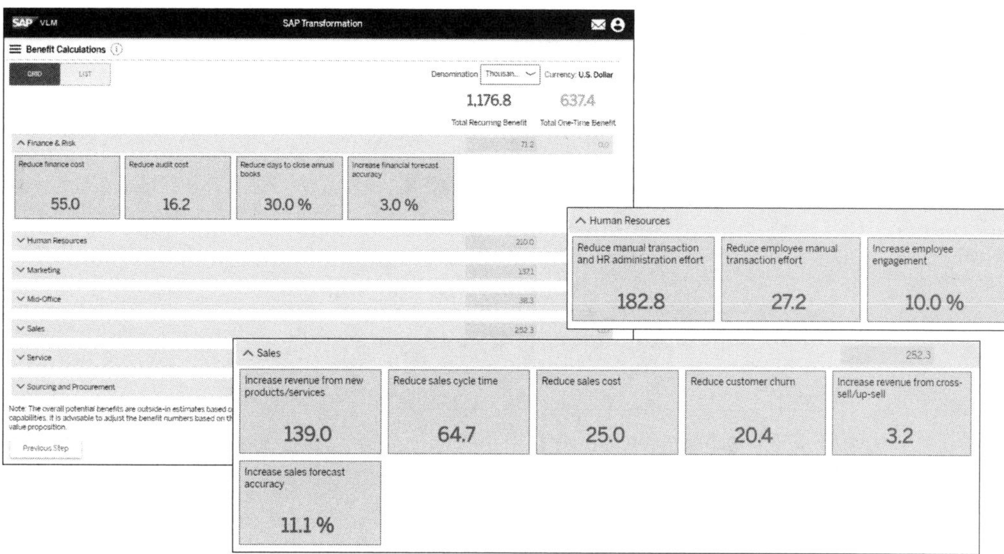

Figure 5.7 SAP Value Lifecycle Manager

- **SAP Transformation Navigator**
  This self-service tool enables a business to plan for the upgrade and build the detailed roadmap of its digital transformation journey to SAP S/4HANA. The roadmap is tailored to specific business needs and answers the following question: "What services and products do we need in this digital transformation journey?" Figure 5.8 shows the transformation journey of a sample banking application in SAP with capabilities such as financial reporting, deposit management, entity close, and bad debt reserve.

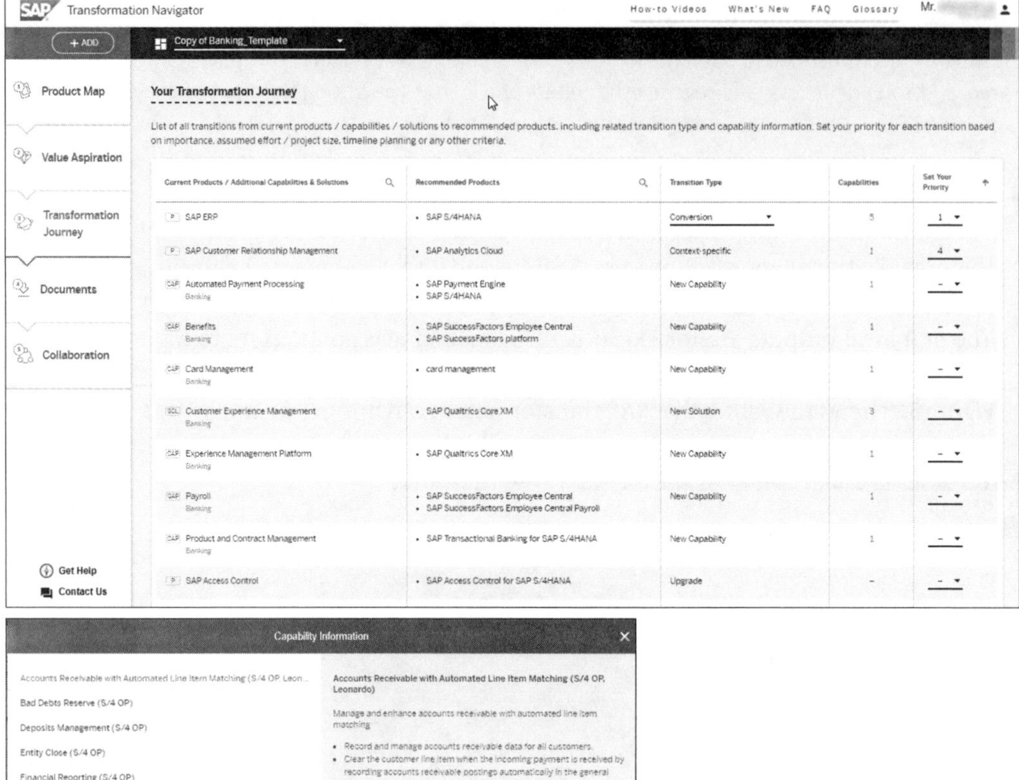

Figure 5.8 SAP Transformation Journey

Accelerators

There are several accelerators for the solution adoption workstream. Figure 5.9 shows a set of accelerators for SAP S/4HANA Cloud, extended edition.

In this section, we'll focus on the following two key accelerators:

- **Stakeholder identification guide**
  We all understand the basic concepts of stakeholders and how can they influence the project. This accelerator will help the project team identify and list stakeholders in a template provided with the SAP Activate methodology.
- **Value audit guide**
  The value audit is executed in the realize phase of the project to ensure that VM processes are aligned with the project implementation. Along with ensuring that the solution scope is continuously aligned with the business objective, it also identifies and mitigates any risks before the system goes live. It continuously tracks the value enablers such as training and infrastructure against the milestone plan and tests the readiness of the value dashboards.

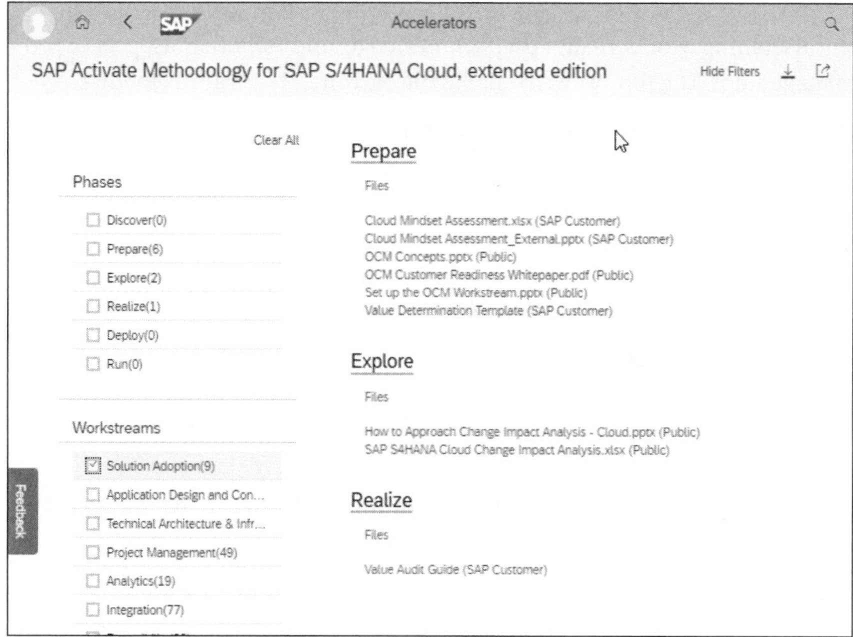

Figure 5.9 Accelerators: SAP S/4HANA Cloud, Extended Edition

Customer Team Enablement

This workstream enables the stakeholders, key users, and administrators, as applicable to the specific deployment options, to perform their duties and activities through the project lifecycle. For example, the customer team needs to execute standard business processes during the explore phase of the cloud deployment. However, to do so, the team must have a detailed understanding of and access to SAP Best Practices. This workstream ensures that the customer team executes these processes seamlessly and that all the prerequisites of a given process are fulfilled.

In the following sections, we'll explore the key concepts, roles, tools, and accelerators involved in the customer team enablement workstream.

Concepts

Following are the major enablement areas for the customer team:

- Project management
- Technical expertise
- Solution expertise

Most of the enablement activities should complete in the prepare phase of the project before the start of the solution validation workshops in the explore phase. These enablement activities include the overview training of SAP Activate to all the members of the customer team, solution validation guidelines, solution and technical training, workstream-specific knowledge, and few other aspects of project management. The four ways to enable the customer team are as follows:

- **Customer-specific workshops by SAP Training and Adoption**
  SAP Training and Adoption, based on the input from the customer, develops courses that meets specific customer needs.
- **Public workshops by SAP Training and Adoption**
  Customers can opt for several of the courses and training materials developed by SAP Training and Adoption. However, these aren't customer-specific courses.
- **Partner-led education**
  Implementation partners may devise their own enabling methodology based on their experience, partner-specific solutions, or their domain expertise.
- **Self-service education**
  The customer team will follow several educational materials that are available on openSAP, SAP Learning Hub, SAP Best Practices, and the Roadmap Viewer.

Roles

The following list provides the roles and responsibilities of the customer team enablement workstream:

- **Education service experts**
  This role is generally filled by the implementation partner with someone who has a broad knowledge of SAP and the customer-specific business domain, sound interviewing and judgement skills, and the ability to build their own questionnaire for the project roles. This person conducts the learning needs analysis, as shown in Figure 5.10, by considering the project scope of the work, roles, and the current information related to SAP Training and Adoption.
- **Team training coordinator**
  This role is generally filled by the customer organization who works closely with the customer team to ensure their availability, avoid scheduling conflicts, control training, provide certification, record attendance, and provide feedback to the trainer and inputs to the participants.
- **Trainer**
  The trainer is a subject matter expert (SME) generally brought in by the implementation partner who has an excellent course delivery persona and expertise in the use of the educational tools.
- **Trainee**
  Trainees are the customer team members who must attend all the designated trainings; appear for the quizzes and tests; complete courses, exercises, and identified scenarios; and pass the certification tests and/or exams as identified by the team training coordinator to achieve the required competence level.

They also provide timely feedback on the trainer, pace, and quality of the training, which act as inputs received from the trainer.

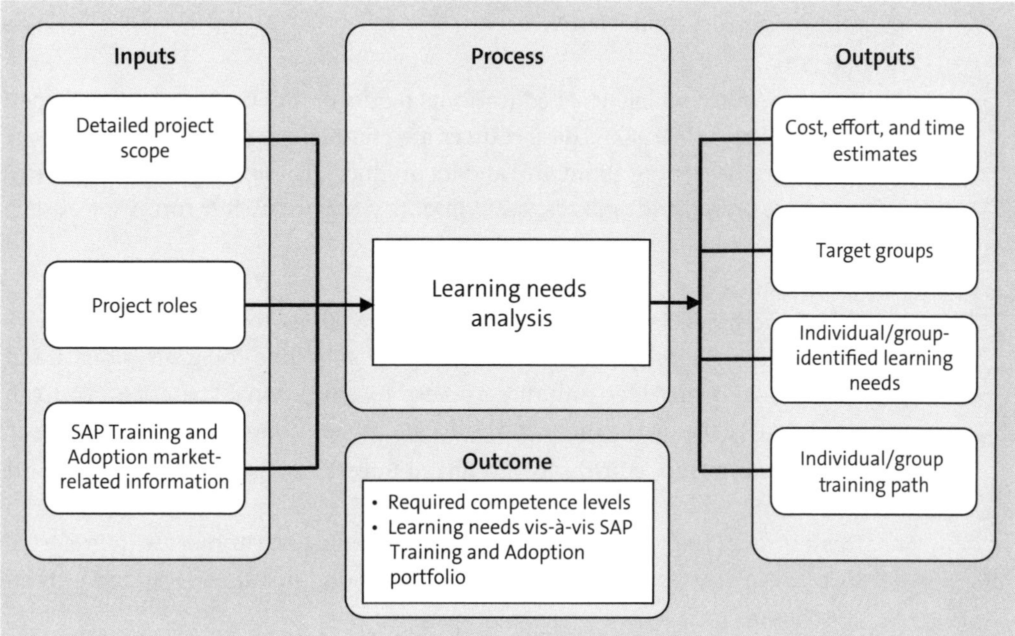

Figure 5.10 Learning Needs Analysis

Tools

Some of the tools used in the customer team enablement workstream are as follows:

- **SAP S/4HANA Cloud trial**
  The SAP S/4HANA Cloud trial will help the customer team understand the details of the processes. The trial is valid for only 14 days, but the user can renew it as many times as needed. You can assess the cloud trial from *www.sap.com/cmp/td/sap-cloud-platform-trial.html.*
- **SAP S/4HANA trials on SAP Cloud Appliance Library**
  SAP Cloud Appliance Library offers several preconfigured, ready-to-use SAP solutions for trial, test, and demo that the customer can consume instantly. You can access SAP Cloud Appliance Library by going to *https://cal.sap.com/* (refer to Chapter 1, Figure 1.15). You can easily and quickly kick-start your SAP project by deploying the solution instantly on your choice of cloud provider such as Amazon Web Services (AWS), Microsoft Azure, or Google Cloud.
- **SAP Best Practices**
  SAP Best Practices provides the ready-to-use preconfigured SAP solutions along with all the relevant business process diagrams, scope item descriptions, documentation, and dependencies. You can access SAP Best Practices at *https://rapid.sap.com/bp/* (refer to Chapter 1, Figure 1.12).

- **Roadmap Viewer**
  This tool provides the solution-specific roadmap with detailed descriptions of activities, accelerators, and artifacts. You can access it at *https://go.support.sap.com/roadmapviewer/*.
- **openSAP**
  This is the most widely used educational platform that provides massive open online courses (MOOCs). These courses are completely free to everyone who is interested in learning about SAP and its products. These courses include learning videos, unit end quizzes, assignments, and discussion forums. You can access it at *https://open.sap.com/*.
- **SAP Learning Hub, professional edition**
  This cloud-based learning platform has capabilities to provide full lifecycle learning management and SAP enablement solutions for professionals and enterprises. It provides unlimited access to educational materials. You can access SAP Learning Hub at *https://learninghub.sap.com/*.
- **SAP Learning Hub, edition for Preferred Success or SAP Enterprise Support customers**
  This subset of the professional version is available to customers with Preferred Success—it's the go-to success plan for public cloud customers—and SAP Enterprise Support.
- **SAP Enterprise Support value maps**
  This tool provides direct access to experts and collaboration forums, and it's available to customers with SAP Enterprise Support contracts. Recommended value maps are for SAP S/4HANA, SAP S/4HANA Cloud, and SAP's application lifecycle management (ALM) functionality.
- **SAP ecosystem and partners**
  This is a chain of partners, vendors, and others who can contribute to the effectiveness of the SAP platform. You can get in contact with them for detailed information on SAP solutions, forums, and user groups.
- **Learning journeys**
  Learning journeys are visual aids that help professionals or users complete the learning path for a specific SAP solution. They are available on the SAP Help Portal. A professional or user can act on this visual step-by-step playbook to complete the journey.

Accelerators

There are no accelerators provided with the customer team enablement workstream.

Application Design and Configuration

The focus of this workstream is all the aspects of the application design and configuration. From discover to deploy, the project team conducts the strategic planning, solution scoping, identification of gaps, and finalization of the scope after rigorous fit-to-standard or fit-gap analysis, finalizing the product backlog, creating the functional and technical design documents, completing the solution configuration, and conducting the dress rehearsal and production cutover. The project team also conducts the periodic update and continuous innovation as a part of this workstream in the run phase of the project. The application design and configuration workstream touches many other workstreams such as extensibility, testing, and integration, which we'll discuss subsequently in this chapter.

In the following sections, we'll explore the key concepts, roles, tools, and accelerators involved in the application design and configuration workstream.

Concepts

After conducting the fit-to-standard or fit-gap analysis and planning the various configuration approaches, the project team will start the configuration processes. Let's understand the configuration processes for on-premise SAP S/4HANA; SAP S/4HANA Cloud, essentials edition; and SAP S/4HANA Cloud, extended edition.

SAP S/4HANA Cloud

The project team conducts the fit-to-standard process for SAP S/4HANA Cloud, essentials edition. Figure 5.11 shows the deliverables in the application design and configuration workstream for the new implementations of SAP S/4HANA Cloud, essentials edition and extended edition. We'll discuss these deliverables and the corresponding activities in Chapter 7 and Chapter 8, but, for now, let's look into some high-level concepts.

The prepare phase starts with customer team enablement, which helps the customer understand the different elements of the SAP system and the SAP Activate methodology. The customer can use several materials for the enablement, including but not limited to SAP Best Practices, Roadmap Viewer, SAP trial system, openSAP, and several other tools available through SAP and the implementation partner. The purpose of these deliverables is to provide hands-on experience to the customer as this experience will help the SME drive the fit-to-standard discussions with the configuration experts.

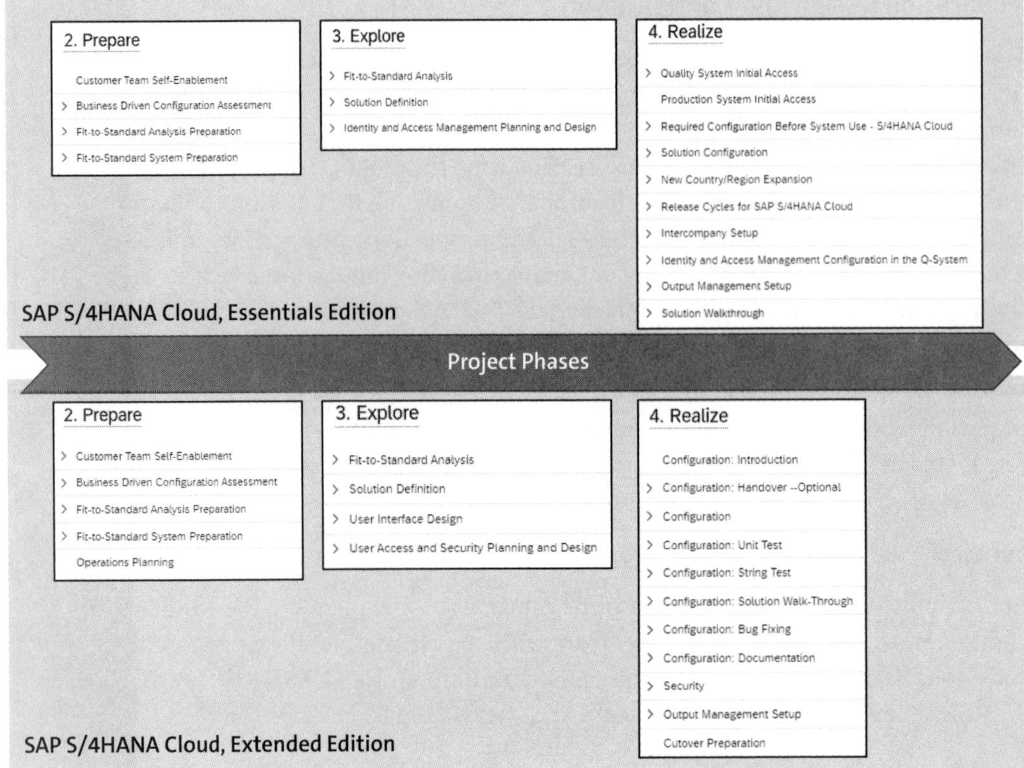

Figure 5.11 Design and Configuration

In the prepare phase of the project, the project team takes the first configuration step, which is the *business-driven configuration questionnaire*. The purpose is to gather insight and additional information based on the solution scope and the customer's current business operations. The configuration expert can download the questionnaire from the **Accelerators** section of the Roadmap Viewer for SAP S/4HANA Cloud, essentials edition, or SAP S/4HANA Cloud, extended edition, as shown in Figure 5.12.

Based on the project scope, the team should update the **Project Relevant? (Y/N)** field shown in Figure 5.12. It's also important to understand that the same questionnaire is applicable to both the essentials edition and the extended edition, as shown in the **Systems** field.

There are two levels of questions in this questionnaire, L2 and L3. The sales and presales team has already covered the L1 questions during the discover phase of the project. The L2 questions are required for execution of the fit-to-standard processes, whereas the L3 questions are designed to gather granular information about a specific process to make a business decision. Essentially, the business team should answer the L2 questions before the L3 questions.

Accelerators

Files

Business Driven Configuration Questionnaire - AI Automation.xlsx (SAP Customer)
Business Driven Configuration Questionnaire - Asset Management.xlsx (SAP Customer)
Business Driven Configuration Questionnaire - Finance.xlsx (SAP Customer)
Business Driven Configuration Questionnaire - Human Resources.xlsx (SAP Customer)
Business Driven Configuration Questionnaire - Integration.xlsx (SAP Customer)
Business Driven Configuration Questionnaire - Manufacturing.xlsx (SAP Customer)
Business Driven Configuration Questionnaire - R&D Engineering.xlsx (SAP Customer)
Business Driven Configuration Questionnaire - Sales.xlsx (SAP Customer)
Business Driven Configuration Questionnaire - Service.xlsx (SAP Customer)
Business Driven Configuration Questionnaire - Sourcing & Procurement .xlsx (SAP Customer)
Business Driven Configuration Questionnaire - Supply Chain.xlsx (SAP Customer)
How to Approach Fit-to-Standard Analysis - Cloud, extended.pptx (Public)

SAP Run Simple usiness Driven Configuration Questionnaire - Finance

Process	Project Relevant? Y/N	Ref	SAP ID	SSCUI Reference	Area	Topic	Topic Definition	Question	Level	Systems	Customers'
Finance	Y	J58	120100	Document Splitting Characteristics	Accounting and Financial Close	G/L Accounts	Each business transaction entered into SAP S/4HANA Cloud is analyzed and split by the profit center or segment using document splitting. With this function, the document splits the line items based on the "characteristics" we define in the system. To support the correct classification of each individual document during the splitting process, G/L accounts need to be classified into different categories - Revenue, Expense, Bank, Cash and Balance Sheet. SAP S/4HANA Cloud is delivered with an SAP Best Practices Chart of Account which have been categorized accordingly.	Do you have additional G/L accounts which will be added to the SAP Best Practices chart? If so, please provide the list and categorize into Revenue, Expense, Bank, Cash, or Balance Sheet.	L3	SAP S/4HANA Cloud, essentials edition SAP S/4HANA Cloud, extended edition	
Finance	Y	J55	101041	Define Profit Center Standard Hierarchy in Controlling Area	Profitability and Cost Analysis	Profit Centers	Per the accounting principles IFRS and US GAAP, companies are required to report on their operating segments. In order to comply with this requirement, SAP offers the possibility to create segments. From an SAP point of view, segments represent divisions of the company for which financial statements and external reports can be created.	Please define the hierarchy required to organize your profit centers to align with your organizational structure within the controlling area.	L2	SAP S/4HANA Cloud, essentials edition SAP S/4HANA Cloud, extended edition	
Finance	Y	19M	101304	Define Disallowed Status Changes	Accounts Receivable	SEPA	If you are using SEPA mandates to collect cash from customer accounts, SAP S/4HANA Cloud comes with settings that enables the same. During the general business process of cash collection, you might be required to change the status of SEPA mandates created. However, you might want to restrict users from changing SEPA mandates to something that it should not be changed to. Here you define the statuses to which you cannot change a current mandate's status to.	SAP S/4HANA Cloud has defined statuses that an existing mandate's status cannot be changed to. Review the list and indicate if any changes are required.	L3	SAP S/4HANA Cloud, essentials edition SAP S/4HANA Cloud, extended edition	

Figure 5.12 Business-Driven Configuration Questionnaire

Another key aspect is preparedness. For effective and efficient fit-to-standard workshops, the project team must follow a high degree of preparedness. The team should review the "how to" accelerators such as "How to approach fit-to-standard analysis" or "How to approach remote fit-to-standard workshops" available on the Roadmap Viewer, review the questions in the questionnaire, understand and download the process contents (e.g., test scripts, processes flow etc.), review the required configurations, and adjust the system to reflect customer's business processes. As a part of preparation, it's also advisable to execute a couple of dry runs with the internal team for the fit-to-standard workshops.

The last step in the prepare phase is the readiness of the working system on which the project team will demonstrate the functionality of the solution. It's highly recommended that the project team use the customer-specific data instead of the predelivered SAP Best Practices data.

In SAP S/4HANA Cloud, extended edition, the team should make themselves familiar with the golden rules of implementation:

1. Foster a cloud mind-set by adhering to the fit-to-standard approach and agile framework for deployments, as detailed in SAP Activate.
2. Leverage the preconfigured solutions and SAP Fiori UX.
3. Use the latest integration technologies and methodologies.
4. Use the latest extensibility technologies.
5. Provide complete transparency on deviations.

We'll discuss these golden rules further in Chapter 8.

Furthermore, in SAP S/4HANA Cloud, extended edition, the team will also define the objective and create a plan to transition the new solution to the operations team. The project team will carry out the transition planning in the project management workstream; however, the team should define the requirements in this workstream. The customer is highly encouraged to work closely with the field implementation partner and SAP to define the target operating model and leverage their tools and resources to operate the delivered solution safely.

It's important to understand that before the fit-to-standard process, the business has already provided the answers to the L2 and L3 questionnaire during the prepare phase of the project. In the explore phase, the configuration specialist will demo the scope items based on the answers to L2 questions, and then gather and validate the L3 answers to facilitate the Self-Service Configuration User Interface (SSCUI) configurations.

Let's move to the explore phase where the team conducts the fit-to-standard process. You have a high-level understanding of the process from Chapter 1, so let's review the process one more time here with a focus on design and configuration work. Figure 5.13 shows the high-level view of the process:

❶ **Review SAP Best Practices**
This is the first step of the fit-to-standard process in which the project team will work closely with the customer's team, including their process owners, reviewing the scope items using the SAP Best Practices detailing the process flow. Additionally, this is the perfect time to ask any final clarification questions on the answers received from the business-driven configuration questionnaires.

❷ **Demo business scenarios**
The project team will demo the detailed business scenarios to the customer's process owners on the starter system using the master data. During this demonstration, be sure to highlight the areas where you think further configuration is needed; it will help drive the discussion and ensure the right understanding.

❸ **Fit with customer's requirements**
In this step, the team encourages detailed discussions to understand the fit and help explain the differences using the question/answers from the business-driven questionnaire.

❹ **Identify gaps**
The team identifies the gaps between the customer's requirements and SAP Best Practices, records them for further analysis, and ensures that the solution will meet the requirements if the team can fill the gaps with additional configurations and extensions.

❺ **Required configurations**
In this step, the team identifies all the configuration value requirements and

in-app extensions. These configuration requirements become part of the product backlog.

❻ **Enable customers**
In this step, the team enables the process owner so that they can execute the processes in the starter system on their own.

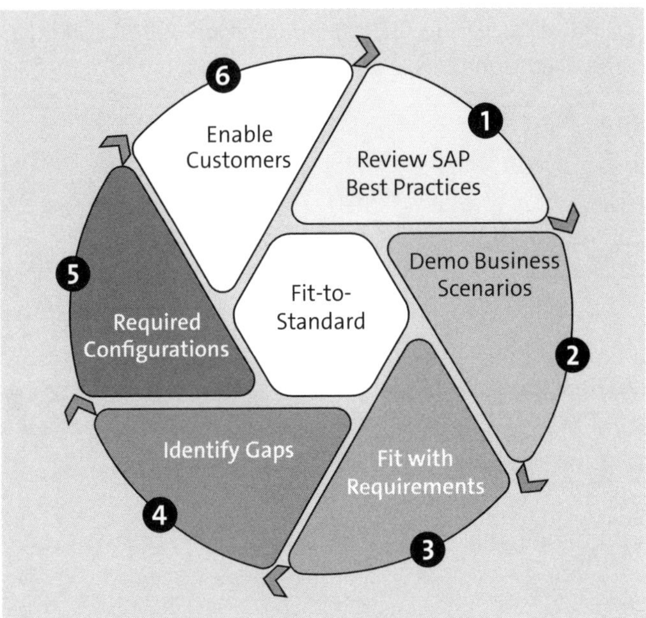

Figure 5.13 Fit-to-Standard Iterative Approach

The primary goal of the fit-to-standard process is to identify and validate any gaps between SAP Best Practices and the customer's requirements without modifying the SAP codes. To execute the fit-to-standard processes effectively, the team should follow the customer enablement process in detail to foster a rich and diversified discussion with the business throughout the process. The technical team further reviews the delta business requirements for feasibility and technical dependencies. We'll continue to discuss the process in upcoming chapters.

After the project team completes the fit-to-standard analysis, the team will have the product backlog ready. After the phase gate approval, the product backlog will become the basis of development and configuration. The quality, completeness, and accuracy of the configuration and the solution itself will depend directly on the quality of the product backlog, which, in turn, is dependent on the fit-to-standard analysis.

The team completes the configuration in the realize phase of the project. This is done in a series of sprints, starting with the prerequisites, such as the customer's fiscal year configuration, profit or cost center configuration, and so on, and subsequently the functional requirements. The project management team should also consider some other factors such as the quarterly innovation cycle from SAP or additional geographical requirements while planning the release and sprint cycle.

The team will release the working software, called increments, at the end of each sprint, which we reviewed in detail in Chapter 3. From a Scrum perspective, do understand that the team doesn't need to deploy every release to production, but each release should be deployable—it's a decision made by the product owner. Figure 5.14 shows the configuration cycle in the implementation of SAP S/4HANA Cloud, essentials and extended editions.

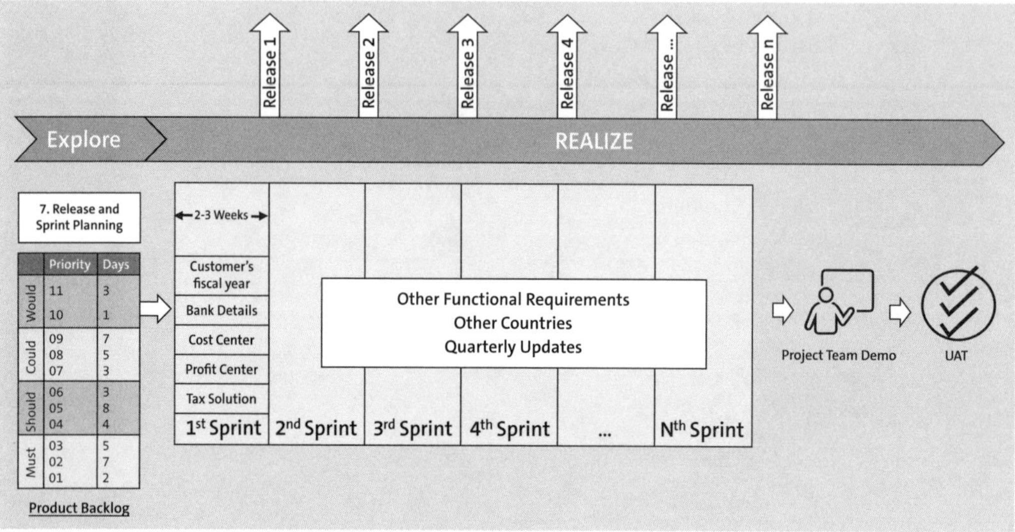

Figure 5.14 Configuration in SAP S/4HANA Cloud, Essentials and Extended Editions

Each sprint follows the iterative approach of configure, test, and verify (with the business users). At the end of the final sprint, the team demos the working software to the process owners and other stakeholders and then moves forward with the user acceptance testing (UAT). For SAP S/4HANA Cloud, extended edition, keep in mind the five golden rules throughout this process.

SAP S/4HANA

In on-premise SAP S/4HANA implementations, the team conducts the fit-gap analysis as compared to the fit-to-standard approach in the SAP S/4HANA Cloud editions. Figure 5.15 shows the application design and configuration workstream deliverables in the prepare, explore, and realize phases of the project.

The configuration planning begins with the prototyping, transition planning, and preparing the transition. Prototyping is a small optional project in itself, which runs in parallel with the main implementation. The idea is to demonstrate the SAP S/4HANA capabilities in a complex scenario and to de-risk the implementation.

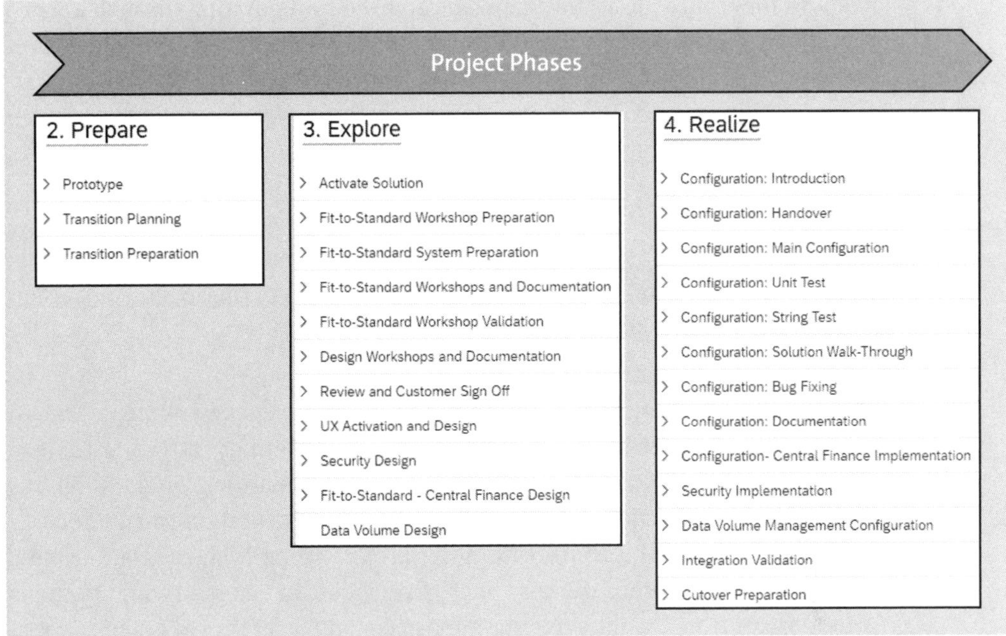

Figure 5.15 Design and Configuration: SAP S/4HANA

The project team plans for the transition during the prepare phase of the project and creates the first version of such plan. This transition plan identifies the action items that the project team should execute to transition from the current system to the new SAP S/4HANA solution. Throughout the implementation, the team will continue to review the transition plan to improve and improvise, including defining the scope and execution plan, UI/UX strategy, cutover approach, conversion readiness, operational readiness, infra readiness, plans to adapt or develop custom code (an integral part of the application design and configuration workstream), and several other activities.

The team executes the preparation activities, such as performing follow-ups or importing the best practice content to SAP Solution Manager. You can refer to the Roadmap Viewer to understand the details of this deliverable. We'll also discuss these topics in more detail in Chapter 6.

In the explore phase, the team conducts the fit-gap analysis in the sandbox environment. Note that the activities to prepare the sandbox environment differ based on which of the three transition paths—new implementation, system conversion, or selective data transition—is used; we'll discuss these in detail in Chapter 6, Chapter 9, and Chapter 10, respectively. At the end of the explore phase, the product backlog is ready, which is a prioritized list of gaps. Additionally, for SAP S/4HANA implementations, the team will conduct the fit-gap analysis for UI/UX, security, data volume, and so on before finalizing the product backlog in the explore phase.

Finally, in the realize phase, the team executes the configuration through a series of sprints that incrementally build the solution. At the end of each sprint, the team conducts the unit testing and string testing, which tests specific business scenarios. The project team conducts the integration testing later in the phase, which tests the end-to-end solution.

Roles

The following list provides the roles and responsibilities of the application design and configuration workstream:

- **Business solution architect**
  The business solution architect ensures the optimum and best strategic system landscape for the customer based on the latest SAP offerings and the customer's requirements. Customer IT and the implementation partner should fulfill this role. The business solution architect from the implementation partner focuses on the solution architecture within the project scope, whereas the business solution architect from the customer IT provides the necessary inputs to his counterpart from the implementation partner and takes care of organizational security requirements, segregation of duties (SoD), process management standards, and application configurations.
- **Application consultants**
  These consultants work closely with the business, customer IT, implementation team, SAP, and several others to gather the requirements; design, develop, and implement them in the system; provide quality documentation; train users; and so on. The implementation partner generally fills this role, but the customer IT can also include its resources to develop in-house competencies, which in turn will lower the total cost of ownership (TCO).
- **Process owner**
  The customer business unit should fill this role with a person who has sound knowledge of the specific business process. Depending on the size of the organization, there can be multiple hierarchies such as chief process owner, modular process owner, business process owner, and the business process expert. The key difference between these levels is the span of their responsibilities. The business process expert should have deep expertise in one or multiple similar processes such as payments or maintenance scheduling. On the other hand, the modular process owner should have expertise in all the processes within an SAP module such as the financial accounting process owner or the materials management process owner; while the business process owner should have sound knowledge of a specific end-to-end process such as order to cash or procure to pay. The chief process owner is someone who has knowledge of these processes,

awareness of the integration points, and a thorough understanding of the organizational operations. These roles surely overlap each other, and the customer must define these roles to remove these overlaps by properly documenting the roles and assigning responsibilities by using a Responsible, Accountable, Consulted, Informed (RACI) chart.

- **Key users**
  These users are the customer's business leads who have accumulated sound business process operational knowledge over the course of SAP implementations and become the "go-to" people for end users. At times, they also help the implementation team with design documentation and testing, including functional and integration tests.
- **Product owner**
  This position is the key to finalize the requirement and forms the bridge between the implementation team and the business when it comes to functional requirements. The product owner works closely with the process owners to identify the features and functionalities, and prioritize them in a clear and concise way to gain maximum value. Additionally, depending on the organizational and the implementation project size and span, there can be multiple product owners, such as one for each module or one for each module and geography for global implementations.
- **Scrum teams**
  This is cross-functional team composed of developers, testers, ABAPers, and several other key functionalities to complete the required configurations, enhancements, testing, documentation, and other aspects of implementation. Remember that the Scrum master and product owner are part of the Scrum team. There can be multiple Scrum teams, called Scrum of Scrums, which depend on the size of the implementation.

We discussed the product owner and Scrum team roles in detail in Chapter 3 and Chapter 4.

Tools

In Chapter 2, we studied self-service configuration, expert configuration, the SAP solution builder tool, and SAP Solution Manager. In this section, we'll review these tools and some of the additional tools that you can use in the application design and configuration workstream. Let's take a closer look at each:

- **Guided configuration**
  In Chapter 1, we looked at guided configuration as one of the three pillars of the SAP Activate methodology. Let's quickly review guided configuration, as shown in Figure 5.16. The left block shows the guided configuration on cloud deployments while the right side shows the on-premise implementations.

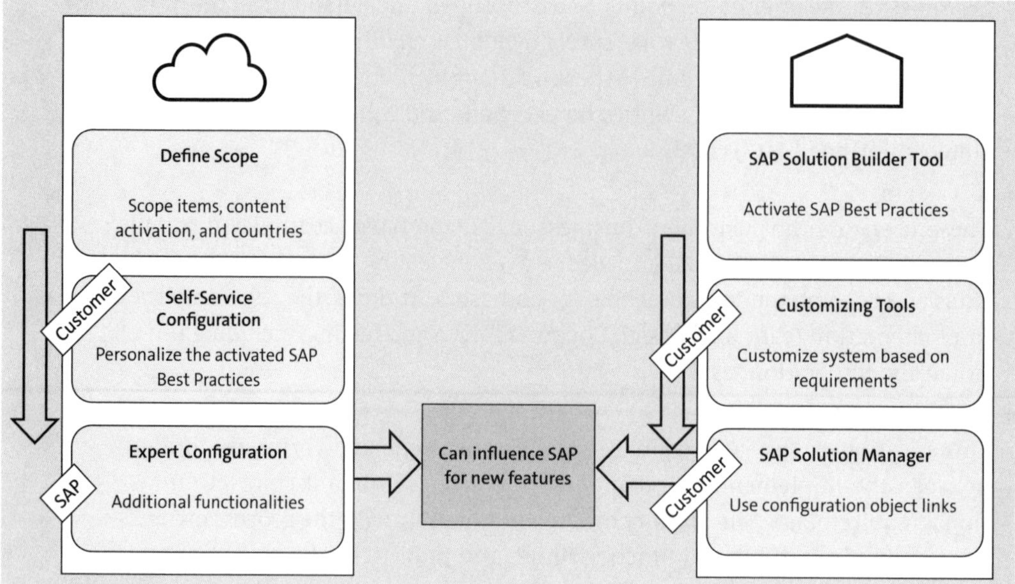

Figure 5.16 Guided Configuration Overview

Guided configuration is available through the Manage Your Solution SAP Fiori app, where a user takes advantage of the following features:

- Initial configuration of the solution for continuous innovations
- Process-driven approach to test the configured processes
- Easily evaluate the activated business process for the specific country
- Easy migration and simple end-user training and onboarding

- **SAP solution builder tool**
  This is the first point of entry to manage configuration and activate the best practices configurations in SAP S/4HANA. You can access the application in the SAP S/4HANA system by using Transaction /N/SMB/BBI. However, to manage the scope items, you can use the Implementation Assistant, which is a function within the SAP solution builder tool.
- **SAP Build**
  You can access SAP Build at *www.build.me*. You can get trial access to the site and learn the design principles. The purpose is to build interactive prototypes in collaboration with the business. One of the salient features is that you can leverage SAP Fiori UI controls and add real sample data.
- **SAP Transformation Navigator**
  SAP Transformation Navigator is a self-service tool that will guide you through your digital transformation journey by consuming your current IT landscape and business strategy, taking market trends into consideration, and delivering

a comprehensive report containing customized recommendations for SAP products and solutions. You can access SAP Transformation Navigator at *http://s-prs.co/v519407*. Concisely, it's a five-step process, which you start by creating a product map. Be sure to go through the **How-to Videos**, **What's New**, **FAQ**, and **Glossary** areas, as shown in Figure 5.17, before you proceed with step ❶.

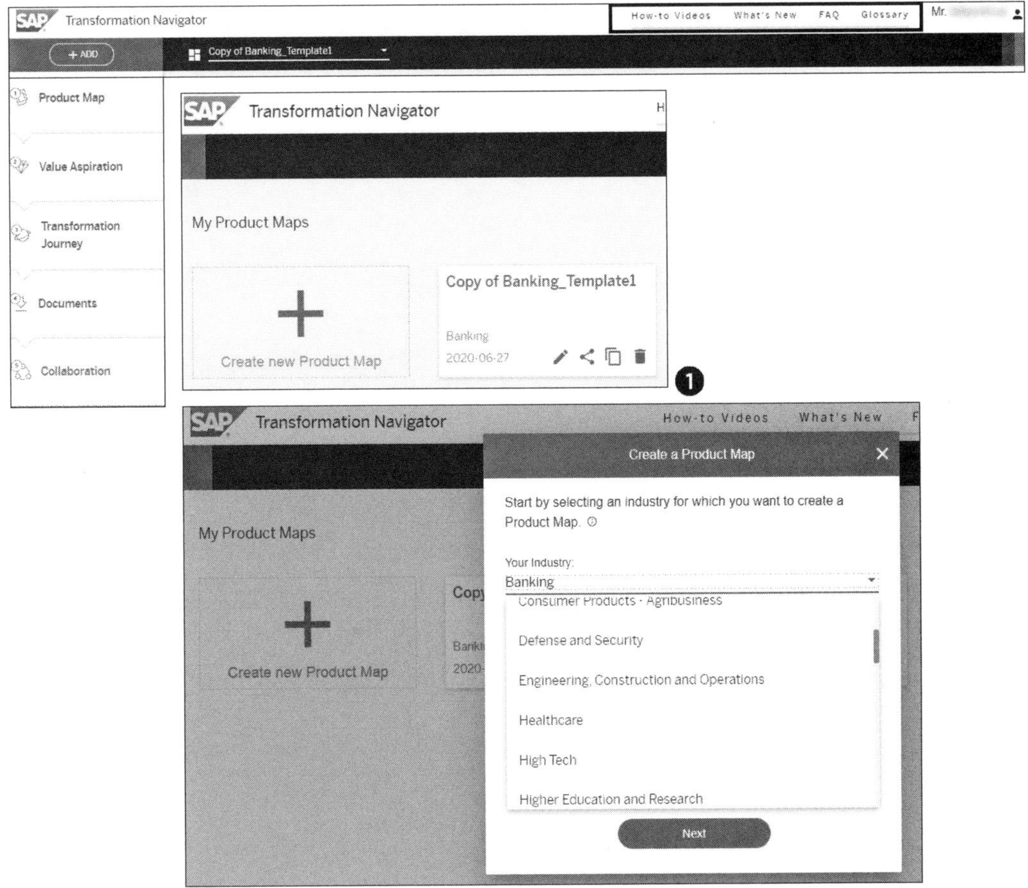

Figure 5.17 SAP Transformation Navigator: My Product Map

Based on your value aspirations in the next step (Figure 5.18 ❷), the navigator will populate **Your Transformation Journey** ❸, and the navigator will further create several documents that you can download ❹. Figure 5.19 shows the three sample presentations (the business guide, technical guide, and transformation guide) created by the navigator.

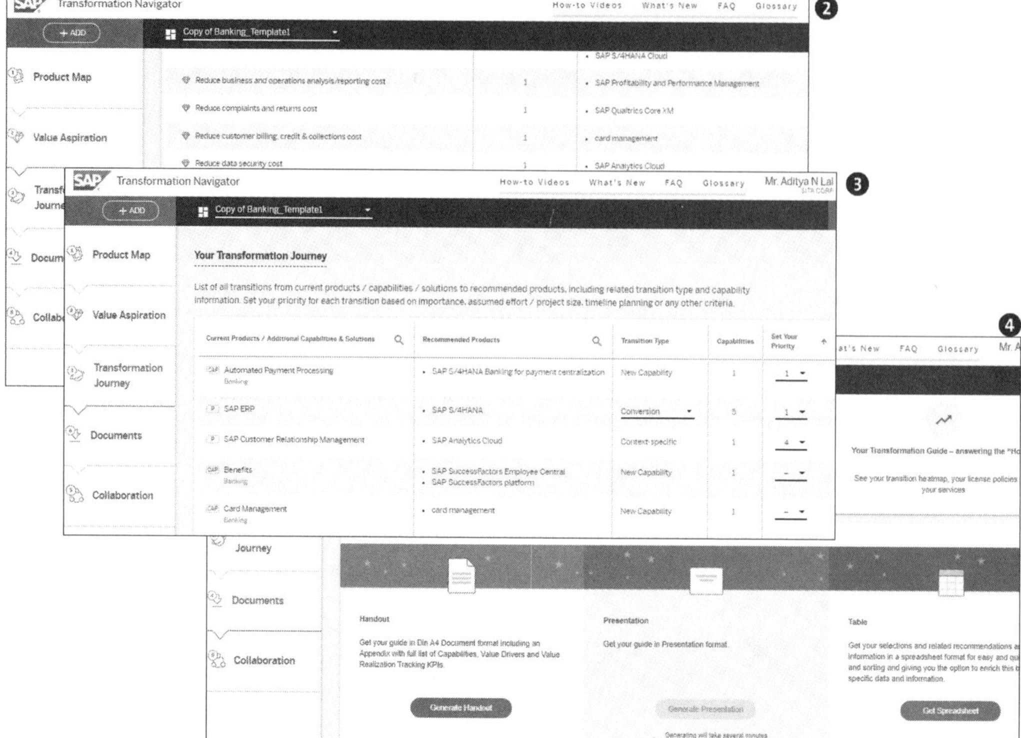

Figure 5.18 Steps 2 through 4 of SAP Transformation Navigator

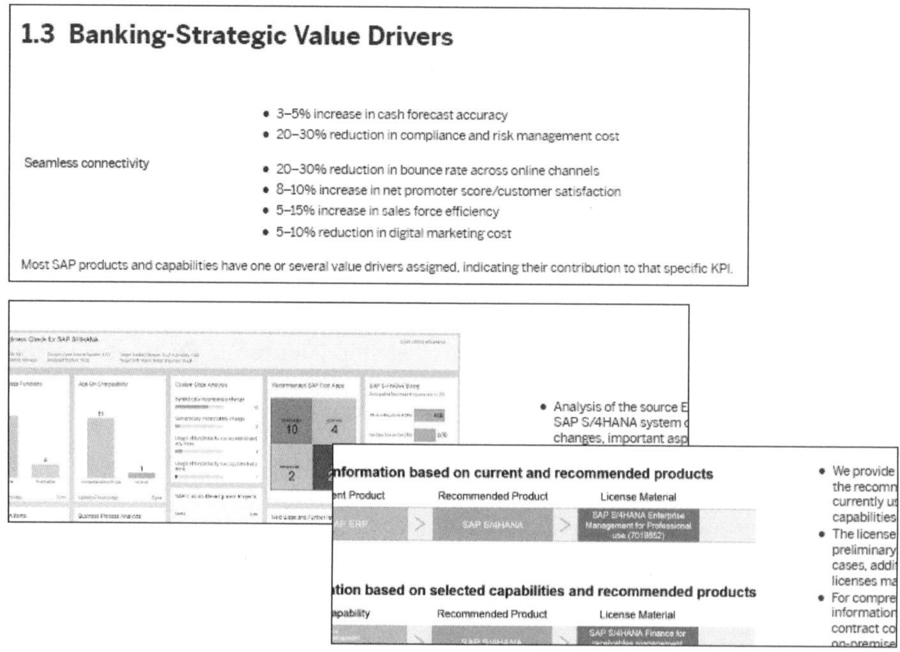

Figure 5.19 Outputs of SAP Transformation Navigator

You can also go through the openSAP course on SAP Transformation Navigator at *https://open.sap.com/courses/tn1*.

- **SAP Best Practice Explorer**
  Throughout this book, we'll continue to review SAP Best Practices Explorer. It delivers standardized business practices, implementation methods, and accelerators for a wide variety of SAP S/4HANA software solutions. Figure 5.20 shows the detailed information structure that is available in SAP Best Practices Explorer.

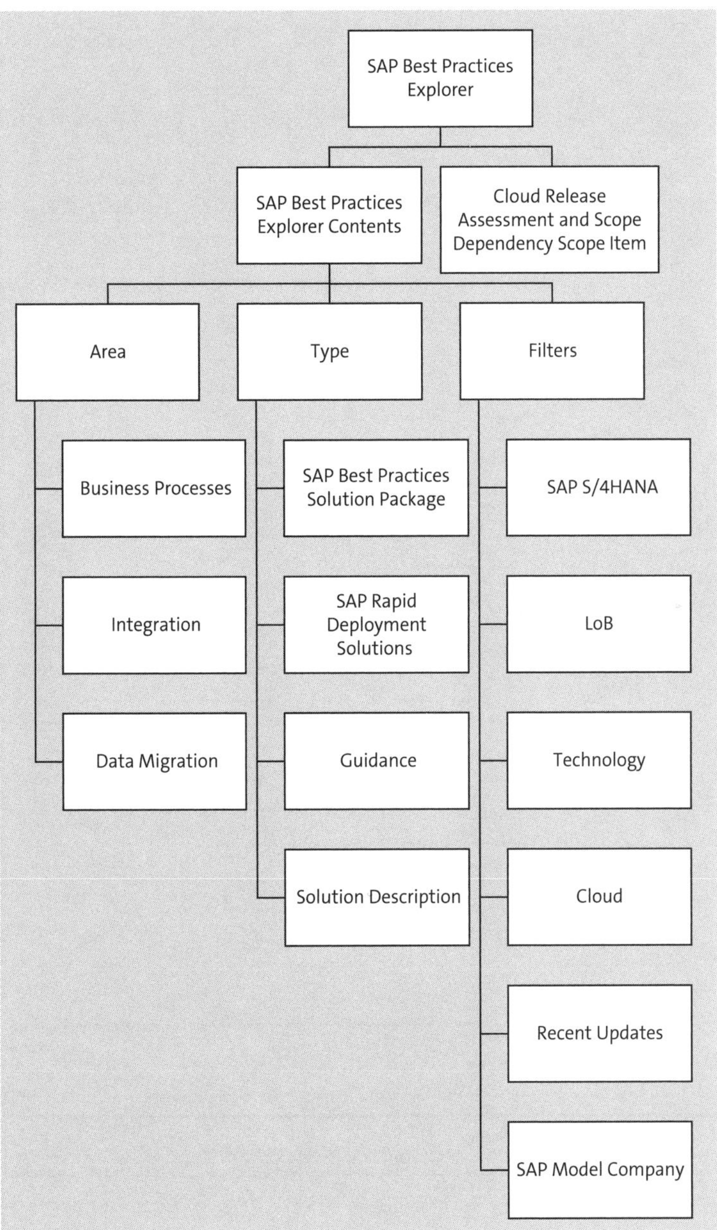

Figure 5.20 SAP Best Practices Explorer Information Structure

It's important that you use your S-user ID to log in to SAP Best Practices Explorer to get complete information. In Figure 5.21, you can see the screen before login on the top and after login on the bottom. The boxes represent the additional information available to the logged-in users.

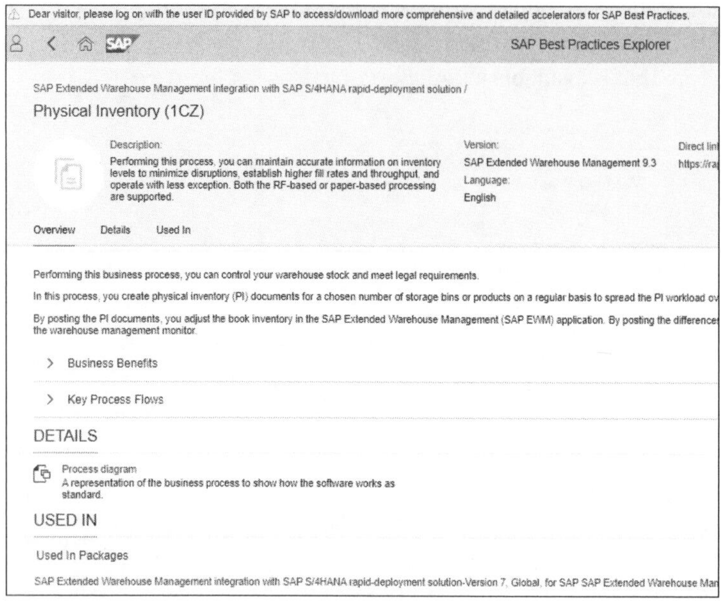

SAP Extended Warehouse Management integration with SAP S/4HANA rapid-deployment solution /
Physical Inventory (1CZ)

Description:
Performing this process, you can maintain accurate information on inventory levels to minimize disruptions, establish higher fill rates and throughput, and operate with less exception. Both the RF-based or paper-based processing are supported.

Version:
SAP Extended Warehouse Management 9.3
Language:
English

Direct link to scope item:
https://rapid.sap.com/bp/scopeitems/1CZ

Overview Details Configuration Used In

Performing this business process, you can control your warehouse stock and meet legal requirements.

In this process, you create physical inventory (PI) documents for a chosen number of storage bins or products on a regular basis to spread the PI workload over the year. You carry out the counting using a radio frequency (RF) device or paper.

By posting the PI documents, you adjust the book inventory in the SAP Extended Warehouse Management (SAP EWM) application. By posting the differences to the SAP S/4HANA application, you balance the stock accounts. You can monitor the progress of y

> Business Benefits

> Key Process Flows

DETAILS

Process diagram
A representation of the business process to show how the software works as standard.

Test script
A procedure for testing the activated system according to the defined business process.

CONFIGURATION

Building Blocks

Name	Description	Assets
Settings in SAP S/4HANA for EWM Integration (EW0)	This building block contains configuration for RFC-based integration between SAP S/4HANA and SAP EWM. The settings have to be made in SAP S/4HANA. The steps described in the configuration guide are essential for the successful integration of the two systems and need to be carried out completely before you proceed with the configuration of further building blocks. This building block is a prerequisite for the installation of all business processes delivered with the SAP Extended Warehouse Management integration with SAP S/4HANA rapid-deployment solution.	Configuration g
	This building block contains the activities for configuration and sample master data in SAP S/4HANA. This building block builds on a SAP S/4HANA system where the business processes for procurement and sales are up and running. The building block only describes additional configuration and sample master data required for the SAP EWM integrated business processes supported with this solution package.	Configuration gu

Figure 5.21 SAP Best Practice Explorer: Before and After Login

- **Solution administration**
  Solution administration scenarios in SAP Solution Manager help you import the SAP Best Practices content from SAP Best Practices Explorer. Figure 5.21 shows the authorization if you use your S-user ID to log in to SAP Best Practices Explorer. After importing, you can edit Business Process Model and Notation (BPMN) process models, accelerators are stored in the SAP Solution Manager, and the process hierarchy and links are preserved. Figure 5.22 shows the content from the SAP Solution Manager basket.

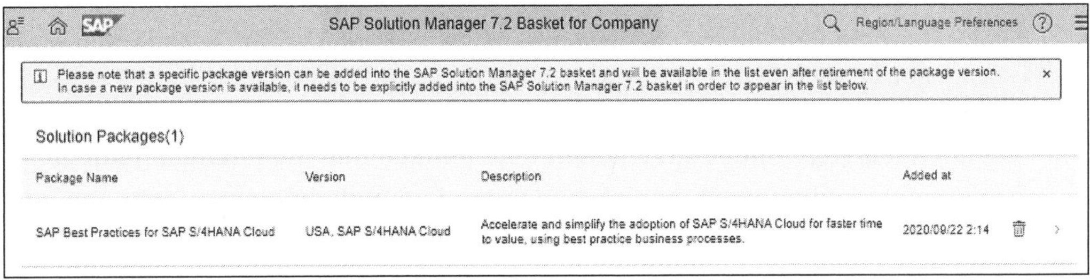

Figure 5.22 SAP Best Practices: SAP Solution Manager Basket

- **SAP Fiori apps reference library**
  The SAP Fiori apps reference library is a comprehensive web-based repository of all relevant SAP content for the SAP Fiori launchpad, as shown in Figure 5.23. You can see the home page ❶, list view ❷, and detail view ❸.

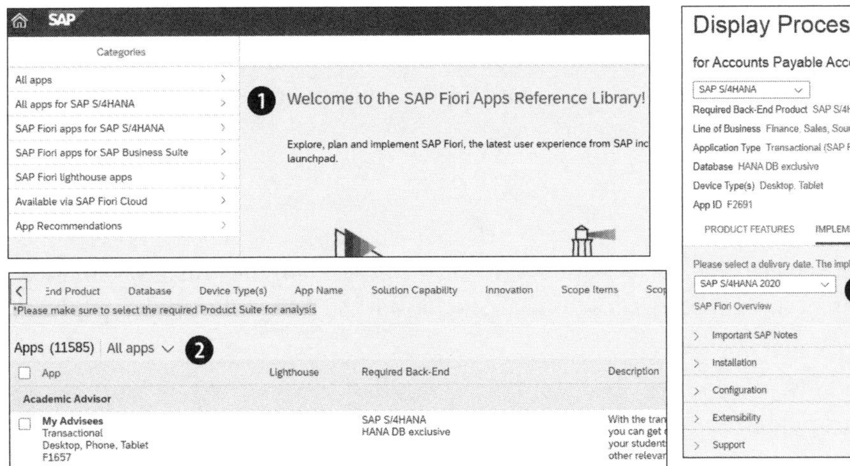

Figure 5.23 SAP Fiori Apps Reference Library

Accelerators

In this section, we'll review the following accelerators:

- **Business Process Master List (BPML) template**
  This is the master list of in-scope business processes documented in a file named *Business Process Description Template*. The purpose of this template is to

capture all requirements, including detailed descriptions, input, output, dependencies, access, upstream and downstream processes, and so on, related to the process. You can download the template from the Roadmap Viewer.

- **Business-driven configuration questionnaire**
  We've covered this in detail in the "SAP S/4HANA Cloud" section. Refer to Figure 5.12 to see the business-driven configuration questionnaire.
- **Business process maps**
  This template shows the activities involved in a business process, who is responsible for the activity, and the process success criteria. It's available on the Roadmap Viewer and can be downloaded. The file name is *Agile Implementations Business Process Management*.
- **Definition of ready**
  This is a standard definition that the user stories must meet so that the development team can start working. Remember the INVEST framework from Chapter 3.
- **Definition of done**
  This was discussed at length in Chapter 3. The definition of done defines all the criteria that a sprint must meet to declare it as "done" or "complete." The definition becomes stringent as the team progresses by adding learned criteria through sprint retrospective ceremonies.

Testing

The testing workstream, as the name suggests, focuses on the different types of testing throughout the application lifecycle.

In the following sections, we'll explore the key concepts, roles, tools, and accelerators involved in the testing workstream.

Concepts

We introduced testing in Chapter 4 (refer to Figure 4.6 in the "Testing Activities" section of that chapter). Let's take a closer look at the different testing types here, as follows:

- **Unit test**
  The implementation partner performs this test to ensure the correct configuration of individual transactions and reports, interfaces, conversions, enhancements, forms, and workflows (RICEFW) development and to check the desired results of the business process in accordance with the business process documents.
- **String test**
  The customer IT performs this test to verify and validate the working of the system components in accordance with the solution documentation. It checks for the correctness, completeness, and synchronization of the system based on documentation.

- **Integration test**
  The customer performs this test to ensure that all inter-module integration points are working correctly. In addition, the customer also ensures that any third-party integration or extensions are working as desired. At times, the customer business also executes such tests to ensure the correct information and business data flow between modules, integration points, and extension apps.
- **User acceptance testing (UAT)**
  The business users from the customer organization execute this test to ensure that the solution provides the desired functionalities per the approved business specification documents.
- **Regression test**
  This test ensures that any new functionalities aren't causing any new defects in the existing and working functionalities. The customer IT performs such tests.
- **Security test**
  This test confirms that the roles and authorizations are sufficient to run the business process and are in accordance with the approved SoD. The team must also ensure that no users have extra privileges and permissions that may affect the system or data security. The customer IT performs the security tests.
- **Performance test**
  The customer IT performs this test to ensure that the solution is providing the outcome as desired. The team performs this test by simulating the desired concurrent login, system load, number of documents processing, and some other parameters. It ensures the scalability and the reliability of the system, the optimal resource usage, and that data-driven decisions are made in relation to the system.
- **Technical infrastructure test**
  The customer IT team performs such testing to ensure the infrastructure availability, disaster recovery and business continuity planning, infrastructure security to ensure compliance with the organizational policies, and backup and restore.

Tip

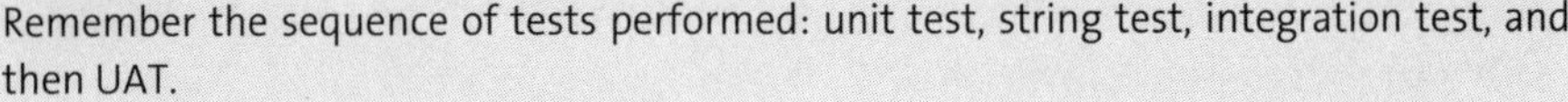

Remember the sequence of tests performed: unit test, string test, integration test, and then UAT.

Roles

The following list provides the roles and responsibilities of the testing workstream:

- **Tester**
  The tester executes the test cases developed by the test case developer and shares the findings with the test leads.

- **Test case developer**
  Test developer roles are fulfilled by the implementation partner who develops the test cases, sometimes using tools for automated testing, performance testing, security testing, and so on, based on the test strategy.
- **Testing lead**
  These roles are generally fulfilled by the implementation partner, and, depending on the project, there can be multiple leads such as performance test lead, automation test lead, security test lead, and others. These leads, however, are experts in their area of testing with sound knowledge and extensive experience and expertise in the given area. They provide guidance to their team and work closely with the testing manager in building the testing strategy and test plan. They are the executioners of the test strategy and share the test results with the team.
- **Testing manager**
  The person in this role owns the creation and execution of the test strategy. The testing manager works with various stakeholders, including project managers, testing leads, Scrum masters, and product owners, to develop and manage the testing activities within the project lifecycle.
- **Test data coordinator**
  This role requires sound understanding of the test data requirement and is generally fulfilled by the implementation partner. The person works closely with the testing leads and testers to identify and define the data requirements, verifies the quality and the completeness of data to load the data in the target system, and may also help the customer IT team extract the test data, if needed, from the source or legacy system.
- **Test coordinator**
  This person, generally from the customer IT organization, works closely with the testing leads, customer IT, and the business to coordinate and ensure the business participation in the testing activities per the test plan.

Tools

Some of the tools use in the testing workstream are as follows:

- **SAP Best Practices Explorer**
  This tool provides you with the complete test scripts for the given scope item.
- **SAP Solution Manager (Focused Build/Test Suite)**
  Focused Build for SAP Solution Manager provides the ready-to-use environments to manage the project requirements and software development projects. From the testing workstream perspective, it's important to understand that Focused Build for SAP Solution Manager provides complete test lifecycle management, including automated test planning and change and release management that supports continuous delivery, integration, and DevOps.

On the other hand, the SAP Solution Manager Test Suite group provides central access to prepare, create, manage, and evaluate test plans, test scripts, test configurations, and so on. The capability includes both manual and automated testing for SAP and non-SAP solutions, customized tests, and test suite analytics, including dashboards, status reporting, gaps reporting, defect management, and more.

- **Component-based test automation (CBTA)**
  CBTA is a test automation tool available with SAP Solution Manager that allows you to create automatic testing for two types of components: default and screen components.
- **Business Process Change Analyzer (BPCA)**
  This tool compares the objects in the transports with the target objects and identifies the impacted business processes, significantly reducing the regression testing efforts. It's an important tool for the system conversion transition and selective data transition paths. You can access the BPCA tool from the SAP Solution Manager launchpad.
- **SAP Test Data Migration Server (SAP TDMS)**
  This high-speed data extraction tool will help you create nonproduction environments from the PROD system by migrating relevant and desired business data.
- **Scope and Effort Analyzer (SEA)**
  This functionality of SAP Solution Manager 7.2 allows you to estimate the scope of change with each software upgrade before the actual installation. Once again, it's an important tool for system conversion and the selective data transition path. It analyzes the SAP environment, identifies and documents the impact, and creates a summary report that provides a wealth of detail, including adjustment for custom codes, estimated time to complete the adjustment, time needed to complete the testing, and much more valuable and time-saving information.

Tip

It's important to be able to identify these estimation tools and to be comfortable identifying which tools are needed for specific transition paths.

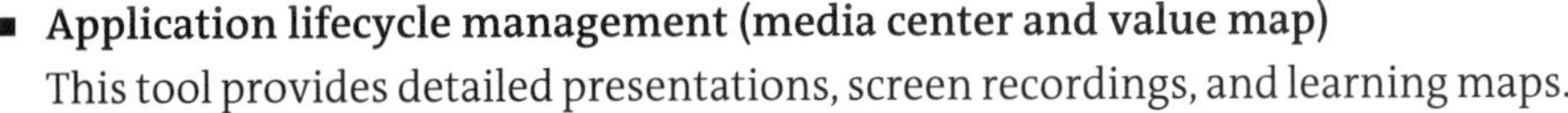

- **Application lifecycle management (media center and value map)**
  This tool provides detailed presentations, screen recordings, and learning maps.
- **Getting started guide for SAP S/4HANA Cloud**
  This guide provides the overview of the test functionalities built in to SAP S/4HANA Cloud. Refer to *https://help.sap.com/s4hana_op_2020* for the necessary documentation and learning guide to kick-start your journey on SAP S/4HANA 2020.

- **SAP support standard for test management**
  This is a set of standard processes, procedures, and practices to enhance the test management processes in a deployment or operation. You can get more information about SAP consulting services and functional enhancements for manual, automated, and performance testing by going to *http://s-prs.co/v519408*.
- **SAP Solution Manager Wiki – Test Suite**
  This Wiki provides a detailed presentation of the Test Suite group tools. Access the Wiki at *https://wiki.scn.sap.com/wiki/display/SM/*, navigate to the bottom-right corner of the page, and find the **Test Suite** section.

Accelerators

Some of the key accelerators for the testing workstream are as follows:

- **SAP Best Practices Explorer test cases**
  SAP Best Practices Explorer contains test scripts for specific scope items such as for Intercompany Reconciliation Process (40Y). After you activate the scope items and import the package into SAP Solution Manager, the scripts will become part of the solution documentation. Figure 5.24 shows test cases for the make-to-order process.

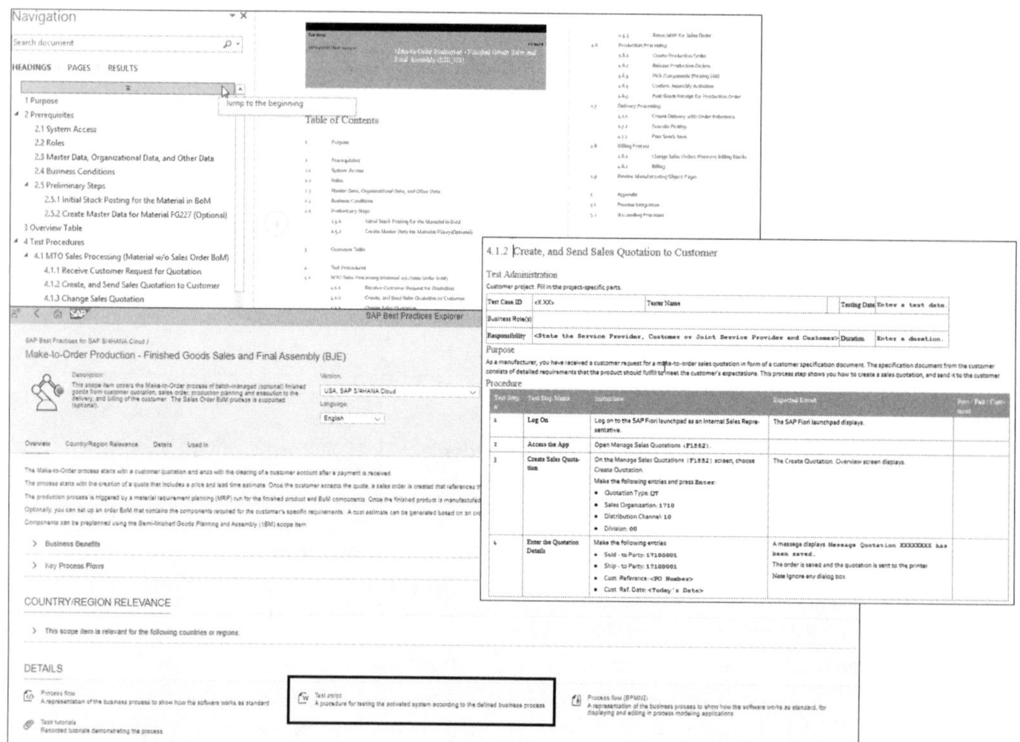

Figure 5.24 Test Cases

- **SAP support standard for test management**
  The SAP support standard for test management defines the principles, functionality, and tools of test management. You can access the functionality from SAP Solution Manager to get the complete lifecycle—plan, define, prepare, identify, build, run, execute, and optimize—of test management. It also defines the quality assurance tasks, KPIs, training needs, and many other aspects of testing.
- **Test strategy**
  This accelerator, which is available on the Roadmap Viewer, provides the strategy for all the applicable tests within the given project. It includes the strategy for unit test, string test, integration test, regression test, performance test, and UAT, along with the in-scope and out-of-scope items, objective of the tests, and functional testing approach. Figure 5.25 shows the test strategy accelerator in the **Explore** section of the SAP S/4HANA Cloud implementation Roadmap Viewer.

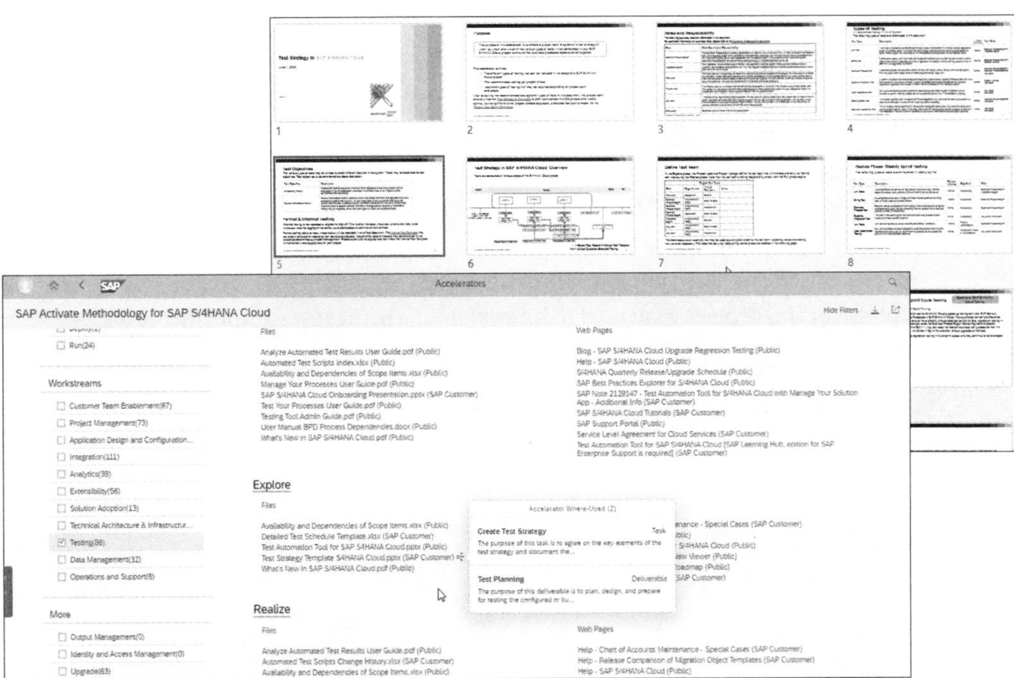

Figure 5.25 Test Strategy

Technical Architecture and Infrastructure

The activities related to the infrastructure and the "to-be" technical architecture start from the discover phase of the project and continue until the deploy phase. Furthermore, certain infrastructure maintenance activities will continue during the run phase of the project.

In the following sections, we'll explore the key concepts, roles, tools, and accelerators involved in the technical architecture and infrastructure workstream.

Concepts

In this section, we'll discuss the technical architecture and infrastructure-related activities, explain the system lifecycle in the three transition paths, and dive deeper into the sizing activities.

Activities

The activities in this workstream start in the discover phase of the project and will continue until the end of the implementation. Figure 5.26 shows a partial list of activities that will start during the discover phase, when the team devises the high-level to-be architecture of the proposed SAP solution, identifies scalability, and notes the availability requirements. Furthermore, the team will complete the sizing activity as discussed later in this section. Equipped with these inputs and based on the organizational needs, the corresponding point of view document, and the best practices, the team will create the data center strategy.

During this phase, the team will create the hardware specification based on the strategy and the point of view document for procuring the infrastructure. However, the team will execute activities such as detailed solution requirements and design in the explore phase of the project, or the performance testing in the realize phase of the project may lead to an update of the hardware specifications.

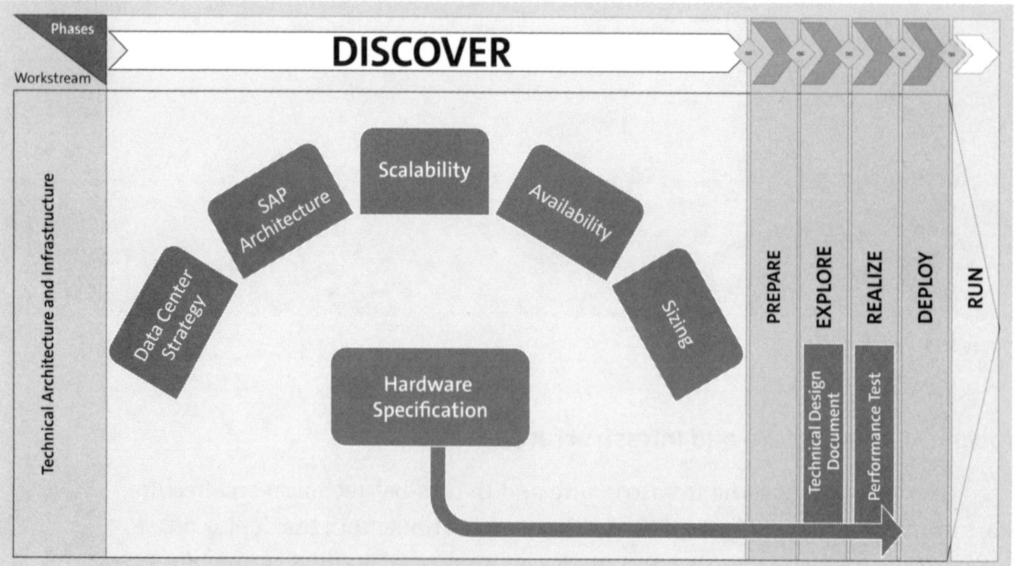

Figure 5.26 Technical Architecture and Infrastructure Activities

Infrastructure Lifecycle

It's important to understand the system lifecycle for the successful outcome of the project. The technical team, project managers, and customer should be in alignment on the availability of the infrastructure. Depending on the transition paths, the lifecycle of the trial system, sandbox, development (DEV) environment, QA system, or PROD box will be different. The simplest of all is the lifecycle for the new implementations: on-premise SAP S/4HANA, as shown in Figure 5.27, or SAP S/4HANA Cloud, essentials edition or extended edition (see Figure 5.28). Although the DEV and QA systems are shown separately for SAP S/4HANA Cloud, essentials edition, they are essentially the same system with different purposes, which we'll discuss in Chapter 7.

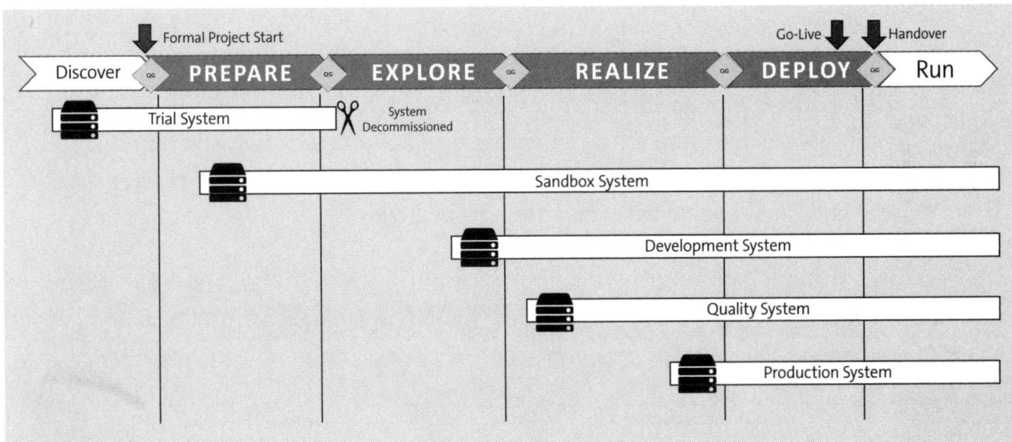

Figure 5.27 Infrastructure Lifecycle (On-Premise SAP S/4HANA New Implementation)

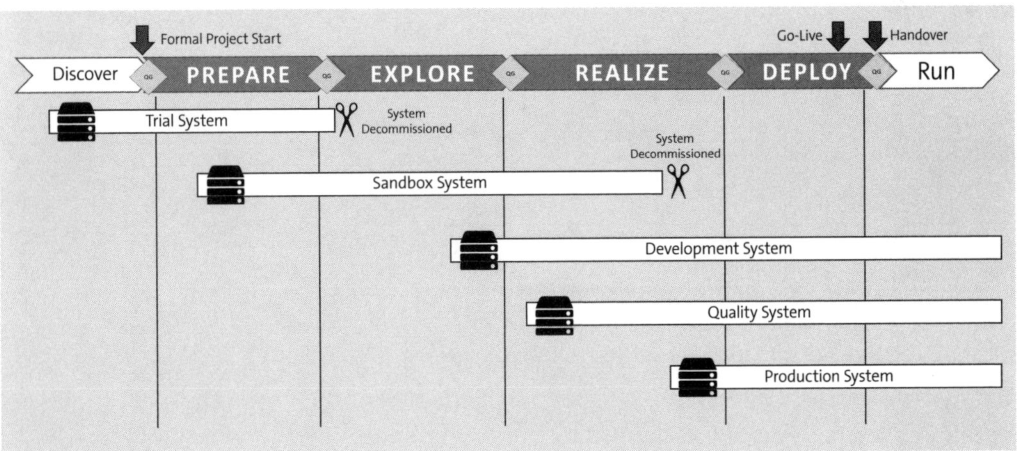

Figure 5.28 Infrastructure Lifecycle (SAP S/4HANA Cloud, Essentials and Extended Editions Implementation)

For new implementations, the team will start with the trial system for customer enablement and the initial best practices walkthrough during the discover phase, which you should decommission toward the end of the prepare phase. At times, you can keep the trial system until the beginning of the explore phase. You receive the sandbox during the prepare phase, the primary purpose of which is to complete the fit-to-standard process in the cloud environment and fit-gap analysis in the SAP S/4HANA implementation. Although you decommission the sandbox environment during the realize phase in SAP S/4HANA Cloud, you'll continue with the same until the end of the project in the on-premise SAP S/4HANA environment. You commission the DEV, QA, and PROD environments in the explore phase, beginning of the realize phase, and toward the end of the realize phase, respectively. We'll discuss new implementation lifecycles further in Chapter 6 (SAP S/4HANA), Chapter 7 (SAP S/4HANA Cloud, essentials edition), and Chapter 8 (SAP S/4HANA Cloud, extended edition).

The infrastructure lifecycle of the system conversion and the selective data transition paths are shown in Figure 5.29 and Figure 5.30, respectively. The lifecycle for these paths is much more complex as the team needs to complete a multitude of activities between the existing systems and the newly commissioned systems. We'll discuss this topic in detail in Chapter 9 and Chapter 10 for the system conversion and the selective data transition, respectively.

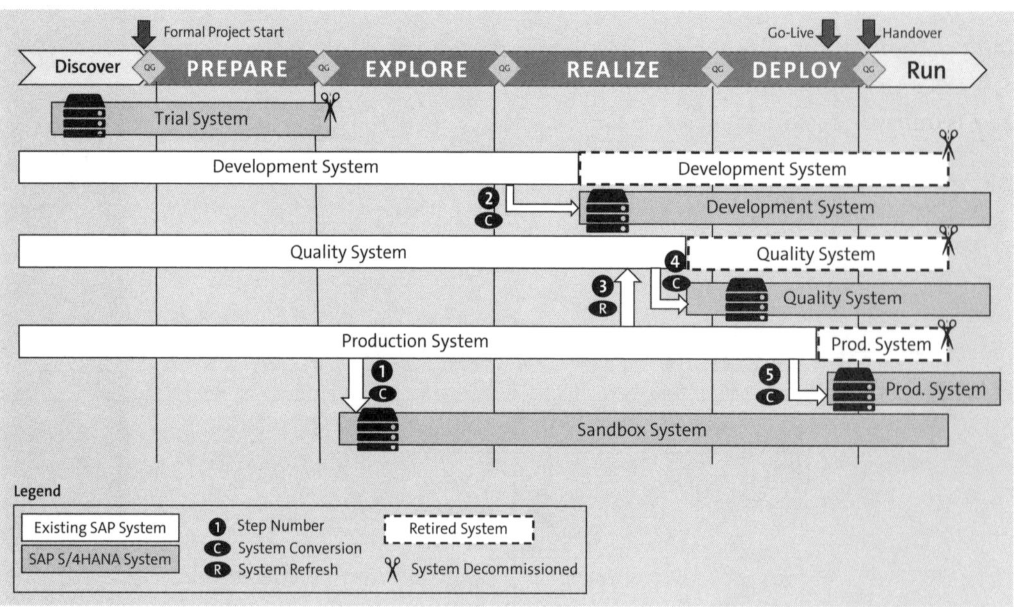

Figure 5.29 Infrastructure Lifecycle (System Conversion)

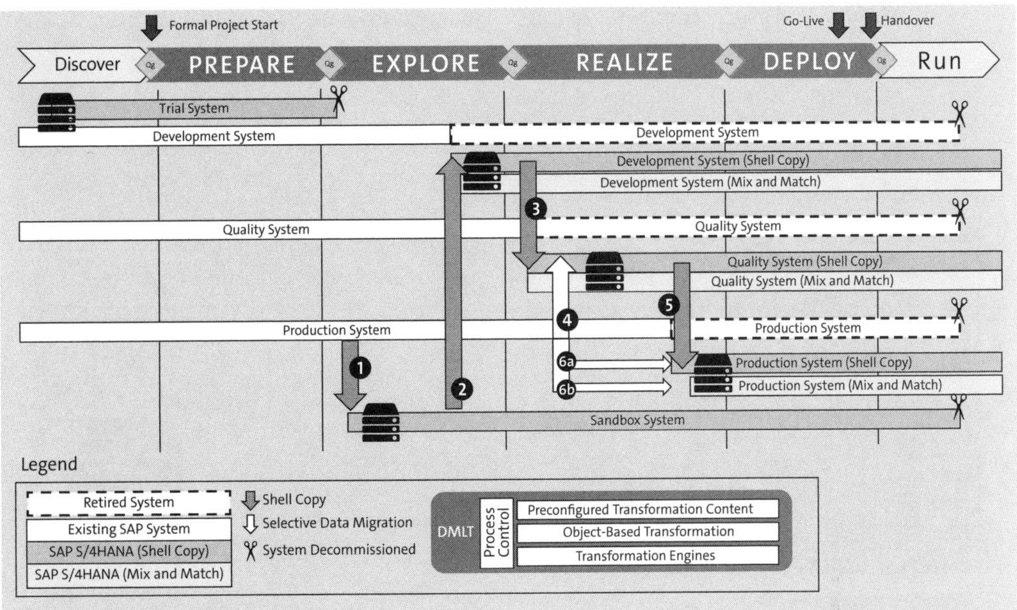

Figure 5.30 Infrastructure Lifecycle (Selective Data Transition)

Infrastructure Sizing

SAP S/4HANA uses SAP HANA, an in-memory database, for which the sizing exercise is different as compared to traditional database. Although memory is the primary driver for SAP S/4HANA sizing, there are several other factors that affect the sizing exercise, as shown in Table 5.4.

Sizing KPIs	Description
Memory	▪ This is the primary driver. ▪ The most important factor is the data footprint. ▪ Other factors include desired response time.
CPU	▪ Desired parallel processing capabilities are available. ▪ There's more CPU for SAP HANA as compared to anyDB.
Disk I/O	▪ Although SAP HANA is an in-memory database, it does require a disk for data persistence. ▪ I/O performance is required for the acceptable data throughput.
Network load	▪ The load focuses on bandwidth.

Table 5.4 Sizing KPIs

Sizing is a three-party collaborative model, as shown in Figure 5.31. In this model, the customer provides the benchmarking requirements, optimal performance, response time, and other expectations from the infrastructure. SAP provides the sizing guidelines, verification processes, benchmarking tools, and so on. The hardware vendor, who has the main responsibility, provides different configurations, service-level agreements (SLAs), and scalable hardware that fulfills the benchmarking needs.

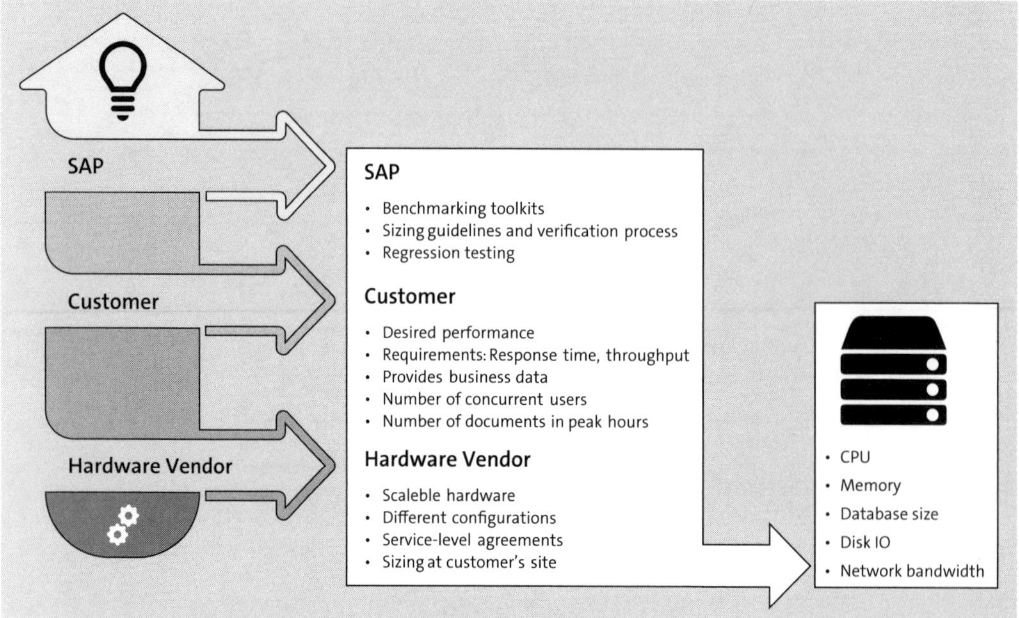

Figure 5.31 Three-Party Collaboration Model

Tip

SAP provides several sizing-related tips and techniques at *http://s-prs.co/v519409*.

The Quick Sizer is SAP's online sizing tool that converts your business requirements into technical requirements, including CPU, disk I/O, and memory.

Note

Data aging is an important concept in SAP HANA where you can move the data from the "hot" area to the "cold" area. For further information, refer to the SAP Help Portal.

Roles

The following list provides the roles and responsibilities of the technical architecture and infrastructure workstream:

- **IT infrastructure administrator**
  The customer IT will fulfill this role with an individual who is responsible for the overall IT infrastructure and system software at the customer organization. The responsibilities include the upkeep of the operating system, network, hardware, database, backups, and so on.

- **Technical SME**
  The customer IT will fulfill the role with an individual who acts as the bridge between the SAP S/4HANA solution and the existing infrastructure setup. The person in this role will provide the requirements from the existing infrastructure side and implement the SAP S/4HANA project requirements.
- **Technology architect**
  Both the customer and the implementation partner fulfill the role with individuals who define the standards and policies for the infrastructure and security measures. This person will also approve the technical design documents.
- **Basis administrator**
  Both the customer and the implementation partner will fulfill this role with an individual who is responsible for the installation and the technical setup of the SAP applications, databases, and other apps. They are also responsible for transport management, user and role creation, and assigning the roles and responsibilities to the users in the system based on the approved SoD.
- **Technical security consultant**
  The implementation partner fulfills the role with an individual who can provide the project security requirements and work closely with the customer security team.
- **Database administrator**
  Customer IT fulfills this role with a person who has sound knowledge of SAP HANA and ensures the correct configuration and reliable operation of the database.

Tools

Some of the tools used in the technical architecture and infrastructure workstream are as follows:

- **SAP Cloud Appliance Library**
  This is a cloud-based repository of SAP S/4HANA solutions for customers to discover and adopt innovations by providing systems for trial and sandbox environments.
- **SAP S/4HANA fully activated appliance**
  This fully activated appliance focuses on the core SAP S/4HANA capabilities and is designed for sandbox usages. You can access the fully activated appliance in SAP Cloud Appliance Library or order it on Blu-ray for on-premise usage.
- **SAP Model Company**
  This tool provides a preconfigured sandbox system that supports the end-to-end processes for specific industries to minimize the risk, effort and cost for the SAP S/4HANA implementation. It provides a kick-start to the team. See Chapter 1 for more details.

- **SAP S/4HANA Cloud trial**
  You can access this cloud-based trial system for a limited period. You can start the trial by going to the product page of the SAP website.
- **SAP EarlyWatch Alert**
  This self-service tool provides a holistic view of system operations.

Accelerators

Two key accelerators for the technical architecture and infrastructure workstream are the technical design document template and the **Enterprise Storage Architecture – Planning** document, as shown in Figure 5.32 (left-hand side and right-hand side, respectively). You can download these accelerators from the Roadmap Viewer.

The technical design document template will help you create the detailed technical design faster. Be sure to include the technical solution, landscape details, software change management landscape, sizing, scalability, availability, data center strategy (if any), overall architecture, and other aspects of the architecture. On the other hand, the storage architecture will include the details of the storage system, storage management, and other aspects of storage.

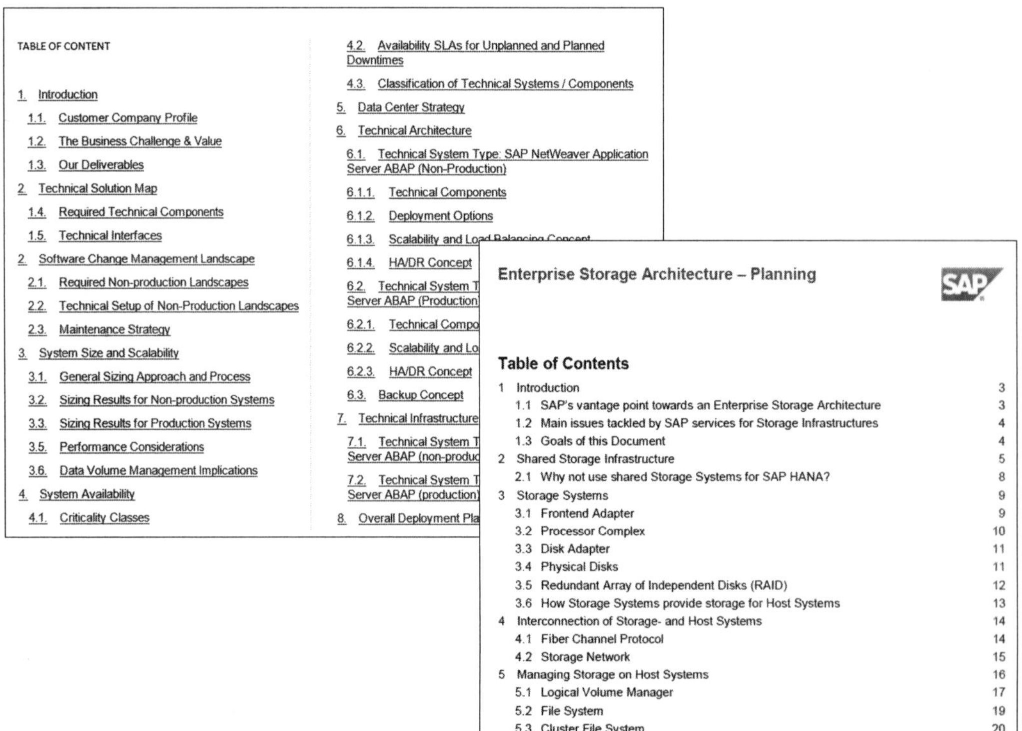

TABLE OF CONTENT

1. Introduction
   1.1. Customer Company Profile
   1.2. The Business Challenge & Value
   1.3. Our Deliverables
2. Technical Solution Map
   1.4. Required Technical Components
   1.5. Technical Interfaces
2. Software Change Management Landscape
   2.1. Required Non-production Landscapes
   2.2. Technical Setup of Non-Production Landscapes
   2.3. Maintenance Strategy
3. System Size and Scalability
   3.1. General Sizing Approach and Process
   3.2. Sizing Results for Non-production Systems
   3.3. Sizing Results for Production Systems
   3.5. Performance Considerations
   3.6. Data Volume Management Implications
4. System Availability
   4.1. Criticality Classes
   4.2. Availability SLAs for Unplanned and Planned Downtimes
   4.3. Classification of Technical Systems / Components
5. Data Center Strategy
6. Technical Architecture
   6.1. Technical System Type: SAP NetWeaver Application Server ABAP (Non-Production)
   6.1.1. Technical Components
   6.1.2. Deployment Options
   6.1.3. Scalability and Lo
   6.1.4. HA/DR Concept
   6.2. Technical System T Server ABAP (Production
   6.2.1. Technical Compo
   6.2.2. Scalability and Lo
   6.2.3. HA/DR Concept
   6.3. Backup Concept
7. Technical Infrastructure
   7.1. Technical System T Server ABAP (non-produc
   7.2. Technical System T Server ABAP (production)
8. Overall Deployment Pla

Enterprise Storage Architecture – Planning

SAP

Table of Contents

1	Introduction	3
1.1	SAP's vantage point towards an Enterprise Storage Architecture	3
1.2	Main issues tackled by SAP services for Storage Infrastructures	4
1.3	Goals of this Document	4
2	Shared Storage Infrastructure	5
2.1	Why not use shared Storage Systems for SAP HANA?	8
3	Storage Systems	9
3.1	Frontend Adapter	9
3.2	Processor Complex	10
3.3	Disk Adapter	11
3.4	Physical Disks	11
3.5	Redundant Array of Independent Disks (RAID)	12
3.6	How Storage Systems provide storage for Host Systems	13
4	Interconnection of Storage- and Host Systems	14
4.1	Fiber Channel Protocol	14
4.2	Storage Network	15
5	Managing Storage on Host Systems	16
5.1	Logical Volume Manager	17
5.2	File System	19
5.3	Cluster File System	20

Figure 5.32 Accelerators in the Technical Architecture and Infrastructure Workstream

Extensibility

Every business is different, requiring SAP Best Practices to align with the company's own custom practices and processes. In our experience, most SAP S/4HANA deployments are "extended" to cater to the client's custom requirements. Extensibility, therefore, is a broad range of adaptation processes and methods that allow changing software behavior. This workstream provides the extensibility concepts, roles, tools, and accelerators for SAP S/4HANA deployments.

In the following sections, we'll explore the key concepts, roles, tools, and accelerators involved in the extensibility workstream. We'll also touch on some relevant additional topics.

Concepts

To facilitate quick business process changes, SAP S/4HANA Cloud supports in-app extensibility and side-by-side extensibility. SAP S/4HANA deployments, in addition to the in-app and side-by-side extensibility, also provide the classic ABAP code-based full flexibility extension through ABAP in the Eclipse integrated development environment (IDE).

Figure 5.33 shows the capabilities of key users who can add or change a number of objects.

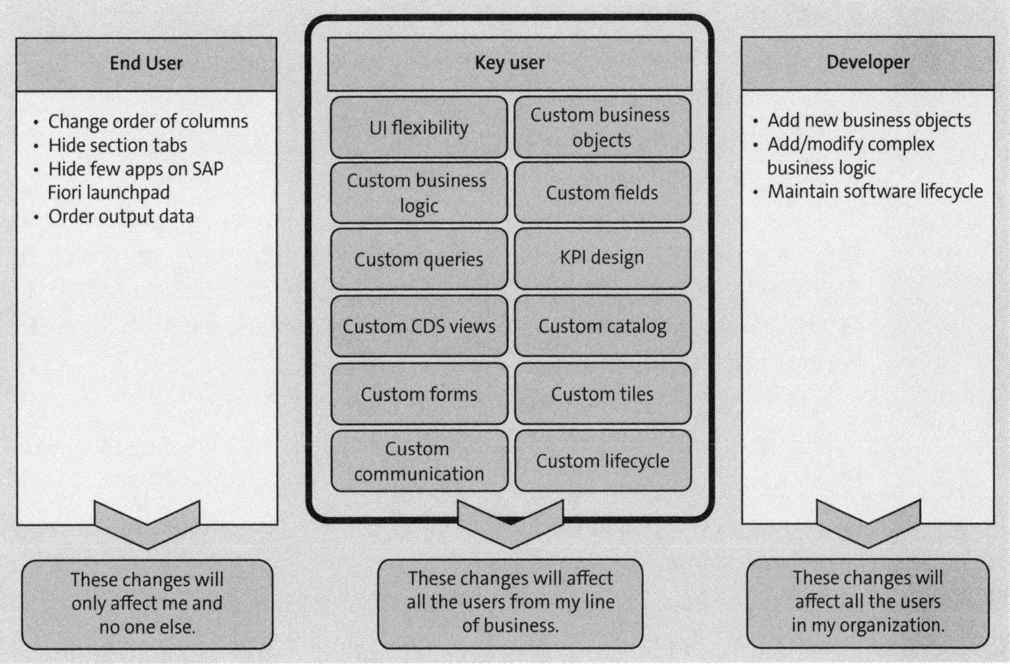

Figure 5.33 Key Users

The in-app extensibility supports these changes, facilitating quick business process changes. For example, if a key user wants to change the order in a report, the user doesn't need to go through the development process—approval and implementation, testing, and deployment—to ask for the change. The user can make such changes themselves through in-app extensibility, saving time, money, and effort.

Let's take a closer look at in-app extensibility versus side-by-side extensibility:

- **In-app extensibility**
  This type of extensibility adapts the built-in apps to provide the extensibility capabilities, with a focus on tight integration. Based on the deployment platform, the project team will have the following options available for in-app extensibility:
  - Key user extensibility:
    - Includes custom fields, forms, analytics, business objects, customer business rules, and so on
    - Modifies or adds business logic and/or business rules
    - Available in both cloud and on-premise deployments
  - Classic extensibility:
    - Full ABAP access (with the Eclipse IDE)
    - Available only in on-premise implementations
  - Managed extensibility:
    - Designed with ABAP programming language
    - Cloud-lifecycle stable
    - Available only in cloud deployments
- **Side-by-side extensibility**
  This type of extensibility provides capabilities to build new apps on SAP Cloud Platform—covered in detail in the integration workstream—consuming the SAP S/4HANA Cloud SDK and application programming interfaces (APIs). This approach weaves external content into the implementation. It includes the following capabilities:
  - Enables SAP Fiori and the mobile UX
  - Integrates with both SAP and non-SAP cloud solutions, including third-party solutions
  - Uses the development platform to build extension applications (SAP HANA native development, Java, etc.)
  - Takes advantage of application services for SAP Cloud Platform

You can visit the SAP Extensibility Explorer for SAP S/4HANA Cloud at *http:///www.sap.com/extendS4*. Table 5.5 shows the major differences between the two pillars of the extensibility strategy.

In-App Extensibility	Side-by-Side Extensibility
■ It's implemented using key-users tool inside the SAP S/4HANA system. ■ Remote communication isn't required between the app and the extension. ■ An enabler for key users doesn't require deep technical expertise but still can create business objects (reports, forms, business logic) and custom fields. ■ Although critical for cloud platforms, we recommend following the same principles for the on-premise implementations as well.	■ It leverages the SAP Cloud Platform as an extension platform. ■ This is an alternative approach to in-app extensibility. ■ It's technically decoupled from the core SAP S/4HANA solutions. ■ It requires deep technical expertise and a sound understanding of SAP Cloud Platform. ■ You can create web-based UIs using SAP Fiori and SAPUI5. Alternatively, you can also create a completely new application. ■ Some other usages are side-by-side services and events, and data mart extensions.

Table 5.5 Difference between In-App and Side-by-Side Extensibility

Roles

The following list provides the roles and responsibilities of the extensibility workstream:

- **Developer**
  The implementation partner fulfills this role with the person who has deep knowledge, understanding, experience, and expertise of development tools, custom code development, and unit testing. This person follows the development lead and creates technical specifications based on the templates provided by the lead.
- **Development lead**
  This role is also fulfilled by the implementation partners with a person who has multiple years of experience as a developer and experience in leading technology teams. The development lead develops the templates and standards, such as development standards, naming conventions, and so on, and gets the buy-in from the project/program manager and quality manager. This person leads the development team, provides technical guidance, enforces standards, ensures quality work, maintains schedules, and collaborates with the development team.
- **Release manager**
  This role is fulfilled by the customer from their IT department with a person who is well versed with the IT landscape within the organization, understands system dependencies, and has the sole ownership of release and change control for the IT systems. The release manager works closely with the other release managers of different IT projects in progress.

- **Quality manager (extensibility)**
  This is another role that is fulfilled by the customer IT organization with a person who has experience in and knowledge of quality assurance as well as quality control. The quality manager sets up the code quality checks, informs code quality issues, and prioritizes code corrections. This person also works with the development lead to provide feedback and approve development standards and templates. The quality manager also ensures code security measures.

Tools

Some of the tools use in the extensibility workstream are as follows:

- **Application lifecycle management (ALM)**
  The media center provides a lot of learning materials on custom code management. You can access ALM at *https://support.sap.com/en/alm.html*. To view learning videos on custom code management, go to **Application Lifecycle Management • Media Center & Demos • ALM Media Center • Access ALM Media Center • Custom Code Management**.
- **SAP Solution Manager processes**
  SAP Solution Manager processes within the ALM portal provide a lot of learning materials and videos for custom code lifecycle management (CCLM) and change control management.
- **SAP Developer Center**
  You can access SAP Developer Center at *https://developers.sap.com/* for various tutorials and trials relevant to developers. You can also communicate with the developer's community by blogs, Q&A, and events.
- **Code Inspector**
  This generic tool performs static code checks on SAP repository objects for security, performance, syntax, adherence to naming conventions, and metrics. You can use the Code Inspector to check a single object, a set of objects, statistical information, or for a specific ABAP word. You can access the Code Inspector by Transaction /NSCI.
- **SAP support standards for custom code management**
  These are the procedures, tools and techniques, documentations, and roles used within the implementation project for establishing the custom code management process. You can access the custom code management guide at *http://s-prs.co/v51410*.

Accelerators

There are several accelerators for the extensibility workstream. However, the two accelerators that are mostly used are as follows:

- **ABAP development standards**
  You can find this accelerator on the Roadmap Viewer for on-premise implementations. It defines the ABAP standard, naming conventions, quality standards, security standards, data dictionary standards, and so on.
- **SAP support standard for custom code management**
  This support standard for custom code is available on the SAP Support Portal. This accelerator defines the overview standard for custom code management, lifecycle of custom code, and continuous improvement, including quality assurance and quality control processes.

Additional Topics

In this section, we'll review a couple of additional topics that are important for project management in the area of extensibility. In the certification exam, although rare, you may get a couple of questions from these topics.

Custom Code Lifecycle Management

Custom code lifecycle management (CCLM) was developed to accompany the custom ABAP code throughout its lifecycle, from requirement to retirement, as shown in Figure 5.34. The lifecycle begins when an ABAP programmer creates an object such as a class or a program, follows through the development and test activities, and deploys the object in the PROD environment. Throughout the object's life in the PROD environment, you monitor the object and optimize it until it completes is lifecycle and is rendered retired.

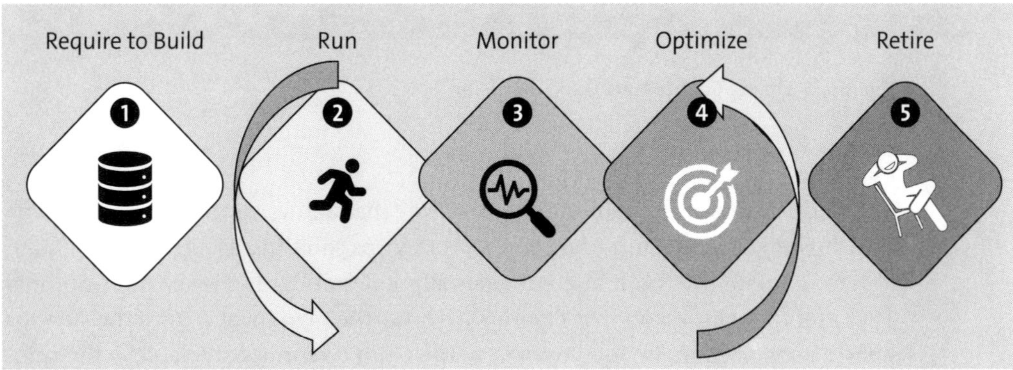

Figure 5.34 Custom Code Lifecyle Management

Change Control Management

A central change and transport system (central CTS) enhances the classic CTS by providing functions for a complex heterogeneous system landscape. In turn, it allows you to control the transports within the complex transport landscape centrally. Two of the features are as follows:

- Combine systems with content dependencies into a system cluster:
  - You can combine ABAP and non-ABAP systems into a system cluster.
  - You can combine systems with the same role into a system cluster.
  - You can define a system cluster centrally in the central CTS server.
- Combine transports into collections:
  - You can combine transports from different systems into a transport collection.

Figure 5.35 shows the building blocks of change control management, which extends from the extensibility workstream where you develop and manage custom code to the technical architecture and infrastructure workstream where the team manages the transports.

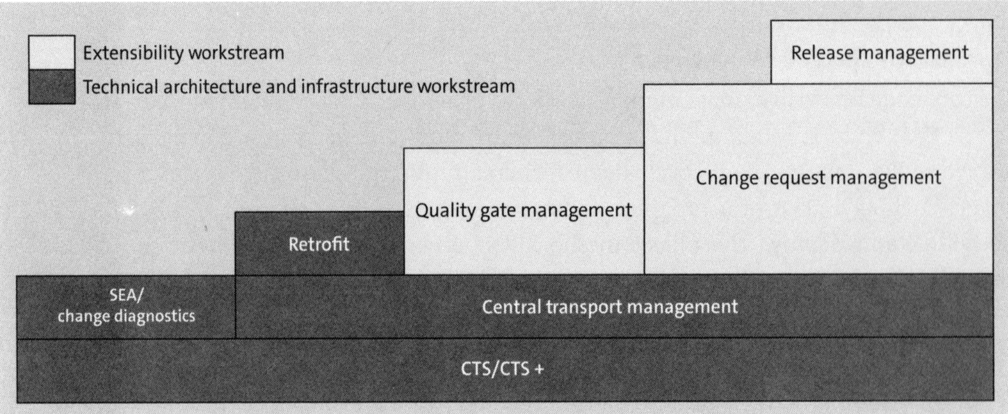

Figure 5.35 Change Control Management Building Blocks

DevOps

SAP understands the capabilities of DevOps—that allows continuous delivery by the implementation team—and supports DevOps tools inside SAP Solution Manager and SAP S/4HANA. It also provides support standards that ensures optimal TCO after the solution go-live. Figure 5.36 shows the high-level view of the DevOps phases supported in SAP deployments. The team continuously deploys the solutions built from the release to feedback phase while the plan, develop, and verify phases continuously integrate the solution.

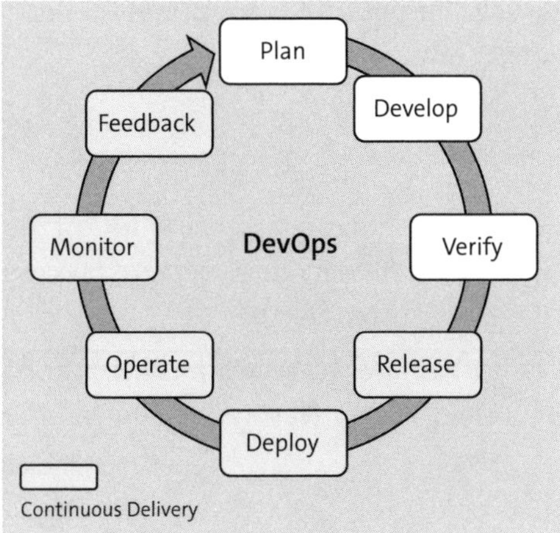

Figure 5.36 DevOps in SAP Deployments

Data Management

The data management workstream has three substreams, as shown in Figure 5.37:

❶ **Master data management**
Aims to unify the master data, resulting in high data quality in the target system.

❷ **Data volume management**
Always aims for limited transactional data. High data volume creates higher risks.

❸ **Data migration**
Deals with the migration policy, strategy, and its execution to migrate the legacy data (both master and limited transactional data) from the source system to the target system.

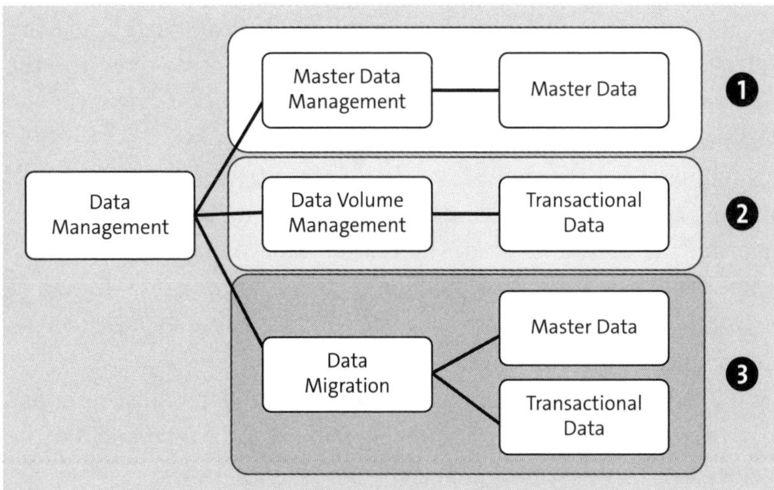

Figure 5.37 Data Management Substreams

In the following sections, we'll explore the key concepts, roles, tools, and accelerators involved in the data management workstream.

Concepts

Incomplete or incorrect master data will lead to easy but catastrophic failure of the solution. A consistent, coherent, and optimized master data management process will provide for higher data quality, which is a key success factor.

Data volume management, on the other hand, handles the relevant transactional data in the "right" volume for the given system. The four features of data volume management are as follows:

- Data avoidance
- Data summarization
- Data deletion
- Data archiving

Data migration provides the tools, technologies, processes, and procedures to migrate the data from the heterogeneous source systems to the target SAP system.

Roles

The following list provides the roles and responsibilities of the data management workstream:

- **Master data sponsor (master data management)**
  This role is fulfilled by the customer business organization with a candidate who has sound knowledge of master data management policies and procedures and a strong understanding of the business strategy. This person enforces these policies and procedures across all the lines of business.
- **Business data owner (master data management)**
  This role is also fulfilled by the customer business with a candidate who has a sound understanding of data structure and its usages in order to ensure the resultant data set aligns with the requirements across business functions.
- **Master data manager (master data management)**
  This role is fulfilled by the customer IT with a candidate who has the detailed understanding of the customer IT landscape along with the available tools and technologies for the data migration. The master data manager will help the project team identify these tools and define the security measures, as well as accept the master data management operation from the project team.
- **Master data change requestor (master data management)**
  This role is fulfilled by the customer business with a candidate whose responsibility is to request for changes in the master data set using the tools and the processes supplied by the master data manager.

- **Master data maintainer (master data management)**
  Based on the change request received by the requestor, the master data maintainer, fulfilled by the customer business organization, will make changes in the data set using the tools and processes identified by the master data manager.
- **Data migration architect (data migration)**
  This role is fulfilled by the implementation partner with a person with sound knowledge of SAP and other relevant data migration tools. In this role, the person will develop and define the migration strategy, select the migration tools, work closely with the solution architect, and oversee the strategy execution.
- **Data extraction expert (data migration)**
  This role is generally fulfilled by the customer IT organization with a person who has extensive knowledge of the legacy system and the extraction tools as identified by the master data manager. This person extracts the data in the format specified by the data migration architect.
- **Data preparation expert (data migration)**
  This role is fulfilled by the customer business organization with a person who is proficient in the business processes. The data preparation expert cleanses the data per the business logic supplied by the data extraction expert.
- **Data migration developer (data migration)**
  The developer role is fulfilled by the implementation partner with a person who develops, tests, and executes the extraction and transformation program code.
- **Data volume ALM process owner (data volume management)**
  The data volume management ALM process owner is from the customer IT organization and ensures the implementation of the processes, programs, and procedures developed by the data volume management consultant.
- **Data volume consultant (data volume management)**
  This consultant is from the implementation partner with comprehensive knowledge of data volume management strategy. This person will develop the data volume management strategy, configure archiving objects and deletion jobs, and create relevant functional specifications.

Tools

The master data management tools are as follows:

- **openSAP courses**
  openSAP is a free platform for all that hosts MOOCs. You may find a number of master data management courses on the openSAP platform.
- **SAP Enterprise Information Management (SAP EIM)**
  SAP EIM is a technology platform that helps you manage your enterprise information and converts it into a set of strategic assets.

- **Blogs**
  Several blogs on SAP Community provide valuable information about the master data management processes, procedures, challenges, to-dos, steps, playbooks, and other assets.
- **SAP Master Data Governance**
  This state-of-the-art software product provides an out-of-the-box, domain-specific master data management solution that will help improvise the information quality and consistency across the organization.
- **SAP Information Lifecycle Management**
  This software product helps you streamline your IT infrastructure by automating the data archiving and retention processes and reduces the business risk with compliant data. Another key feature of the software is system decommissioning, whereby data is moved to a central warehouse, and the legacy system is shut down.
- **SAP Information Steward**
  This is another software product from SAP that helps analyze the data quality of data coming from multiple sources. It improves the integrity of the enterprise data model by gaining valuable insights and analytics of enterprise data.

The data migration tools are as follows:

- **Blogs**
  Several blogs provide valuable information about the data migration processes, procedures, challenges, to-dos, steps, playbooks, and other assets.
- **SAP Data Services**
  This is an extract, transform, and load (ETL) tool that provides an enterprise-level solution for data migration from heterogeneous sources into a central data warehouse.
- **Rapid data migration to SAP S/4HANA**
  This approach accelerates the data migration processes—from data cleansing to loading—from many sources to SAP S/4HANA. You'll find this accelerator on SAP Best Practices Explorer, which provides you with prebuilt best practice content.
- **SAP Agile Data Preparation**
  This software product from SAP follows the agile approach for data preparation, cleansing, integration, and deduplication of data.

The data volume management tools are as follows:

- **SAP Help Portal**
  This portal enables you to find the documentation, approach, learning journeys, content, and other accelerators for data volume management.
- **SAP Solution Manager**
  This tool provides the step-by-step process to implement data volume management and the detailed data volume management process descriptions on the SAP Support Portal.

- **SAP Wiki**
  On the Wiki hub, you can find useful links on data volume management topics at *http://s-prs.co/v519411*.

Accelerators

The two main accelerators are as follows:

- **Data governance plan**
  The data governance plan is a communication accelerator to manage and monitor the enterprise data. The plan identifies the data policies, standard, data lifecycle and procedure, different organizational levels, and the corresponding access, data security, and so on.
- **Data migration strategy and approach**
  The data migration approach identifies the steps and processes to migrate the data from the source system to the target system. The approach details the data that should be migrated, how the data will be migrated, details of the ETL process, data cleansing, migration tools, testing methodologies, and so on.

Integration

These workstream activities are relevant for integration implementation experts covering integration requirements, integration points, approach, solution design, and middleware setup between the SAP solution and the external system.

In the following sections, we'll explore the key concepts, roles, tools, and accelerators involved in the integration workstream.

Concepts

Let's start with understanding the SAP Cloud Platform Integration Suite and then review the integration options in the subsequent sections.

SAP Cloud Platform Integration Suite

There are several different cloud service models, so let's review those first:

- **Infrastructure-as-a-service (IaaS)**
  In its simplest form, you're using someone else's infrastructure—servers, virtual machines, networking, and storage—for a yearly subscription fee.
- **Platform-as-a-service (PaaS)**
  This provides you a platform such as Java Runtime Environment (JRE), web server environment, middleware, or similar services where you pay based on consumption. The user develops the code to run it on the available runtime environment. This is the key concept that you need to understand for SAP Cloud Platform Integration Suite.

- **Software-as-a-service (SaaS)**
  In this case, the user will get the preconfigured software and pay the provider based on either consumption or a flat yearly subscription fee. Some SaaS examples are SAP SuccessFactors, SAP Concur, and SAP Ariba.

You can access SAP cloud solutions and services at *http:///www.sap.com/trends/cloud-solutions.html.*

Now, let's consider the integration platform-as-a-service (IPaaS), which is a collection of services, in this case provided by SAP, for the sole purpose of integration. IPaaS has several integration services, including APIs, cloud integration, enterprise messaging, SAP HANA smart data integration, OData, open connectors, and RabbitMQ. It's important to understand that SAP Cloud Platform Integration Suite isn't a tool; rather, it's a collection of tools and services that is available to an enterprise to integrate cloud-to-cloud systems and on-premise applications. Figure 5.38 shows the available tools and services within SAP Cloud Platform Integration Suite and how can you access the trial version of SAP Cloud Platform Integration Suite via the **Start free trial** button.

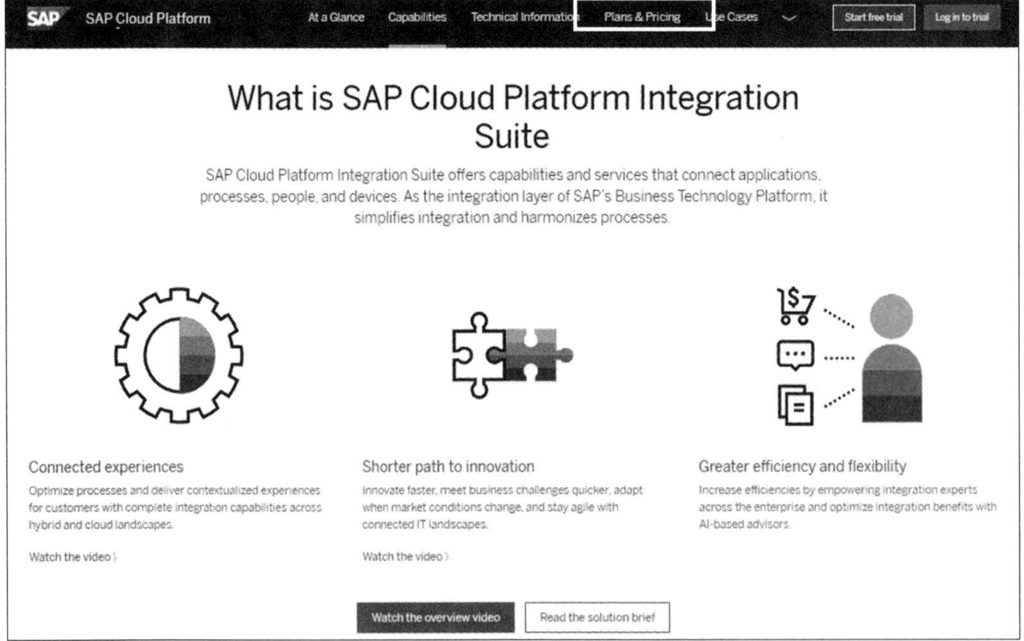

Figure 5.38 SAP Cloud Platform Integration Suite

There are several integration options that an enterprise can use via SAP Cloud Platform Integration Suite:

- **Social network integration**
  You can connect with social media using the new adopters.

- **On-premise integration**
  You can even connect to on-premise applications using several third-party and SAP connectors.
- **Cloud integration**
  This is cloud-to-cloud integration; we'll dive deeper into these integration concepts in the next section.
- **APIs, connectors, and OData**
  These adopters are available to connect to several third-party applications.
- **SAP HANA smart data integration**
  This enables you to sync data between two systems in real time.
- **SAP Cloud Platform Workflow Management**
  SAP Cloud Platform Workflow Management is business process modeling in the cloud that allows you to build the workflows spanning business units and organizations. You can use the tool for workflow modeling, APIs for consumption, SAP Fiori-based tool for end users, and monitoring tools.
- **RabbitMQ**
  This open-source tool manages the advanced messaging queuing protocol and can connect with the JMS servers.
- **iFlow, Eclipse, Groovy**
  iFlow is a development tool, Eclipse is a software development kit (SDK), and Groovy is a dynamic language that uses all the features of Java.
- **Predefined integration content**
  This predefined content is provided either by SAP or by a third party to connect several applications such as SAP SuccessFactors, SAP Concur, and so on. Therefore, before you start developing an integration connector, you should check the prepackaged content; it's highly likely that you'll get one that suits your need. If not, you can still start with a relevant connector and customize it to save a lot of effort. To access prepackaged content, go to *https://api.sap.com/* and *http://s-prs.co/v519412*.

Note

For further technical help on the SAP Cloud Platform Integration Suite (beyond the scope of the exam), refer to the following:

- SAP Cloud Platform Integration Help at *http://s-prs.co/v519413*
- SAP Cloud Platform Adopters *http://s-prs.co/v519414*

Integration Options

In today's technological era of advancement, enterprise applications can scatter around the cloud and within the enterprise network. There are multiple options, as shown in Figure 5.39, that you can leverage to integrate these scattered applications:

- **Cloud to cloud**
  To integrate applications on the cloud, SAP Cloud Platform Integration Suite is the recommended option.
- **On-premise to on-premise**
  SAP Process Orchestration is the recommended choice for such integrations, and APIs should be considered.
- **Hybrid**
  For hybrid scenarios, it's possible to choose SAP Cloud Platform Integration Suite or SAP Process Orchestration.

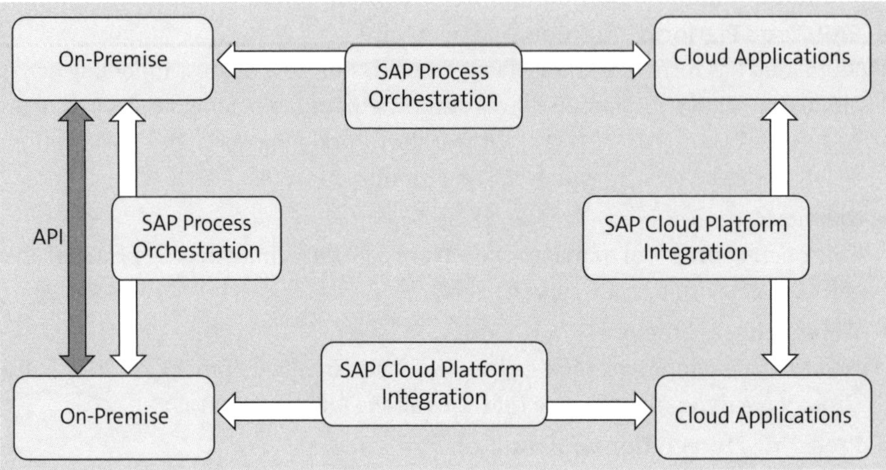

Figure 5.39 Integration Options

Table 5.6 summarizes the differences between SAP Cloud Platform Integration Suite and SAP Process Orchestration.

	SAP Cloud Platform Integration Suite	SAP Process Orchestration
Responsibility	SAP	Customer
Deployment	Cloud	On-premise
Licensing	Subscription based	Product license and annual maintenance
Software maintenance	■ Automated failover ■ Multitenancy, data isolation, virtualization ■ Regular software update	■ No built-in virtualization capabilities ■ Customer-configured failover mechanism
Prepackaged	SAP cloud solutions	Wide range of (on-premise) SAP and non-SAP applications
Preferred use cases	■ Cloud to cloud ■ Cloud to on-premise	■ On-premise to on-premise ■ On-premise to cloud

Table 5.6 Difference between SAP Cloud Platform Integration Suite and SAP Process Orchestration

Roles

The following list provides the roles and responsibilities of the integration workstream:

- **Integration lead**
  This role is generally fulfilled by the customer IT by an individual who has sound knowledge of the integration requirements from the legacy systems and also has a good understanding of the SAP integration interfaces. The integration lead will work closely with the integration consultants and the security SME to provide the necessary details.
- **Integration security SME**
  Customer IT generally fulfills this role with an individual who has a good understanding of the organization's security requirements and current security threats, and, may be a member of the organizational security team.
- **Integration consultant**
  The implementation partner will generally fulfill this role with individuals who have sound knowledge of and experience with using integration tools, conducting integration workshops to understand the customer's need, developing integration strategies, using functional and technical specifications, and creating and testing the integration programs.

Tools

Some of the tools used in the integration workstream are as follows:

- **SAP Best Practices Explorer**
  This tool provides the integration-related scope items.
- **SAP Cloud Platform Integration Suite**
  This tool provides valuable information about the value of integration, SAP Cloud Platform Integration, and the simplification of integration.
- **SAP API Business Hub**
  This tool is the enabler for developers to discover, customize, and use public APIs from SAP. You can access SAP API Business Hub at *https://api.sap.com/*.
- **Roadmaps**
  The roadmaps for SAP Cloud Platform Integration Suite and SAP Process Orchestration will help you maintain up-to-date information about products and recent innovations. You can access the product roadmap at *www.sap.com/products/roadmaps.html*.
- **SAP Help Portal**
  This tool provides detailed documentation on the SAP Cloud Platform Integration Suite and its accelerators, as well as SAP Process Orchestration.
- **Cloud Integration Automation service**
  This tool provides the guided workflow to integrate cloud solutions to on-premise solutions. You can access this service from the maintenance planner.

You can download the user guide from the SAP Help Portal at *http://s-prs.co/v519415*.

Accelerators

You can find the integration-related accelerators on the Roadmap Viewer. The main accelerators are as follows:

- **Interface documentation in SAP Solution Manager 7.2**
  This accelerator is used in the prepare phase of the project to create the interface, interface library, and related documentation in the solution documentation.
- **Interface register templates**
  This template is also used in the prepare phase of the project to determine the interfacing fields, their structure, and the links to the business process master list.
- **Interface functional specification template**
  This functional specification template is useful in the prepare phase of the project and defines all the required functionalities of the interface that will form the basis of development in the realize phase.
- **Technical specification – enhancement template**
  This technical specification template identifies the technical characteristics of the interface.

Analytics

SAP has added the analytics workstream to highlight the importance of the activities needed to establish a strong analytical solution for the client. It includes data connection and modeling, design, building and testing the reporting and analytics embedded in the solution, and predictive analytics.

In the following sections, we'll explore the key concepts, roles, tools, and accelerators involved in the analytics workstream.

Concepts

Before we start looking into SAP's analytics platform and solution, let's understand the three approaches of data integration in a two-tier ERP setup:

- **Data extraction**
  This is the process to extract (or retrieve) data from various sources either to store the data or to process it further to gather meaningful information. It's imperative to understand that the information is derived from data; data may or may not be structured.

- **Data replication**
  This is a process of syncing the data from the source systems to the target systems.
- **Virtual data access**
  In this approach, there is no movement of actual data but the source system reads the data on the target system virtually. It's most suitable for lower data volumes.

Figure 5.40 shows the different analytics options that are available to customers to consume via key solutions like SAP Analytics Cloud. SAP analytics has three focused areas: business intelligence (BI), planning, and predictive analytics. You can select a host of products from BI such as SAP Crystal Reports and SAP BusinessObjects Business Intelligence. For planning, you have SAP Business Planning and Consolidation (SAP BPC), and for predictive analytics, you can use the machine learning integration and other predictive models. For analytics apps, you can choose either SAP S/4HANA for embedded analytics or SAP BW/4HANA for data extraction and data lifecycle management. You can access analytics offering details at *http://s-prs.co/v519416*.

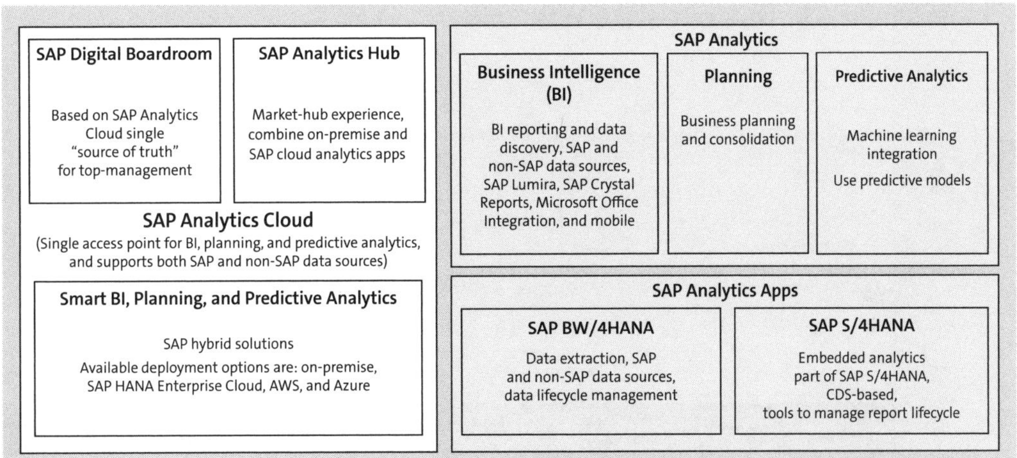

Figure 5.40 Analytics and Reporting Options

Roles

The following list provides the roles and responsibilities of the analytics workstream:

- **Consultants**
  The implementation partner generally provides the analytics consultants. These individuals are experts in the design and implementation of data integration approaches, have sound experience and knowledge in the selected applications, and have prior experience in designing and implementing dashboards and reports.

- **Architect**
  The customer IT generally fills this role with individuals who have the big picture understanding of the analytical requirements, can build and implement the analytics strategy, and can define a detailed roadmap in alignment with the organizational strategy and with the SAP implementation roadmap.

Tools

The following two tools are relevant for the analytics workstream:

- **SAP Analytics Hub interactive demo**
  This is a great tool that provides multiple interactive demos of analytics solutions. You can access the tool at *www.sap.com/products/analytics-hub.html*. Figure 5.41 shows the demo screen. You can also request a free trial of the hub by clicking on the **Request a Trial** button.

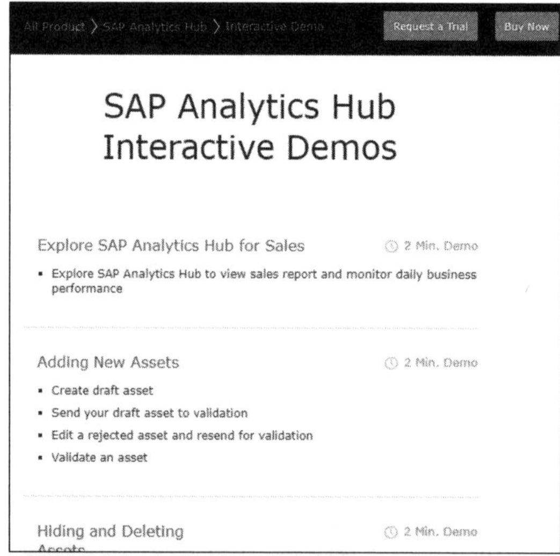

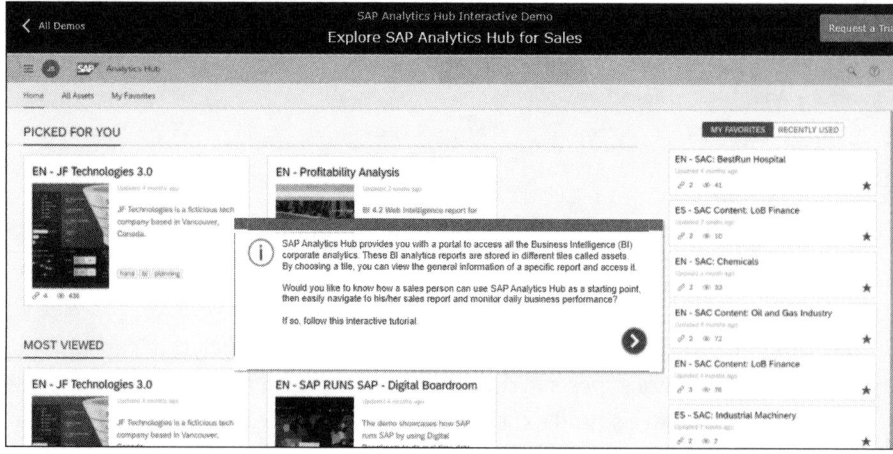

Figure 5.41 SAP Analytics Hub Demo

- **SAP Analytics Hub**
  This is the single source of truth for all analytics requirements. You can access the hub at *http://s-prs.co/v519417*. Figure 5.42 shows the SAP Analytics Hub and the menu items. Inside the hub, you can create any analytics model, applications, data set, or processes.

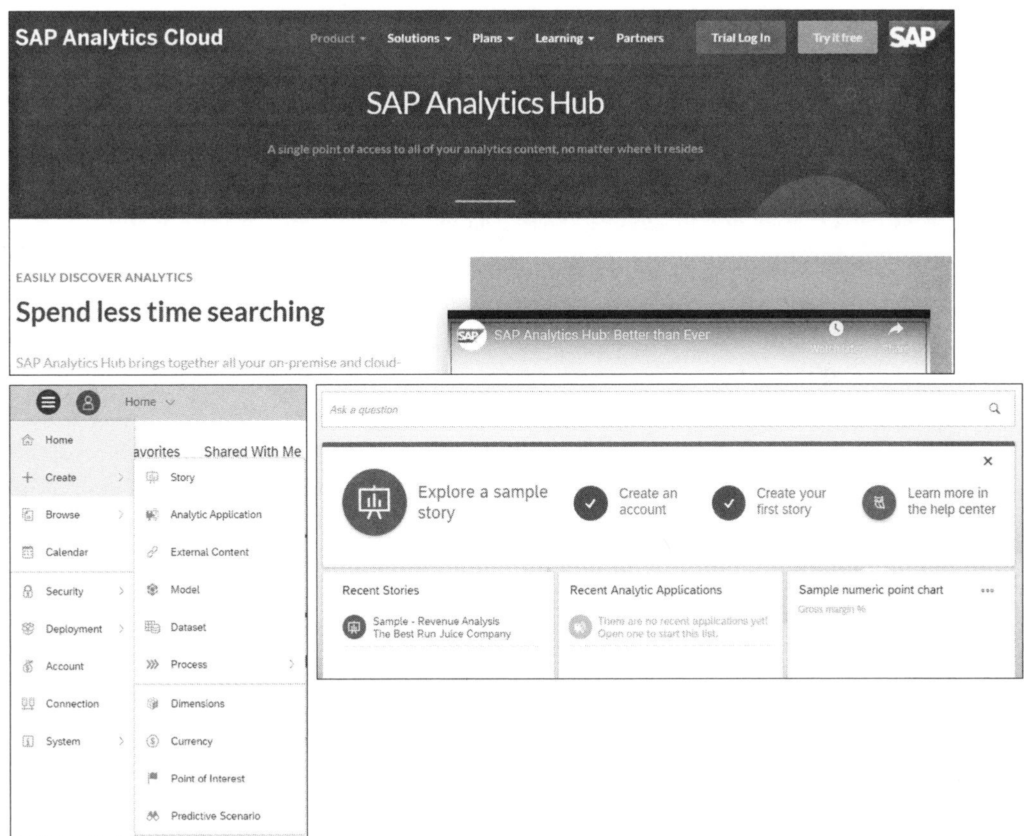

Figure 5.42 SAP Analytics Hub

Accelerators

The key accelerator is as follows:

- **SAP Best Practices for analytics with SAP S/4HANA**
  SAP Best Practices for analytics provide guidance for analytical content activation in the proposed solutions from SAP's analytics and reporting portfolio. You can access the solution available on SAP Best Practices at *https://rapid.sap.com/bp/#/BP_S4H_ANA*. Remember to log in using you S-user ID to maximize the benefit.

Operations and Support

The operations and support workstream helps the organization run the implemented solution effectively and efficiently with an agenda to continuously improve the services by defining the relevant standards, policies, standard operating procedures (SOPs), and so on. Establishing operations for on-premise implementations is much more involved than for cloud-based implementations. Some of the operations and support workstream activities include the following:

- Facilitating the setup of "run" or "operations" organization.
- Setting up the help-desk and the relevant processes.
- Incident management, including post go-live change management
- SLA management, operational excellence, and continuous improvement

In the following sections, we'll explore the key concepts, roles, tools, and accelerators involved in the operations and support workstream.

Concepts

The activities in this workstream, surprisingly, start from the discover phase of the project when the team works on the strategic planning, and continue through the project phases until the final run phase. So far, you've learned about the possible deployment platforms: SAP S/4HANA; SAP S/4HANA Cloud, essentials edition; and SAP S/4HANA Cloud, extended edition. Now let's take a quick look at the operations for the plausible deployment options. Figure 5.43 shows the responsibilities of customers and SAP across the different options.

It's evident that the customers will own and operate the business context. Furthermore, depending on the deployment options, SAP and customers share the responsibilities in varying degrees. One important point to note here is that SAP S/4HANA Cloud, extended edition and SAP S/4HANA Cloud, essentials edition have the same operating model, but they run on different infrastructures.

In Chapter 1, you learned about premium engagement ready, which is a key characteristic of the SAP Activate methodology. The operations and support workstream extensively leverages this characteristic. Figure 5.44 shows a basic model of the Customer Center of Expertise (Customer COE)—a single source of truth because all support and communication activities should be managed by the Customer COE. The primary function of the Customer COE is to collaborate between the business and the IT organization within the customer's organization and between SAP and the customer's organization. The Customer COE acts a liaison across multiple stakeholders from different business units and brings them in cohesive alignment to meet the organizational objectives. In the proposed model, the SAP Innovation Control Center manages the custom development, solution design, and documentation, while the SAP Operations Control Center focuses on application management and operations.

		SAP S/4HANA Cloud, Essentials Edition	SAP HANA Enterprise Cloud	SAP S/4HANA Cloud, Extended Edition	On-Premise
Business Process Management	Business Context	Customer Always Manages Business Context			
Application Management	Applications				
	Middleware, Platform				
System Management	System				
	Database				
	Operating System				
	Virtualization				
IT Infrastructure Management	Server				
	Storage				
	Networking				

Legend

Completely Managed by SAP, No Transparency to Customer — Managed by SAP with Predefined SLAs and Transparency to Customer on Critical Events — Completely Managed by Customers without Any Transparency to SAP

Figure 5.43 Ownership in Different Cloud Deployment Options

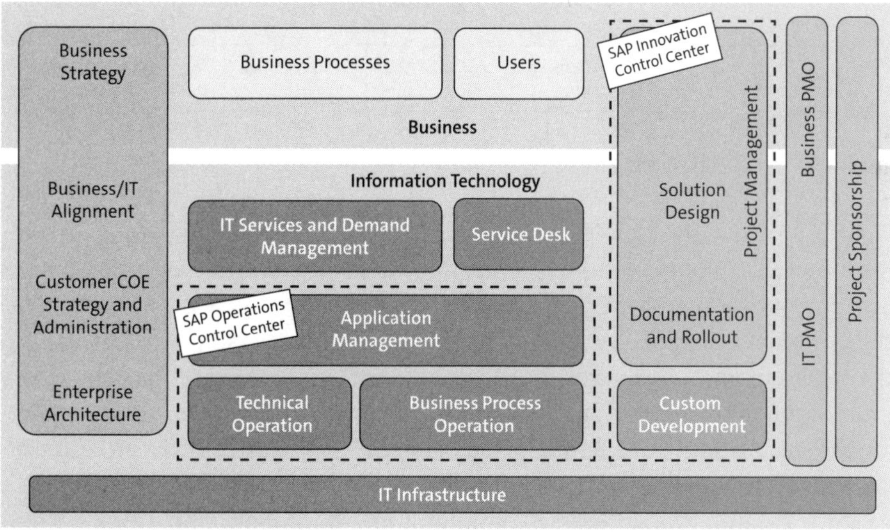

Figure 5.44 Customer COE Model

SAP offers two levels of maturity for the Customer COE: primary and advanced. Customers generally start with the primary level, and, in partnership with SAP, they embark on their journey of continuous improvements and KPI-based measurements that will transform their Customer COE to the advanced maturity level.

Figure 5.45 shows the benefits of establishing the Customer COE model, which promotes the concepts "build SAP like a factory" and "run SAP like a factory." To build SAP like a factory means that via partnership with the SAP Innovation Control Center, you can improve the value chain, reduce innovation cost, and accelerate time to value. To run SAP like a factory means that via partnership with the SAP Operations Control Center, you can reduce the total cost of operations if run with end-to-end integrated lifecycle management. As a whole, it increases the transparency of the business processes, reduces implementation efforts, aligns stakeholders, clearly defines the governance, accelerates time-to-value, and reduces risk and TCO.

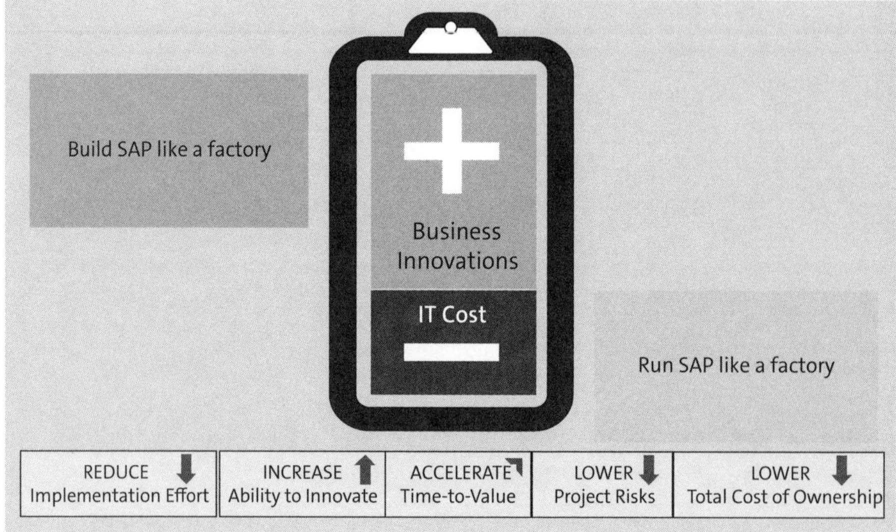

Figure 5.45 Customer COE Benefits

Figure 5.46 shows the high-level approach in the Customer COE model versus non-Customer COE model. There are two paths that an organization can take—either implement the Customer COE model or not. The better approach is to implement the Customer COE model, in which case, the team in partnership with SAP defines the requirements, procedures, and acceptance criteria leading to the continuous monitoring of the project outcomes. In this approach, the organization gets predictable results with enhanced efficiency and lowered TCO. However, an organization can decide not to go with the Customer COE model, in which case there won't be any standards, tools, processes, or procedures, which may in turn lead to parallel projects and enhanced TCO.

One key activity of this workstream is hypercare, during which the team fast-tracks all critical issues and ensures timely resolution for the continued business operation. The team mostly faces clarification questions on the business functionalities that can be resolved by refresher trainings, short videos, or quick conversations or meetings. During this period, the team also faces authorization issues that can be resolved immediately by implementing temporary provisions of emergency authorization.

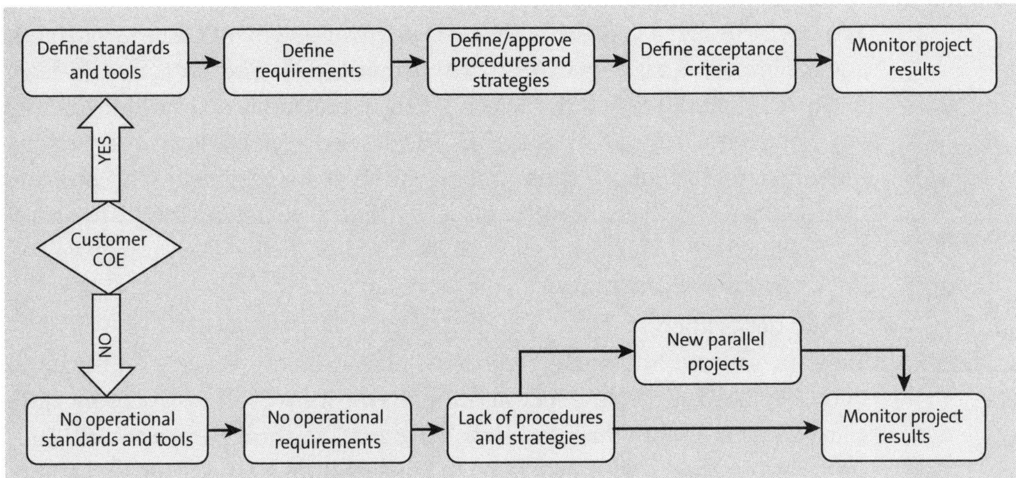

Figure 5.46 Approaches to Operations and Support

Roles

The following list provides the roles and responsibilities of the operations and support workstream:

- **Head of Customer COE**
  The customer organization fills this leadership position with individuals who have extensive knowledge of SAP, SAP support models, and ALM in general. This person is the sponsor of the Customer COE and provides the necessary resources, ensures alignment with organizational strategies, and certifies ALM processes to ensure the optimum TCO. The head of the Customer CoE also ensures the continuous improvement and monitoring of the processes so that the product of the implementation meets the benefit realization.
- **ALM process owner**
  This role is fulfilled by the customer IT organization; often, the ALM process owner works closely with the ALM consultants whose role and responsibilities are discussed next. This person is an expert in the ALM processes, has a sound understanding of and strong experience in ALM, and is well versed with the customer organization. The process owner defines the requirement for the ALM process in the partnership with other stakeholders, including business users.
- **ALM consultant**
  The implementation partner fulfills this role with resources who have prior experience in building Customer COE strategies, multiyear operation plans, and organizational structures and their roles and responsibilities. They are also the SMEs in the relevant areas to define the functional and process models. They

leverage their industry know-how and connections to identify the right set of tools needed and rightly suited for the customer organization.

- **Service desk manager**
  The service desk manager works closely with the Customer COE head, business, and the implementation partner to define the SLAs. As a best practice, the leadership team should review the SLAs frequently, preferably quarterly, to identify any improvements and adjustments. The service desk manager has a strong influence in the tool selection process, incident management, and problem management. This person works closely with the change manager to implement the change management processes and with the release manager to implement the release management processes.
- **Service desk expert**
  They are the front-line workers who are mostly from the customer IT organization. They take the first level of calls from the business users in case of any difficulty. Sometimes, the service desk is outsourced to third parties as well. They work with end users, work according to the operation manual, and many times help resolve minor issues such as password resets.
- **Security manager**
  Customer IT fulfills this role with an individual who ensures that the organizational policies in regards to security are followed. In addition, if needed, this person establishes additional security measures.
- **SAP Solution Manager administrator**
  This role is also fulfilled by customer IT with an administrator who extends any templates or process flow updates in SAP Solution Manager.
- **SAP Solution Manager consultant**
  The implementation partner fulfills this role with a person who is responsible to configure and support the SAP Solution Manager processes.

Tools

Some of the tools used in the operations and support workstream are as follows:

- **Customer COE**
  The Customer COE aims for the following objectives:
  - Optimum IT operation: Proactive monitoring, KPI-based models, metrics-driven governance, and continuous improvements are vital.
  - Integrated quality management: Strong collaboration with business and IT is the key for a robust and results-oriented Customer COE.
  - One team: Business and IT are one team whose focus and objectives are aligned with themselves as well as with the organizational goals.
  - Transparent, conscious, and data-driven decisions: Any decisions made should be transparent and strongly based on the monitored data.

  - Clear roadmap and value realization: The roadmaps should be based on the current KPI state and the future state.

  The tools and knowledgebase are as follows:

  - Prior experience and discussions on the Customer COE.
  - Blogs and articles on SAP Community.
  - Getting started with the Customer COE (*https://support.sap.com/en/offerings-programs/ccoe.html*). You can review the three offerings (**Primary Customer COE**, **Advanced IT Operations Self-Assessment**, and **Advanced Customer COE**) as three tabs on the webpage.

- **Maintenance planner**
  SAP Solution Manager's cloud-based maintenance planner enables efficient planning of all changes in the customer's SAP system landscape. Figure 5.47 shows the maintenance planner.

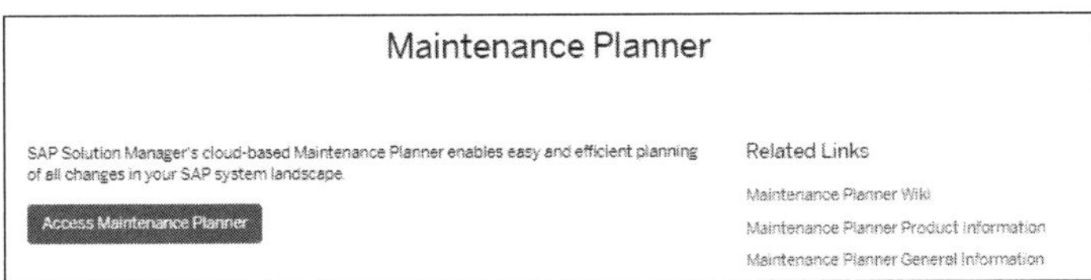

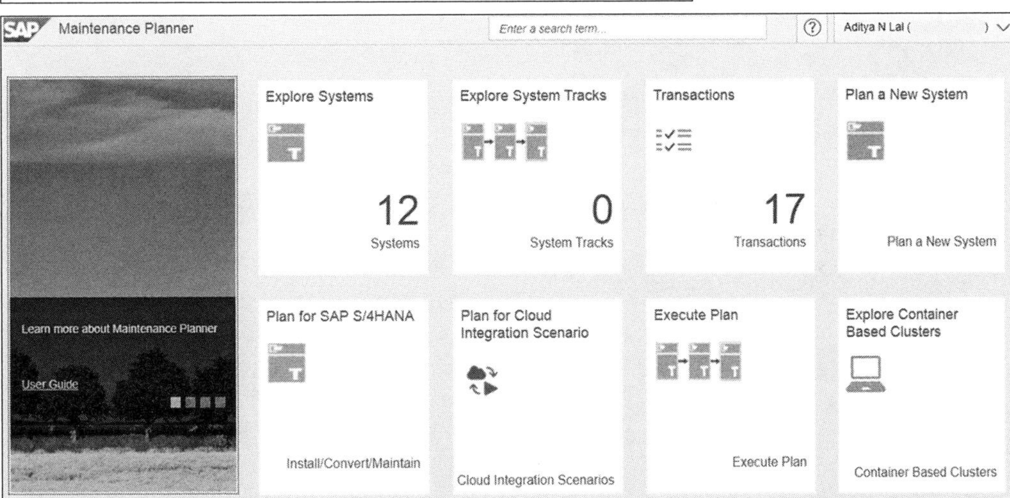

Figure 5.47 Maintenance Planner

Note

Many minor tools are involved in this workstream that we've mentioned throughout the chapter, including the following:

- SAP Cloud ALM
- SAP Enterprise Support
- SAP ONE Support Launchpad
- SAP S/4HANA Cloud service specifications

- SAP Solution Manager
- SAP support offerings
- SAP Support Portal
- SAP Standard Support
- SAP Enterprise Support value maps
- Support policy for cloud offerings

Accelerators

The accelerators for the operations and support workstream are as follows, as shown in Figure 5.48:

- **SAP ONE Support Launchpad**
  SAP ONE Support Launchpad is the central point to access all support-related information and activities. You can report an incident and access tools such as the maintenance planner, SAP Readiness Check, or SAP EarlyWatch Alert.
- **SAP Support Portal**
  From the SAP Support Portal, you can search for the latest knowledgebase, SAP Notes, and so on.

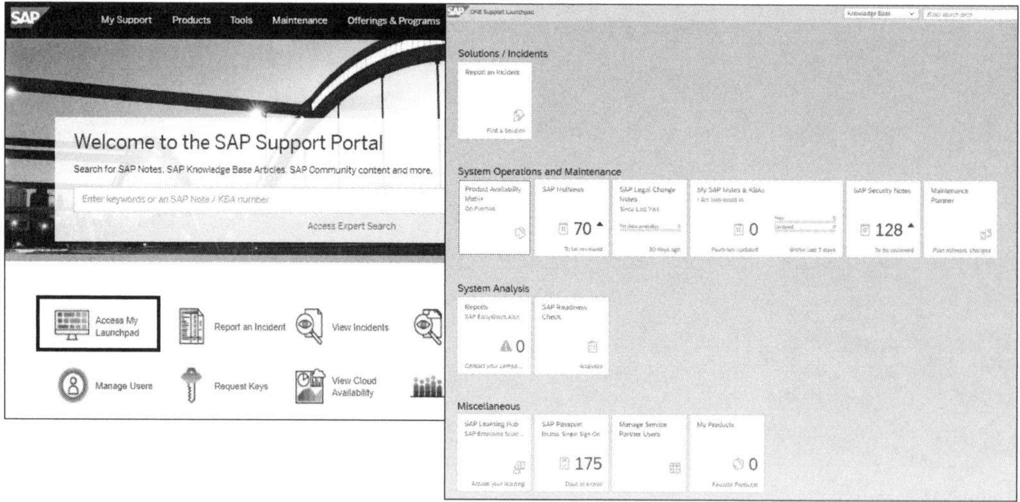

Figure 5.48 Operations and Support Accelerators

Security

During the fit-to-standard processes, several security-related questions come up. It's important to have a good understanding of the various security tasks and responsibilities, which are distributed among the workstreams (because there is no security workstream) and are carried out by the security manager in the operations and support workstream. Table 5.7 shows the five main categories that spread across six workstreams with 16 different security tasks. Note that the task "users and authorization" spans both the application design and configurations workstream and the technical architecture and infrastructure workstream.

	Infrastructure Security	**Secure Code**	**Secure Setup**	**Secure Operations**	**Security Compliance**
Application design and configuration			Secure configuration	Users and authorization	
Technical architecture and infrastructure	▪ Network security ▪ Operating system and database security ▪ Frontend security			▪ Users and authorization ▪ Authentication and single-sign on (SSO)	
Extensibility		▪ Security maintenance of SAP code ▪ Custom code security			
Data management			Data security		
Integration			Integration security		
Operations and support				▪ Support security ▪ Security review and monitoring	▪ Security governance ▪ Audit ▪ Cloud security ▪ Emergency concepts

Table 5.7 Security Tasks

Let's review these categories and the security tasks:

- **Infrastructure security**
  This category deals with all servers, networks, and frontends. It ensures that the network is secured, operating systems and databases are secured with the latest patches, and the devices accessing the system (e.g., workstations and mobile devices) are secured.

- **Secure code**
  This ensures that the SAP code is secured as well as any custom code that is part of the application. It also ensures that the SAP software has the latest mandated security patches.
- **Secure setup**
  This deals with securing the data, configurations, integration, and communication.
- **Secure operations**
  This ensures the correct and rightful authorizations, proper authentication using SSO, and resolution of incidents in a secure manner. Furthermore, it also ensures the timely review and the monitoring of SAP systems.
- **Security compliance**
  This group ensures that the SAP applications, teams, and processes comply with several processes, such as security audits and governance, cloud security, and emergency concepts and the related drills laid out by the organizations.

Important Terminology

For this exam objective, you're expected to understand the following terms:

- **Agile release trains (ARTs)**
  This is the process through which the SAFe team continuously delivers in a predefined cadence.
- **Build sprint**
  In this sprint, the team works on building the software product.
- **Business-driven configuration questionnaire**
  This accelerator is used in the prepare phase of the project to gather insight about the project scope.
- **Customer Center of Expertise (Customer COE)**
  This service model by SAP collaborates with IT and the business within the organization to provide SAP operations and support processes.
- **Data aging**
  This is an option to move a large amount of less frequently used data from memory to the hard drive.
- **DevOps**
  These are modern-day software development practices that combine development and IT operations.
- **Firm-up sprint**
  The firm-up sprint is used to complete the string testing, perform any bug fixes, or for the application security test protocol.

- **Foundation sprint**
  This is the very first sprint at the beginning of the realize phase where the team sets up the organizational structure, chart of accounts, and some other basic configurations.
- **Guided configuration**
  This step-by-step guided process is used to configure organizational structure, logos, and so on in an SAP S/4HANA Cloud system.
- **In-app extensibility**
  This process is used to extend the solution's functionality by making changes within the application.
- **Information radiators**
  This is an agile term for any material, manual or computer based, that shows information about the project, product, or progress.
- **Infrastructure-as-a-service (IaaS)**
  This is an infrastructure service provider that provides infrastructure over the Internet to use by another party.
- **Integration platform-as-a-service (IPaaS)**
  This specific type of PaaS is used for integration purposes.
- **Platform-as-a-service (PaaS)**
  This refers to a service provider providing a cloud computing platform, such as a Java runtime, that can be used by another party.
- **Side-by-side extensibility**
  This provides the capability to build new functionality on SAP Cloud Platform and integrate it with the solution.
- **Software-as-a-service (SaaS)**
  A third-party provides host applications (or software) and makes it available to customers over the Internet for a fee.

Practice Questions

These practice questions will help you evaluate your understanding of the topics covered in this chapter. The questions shown are similar in nature to those found on the certification examination. Although none of these questions will be found on the exam itself, they will allow you to review your knowledge of the subject. Select the correct answers, and then check the completeness of your answers in the "Practice Question Answers and Explanations" section. Remember that on the exam, you must select all correct answers and only correct answers to receive credit for the question.

1. The SAP Activate methodology supports three transition paths—new implementations, system conversions, and selective data transition. Which one of the following workstreams doesn't support the system conversion transition path?

☐ **A.** Extensibility

☐ **B.** Data migration

☐ **C.** Analytics

☐ **D.** None of the above

2. You're working as a project manager for a major chemical distribution company when you find out that the company has decided to implement SAP S/4HANA Cloud, essentials edition. You were excited to hear about it as you have a sound knowledge of SAP S/4HANA. You decided to share the information with your team when one of the senior team members asked about the organizational change management (OCM) processes. Which workstream of SAP Activate covers the OCM processes?

☐ **A.** A separate workstream for OCM named "organizational change management"

☐ **B.** OCM spans two workstreams: project management and solution adoption

☐ **C.** Solution adoption

☐ **D.** Project management

3. What is the purpose of customer team enablement?

☐ **A.** To empower end users for the rightful utilization of the solution.

☐ **B.** To empower the project team for the rightful utilization of the solution.

☐ **C.** To conduct training in the deploy phase.

☐ **D.** To support the project team by providing training presentations.

4. You're an SAP S/4HANA Finance functional consultant and have suggested that an SAP user could better understand many of the SAP S/4HANA features by reviewing tools such as SAP Best Practices, Roadmap Viewer, SAP Learning Hub, openSAP, and the training services provided by your organization. Which most accurately describes the activity you're involved in from the following list?

☐ **A.** You're cross-selling your services, which is forbidden and against SAP policies.

☐ **B.** You're explaining the enablement services to the customer, which is part of the customer team enablement workstream.

☐ **C.** You're helping the customer enhance the adoptability of the solution within the customer's organization.

☐ **D.** Indirectly, you're telling the user about SAP S/4HANA's complexity.

5. You're working as a service delivery manager for a platinum SAP partner, and your client is undergoing an SAP S/4HANA transformation. They asked you about the benefits of "build SAP like a factory" and "run SAP like a factory." Which two options will you choose? (There are two correct answers.)

☐ **A.** They are marketing terms that help clients lower their TCO.

☐ **B.** Build SAP like a factory reduces the innovation cost and accelerates the time to value.

☐ **C.** Run SAP like a factory is part of the Customer COE model, which engages SAP Innovation Control Center to use innovative ideas to reduce the operating cost.

☐ **D.** Run SAP like a factory reduces the IT cost.

☐ **E.** Build SAP like a factory refers to the agile approach where the software development lifecycle (SDLC) works like an "assembly line" approach.

6. What are the three substreams of the data management workstream?

☐ **A.** Master data migration, data volume management, data migration

☐ **B.** Master data management, data volume management, data migration

☐ **C.** Master data management, transaction data management, data migration

☐ **D.** Master and transaction data, data migration, data cleansing

7. You and your team are busy using the Code Inspector. What is the purpose of the tool, and in which workstream will you use this tool?

☐ **A.** It's used to check custom code for the innovations in the analytics workstream.

☐ **B.** It's used to analyze the quality of the code only to ensure the naming convention in the application design and configuration workstream

☐ **C.** It's helpful to detect syntax errors in the data migration ABAP code. This tool is generally use in the testing workstream.

☐ **D.** It's used to perform static code checks such as security, performance, and so on in the extensibility workstream.

8. What are some of the activities that the project team performs in the testing workstream?

☐ **A.** The test case developer develops test cases in the realize phase of the project.

☐ **B.** The project manager works with the test manager to ensure that the test cases are prepared for the unit testing.

☐ **C.** The team prepares the test assignment and test strategy, identifies and sets up testing tools, and develops the test case.

☐ **D.** The team prepares the test assignment and test strategy, identifies and sets up testing tools, and develops the change impact analysis.

9. You're doing system conversion for a major real estate company based in New Jersey, USA. You've just created a training plan outlining the schedule and approach, identifying the participants and training materials, and determining the training system. The intention is to discuss the plan with the customer's key stakeholders and execute the plan. What is the deliverable, project phase, and workstream?

☐ **A.** Learning realization, run, operations and support

☐ **B.** Learning realization, deploy, technical architecture and infrastructure

☐ **C.** Learning realization, run, application design and configurations

☐ **D.** Learning realization, deploy, solution adoption

10. You're in the discover phase of a project working closely with many key stakeholders of the customer's organization. Currently, they have a global setup of outdated non-SAP ERP software, and they want to move to SAP. Which of the following tools will you use to show the transformation journey?

☐ **A.** Roadmap Viewer

☐ **B.** SAP Best Practices Explorer

☐ **C.** SAP Transformation Navigator

☐ **D.** SAP Enable Now

11. You're working as a project manager for an SAP implementation partner. You were explaining the concept of agile in SAP to the client and the client's advisor who is new to SAP but has extensive experience with agile, Scrum, and Scaled Agile Framework (SAFe). During this discussion, the advisor stopped you to counter the foundation sprint concept and especially the firm-up sprint concept. Which is the correct choice to explain the firm-up sprint?

☐ **A.** It's required to revisit the release and sprint plan.

☐ **B.** It's required for the string and/or integration testing.

☐ **C.** It's a "test sprint" to resolve all bugs and provide an error-free experience.

☐ **D.** It's where we'll involve end users for their training.

12. Which one of the following activities will be performed in the data management workstream and by whom?

☐ **A.** The data migration architect will work closely with the solution architect to develop and define the migration strategy and select the migration tools.

☐ **B.** The test manager will work closely with the functional consultants to cleanse the data in a large global project of 150 resources.

☐ **C.** The project manager defines the cutover approach.

☐ **D.** The technical architect defines the security architecture for the solution.

13. What are the purposes of transition planning? (There are two correct answers.)

☐ **A.** To define the scope and execution plan of the project

☐ **B.** To define the UI/UX strategy

☐ **C.** To identify the operations manager

☐ **D.** To identify the tools that migrate the data from the legacy system

14. You're a project manager for a major system conversion project and are working closely with the technical architect to define the virtualization strategy, network design, hardware selection, and similar activities. In which workstream are you spending your effort?

☐ **A.** Project management because you're a project manager

☐ **B.** Technical architecture and infrastructure because you're working with an architect

☐ **C.** Technical architecture and infrastructure because you're involved in technical architecture and infrastructure definition

☐ **D.** None of the above

15. Which of the following tools are used in the data management workstream? (There are three correct answers.)

☐ **A.** Roadmap Viewer

☐ **B.** SAP Data Services

☐ **C.** SAP Best Practices Explorer

☐ **D.** SAP Landscape Transformation

☐ **E.** SAP S/4HANA migration cockpit

16. Which of these are SAP Activate workstreams? (There are three correct answers.)

☐ **A.** Project development

☐ **B.** Testing

☐ **C.** Data migration

☐ **D.** Customer team enablement

☐ **E.** Technical architecture and infrastructure

17. One of your team members sent you a weekly report that includes resource consumption per task type, resource consumption per transaction/process, duration of background jobs, response time per dialog transaction, and most expensive SQL. Explain why you were very unhappy to see this report.

☐ **A.** You're in the realize phase of the project, and certain KPIs are wrongly calculated; you weren't expecting such a mistake from a senior team member.

☐ **B.** These KPIs are for the run phase of the project in the operations and support workstream; these KPIs were very high and about to breach the SLAs.

☐ **C.** The team member sends the KPIs in Microsoft Excel format rather than the Word document that you were expecting.

☐ **D.** The team member delayed sending the report by more than an hour, and you missed the meeting with the client.

18. You and your team were discussing the sprint duration with the product owner for a 12-month implementation project in the United States, Britain, and Germany. The modules include SAP S/4HANA Finance, materials management, sales and distribution, and SAP Business Warehouse. What would be the best-suited team structure for the project?

☐ **A.** You proposed four Scrum teams of four members for each location and a sprint duration of three weeks; this is the most efficient team setup.

☐ **B.** You proposed a large team of 15 members for each location and a sprint duration of three weeks; this is the most cost-effective option.

☐ **C.** You proposed four Scrum teams of four members for each location and a sprint duration of one week; this is the fastest time-to-market option.

☐ **D.** You proposed a large team of 15 members for each location and a sprint duration of two weeks. This option has the best of both worlds—faster time to market and cost effective.

19. You're working with a team to review the fit-to-standard preparation. What is the workstream and project phase?

☐ **A.** Application design and configuration, explore

☐ **B.** Integration, realize

☐ **C.** Extensibility, prepare

☐ **D.** Technical architecture and infrastructure, discover

20. What is the difference between fit-to-standard and fit-gap analysis?

☐ **A.** Fit-to-standard is for on-premise implementations, whereas fit-gap is for cloud implementations.

☐ **B.** Fit-to-standard is for cloud implementations, whereas fit-gap is for on-premise implementations.

☐ **C.** Fit-to-standard is for the system conversion transition path, while fit-gap is for the selective data transition.

☐ **D.** Fit-to-standard is for the new implementations transition path, while fit-gap is for selective data transition.

Practice Question Answers and Explanations

1. Correct answer: **D**
   All of the workstreams listed support the system conversion implementation path. There is no workstream that doesn't support all of the transition paths.
2. Correct answer: **C**
   The solution adoption workstream covers OCM processes along with VM and end-user training.
3. Correct answer: **A**
   Customer team enablement, as the name suggests, enables the project team, including end users, to ensure the solution utilization post go-live. It is concerned with the enablement of customers and users, not the project team.
4. Correct answer: **B**
   The tools in question are relevant for the customer team enablement workstream. You can also use the process of elimination by removing option A and D right away. Between B and C, B is the right choice.
5. Correct answers: **B, D**
   You can eliminate option A and E directly as these are false statements. Option C is incorrect because "run SAP like a factory" engages the SAP Operations Control Center, while "build SAP like a factory" engages SAP Innovation Control Center for innovations.

6. Correct answer: **B**

   This is a straightforward question. Master data migration, transaction data management, and data cleansing aren't substreams.

7. Correct answer: **D**

   The Code Inspector isn't a tool for the analytics workstream, so option A is incorrect. Option B is incorrect because it limited the usage *only* to check the naming convention. Although the usage is correct in option C, it's still an incorrect choice because it's not used in the testing workstream. Both the usage and the workstream name is correct in option D.

8. Correct answer: **C**

   Options A and B are incorrect. Develop change impact analysis in option D is part of the solution adoption workstream, making it an incorrect choice as well. The correct choice is option C.

9. Correct answer: **D**

   Option D is the right choice; the identified activity is part of the deploy phase and isn't part of the technical architecture and infrastructure workstream.

10. Correct answer: **C**

    This is another straightforward question. Options A and B are incorrect, and SAP Enable Now in option D is a learning tool, so it's also incorrect. The only correct choice is option C—SAP Transformation Navigator.

11. Correct answer: **B**

    The firm-up sprint is required for bug fixing and string/integration testing, so option B is the right choice.

12. Correct answer: **A**

    None of the mentioned activities are from the data management workstream except option A.

13. Correct answers: **A, B**

    Options A and B are the right choices. Options C and D are factually incorrect; transition planning isn't used to identify the operations manager or for data migration.

14. Correct answer: **C**

    This is another straightforward question where the activities are identified in the question and you're asked to identify the workstream. Option B is incorrect; just because you're working with an architect doesn't mean that you're in the technical architecture and infrastructure workstream.

15. Correct answers: **B, D, E**

    This is a simple question, and the correct options are SAP Data Services, SAP Landscape Transformation, and SAP S/4HANA migration cockpit.

16. Correct answers: **B, D, E**
    This is also a straightforward question; you just need to remember the workstream names. Data migration and project development aren't SAP Activate workstreams.
17. Correct answer: **B**
    This is a tricky question; don't focus on the reason for unhappiness. The question is indirectly asking you for the project phase and the workstream, which are the run phase and operations and support workstream, making option B correct.
18. Correct answer: **A**
    Options B and D are incorrect. Option C is incorrect because the recommended sprint duration is two to four weeks.
19. Correct answer: **A**
    This is a straightforward question; the fit-to-standard process is a part of the explore phase activity in the application design and configuration workstream.
20. Correct answer: **B**
    This is also a straightforward question, and option B is the correct choice. Fit-to-standard is for cloud deployments, whereas fit-gap analysis is for on-premise implementations.

Takeaway

This chapter laid the foundation of the SAP Activate deliverables and the corresponding activities across the eleven workstreams. We started with the project management workstream, understood the basic concepts, including agile and the Scrum approach, and reviewed the tools and accelerators available in the workstream. We continued our journey and looked into the different deliverables, activities, and the concepts for each workstream. Furthermore, we reviewed the tools and accelerators of these workstreams.

In this chapter, we've covered several tools and their usages throughout the implementations across the workstream. However, one important tool is SAP Solution Manager 7.2. We've covered SAP Solution Manager to a certain degree in this chapter and throughout the book, which is sufficient from the certification exam perspective.

Summary

In this chapter, we've covered the deliverables, concepts, tools, activities, and accelerators across the three transition paths of the eleven workstreams. These deliverables and activities are critical to understand because they will form the basis of your knowledge and further success in the certification exam and in real-world projects.

Next, we'll move on to the first of the implementation paths that we'll cover in this book: an on-premise new implementation.

Chapter 6
New Implementation SAP S/4HANA Transition Path

6

Techniques You'll Master

- Understand the three implementation paths
- Explain fit-gap analysis
- Describe transition planning—a key deliverable in new implementation, system conversion, and selective data transition
- Review prototypes—a smaller project to evaluate a specific innovation
- Explain the discover phase of the project and its deliverables
- Explain the prepare to run phases of the project and corresponding deliverables

You now have extensive knowledge about the SAP Activate methodology, its eleven workstreams, six phases, and detailed taxonomy. In Chapter 3 and Chapter 4, we also studied, in detail, the agile framework, its value and composition, key agile terminologies, SAP Activate vis-à-vis Scrum, release planning, and several other agile concepts. We'll start this chapter by revisiting the three transition paths, introduced in Chapter 1, which will reinforce the foundation for the remainder of the book.

The Roadmap Viewer is one of the key tools you need to know about, and you'll see how you can access the deliverables for an SAP S/4HANA new implementation. Before we immerse ourselves in the deliverables and tools, it's important to understand transition planning, which is a key plan to transition from the current state to on-premise SAP S/4HANA; prototypes, which are smaller projects that may require evaluation of a specific or complex scenario; and fit-gap analysis, which is a key process in the explore phase of the project. We'll refer to these three deliverables in this chapter and in the last two chapters of the book.

Subsequently, we'll explore and understand the activities performed during the discover phase of the project and establish the project as a greenfield implementation. This will set us on our journey for project deployment, and we'll review the subsequent phases—prepare, explore, realize, and deploy—to better understand the activities and the related deliverables specific to the on-premise SAP S/4HANA new implementation transition path. In the final section of this chapter, we'll review the run phase of the project and discuss how the team can optimize the operation during this phase. Many of the deliverables and tools are common across new implementations of SAP S/4HANA, system conversions (discussed in Chapter 9), and selective data transitions (discussed in Chapter 10).

Real-World Scenario

You're an SAP sales executive working with a global SAP partner located in the Midwest region of the United States. Next week, you have a critical meeting with the chief information officer (CIO) of a prospective client that manufactures faucets. Although you're meeting the CIO for the first time, you have strong SAP sales experience across a wide variety of SAP products. In addition to your experience and expertise, you reviewed the company's past performances, growth, IT systems, and other information that is publicly available.

You felt comfortable on the day of the meeting and arrived on time. The CIO of the company and the head of business development greeted you in the conference room. You were excited and started the discussion to understand their needs and wants, their current IT setup, related challenges and budgets, their strategy and roadmap (if any), and the driving factors behind the change. You vigorously took notes and meticulously listened their demands.

At the end of the meeting, you thanked them for the wonderful meeting, their precious time, and the valuable information they shared. You committed that within seven business days, you, along with SAP solution experts, would come back with any follow-up questions to fine-tune the capability presentation schedule early next month.

On your way back, you were trying to remember the following salient features of their requirements:

- Reduced infrastructure cost but in-house hosting
- Enhanced business capabilities to increase sales and get faster reporting
- Better performance
- Lower total cost of ownership (TCO)
- Non-SAP legacy system

Because the prospective client is on a non-SAP system and they want in-house hosting, it's a clear case of the need for an SAP S/4HANA new implementation.

Objectives of This Portion of the Test

The certification examination will test your knowledge about the following topics:

- Three transition paths
- Sound understanding of key deliverables for an SAP S/4HANA implementation
- Activities during the SAP S/4HANA implementation
- Deliverables of an SAP S/4HANA deployment

In the following sections, you'll learn and understand these key concepts followed by some questions and answers.

Note
The new implementation SAP S/4HANA transition path topic carries a <8% weightage on the exam. You can expect around 6 questions from these topics.

Key Concepts Refresher

This section will help you understand the implementation methodology focusing on the SAP S/4HANA deployment and will advance your abilities to carry out given activities and deliver the desired deliverables. These concepts are critical for you to pass the exam.

Navigating the Roadmap Viewer

You can navigate in the Roadmap Viewer by following the steps shown in Figure 6.1:

❶ Go to the Roadmap Viewer, and click on **Solution Specific**.

❷ Navigate right, and click on **Roadmap: SAP Activate Methodology for Transition to SAP S/4HANA** to go to the overview page.

❸ Click on the **Content** menu shown in the upper-left portion of the screen to go to the content page.

❹ Scroll down until you see **More** on the left pane of the window. Check the **New Implementation** checkbox (see Figure 6.2) to include only the deliverables, tasks, and accelerators from the new implementation transition path.

Figure 6.1 Navigation in the Roadmap Viewer

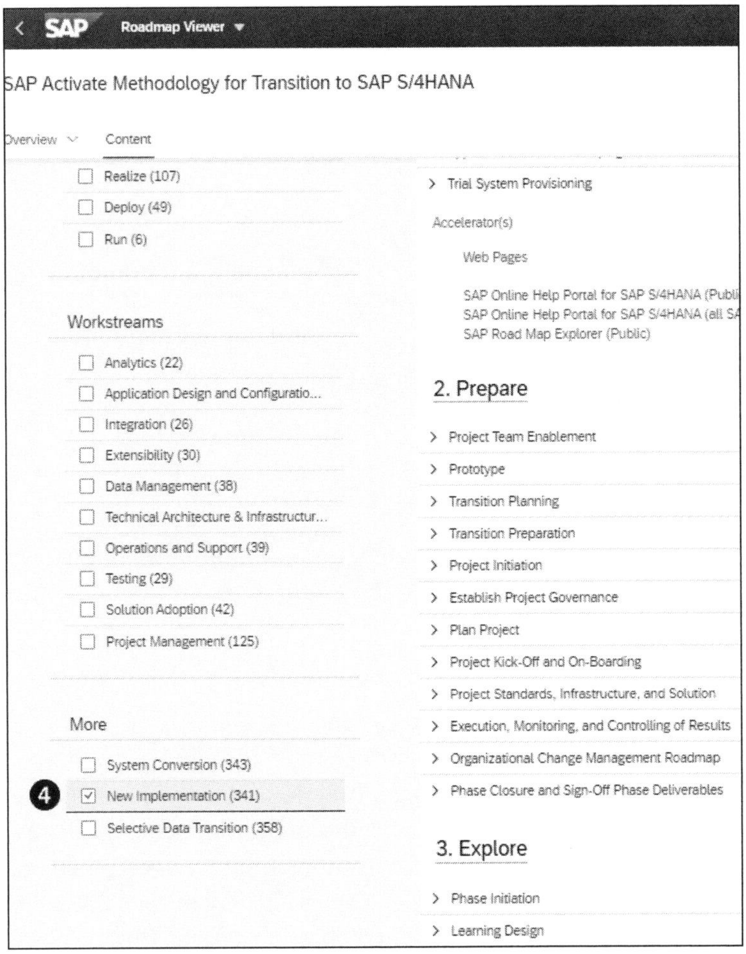

Figure 6.2 Selecting New Implementation

Three Transition Paths

In Chapter 1, we introduced the three transition approaches—new implementations, system conversions, and selective data transitions—that are available for the SAP S/4HANA customer. However, it's of paramount importance to understand the scenario and the customer's need to devise the suitable transition approach and subsequently a functioning, efficient, and effective solution. Let's explore our real-world scenario where we're an SAP sales executive from the Midwest US region.

Now, we know the customer's requirements in terms of their business need (increased sales and faster reporting) and IT requirements (in-house hosting, cost reduction, better performance, and lower TCO). Moreover, we're also aware that the customer is currently on the non-SAP environment, which means a new SAP installation is clearly needed. However, let's explore the three implementation paths with a little extra detail, as shown in Figure 6.3.

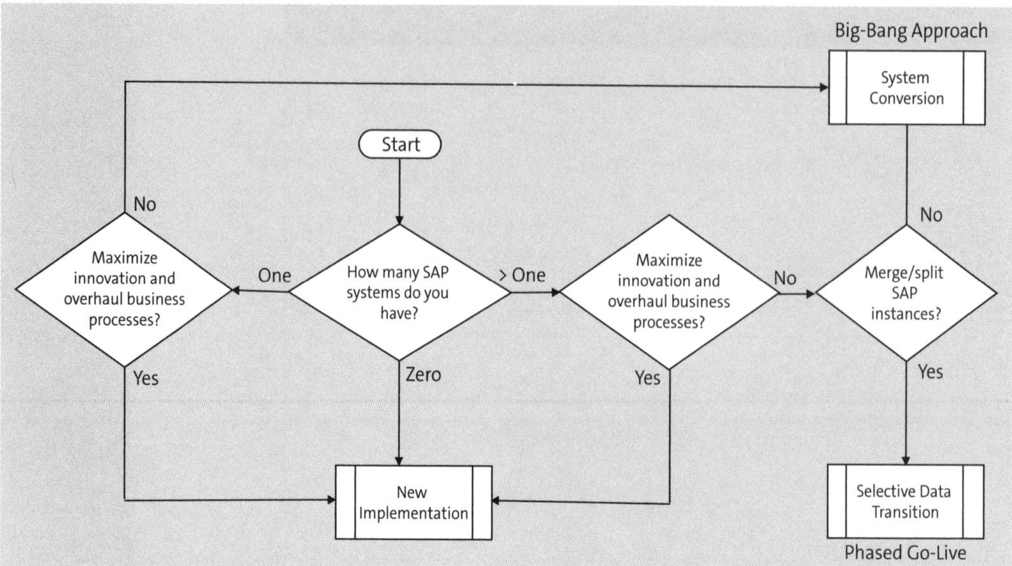

Figure 6.3 Three Transition Paths

To review, the following three transition paths are available:

- **New implementation**
  If you're new to SAP, then the choice is very clear and that will be a new implementation. However, if you're already using SAP systems, then you can choose from one of the three transition paths. Irrespective of the number of instances, if you want to take advantage of the latest innovations, improved best practices, and efficient and effective data management, then it's best to maximize the innovations by adopting the new implementation approach. However, we strongly recommend migrating only master data and the essential transactional data. Additionally, if you are currently on an on-premise version and want to use the latest cloud technology, you should follow the new implementation approach. We'll discuss new implementations in this chapter (specifically for SAP S/4HANA implementations), followed by the two SAP S/4HANA Cloud options in Chapter 7 and Chapter 8. Figure 6.4 shows the high-level approach with activities in the new implementation transition path.
- **System conversion**
  You can't utilize the system conversion approach if you're currently on a non-SAP system. However, if you want to convert the existing SAP solution or merge/split the SAP instances, then choose this path. In this path, you should minimize the initial changes, keep the existing configurations and business data, and go live with a big-bang approach. However, it's highly recommended that you innovate slowly after the go-live to take full advantage of SAP S/4HANA. We'll discuss this in Chapter 9.
- **Selective data transition**
  If you have multiple SAP instances, and you want to consolidate those

instances, then choose this approach. Alternatively, if you want to merge or split instances, then you can also choose this approach provided you want to go live in a phased approach. This approach is extremely useful for selective geography go-live or phased go-live based on the business processes. We'll discuss this in Chapter 10.

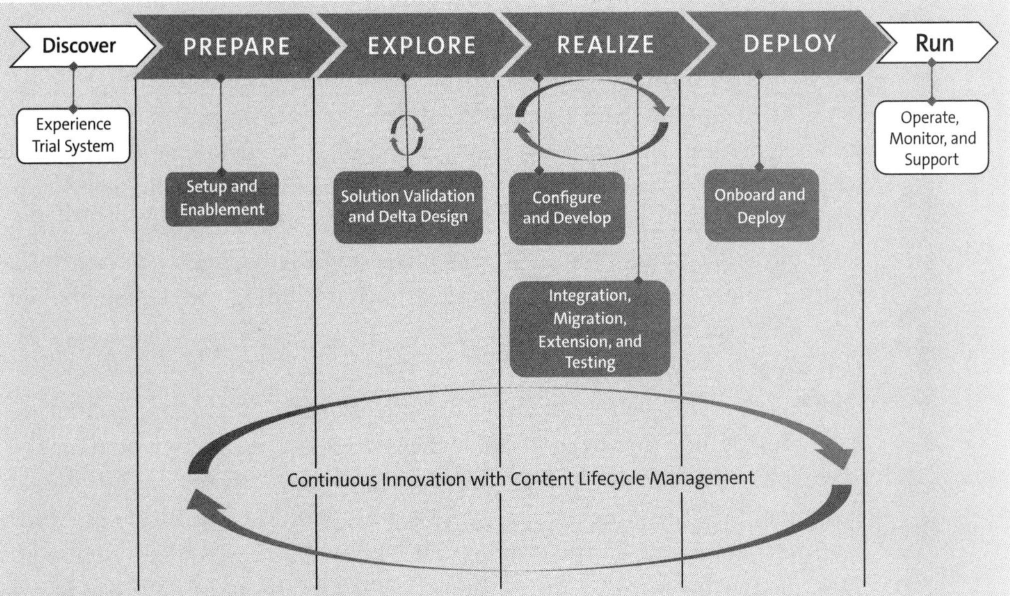

Figure 6.4 New Implementation Approach

Now that you know, at least at a high level, how to select the transition approach, let's look at the faucet manufacturing company from the previous example. The company is currently using a non-SAP system and wants to host the infrastructure in-house, meaning the company wants to go for on-premise SAP S/4HANA.

Key Deliverables

In this section, we'll review some of the key deliverables that are important from the exam perspective. However, it doesn't mean you won't get any questions related to the other deliverables or that other deliverables are unimportant. It's important to understand all the deliverables and their significance.

Transition Planning

Transition planning, although a confusing name for new implementations, is a set of processes and steps that uses numerous tools to define the overall project scope and the subsequent execution plan. The transition plan, an output of the process, is an action plan defining cutover to the user interface/user experience (UI/UX) strategy, but it's by no means a replacement for the project plan; rather, it feeds into the project plan, which has a much larger scope of managing cost, risks, issues, and so on.

Transition planning is a prepare phase deliverable that spans all the workstreams. Several documents from the discover phase feed into the transition plan. The steps to complete the transition planning are available on the Roadmap Viewer, so we won't go into the details of every step. However, at a high level, let's review the planning process components and tools:

- **SAP S/4HANA transition project: scope definition and objectives**
  In the discover phase, the transition path the project team has identified—new implementation, system conversion, or the selective data transition—along with the identified changes to the solution, should form the preliminary scope statement of the project. This statement should be objectively built, as a part of this deliverable, describing the IT objectives and the business objectives. The team should also identify the target platform, including the release and any related SAP systems.
- **Define cutover approach**
  Contrary to many beliefs, defining the preliminary cutover approach at the beginning of the project is crucial for the success of the implementation. This playbook-like document will list the sequential steps to execute the cutover, document the downtime requirement vis-à-vis permitted business downtime, interim states based on the Product Availability Matrix (PAM), any prerequisites, such as the year-end process or reconciliation processes, data load framework, and a few other details.

  Note that this is a preliminary document that the team will continue to update throughout the explore and realize phases of the project. During the deploy phase, the team will follow the steps during the mock cutover and adjust the document accordingly.
- **Define custom code adaption**
  Custom code adaption isn't applicable for new implementation projects when moving from a non-SAP system. However, it's a required step if you currently have an SAP system, and you're going with the new implementation transition path because you want to reengineer your business process or you're using the other two transition paths. The end objective is to ensure that the existing custom code works in SAP S/4HANA. However, most of the time, it may not be the case, because of the change in the table structure in SAP HANA, among other reasons. Using the Code Inspector, the team can analyze the custom code, which can be either retired or adjusted.

  Because this is a planning step, the team needs to understand and document the scope of custom code, the compatibility check with SAP HANA using the ABAP Test Cockpit, and finally the functionality adaptation.
- **Clarify operational readiness**
  The new system will go live in the deploy phase of the project, and the project

team will ensure the optimum hypercare before handing over the new solution to the operation team. The operational readiness of the transition planning will identify all such requirements and recommendations such as setting up a Customer Center of Expertise (Customer CoE). The operational readiness plan will include organizational structure, roles and responsibilities, service-level agreements (SLAs), ticketing tool, processes, incident and change management processes, and so on.

- **Define technical architecture**
  The organizational IT structure will change as the team moves from the discover phase to the deploy phase of the project with the addition of productive systems. This preliminary document on the architecture will include to-be architecture, virtualization, sizing information, high availability, disaster recovery and business continuity plan, backup and recovery strategy, data center strategy, downtime requirements (if any), and several other pieces of architectural information.
- **Define the data migration architecture**
  This particular step, needed for new implementations and selective data transitions, will ensure the assessment of the source system, data availability, and data requirements. In addition, based on several factors, such as complexity, quality, and completeness of the data, this step will define the extract, transform, and load (ETL) approach. SAP provides the following two solutions to carry out the data migration:
  - **SAP Data Services with rapid data migration services**
    This data integration tool, although it comes with an additional license fee, provides many functionalities, including matching, consolidating, standardizing, parsing, cleansing, address correcting, geocoding and reverse geocoding, and data cleansing.
  - **SAP S/4HANA migration cockpit**
    This tool is part of the SAP S/4HANA solution and has the capability to transfer master and transactional data from your SAP as well as non-SAP systems.
- **Define the UI/UX strategy**
  This task will ensure that the project defines the UI/UX strategy to include the SAP Fiori UI. The strategy will describe the need for a broad understanding of SAP Fiori and to collect the UI requirements.
- **Prepare interface register**
  The interface register will identify all the external systems, applications, and business objects that the team should integrate with the new SAP S/4HANA system. This interface list will form the overall scope of the interface needed and will help complete the project estimation.
- **Run a legacy impact analysis on interface inventory and data integration**
  Similar to custom code, if you're moving from an existing SAP system, the team should analyze the legacy interfaces to ensure the proper understanding of changes, if any, in those interfaces.

- **Run a first assessment on output management**
  Output management is the way you manage business documents such as alerts, emails, printouts, and print forms. SAP S/4HANA brings you a new way to manage your output. It's not mandatory to use the new SAP S/4HANA output management, but it will be the successor to current output management solutions in the future. This task ensures that the team identifies any such needs for the output such as sending an approved purchase order to the vendor.
- **Run a first assessment on training requirements**
  This task will identify the training needs for end users and document the requirements.
- **Run a technical security self-check (optional)**
  This optional task will review any security requirements, such as security settings and role changes.

The transition plan, in a nutshell, is collecting the high-level requirements from all the workstreams and building the strategy to implement the requirements in the proposed solution.

Transition Preparation

Transition preparation is the list of prerequisite activities that the team must perform before project start. The preparation work will help reduce downtime, provided the team discussed each of these individual items in the respective planning workshops in the transition planning deliverable. Some of the prerequisite activities are as follows:

- Migrate customers and vendors to business partners.
- Review the simplified logic of material requirements planning (MRP) in SAP S/4HANA.
- Review SAP Global Trade Services (SAP GTS), which is your new foreign trade solution.
- Review the new asset accounting.

Note
You can find the comprehensive list on the Roadmap Viewer. From an exam perspective, you won't get any questions related to these prerequisite activities; however, it's important to understand for the bigger picture.

The concept is that the team completes the transition planning activities, discusses specific prerequisites, prepares for the transition, and then executes the transition plan subsequently.

Prototype

At this point, we're still in the prepare phase of the project with a lot of uncertainty about the new and complex functionalities, performance of the system, effort requirement for system conversion, and several other concerns. To overcome such situations and minimize the uncertainty, the team should build a prototype using the real business data for a successful evaluation of the value addition.

Prototyping is a project that starts in the prepare phase and is completed in the explore phase, with a purpose to evaluate the functionality. The prototype should be separate from the main project and be done with minimal effort. The following is a list of benefits that the team and customer can get with a prototype:

- Customers will better understand the functionality in detail.
- The project team will better understand the implementation roadblocks.
- The project team will understand key characteristics of the customer organization, such as data quality, operational readiness, degree of documentation, and so on, which will help in further planning.
- Customers will better understand SAP S/4HANA innovations, transition tools, simplification lists, and so on.
- A go/no-go decision can be made based on the outcome of the prototype.

Figure 6.5 shows the plan and prototype (PLPT) service lifecycle. The steps are defined in the boxes, and the high-level milestones are shown in the top portion of the diagram.

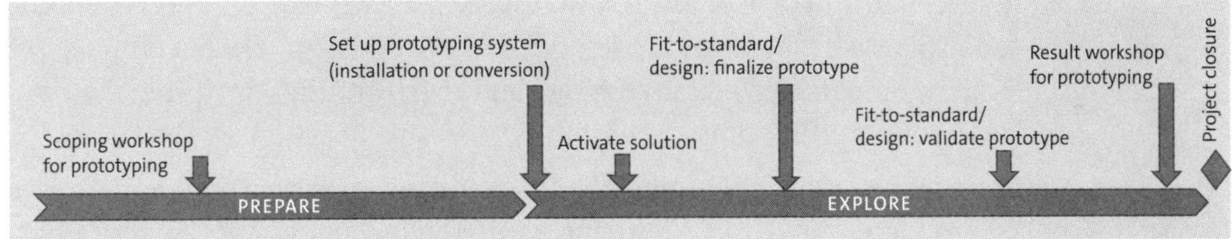

Figure 6.5 Plan and Prototype Service Lifecycle

It's important to understand that a prototype is a mini project, and it may fail as well. Additionally, the idea for the prototype is to evaluate new and complex functionalities but not all the functionalities. It's important to limit the scope of the prototype to two to three complex or new functionalities. Involve key stakeholders, define the minutest scope of the work during the scoping workshop, and correlate it with the work done during the result workshop. To take full advantage of the prototype, be sure to leverage the project team and make full use of what is learned during the prototyping.

Fit-Gap Analysis

We reviewed fit-gap analysis in Chapter 1, understood the related agile concepts such as the product backlog in Chapter 3, and described release planning in Chapter 4. Fit-gap analysis is an explore phase deliverable and is significant both in the exam and in real-life project delivery.

Note

Note the following information about fit-gap/fit-to-standard analysis:

- Fit-to-standard is the nomenclature used across SAP Activate and on the exam. We've used the same nomenclature in this chapter, although, technically, you'll do fit-gap analysis during the explore phase of an on-premise SAP S/4HANA implementation.
- Delta design is mandatory for SAP S/4HANA installations but is an optional step for SAP S/4HANA Cloud, essentials edition, which we'll study in Chapter 7.

Cutover Planning

We've reviewed the cutover plan and mock cutover (also known as dress rehearsal) in Chapter 4. Let's now take a quick glance at the cutover plan, a realize phase deliverable, as many of the deliverables in the subsequent sections will refer back to this section. The preparation activities for the cutover span all the workstreams except for the solution adoption workstream.

The project team creates the cutover plan, a series of activities arranged in the order of execution, in the realize phase of the project. The team then executes these steps in the deploy phase first to test the plan and subsequently to execute the tested plan as a part of production cutover. Depending upon the complexity of the project, outcome of dress rehearsal, and many other factors, the team may decide to have multiple dress rehearsals.

As a part of the cutover planning, the team ensures the setup and preparedness of the production (PROD) system, including the installation of the desired SAP products, and then creates the cutover plan. The content of the cutover planning will differ based on the chosen transition path; for a detailed listing of the activities, refer to the Roadmap Viewer.

Note

There won't be any questions related to the detailed activities in the cutover plan, but it's important to understand the cutover plan, dress rehearsal, production cutover, and other similar deliverables and activities.

Landscape

In the discover phase of the project, the team will access the trial system using SAP Cloud Appliance Library to understand the needed functionalities and innovations in SAP S/4HANA. After the team decides to move forward with the SAP

S/4HANA implementation, the team can decommission the trial system, as shown in Figure 6.6.

The team will receive the sandbox environment with preconfigured solution in the prepare phase of the project, activate the desired best practices, and use the customer data to show and tell the business functionalities as a part of fit-gap analysis in the explore phase. The team can use SAP Model Company, SAP S/4HANA fully activated appliance, or manual setup with or without SAP Best Practices to set up the sandbox.

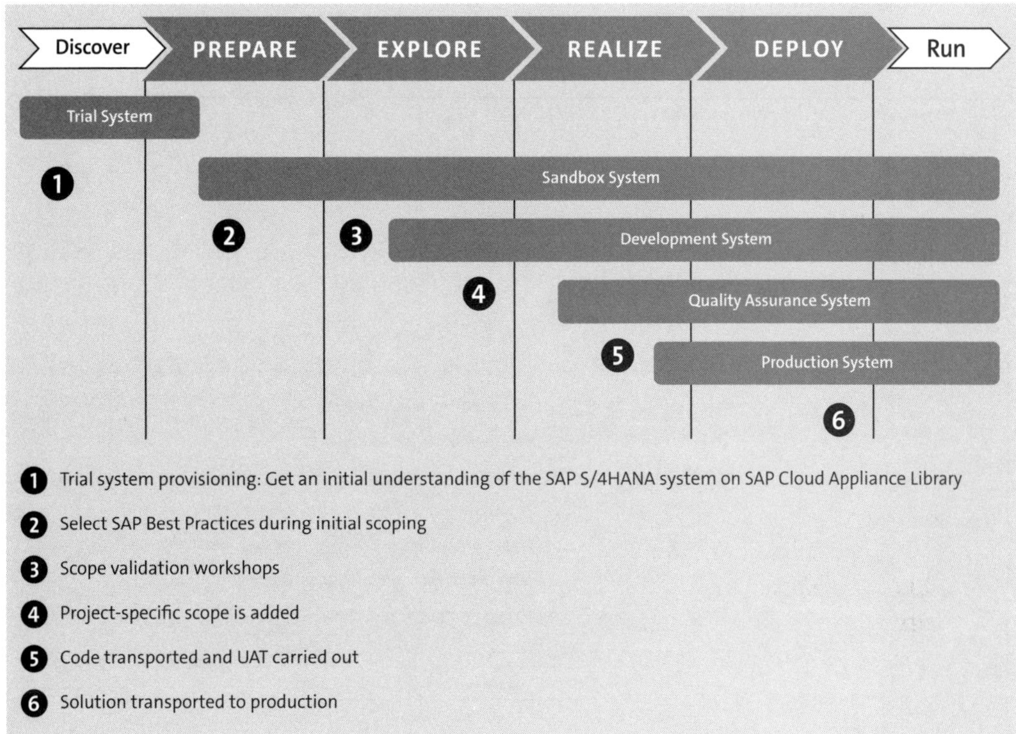

Figure 6.6 Landscape in New Implementations

The team will receive the development (DEV) system in the explore phase of the project on which they will configure the solution during the realize phase. The team will transport the unit tested configuration to the quality assurance (QA) environment to complete the user acceptance testing (UAT) and finally to the PROD environment for use by end users.

Discover Phase

The discover phase starts with the strategic planning activities and concludes when the client decides that SAP S/4HANA is the right ERP system for them, backed up by the detailed business case and point of view (POV) document, which summarizes the user's view and challenges, and how an SAP implementation can overcome those challenges. It's important to understand that the project hasn't started yet; in fact, the project is nonexistent during this phase. Throughout this phase, the leadership team will build the digital transformation strategy and multiyear roadmap and will exit the phase after deciding on the delivery approach—one of the three transition paths—and possibly the delivery partner. By the end of the discover phase, the sponsor approves the project, and the resource assignment starts.

Figure 6.7 shows the three deliverables that we'll explore in this section.

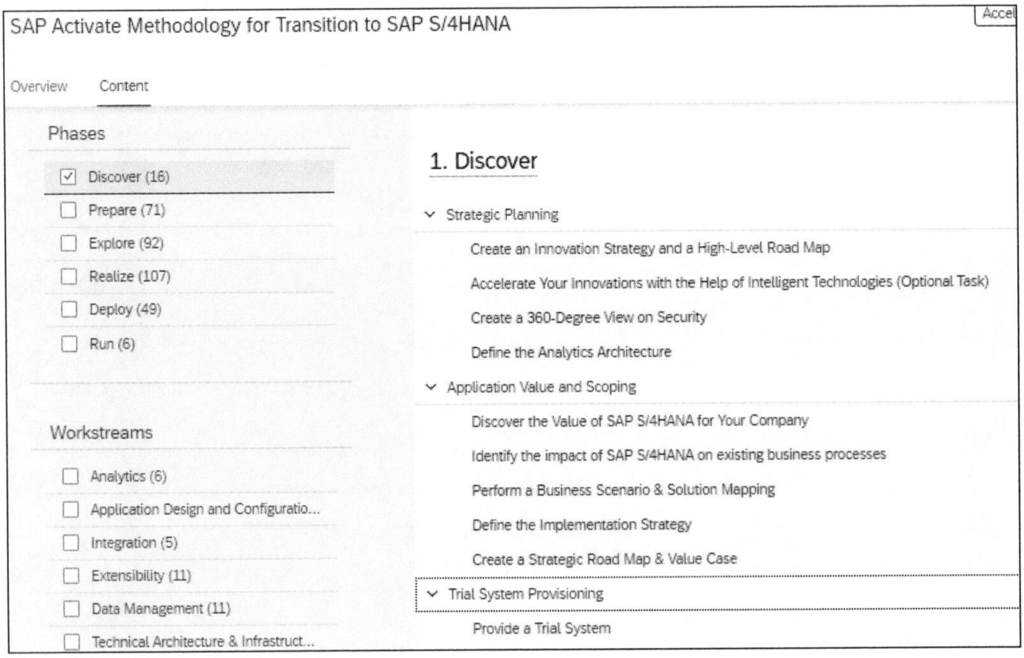

Figure 6.7 Discover Phase Deliverables

Strategic Planning

The SAP S/4HANA movement page, available at *http://s-prs.co/v519418*, provides valuable information about transitioning to SAP S/4HANA, starting from defining your strategy. The strategic planning itself has two major parts—building the strategy and planning the roadmap. Remember that it's not your typical multiyear project plan but a strategy document and the implementation roadmap weighing multiple options, such as adapting innovations, retaining data, balancing between reengineering and retaining processes, and so on.

The strategy-building exercise involves making tough decisions, enhancing the chance to succeed, reducing risks, and, subsequently, planning at the detail level. To build a detail strategy, you must start with the current challenges, create a vision and mission statement, and then weigh your options. At the end of the strategy building exercise, you decide the most suitable option that fulfills your vision and mission statement.

You build a multiyear roadmap based on the chosen option with as many details as possible. The strategy roadmap should include "what," "how," and "when," along with financials, risks, benefits, and measurement criteria. During the detail planning stage, you can use tools such as SAP Transformation Navigator (see Chapter 5), SAP Business Scenario Recommendations report for SAP S/4HANA (a report based on line of business [LoB] that helps in boosting overall system performance), and SAP Innovation and Optimization Pathfinder and Innovation Guide (helps to identify opportunities for innovations, business process improvements, and optimization).

Application Value and Scoping

Now that you have the strategy and the first cut of the high-level roadmap, it's important to understand the scope of changes and the value that the new SAP S/4HANA system will bring into the client organization. This five-step process is as follows:

1. **Value of the SAP solution**
   This isn't a one-time exercise; rather, it's a continuous process until you have a deep understanding of the value that the client organization will receive by implementing SAP. You must identify the value such as faster reporting, lower TCO, and quick reconciliation that is specific to your organization.
2. **Impact of the SAP solution**
   In this activity, the team will measure the impact of the enhanced business processes consumed through SAP S/4HANA on your existing business processes delivered through an existing ERP system. The best way to compare these two is to consider the simplification list of SAP S/4HANA that is available on the SAP Help Portal (*http://s-prs.co/v519419*). This process will identify any major roadblocks in the roadmap and must be completed during the discover phase of the project using SAP Readiness Check.

   The SAP Readiness Check tool will consume, preferably, the copy of your PROD system and analyze the readiness based on the simplification items. It will check and report the readiness of the current SAP ERP system, based on which the leadership can decide to go for system conversion or a new implementation.

3. **Business scenario and solution mapping**
   This step solidifies the project scope and any relevant adjustments for the system conversion or selective data transition. The team will conduct the workshops with the process experts to analyze for innovations in the given scope item and find the relevancy in the innovation for the organization.
4. **Implementation strategy**
   In this step, you'll devise the strategy to implement SAP S/4HANA and answer some or all of these questions, including single versus multiple instances, global versus regional instances, big-bang versus phased go-live approach, technical architecture and cloud versus on-premise, integration approach, data cleansing and migration, and many more.
5. **Enhance roadmap**
   Enhance the high-level roadmap created earlier with the detailed information and documents that you gathered through steps 1 to 4.

Trial System Provisioning

This is a critical part of the roadmap planning where you get to try out the latest SAP system. SAP will provision the trial system specifically for you using the SAP Cloud Appliance Library, as discussed in the "Key Characteristics" section of Chapter 1, which can host on Amazon Web Services (AWS), Google Cloud, or Microsoft Azure.

Prepare Phase

In the prepare phase, as the name suggests, the project team will plan and prepare several planning documents from kick-off to phase closure. In this section, we'll review the prepare phase activities and the corresponding deliverables for the SAP S/4HANA new implementations.

Before the start of this phase, the sponsor has approved the project, and the team is already assigned. During this phase of the project, the team will work closely with the customer's project manager to create several planning documents as described in the following sections, which are organized based on the workstream. Figure 6.8 shows the deliverables in the prepare phase of the project, which we'll walk through in the following sections.

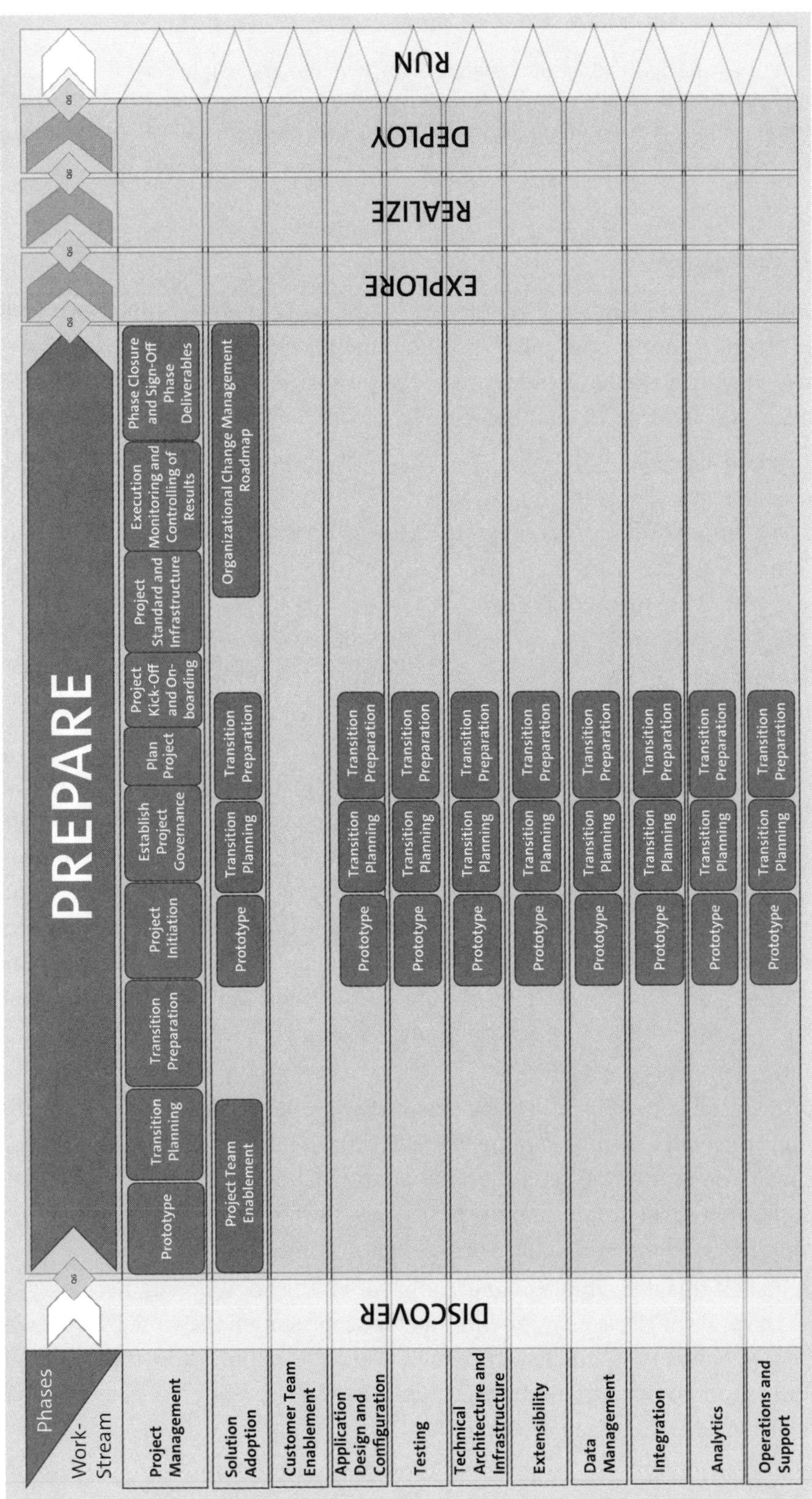

Figure 6.8 Prepare Phase Deliverables

Tip

From the exam perspective, assume that all team members are assigned before the start of the prepare phase. However, in reality, we've seen that many members, specifically the technical members (e.g., ABAP lead/consultant) or sometimes even a functional member (e.g., SAP treasury functional lead) will onboard at a later stage of the project.

Project Management

The project management workstream covers all aspects of project initiation, planning, execution, monitoring and controlling, and the closure activities. It includes the following deliverables, in addition to the prototype, transition planning, and transition preparation deliverables we discussed in the "Key Deliverables" section:

- **Project initiation**
  This is the very first step that formally recognizes the existence of the project. The key purpose of this process group is to ensure that the stakeholder's expectations are aligned with the initiative, identify any gaps, and work closely with the sponsor to close the alignment gaps.

  During this process group, the sales team will hand over the project, and the customer will sign the contract and place the purchase order. The assigned project manager will create the project charter, enhance the stakeholder's list identified earlier, capture their expectations and requirements, and create the deliverable and project acceptance criteria. Finally, during this process group, the project manager will create the detail project plan, including all its management plans such as cost management, scope baseline, scope management plan, requirement management plan, schedule management plan, stakeholder and communication management plan, risk and issue management plan, procurement management plan, change management plan, and human resource management plan. The project plan should also include the project constraints, assumptions and standards, and sign-off procedure.

- **Establish project governance**
  This deliverable establishes the oversight that provides the framework for the monitoring and controlling of the project. During this process group, the project team will be established, project hierarchy will be defined, roles and responsibilities will be identified, and the project plan will be reviewed.

- **Plan project**
  The goal of this deliverable is to account for all the components necessary to plan the project. These components include scope statement, work breakdown, schedule, constraints, budget, stakeholders and communication, risk and issue handling, and procurement management. This will feed into the project initiation deliverable discussed earlier.

- **Project kick-off and onboarding**
  In this deliverable, the project manager will kick off the project signaling the official start date of the project. The purpose of this kick-off meeting is to share all the necessary information with the project stakeholders, including the team members. The project manager will use this platform to communicate the overall objective of the project, project structure, decision-making processes, timeline, resources requirements with their roles and responsibilities, and overall plan along with many other aspects. It also seeks the consent for the stakeholder's commitment throughout the project, outlining key areas where higher involvement is required such as the involvement of the end-user community during the explore phase or for UAT, IT services during data migration or go-live, and so on.
- **Project standard, infrastructure, and solution**
  This deliverable will ensure that the team has a detailed understanding of the project standard, including documentation, coding, extensibility, configuration, process flow, requirement management, and any other standard required for the given client. This deliverable will also ensure the availability of tools such as project planning software, SAP Solution Manager, video conferencing tools, conference rooms and laptops, Internet connectivity, or any other infrastructure need. The SAP S/4HANA server requirement is *not* part of this deliverable; instead, we'll discuss it in the "Technical Architecture and Infrastructure" section.
- **Execution monitoring and controlling of results**
  This deliverable will ensure that the team has access, necessary privilege, required tools, and appropriate techniques to monitor and control the project execution throughout the project lifecycle.
- **Phase closure and sign-off phase deliverables**
  This is the last deliverable of the prepare phase that will ensure the timely delivery of all committed deliverables. The phase is closed, and the team can move to the next phase subject to the sign-off from the client.

Solution Adoption

The solution adoption workstream ensures the high adoptability of the solution within the organization. It includes the following deliverables, in addition to the prototype, transition planning, and transition preparation deliverables we discussed in the "Key Deliverables" section:

- **Project team enablement**
  The team needed several enablement activities, including the training for SAP solution, understanding the SAP Activate methodology, using the trial system, and more. This deliverable will ensure that the project team undergoes identified SAP Solution Manager training and knowledge-sharing sessions.

This deliverable will ensure that the project team has a sound understanding of the working methodology during the explore phase and the rest of the project. If needed, the project team should undergo Scrum framework training to understand its value and principles, approach, tools, and techniques. Team enablement may also require training and/or knowledge-sharing sessions on a multitude of topics, including the SAP Activate methodology, SAP Solution Manager, SAP Best Practices, and other tools. It's also advisable that the project team members should engage in self-learning exercises through blogs, openSAP, online demo sessions, trial environments, and so on.

- **Organizational change management (OCM) roadmap**
  We've reviewed OCM in Chapter 5. This deliverable will ensure that the fine details, such as consistency in the project plan, traceability of the OCM activities, and relationship between each activity, are appended to the high-level OCM roadmap created earlier in the discover phase of the project.

Application Design and Configuration

This workstream ensures the seamless application design and configuration. It includes the prototyping, transition planning, and transition preparation deliverables that we've discussed previously.

Testing

This workstream covers all the aspects of testing the solution. It includes the prototyping, transition planning, and transition preparation deliverables that we've discussed previously.

Technical Architecture and Infrastructure

This workstream covers all aspects of the infrastructure requirements and architecture. It includes the prototyping, transition planning, and transition preparation deliverables that we've discussed previously.

Extensibility

This workstream covers all the aspects of extension-related activities. It includes the prototyping, transition planning, and transition preparation deliverables that we've discussed previously.

Data Management

This workstream covers all aspects of the master data, transaction data, and data migration activities. It includes the prototyping, transition planning, and transition preparation deliverables that we've discussed previously.

Integration

This workstream covers all aspects of the integration with other SAP or third-party systems. It includes the prototyping, transition planning, and transition preparation deliverables that we've discussed previously.

Analytics

This workstream covers all aspects of the analytics. It includes the prototyping, transition planning, and transition preparation deliverables that we've discussed previously.

Operations and Support

This workstream covers all aspects of the operation and support post hypercare. It includes the prototyping, transition planning, and transition preparation deliverables that we've discussed previously.

Explore Phase

During the explore phase of the project, the team performs the fit-gap analysis and prepares the product backlog. Most of the planning is completed during the prepare phase; the customer has now signed off the phase, and the project has progressed to the next phase, that is, the explore phase. In this phase, the team will focus on the requirements through fit-gap analysis across multiple workstreams. Furthermore, the project team will receive the development system, ensuring its readiness before moving to the next phase of the project. Figure 6.9 shows the deliverables in the explore phase of the project, which we'll walk through in the following sections.

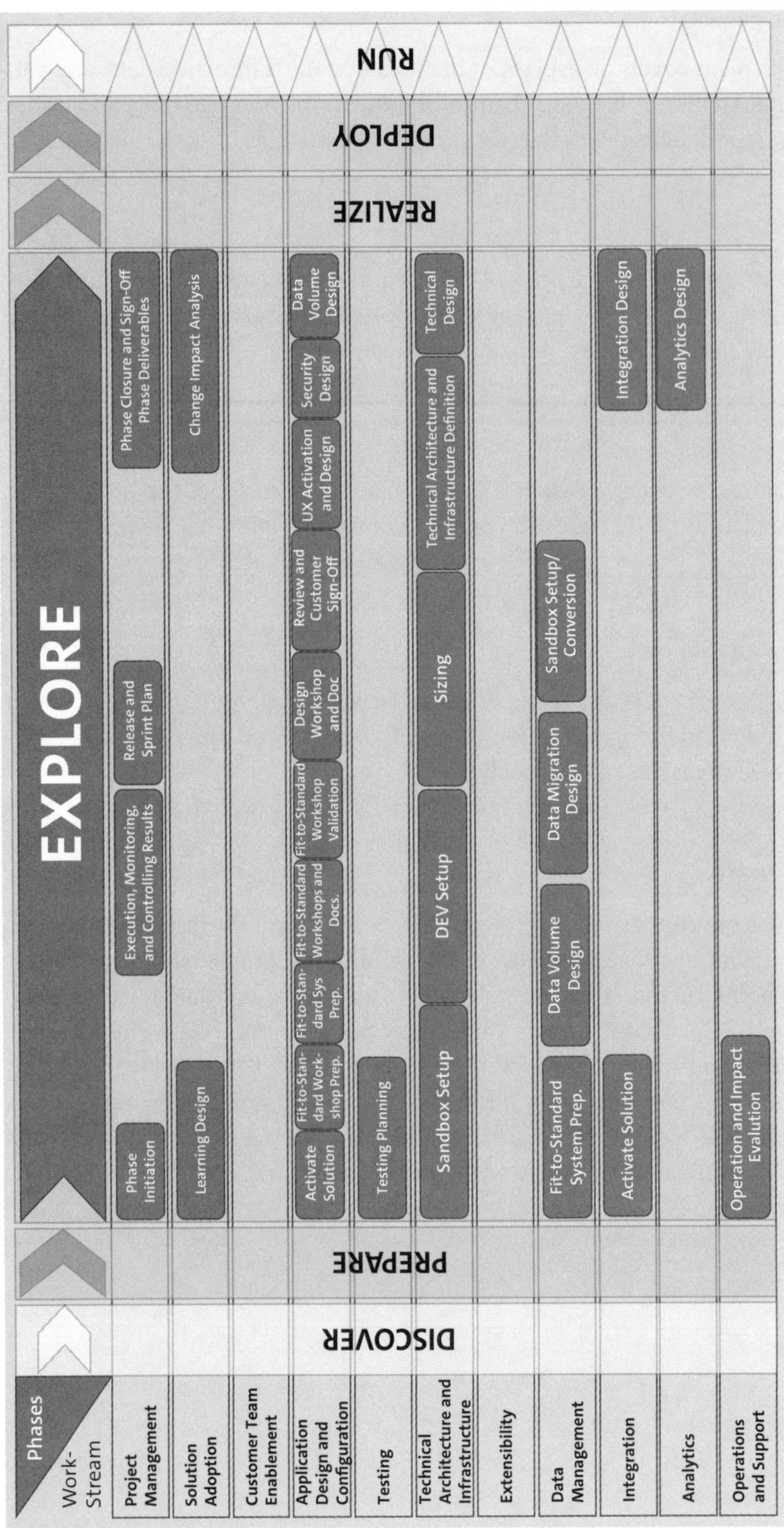

Figure 6.9 Explore Phase Deliverables

Project Management

The project management workstream covers all the aspects of project initiation, planning, execution, monitoring, and controlling, as well as the closure activities. It includes the following deliverables:

- **Phase initiation**
  The objective of this deliverable is to recognize formally the start of the explore phase of the project. During this deliverable, the project manager will work with the client manager to review the upcoming deliverables in the current phase and its timeline, revisit the client's commitment, and review the responsibility matrix to deliver the deliverables.
- **Execution, monitoring, and controlling results**
  This deliverable ensures the continuous monitoring of the project execution and controlling the execution in case of any deviation from the planned activities, schedule, costs, or any other constraints.
- **Release and sprint plan**
  The objective of this deliverable is to plan the sprint based on the prioritized backlog items, estimate the effort, develop the software, and release the sprint per the agreed-upon timeline after the sprint review and the approval from the respective product owner. We've reviewed the sprint planning and release planning in Chapter 4.
- **Phase closure and sign-off phase deliverables**
  This deliverable ensures the timeliness and quality of deliverables, signifying the completion of the explore phase of the project.

Solution Adoption

The solution adoption workstream ensures the high adoptability of the solution within the organization. It includes the following deliverables:

- **Learning design**
  The customer is moving onto a new ERP system, that is, SAP S/4HANA, from either a legacy system or a prior version of SAP. In either case, the end users and key users will need detailed training to use the system flawlessly. This deliverable, based on the initial assessment as a part of the transition plan, will design the learning methods for the end users and key users.
- **OCM impact analysis**
  This deliverable ensures that the OCM steps and processes are documented properly. The team should create as-is and to-be business processes and demonstrate the comparison to stakeholders, ensuring the organizational alignment of the approach. Additionally, the team will establish the baseline of the current state against which the team can measure the project progress and success of change management.

Application Design and Configuration

This workstream ensures the seamless application design and configuration. In this particular phase, the focus of this workstream is the fit-to-standard process that we've discussed earlier. The workstream includes the following deliverables:

- **Activate solution**
  This deliverable focuses on the availability of the functional system for the fit-to-standard workshops on the sandbox—set up by the technical team in the technical architecture and infrastructure workstream. In this case, the team will reconfirm the activation scope and ensure the configuration of SAP Fiori in the sandbox environment.
- **Fit-to-standard workshop preparation**
  This deliverable ensures that the project team is familiar with the fit-to-standard processes and logistics, such as the meeting room, availability of process owner, meeting invite, relevant participation, checklists, accelerators, other shared documentation, and any other similar activities.
- **Fit-to-standard system preparation**
  This deliverable ensures that the sandbox system is fully ready for workshops by ensuring that the customer data is loaded and the team has enhanced the system by completing any additional configuration and testing needed for the successful fit-to-standard process.
- **Fit-to-standard workshops and documentation**
  This deliverable ensures that the team conducts the workshops for each LoB. During the workshop, the team should present the target solution to the process owners and subject matter experts (SMEs). The outcome of the process will be a set of validated business processes and an initial delta requirement.
- **Fit-to-standard workshop validation**
  This workshop is to confirm the delta requirements before moving forward with design workshops. The team will ensure the quality and completeness of the identified delta requirements.
- **Design workshops and documentation**
  These are the design workshops conducted to detail the solution and document delta requirements. These workshops are conducted iteratively to ensure that the team captured the complete solution design.
- **Review and customer sign-off**
  As a part of this deliverable, the team performs the design review with the respective business SME and other stakeholders for their validation and sign-off from the customer.
- **UX activation and design**
  This deliverable is to compare the customer-specific requirements for UX with the SAP standard configuration for SAP Fiori. SAP Fiori items without any deviation are activated, while the team documents the gaps with other SAP Fiori items. Based on the prioritized gaps and after confirmation and approval from the client, the team drafts the mock-ups.

- **Security design**
  This deliverable builds the security roadmap per the customer's requirement. User management for SAP S/4HANA and authorization management are a couple of examples that should be included in the security design.
- **Data volume design**
  SAP S/4HANA is built on SAP HANA, an in-memory database. The strategy and management of the data volume is critical, which includes business data needs, internal and external data requirements, data privacy, and dependency between data archiving and document management. The customer should consider data deletion and data archiving apart from data aggregation and data avoidance to manage the data volume effectively. As a result, the team has a documented strategy to manage data volume.

Testing

This workstream covers all the aspects of testing the solution and includes the following deliverable:

- **Test planning**
  This deliverable will help prepare the solution test plan that should include testing objectives, testing scope, approach, deliverables, any automation strategy and relevant tools, testing tools, defect management, and expectations from the customer, including roles and responsibilities. The test plan should also include different types of tests that the team should conduct, including unit, string, integration, data migration, and user acceptance.

Technical Architecture and Infrastructure

This workstream covers all aspects of the infrastructure requirements and the architecture, and it includes the following deliverables:

- **Sandbox setup/conversion**
  This deliverable will ensure that the sandbox environment has all the necessary software, user access and privileges, and the customer sample data for the fit-to-standard process. If SAP Best Practices seems a better fit for the customer's needs, then the team should include SAP Model Company or the fully activated appliance. However, the team should start from a new and empty SAP S/4HANA system in case SAP Best Practices doesn't fit the customer's requirements.
- **Development (DEV) system setup/conversion**
  Before the start of the realize phase, the team should set up the DEV environment. Based on multiple factors, which won't be covered in the exam, the team can decide to repurpose the sandbox environment or set up a new DEV environment. If there are additional systems, such as preproduction or training environment, the team should adjust the roadmap and plan accordingly.

- **Sizing**
  We've discussed the sizing process in detail in Chapter 5. The team should estimate the infrastructure capacity such as RAM size, CPU requirements, network capabilities, and storage needs. The team should deliver this for the nonproduction systems in the explore phase and for the PROD system in the realize phase of the project.
- **Technical architecture and infrastructure definition**
  This deliverable will detail the technical architecture and the infrastructure landscape by identifying technical boundaries, creating the technical solution map, choosing integration options, making hardware selections, virtualizing the strategy, designing the network, and performing infrastructure test preparation.
- **Technical design**
  This activity will result in a technical solution design document that is developed using a series of workshops to understand and document technical components, scalability, backup and restore, high availability and disaster recovery, sizing, third-party integrations, load balancing, and other technical requirements.

Data Management

This workstream covers all aspects of the master data, transactional data, and data migration activities. It includes the following deliverables:

- **Fit-to-standard system preparation**
  This deliverable is part of the overall fit-to-standard process that feeds into the application design and configuration workstream by setting the sample data in the sandbox environment.
- **Data volume design**
  We've discussed the data volume design in the application design and configuration workstream. The objective of this deliverable is to build the data volume strategy and balance the business need to access data versus IT effort to maintain database and storage.
- **Data migration design**
  The team will build the data migration design by conducting migration assessment, auditing, and identifying migration scope, data quality, data source, data specification, and a few other parameters. This strategy document will outline the data migration object. It's an enhanced version of the data migration architecture built as a part of transition planning during the prepare phase of the project. It's applicable to the new implementation approach and the selective data transition approach.
- **Sandbox setup/conversion**
  We've discussed this in the technical architecture and infrastructure workstream.

Integration

This workstream covers all the aspects of integration activities and includes the following deliverables:

- **Activate solution**
  This deliverable will ensure that the team activates any integration-related requirements, including business-to-business (B2B), application-to-application (A2A), SAP Solution Manager integration, output management, UIs, and Internet of Things (IoT) integrations.
- **Integration design**
  This deliverable is a part of the fit-to-standard design workshops and is specific for the understanding and solution designing from an integration perspective.

Analytics

This workstream covers all the analytics aspects and includes the following deliverable:

- **Analytics design**
  This deliverable is a part of the fit-to-standard design workshops and is specific for the understanding and solution designing from an analytics perspective.

Operations and Support

This workstream covers all aspects of the operation and support post-hypercare. It includes the following deliverable:

- **Operations impact evaluation**
  With the introduction of the SAP S/4HANA solution, the operation landscape will change for sure. To understand the impact of this change, the team must analyze the target framework, recommend best practices for support, help the customer build the target operating model, assign roles and responsibilities, and so on.

Realize Phase

The purpose of the realize phase is to realize the build incrementally and iteratively based on the business requirements and scenarios identified during the previous phases of the project.

During the realize phase, the team is deep into system configuration based on the fit-gap analysis and the prioritized product backlog. In addition, during this phase, the legacy data load starts, solution adoption continues, and operation planning happens. Figure 6.10 shows the deliverables in the realize phase of the project, which we'll discuss in the following sections.

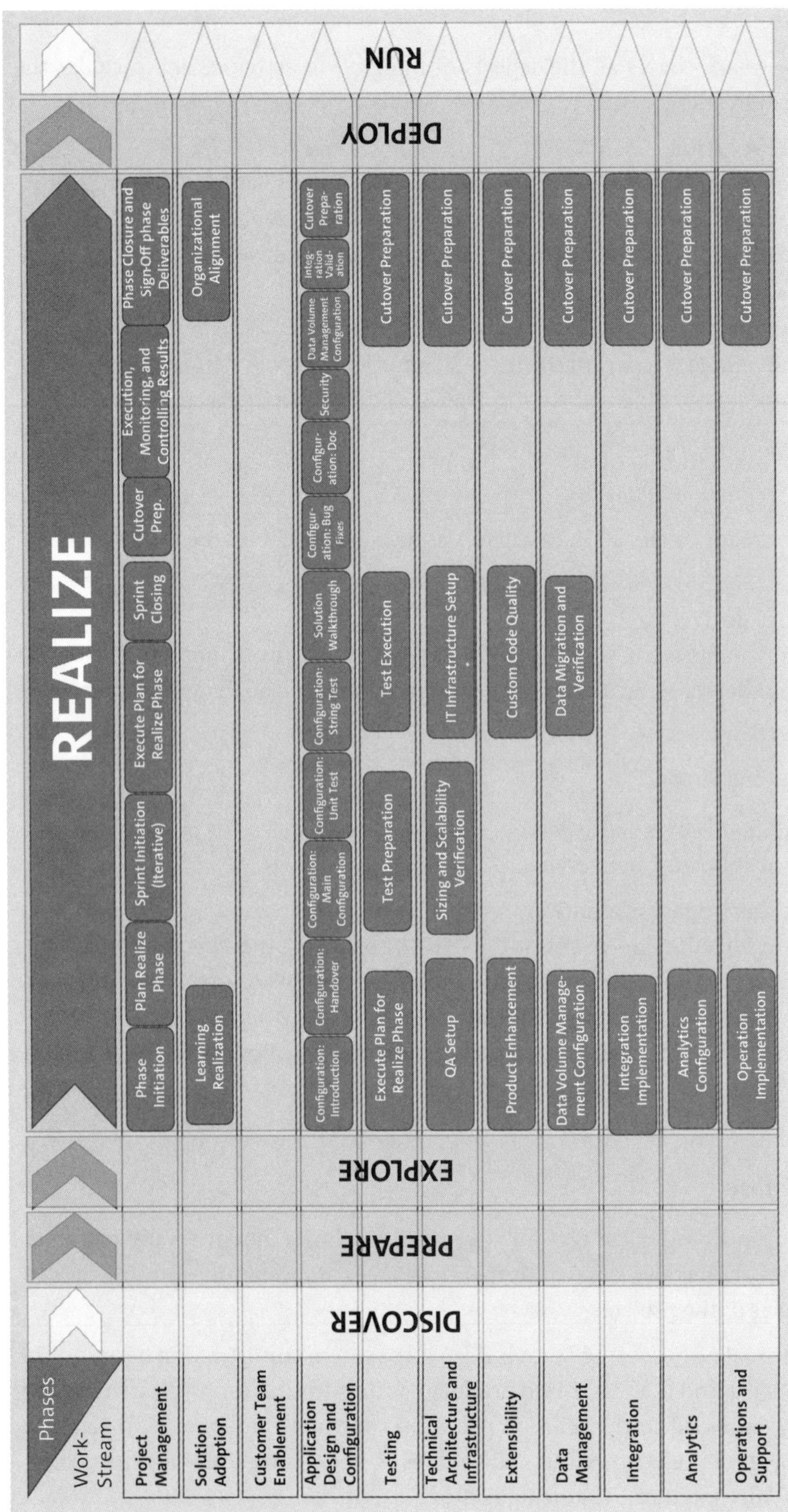

Figure 6.10 Realize Phase Deliverables

Project Management

The project management workstream covers all the aspects of project initiation, planning, execution, monitoring, and controlling, as well as the closure activities. It includes the following deliverables:

- **Phase initiation**
  The objective of this deliverable is to recognize formally the start of the realize phase of the project. During this deliverable, the project manager will work with the client manager to review the upcoming deliverables in the current phase and its timeline, revisit the client's commitment, and review the responsibility matrix to deliver the deliverables.
- **Plan realize phase**
  This planning, specific to the realize phase, is required to identify the sprint cycle, sprint planning, and other sprint ceremonies. See Chapter 4 for more details on sprints.
- **Sprint initiation (iterative)**
  This deliverable formally initiates a sprint in the sprint ceremony—sprint planning. We've discussed this in Chapter 3 and Chapter 4.
- **Execute plan for realize phase**
  This is the execution of the realize phase plan to manage the sprint and deliver the workable solution at the end of each sprint.
- **Sprint closing**
  After the formal sprint retrospective and sprint review ceremonies, this deliverable ensures the sprint closure.
- **Cutover preparation**
  We've discussed cutover preparation in detail at the beginning of this chapter and in Chapter 4.
- **Execution, monitoring, and controlling results**
  This deliverable ensures the continuous monitoring of the project execution and controlling the execution in case of any deviation from the planned activities, schedule, costs, or any other constraint.
- **Phase closure and sign-off phase deliverables**
  This deliverable ensures the timely and quality deliverables, signifying the completion of the realize phase of the project.

Solution Adoption

The solution adoption workstream ensures the high adoptability of the solution within the organization. It includes the following deliverables:

- **Learning realization**
  This deliverable is the realization of the learning assessment that the team did in the explore phase of the project. The team will create the training document and train the key users during this deliverable.

- **Organizational alignment**
  The objective of this deliverable is to align the end users' roles and responsibilities to ensure their activities are aligned with the project's objective.

Application Design and Configuration

This workstream ensure the seamless application design and configuration. It includes the following deliverables:

- **Configuration**
  Configuration isn't an actual deliverable but is a group of deliverables as listed here. However, it's important to understand that this group caters to all the configuration-related work, from becoming familiar with configuration activities to making the configuration changes, completing the unit testing, string testing, documenting, bug fixing, and doing the solution walkthrough.
- **Configuration: Introduction**
  We discussed the foundation sprint in Chapter 5. This deliverable translates to the foundation sprint because the purpose of this deliverable is to configure the mandatory settings, for example, legal entities, organizational structure, other general settings, and preparation of master data.
- **Configuration: Handover**
  Although it's an optional deliverable, the structured handover is critical for the subsequent configuration. The fit-to-standard workshop teams will hand over the learning, product backlog, and other documentation to the configuration team by organizing handover sessions for each LoB and solution.
- **Configuration: Main configuration**
  The objective of this work is to configure the exploration system based on the handover received from the fit-to-standard team. It includes master data configuration, core finance, and other relevant configurations.
- **Configuration: Unit test**
  The team will complete the unit testing as a part of this deliverable, document the findings, and resolve the issues, if any, before moving forward.
- **Configuration: String test**
  In Chapter 5, you learned about the firm-up sprint and string testing. This is the deliverable where the team performs the string testing—a test to integrate different sprints specifically for epics. This can happen only after the completion of unit testing and follows the same process of documentation and issue resolution before moving forward.
- **Configuration: Solution walkthrough**
  Through the iterative process, this deliverable ensures that the project team completes the walkthrough of the solution for each process across the business and gets the business feedback and necessary approvals.
- **Configuration: Bug fixing**
  The purpose of this deliverable is to resolve any issues that the team has

identified during the solution walkthrough. Any leftover issues from unit testing and string testing must be fixed during this deliverable. It's recommended to fix unit test-related issues before moving to the string test and to fix string testing-related issues before moving to the solution walkthrough.

- **Configuration: Documentation**
  This deliverable is to complete the configuration document and upload the same in SAP Solution Manager.
- **Security implementation**
  Any security-related requirements captured during the fit-to-standard processes are performed in this deliverable.
- **Data volume management configuration**
  Based on analysis conducted in the explore phase of the project, the team configures the data volume requirements.
- **Integration validation**
  Integration validation is a process to validate the necessary integrations between multiple applications, and it addresses data consistency, performance and scalability, and business process management and exception handling. The team should identify the integration validation scope, initiate the support activities, and initiate the SAP going-live check. This will continue until the deploy phase of the project.
- **Cutover preparation**
  We've discussed cutover preparation in detail at the beginning of this chapter and in Chapter 4.

Testing

This workstream covers all aspects of testing the solution. It includes the following deliverables:

- **Execute plan for the realize phase**
  The objective of this deliverable is to execute the plan defined in the realize phase and manage the sprints and testing according to previously defined plans. During test execution, all issues must be logged and documented in the system for traceability purposes. The tests include integration testing, security testing, and UAT.
- **Test preparation**
  The objective is to prepare the test per customer-specific requirements.
- **Test execution**
  Testing can start after the planning in the test preparation deliverable and the availability of test data. The test execution includes all three testing types identified earlier.
- **Cutover preparation**
  We've discussed cutover preparation in detail at the beginning of this chapter and in Chapter 4.

Technical Architecture and Infrastructure

This workstream covers all aspects of the infrastructure requirements and the architecture. It includes the following deliverables:

- **Quality assurance (QA) system setup/conversion**
  The purpose of the quality assurance environment is to install a viable, correctly configured technical QA system environment that is available for use by the project team to perform QA system testing.
- **Sizing and scalability verification**
  The sizing and scalability exercise done during the explore phase of the project should be verified again in the realize phase. This deliverable ensures that the team verifies the sizing and scalability of the infrastructure.
- **IT infrastructure setup**
  The purpose of the PROD infrastructure and environment design and setup deliverable is to install a viable, correctly configured technical PROD environment to support productive operations of the delivered solution. It also includes the related infrastructure testing such as performance tests, backup and recovery tests, high availability and disaster recovery tests, and so on.
- **Cutover preparation**
  We've discussed cutover preparation in detail at the beginning of this chapter and in Chapter 4.

Extensibility

This workstream covers all the aspects of extension-related activities and includes the following deliverables:

- **Product enhancement**
  Based on the fit-to-standard analysis and the extension requirements of the functionalities, the team will develop the custom code to close the delta requirements. It includes the adjustment of custom code and development of report, interface, conversion, enhancement, form, and workflow (RICEFW) objects and UIs.
- **Custom code quality**
  This deliverable ensures the desired level of quality work in the custom code.
- **Cutover preparation**
  We've discussed cutover preparation in detail at the beginning of this chapter and in Chapter 4.

Data Management

This workstream covers all aspects of the master data, transactional data, and data migration activities. It includes the following deliverables:

- **Data volume management configuration**
  The objective of this deliverable is to configure the solution based on the data volume strategy developed earlier.
- **Data migration and verification**
  The objective of this deliverable is to develop, implement, and test the data migration programs as defined earlier in the explore phase. The development is done through the iterative cycles of code building and testing. It focuses on data analysis, continuous refinement of business rules, and deployment of programs that will extract, cleanse, transform, and enrich legacy data. The process is repeated multiple times for various test cycles and finally for the production cutover.
- **Cutover preparation**
  We've discussed cutover preparation in detail at the beginning of this chapter and in Chapter 4.

Integration

This workstream covers all aspects of the integration activities and includes the following deliverables:

- **Integration implementation**
  The team implements the integration requirements specific to the customer needs as identified in the explore phase of the project.
- **Cutover preparation**
  We've discussed cutover preparation in detail at the beginning of this chapter and in Chapter 4.

Analytics

This workstream covers all aspects of the analytics and includes the following deliverables:

- **Analytics configuration**
  The team configures the analytics requirements specific to the customer needs as identified in the explore phase of the project.
- **Cutover preparation**
  We've discussed cutover preparation in detail at the beginning of this chapter and in Chapter 4.

Operations and Support

This workstream covers all aspects of the operation and support post-hypercare. It includes the following deliverables:

- **Operations implementations**
  The team implements the strategy and recommendations based on the operations impact evaluation conducted during the explore phase of the project. IT should be ready to accept the handover at the start of the run phase.
- **Cutover preparation**
  We've discussed cutover preparation in detail at the beginning of this chapter and in Chapter 4.

Deploy Phase

In the deploy phase of the project, the business switches the operation to the new PROD environment. This is the final phase of the project—where the "rubber meets the road." The team will close all the open issues, ensure the organizational readiness, and execute the production cutover so that the business can realize the benefits of the newly implemented solution. Figure 6.11 shows the deliverables in the deploy phase of the project, which we'll discuss in the following sections.

Project Management

The project management workstream covers all aspects of project initiation, planning, execution, monitoring, and controlling, as well as the closure activities. It includes the following deliverables, in addition to the dress rehearsal and production cutover deliverables we discussed in the "Key Deliverables" section:

- **Phase initiation**
  The objective of this deliverable is to recognize formally the start of the deploy phase of the project. During this deliverable, the project manager will work with the client manager to review the upcoming deliverables in the current phase and its timeline, revisit the client's commitment, and review the responsibility matrix to deliver the deliverables.
- **Execution, monitoring, and controlling results**
  This deliverable ensures the continuous monitoring of the project execution and controls the execution in case of any deviation from the planned activities, schedule, costs, or any other constraint.
- **Release closing**
  The purpose of this deliverable is to formally close the release and prepare for the next release or sprint planning meeting.
- **Project closure and sign-off project deliverables**
  This deliverable ensures the timely and quality deliverables, signifying the completion of the deploy phase of the project.

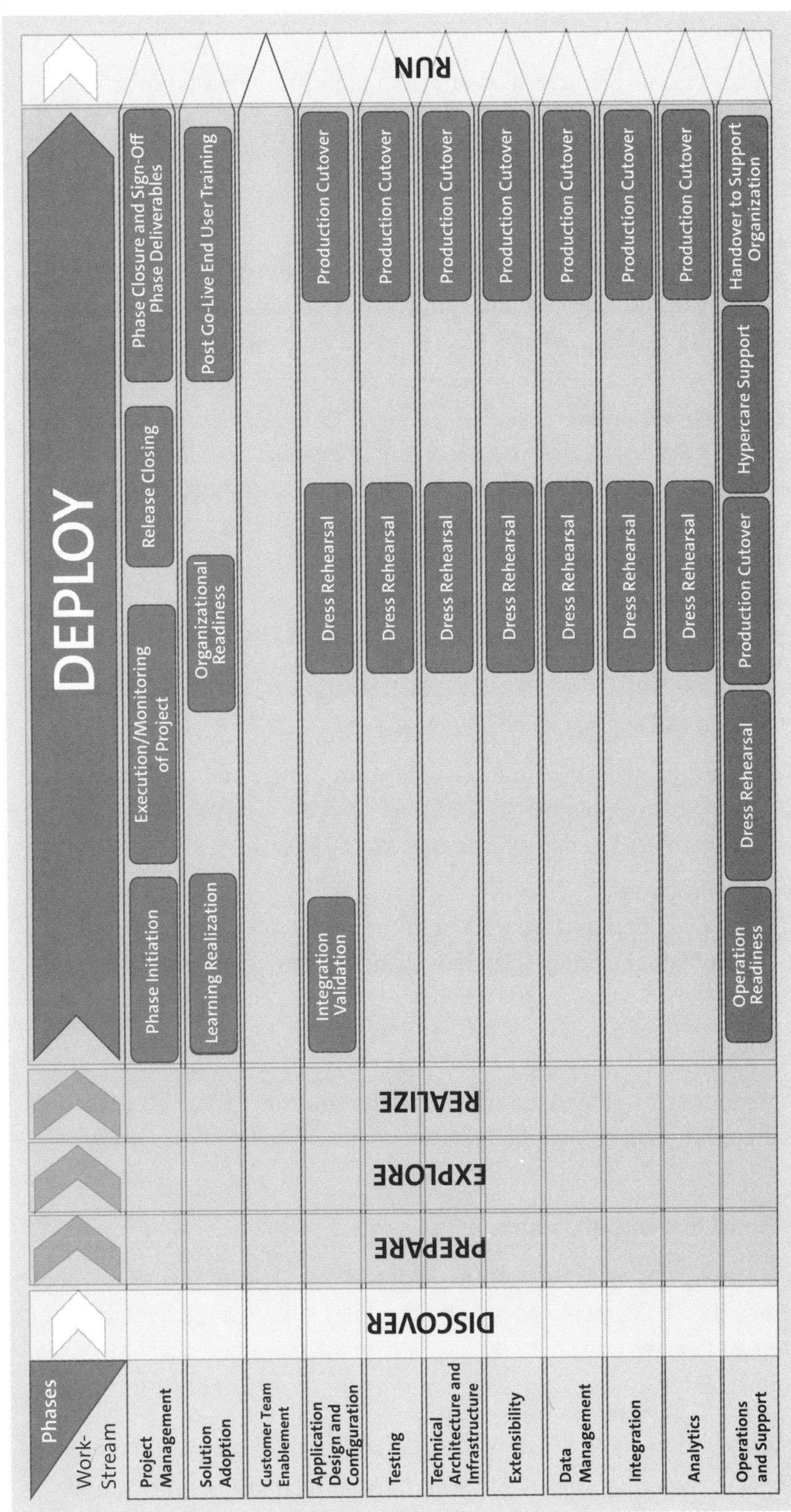

Figure 6.11 Deploy Phase Deliverables

Solution Adoption

The solution adoption workstream ensures the high adoptability of the solution within the organization. It includes the following deliverables, in addition to the dress rehearsal and production cutover deliverables we discussed in the "Key Deliverables" section:

- **Learning realization**
  This deliverable is the execution of the learning assessment that the team did in the explore phase of the project and delivers the end-user training with the aid, documents, scenarios, and other artifacts created by the team during the realize phase.
- **Organizational readiness**
  This deliverable is used to measure the organization readiness in terms of adoption and adaption of the new solution across the organization, user readiness, system know-how, and so on. More focused OCM activities may be required if the readiness is below a predetermined level.
- **Post go-live end-user training**
  This deliverable ensures that the end users have adopted the solution.

Application Design and Configuration

This workstream ensures the seamless application design and configuration. It includes the following deliverable, in addition to the dress rehearsal and production cutover deliverables we discussed in the "Key Deliverables" section:

- **Integration validation**
  The integration validation work started in the realize phase of the project will continue to validate the integration requirements until the deploy phase.

Testing

This workstream covers all aspects of testing the solution. It includes the dress rehearsal and production cutover deliverables that we discussed previously.

Technical Architecture and Infrastructure

This workstream covers all aspects of the infrastructure requirements and architecture. It includes the dress rehearsal and production cutover deliverables that we discussed previously.

Extensibility

This workstream covers all aspects of the extension-related activities. It includes the dress rehearsal and production cutover deliverables that we discussed previously.

Data Management

This workstream covers all aspects of the master data, transactional data, and data migration activities. It includes the dress rehearsal and production cutover deliverables that we discussed previously.

Integration

This workstream covers all aspects of the integration with other SAP or third-party systems. It includes the dress rehearsal and production cutover deliverables that we discussed previously.

Analytics

This workstream covers all aspects of the analytics and includes the dress rehearsal and production cutover deliverables that we discussed previously.

Operations and Support

This workstream covers all aspects of the operation and support post-hypercare. It includes the following deliverables, in addition to the dress rehearsal and production cutover deliverables we discussed in the "Key Deliverables" section:

- **Operational readiness**
  This activity checks the customer's ability to operate the newly built SAP S/4HANA solution. Operational readiness is different from organizational readiness in terms of what you're measuring, such as operational capacity (roles and responsibility, support tools, operation documentation, knowledge transfer, etc.) of the team versus end-user adoption of the solution, their preparedness to run the business process, and so on.
- **Hypercare support**
  During this part of the project, the solution is operational, and the project team supports any end-user needs.
- **Handover to support organization**
  At the end of the hypercare support, the team will hand over the operation to the operation team of the customer organization.

Run Phase

This phase starts after the hypercare, during the previous phase of the project, to optimize the overall operation. During this phase, support is provided by the customer IT team who continue to strive for optimization, automate the application processes, ensure system availability, and provide system performance. Figure 6.12 shows the deliverables in the run phase of the project, which we'll discuss in the following sections.

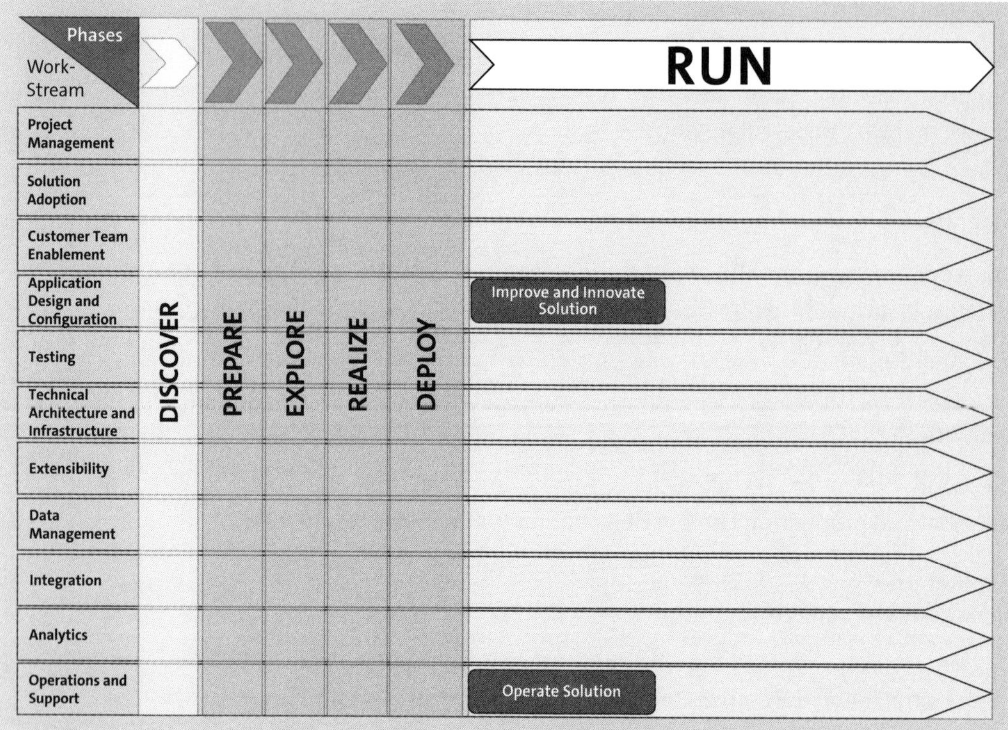

Figure 6.12 Run Phase Deliverables

Application Design and Configuration

This workstream ensures the seamless application design and configuration. It includes the following deliverable:

- **Improve and innovate solution**
  The task in this workstream focuses on the periodical updates and preparedness of the team to accept new updates.

Operations and Support

This workstream covers all aspects of the operation and support post-hypercare. It includes the following deliverable:

- **Operate solution**
  The operations maturity assessment evaluates the SAP customer's support operations to determine areas in need of optimization.

Important Terminology

For this exam objective, you're expected to understand the following terms:

- **Output management**
  This is a way to manage business documents such as printouts, emails, alerts, and so on, which will eventually replace multiple output control processes.
- **Prototype**
  This is a small project that spans from the prepare to explore phase of the project to evaluate the complex or latest innovations from SAP with the customer's data.
- **SAP Fiori**
  The new UI and design language for SAP S/4HANA.
- **Transition planning**
  This is the process to build a detailed transition plan from the current setup to the desired platform. The transition planning is applicable to the new implementation of SAP S/4HANA, system conversion, and selective data transition.
- **Trial system provisioning**
  This cloud-based system is provided by SAP for the initial discovery of the project objectives.

 Practice Questions

These practice questions will help you evaluate your understanding of the topics covered in this chapter. The questions shown are similar in nature to those found on the certification examination. Although none of these questions will be found on the exam itself, they will allow you to review your knowledge of the subject. Select the correct answers, and then check the completeness of your answers in the "Practice Question Answers and Explanations" section. Remember that on the exam, you must select all correct answers and only correct answers to receive credit for the question.

1. What are the project management deliverables from the prepare phase of the SAP S/4HANA new implementation project? (There are three correct answers.)

☐ **A.** Phase initiation

☐ **B.** Project initiation

☐ **C.** Plan project

☐ **D.** Organizational change management (OCM)

☐ **E.** Project standard, infrastructure, and solution

2. What are the three deliverables from the testing workstream in the prepare phase of the SAP S/4HANA new implementation project?

☐ **A.** Initiate testing, prepare testing policy, and prepare testing strategy

☐ **B.** Prototype, transition planning, and transition preparation

☐ **C.** Initiate testing, define testing strategy, and create test plan

☐ **D.** Prototype, transition preparation, and prepare policy for performance testing

3. What are the deliverables that aren't from the data management workstream in the prepare phase of the SAP S/4HANA new implementation project? (There are two correct answers.)

☐ **A.** Business process map

☐ **B.** Legacy data migration

☐ **C.** Transition planning

☐ **D.** Prototype

☐ **E.** Transition preparation

4. What are the activities in the explore phase of the SAP S/4HANA new implementation? (There are two correct answers.)

☐ **A.** Fine-tune business requirements.

☐ **B.** Explore the solution and build the strategy.

☐ **C.** Conduct fit-gap analysis.

☐ **D.** Conduct sprint review.

☐ **E.** Build product backlog.

5. Which of the following is a purpose of the explore phase?

☐ **A.** Onboard project resources.

☐ **B.** Learn the agile approach.

☐ **C.** Explore business functionalities.

☐ **D.** Finalize the product backlog.

6. Which of the following are correct statements about the SAP S/4HANA new implementation? (There are two correct answers.)

☐ **A.** Fit-gap analysis overlaps between the explore and realize phases of the project.

☐ **B.** The team performs the fit-gap analysis during the explore phase of the project.

☐ **C.** Delta design workshops follow the solution validation workshops.

☐ **D.** Workshop B is optional in an SAP S/4HANA implementation. It's mandatory for the SAP S/4HANA Cloud implementations.

☐ **E.** The team conducts workshop A in the explore phase of the project and workshop B in the realize phase of the project.

7. You presented a set of findings and recommendations to the customer project manager for review and approval after a series of activities, such as performance testing, high availability, disaster recovery test, backup and restore test, and some additional testing. What is the project phase, workstream, and deliverable from an SAP S/4HANA implementation standpoint?

☐ **A.** Deploy phase, technical architecture and infrastructure workstream, IT infrastructure setup

☐ **B.** Deploy phase, testing workstream, approve technical system tests deliverable

☐ **C.** Realize phase, testing workstream, approve technical system tests deliverable

☐ **D.** Realize phase, technical architecture and infrastructure workstream, IT infrastructure setup

8. You're in the deploy phase of the SAP S/4HANA implementation project. You just came out of a training room full of participants praising the post go-live end-user training. What did you just deliver?

☐ **A.** Learning realization

☐ **B.** Post go-live training planning discussion

☐ **C.** Post go-live change readiness check

☐ **D.** Post go-live party

9. When will the customers get access to the trial environment?

☐ **A.** Discover phase

☐ **B.** Realize phase

☐ **C.** Run phase

☐ **D.** Prepare phase

10. When does the project team prepare the sandbox environment?

☐ **A.** Discover phase

☐ **B.** Realize phase

☐ **C.** Run phase

☐ **D.** Prepare phase

11. What is the available target solution for the system conversion transition path?

☐ **A.** SAP S/4 HANA Cloud, essentials edition

☐ **B.** SAP S/4 HANA Cloud, extended edition

☐ **C.** On-premise SAP S/4HANA

☐ **D.** None of the above

12. SSCUIs provide customers with access to on-premise SAP S/4HANA configuration. True or false?

☐ **A.** True

☐ **B.** False

13. During a new implementation of SAP S/4HANA, sizing exercises are important to estimate hardware budget. True or false?

☐ **A.** True

☐ **B.** False

14. Which of the following media is used by SAP to provide ready-to-run systems for on-premise deployments? (There are two correct answers.)

☐ **A.** SAP Cloud Appliance Library

☐ **B.** Floppy disk

☐ **C.** Blu-ray disks

☐ **D.** USB drive

15. What is the recommended choice for on-premise to on-premise integration scenarios?

☐ **A.** SAP Cloud Platform Integration Suite

☐ **B.** SAP Process Orchestration

☐ **C.** Roadmap Viewer

☐ **D.** SAP Best Practices

Practice Question Answers and Explanations

1. Correct answers: **A, C, E**
   There are no deliverables named "project initiation" or "organizational change management." Organizational change management (OCM) is one of the substreams of solution adoption.
2. Correct answer: **B**
   The three deliverables are prototype, transition preparation, and transition planning. Initiate testing as mentioned in options A and C, prepare testing policy as mentioned in option A, and the prepare policy for performance testing as mentioned in option D are incorrect because there are no such deliverables.

3. Correct answers: **A, B**

   The three deliverables in the data management workstream in the prepare phase of the project are prototype, transition preparation, and transition planning. Options A and B list others, so they are the right choices.

4. Correct answers: **C, E**

   During the explore phase, the team conducts fit-gap analysis and builds the product backlog.

5. Correct answer: **D**

   During the explore phase, the project team completes the fit-gap analysis to validate the solution and, as a result, builds the product backlog. Therefore, option D is the correct choice.

6. Correct answers: **B, C**

   The team performs the fit-gap analysis during the explore phase of the project. As a part of this exercise, the team conducts two workshops—solution validation (aka workshop A) and delta design (aka workshop B).

7. Correct answer: **D**

   From the situation provided, it's clear that the project team has performed the IT infrastructure tests and presented the findings to the client for review and approval. These tests are part of the IT infrastructure setup, which is conducted during the realize phase of the project as a part of the technical architecture and infrastructure workstream.

8. Correct answer: **A**

   Options B and C are incorrect while option D is reasonable, but incorrect from an SAP Activate perspective. The team does celebrate the go-live, but the scenario presented is for the learning exercise.

9. Correct answer: **A**

   SAP completes the trial system provisioning in the discover phase of the project. Based on the trials and the corresponding learning, the team builds the initial scope, strategy, and implementation roadmap in the discover phase.

10. Correct answer: **D**

    The team prepares the sandbox environment in the prepare phase of the project. The discover phase would be too early to build a sandbox solution, and it would be too late to build a sandbox in other phases.

11. Correct answer: **C**

    The only target platform for system conversion is an on-premise deployment. You can't move the current on-premise deployment to SAP S/4HANA Cloud as that will be a new implementation.

12. Correct answer: **B**

    False. SSCUI is available for cloud deployments. You'll use the IMG to configure on-premise deployments.

13. Correct answer: **A**

    True. The sizing exercise is required to determine the hardware sizing for on-premise implementations. It's a part of the technical architecture and infrastructure workstream.

14. Correct answers: **A, C**

    To use ready-to-run systems for the on-premise implementations, you can use either SAP Cloud Appliance Library or the Blu-ray shipped by SAP. Remember that the shipment can take a few days, but access to SAP Cloud Appliance Library is instant.

15. Correct answer: **B**

    For on-premise to on-premise integration, SAP Process Orchestration is the recommended choice. You can use SAP Cloud Platform Integration Suite to integrate cloud solutions with on-premise solutions. The Roadmap Viewer outlines the SAP Activate methodology, while SAP Best Practices is a cloud-based repository of SAP solutions.

Takeaway

This chapter built on the three transition paths discussed earlier. The chapter focused on the SAP S/4HANA new implementation, discussed the detailed steps in the discover phase of the project to build the strategy, and the roadmap to execute the strategy.

You also learned about the different deliverables and the high-level activities necessary to deliver them during each phase of the project. Contrary to Chapter 5, this chapter and subsequent chapters are arranged based on the deliverables and workstreams. You learned about all phases of SAP S/4HANA implementations.

Summary

In this chapter, we covered the concepts of SAP S/4HANA new implementations and learned about the different deliverables and the corresponding activities during the SAP S/4HANA new implementation project. We'll focus on the deliverables for SAP S/4HANA Cloud, essentials edition implementation and activities in the next chapter.

Chapter 7

New Implementation SAP S/4HANA Cloud, Essentials Edition Transition Path

7

Techniques You'll Master

- Explain an overview of cloud implementations
- Differentiate between SAP S/4HANA Cloud, essentials edition and SAP S/4HANA Cloud, extended edition
- Understand the fit-to-standard process
- Know the deliverables, tools, and techniques in the project implementation phases

In the previous chapter, our focus was on the new implementation of SAP S/4HANA. In this chapter, we'll dive deeper to understand the implementation process in SAP S/4HANA Cloud, essentials edition (previously known as the multitenant edition). We'll start, however, with understanding the concept of multitenant and single-tenant and review the differences between them.

Similar to the previous chapter, we'll review the deliverables, activities, tools, and techniques required to complete the SAP S/4HANA Cloud, essentials edition implementation. We'll start with the discover phase of the project and go until the run phase of the implementation. It's important to understand the objective of the discover phase—discover the solution, build the implementation strategy, and plan the implementation roadmap—remains unchanged. During this phase, the team, based on several factors, decides to go for the on-premise, multitenant, or single-tenant implementation. The concepts presented in this chapter are for the multitenant version, that is, SAP S/4HANA Cloud, essentials edition.

Note

Whenever you see SAP S/4HANA Cloud, you can assume that the context is for SAP S/4HANA Cloud, essentials edition. This edition was previously known as SAP S/4HANA Cloud, multitenant edition, but it's still, as of the writing of this book, referred to as simply "SAP S/4HANA Cloud" on the C_ACTIVATE12 exam, which is the terminology we'll use in this chapter accordingly. Previously, it was known as SAP S/4HANA public cloud, and, prior to that, it was known as SAP S/4HANA public option.

The single-tenant edition is now called SAP S/4HANA Cloud, extended edition, and the on-premise edition is simply referred to as SAP S/4HANA.

Real-World Scenario

Let's continue with the SAP sales executive example from Chapter 6. You're in pursuit of several SAP implementations and contacting many of your prior clients to explain the features and benefits of SAP S/4HANA.

You're a pizza lover, and a particular fan of a local chain that, five years back, you sold SAP Business One to. Now, times have changed, and it's time for this local chain to upgrade their enterprise resource planning (ERP) system. You call Ms. Eleonora D. Esposito, co-CEO and the head of the IT department, to talk about the transition from SAP Business One to SAP S/4HANA Cloud.

During the call, you get directly to the matter at hand: reviewing the requirements of the business. Their needs are lower total cost of ownership (TCO), legacy data migration to the new environment, and a minimal IT budget. They also have a minimal need to customize their ERP system. A question is raised: What can they expect from a cloud implementation?

Objectives of This Portion of the Test

The certification examination will test your knowledge about the following topics:

- Cloud deployment editions
- Differences between the SAP S/4HANA Cloud editions
- Activities during the SAP S/4HANA Cloud implementation
- Deliverables of SAP S/4HANA Cloud deployment

In the subsequent sections, you'll learn about these key concepts followed by some questions and answers.

Note

The new implementation SAP S/4HANA Cloud, essentials edition transition path topic carries an 8 – 12% weightage on the exam. You can expect 6 to 10 questions from these topics.

Key Concepts Refresher

This section will help you understand the implementation methodology by focusing on the SAP S/4HANA Cloud deployment and will advance your abilities to carry out given activities and deliver the desired deliverables. These concepts are critical for you to pass the exam.

Cloud Deployments

Let's look at the options for SAP S/4HANA Cloud: SAP S/4HANA Cloud, essentials edition, and SAP S/4HANA Cloud, extended edition.

Architecture

SAP S/4HANA Cloud, essentials edition architecture means that a single instance of SAP S/4HANA software on a large infrastructure supports multiple numbers of SAP customers. All the customers share the single database, although the data for each customer is isolated from other customer to provide the necessary data security for the clients. Table 7.1 lists the potential benefits and drawbacks of the multitenant architecture.

Benefits	Drawbacks
▪ Lower TCO ▪ No challenges related to infrastructure and database resource requirement ▪ Standardized core ERP and select line of business (LoB) processes ▪ Quarterly innovation cycle ▪ SAP S/4HANA extensibility framework and extensions	▪ Multiple users from other tenants with access to the same database where your data is residing, although they can't access the data ▪ Limited customizations ▪ Possible interference of quarterly update with integration of other software-as-a-service (SaaS) products

Table 7.1 Benefits and Drawbacks of Multitenant Architecture

SAP S/4HANA Cloud, extended edition architecture, on the other hand, allows a single customer to use an instance of SAP on the suited infrastructure. Unlike multitenant, there are no other users from other customers on the same database, which provides better data security. Table 7.2 list the potential benefits and drawbacks of the single-tenant architecture.

Benefits	Drawbacks
▪ Lower TCO, although higher than multitenant environment ▪ Better data security because of dedicated database ▪ High availability of resources and infrastructure ▪ No challenges related to infrastructure and database resource requirement ▪ Standardized core ERP and select LoB processes ▪ Half-yearly innovation cycle ▪ SAP S/4HANA extensibility framework and extensions	▪ Higher maintenance cost ▪ Limited customization, although better than multitenant

Table 7.2 Benefits and Drawbacks of Single-Tenant Architecture

Figure 7.1 shows the two architectures and their salient features.

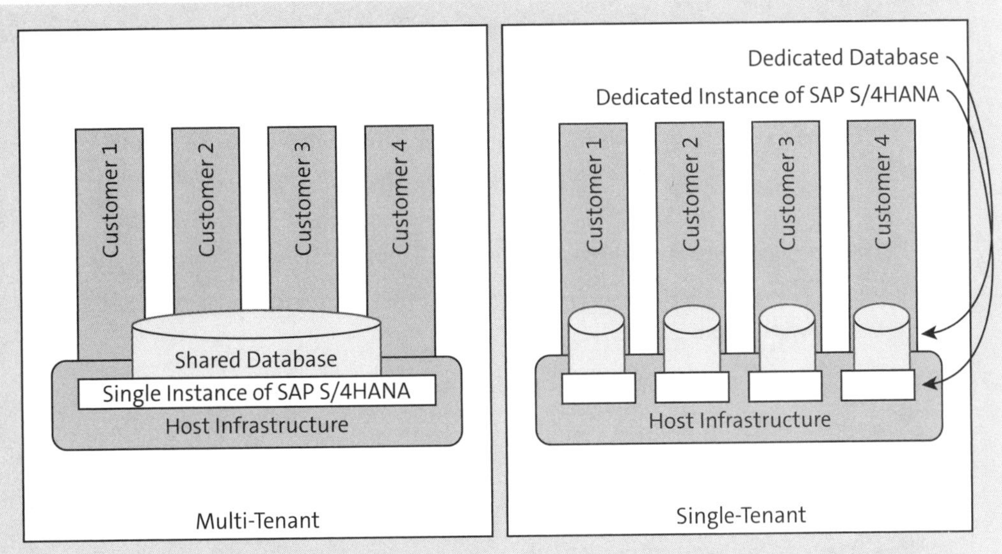

Figure 7.1 Multitenant Architecture versus Single-Tenant Architecture

Comparison

Let's compare the two cloud implementation options with the on-premise implementation. Table 7.3 shows the comparison.

Items	SAP S/4HANA Cloud, Essentials Edition	SAP S/4HANA Cloud, Extended Edition	SAP S/4HANA
TCO	Lowest	Lower	Highest
Customization	Lowest	Lower	Highest
Standardization	Standard core ERP	Extended ERP	Extended ERP
Security	Lowest	Lower	Highest
Implementation options	New implementation with data migration	New implementation	New implementation, system conversion, or selective data transition
Functional area	Standard core ERP with select LoB	Core ERP and extended LoB and industry processes	Core ERP and extended LoB and industry processes
Innovation frequency	Quarterly	Half-yearly with one mandatory consumption	Annual, driven by customer

Table 7.3 Comparison of Multitenant, Single-Tenant, and On-Premise Implementations

Items	SAP S/4HANA Cloud, Essentials Edition	SAP S/4HANA Cloud, Extended Edition	SAP S/4HANA
Governance	SAP driven	SAP + Customer	Customer driven
Benefits	Lowest TCO and fastest return on investment (ROI)	Low TCO and fast ROI	Customer-controlled deployment

Table 7.3 Comparison of Multitenant, Single-Tenant, and On-Premise Implementations (Cont.)

Value Proposition

Briefly, the cloud deployment options have the following benefits:

- Reduce TCO
- Faster time to value
- Better ROI
- Lower IT expenditure

Figure 7.2 shows the value adds of cloud deployments:

- **Lower TCO**
  Cloud deployments have a lower TCO for the following reasons:
  - SAP Best Practices implementation
  - Lower customization
  - Easy maintenance
  - No infrastructure cost
  - Multitenant options
- **Quicker ROI**
  Cloud deployments have a quicker ROI for the following reasons:
  - Shorter implementation cycle
  - Need-based activation
- **Better business agility**
  Cloud deployments have better business agility for the following reasons:
  - Strong integration options
  - Consumes regular innovations quarterly in multitenant environments and half-yearly in single-tenant environments
  - Enhanced value with continuous innovations
- **Stronger governance**
  Cloud deployments have stronger governance for the following reasons:
  - SAP-managed solution
  - Stronger security and enhanced flexibility

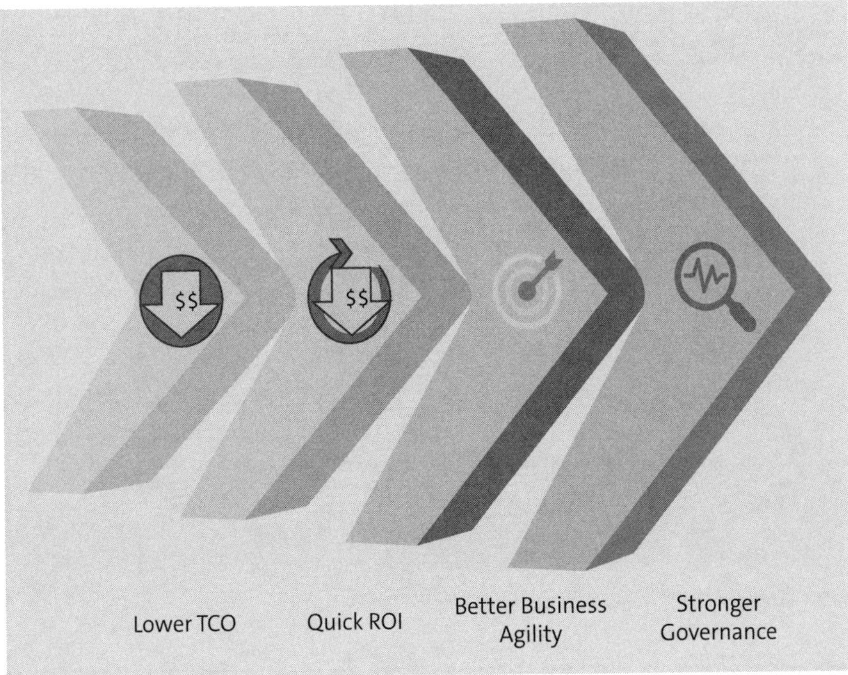

Figure 7.2 Value Proposition

Overview

Figure 7.3 shows the overview of an example new implementation of SAP S/4HANA Cloud, essentials edition. For instance, you currently have a non-SAP system and want to move to SAP S/4HANA Cloud. In a series of joint exercises with SAP and the implementation partner in the discover phase, the leadership decides to implement SAP S/4HANA Cloud, essentials edition.

In the discover phase of the project, you can access the trial system, which is available for a limited period of 14 days at *www.sap.com/cmp/oth/crm-s4hana/index.html*. You can get access for unlimited times every 14 days; however, you can't carry forward any data/configuration from one trial to next. It's important to access and use the trial system, not only for learning but also for impact evaluation and value determination—additional deliverables to help the leadership make the decision.

After the decision is made, your journey to an intelligent ERP moves to the prepare phase. In this phase of the project, the project manager performs many project management activities, including initiation, kick-off, planning, scheduling, and so on. The objective of this phase is to prepare for the project, initial setup and system access, and team enablement. In this phase, the project team also prepares for the fit-to-standard analysis, a key set of activities in the next phase of the project. From the landscape perspective, you receive the starter system where the team will perform the fit-to-standard process.

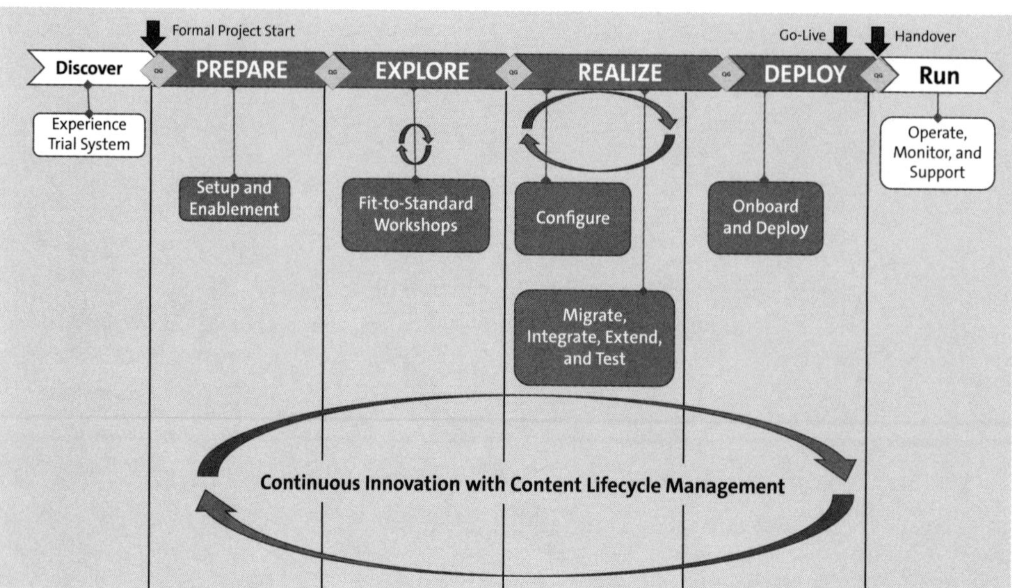

Figure 7.3 Overview

Tip

It's important to remember that in SAP S/4HANA Cloud, essentials edition, the team performs the fit-to-standard analysis in the *starter system*. The starter system isn't your trial system or development environment.

After the quality gate approval, the project progresses to the explore phase where the team completes the fit-to-standard workshops for the activated scope items and creates the product backlog; integration, extension, and analytics design; test planning; learning analysis; and organizational change management (OCM) impact analysis. If you need to migrate the data from your current non-SAP systems, you complete the data migration activities as well. Finally, from the landscape perspective, you request quality assurance (QA) system provisioning from SAP.

Figure 7.4 shows the details of the fit-to-standard process for the new implementation in SAP S/4HANA Cloud, essentials edition. The team shares the business-driven configuration questionnaire, which we discussed in Chapter 5, with the customer, and, based on the answers, the team prepares for the fit-to-standard analysis. Additionally, based on the integration, extension, interface, and analytics requirements, the team will prepare for the starter system readiness. The team carries out the fit-to-standard analysis, as discussed in Chapter 1, and creates the product backlog while the customer is enabling themselves through the learning and the execution of the standard scenarios.

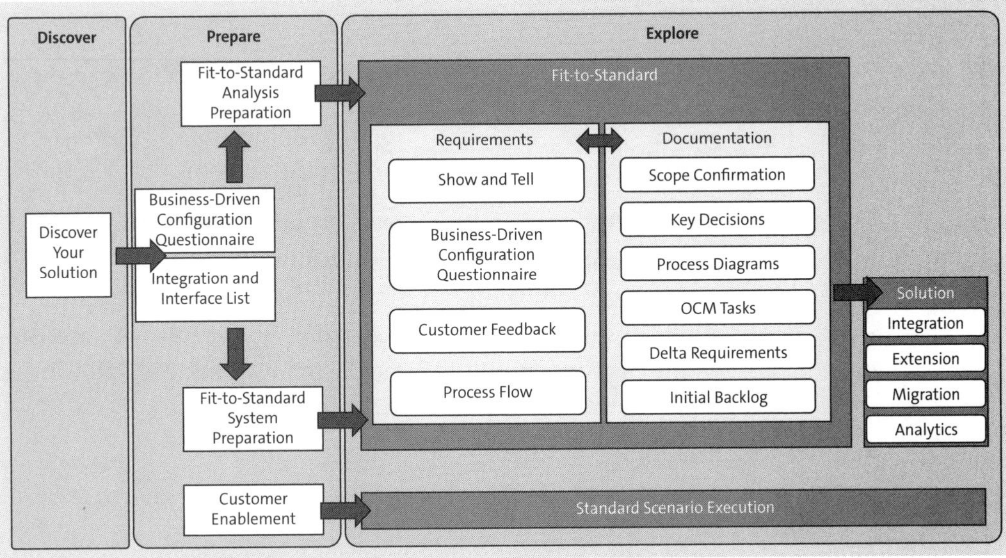

Figure 7.4 Fit-to-Standard Process

After the product backlog is ready, the team enters into the realize phase where they will focus on the configuration, migration, integration, extension, and testing. During this phase, the team will also receive the QA system and request the production (PROD) environment from SAP, which the team will receive toward the end of the phase. The team will also carry out the OCM processes and integrate with the other SAP systems such as SAP Ariba, SAP SuccessFactors, SAP Fieldglass, SAP Concur, and non-SAP systems through the SAP Cloud Platform Integration Suite, as discussed in Chapter 5. Table 7.4 describes the high-level purpose of the three systems available for SAP S/4HANA Cloud, essentials edition.

Starter System	■ Host environment for the fit-to-standard workshop ■ Preconfigured with master data for the selected cloud solution
Quality Assurance (QA) System	■ Acts as a development environment during implementation ■ Acts as a test environment after go-live ■ Quality assurance check during quarterly update process
Production (PROD) System	■ Production environment ■ Automatic quarterly update consumed automatically by customer

Table 7.4 SAP S/4HANA Cloud, Essentials Edition Landscape

Tip

There may be at least one question on the exam about the SAP S/4HANA Cloud, essentials edition landscape. Remember the following:

1. There is *no* separate development environment.
2. During the quarterly update, the QA system will be updated two weeks before the PROD update to allow the customer time to check the added functionalities.
3. Customers must consume the quarterly update from SAP.

SAP S/4HANA Cloud, essentials edition is updated every quarter with the latest innovations, and the customer must consume the innovations. The following is a list of salient points related to the release cycle:

- Upgrades are quarterly.
- All customers must consume the release. They are all on the same release and hotfix package.
- Contents corrections are scheduled on a two-week period and deployed over the weekend during normal downtime.
- Service level for the cloud services are applicable.
- The upgrade schedule is shared at least six weeks in advance.
- Adopt the upgrade cycle in your project plan.

Finally, in the deploy phase, the project team will ensure that there is end-user learning, continue to execute the OCM processes, and execute the production cutover to go live. During the deploy phase of the project, the team will provide the hypercare support and finally hand over the solution to the operate organization to carry out the run phase of the project.

Discover Phase

In the discover phase, although it's not a project phase, the customer will seek to discover the right solution choice. The objective is to ensure that the customer understands the transformation journey and transition path, and then build the strategy and implementation roadmap in partnership with the implementation partner. Figure 7.5 shows the discover phase deliverables.

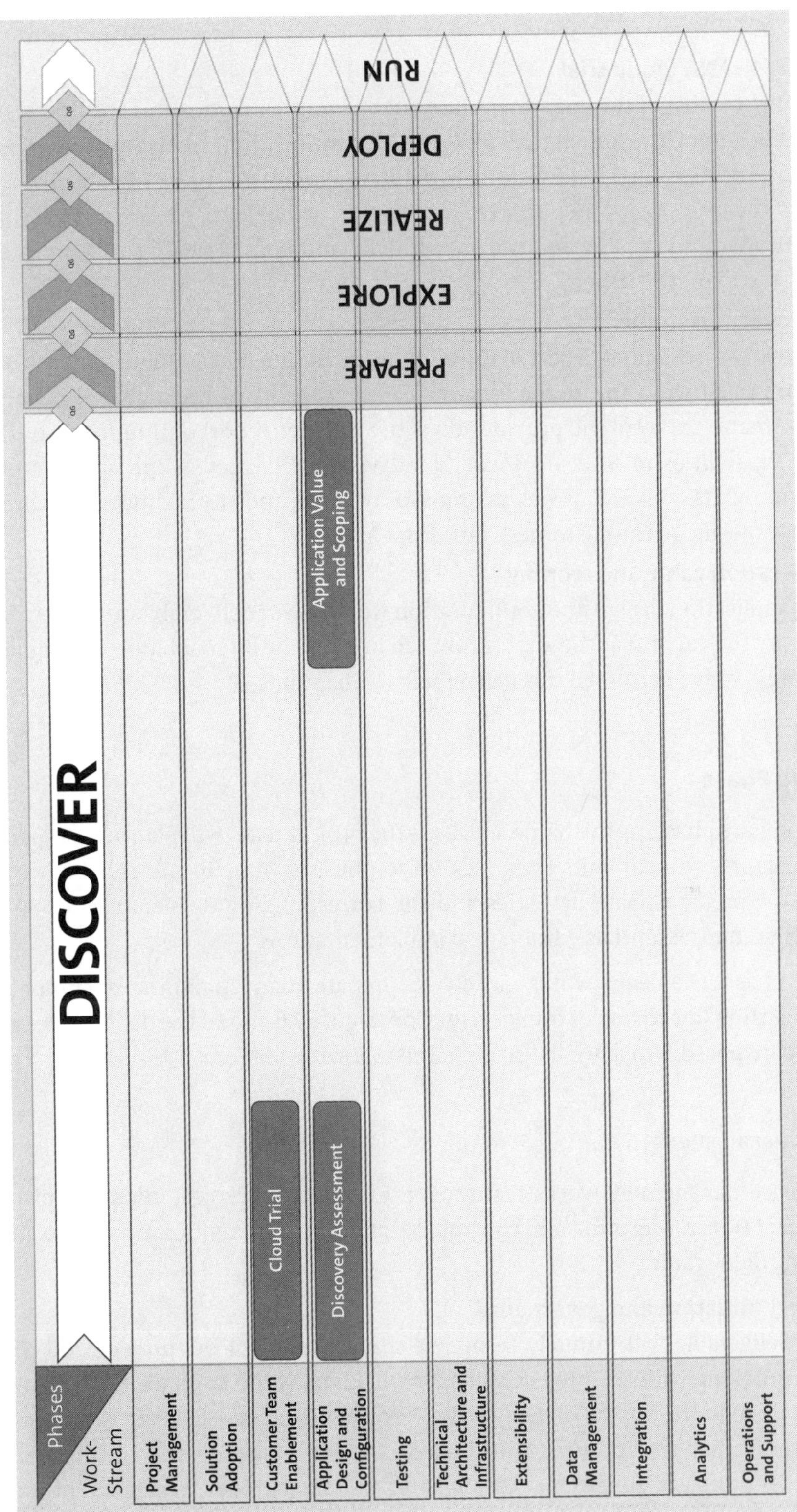

Figure 7.5 Discover Phase Deliverables

Let's review them one by one:

- **SAP S/4HANA Cloud trial**
  This deliverable of the customer team enablement workstream is the first step to understand the intelligent ERP and the innovations that SAP S/4HANA brings. Through this cloud system, you'll start your learning journey and understand the processes. The purpose is to review the business processes that you want for your company and engage with SAP and possibly with a system integrator to explore further.
- **Discovery assessment**
  Discovery assessment is part of the application design and configuration workstream that helps capture the project's initial scope using the digital discovery assessment. This tool will provide you with a detailed report outlining the available capabilities of SAP S/4HANA Cloud vis-à-vis desired scope, integration requirements with SAP as well as non-SAP systems, and any additional requirements specific to the customer's landscape.
- **Application value and scoping**
  This application design and configuration workstream deliverable will help you identify the value that the application can bring, identify roadblocks, and build strategy. We've discussed this deliverable in Chapter 6.

Prepare Phase

In the prepare phase, as the name suggests, the project team will plan and prepare several planning documents from kick-off to phase closure. In this section, we'll review the prepare phase activities and the corresponding deliverables for SAP S/4HANA Cloud, essentials edition new implementations.

In this phase, the team works closely to prepare many planning documents needed during the course of implementation. Figure 7.6 shows the deliverables in the prepare phase, which we'll discuss in the following sections.

Project Management

The project management workstream covers all aspects of project initiation, planning, execution, monitoring and controlling, and closure activities. It includes the following deliverables:

- **Project initiation and governance**
  This deliverable will formally recognize the existence of the project, and the sponsor along with the project manager will identify the key stakeholders and align them to the overall objectives. The project manager will create the project charter, in partnership with the sponsor and key stakeholders, which establishes the project governance and creates the stakeholder management and communication plan. Remember that the communication plan must include

the target audience and who will send the communication via which media, among other details.

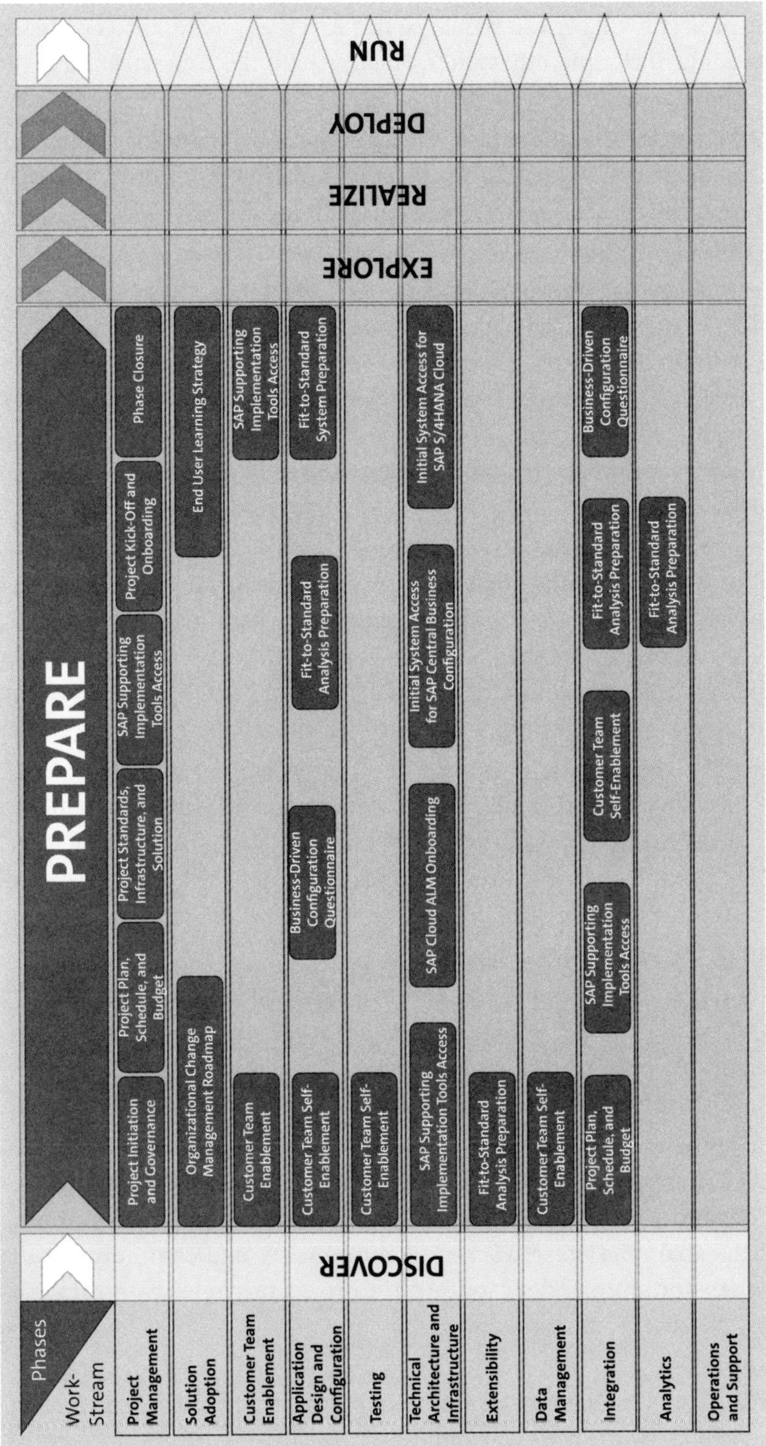

Figure 7.6 Prepare Phase Deliverables

- **Project plans, schedule, and budget**
  Subsequent to the authorization of the project charter, the project manager will refine the business requirements and create the work breakdown structure (WBS). The project manager will sequence the activities and tasks to create the project schedule, including milestones. Finally, the project manager adds the resources to create the project budget.

  It's in this deliverable that the project manager works on additional plans such as the risk management plan, cost management plan, and any other management plans needed for the successful execution of the project.
- **Project standards, infrastructure, and solution**
  The project manager, in partnerships with leads, will create the rules and conventions for several areas such as custom code, requirement management, and so on. In addition, they must identify and set up the infrastructure requirements to execute the project successfully. These requirements include videoconferencing tools and software; conference rooms; licenses for Jira, Microsoft Project, or any other tools; physical security; phones; laptops; Internet access with bandwidth; and so on.
- **SAP supporting implementation tools access**
  In general, the SAP supporting implementation tools access deliverable ensures that the project team has access to all the required tools throughout the project lifecycle. These tools include the Roadmap Viewer, SAP Best Practices, SAP Support Portal, SAP customer communities, and SAP Jam. If members of the team don't have access, then the project manager should get the proper access for those members.

  You'll see this deliverable throughout the prepare phase of the project in four different workstreams—project management, customer team enablement, technical architecture and infrastructure, and integration. Although the overall purpose of this deliverable remains the same, the specific task changes and focus shifts to the related task.

  As a part of this deliverable in the project management workstream, the team will request access to SAP S/4HANA Cloud Release Assessment and Scope Dependency tool, which will allow you to assess the new features and enhancements in the latest release vis-à-vis your solution scope.
- **Project kick-off and onboarding**
  The project manager will schedule the kick-off meeting with the sponsor, key stakeholders, and other L2/L3 stakeholders. The purpose is to advertise the project, share the goals and objective, seek commitments, and communicate the schedule, risks, and any other constraints. The project manager also ensures the onboarding of other team members.
- **Phase closure**
  This deliverable will validate the deliverables prepared and presented throughout the prepare phase to ensure the sign-offs from the customer. After the quality gate, the project is ready to move to the next phase of the project.

Solution Adoption

The solution adoption workstream ensures the high adoptability of the solution within the organization. It includes the following deliverables:

- **Organizational change management (OCM) roadmap**
  This deliverable will ensure that the fine details are appended, such as consistency in the project plan, traceability of the OCM activities, and relationship between each activity to the high-level OCM roadmap created earlier in the discover phase of the project. See the "Discover Phase" section in Chapter 6 for more details. To complete this deliverable, you set up the OCM team, define the roles and responsibilities, and agree on the OCM concepts that include OCM network, stakeholder engagement, communication, organizational transition, learning, change effectiveness, and sustainability.
- **End-user learning strategy**
  This deliverable will develop and implement the best practices for end-user learning. This deliverable will outline the continuous learning approach, scope of knowledge and learning management, current learning culture, current capabilities and capacities, required skill levels, gaps, and fulfillment strategy. This learning strategy is the foundation for effective end-user enablement.

Customer Team Enablement

This workstream enables the key users and administrators to perform their specific duties and includes the following deliverables:

- **SAP supporting implementation tools access**
  As a part of this deliverable in customer team enablement workstream, the focus is on SAP Learning Hub. The task is to ensure that the team has access to SAP Learning Hub—a centralized location that has different learning opportunities and learning rooms.
- **Customer team self-enablement**
  The primary purpose of this deliverable is to enable the customer team in various aspects of the SAP S/4HANA Cloud implementation. This deliverable spans five workstreams—customer team enablement, application design and configuration, testing, data management, and integration.

  In this particular workstream, the deliverable ensures that the customer team understands the different elements of the SAP systems such as getting started tutorials, SAP S/4HANA Cloud learning room, SAP Central Business Configuration, business-to-business (B2B) integration learning, and artificial intelligence (AI) learning using links and materials to the enablement content. Make sure to check the SAP bot store for available bots at *http://s-prs.co/v519420*.

Application Design and Configuration

This workstream ensures the seamless application design and configuration. It includes the following deliverables:

- **Customer team self-enablement**
  Deliverables from the integration, testing, data management, and customer team enablement workstream feed into the customer team self-enablement deliverable in the application design and configuration workstream to ensure that the customer has all necessary access and has learned from these enablement programs.
- **Business-driven configuration questionnaire**
  This deliverable ensures that the project team will get accurate insight into the customer's business processes through the assessment questionnaire and the corresponding answers from the client. The integration-related questions will feed into the overall questionnaire. We've discussed this process in Chapter 5.
- **Fit-to-standard analysis preparation**
  The overall objective of fit-to-standard analysis preparation is to facilitate the fit-to-standard workshops that the team will execute in the explore phase of the project. As a part of the preparation work, the team needs to understand the current scope of work by analyzing the contract and other sources. The team should also keep the SAP Best Practices content available and review the configuration possibilities in conjunction with the scope of work. As a part of preparation, the team should thoroughly understand how to approach fit-to-standard analysis and carry out a couple of dry-run analyses.

  This deliverable, like a few others, is also repeated throughout the prepare phase of the project and spans the application design and configuration, extensibility, integration, and analytics. The deliverable focuses on the specific tasks related to the respective workstreams only.

  In this workstream, the focus is to create the initial application workplace list, which determines the application for each scope item and collects all required applications for the given project scope, from the digital discovery assessment report that was created in the discover phase of the project.
- **Fit-to-standard system preparation**
  This deliverable focuses on the system where the team will perform the fit-to-standard analysis. The starter system comes with standard predelivered master and sample data. However, it's strongly recommended to use the customer's data, such as chart of accounts, materials master, house bank, and so on. Starter system readiness with the client-provided sample data is important and one of the key success factors of the SAP S/4HANA Cloud implementation.

Testing

This workstream covers all aspects of testing the solution and includes the following deliverable:

- **Customer team self-enablement**
  The deliverable in this workstream focuses on self-enabling the test automation tool, which is only available in the QA system, for SAP S/4HANA Cloud.

Technical Architecture and Infrastructure

This workstream covers all aspects of the infrastructure requirements and architecture. It includes the following deliverables:

- **SAP supporting implementation tools access**
  As a part of this deliverable, the team will request access to the SAP S/4HANA Cloud Release Assessment and Scope Dependency tool, which will allow you to assess the new features and enhancements in the latest release vis-à-vis your solution scope.
- **SAP Cloud ALM onboarding**
  The purpose of this deliverable is to request the SAP Cloud ALM tenant, set up the project users, and ensure the proper access. SAP Cloud ALM is a cloud-based ALM offering that will help you manage the intelligent enterprise from implementation to operation.
- **Initial system access for SAP Central Business Configuration**
  SAP Central Business Configuration is yet another tool from SAP that aims to reduce the configuration efforts and provide higher flexibility, faster rollouts, and partner extensions by providing the capability to configure a business process that spans multiple SAP solutions. This deliverable is meant to ensure that the project team has access to SAP Central Business Configuration.
- **Initial system access for SAP S/4HANA Cloud**
  The team is in the prepare phase and will receive the starter system. This deliverable will ensure the execution of the process to set up initial users and complete the initial setup, such as for the local printer and printing queue.

Extensibility

This workstream covers all aspects of the custom code requirement and extensibility features. It includes the following deliverable:

- **Fit-to-standard analysis preparation**
  This deliverable under the extensibility workstream will create a list of application programming interfaces (APIs) and other extensibility requirements from the scope items.

Data Management

This workstream covers all aspects of the master data, transactional data, and data migration activities. It includes the following deliverable:

- **Customer team self-enablement**
  The focus of this deliverable is to ensure that the key users have access to the SAP S/4HANA migration cockpit.

Integration

This workstream covers all aspects of the integration with other SAP or third-party systems and includes the following deliverables:

- **SAP supporting implementation tools access**
  As a part of this deliverable, in the integration workstream, the customer requests access to the Cloud Integration Automation service, a cloud service that allows integrating SAP cloud solutions with other SAP cloud and on-premise solutions.
- **Customer team self-enablement**
  The focus of customer team self-enablement in the integration workstream is to ensure that the project team has self-enabled themselves by accessing and learning how to use the Cloud Integration Automation service, open connectors on SAP Cloud Platform, B2B integrations using electronic data interchange (EDI), and AI.
- **Project plan, schedule, and budget**
  This particular deliverable in the integration workstream caters to the Project Management Institute (PMI) knowledge area of project integration management where the project management team aligns the project schedule based on some key project deliverables, such as landscape provisioning, testing, system operations, key dates, and so on.
- **Business-driven configuration questionnaire**
  In this particular workstream, the team reviews the questions specific to the integration activities, such as source and target details, integrating third-party business process, and so on. Note that the team focuses only on the questions in this workstream. The customer provides answers to these questions in the application design and configuration workstream. The complete process related to the business process configuration questionnaire is discussed in Chapter 5.
- **Fit-to-standard analysis preparation**
  This deliverable under the integration workstream will create initial integration and API lists and other known integrations such as third-party and B2B from all sources. The team also works on the integration requirements for AI and creates the list.

Analytics

This workstream covers all aspects of the analytics and includes the following deliverable:

- **Fit-to-standard analysis preparation**
  This deliverable under the analytics workstream focuses on creating the initial analytics list by downloading the template from the Roadmap Viewer and distributing it to the proposed participants of the workshops.

Explore Phase

During this phase of the project, the team performs the fit-to-standard analysis and prepares the product backlog. All the planning is done during the prepare phase, and the customer has signed off on the phase. In the explore phase, the team will focus on the requirements. Figure 7.7 shows the deliverables in the explore phase of the project, which we'll discuss in the following sections.

Project Management

The project management workstream covers all aspects of project initiation, planning, execution, monitoring and controlling, and closure activities. It includes the following deliverables:

- **Execution/monitoring of project**
  This deliverable ensures the seamless execution of the project per the approved plan; continuous monitoring of the project, including risks and issues; regular updates to the planning documents; change management; and constant communication.
- **Phase closure and sign-off phase deliverables**
  This deliverable checks and validates for the timely and quality deliverables, signifying the completion of the explore phase of the project. The team can move on to the next phase by completing the quality gate.

Solution Adoption

The solution adoption workstream ensures the high adoptability of the solution within the organization and includes the following deliverables:

- **End-user learning needs analysis and plan**
  The objective of this deliverable is to understand the end-user's training needs and gaps based on the as-is and to-be business processes and develop the training plan.

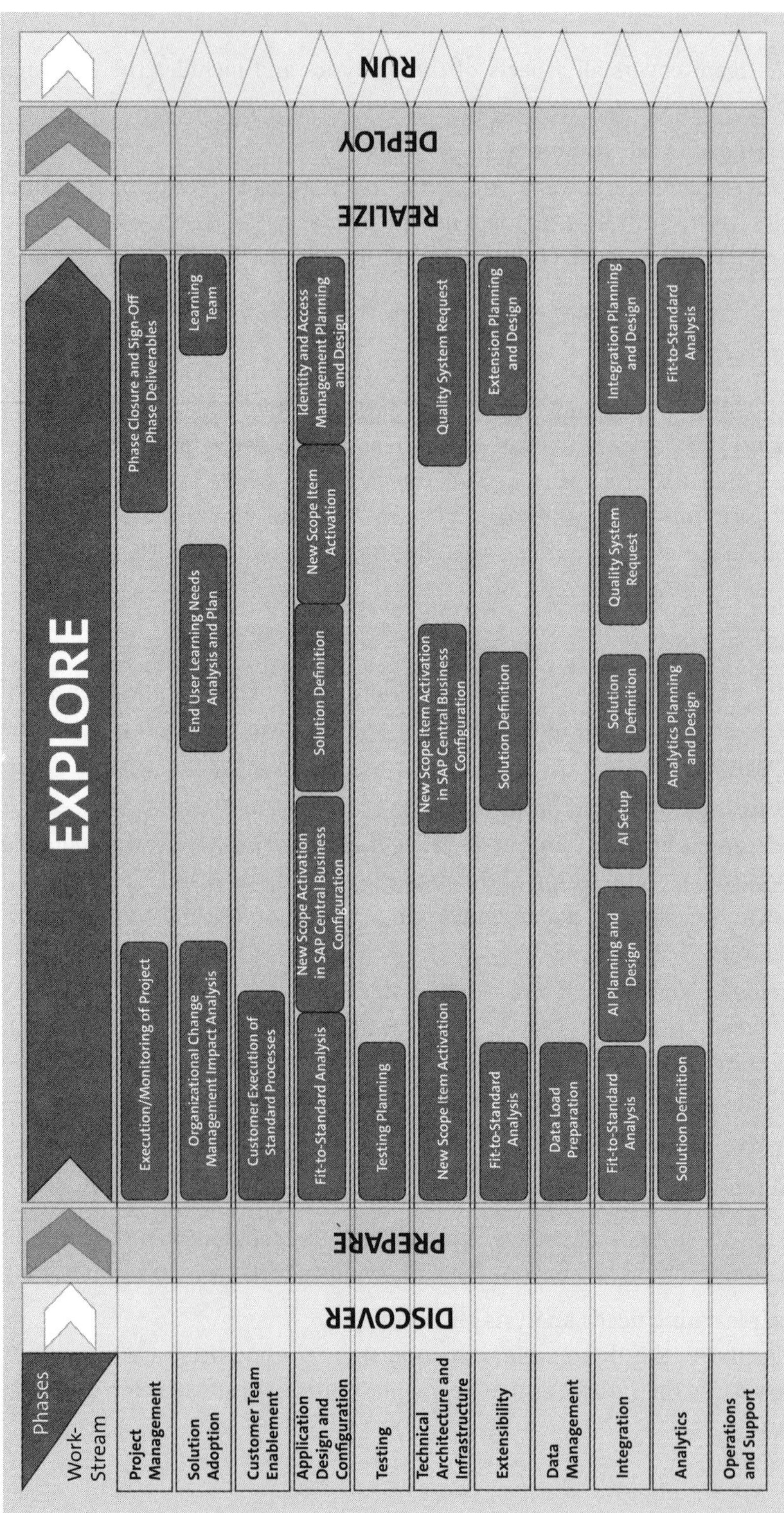

Figure 7.7 Explore Phase Deliverables

- **OCM impact analysis**
  To create this deliverable, the team analyzes the change impact, stakeholder and communication needs, and learning requirements, and then creates the OCM activities. The deliverable ensures that the OCM steps and processes are documented properly. The team should create as-is and to-be business processes and demonstrate the comparison for a better understanding of the change.
- **Learning team**
  The objective of this deliverable is to prepare the necessary training content, including any documentation, PowerPoint presentations, training environments, and so on. A mobilization workshop is conducted to ensure the understanding of the timeline, objective, next steps, and other fundamental information while the development workshop ensures that the team creates quickly digestible learning content—probably interactive, definitely creative—to ensure all-around learning.

Customer Team Enablement

This workstream enables the key users and administrators to perform their specific duties and includes the following deliverable:

- **Customer execution of standard processes**
  The starter system delivers the standard processes; this deliverable ensures that the customer's business subject matter expert (SME) must execute the standard process before they come to the fit-to-standard analysis. The objective is to ensure that they understand the differences and similarities between the standard processes and their business processes.

Application Design and Configuration

This workstream ensures the seamless application design and configuration. It includes the following deliverables:

- **Fit-to-standard analysis**
  The team performs the fit-to-standard analysis to understand the fit of SAP Best Practices with the customer's business processes and identify the gaps between them, if any. The delta requirements, which can fill these gaps, are identified, discussed, and appended to the product backlog.

  The work on this deliverable starts by scheduling the workshops; remember, all preparation work is complete in the prepare phase of the project. Chart of accounts and organizational structure are the first two workshops that the team should conduct—the team will complete the configuration work for the chart of accounts and organizational structure in the foundation sprint. Depending on the scope of work, the team will conduct different workshops, such as for finance, manufacturing, sales, human resources, or any other business function.

This deliverable spans application design and configuration, extensibility, integration, and analytics workstreams. See Chapter 1 for more information about fit-to-standard analysis.

- **Solution definition**
  In Figure 7.4, you saw that the team defines the solution after the fit-to-standard process. During the fit-to-standard processes, the business will provide requirements for integration, extension, identity and access, and many others. The general purpose of this deliverable is to document all such requirements that define and further form the basis of the solution and also include defining the master data requirements, and configuration values, including expert configuration, analytics requirements, and others.

  This deliverable requires the team to execute tasks in extensibility, integration, and analytics workstreams that will feed into the application design and configuration workstream. The team starts by documenting initial configuration requirements such as fiscal year, chart of accounts, organizational structure, and so on for SAP Central Business Configuration. The team should document every requirement, including master data, analytics, integration, identity and access management, and more. The team should also document any need for expert configuration. One important activity to ensure the correct solution definition is to confirm the product backlog created as a part of the fit-to-standard process.

- **Identity and access management planning and design**
  The objective of this deliverable is to ensure the right setup of the roles and authorizations to meet customer requirements. The authorization concept should be based on correctness, completeness, confirmability, variability, availability, and protection from misuse and manipulation.

- **New scope item activation in SAP Central Business Configuration**
  This deliverable is applicable to customers with SAP Central Business Configuration, and the general purpose of this deliverable is to activate the new solution scope in the starter system and QA system using SAP Central Business Configuration, especially for the quarterly update during the project lifecycle. This deliverable spans two workstreams—the application design and configuration workstream and the technical architecture and infrastructure workstream.

  The deliverable in this workstream focuses on ensuring that new country requirements are consistent with existing cross-country configuration, exchange rate setup, and requests for new country scopes, if needed.

- **New scope item activation**
  This deliverable is different from the new scope activation in SAP Central Business Configuration because of its applicability to all customers and the exclusion of the country/region extension. However, the purpose of this deliverable remains the same as that of the new scope to ensure that the new scope items

are activated, if needed, due to the quarterly release during the project lifecycle. This deliverable also spans two workstreams—the application design and configuration workstream and the technical architecture and infrastructure workstream.

The deliverable in this workstream focuses on reviewing and activating the new and required scope items.

Testing

This workstream covers all aspects of testing the solution and includes the following deliverable:

- **Test planning**
  The objective of this deliverable is to build a complete test strategy for the solution, including test approach and methodology, test standards and guidelines, test case development, defect management, reporting and analysis, roles and responsibilities, functional testing (unit, string, integration, scenario, user acceptance, regression, etc.), and performance testing.

Technical Architecture and Infrastructure

This workstream covers all aspects of the infrastructure requirements and the architecture. It includes the following deliverables:

- **New scope activation in SAP Central Business Configuration**
  In this workstream, the objective of this deliverable is to adopt the addition of business catalogs and business roles resulting from the new scope activation or quarterly update. This is applicable to customers using SAP Central Business Configuration.
- **New scope item activation**
  As mentioned earlier in this chapter, the project team should consider the quarterly update while planning the project. It's common that at least one quarterly update will fall during the implementation phase, and the project team should be able to consume the added scope items from the latest release. The deliverable is necessary to activate any such added scope items in the QA system. The project team should also consider the overall impact on the project schedule, cost, and other metrics while adding these additional scope items, if any.

  The objective in this workstream is to adopt the addition of business catalogs and business roles resulting from the new scope activation or quarterly update. This is applicable to the customers who aren't using SAP Central Business Configuration.
- **QA system request**
  A request form must be filled by the project manager and submitted to SAP for the QA system provisioning. To get timely access during the realize phase, the

team must complete the request as prescribed by SAP. Another aspect of this deliverable is part of the integration workstream, which will be explained subsequently.

Extensibility

This workstream covers all aspects of the custom code requirement and extensibility features and includes the following deliverables:

- **Fit-to-standard analysis**
  It's the same as that of the application design and configuration workstream; however, any extensibility related options are also considered here per the extension planning and design explained subsequently.
- **Solution definition**
  This particular deliverable is specific to the extension requirements, meaning it will define and document the solution from an extensibility perspective. This deliverable will feed into the solution definition deliverable within the application design and configuration workstream.
- **Extension planning and design**
  This deliverable ensures that gaps, if any, identified during the fit-to-standard process can (or can't) be fulfilled by the business process extensions. The steps are as follows:
  - Complete the requirement for extension from fit-to-standard and hand it over to the developer.
  - Collect the extension details.
  - Check for any available apps (in SAP App Center) or solutions (in the SAP solution store).
  - Design side-by-side extensibility.
  - Review the information, including estimates, and get the customer's sign-off.

Data Management

This workstream covers all aspects of the master data, transactional data, and data migration activities. It includes the following deliverable:

- **Data load preparation**
  For the multitenant environment, you can download the data load templates from SAP Best Practices, and the cleansed data should be provided in the specified template to load on the cloud environment.

Integration

This workstream covers all aspects of the integration with other SAP or third-party systems and includes the following deliverables:

- **Fit-to-standard analysis**
  This is similar to the application design and configuration workstream, but with a focus on integration options. Any integration-related options are considered here per the integration planning and design as explained in this list.
- **Solution definition**
  This particular deliverable is specific to the integration requirements, meaning it will define the solution from an integration perspective. This deliverable will feed into the solution definition deliverable within the application design and configuration workstream.
- **Integration planning and design**
  This deliverable ensures that gaps, if any, identified during the fit-to-standard process can (or can't) be fulfilled by the business process extensions. The steps are as follows:
  - Complete the requirement for integration, and hand it over to the expert.
  - Determine the integration scenario options.
  - Optimize and align the integration scenario.
  - Determine the details for customer-driven integration.
  - Review the information, including estimates, and get the customer's sign-off.
- **AI planning and design**
  The purpose of this deliverable is to start the planning activities for the AI requirements, including robotic process automation (RPA) and machine learning.
- **AI setup**
  The setup process will ensure the team installs the RPA components.
- **QA system request**
  The request for the QA system provisioning is made in the technical architecture and infrastructure workstream. However, in this workstream, this deliverable focuses on integration with SAP SuccessFactors Employee Central.

Analytics

This workstream covers all aspects of the analytics and includes the following deliverables:

- **Fit-to-standard analysis**
  The general purpose for this deliverable is explained in the application design and configuration workstream. Additionally, if the team identifies any analytics

requirements, then the team should perform the fit-to-standard analysis for the analytics scope item.

- **Solution definition**
  This deliverable will identify any requirements related to the analytics and document them in the solution definition.
- **Analytics planning and design**
  The objective of this deliverable is to plan and design any analytics-related requirements captured in the solution definition.

Realize Phase

The purpose of this phase is to realize the build incrementally and iteratively based on the business requirements and scenarios identified during the previous phases of the project. During the realize phase of the project, the team will build and test the business and system environment based on the fit-to-standard analysis. In addition, during this phase, legacy data load starts, solution adoption continues, and operation planning happens. Figure 7.8 shows the deliverables in the realize phase, which we'll discuss in the following sections.

Project Management

The project management workstream covers all aspects of project initiation, planning, execution, monitoring and controlling, and closure activities. It includes the following deliverables:

- **Execution/monitoring of project**
  This deliverable ensures the seamless execution of the project per the approved plan; continuous monitoring of the project, including risks and issues; regular updates to the planning documents; change management; and constant communication.
- **Phase closure and sign-off phase deliverables**
  This deliverable ensures the timely and quality deliverables are checked and validated, signifying the completion of the explore phase of the project. The team can move on to the next phase by completing the quality gate.

Solution Adoption

The solution adoption workstream ensures the high adoptability of the solution within the organization and includes the following deliverables:

- **OCM alignment activities**
  The purpose of this deliverable is to identify any further OCM activities related to the OCM execution. To complete this deliverable, the OCM team will execute and monitor the activities related to the stakeholder and communication plan, organizational transition plan, and post go-live OCM activities.

- **Learning content**
  The objective of this deliverable is to assess and develop the learning materials on the SAP products and business solutions, as well as equip trainers to conduct the training sessions to deliver the learning contents to the customer.

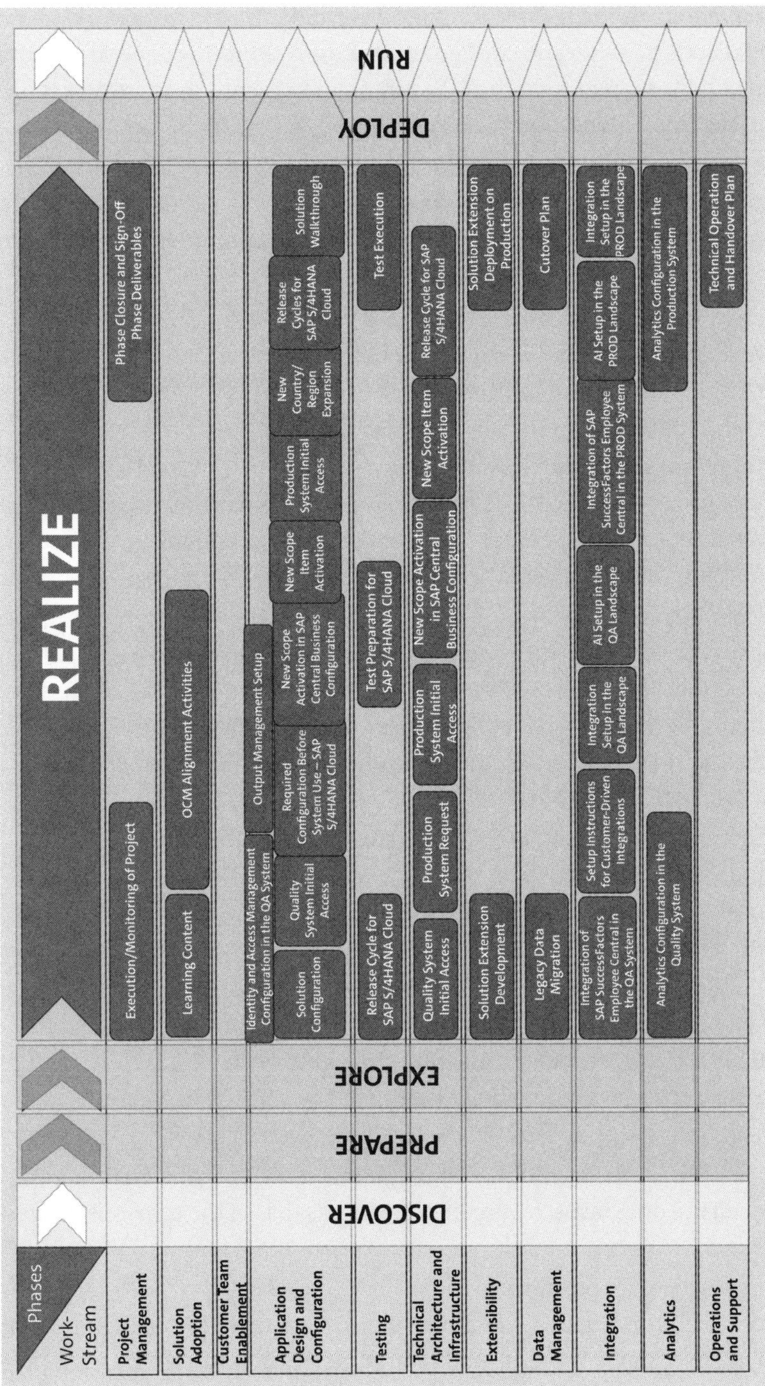

Figure 7.8 Realize Phase Deliverables

Application Design and Configuration

This workstream ensure the seamless application design and configuration. It includes the following deliverables:

- **QA system initial access**
  This deliverable spans the technical architecture and infrastructure workstream and the application design and configuration workstream. The general purpose of this deliverable is to receive the QA system and prepare the system for further use in the implementation.
  In this workstream, however, the focus is to adopt the chart of accounts, developed in the explore phase, in the QA system. Remember that for SAP S/4HANA Cloud, essentials edition, the QA system acts as a development environment during implementation.
- **PROD system initial access**
  This deliverable is to ensure that the team has initial access to the PROD system. This deliverable has more significance in the technical architecture and infrastructure workstream.
- **Required configuration before system use – SAP S/4HANA Cloud**
  The purpose of this deliverable is to configure the initial functionalities that include tax solution, profit center, cost center master data, takeover date for asset accounting, and fiscal year variant.
- **Solution configuration**
  The purpose is to configure the requirements identified in the scope validation workshops and listed in the product backlog across all scope areas, create sample data, and unit test the business processes based on the sample data. In this deliverable, the team is building the solution on the QA system based on the identified solution and product backlog.
- **New scope item activation in SAP Central Business Configuration**
  In the explore phase, we activated the scope item in SAP Central Business Configuration, documented the requirements of additional scope items during fit-to-standard processes, and updated the product log. Now, in the realize phase, we're configuring the same based on the updated product log.
  The deliverable in this workstream focuses on ensuring that new country requirements are consistent with existing cross-country configuration and the exchange rate setup, and requesting a new country scope, if needed.
- **New scope item activation**
  This is applicable for the customers who don't have SAP Central Business Configuration. All the other aspects remain the same as that of the previous deliverable.
- **New country/region expansion**
  This deliverable is to include the scope items for the additional country or regions. The first step is to verify the requirement, then set up the exchange

rate, and finally to extend the solution in the QA system to include the new country/region and the related base configuration.

- **Release cycles for SAP S/4HANA Cloud**
  We understood that there would be at least one quarterly update cycle during the implementation project lifecycle. SAP provides these innovations in the QA system two weeks prior to the production upgrade. The focus of this deliverable is to synchronize the PROD system with the QA system by releasing the change projects and transporting via the adaptation transport organizer (ATO). The team should complete this process prior to the quarterly upgrade process.
- **Identity and access management configuration in the QA system**
  Based on the segregation of duties (SoDs), this deliverable focuses on the rightful access to the users. The project team creates and tests the business roles in the QA system.
- **Output management setup**
  Printers, emails, forms, and so on are the examples of different output media available to the users of SAP S/4HANA Cloud, essentials edition. This deliverable ensures that the outputs are configured in the QA system.
- **Solution walkthrough**
  Through the iterative process, this deliverable ensures that the project team completes the walkthrough of the solution for each process across the business and gets the business feedback and necessary approvals.

Testing

This workstream covers all aspects of testing the solution and includes the following deliverables:

- **Release cycle for SAP S/4HANA Cloud**
  The focus of this deliverable is to complete the regression test in the QA system and ensure that the functionality works as expected after the quarterly release.
- **Test preparation for SAP S/4HANA Cloud**
  In this deliverable, the team prepares to test the end-to-end solution with the customer. The preparation includes defining the test cases, test scripts, and relevant test data. The team also creates an elaborate plan, including the resource requirements, timeline, and any contingencies.
- **Test execution**
  The team executes the plan in an iterative fashion and fixes any issues noticed during the testing. The team should also monitor the progress, take corrective actions if needed, and report the status to the stakeholders.

Technical Architecture and Infrastructure

This workstream covers all aspects of the infrastructure requirements and the architecture. We've reviewed the purpose of these deliverables in the previous sections:

- **QA system initial access**
  This deliverable ensures that the team received the QA system system and created the users along with other tasks.
- **PROD system request**
  By virtue of this deliverable, the team is requesting that SAP provision the PROD system. After the PROD system is available, the configurations between the PROD and the QA systems are synchronized using a change project and sprints.
- **PROD system initial access**
  This deliverable ensures that the team received the PROD system and created the users along with other tasks. In addition, the team also transports the initial change project from the QA system to the PROD system.
- **New scope item activation in SAP Central Business Configuration**
  This deliverable is applicable to the customers with SAP Central Business Configuration. The purpose of this deliverable in this workstream is to adapt the existing business catalog and roles resulting from new scope or quarterly update.
- **New scope item activation**
  This is a similar deliverable to the preceding, except that it's applicable to the customers who don't have SAP Central Business Configuration.
- **Release cycle for SAP S/4HANA Cloud**
  The purpose in this workstream is to ensure the proper preparation to consume the quarterly upgrade, evaluate the functionalities in the QA system, and revise business roles and catalog due to the upgrade.

Extensibility

This workstream covers all aspects of the custom code requirement and extensibility features. It includes the following deliverables:

- **Solution extension development**
  The purpose of this deliverable is to realize the extensions to the solution by extending user interfaces; adding fields, business objects, and business logic; and adapting UIs according to the customer requirements. Additionally, the team transports the extension from the QA system to the PROD system.
- **Solution extension deployment on production**
  This deliverable will ensure the solution deployment on the PROD environment.

Data Management

This workstream covers all aspects of the master data, transactional data, and data migration activities. It includes the following deliverables:

- **Legacy data migration**
  The objective of this deliverable is to ensure the successful migration of the legacy data. To achieve the objective, the team needs to validate the data load based on the data received from the customer in the specified format shared with the customer during the explore phase of the project. The project team will identify any issues in the data load process and work closely with the customer to resolve the issues. Finally, after resolving all the known issues, the team will conduct the quality assessment of the data, report the key findings to the stakeholders, and load the data in the PROD environment after receiving all the requisite approvals.
- **Cutover plan**
  The deliverable documents the cutover activities that the team will execute subsequently. The plan must include the detailed timeline, activities (e.g., production system initialization, interface connections, data migrations, user ID creations, communications, decommissioning legacy system and other tasks), status, owner and prerequisites of each task, and any known constraints to move the system from an as-is to a to-be solution.

Integration

This workstream covers all aspects of the integration with other SAP or third-party systems. In the previous sections, we've seen the purpose of these deliverables, which we'll review here as well:

- **Integration of Employee Central in the QA system**
  The purpose of this deliverable is to set up Employee Central integration in the QA system.
- **Setup instruction for customer-driven integrations**
  For this deliverable, the team creates a detailed instruction for customer-driven integration.
- **Integration setup in the QA landscape**
  The project team performs any integration-related setup required in the QA system and deliver the QA system landscape. The project team will create the integration mapping, perform the integration setup, perform the integration setup in the on-premise system, and finally execute the initial data load.
- **AI setup in QA landscape**
  The purpose of this deliverable is to set up available RPA bots in the QA system.

- **Integration of Employee Central in the PROD system**
  The purpose of this deliverable is to set up Employee Central integration in the PROD system.
- **Integration setup in the PROD landscape**
  The project team performs any integration-related setup required in the PROD system. Alternatively, you can include it in the cutover list. The project team will create the integration mapping, perform the integration setup, perform the integration setup in the on-premise system, and finally execute the initial data load.
- **AI setup in PROD landscape**
  The purpose of this deliverable is to set up available RPA bots in the PROD system.

Analytics

This workstream covers all aspects of analytics and includes the following deliverables:

- **Analytics configuration in the QA system**
  The purpose of this deliverable is to configure analytics in the QA system.
- **Analytics configuration in the PROD landscape**
  The purpose of this deliverable is to configure analytics in the PROD system.

Operations and Support

This workstream covers all aspects of the operation and support post-hypercare. It includes the following deliverable:

- **Technical operation and handover plan**
  This planning deliverable is to ensure the creation of the handover plan to the run organization and then continuous technical operation of the solution.

Deploy Phase

In the deploy phase of the project, the business switches the operation to the new PROD environment. This is the final phase of the project where the "rubber meets the road." The team will close all the open issues, ensure the organizational readiness, and execute the production cutover so that the business can realize the benefits of the newly implemented solution. Figure 7.9 shows the deliverables in the deploy phase of the project, which we'll discuss in the following sections.

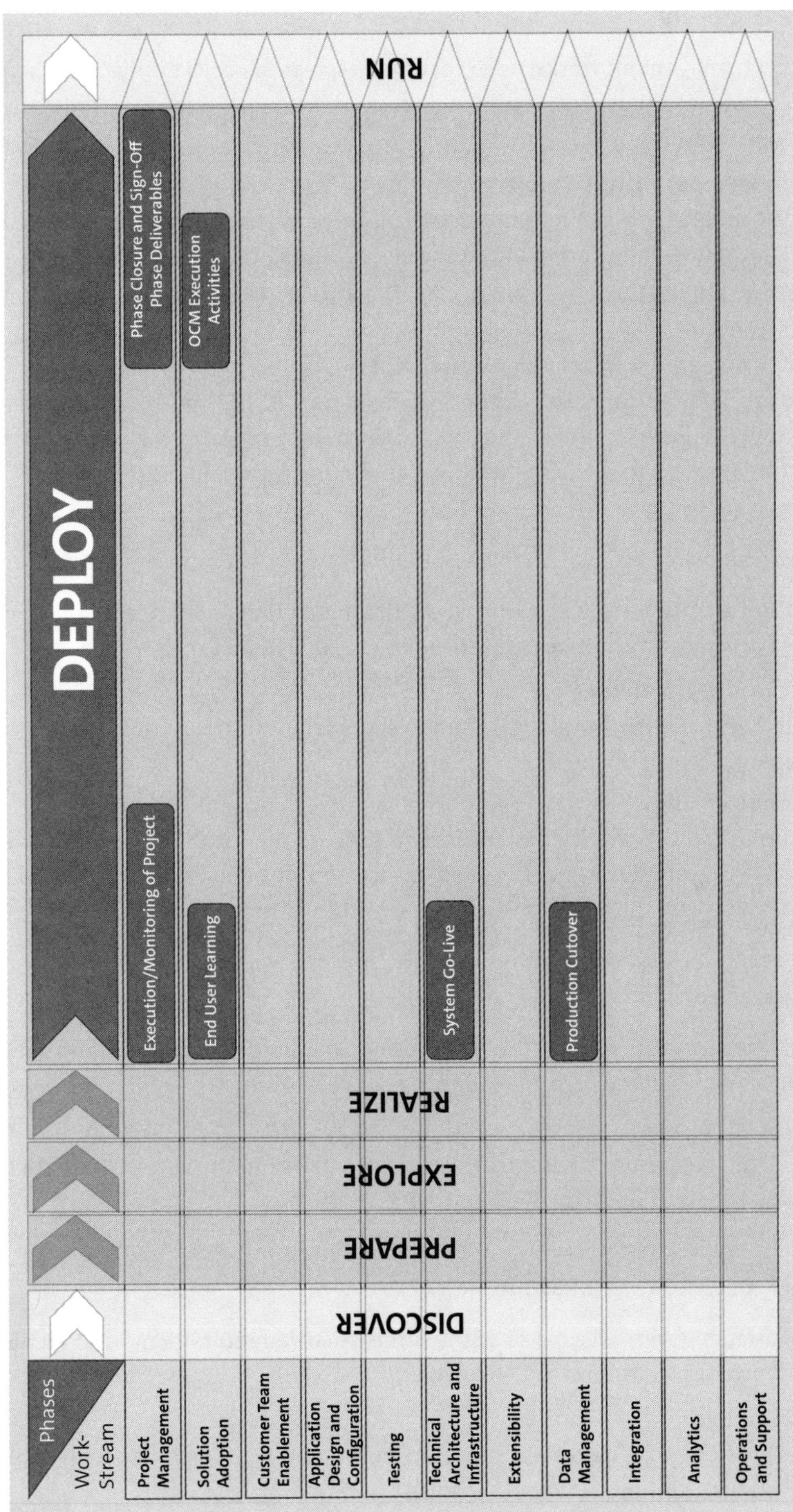

Figure 7.9 Deploy Phase Deliverables

Project Management

The project management workstream covers all aspects of project initiation, planning, execution, monitoring and controlling, and closure activities. It includes the following deliverables:

- **Execution/monitoring of project**
  This deliverable ensures the seamless execution of the project per the approved plan; continuous monitoring of the project, including risks and issues; regular updates to the planning documents; change management; and constant communication.
- **Phase closure and sign-off phase deliverables**
  This deliverable ensures the check and validation of the timely and quality deliverables, signifying the completion of the deploy phase of the project. The team can move on to the next phase by completing the quality gate.

Solution Adoption

The solution adoption workstream ensures the high adoptability of the solution within the organization and includes the following deliverables:

- **OCM execution activities**
  This deliverable ensures that the team executes the OCM activities specific to the deploy phase of the project.
- **End-user learning**
  The purpose of the end-user learning is to execute the learning plan that was developed earlier for the end users and ensures that the end users have the necessary skills to get the benefits from the newly implemented solution.

Data Management

This workstream covers all aspects of the master data, transactional data, and data migration activities. It includes the following deliverable:

- **Production cutover**
  This deliverable ensures that the project team carries out the cutover activities and takes the solution to the PROD system.

Technical Architecture and Infrastructure

This workstream covers all aspects of the infrastructure requirements and architecture. It includes the following deliverable:

- **System go-live**
  This is where all your hard work comes to fruition by marking the system with a "run" status, notifying SAP that the PROD system is in use.

Run Phase

This phase starts after the hypercare, during the previous phase of the project, to optimize the overall operation. During this phase, the support is provided by the customer IT team, which continues to strive for optimization, automate the application processes, ensure system availability, and provide system performance. Figure 7.10 shows the deliverables in the run phase of the project, which we'll discuss in the following sections.

Solution Adoption

The solution adoption workstream ensures the high adoptability of the solution within the organization and includes the following deliverables:

- **OCM activities**
  This deliverable focuses on the continuous improvement of organizational efficiency by expanding the use of solution through continuous adoption of the new system functionality.
- **Continuous learning**
  This deliverable will ensure the continuous monitoring of the end users, their skills, and the learning path to ensure that the training contents are up to date as well as the end user's skillsets. The deliverable spans solution adoption, customer team enablement, and operations and support throughout the run phase of the project.

Customer Team Enablement

This workstream enables the key users and administrators to perform their specific duties and includes the following deliverables:

- **Continuous learning**
  This deliverable focuses on the efficient system usages after the training and updates the training materials as needed.
- **SAP Trust Center**
  The purpose of this deliverable is to use SAP Trust Center services, such as cloud service status, security, data protection and privacy, compliance, and agreement.
- **SAP support services for SAP S/4HANA Cloud**
  SAP provides basic cloud support post go-live with the subscription. The purpose of this deliverable is to keep yourself up to date with the four dimensions of SAP Enterprise Support.

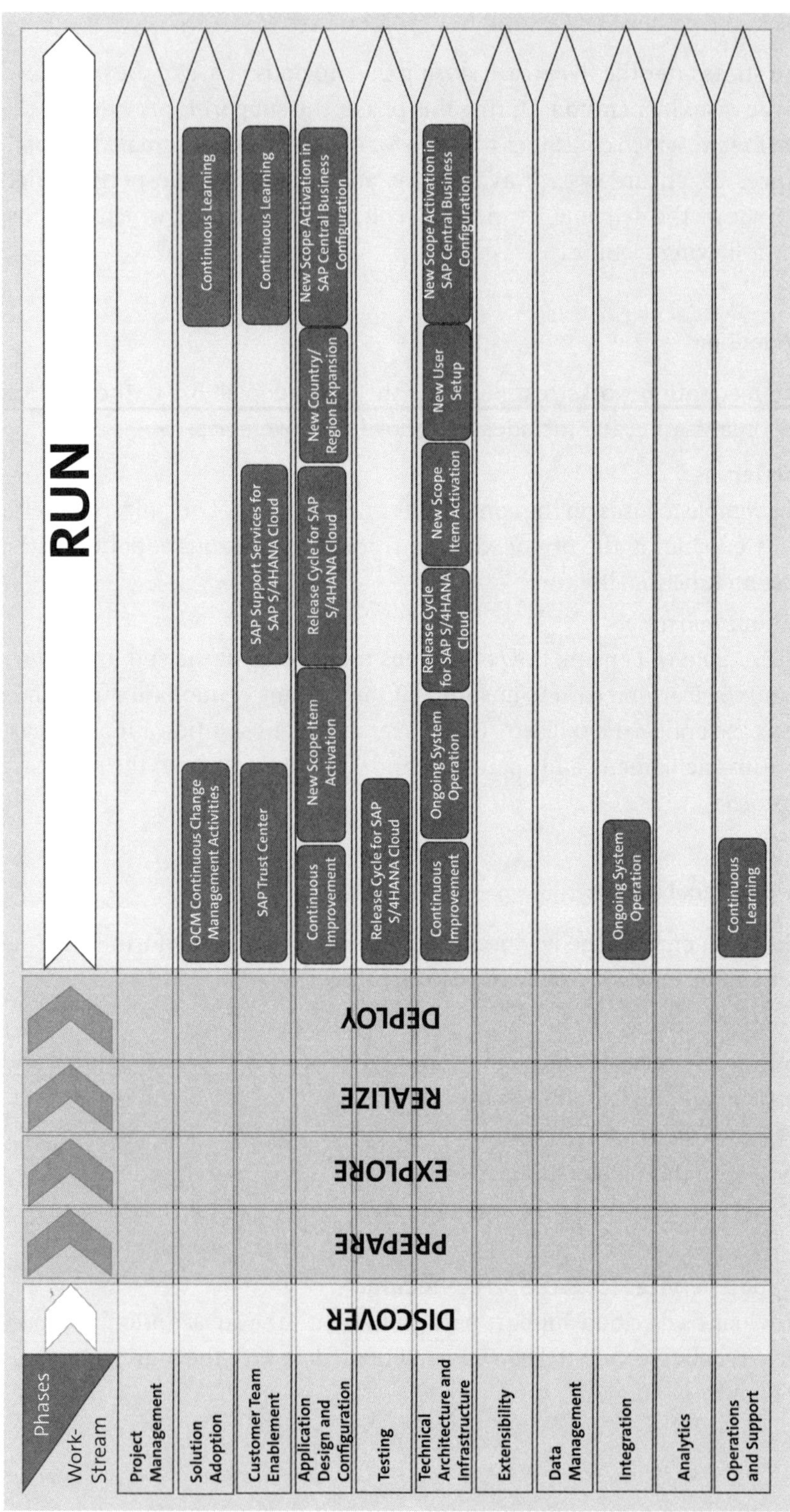

Figure 7.10 Run Phase Deliverables

Application Design and Configuration

This workstream ensures the seamless application design and configuration. We've reviewed the details and the purpose of the following deliverables that are also relevant in the run phase:

- Continuous improvement
- Release cycle for SAP S/4HANA Cloud
- New scope activation in SAP Central Business Configuration
- New scope item activation
- New country/region expansion

Testing

This workstream covers all aspects of testing the solution and includes the following deliverable:

- **Release cycle for SAP S/4HANA Cloud**
  We've reviewed this deliverable previously and understand its general purpose. Specific to this workstream, the deliverable ensures that all the necessary testing is completed for the new scope items post quarterly update, including the regression testing for the existing functionalities.

Technical Architecture and Infrastructure

This workstream covers all aspects of the infrastructure requirements and architecture. Throughout the solution operation, the team needs to ensure the effectiveness, work through to improve the operational excellence, consume the quarterly updates with new functionalities, and add/change the users. We've reviewed the details and the purpose of the following deliverables that are also relevant in the run phase:

- Ongoing system operations
- Continuous improvement
- Release cycle for SAP S/4HANA Cloud
- New scope activation in SAP Central Business Configuration
- New scope item activation
- New user setup

Integration

This workstream covers all aspects of the integration with other SAP or third-party systems and includes the following deliverable:

- **Ongoing system operations**
  This deliverable focuses on the integration aspect of system operations.

Operations and Support

This workstream covers all aspects of the operation and support post hypercare. It includes the following deliverable:

- **Continuous learning**
  As a part of continuous learning, it's recommended that the customer participates in the SAP S/4HANA Cloud customer community, which can be accessed at *https://s4hanacloud.community.sap/home*.

Important Terminology

For this exam objective, you're expected to understand the following terms:

- **Digital discovery assessment tool**
  Digital discovery assessment is a tool that captures the project's initial scope in the discover phase of the project.
- **Multitenant architecture**
  In this cloud architecture, many customers share the same cloud infrastructure and database but have different environments.
- **PROD system**
  This is the production system where the solution is running for the production purpose, and end users will use the system for their business purpose.
- **QA system**
  This is the quality assurance system where the project team will make configurations initially and then test any changes, including quarterly updates, before moving the changes to the PROD system.
- **SAP Central Business Configuration**
  This new cloud-based tool will help you configure a business that spans multiple SAP solutions.
- **SAP Cloud ALM**
  This is another cloud-based tool that will help you manage the intelligent enterprise from implementation to operation.
- **SAP S/4HANA Cloud Release Assessment and Scope Dependency tool**
  This tool will allow you to compare the new features and enhancements with your solution scope.
- **Single-tenant architecture**
  As the name implies, only one customer will have access to the given infrastructure and the database.

Practice Questions

These practice questions will help you evaluate your understanding of the topics covered in this chapter. The questions shown are similar in nature to those found on the certification examination. Although none of these questions will be found on the exam itself, they will allow you to review your knowledge of the subject. Select the correct answers, and then check the completeness of your answers in the "Practice Question Answers and Explanations" section. Remember that on the exam, you must select all correct answers and only correct answers to receive credit for the question.

1. An existing SAP ERP 6.0 customer wants to forgo the current implementation and start from scratch. The customer is convinced that SAP Best Practices is the most suitable option, and the company can perform its business activities without any major customization except for business logos, chart of accounts, general ledgers, number ranges, and a few others. However, the company must transfer its master data and a portion of the transaction data to the new environment. The company has a highly profitable business and a cash reserve of one billion plus USD. What is the implementation path?

☐ **A.** New implementation of SAP S/4HANA because the client has a huge cash pile

☐ **B.** New implementation of SAP S/4HANA Cloud, extended edition, because the client wants to customize its environment such as business logo, chart of accounts, general ledgers, and number range

☐ **C.** New implementation of SAP S/4HANA Cloud because the client is sure that the company doesn't need major customization

☐ **D.** Selective data migration as the client wants to migrate transactional data

☐ **E.** None of the above

2. What are three benefits of cloud deployments as compared to the on-premise implementations of SAP S/4HANA? (There are three correct answers.)

☐ **A.** Lower TCO.

☐ **B.** Slower ROI.

☐ **C.** Faster time to value.

☐ **D.** No infrastructure cost.

☐ **E.** No need to migrate data; we can use SAP Model Company.

3. What are the three tasks that you'll perform during the prepare phase of the SAP S/4HANA Cloud deployment to deliver the project initiation and governance? (There are three correct answers.)

☐ **A.** Establish project governance.

☐ **B.** Create project charter and scope statement.

☐ **C.** Authorize project charter.

☐ **D.** Create project plan, schedule, and budget.

☐ **E.** Define project communications and reporting.

4. You're implementing SAP S/4HANA Cloud for a major fast-food chain, and today is the first day of the prepare phase. The client project manager is new to the SAP Activate methodology and asked you about the SAP supporting tools that the team may need throughout the project lifecycle. What is the best response?

☐ **A.** You explain tools such as videoconference, communication and email tools, and the project management tools (e.g., Scrum board). You explained the project standards, infrastructure, and solution deliverable.

☐ **B.** You explain the SAP supporting tools access deliverables, such as SAP Best Practices, Roadmap Viewer, SAP Activate on SAP Jam, and SAP Support Portal.

☐ **C.** You describe SAP Solution Manager, as that is the only tool needed for the SAP S/4HANA Cloud.

☐ **D.** None of the above.

5. You're in the middle of the SAP S/4HANA Cloud implementation project. You're executing a set of processes such as production system request, production system initial access, user creation, decommissioning the legacy system, and so on to move to the to-be solution. When will you create such a plan, and what is your current project phase?

☐ **A.** Deploy and realize

☐ **B.** Explore and deploy

☐ **C.** Realize and deploy

☐ **D.** Prepare and deploy

☐ **E.** Realize and run

6. You're currently reviewing the available authorization roles and mapping them to the business user roles. What is the project phase?

☐ **A.** Prepare

☐ **B.** Explore

☐ **C.** Realize

☐ **D.** Deploy

☐ **E.** Run

7. You're preparing the cutover communication document. What are the areas that you would like to include in this communication plan? (There are three correct answers.)

☐ **A.** Target audience

☐ **B.** Why should you send the communication

☐ **C.** Who is responsible for the communication

☐ **D.** Communication method

☐ **E.** A note stating that "you must review all communications"

8. You're in the realize phase of the SAP S/4HANA Cloud implementation. What are the deliverables that you've already completed and had signed off by the customer? (There are two correct answers.)

☐ **A.** Organizational change management impact analysis

☐ **B.** Solution walkthrough

☐ **C.** End-user learning needs analysis and plan

☐ **D.** Learning content

9. You're implementing SAP S/4HANA Cloud for a furniture manufacturing company. You, the customer's project manager, some key stakeholders, and the sponsor of the project are reviewing deliverables such as system go-live, production cutover, and a few other deliverables. What is your current project phase?

☐ **A.** Explore

☐ **B.** Realize

☐ **C.** Review

☐ **D.** Run

☐ **E.** Deploy

10. You've requisitioned the QA system in the previous phase. What deliverables will you work on during the current phase within the technical architecture and infrastructure workstream? (There are two correct answers.)

☐ **A.** QA system initial access

☐ **B.** Sign-off quality system

☐ **C.** Receive trial system

☐ **D.** PROD system request

☐ **E.** Starter system initial access

11. The financial SME and the project manager from the implementation partner are communicating the lack of equipment and necessary infrastructure for an event that started today. They were unhappy and clearly frustrated, but they professionally asked the client project manager to fulfill the necessary requirements communicated earlier. What is the deliverable, workstream, and project phase, respectively, in the given scenario for an SAP S/4HANA Cloud deployment project?

☐ **A.** End-user training, solution adoption, deploy phase

☐ **B.** Learning content, solution adoption, realize phase

☐ **C.** Stakeholder analysis, solution adoption, explore phase

☐ **D.** Communication plan, solution adoption, deploy phase

☐ **E.** End-user training strategy and plan, solution adoption, realize phase

12. You're implementing SAP S/4HANA Cloud for a regional company that manufactures doors. The company is currently using a 15-year-old legacy ERP system that doesn't exist anymore. Due to the local regulations, the company must move any open invoices, payment advices, customer complaints, purchase orders, requisitions, good receipts, sales orders, and other transactions. You've downloaded the templates from the SAP Best Practices and shared them today with the clients after proper review. Until yesterday, you and your team were helping the customer's IT organization cleanse the legacy data. Based on the given scenario, what is the next activity?

☐ **A.** Prepare the data load.

☐ **B.** Perform data cleansing.

☐ **C.** Execute and validate the data load.

☐ **D.** Provide a template and instructions for the data load.

☐ **E.** Define specifications for the data extraction programs.

13. You and your team are working closely with the business from a generic drug manufacturing company, a regional company based out of Chicago, IL, USA. The process leads of your team are working closely with the customer's SMEs and have conducted many sessions to identify gaps, if any, between SAP Best Practices and the business processes. After one such meeting where the functional lead was unable to log in, the infra lead of your team, who attended the meeting, complained that the production system isn't ready yet. Furthermore, the functional leads haven't requested any system where they can provide such a demo. What is wrong in the given scenario?

☐ **A.** The functional leads should have given enough notice to the infra lead so that he can set up the credentials accordingly.

- ☐ **B.** Nothing is wrong with this scenario except that the user credentials weren't set up properly. The project is in the deploy phase, and they were conducting UAT.
- ☐ **C.** The project manager should not invite the infra team in any such meetings where the team will discuss the business functionality.
- ☐ **D.** The project is in the explore phase, and the team is doing fit-to-standard analysis. The infra lead should not worry about the production system. They first need to request a QA system in the explore phase and then a PROD system in the realize phase.
- ☐ **E.** The project is in the explore phase, and the team is doing fit-to-standard analysis. The infra lead should not interfere in this process.

14. Arrange the following four tasks sequentially.

- ☐ **A.** Apply a nontransportable setup.
- ☐ **B.** Receive the production system.
- ☐ **C.** Set up user IDs for project team members in the production system.
- ☐ **D.** Request the production system.

15. Match the deliverables with the workstreams, and fill in the project phase for an SAP S/4HANA Cloud implementation project in Table 7.5.

Deliverable	Workstream	Phase
New scope item activation	Solution adoption	______
Learning team	Technical architecture and infrastructure	______
Extension planning and design	Operations and support	______
Production cutover	Extensibility	______

Table 7.5 Question 15

Practice Question Answers and Explanations

1. Correct answer: **C**

   This is clearly a new implementation as the customer is moving away from the SAP ERP 6.0 implementation to the cloud implementation; therefore, option D is incorrect. Just because the customer has a huge cash pile doesn't mean the company has a huge budget for the implementation. Additionally, option A is an unethical choice. Option B is incorrect because the said configurations are possible in the multitenant environment as well. Option C is the right choice because the customer is clearly communicating that they can achieve their business goal with SAP Best Practices.

2. Correct answers: **A, C, D**
   Option B, slower ROI, isn't a benefit, and option E is incorrect. The right choices are lower TCO, faster time to value, and no infrastructure costs for the cloud deployments.
3. Correct answers: **A, B, E**
   Authorize project charter, option C, is incorrect as there is no such task. On the other hand, option D, create project plan, schedule, and budget is another deliverable and isn't a task to deliver project initiation and governance.
4. Correct answer: **B**
   You're starting the prepare phase of the project. Although option A is correct in itself, if you read the question carefully, you'll notice that the question is about "SAP supporting tools," which refers to SAP Jam, the Roadmap Viewer, SAP Best Practices, and SAP Support Portal. Therefore, option B is correct. Option C is incorrect.
5. Correct answer: **C**
   The tasks mentioned in the question are related to the cutover plan and production system initial setup. You create the cutover plan in the realize phase of the project and execute it in the deploy phase; therefore, option C is the correct choice.
6. Correct answer: **B**
   During the explore phase, the team reviews the available authorization roles and maps them to the business user roles to deliver "identity and access management planning and design." Option B is the right choice.
7. Correct answers: **A, C, D**
   Any communication plan must include the target audience, the owner, or the responsible party to send the communique, as well as how the communication will be provided. Generally, you don't include the reasoning for the communication, and you never include a note to mandate all communication reviews.
8. Correct answers: **A, C**
   Read the question carefully. The question states that you're in the realize phase and asks you to list the deliverables that are signed off by the client, meaning the deliverables from the prepare and explore phases. The solution walk-through and learning content are the realize phase deliverables, whereas options A and C are from the explore phase.
9. Correct answer: **E**
   These deliverables are from the deploy phase, so option E is the right choice.
10. Correct answers: **A, D**
    The QA system is requisitioned in the explore phase. It means that you're in the realize phase of the project. The two deliverables in the realize phase from the

technical architecture and infrastructure workstream are QA system initial access and PROD system request.

11. Correct answer: **A**

    The event that started today and will continue at least for tomorrow is the end-user training. They are talking about the lack of essential infrastructure such as projector, board, marker, and so on, which are specific to the training. The end-user learning is a part of the solution adoption during the deploy phase of the project. The team isn't building the communication plan, creating the training strategy, or analyzing stakeholders.

12. Correct answer: **E**

    The team has completed the data cleansing activities and shared the templates with the client. The subsequent activity is to define the specifications for the data extraction programs. Option A is the deliverable that the team can accomplish by executing these three steps. Option C is an activity from the realize phase. In addition, all the information about regulations, data migrations for certain specific processes, and so on are to divert your attention.

13. Correct answer: **D**

    It's evident that the team is doing the fit-to-standard analysis, meaning they are in the explore phase of the project. At this time, the team has access to the starter system; they will request the QA system first and then the PROD system. Option D is the correct choice.

14. Correct answer: **D-B-C-A**

    The sequence of the given tasks is:

    - Request the PROD system.
    - Receive the PROD system.
    - Set up user IDs for project team members in the production system.
    - Apply a nontransportable setup.

15. Correct answer: See Table 7.6.

Deliverable	Workstream	Phase
New scope item activation	Technical architecture and infrastructure	Explore
Learning team	Solution adoption	Explore
Extension planning and design	Extensibility	Explore
Production cutover	Data management	Deploy

Table 7.6 Answer to Question 15

Takeaway

We started the chapter with the understanding of the multitenant and single-tenant cloud architecture and reviewed the value proposition of the cloud environment. In the subsequent sections, you learned about the different deliverables and the high-level activities necessary to deliver the deliverables during each phase of the project.

Summary

In this chapter, you learned the concepts, deliverables, and relevant tasks related to the greenfield implementations of the SAP S/4HANA Cloud environment. Our focus in the next chapter will be to understand the tasks and deliverables of new implementations of SAP S/4HANA Cloud, extended edition.

Chapter 8

New Implementation SAP S/4HANA Cloud, Extended Edition Transition Path

Techniques You'll Master

- Understand SAP S/4HANA Cloud, extended edition (formerly known as single-tenant edition)
- Know the five golden rules of cloud implementation
- Explain landscape details for SAP S/4HANA Cloud, extended edition
- Know the deliverables and activities during the project implementation phases of SAP S/4HANA Cloud, extended edition

In the previous chapter, our focus was on the new implementation of SAP S/4HANA Cloud, essentials edition. This chapter focuses on the implementation process in the single-tenant environment, that is, SAP S/4HANA Cloud, extended edition.

Similar to the previous chapters, we'll review the deliverables, activities, and tools and techniques required to complete the SAP S/4HANA Cloud, extended edition implementation. We'll start with the overview of SAP S/4HANA Cloud, extended edition, and then review the deliverables and activities from the discover phase to the run phase of the project.

Note

SAP renamed SAP S/4HANA Cloud, single-tenant edition, to SAP S/4HANA Cloud, extended edition. However, the C_ACTIVATE12 exam still refers to "single-tenant edition" or "STE" as of the writing of this book.

Throughout this book, we use SAP S/4HANA Cloud, extended edition, as the most updated terminology.

Real-World Scenario

As an SAP sales executive, you continue contacting as many current and prospective customers as possible to help them understand that technology is advancing toward the cloud and the role of SAP S/4HANA in achieving their business and IT goals.

In a recent conversation with Ms. Anitha Shah, who is the IT director of a fishing products company, she pointed out the need for certain data, security features, a dedicated landscape, and full integration options with the on-premise implementation.

Sounds like the perfect opportunity to walk her through the SAP S/4HANA Cloud, extended edition version and explain its capabilities and constraints.

Objectives of This Portion of the Test

The certification examination will test your knowledge about the following topics:

- Concepts, characteristics, and landscape overview of SAP S/4HANA Cloud, extended edition
- Five golden rules of the cloud implementations and the corresponding benefits
- Activities during the SAP S/4HANA Cloud, extended edition implementation
- Deliverables of the SAP S/4HANA Cloud, extended edition deployment

In the following sections, you'll learn about these key concepts followed by some questions and answers.

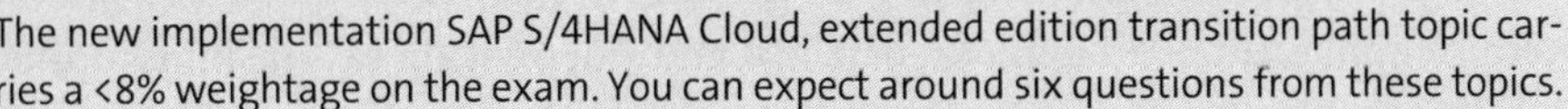

Note

The new implementation SAP S/4HANA Cloud, extended edition transition path topic carries a <8% weightage on the exam. You can expect around six questions from these topics.

Key Concepts Refresher

This section will help you understand the implementation methodology by focusing on the SAP S/4HANA Cloud, extended edition deployment, as well as advance your abilities to carry out given activities and deliver the desired deliverables. These concepts are critical for your success in the exam.

Overview

The implementation process for SAP S/4HANA Cloud, extended edition follows the five golden rules for cloud deployments, which we'll discuss in this section. The SAP S/4HANA Cloud, extended edition deployment uses the same fit-to-standard process and has the same process flows as that of SAP S/4HANA Cloud, essentials edition. If you're looking to deploy a cloud-based SAP solution with additional capabilities to configure, extend, and integrate, then SAP S/4HANA Cloud, extended edition is the right choice as it provides configuration capabilities with the implementation guide (IMG), which isn't available in SAP S/4HANA Cloud, essentials edition.

Throughout this chapter, we'll review the process and tools required to implement SAP S/4HANA Cloud, extended edition. However, we'll often refer back to SAP S/4HANA Cloud, essentials edition (covered in Chapter 7), especially to review certain common deliverables and, at times, to contrast the tool usages for configuration and during the integration and extensibility workstream.

Figure 8.1 summarizes the SAP S/4HANA Cloud, extended edition processes and clearly indicates the similarity in the process and activities to deploy SAP S/4HANA Cloud, extended edition, as compared to that of SAP S/4HANA Cloud, essentials edition. The process starts with the trial system provisioning, value discovery, and strategy building during the discover phase, and then continues through the project preparation and fit-to-standard preparation in the prepare phase. The team evaluates SAP Best Practices through the fit-to-standard process, defines the solution, builds the product backlog, completes the data load preparation, and performs test planning in the explore phase of the project.

We can use the IMG instead of Self-Service Configuration User Interface (SSCUI; similar to on-premise implementations) to configure the business processes and complete the migration, integration, extension, and testing in the realize phase. However, any such decisions to extend the preconfigured solution should be documented completely. SAP provides a host of integration capabilities such as predelivered standard integration scenarios for SAP cloud and on-premise products, open application programming interfaces (APIs) published on SAP API Business Hub, and SAP Cloud Platform Integration Suite to integrate other cloud and on-premise applications. In-app extensibility and side-by-side extensibility options are preferred options to extend the solution over the classic extensibility where the team can create custom code. We'll review these concepts in greater detail in the realize phase of the project.

We'll cruise through the production cutover, end-user training, onboarding, and deployment processes in the deploy phase, and then we'll finally operate, monitor, support and improve, during the run phase of the project. The project team should consider the release upgrade and continuous enhancements to consume the new capabilities and innovations. The longer release cycle is another notable difference of SAP S/4HANA Cloud, extended edition, as compared to that of SAP S/4HANA Cloud, essentials edition. Additionally, in SAP S/4HANA Cloud, extended edition, you can use a customer evaluation system (CES), discussed in the "Landscape" section, for the sandbox.

In the following sections, let's look closely at certain key characteristics of SAP S/4HANA Cloud, extended edition, and study the system landscape.

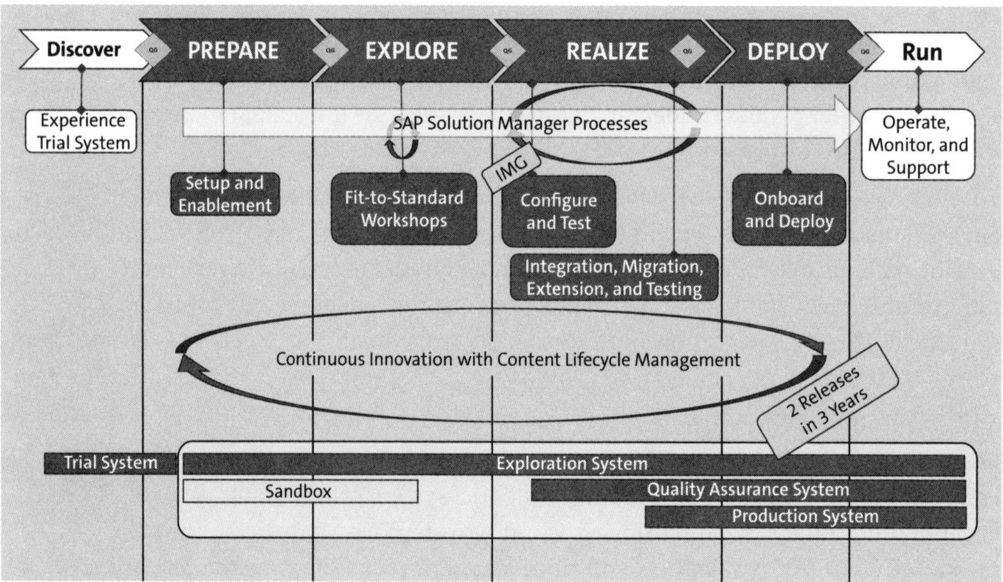

Figure 8.1 Overview

Characteristics

The processes, which are based on the five golden rules (explained later in this section), and the high-level activities are similar for SAP S/4HANA Cloud, essentials edition and SAP S/4HANA Cloud, extended edition. However, some of the key characteristics of SAP S/4HANA Cloud, extended edition are critical for the overall understanding and reviewing of the process deltas. These key characteristics are categorized in four different parts:

- **Scoping and configurations**
  - Fit-to-standard is used for the scoping and business-driven configurations.
  - The basis is SAP Best Practices or SAP Model Company.
  - Business-driven innovation is used in extension and integration.
- **Services and upgrades**
  - Two upgrades are performed in every three-year period.
  - Customers have a strong say in the update time slots.
- **Flexibility**
  - SAP S/4HANA Cloud, extended edition is the on-premise version deployed in the SAP HANA Enterprise Cloud infrastructure.
  - Full IMG configuration is available.
  - Full extension is possible with an exception of modifying SAP standard codes.
- **Landscape**
  - A dedicated landscape is used.
  - Data migration is possible.

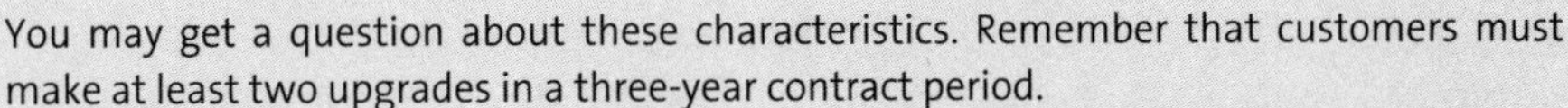

Note

You may get a question about these characteristics. Remember that customers must make at least two upgrades in a three-year contract period.

Landscape

Figure 8.2 shows the system landscape for SAP S/4HANA Cloud, extended edition. The configuration requirements are captured through the business-driven configuration questionnaire—an accelerator available on the Roadmap Viewer—applied to development box that will transport to the higher environments.

The SAP S/4HANA Cloud, extended edition landscape includes the following:

- The three systems in the production landscape are the exploration system, quality assurance (QA) system, and production (PROD) system.
- Customers can also include a sandbox system, also referred to as a customer evaluation system (CES) as mentioned earlier, to evaluate the functionality before activating it in the exploration system.
- The transport management system is set up to transport changes from exploration to QA and finally to PROD. There is no transport system to transport objects from a sandbox or CES environment to any of the systems in the production landscape (exploration, QA, and PROD).
- In a smaller setup, a customer can combine the exploration and QA environments, resulting a two-tier environment where the QA environment is used to configure and test the changes before moving to the higher environment.

- Some other usages of the CES are for training and implementing SAP Model Company and proof of concepts.

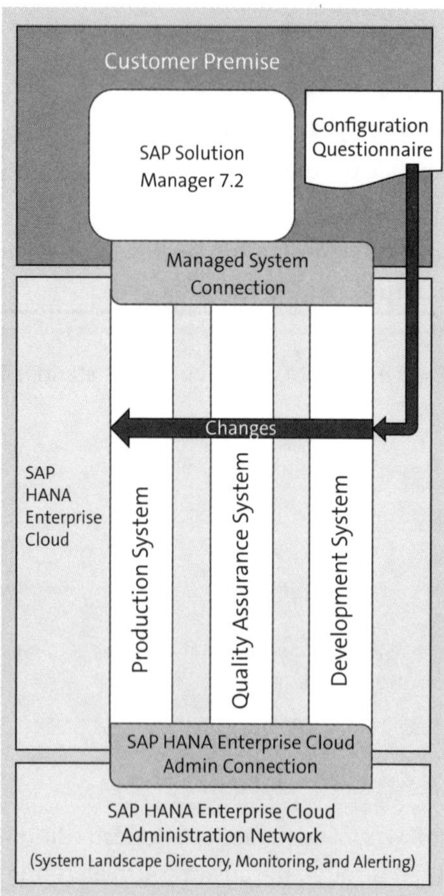

Figure 8.2 Landscape Overview

Five Golden Rules

SAP S/4HANA Cloud, extended edition deployments leverage the five golden rules of deployment to provide greater flexibility, enhanced extensibility, and better integration compared to SAP S/4HANA Cloud, essentials edition implementations. In fact, these capabilities are comparable to the on-premise implementations. However, these additional capabilities come at a cost of increased total cost of ownership (TCO) during the regular updates. To balance the enhanced capabilities and TCO, SAP published the "five golden rules" for SAP S/4HANA Cloud, extended edition implementations. Let's walk through each one:

❶ **Foster a cloud mind-set by adhering to the fit-to-standard approach and agile framework for deployment**
The cloud mind-set means staying as close to the standard as possible and using the software as a service. The fit-to-standard approach in the explore phase of

the project will keep the implementing organizations closer to the SAP Best Practices, SAP Model Company, or partner package qualified by SAP. Figure 8.3 shows the usages of the first two rules.

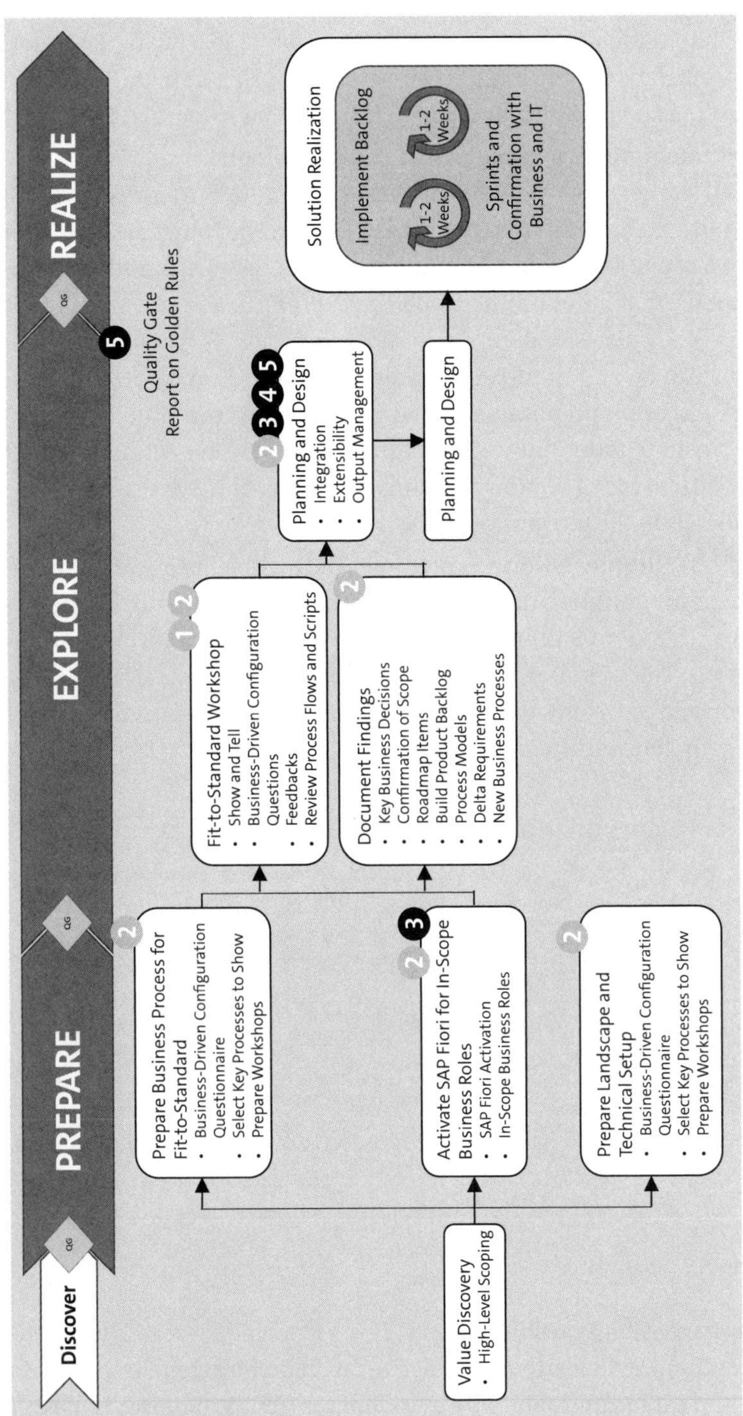

Figure 8.3 Golden Rules 1 and 2

The agile framework ensures the prioritization of the features in descending order of business value and supports incremental delivery of the solution with higher business values first.

❷ **Leverage the preconfigured solutions and SAP Fiori user experience (UX)**
Preconfigured solutions provide standardization, while leveraging SAP Fiori enhances the efficiency of business processes by exposing both analytics and transactional data and providing intelligent insights that helps take action.

❸ **Use the latest integration technologies and methodologies**
As mentioned earlier, SAP provides a host of solutions to integrate SAP S/4HANA Cloud, extended edition with other systems. The "other systems" can be the other SAP solutions such as SAP SuccessFactors, SAP Ariba, and SAP Concur, which are hosted either on the cloud or on-premise. For such cases, you should use predelivered standard integration scenarios. Furthermore, these other systems can be any third-party system, including homegrown applications that are either on premise or hosted on the cloud. You should use SAP Cloud Platform Integration Suite to integrate such systems with your SAP S/4HANA Cloud, extended edition solution. In Chapter 5, we've explained the integration details in the integration workstream.

The team collects the integration requirements during the fit-to-standard processes, and after optimization of the list, the team should use standard integration scenarios for SAP-to-SAP integrations; SAP also provides various out-of-box integrations. The technical consultant adds the technical details regarding the integration and completes the documentation. Figure 8.4 shows the activity flow used to complete the integration scenario as well as the interface list accelerators.

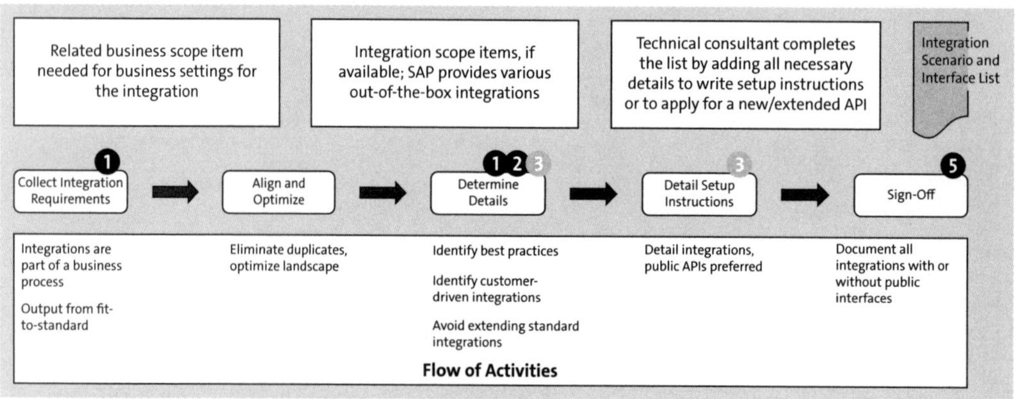

Figure 8.4 Golden Rule 3

❹ **Use the latest extensibility technologies**
SAP S/4HANA Cloud, extended edition has the capability to extend the solution with both in-app extensibility and side-by-side extensibility. We discussed both concepts in the extensibility workstream in Chapter 5.

The steps to complete the extensibility requirements are similar to that of the integration required discussed previously. The team collects the extension requirements during the fit-to-standard process; optimizes the extension list; collects the design details to decide whether to use in-app, side-by-side, or classic extensibility; and finally develops, tests, documents, and gets sign-off on the extension. SAP Extensibility Explorer and SAP S/4HANA Cloud extensibility tools are the primary tools for the extension. Figure 8.5 shows the process flow to complete the extension; it also shows the available extensibility tools.

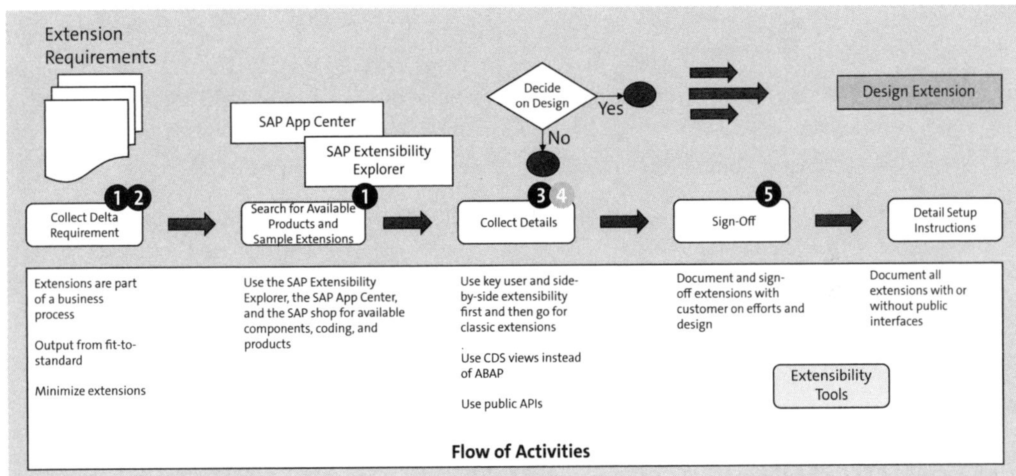

Figure 8.5 Golden Rule 4

❺ Complete transparency on deviations

The fifth and the final golden rule ensures complete documentation and transparency of any deviation from rules ❶–❹.

Benefits

Organizations that adopt the five golden rules can garner the following benefits:

- Faster time to value is realized.
- TCO is reduced due to lower initial deployment cost, lower ongoing operation cost, and lower infrastructure cost.
- The organization is poised to consume SAP- and partner-delivered innovations faster.
- The use of the latest technologies leads to a future-proof deployment.
- By adopting SAP Best Practices, organizations can de-risk deployment challenges, including security risks introduced by custom code.
- Documenting and understanding deviations will reduce dependence on one implementation partner.

Key Differences

Before we dive deeper into the trenches, let's review the key differences between the three new implementations that we've studied so far in Table 8.1.

SAP S/4HANA	SAP S/4HANA Cloud, Essentials Edition	SAP S/4HANA Cloud, Extended Edition
SAP Activate transitions to SAP S/4HANA (supporting new implementation, system conversion, and selective data transformation)	▪ SAP Activate methodology ▪ SAP S/4HANA Cloud	▪ SAP Activate methodology ▪ SAP S/4HANA Cloud, extended edition
▪ SAP Best Practices for SAP S/4HANA ▪ SAP Model Company	SAP Best Practices for SAP S/4HANA Cloud	SAP Best Practices for SAP S/4HANA
▪ IMG ▪ Focused Build for SAP Solution Manager 7.2	Guided configuration	▪ IMG ▪ Focused Build for SAP Solution Manager 7.2
Fit-gap analysis	Fit-to-standard	Fit-to-standard

Table 8.1 New Implementation Comparison

Discover Phase

The objective of this phase is for customers to understand the business functionality of SAP S/4HANA Cloud, extended edition and the benefits that the customer can reap by using this ERP. Once determined, the team will build the strategy and implementation roadmap.

Figure 8.6 shows the deliverables and the activities, which we'll discuss in the following sections.

Solution Adoption

The solution adoption workstream ensures the high adoptability of the solution within the organization and includes the following deliverables:

- **Stakeholder identification**
  The objective of this deliverable is to identify key stakeholders that are critical to the success of the project, including the discovery sessions. The deliverables identified in the discover phase are highly dependent on the successful identification of decision makers, influencers, and other key stakeholders as follows:
  - **Core team and executive sponsors (L1 stakeholders)**
    This group comprises the change promoters who will analyze the business needs, conceptualize the solution, and drive the change.

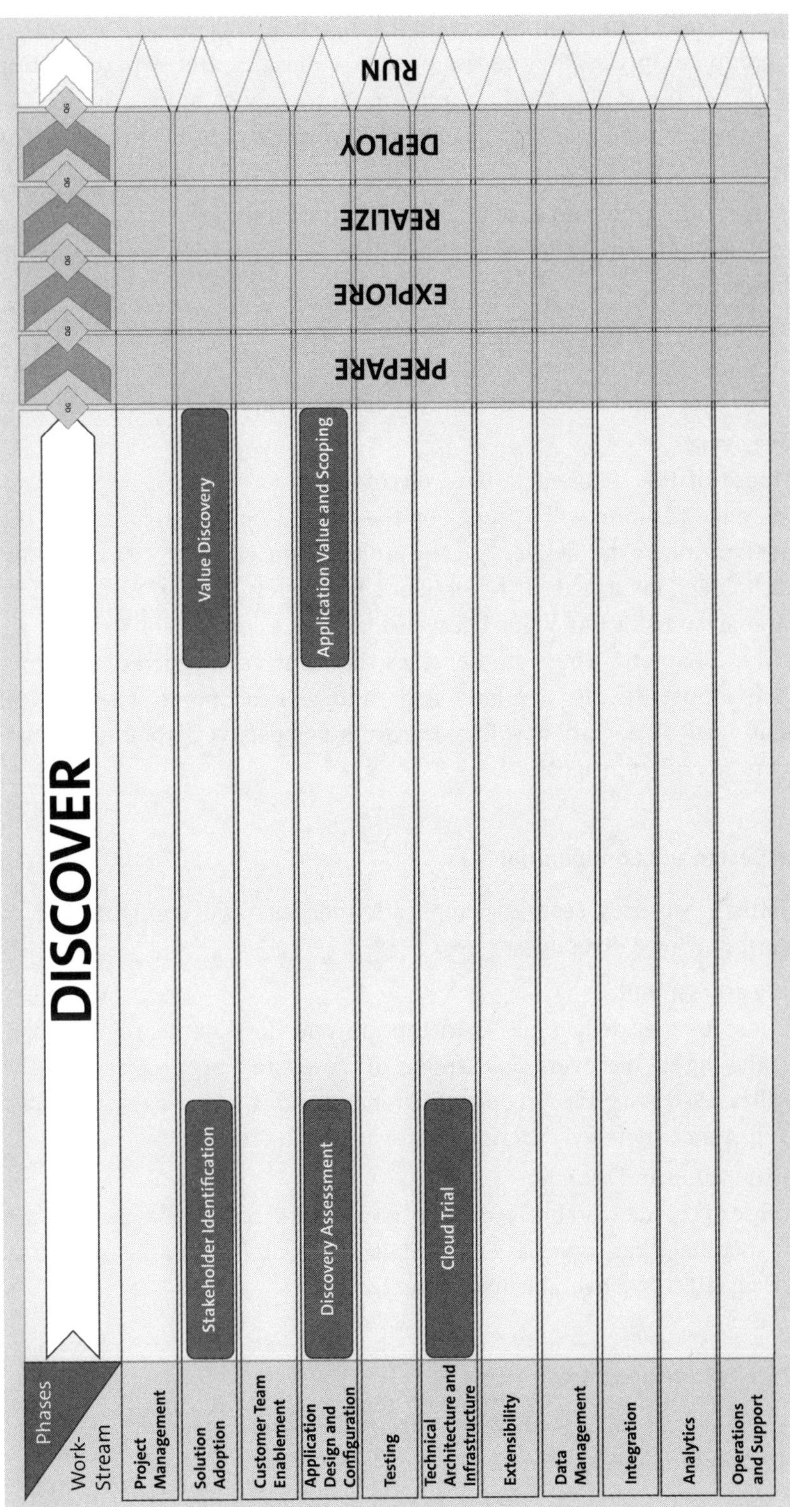

Figure 8.6 Overview of the Discover Phase

  - **Key users and extended project team (L2 stakeholders)**
    This group comprises key process owners, subject matter experts (SMEs), probable key users, IT executives, auditors, and analysts, among others. The project team should identify the change advocates and foster them in the group.
  - **Consumers (internal and external) (L3 stakeholders)**
    This group comprises other individuals, such as end users, who are affected by the change.
  - **Implementation project team (L4 stakeholders)**
    This group comprises the individuals who are part of the project team and tasked to execute one or another aspect of the implementation.
- **Value discovery**
  The purpose of this deliverable is to discover the value that SAP S/4HANA Cloud, extended edition will bring given the current business scenario at the customer location. In this deliverable, the project team will work with the different stakeholders, identified in the previous bullet item, to perform a benchmarking analysis using SAP Value Lifecycle Manager, a comparison tool that we discussed in Chapter 5. The team develops the value case, which can be converted into a business case at a later stage, and creates a point of view (POV) document. The POV document will list the users' perspective of their need, challenges, and any other insights.

Application Design and Configuration

This workstream ensures seamless application design and configuration. It includes the following deliverables:

- **Discovery assessment**
  The purpose of this deliverable is to capture and document project scope, through the digital discovery assessment, to generate a scoping report. The report will be used as a project scoping reference during the phases of the implementation. A more detailed description is available in Chapter 7.
- **Application value and scoping**
  The purpose of this deliverable is to identify values and roadblocks, and create a strategic roadmap that serves as a key input into the customer business case. We've discussed this deliverable in Chapter 6.

Technical Architecture and Infrastructure

This workstream covers all aspects of the infrastructure requirements and architecture. It includes the following deliverable:

- **SAP S/4HANA Cloud trial**
  The purpose of this deliverable is to get access to an SAP S/4HANA Cloud trial system via the SAP S/4HANA Cloud trial. As a result, project members have access to the trial system for demoing, identifying value, and evaluating impact. You can create the trial environment using SAP Cloud Appliance Library, which we've discussed in Chapter 5 in detail.

Prepare Phase

In the prepare phase, the project team will plan and prepare several planning documents from kick-off to phase closure, receive the starter system where the team will perform the fit-to-standard process in the explore phase, and plan for fit-to-standard. In this section, we'll review the prepare phase activities and the corresponding deliverables for new implementations of SAP S/4HANA Cloud, extended edition.

In this phase, the team works closely to prepare many planning documents needed during the course of the implementation. The prepare phase of SAP S/4HANA Cloud, extended edition is similar to that of SAP S/4HANA Cloud, essentials edition. Figure 8.7 shows the deliverables in the prepare phase, which we'll discuss in the following sections.

Note

In the following sections, many deliverables are identical to SAP S/4HANA Cloud, essentials edition, which we discussed in Chapter 7. Rather than repeating descriptions for each here, we'll focus on explaining the deliverables specific to SAP S/4HANA Cloud, extended edition.

Project Management

The project management workstream covers all aspects of project initiation, planning, execution, monitoring and controlling, and closure activities. We've discussed most of the deliverables in Chapter 7, except for the following two deliverables:

- **Getting started with the implementation of SAP S/4HANA Cloud, extended edition**
  The objective of this deliverable is to ensure that everyone associated with the project becomes familiar with the SAP Activate methodology to implement SAP S/4HANA Cloud, extended edition. You can access the Roadmap Viewer at *https://go.support.sap.com/roadmapviewer/* and navigate to **SAP Activate Methodology for SAP S/4HANA Cloud, extended edition**.

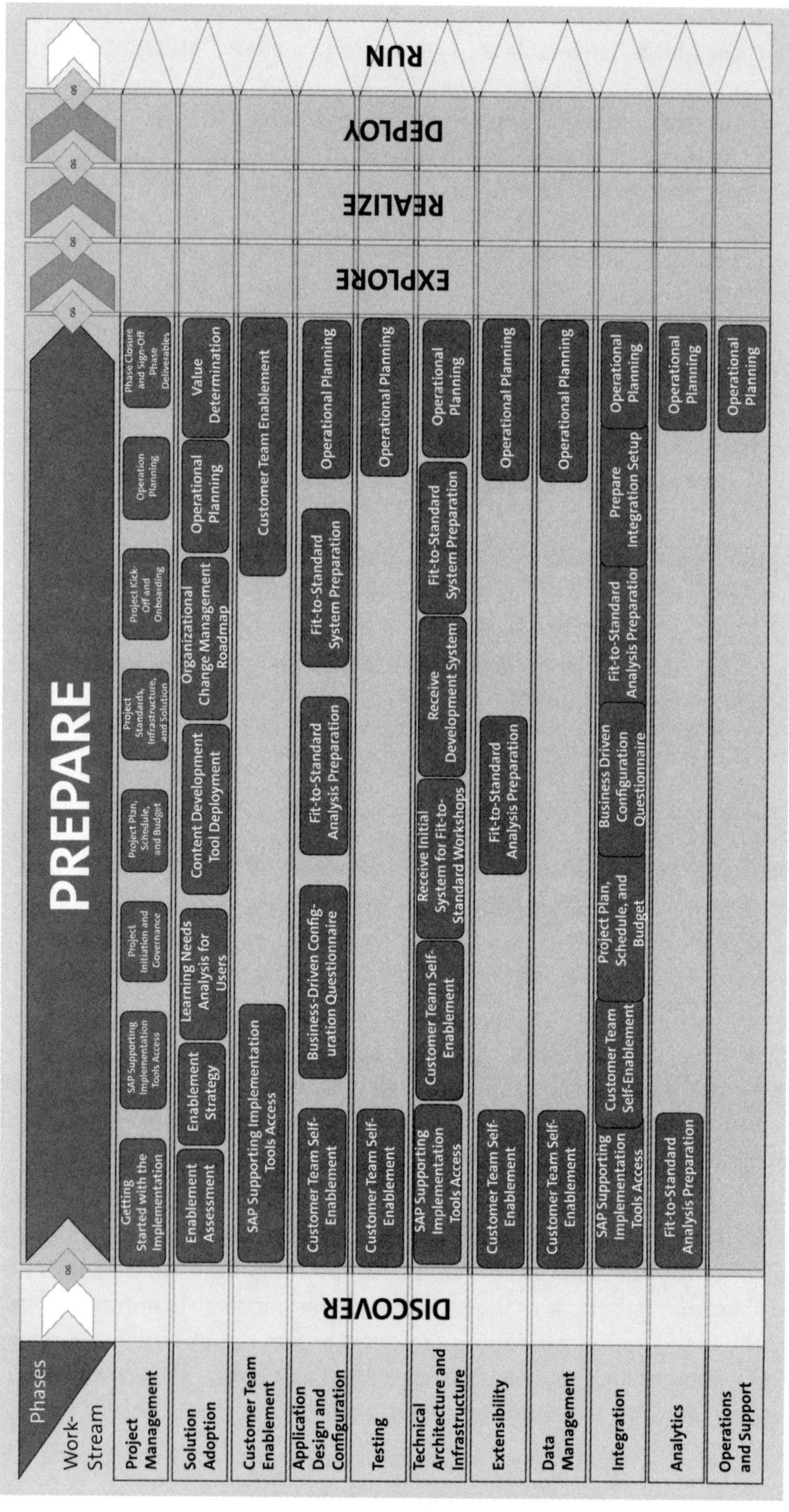

Figure 8.7 Overview of the Prepare Phase

- **Operation planning**
  This planning deliverable ensures the proper transition of the operation, due to the change in the IT framework with the new solution, to the operations team. SAP provides the necessary support, tools, and resources to build and operate the target-operating model in an efficient and effective manner. It's important to understand that this deliverable isn't applicable in SAP S/4HANA Cloud, essentials edition, because SAP provides the necessary basic support for the implementation post go-live. This deliverable requires input from all the workstreams and will appear as a deliverable throughout the prepare phase across the eleven workstreams. However, we won't discuss this deliverable subsequently in the prepare phase.

The following deliverables are also applicable for SAP S/4HANA Cloud, extended edition, which were discussed in detail in Chapter 7:

- SAP supporting implementation tools access
- Project initiation and governance
- Project plans, schedule, and budget
- Project standards, infrastructure, and solution
- Project kick-off and onboarding
- Phase closure and sign-off phase deliverables

Solution Adoption

The solution adoption workstream ensures the high adoptability of the solution within the organization and includes the following deliverables:

- **Enablement assessment**
  The purpose of the solution adoption workstream is to enhance the new solution adoption throughout the organization. To do so, the team needs to understand the current situation and capabilities across the customer organization by researching and interviewing stakeholders. Based on their research and interviews, the team completes the assessment report, outlining the digital learning approach methodology that is specific to this customer, action items along with the owners, and the execution plan. This report will feed into other deliverables.
- **Enablement strategy**
  The digital learning approach, just identified, and the detail assessment report will help create the enablement strategy and roadmap for the duration of the project.
- **Learning need analysis for users**
  The objective of this deliverable is to analyze the digital learning opportunities and ensure the availability of the right learning when needed.

- **Content development tool deployment**
  The purpose of this deliverable is to identify a content development tool that the team can use to edit and distribute the organizational enablement assets.

Note

SAP Enable Now is one such tool, and there may be a question from this topic on the exam.

- **Organizational change management (OCM) roadmap**
  This deliverable is discussed in Chapter 7.
- **Operational planning**
  This deliverable is discussed in the project management workstream of this chapter.
- **Value determination**
  During the discover phase of the project, the team created the business case and POV document. In this deliverable, the team will ensure the alignment of the business case and POV with the key process changes and functionality and then establish a tracking framework.

Customer Team Enablement

This workstream enables the key users and administrators to perform their specific duties. We've discussed the following two deliverables in Chapter 7:

- SAP supporting implementation tools access
- Customer team self-enablement

Application Design and Configuration

This workstream ensure seamless application design and configuration. We've discussed the following deliverables in Chapter 7:

- Customer team self-enablement
- Business-driven configuration assessment
- Fit-to-standard analysis preparation
- Fit-to-standard system preparation

We've discussed the following deliverable previously in this chapter:

- Operational planning

Testing

This workstream covers all aspects of testing the solution and includes the following two deliverables, which have been discussed previously:

- Customer team self-enablement
- Operational planning

Technical Architecture and Infrastructure

This workstream covers all aspects of the infrastructure requirements and architecture. The new deliverables are as follows:

- **Receive initial system for fit-to-standard workshops**
  As discussed in the "Landscape" section earlier, the team will receive a system in which they will carry out the fit-to-standard analysis. If the customer has a sandbox system, then the team will receive this system. However, in case of a non-sandbox environment, the team will receive the exploration system (aka the development (DEV) system) for the fit-to-standard process, which will be used as a DEV system after the fit-to-standard process.

  SAP will deliver the starter system with preconfigured content to conduct the fit-to-standard processes. It will contain the necessary configuration and master data for the seamless execution of the business processes. After the team receives the system, the administrator will set up the users and assign relevant authorizations.
- **Receive DEV system**
  If you have a sandbox environment, you'll receive a DEV system (aka exploration system) with preconfigured business processes for use in the fit-to-standard process. The project team, after receiving the exploration system, will create the necessary users and grant them relevant access and privileges.

The following deliverables are also applicable for SAP S/4HANA Cloud, extended edition, which we've already discussed in detail:

- SAP supporting implementation tools access
- Customer team self-enablement
- Fit-to-standard system preparation
- Operational planning

Extensibility

This workstream covers all aspects of the custom code requirement and extensibility features. The deliverables are as follows, which have been discussed previously:

- Customer team self-enablement
- Fit-to-standard analysis preparation
- Operational planning

Data Management

This workstream covers all aspects of the master data, transactional data, and data migration activities. The deliverables are as follows, which have been discussed previously:

- Customer team self-enablement
- Operational planning

Integration

This workstream covers all aspects of the integration with other SAP or third-party systems. The deliverables are as follows, which have been discussed previously:

- SAP supporting implementation tools access
- Customer team self-enablement
- Project plan, schedule, and budget
- Business-driven configuration assessment
- Fit-to-standard analysis preparation
- Prepare integration setup
- Operational planning

Analytics

This workstream covers all aspects of the analytics. The deliverables are as follows, which have been discussed previously:

- Fit-to-standard analysis preparation
- Operational planning

Operations and Support

This workstream covers all aspects of the operations and support. The only deliverable in this workstream is operational planning, which we discussed earlier in this chapter.

Explore Phase

During this phase of the project, the team performs the fit-to-standard analysis and prepares the product backlog. All the planning is done during the prepare phase, and the customer has signed off the phase. In this phase, the team will focus on the requirements. The explore phase of SAP S/4HANA Cloud, extended edition is similar to that of SAP S/4HANA Cloud, essentials edition. Figure 8.8 shows the deliverables in the explore phase, which we'll discuss in the following sections.

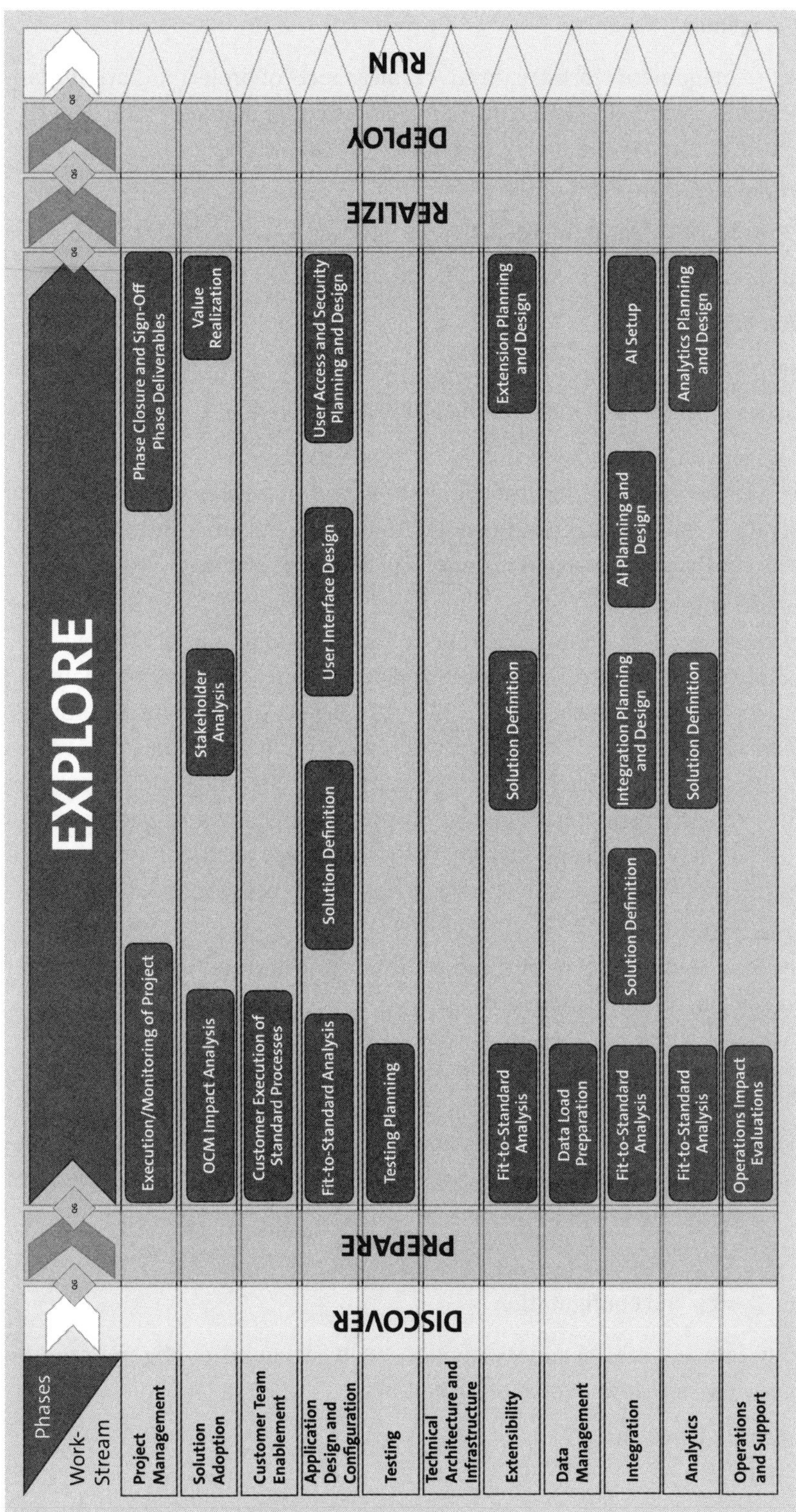

Figure 8.8 Overview of the Explore Phase

Project Management

The project management workstream covers all aspects of project initiation, planning, execution, monitoring and controlling, and closure activities. The deliverables, which we've already discussed in Chapter 7, are as follows:

- Execution/monitoring of project
- Phase closure and sign-off phase deliverables

Solution Adoption

The solution adoption workstream ensures the high adoptability of the solution within the organization and includes the following deliverables:

- **OCM impact analysis**
  This deliverable ensures that the OCM steps and processes are documented properly. The team should create as-is and to-be business processes and demonstrate the comparison for a better understanding of the change.
- **Stakeholder analysis**
  This deliverable will provide an idea about the stakeholder's level of acceptance and their attitude toward the project and its success. One way of analyzing stakeholders is to assign them into different buckets of advocate, supporters, detractors, and neutrals. In this case, the team should also plan to move the stakeholders from one bucket to another by understanding their reasoning until they are either supporters of your work or openly advocate your work. As a part of the analysis, you also identify their role as an executive, business decision maker, process expert, key user, end user, or any other role.
- **Value realization**
  This deliverable ensures the continuous monitoring and controlling of the predefined key performance indicators (KPIs).

Customer Team Enablement

This workstream enables the key users and administrators to perform their specific duties. We've already discussed the only deliverable—customer execution of standard processes—in Chapter 7.

Application Design and Configuration

This workstream ensures seamless application design and configuration. The deliverables we've already covered are as follows:

- Fit-to-standard analysis
- Solution definition

The following new deliverables are also relevant:

- **User interface (UI) design**
  The objective of this deliverable is to complete the UI design as agreed upon during the fit-to-standard process. You can use the SAP Build tool at *www.build.me/* to complete the wireframe.
- **User access and security planning and design**
  The objective of this deliverable is to ensure the right setup of the roles and authorizations that meets the customer requirements.

Testing

This workstream covers all aspects of testing the solution. We've already discussed the only deliverable—test planning—in Chapter 7.

Extensibility

This workstream covers all aspects of the custom code requirement and extensibility features. It includes the following deliverables, which we've already discussed in Chapter 7:

- Fit-to-standard analysis
- Solution definition
- Extension planning and design

Data Management

This workstream covers all aspects of the master data, transactional data, and data migration activities. We've already discussed the only deliverable—data load preparation—in Chapter 7.

Integration

This workstream covers all aspects of the integration with other SAP or third-party systems and includes the following deliverables, as discussed in Chapter 7:

- Fit-to-standard analysis
- Solution definition
- Integration planning and design
- Artificial intelligence (AI) planning and design
- AI setup

Analytics

This workstream covers all aspects of the analytics and includes the following deliverables, as discussed in Chapter 7:

- Fit-to-standard analysis
- Solution definition
- Analytics planning and design

Operations and Support

This workstream covers all aspects of the operations and support and includes the following deliverable:

- **Operation impact evaluation**
  This deliverable will identify any impact on the changes related to the IT operations post go-live of the solution.

Realize Phase

The purpose of this phase is to realize the build incrementally and iteratively based on the business requirements and scenarios identified during the previous phases of the project. During the realize phase, the team will build and test the business and system environment based on the fit-to-standard analysis. In addition, the team will start legacy data load migration, continue solution adoption processes, and plan for operations. The realize phase of SAP S/4HANA Cloud, extended edition is slightly different from that of SAP S/4HANA Cloud, essentials edition, mainly because of application design and configuration, integration, extensibility, and a subtle difference in analytics. Figure 8.9 shows the deliverables in the realize phase, which we'll discuss in the following sections.

Project Management

The project management workstream covers all aspects of project initiation, planning, execution, monitoring and controlling, and closure activities. It includes the following deliverables, as discussed in Chapter 7:

- Execution/monitoring of project
- Phase closure and sign-off phase

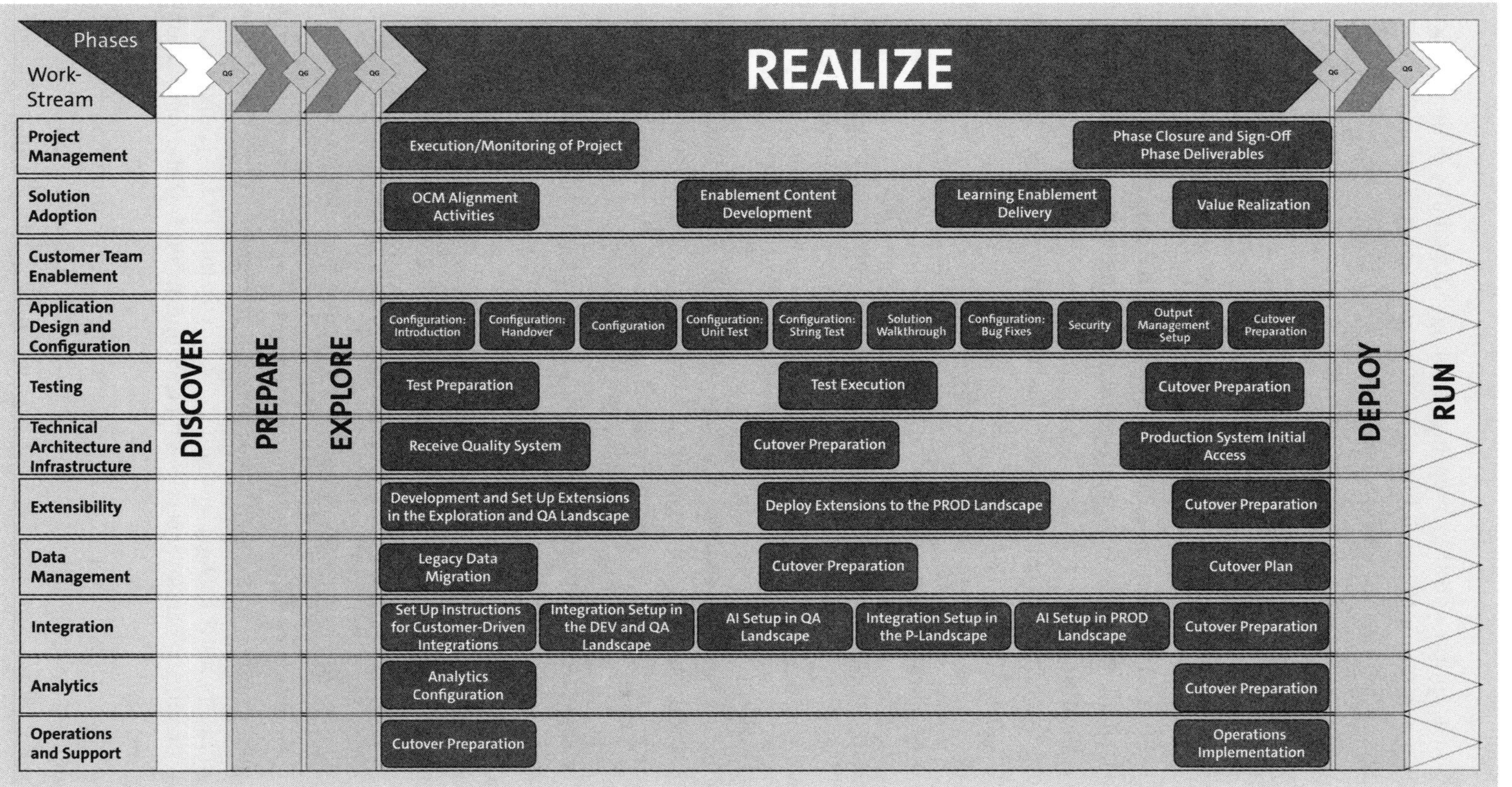

Figure 8.9 Overview of the Realize Phase

Solution Adoption

The solution adoption workstream ensures the high adoptability of the solution within the organization. We've discussed OCM alignment activities in Chapter 7. The other three deliverables are as follows:

- **Enablement content development**
  This deliverable is to ensure that the team creates the learning and enablement content for the end users to consume.
- **Learning enablement delivery**
  This deliverable is to ensure the delivery of the content developed earlier by the team. The delivery options vary from client to client, but general options are in-person training, online classes, self-paced learning, and so on.
- **Value realization**
  The purpose of this deliverable is to monitor constantly and, if needed, control the value enablers identified earlier in the project.

Application Design and Configuration

This workstream ensure seamless application design and configuration. This is one of the workstreams where you'll see major differences as compared to SAP S/4HANA Cloud, essentials edition. The deliverables are as follows:

- **Configuration**
  Configuration isn't an actual deliverable but is a group of deliverables that we'll unpack throughout this list. However, it's important to understand that this group caters to all the configuration-related work, from being familiarized with the configuration activities to actual configuration changes, completing the unit testing, string testing, documentation, bug fixes, and solution walk-through.
- **Configuration: Introduction**
  We discussed the foundation sprint in Chapter 5. This deliverable translates to the foundation sprint because its purpose is to configure the mandatory settings—such as include legal entities, organizational structures, and other general settings—and prepare the master data.
- **Configuration: Handover (optional)**
  Although it's an optional deliverable, the structured handover is critical for the subsequent configuration. The fit-to-standard workshop teams will hand over the learning, product backlog, and other documentation to the configuration team by organizing handover sessions for each line of business and/or solution.
- **Configuration**
  The objective of this deliverable is to configure the exploration system based on the handover received from the fit-to-standard team, and it includes master data configuration, core finance configuration, and other relevant configurations.

- **Configuration: Unit test**
  The team will complete the unit testing as a part of this deliverable, document the findings, and resolve the issues, if any, before moving forward.
- **Configuration: String test**
  In Chapter 5, you learned about the firm-up sprint and string testing. This is the deliverable where the team performs the string testing—a test to integrate different sprints specifically for epics. This can happen only after the completion of unit testing and follows the same process of documentation and issue resolution before moving forward.
- **Configuration: Solution walkthrough**
  Through the iterative process, this deliverable ensures that the project team completes the walkthrough of the solution for each process across the business and gets the business feedback and necessary approvals.
- **Configuration: Bug fixing**
  The purpose of this deliverable is to resolve any issues that the team has identified during the solution walkthrough. Any leftover issues from unit testing and string testing must be fixed during this deliverable. It's recommended, however, to fix unit testing-related issues before moving to string testing and to fix string testing-related issues before moving to the solution walkthrough.
- **Configuration: Documentation**
  This deliverable is to complete the configuration document and upload the same in SAP Solution Manager.
- **Security**
  Any security-related requirements captured during the fit-to-standard processes are performed in this deliverable.
- **Output management setup**
  This deliverable is the same as that of SAP S/4HANA Cloud, essentials edition, which we've discussed in Chapter 7.
- **Cutover preparation**
  Here, the team prepares the steps for cutover. The team sets up the PROD environment as a part of the preparation activity. The team will test the plan in the dress rehearsal during the deploy phase.

Testing

This workstream covers all aspects of testing the solution and includes the following deliverables:

- **Test preparation**
  In this deliverable, the team prepares to test the end-to-end solution with the customer. The preparation includes defining the test cases, test scripts, and relevant test data. The team also creates an elaborate plan, including the resource requirements, timeline, and any contingencies. You can store these test scripts on either SAP Solution Manager or SAP Cloud ALM. The cross-system business

process can be tested using one of the two tools just mentioned. However, to complete the activities, the team should set up the tool, define the solution within the tool, and assign the test cases.

- **Test execution**
  The team executes the plan in an iterative fashion and fixes any issues noticed during the testing. The team should also monitor the progress, take corrective actions if needed, and report the status to the stakeholders. The execution should include all the planned tests, including integration testing, regression testing, and user acceptance testing (UAT).
- **Cutover preparation**
  Here, the team prepares the steps for cutover. The team sets up the PROD environment as a part of the preparation activity. The team will test the plan in the dress rehearsal during the deploy phase.

Technical Architecture and Infrastructure

This workstream covers all aspects of the infrastructure requirements and architecture. It includes the following deliverables:

- **Receive quality system**
  The team accepts the QA system, create users, and ensures the proper and requisite access.
- **Cutover preparation**
  The team prepares the steps for cutover. The team sets up the PROD environment as a part of the preparation activity. The team will test the plan in the dress rehearsal during the deploy phase.
- **PROD system initial access**
  This deliverable ensures that the PROD system is ready before the go-live. The team completes and submits the requisition to SAP, receives the PROD system, ensures the proper access, and finally applies the nontransportable setup. However, to receive the PROD system, the team must pass the explore quality gate.

Extensibility

This workstream covers all aspects of the custom code requirement and extensibility features. It includes the following deliverables:

- **Develop and set up extensions in exploration and QA landscape**
  The objective of this deliverable is to set up the extensions in the DEV landscape. The detailed design of the extension in the explore phase is the input to this deliverable. The team will develop the key-user extensions, side-by-side extensions, and classic extensions in the exploration environment. The team will then transport these extensions to the QA landscape to test the extended scenarios.

- **Deploy extensions to PROD landscape**
  After testing in the QA landscape, the team will deploy the three sets of extensions to the PROD landscape.
- **Cutover preparation**
  From an extensibility perspective, this deliverable will ensure that the team completes the cutover preparation by including the extensibility-related activities.

Data Management

This workstream covers all aspects of the master data, transactional data, and data migration activities. It includes the following deliverables:

- **Legacy data migration**
  The objective of this deliverable is to ensure the successful migration of the legacy data. To achieve the objective, the team needs to validate the data load based on the data received from the customer in the specified format shared with the customer during the explore phase. The project team will identify any issues in the data load process and work closely with the customer to resolve the issues. Finally, after resolving all the known issues, the team will conduct the quality assessment of the data and report the key findings to the stakeholders. After receiving all the requisite approvals, the team will load the data in the PROD environment.
- **Cutover preparation**
  This deliverable focuses on the data-related activities that should be included in the planning work.
- **Cutover plan**
  This deliverable documents the cutover activities that the team will execute subsequently. The plan must include the detailed timeline, activities (e.g., PROD system initialization, interface connections, data migrations, user ID creations, communications, decommissioning the legacy system, and other tasks), statuses, owner and prerequisites of each task, and any known constraints to move the system from the as-is to the to-be solution. See Chapter 5 for more details.

Integration

This workstream covers all aspects of integration with other SAP or third-party systems and includes the following deliverables:

- **Set up instructions for customer-driven integrations**
  This deliverable is specific to the customer-driven integration, meaning those integrations that aren't completely covered by SAP Best Practices. For such integrations, the team should create a detailed setup instruction document.

- **Integration setup in the DEV and QA landscape**
  The project team performs any integration-related setup required in the DEV and QA landscapes. The project team will create the integration mapping and perform the integration setup. You can use the Cloud Integration Automation service to complete the setup.
- **AI setup in the QA landscape**
  The objective of this deliverable is to leverage the existing SAP bots. This deliverable will ensure the robotic process automation (RPA) setup on the QA landscape and document the instructions.
- **Integration setup in the PROD landscape**
  This deliverable will ensure the integration setting in the PROD environment. To complete the deliverable, the team will use the tested instruction guide from the integration setup in the DEV and QA landscapes.
- **AI setup in the PROD landscape**
  The objective is to leverage the tested instruction guide created in the AI setup in the QA landscape and set up the RPA bots in the PROD environment.
- **Cutover preparation**
  The cutover preparation in this workstream ensures that all the activities related to the integration workstream are captured in the cutover preparation.

Analytics

This workstream covers all aspects of the analytics, and the two deliverables are as follows:

- **Analytics configuration**
  This deliverable ensures the configuration of analytics requirements as captured during the fit-to-standard workshop.
- **Cutover preparation**
  The cutover preparation ensures that all the activities related to the analytics workstream are captured in the cutover preparation.

Operations and Support

This workstream covers all aspects of the operation and support post-hypercare. The two deliverables are as follows:

- **Cutover preparation**
  This deliverable ensures that any support-related requirements are captured in the cutover plan.

- **Operations implementations**
  This deliverable ensures the implementation of changes to the support operations.

Deploy Phase

In the deploy phase of the project, the business switches the operation to the new PROD environment. This is the final phase of the project in which the team will close all the open issues, ensure the organizational readiness, and execute the production cutover so that the business can realize the benefits of the newly implemented solution. Figure 8.10 shows the deliverables in the deploy phase, which we'll discuss in the following sections.

Project Management

The project management workstream covers all aspects of project initiation, planning, execution, monitoring and controlling, and closure activities. This workstream includes the following deliverables, as discussed in Chapter 7:

- Execution/monitoring of project
- Phase closure and sign-off phase

Solution Adoption

The solution adoption workstream ensures the high adoptability of the solution within the organization. This workstream includes the following deliverables:

- **UX management tool deployment**
  The objective of this deliverable is to deploy Knoa—a comprehensive tool that generates UX analytics and helps customers manage their UX with SAP solutions.
- **OCM execution activities**
  We've discussed this deliverable in Chapter 7.

Data Management

This workstream covers all aspects of the master data, transactional data, and data migration activities. It includes the following deliverable:

- **Production cutover**
  This deliverable ensures that the cutover activities were completed successfully and the system can cut over to production.

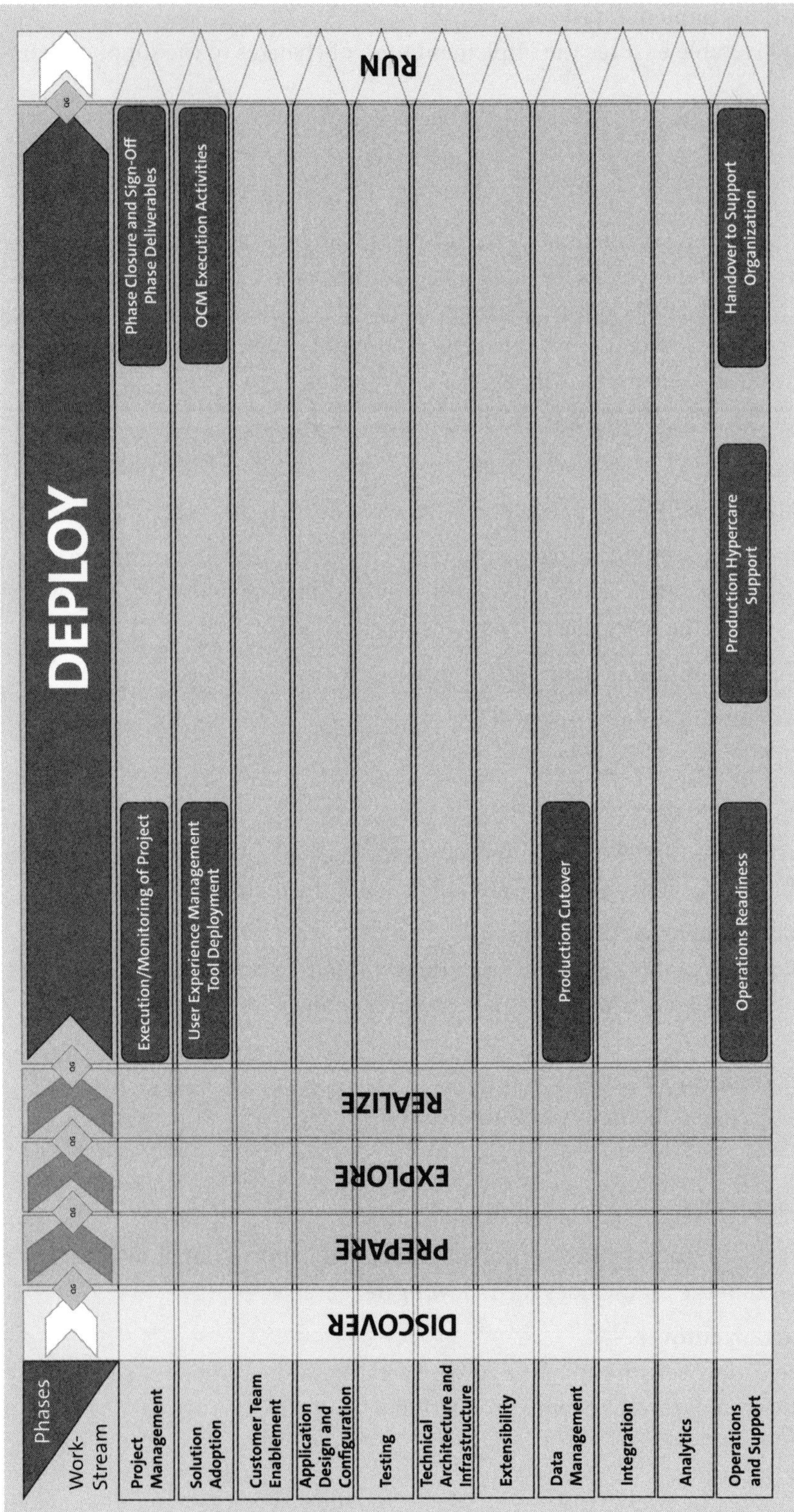

Figure 8.10 Overview of the Deploy Phase

Operations and Support

This workstream covers all aspects of the operation and support post-hypercare. It includes the following deliverables:

- **Operations readiness**
  The objective of this deliverable is to ensure that the customer is ready to operate the SAP S/4HANA Cloud, extended edition solution post go-live. The team carries out a comprehensive check for the operation readiness that includes the roles and responsibilities check, support process and procedure check, operation tools and documentation, and knowledge transition to the client's operation team.
- **Production hypercare support**
  The purpose of this deliverable is to provide the hypercare support during the deploy phase post go-live. It will help to improve the system performance before handing over the solution to the operation team.
- **Handover to support organization**
  This deliverable will ensure the seamless handover of the solution operation to the client's operation team. The project team must close any open issues and hand over the responsibilities to the customer organization.

Run Phase

This phase starts after the hypercare, during the previous phase of the project, to optimize the overall operation. During this phase, the support is provided by the customer IT team, and they continue to strive for optimization, automate the application processes, ensure system availability, and provide system performance. Figure 8.11 shows the deliverables in the run phase, which we'll discuss in the following sections.

Solution Adoption

The solution adoption workstream ensures the high adoptability of the solution within the organization and includes the following deliverables:

- **OCM continuous change management activities**
  This deliverable ensures the continuous monitoring of end users, their skills, and learning paths to ensure that both the training content and the end users' skillsets are up to date.
- **Value management**
  This deliverable ensures that customers build a long-term strategy to manage and measure the business values and KPIs identified earlier in the project.

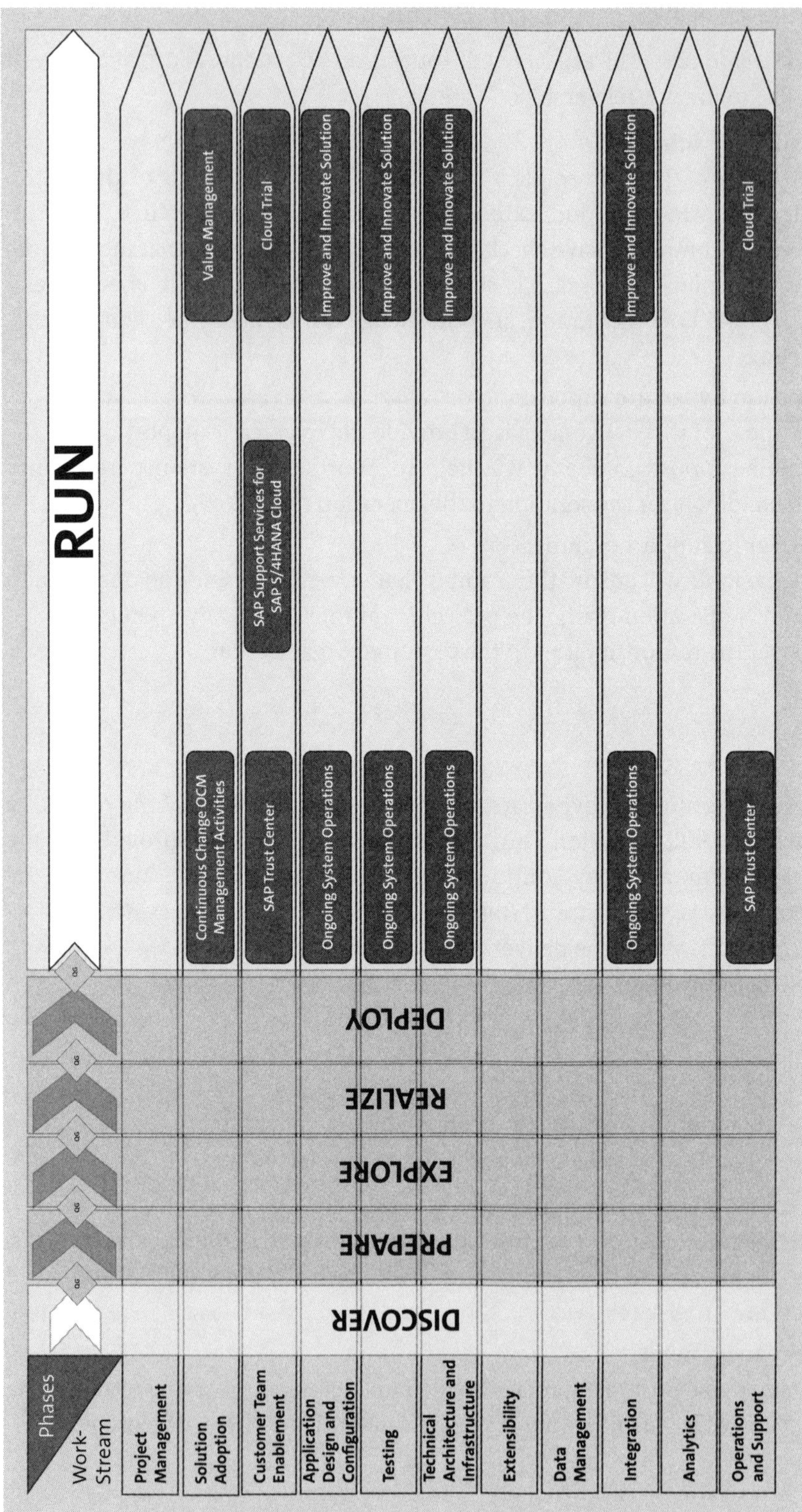

Figure 8.11 Overview of the Run Phase

Customer Team Enablement

This workstream enables the key users and administrators to perform their specific duties:

- **SAP Trust Center**
  We've discussed this deliverable in Chapter 7.
- **SAP support services for SAP S/4HANA Cloud**
  We've discussed this deliverable in Chapter 7.
- **Cloud trial**
  The purpose of this deliverable is to learn the innovations continuously from the SAP S/4HANA Cloud trial.

Application Design and Configuration

This workstream ensure seamless application design and configuration. The two deliverables are as follows:

- **Ongoing system operations**
  The objective of this deliverable is to perform the routine actions required for continued optimum system performance. This deliverable spans the application design and configuration, testing, technical architecture and infrastructure, integration, and operations and support workstreams. The tasks in the different workstreams are different with some overlapping, but they fulfill the goal of continued operations.

  In this workstream, the focus is to operate the new solution and continuously optimize the operations by adopting the Advanced Customer Center of Expertise (Customer COE), an advanced approach to the Customer COE model that we reviewed in Chapter 5.
- **Improve and innovate solution**
  The objective of this deliverable is to improve the solution by performing continued benchmarking assessments, performing business scenarios, and solution mapping. The customer should continue to consume innovations based on the update cycle. Remember that the customer must consume at least two release of the three updates. This deliverable also spans the five workstreams as mentioned in the previous deliverable, and the tasks overlap between these workstreams.

  In this workstream, the team focuses on updating the SAP system, preparing for the yearly innovation cycle, performing business scenarios and solution mapping, and benchmarking assessments for comparison with agreed-upon KPIs.

Testing

This workstream covers all aspects of testing the solution and includes the following deliverables:

- **Ongoing system operations**
  The tasks in this deliverable focus on the continuous operation and optimization of the solution.
- **Improve and innovate solution**
  The tasks in this workstream focus on periodical updates and preparedness.

Technical Architecture and Infrastructure

This workstream covers all aspects of the infrastructure requirements and the architecture. It includes the following deliverables:

- **Ongoing system operations**
  The tasks in this deliverable focus on continuous operation, reviewing legal changes, and optimizing the solution.
- **Improve and innovate solution**
  The tasks in this workstream focus on periodical updates and preparedness.

Integration

This workstream covers all aspects of the integration with other SAP or third-party systems and includes the following deliverables:

- **Ongoing system operations**
  The tasks in this deliverable focuses on the continuous operation, monitoring RPA factory, and optimization of the solution.
- **Improve and innovate solution**
  The tasks in this workstream focuses on the periodical updates and the preparedness.

Operations and Support

This workstream covers all aspects of the operation and support post-hypercare, including the following deliverables:

- **Ongoing system operations**
  The tasks in this deliverable focus on continuous operation, regular system health-checks, and optimizing the solution.
- **Improve and innovate solution**
  The tasks in this workstream focus on periodical updates and preparedness.

Important Terminology

For this exam objective, you're expected to understand the following terms:

- **Customer evaluation system (CES)**
  On this system, the customer can evaluate the business functionalities before activating the same in the exploration system.
- **Exploration system**
  This is the DEV environment where the team can evaluate the in-scope business functionalities. This fit-to-standard system will later be used as a DEV system in a non-sandbox landscape.
- **Five golden rules**
  SAP published a set of five rules that guide an implementation of SAP S/4HANA Cloud, extended edition.
- **SAP S/4HANA Cloud, extended edition**
  SAP S/4HANA is the latest ERP system from SAP that can be deployed as on-premise as well as on the cloud. The version of the ERP that we can deploy is either SAP S/4HANA Cloud, essentials edition or SAP S/4HANA Cloud, extended edition. SAP S/4HANA Cloud, essentials edition is the vanilla flavor SAP S/4HANA system, but you can customize SAP S/4HANA Cloud, extended edition based on your needs.

 Practice Questions

These practice questions will help you evaluate your understanding of the topics covered in this chapter. The questions shown are similar in nature to those found on the certification examination. Although none of these questions will be found on the exam itself, they will allow you to review your knowledge of the subject. Select the correct answers, and then check the completeness of your answers in the "Practice Question Answers and Explanations" section. Remember that on the exam, you must select all correct answers and only correct answers to receive credit for the question.

1. Which one of these is a characteristic of SAP S/4HANA Cloud, extended edition?

☐ **A.** You have the flexibility to modify SAP codes.

☐ **B.** Full IMG configuration is available.

☐ **C.** Data migration isn't an option for SAP S/4HANA Cloud, extended edition.

☐ **D.** The team can migrate only certain data sets that are preapproved by SAP or an SAP partner.

☐ **E.** Only partial IMG configuration is available, which is limited to configuration master data only.

2. Which of these aren't the characteristics of SAP S/4HANA Cloud, extended edition? (There are three correct answers.)

- ☐ **A.** Uses latest integration technologies
- ☐ **B.** Dedicated landscape
- ☐ **C.** Uses latest extensibility technologies
- ☐ **D.** De-risks deployment challenges
- ☐ **E.** The on-premise version deployed on SAP HANA Enterprise Cloud

3. Match the benefits that an organization can achieve with the golden rules that they must follow to achieve the benefits in Table 8.2.

Benefits	Golden Rules
A. Less dependency on one system integrator	Preconfigured solutions
B. Reduce TCO	Documented deviations
C. Future-proof deployments	Adopting SAP Best Practices
D. Faster time to value	Use of latest integration and extensibility technologies
E. Lower deployment risks	Foster cloud mind-set

Table 8.2 Question 3

4. Which two of these aren't the golden rules of cloud deployments for SAP S/4HANA Cloud, extended edition? (There are two correct answers.)

- ☐ **A.** Use the latest technologies for integration and extensions.
- ☐ **B.** Foster a cloud mind-set.
- ☐ **C.** Use the product backlog.
- ☐ **D.** Document deviations.
- ☐ **E.** De-risk deployments.

5. You're the full-time project manager of an SAP S/4HANA Cloud, extended edition deployment for a regional generic drug manufacturing company. Including you, the team has five members. The customer wanted to have all four systems in the landscape, although you think that isn't necessary. The team completed the fit-to-standard analysis on the sandbox environment and transported the changes to the higher environment. What is wrong with the given scenario?

- ☐ **A.** There is nothing wrong in the scenario.
- ☐ **B.** There is no need for a full-time project manager for such a small project.

☐ **C.** The team should complete the fit-to-standard analysis in the exploration system.

☐ **D.** You're right about the extra environment in the landscape.

☐ **E.** You can't transport the changes from the sandbox environment.

6. You're working closely with the key stakeholders of a furniture retail chain who wants to move from a legacy ERP system to SAP S/4HANA Cloud, extended edition. While you and the sponsor of the project were discussing value discovery, stakeholder identification, scoping, and S/4HANA Cloud trial, you noticed that one of your ex-clients who was a Basis lead is working as the technical lead for the organization. You do know that he is very demanding and has a sound knowledge of Basis, but he never took any initiative to learn the new and latest technologies. In the next meeting with the sponsor, he was also present and demanded the timeline for the three-system landscape. What will be your response?

☐ **A.** Ask him "what do you know about the SAP S/4HANA Cloud, extended edition deployment?"

☐ **B.** Tell him, "We'll get you the exploration system in the prepare phase, which is starting next week, and the QA and PROD environment during the realize phase of the project."

☐ **C.** Tell him, "We're in the discover phase of the project assessing the value that the organization can get from SAP S/4HANA Cloud, extended edition deployment. Although, it's not final that this is the implementation path that we'll take, it's very difficult to provide you the infrastructure timeline at this time."

☐ **D.** You ignore him and continue your discussion with the sponsor.

☐ **E.** You recounted to the sponsor the earlier conversation and mentioned, "I told you so."

7. You've just received access to the trial environment. What is the purpose of the trial environment?

☐ **A.** To agree to the SAP terms and conditions

☐ **B.** For the project team to support the value identification and the impact evaluation

☐ **C.** For the project team to check all the available in-scope items

☐ **D.** To build the questionnaire needed for the fit-to-standard analysis

☐ **E.** To enhance team knowledge and skills on SAP S/4HANA Cloud, extended edition

8. You're an aspiring project manager helping a seasoned project manager implement SAP S/4HANA Cloud, extended edition for a semiconductor manufacturing company. The project manager asked you to schedule a workshop with sponsors, all the stakeholders, team members, the business team (with the process subject matter experts [SMEs]), and supporting organizations. What is the purpose of this meeting?

- ☐ **A.** Fit-to-standard workshop A
- ☐ **B.** Delta design workshop
- ☐ **C.** Workshop B
- ☐ **D.** Kick-off workshop
- ☐ **E.** Both A and D

9. Identify the deliverables from the prepare phase of the project.

- ☐ **A.** Organizational change management roadmap, fit-to-standard analysis preparation, operational planning, and customer team self-enablement
- ☐ **B.** Cloud trial, fit-to-standard analysis preparation, operational planning, and customer team self-enablement
- ☐ **C.** Organizational change management roadmap, fit-to-standard analysis preparation, operational planning, and test planning
- ☐ **D.** Organizational change management roadmap, fit-to-standard analysis preparation, cutover preparation, and customer team self-enablement
- ☐ **E.** Organizational change management roadmap, improve and innovate solution, operational planning, and customer team self-enablement

10. Over the past couple of weeks, you worked with key stakeholders, including the lengthy and cumbersome meeting that you had with the change manager to discuss the OCM execution activities; spoke with a senior manager to fine-tune the hypercare support activities; and discussed the production cutover yesterday with the sponsor. Assuming that you're implementing SAP S/4HANA Cloud, extended edition, what is the project phase?

- ☐ **A.** Discover
- ☐ **B.** Prepare
- ☐ **C.** Fit-to-standard
- ☐ **D.** Deploy
- ☐ **E.** Deploy and run

11. The team is working on three key deliverables: (1) develop and set up extensions in QA and exploration landscapes, (2) cutover preparation, and (3) deploy extensions to the PROD environment. What is the project phase and the workstream?

☐ **A.** Extensibility, run

☐ **B.** Realize, extensibility

☐ **C.** Customer team enablement, deploy

☐ **D.** Deploy, integration

☐ **E.** Explore, fit-to-standard

12. You're in the explore phase of the project. What are the deliverables related to the application design and configuration workstream? (There are two correct answers.)

☐ **A.** Test planning

☐ **B.** Cutover preparation

☐ **C.** Fit-to-standard analysis

☐ **D.** Demo system initial access

☐ **E.** User interface design

13. Even though this is your first project as a project manager, you know that the success of a project lies in the successful migration of the legacy data. You're worried about data migration and looking for the ready-made templates for the data loads. Where would you look for these templates?

☐ **A.** Ask the client for the template

☐ **B.** Roadmap Viewer

☐ **C.** SAP Best Practices

☐ **D.** SAP Support Portal

☐ **E.** SAP Cloud ALM

14. You and your team have just received access to SAP Learning Hub while the team is in the process of implementing SAP S/4HANA Cloud, extended edition. You sent the access email to your team asking them to validate the access. Identify the project phase, workstream, and deliverable.

☐ **A.** Prepare, learning, learning plan

☐ **B.** Explore, fit-to-standard, customer team self-enablement

☐ **C.** Run, learning, end-user training

☐ **D.** Prepare, analytics, customer team analytics-enablement

☐ **E.** Prepare, customer team enablement, customer team self-enablement

15. What are three deliverables related to artificial intelligence? (There are three correct answers.)

☐ **A.** Ongoing system operations

☐ **B.** AI setup in productive landscape

☐ **C.** Customer team self-enablement

☐ **D.** Test planning

☐ **E.** Project scoping

Practice Question Answers and Explanations

1. Correct answer: **B**
   Although you'll have full access to the IMG, you can't modify SAP codes. Option C is incorrect because you can migrate data from the legacy system to the cloud environment with certain restrictions. However, you don't need SAP approval, so option D is incorrect. Finally, option E is incorrect regarding the limitation to configure master data only.
2. Correct answers: **A, C, D**
   Option B, dedicated landscape, and option E, on-premise version deployed on SAP HANA Enterprise Cloud, are the characteristics of the SAP S/4HANA Cloud, extended edition deployment. Options A and C are the third and fourth golden rules, respectively, while option D is one of the benefits to following the golden rules.
3. Correct answer: See Table 8.3

Benefits	Golden Rules
A. Less dependency on one system integrator	Documented deviations
B. Reduce TCO	Foster cloud mind-set
C. Future-proof deployments	Use of latest integration and extensibility technologies
D. Faster time to value	Preconfigured solutions
E. Lower deployment risks	Adopting SAP Best Practices

Table 8.3 Answers for Question 3

4. Correct answers: **C, E**
   Using agile framework is a part of golden rule 1 but not the product backlog. Additionally, de-risking deployment is a benefit and not the rule itself.

5. Correct answer: **E**
   SAP doesn't provide the transport management system on the sandbox environment. Option B isn't necessarily correct, especially in this scenario when the scope of work is unknown. Options C and D are incorrect.

6. Correct answer: **C**
   Be aware of these wordy questions. It's simply asking, "Can you provide the infrastructure timeline during the discover phase of the project?" The idea is to identify the project phase that is clear from the key words such as value discovery, stakeholder identification, scoping, and cloud trial.

7. Correct answer: **B**
   Option B is the correct answer. Option C is incorrect because, at this time (you're in the discover phase), no one is certain about the scope items. Options D and E are incorrect.

8. Correct answer: **D**
   You're doing the project kick-off workshop. Options A, B, and C are from the fit-to-standard workshop, which is irrelevant to have with all the stakeholders and supporting organizations. Option E, on the other hand, is to confuse you as the same logic holds true for option A alone or combined with option D.

9. Correct answer: **A**
   Cloud trial in option B is from the discover phase, test planning in option C is from the explore phase, cutover preparation in option D is from the realize phase, and improve and innovate solution in option D is from the run phase.

10. Correct answer: **D**
    OCM execution activities, hypercare support activities, and production cutover are from the deploy phase of the project. Option D is the correct choice.

11. Correct answer: **B**
    The three deliverables are from the extensibility workstream. The only correct answer is option B.

12. Correct answers: **C, E**
    Option A is a testing workstream deliverable, while option B is from the realize phase. Option D is incorrect. Options C and E are the only correct choices.

13. Correct answer: **B**
    You'll find the accelerators in the Roadmap Viewer and SAP Best Practices. If you have prior experience, a key criterion for the certification, you'll know that the data migration templates are available on the Roadmap Viewer.

14. Correct answer: **E**
    The scenario clearly indicates that you're in the prepare phase of the project, so you can discard options B and C. There is no workstream called "learning," so you can discard option A as well. There is no deliverable named "customer team analytics-enablement," so the only available option is E. If you look closely, the SAP Learning Hub access is a part of customer team self-enablement, which, in

turn, is part of the customer team enablement workstream in the prepare phase of the project.

15. Correct answers: **A, B, C**
    Option E is incorrect as there is no deliverable named project scoping, and test planning has no relation to the AI, so options A, B, and C are the correct choices.

Takeaway

We started with the characteristics of SAP S/4HANA Cloud, extended edition, and comprehensively reviewed the two-, three-, and four-system requirements—sandbox or CES, exploration, QA, and PROD environments—and their usages in the client landscape. We also reviewed the key features of the CES environment. Furthermore, we studied the five golden rules published by SAP to help create a seamless implementation of SAP S/4HANA Cloud, extended edition and the benefits that an organization can reap by following these rules.

Similar to the previous chapters, we started reviewing the deliverables and the activities in the discover phase where you saw the five key steps that the project team performs to create the business case. In the prepare phase, apart from the deliverables and activities, you learned more about the fit-to-standard preparation, whereas in the explore phase, we revisited the complete fit-to-standard process along with the deltas. You learned more about the solution configuration, integration, extension, and testing during the realize phase of the project. In the deploy and run phases of the project, you learned about the production cutover, end-user training, release upgrades, and continuous enhancement.

Summary

In this chapter, you learned the concepts, deliverables, and relevant tasks related to the greenfield implementations of SAP S/4HANA Cloud, extended edition. Our focus in the next chapter is to understand the tasks and deliverables of the system conversion of the SAP S/4HANA implementation.

Chapter 9
System Conversion Transition Path

Techniques You'll Master

- Understand system conversion and the applicable scenarios
- Explain the key considerations when doing a system conversion
- Know the deliverables and activities during the conversion phases
- Explain the tools needed during system conversion

Now that you have a sound understanding of the new implementations of SAP S/4HANA and SAP S/4HANA Cloud, we'll next focus on the system conversion approach and its related deliverables and associated tasks.

We'll start by discussing the approach, reviewing the process leading to the system conversion or new implementation in detail—a different and more detailed perspective as compared to the flow chart shown in Chapter 6—and explaining the deliverables and associated tasks.

Real-World Scenario

Ms. Brannon, a senior account executive at SAP, handed over a few of her clients to you as she was transitioning to a bigger role at the company. You reviewed all of her accounts and are interested in a particular account, Global Tools, a tool-manufacturing company with a global presence in 50+ countries and revenue of 2 billion USD.

Ms. Brannon was clear in her transition that Global Tools has a huge SAP landscape with multiple instances spread across the geography. Additionally, due to recent EU regulations, Brexit, and certain litigations in the United States, Global Tools must retain a considerable chunk of data. These factors together make a system conversion seem like the correct transition path for this customer. You were ready to call Ms. Laura J. Smith, senior director (IT) at Global Tools, tomorrow morning to find out any integration requirements of any other IT systems with the SAP instances, project budget, and program sponsorship details.

Objectives of This Portion of the Test

The certification examination will test your knowledge of the following topics:

- Considerations for system conversions
- System conversion processes
- Activities during the system conversion
- Associated deliverables in the system conversion approach

In the following sections, you'll learn about these key concepts followed by some questions and answers.

Note

The system conversion transition path topic carries a <8% weightage on the exam. You can expect around six questions from these topics.

Key Concepts Refresher

This section will help you understand the system conversion transition path from the existing SAP system to SAP S/4HANA and will advance your abilities to carry out given activities and deliver the desired deliverables. These concepts are critical for you to pass the exam.

Navigating the Roadmap Viewer

You can navigate in the Roadmap Viewer by following the steps shown in Figure 9.1:

❶ Go to the Roadmap Viewer, and click on **Solution Specific**.

❷ Navigate right and click on **SAP Activate Methodology for Transition to SAP S/4HANA** to go to the overview page.

❸ Click on the **Content** menu shown in the upper-left portion of the screen to go to the content page.

❹ Scroll down until you see **More** on the left pane of the window. Select the **System Conversion** checkbox (see Figure 9.2) to include only the deliverables, tasks, and accelerators from the system conversion transition path.

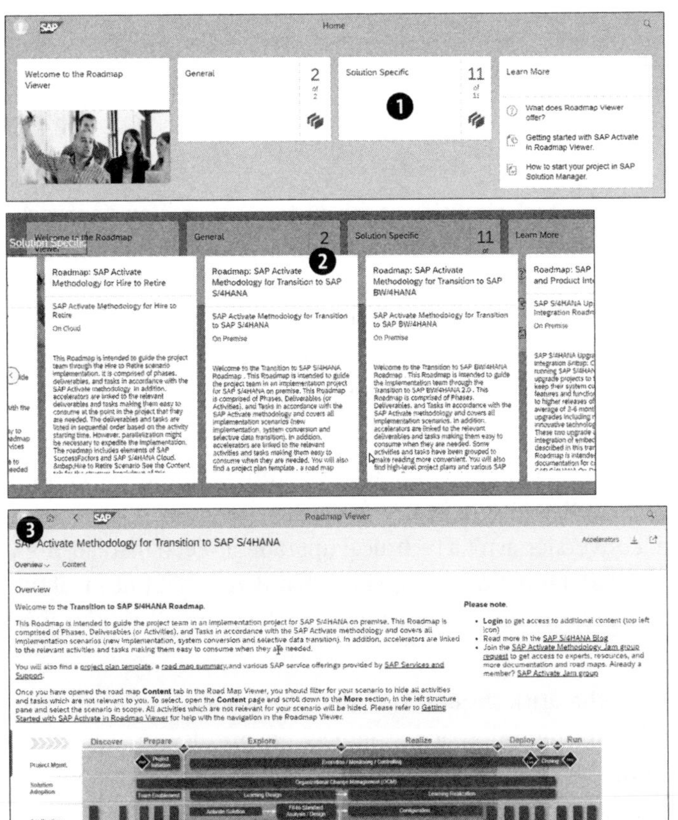

Figure 9.1 Navigation in the Roadmap Viewer

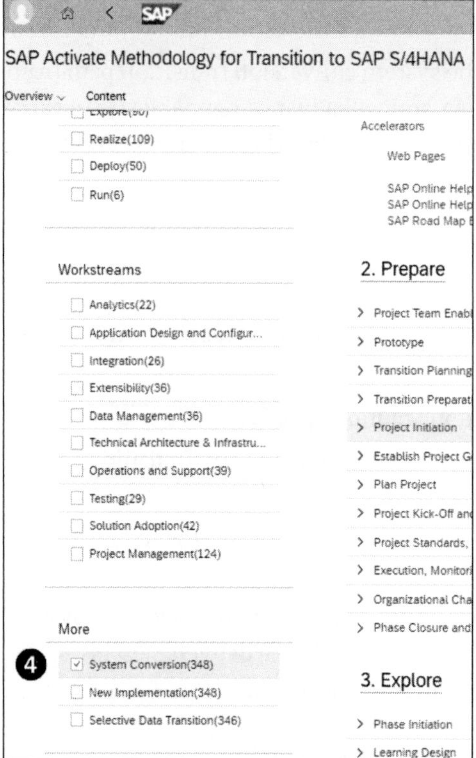

Figure 9.2 Selecting System Conversion

Key Considerations

Before we start diving into the technicalities of the system conversion approach, it's important to understand the process that will help determine the transition path. As you may recall from Chapter 1, when a customer with an existing SAP solution wants to move to SAP S/4HANA, you use the system conversion approach. Let's review this in more detail from the perspective of business processes, SAP Best Practices, data needs, and a few other aspects.

At a high level, a system conversion is a lift-and-shift approach where you move your current business process and data to a new environment and make certain adjustments and minor modifications to fit the changes in the new environment. Remember that system conversion isn't a technical upgrade project; instead, it's a combination of a technical and functional upgrade. What if you don't need all the data or what if the business team wants some changes to the current business processes?

Figure 9.3 shows some of the critical questions that the leadership team must answer to decide on the desired approach. There is no priority or weightage assigned to these questions. We're not going into the detail of each question, as these are self-explanatory. Additionally, there may be hybrid scenarios such as an IT sponsored project with a high number of interfaces that can adopt SAP Best

Practices. In such scenarios, the leadership team will decide subjectively whether to move forward with the system conversion, new implementation, or selective data transition, which is a hybrid approach—explained in Chapter 10—by considering many other factors such as the total cost of ownership (TCO), urgency of the business changes, organizational readiness, and so on.

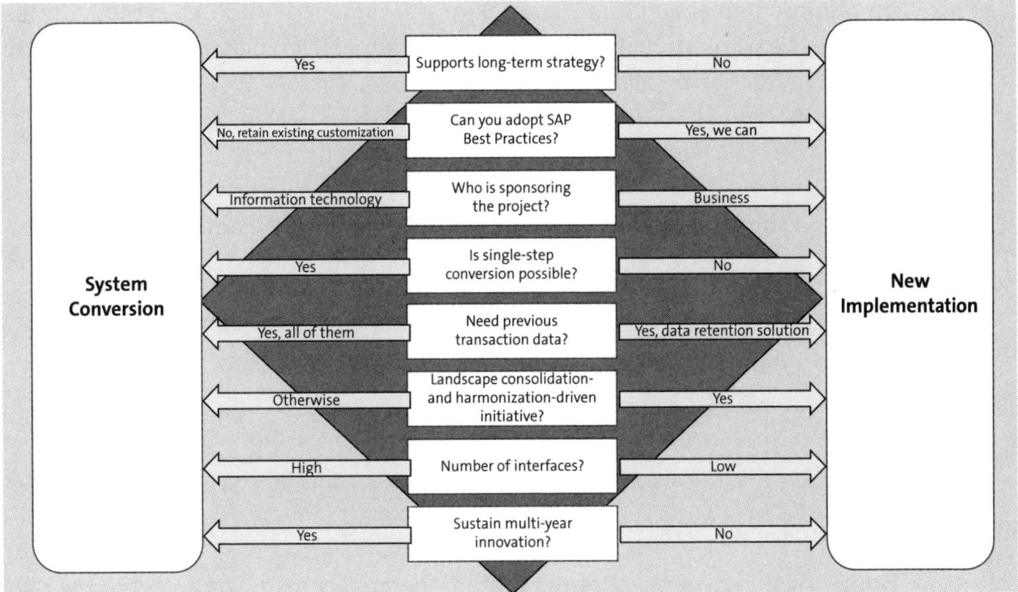

Figure 9.3 Key Considerations

Prerequisites

If the client is okay to retain the current business functionalities with minor modifications, such as adopting business partners rather than vendor and customer masters, or is ready to move to SAP S/4HANA cash management from the current classic cash and liquidity management, then their choice should incline toward system conversion. The leadership team should decide the approach after careful consideration of all aspects in play.

Additionally, it's important to check the current version of the SAP system. If the customer is using an SAP ERP 6.0 EHP 08, Unicode single-stack (SAP NetWeaver Application Server for ABAP) system, then you can convert to SAP S/4HANA in a single step. However, if the customer is on any previous release or the system is non-Unicode, then you first need to upgrade to SAP ERP 6.0 EHP 08. Furthermore, dual-stack systems (combined SAP NetWeaver Application Server for ABAP and SAP NetWeaver Application Server for Java systems) aren't supported for the conversion transition path, which means the team has to split the system before continuing with the conversion.

Lastly, from the general ledger perspective, the team needs to convert the system to the new general ledger before continuing with the system conversion.

What Is System Conversion?

By now, the customer, in partnership with SAP, has decided that the system conversion is the right approach. In this approach, the team converts the existing SAP system to SAP S/4HANA. At this point, it's important to note that the activities and deliverables of the system conversion approach are similar to that of the on-premise implementations and follow the same roadmap. As a result, in this chapter, we won't provide the details of certain deliverables and activities, and, wherever applicable, we'll refer to Chapter 6.

Overview

Figure 9.4 summarizes the key activities carried out by the team in the system conversion approach. One key difference is that the team adjusts the custom code and converts the application and data in the system conversion transition path as compared to developing, configuring, and migrating data in the new implementation of SAP S/4HANA.

Tip

There will most likely be at least one question on the exam asking you to identify the difference between a new implementation and a system conversion.

During the discover phase of the project, the project team has access to the trial system. The project team has reviewed the relevant simplification list to understand the changes.

The system conversion starts with the readiness check in the discover phase of the project, which is a report run on the customer system to identify the relevant simplification items, compare them with the existing solution, identify the gaps, and minimize the showstoppers, if any. At this phase, it's also important to understand the overall scope of the conversion such as the additional license requirements for cash and credit management in SAP S/4HANA. You also need to ensure that the year-end and quarter-end activities are complete, and the data is reconciled.

In the prepare phase, apart from project kick-off and other project management activities, the team starts the transition planning by reviewing the system requirements, running maintenance planner, performing simplification checks, and completing the custom code analysis to identify any changes, retire unused codes, modify incompatible code, and provide high-level estimates of the changes.

In the explore phase, the team carries out the fit-gap analysis and prepares the product backlog based on the delta-design workshops for any additional business requirements. It's not necessary to run the solution validation workshops (workshop A), and the team can directly run the delta design workshops (workshop B).

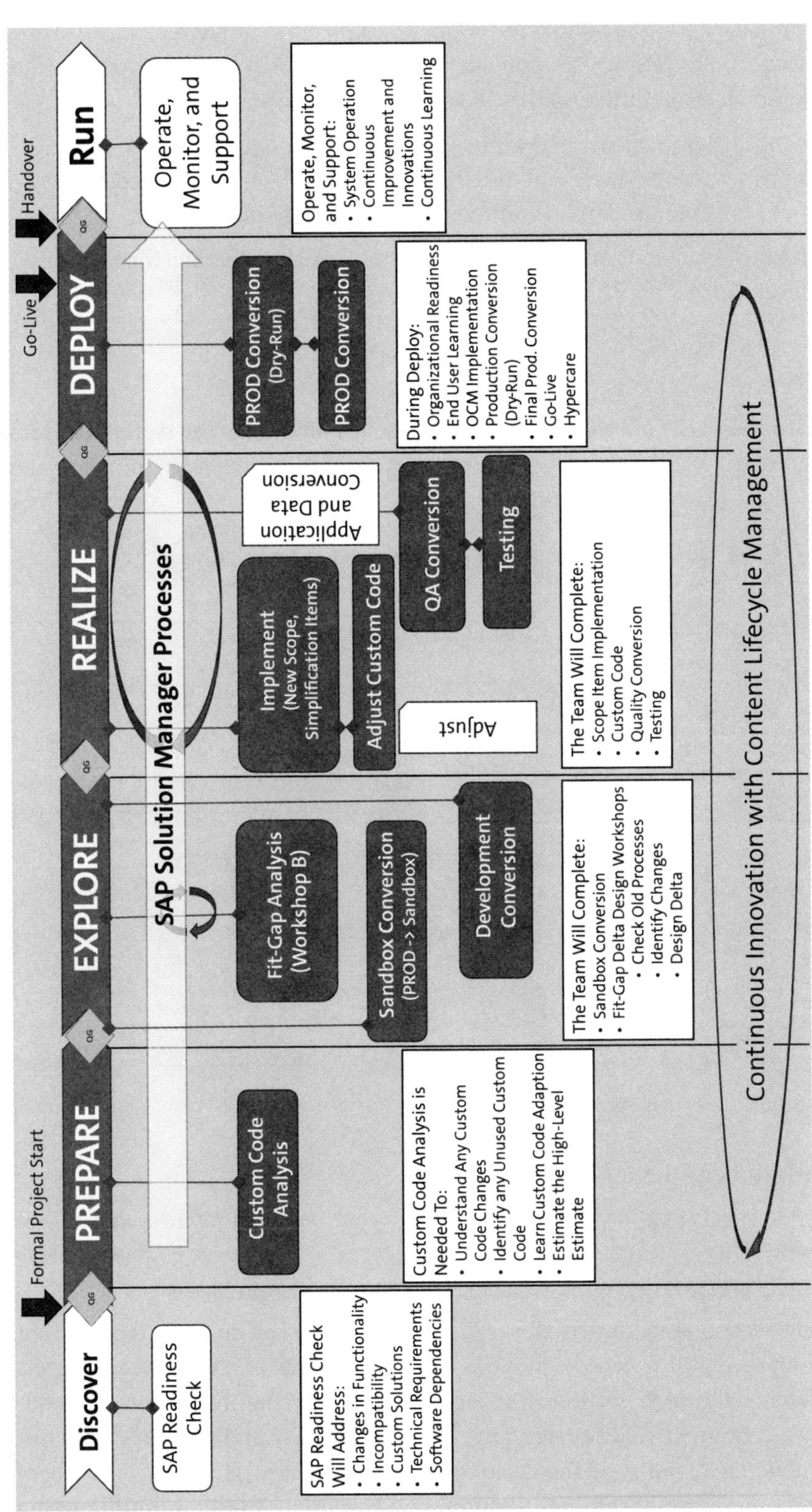

Figure 9.4 Overview of System Conversion

In the realize phase, the team adjusts the custom codes, implements new scope items and simplification lists, converts the quality assurance (QA) system, and tests the converted solution in the QA system environment.

Finally, in the deploy phase, the team completes the production conversion, go-live, and hypercare. At the end of the deploy phase, the build team hands over the solution to the operate team to commence the run phase of the project.

In the following sections, we'll look closely at these deliverables and the associated activities.

Landscape

Figure 9.5 shows the lifecycle of the existing environments in the system conversion approach.

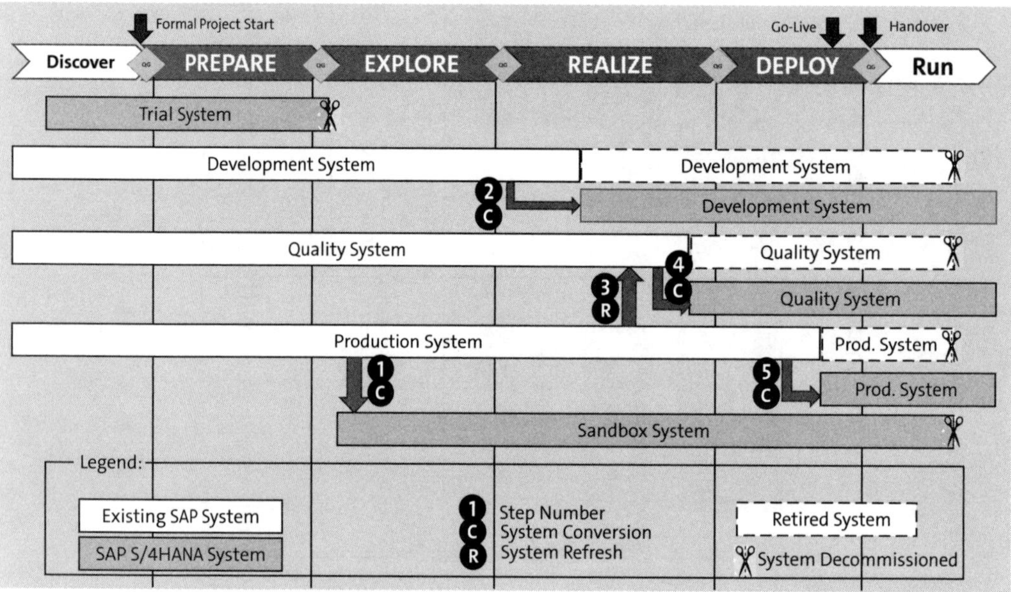

Figure 9.5 Landscape Overview of System Conversion

Let's walk through the key steps:

❶ The first step is to build the sandbox environment by copying the existing production (PROD) environment. The team will use the sandbox system to drive the delta design workshops in the explore phase of the project.

❷ In the second step, during the realize phase, you need to copy the existing development (DEV) environment to the SAP S/4HANA DEV environment. At this point, although not shown in Figure 9.5, you can decommission the sandbox environment. Additionally, after you build the SAP S/4HANA DEV environment, you may not need the existing DEV environment. However, for precautionary measures, we strongly recommend keeping the system until after the go-live and then decommission it, as shown in Figure 9.5.

❸ In the next steps, the project team refreshes the existing QA environment from the PROD environment.

❹ Subsequently, the team builds the SAP S/4HANA QA system by copying from the existing QA system. In the QA system, the team completes all the testing activities. The team should fix any bugs in the SAP S/4HANA DEV environment and transport the fixes to the QA system for further testing.

❺ After successful completion of the user acceptance testing (UAT), the team will transport the solution from the QA system to the PROD system and then perform the system copy from the exiting PROD environment to the new PROD environment.

Figure 9.6 shows an example of the high-level activities to create the landscape.

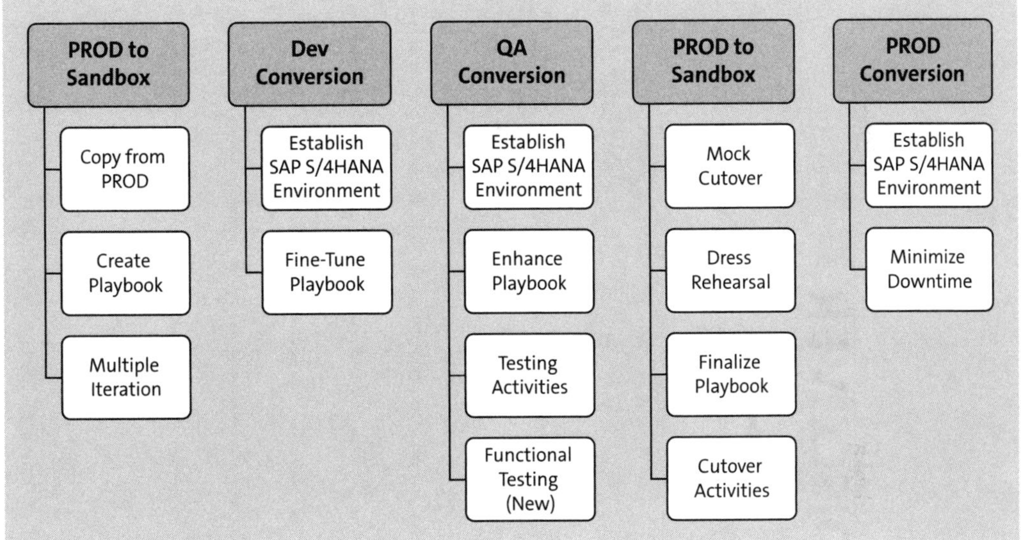

Figure 9.6 High-Level Plan

Benefits

Some of the benefits of the system conversion approach are as follows:

- Faster time to value as compared to the new implementations
- Retain your data
- Ability to consume innovations at your own pace
- Maintain higher number of interfaces

Discover Phase

The objective of this phase is for the customer to understand the business functionality of SAP S/4HANA and the benefits that the customer can reap by using this enterprise resource planning (ERP) system.

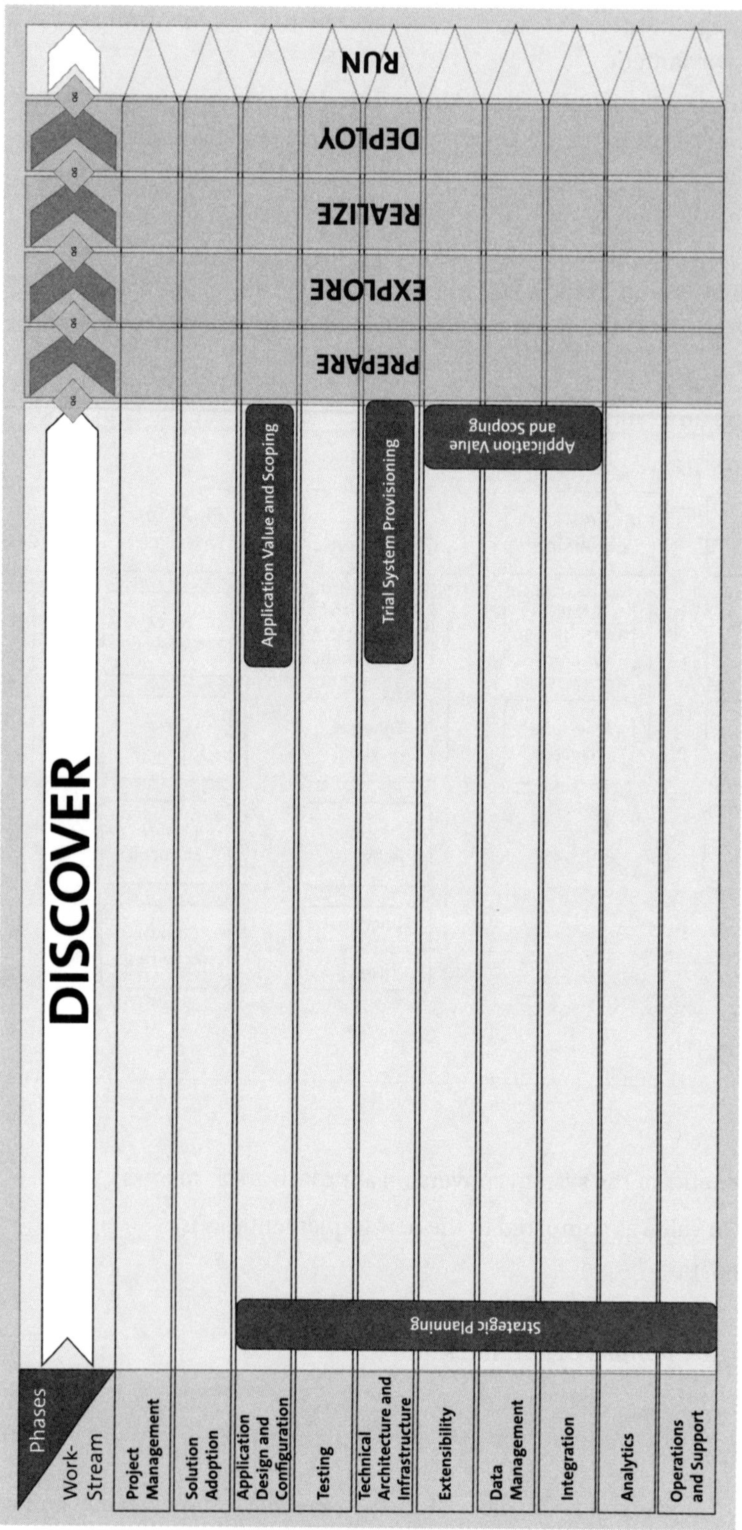

Figure 9.7 Discover Phase Deliverables

The deliverables of the discover phase are as follows:

- Strategic planning
- Application value and scoping
- Trial system provisioning

These deliverables are covered in the "Discover Phase" section in Chapter 6. Figure 9.7 shows the discover phase deliverables.

Prepare Phase

In the prepare phase, the project team will plan and prepare several planning documents from kick-off to phase closure. In this section, we'll review the prepare phase activities and the corresponding deliverables for SAP S/4HANA system conversions.

Before the start of this phase, the sponsor has approved the project and the team is already assigned. During this phase of the project, the team will work closely with the customer's project manager to create several planning documents as described in this section, which is organized based on the workstream. Figure 9.8 shows the deliverables in the prepare phase of the project, which we'll discuss in the following sections.

Project Management

The project management workstream covers all aspects of project initiation, planning, execution, monitoring and controlling, and closure activities. It includes the following deliverables:

- **Prototype**
  We've discussed prototyping in detail in Chapter 6. The overall objective, processes, SAP service, and components are similar except the way the team will set up the system. Instead of setting the SAP Model Company, you need to perform the system copy from the current PROD environment and use that system for the further prototype implementation and business case evaluation.
- **Transition planning**
  The transition planning objective, processes and procedures, and approach, explained in Chapter 6, are similar for the system conversion as that of the new implementation except for a few minor changes. Let's start by reviewing the tasks:
  - Perform the system conversion readiness check (applicable only for the system conversion).
  - Create the scope definition and objectives for the SAP S/4HANA transition project.
  - Define the cutover approach.

- Clarify the custom code adaptation.
- Clarify operational readiness.
- Define the technical architecture.
- Define the data migration architecture.
- Perform data volume planning.
- Define the user interface/user experience (UI/UX) strategy.
- Prepare the interface register.
- Run a legacy impact analysis on the interface inventory and data integration.
- Run a first assessment on output management.
- Run a first assessment on training requirements.
- Run a technical security self-check (optional).

The only task that is applicable to the project management workstream is "define cutover approach." The system conversion readiness check is described in Chapter 6 under the "SAP Readiness Check for SAP S/4HANA" section. We've reviewed the rest of the tasks in Chapter 6 under the "Transition Planning" section.

SAP provides the migration and upgrade planning workshop (MPW) to help customers complete the transition planning. The workshop will help define the overall scope and the detailed execution plan for the system conversion project to SAP S/4HANA.

- **Transition preparation**
  We've reviewed this deliverable in Chapter 6, in the "Transition Preparation" section. The only applicable task in the project management workstream is to prepare SAP Solution Manager 7.2 for project support.
- **Project initiation**
  This is the first step that formally recognizes the existence of the project. The key purpose of this process group is to ensure that the stakeholder's expectations are aligned with the initiative, identify any gaps, and work closely with the sponsor to close the alignment gaps.

  During this process group, the sales team will hand over the project, and the customer will sign the contract and place the purchase order. The assigned project manager will create the project charter, enhance the stakeholder's list identified during the discover phase, capture their expectations and requirements, and create the deliverable and project acceptance criteria. Finally, during this process group, the project manager will create the detailed project plan, including all of its management plans, such as cost management, scope baseline, scope management plan, requirement management plan, schedule management plan, stakeholder and communication management plan, risk and issue management plan, procurement management plan, change management plan, and human resource management plan. The project plan should also include the project constraints, assumptions and standards, and sign-off procedure.

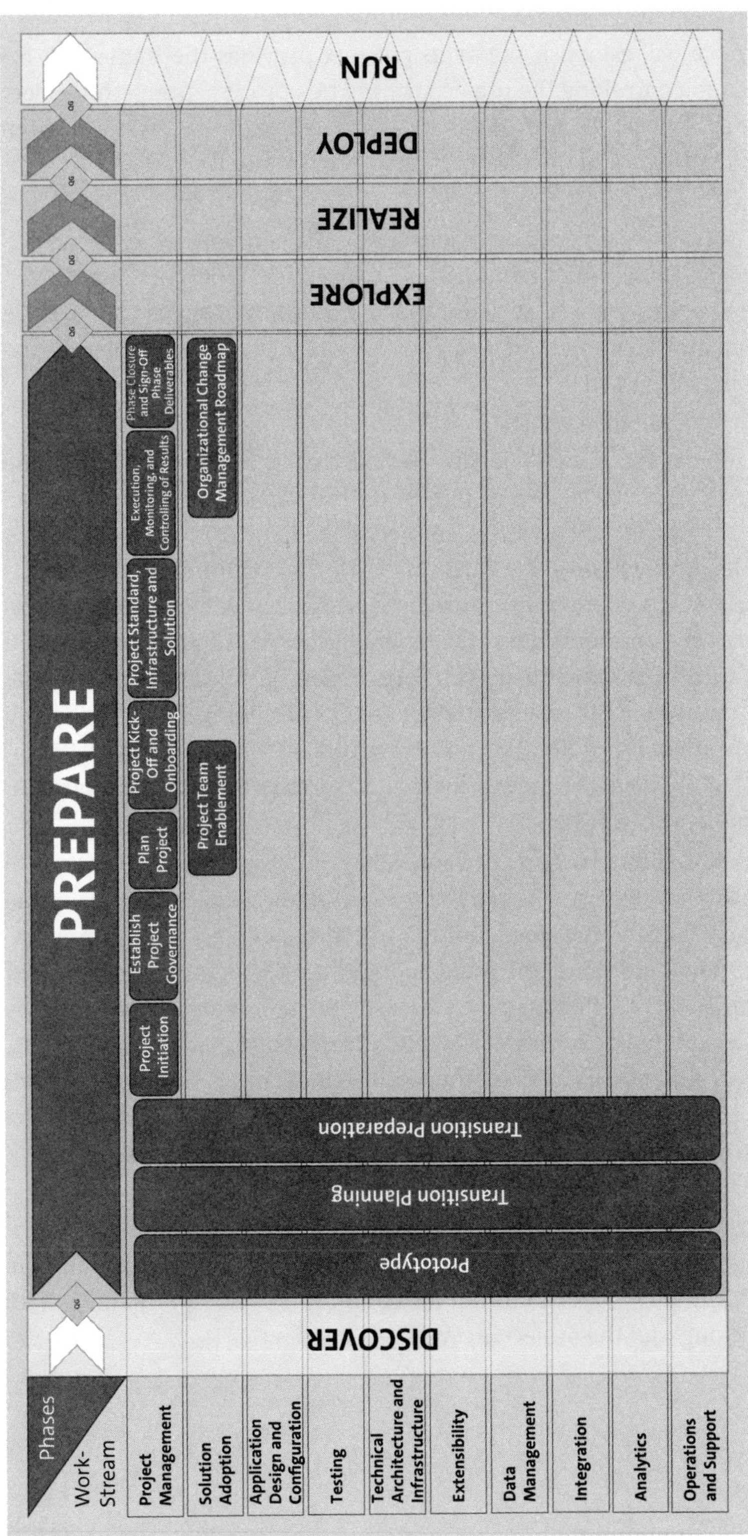

Figure 9.8 Prepare Phase Deliverables

- **Establish project governance**
  This deliverable will establish the oversight that provides the framework for monitoring and controlling the project. During this process group, the project team will be established, project hierarchy will be defined, roles and responsibilities will be identified, and the project plan will be reviewed.
- **Plan project**
  The goal of this deliverable is to account for all the components necessary to plan the project. These components include scope statement, work breakdown, schedule, constraints, budget, stakeholders and communication, risk and issue handling, and procurement management. This will feed into the project initiation deliverable discussed next.
- **Project kick-off and onboarding**
  In this deliverable, the project manager will kick off the project, signaling the official start date of the project. The purpose of this kick-off meeting is to share all the necessary information with the project stakeholders, including the team members. The project manager will use this platform to communicate the overall objectives of the project, project structure, decision-making processes, timeline, resources requirements with their roles and responsibilities, and overall plan, along with many other aspects. It also seeks the consent for the stakeholder's commitment throughout the project by outlining key areas where higher involvement is required, such as the involvement of the end-user community during the explore phase or for UAT, IT services during data migration or go-live, and so on.
- **Project standard, infrastructure, and solution**
  This deliverable will ensure that the team has a detailed understanding of the project standard, including documentation, coding, extensibility, configuration, process flow, requirements management, and any other standard required for the given client. This deliverable will also ensure the availability of tools such as project planning software, SAP Solution Manager, videoconferencing, conference rooms and laptops, Internet connectivity, or any other infrastructure need. The SAP S/4HANA server requirement isn't part of this deliverable; we'll discuss that in the "Technical Architecture and Infrastructure" section subsequently.
- **Execution, monitoring, and controlling of results**
  This deliverable will ensure that the team has access, necessary privilege, required tools, and appropriate techniques to monitor and control the project execution throughout the project lifecycle.

- **Phase closure and sign-off phase deliverables**
  This is the last deliverable of the prepare phase that will ensure the timely delivery of all committed deliverables. The phase is closed, and the team can move to the next phase subject to the sign-off from the client.

Solution Adoption

The solution adoption workstream ensures the high adoptability of the solution within the organization and includes the following deliverables:

- **Project team enablement**
  This deliverable will ensure that the project team has a sound understanding of the working methodology during the explore phase and the rest of the project. If needed, the project team should undergo Scrum framework training to understand its value and principles, approach, tools, and techniques. Team enablement may also require training and knowledge-sharing sessions on a multitude of topics, including the SAP Activate methodology, SAP Solution Manager, SAP Best Practices, and other tools. It's also advisable that the project team members should engage in self-learning exercises through blogs, openSAP, online demo sessions, trial environments, and so on.
- **Organizational change management (OCM) roadmap**
  This deliverable will append the fine details such as consistency in the project plan, traceability of the OCM activities, and relationship between each activity to the high-level OCM roadmap created earlier in the discover phase of the project.

Other deliverables include prototyping, transition planning, and transition preparation, each of which we discussed in Chapter 6 and in the corresponding entries for the project management workstream.

Application Design and Configuration

This workstream ensures seamless application of the design and configuration. It includes the prototype, transition planning, and transition preparation deliverables, which don't differ from the previous workstreams.

Testing

This workstream covers all aspects of testing the solution and includes the prototype, transition planning, and transition preparation deliverables, which don't differ from previous workstreams.

Technical Architecture and Infrastructure

This workstream covers all aspects of the infrastructure requirements and architecture. It includes the prototype, transition planning, and transition preparation deliverables, which don't differ from previous workstreams.

Extensibility

This workstream covers all aspects of the custom code requirement and extensibility features. It includes the prototype, transition planning, and transition preparation deliverables, which don't differ from previous workstreams.

Data Management

This workstream covers all aspects of the master data, transactional data, and data migration activities. It includes the prototype, transition planning, and transition preparation deliverables, which don't differ from previous workstreams.

Integration

This workstream covers all aspects of the integration with other SAP or third-party systems. It includes the prototype, transition planning, and transition preparation deliverables, which don't differ from previous workstreams.

Analytics

This workstream covers all aspects of the analytics and includes the prototype, transition planning, and transition preparation deliverables, which don't differ from previous workstreams.

Operations and Support

This workstream covers all aspects of the continuous operations, support, improvement, and innovations post-hypercare. It includes the prototype, transition planning, and transition preparation deliverables, which don't differ from previous workstreams.

Explore Phase

During this phase of the project, the team performs the fit-gap analysis and prepares the product backlog. All the planning is done during the prepare phase, and the customer has signed off the phase. In this phase, the team will focus on the requirement. Figure 9.9 shows the deliverables in the explore phase of the project, which we'll discuss in the following sections.

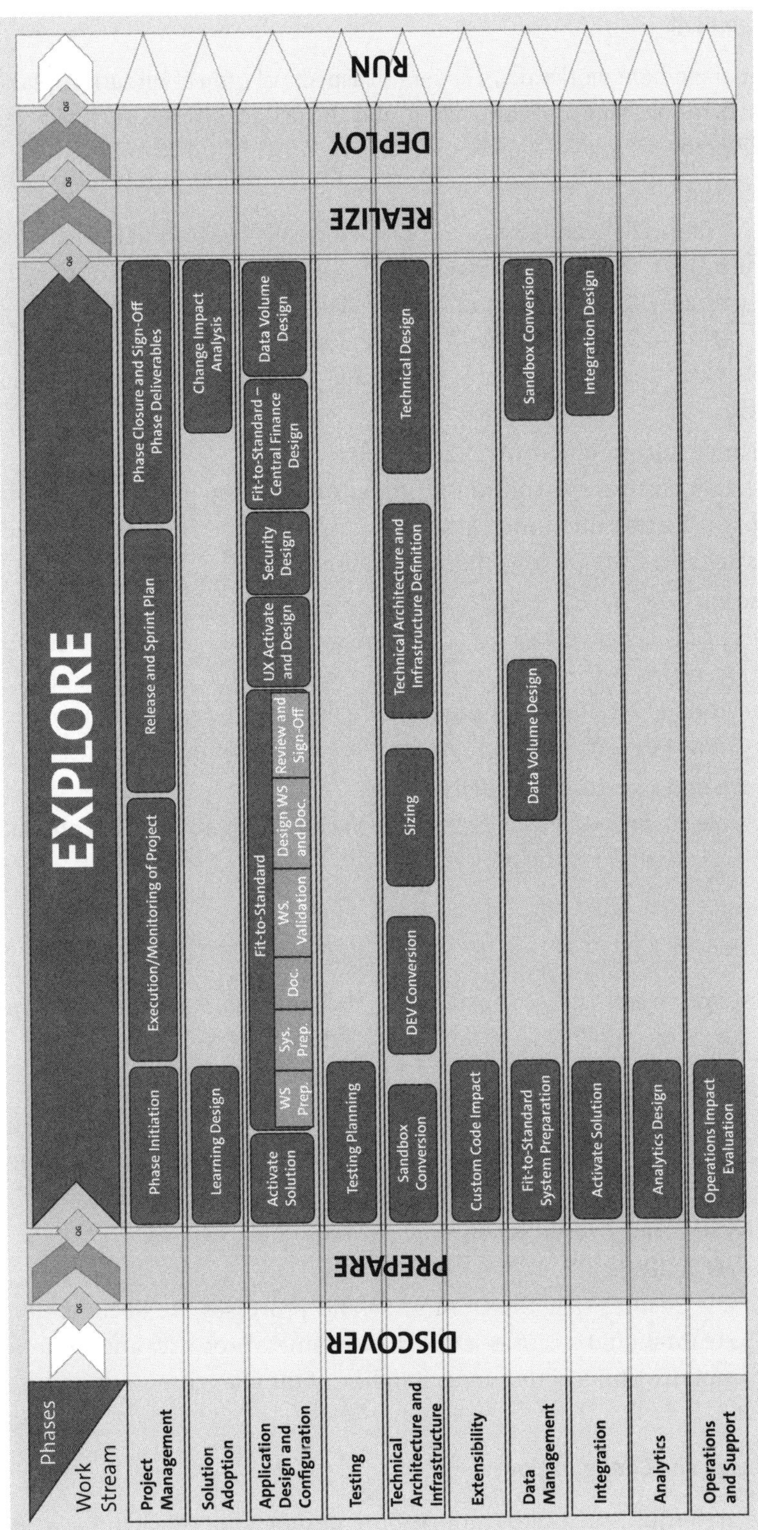

Figure 9.9 Explore Phase Deliverables

Project Management

The project management workstream covers all aspects of project initiation, planning, execution, monitoring and controlling, and closure activities. It includes the following deliverables:

- **Phase initiation**
  The objective of this deliverable is to recognize formally the start of the explore phase of the project. During this deliverable, the project manager will work with the client manager to review the upcoming deliverables during the explore phase and its timeline, as well as revisit the client's commitment (along with the Responsible, Accountable, Consulted, Informed [RACI] chart) to deliver the deliverables.
- **Execution, monitoring, and controlling results**
  This deliverable ensures the continuous monitoring of the project execution and control of the execution in case there is any deviation from the planned activities, schedule, costs, or any other constraints.
- **Release and sprint plan**
  The objective of this deliverable is to plan the sprint based on the prioritized backlog items, estimate the effort, develop the software, and release the sprint per the agreed-upon timeline after the sprint review and the approval from the respective product owner. See Chapter 4 for more information on sprints.
- **Phase closure and sign-off phase deliverables**
  This deliverable ensures timely and quality deliverables, signifying the completion of the explore phase of the project.

Solution Adoption

The solution adoption workstream ensures the high adoptability of the solution within the organization and includes the following deliverables:

- **Learning design**
  This deliverable will document the key-user and end-user training needs and create a training plan to fulfill the need. The plan is created by analyzing the solution and applications on one side and the supply of existing skills, knowledge gaps, locational constraints, and language requirements.
- **Change impact analysis**
  This deliverable ensures that the OCM steps and processes are documented properly. The team should create as-is and to-be business processes and demonstrate the comparison for a better understanding of the change.

Application Design and Configuration

This workstream ensures seamless application design and configuration. It includes the following deliverables:

- **Activate solution**
  The objective of this deliverable is to ensure the availability of a system for the fit-gap workshops. The team activates the preconfigured solutions based on the confirmed scope that becomes the foundation of the complete solution and a key implementation strategy. The scope includes the provisioning of the sandbox system.
- **Fit-to-standard workshop preparation**
  This deliverable aims to prepare the team for the upcoming fit-gap analysis. It includes becoming familiar with the scope items and related processes, testing the business processes, identifying and familiarizing with relevant tools and techniques, performing a dry run, and handling workshop logistics such as conference room, videoconference rooms, presenter, timing, and so on.
- **Fit-to-standard system preparation**
  The objective of this deliverable is to ensure that the sandbox is ready with sample data, and the team has completed the additional configurations and testing. It ensures sandbox readiness.
- **Fit-to-standard system workshops and documentations**
  This deliverable refers to the workshops conducted with the dedicated key users to present the target solutions. Document the suggestions and feedback received from the key users while conducting the workshops, and ensure that they are aware of certain changes and the reasoning behind them. It's critical to make necessary notes and take minutes of the meeting.
- **Fit-to-standard system workshops validation**
  This deliverable ensures the prioritization of the delta requirements captured during the workshops.
- **Design workshops and documentation**
  The project meets iteratively to finalize the design for the captured delta requirements.
- **Review and customer sign-offs**
  The project performs the quality gate review, and the customer's process owner signs off on the delta requirement and the design document.
- **UX activation and design**
  This deliverable aims to identify the gaps between a customer's specific requirements and the SAP standard configuration for SAP Fiori.
- **Security design**
  This deliverable covers the specific security topics, such as user management, authorization management, role management, and so on.
- **Fit-to-standard – Central Finance design**
  This special deliverable for the system conversion to Central Finance allows customers to create a common reporting structure. This deliverable will help customers deep dive into Central Finance topics.
- **Data volume design**
  This deliverable will outline the data volume, storage duration, and archival or

deletion strategy. SAP HANA moves data from memory to the disk, based on certain system settings, which is called data aging. It helps free up in-memory by moving the aged data to the disk.

Testing

This workstream covers all aspects of testing the solution and includes the following deliverable:

- **Test planning**
  The objective of this deliverable is to build a complete test plan for the solution that should include objectives and assumptions, test scope, type of testing (unit, string, integration, scenario, user acceptance, regression, etc.), test approach and methodology, test deliverables, tools, standards and guidelines, test case development, defect management, reporting and analysis, roles and responsibilities, and performance testing.

Technical Architecture and Infrastructure

This workstream covers all aspects of the infrastructure requirements and architecture. It includes the following deliverables:

- **Sandbox conversion**
  For the system conversion, this deliverable ensures that the sandbox system is prepared by copying the PROD environment.
- **DEV conversion**
  The DEV system on SAP S/4HANA must be built from the DEV system of the current environment.
- **Sizing**
  Run a capacity estimation, for example, using the Quick Sizer tool, on the required hardware for application servers and databases (CPU, RAM, storage, network).
- **Technical architecture and infrastructure definition**
  To be able to provide a detailed definition of the technical target architecture and infrastructure, you'll first need to clarify the technical boundary conditions. This is the basis for the creation of the technical solution blueprint.
- **Technical design**
  This activity creates a technical design document.

Extensibility

This workstream covers all aspects of the custom code requirement and extensibility features. It includes the following deliverable:

- **Custom code impact**
  For the system conversion, the team must analyze the custom code using the Code Inspector to determine what code should be retired or adjusted.

Data Management

This workstream covers all aspects of the master data, transactional data, and data migration activities. It includes the following deliverables:

- **Data volume design**
  This deliverable will outline the data volume, storage duration, and archival or deletion strategy. SAP HANA moves data from memory to the disk, based on certain system settings, which is called data aging. It helps free up memory by moving the aged data to the disk.
- **Sandbox conversion**
  For the system conversion, this deliverable ensures that the sandbox system is prepared by copying the PROD environment.

Integration

This workstream covers all aspects of the integration with other SAP or third-party systems and includes the following deliverables:

- **Activate solution**
  This deliverable (1) adjusts and removes any integration settings in the sandbox environment with any other PROD environment (remember that the team created the sandbox environment from the current PROD environment), and (2) integrates the sandbox system with any other SAP/non-SAP systems.
- **Integration design**
  This deliverable documents the detailed aspects of integration identified in the previous project phases. Some key considerations are as follows:
  - Design of the to-be system and solution landscape with interfaces
  - Integration between SAP solutions, for example, between SAP S/4HANA and SAP cloud solutions such as SAP Ariba and SAP SuccessFactors
  - Integration between SAP and non-SAP solutions
  - All other technical, nonbusiness priority-specific topics

  This design document is for communication as well as formal sign-off.

Analytics

This workstream covers all aspects of the analytics and includes the following deliverable:

- **Analytics design**
  The deliverable focuses on the analytics topics such as the predictive analytics, business intelligence (BI), and the corresponding detail requirements.

Operations and Support

This workstream covers all aspects of the continuous operations, support, improvement, and innovations post hypercare. It includes the following deliverable:

- **Operations impact evaluation**
  This deliverable dictates the IT framework after the implementation of the new solution. The customer, in the partnership with the system integrator and SAP, creates a target-operating model to safely operate the new solution.

Realize Phase

The purpose of this phase is to realize the build incrementally and iteratively based on the business requirements and scenarios identified during the previous phases of the project. During the realize phase, the team is deep into system configuration based on the fit-gap analysis and the prioritized product backlog. In addition, legacy data load starts, solution adoption continues, and operation planning happens. Figure 9.10 shows the deliverables in the realize phase of the project, which we'll discuss in the following sections.

Project Management

The project management workstream covers all aspects of project initiation, planning, execution, monitoring and controlling, and closure activities. It includes the following deliverables:

- **Phase initiation**
  The objective of this deliverable is to recognize formally the start of the realize phase of the project. During this deliverable, the project manager will work with the client manager to review the upcoming deliverables during the realize phase and its timeline, as well as revisit the client's commitment (along with the RACI chart) to deliver the deliverables.
- **Plan realize phase**
  This planning is, specific to the realize phase, required to identify the sprint cycle, sprint planning, and other sprint ceremonies. See Chapter 4 for more information on sprints.
- **Sprint initiation (iterative)**
  This deliverable formally initiates a sprint.

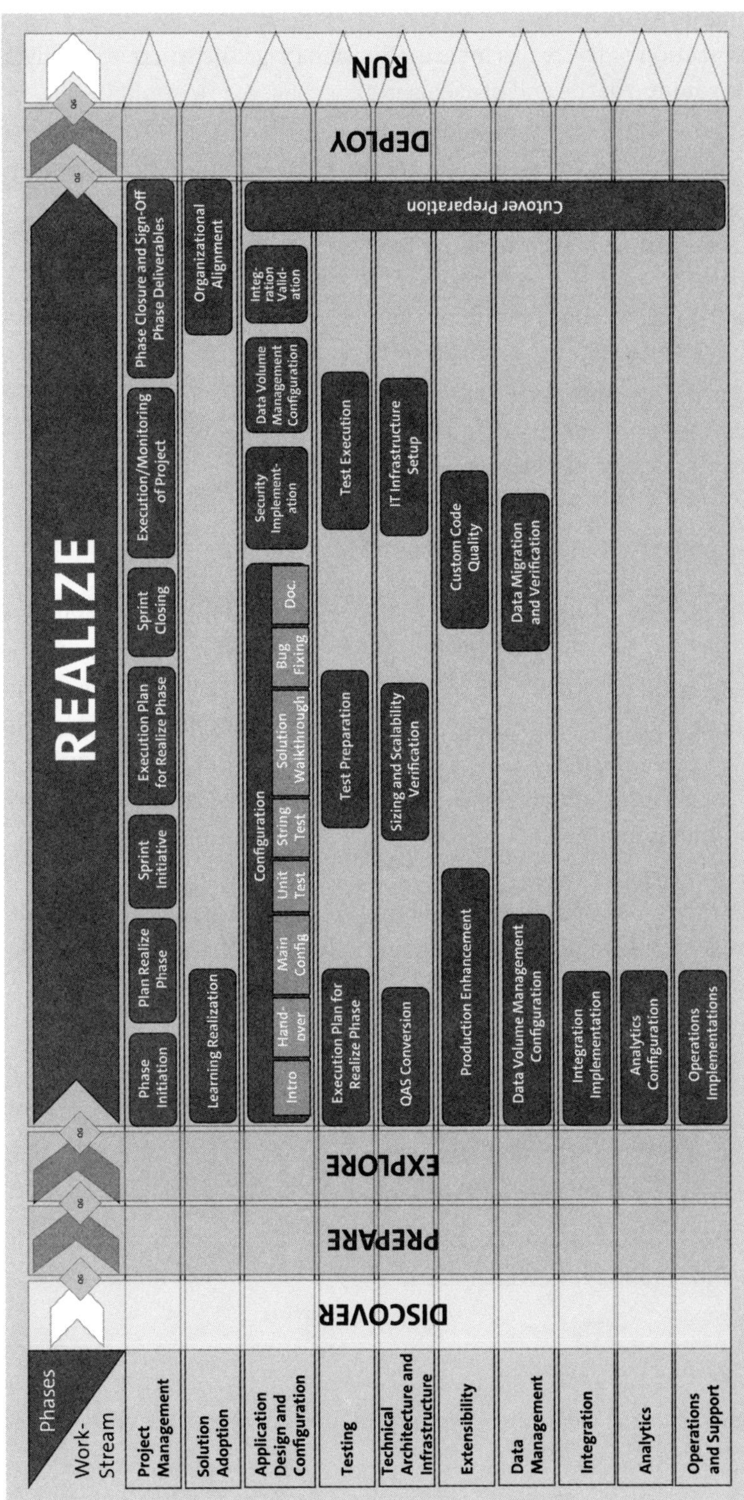

Figure 9.10 Realize Phase Deliverables

- **Execute plan for realize phase**
  This is the execution of the realize phase plan to manage the sprint and deliver the workable solution at the end of each sprint.
- **Sprint closing**
  After the formal sprint retrospective and sprint review ceremonies, this deliverable ensures the sprint closure.
- **Execution, monitoring, and controlling results**
  This deliverable ensures the continuous monitoring of the project execution and controls the execution in case there's any deviation from the planned activities, schedule, costs, or any other constraints.
- **Phase closure and sign-off phase deliverables**
  This deliverable ensures timely and quality deliverables, signifying the completion of the explore phase of the project.

Solution Adoption

The solution adoption workstream ensures the high adoptability of the solution within the organization and includes the following deliverables:

- **Learning realization**
  The team created the learning design in the explore phase. In this phase, the team will implement the design to create the end-user training materials, such as business process documents, PowerPoint presentations, videos, and so on, and train the end users.
- **Organizational alignment**
  The objective of this deliverable is to align the end user's roles and responsibilities to ensure that the end user's activities are match up with the project's objective. The tasks are as follows:
  - Execute role mapping and transition planning.
  - Conduct sounding board and pulse checks.
  - Communicate the sprint scope and plan (iterative).
  - Communicate the sprint result (iterative).
  - Refine and execute the communication plan.
  - Use OCM and testing alignment.
  - Use OCM and data migration alignment.

Application Design and Configuration

This workstream ensures seamless application design and configuration. It includes the following deliverables:

- **Configuration**
  Figure 9.11 shows the configuration deliverables that start from the beginning of the sprint by handover sessions and continue until the documentation. The team familiarizes themselves with the system configuration in the introduction deliverables. At the start of the sprint, the ownership transfers from the design team to the configuration team, ensuring that all the design activities are complete, reviewed, and signed-off on. The configuration team completes the required configurations, and unit tests and spring tests the solution. The team then walks through the configured solution with the business and gets their feedback and approval. Once again, it's a repeated process until the bugs are fixed. In the final step, the team complete the documentation, which will end the sprint cycle.

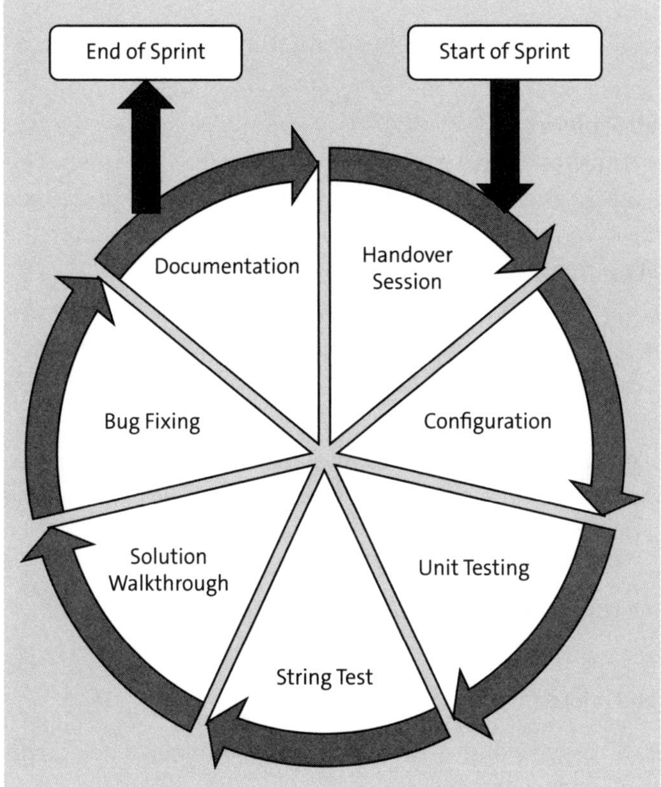

Figure 9.11 Configuration Cycle

- **Security implementation**
  The team implements all the necessary customer-specific security requirements.
- **Data volume management configuration**
  Data volume and data aging, a concept introduced in the explore phase of the project, are configured in this deliverable.

- **Integration validation**
  This key deliverable ensures that the project team completes the integration work per the requirement. The integration validation addresses the following aspects:
  - Data consistency
  - Business process monitoring and exception management
  - Performance and scalability
- **Cutover preparation**
  In this deliverable, the team creates the cutover plan. See the "Testing and Deployment" section in Chapter 4 for more details on cutover plans.

Testing

This workstream covers all aspects of testing the solution and includes the following deliverables:

- **Execute plan for realize phase**
  The purpose of this deliverable is to execute the work defined in the realize phase and manage the sprints and testing according to previously defined plans. During test execution, all issues must be logged and documented in the system for traceability purposes.
- **Test preparation**
  The purpose of this activity is to prepare all business process–related tests according to customer-specific configurations.
- **Test execution**
  The purpose of this activity is to execute the integration test, regression test, and UAT. After the tests have been planned and test data made available on the test systems, testing can begin.
- **Cutover preparation**
  In this deliverable, the team creates the cutover plan.

Technical Architecture and Infrastructure

This workstream covers all aspects of the infrastructure requirements and architecture. It includes the following deliverables:

- **QA system conversion**
  The purpose of the QA system environment (software setup) is to install a viable, correctly configured technical QA system environment that is available for use by the project team to perform QA system testing.

- **Sizing and scalability verification**
  In this activity, the sizing estimation performed in the explore phase is further detailed and verified afterwards. The initial assumptions made are now challenged with real-world KPIs.
- **IT infrastructure setup**
  In the realize phase, the technical infrastructure must be installed and configured as required for the go-live. Prior to the go-live, a technical verification is proposed to ensure that SAP Best Practices are followed. The technical infrastructure follows the technical design document created in the technical design activity.
- **Cutover preparation**
  In this deliverable, the team creates the cutover plan.

Extensibility

This workstream covers all aspects of the custom code requirement and extensibility features. It includes the following deliverables:

- **Product enhancements**
  The product enhancements activity covers the development of custom code to close the delta requirements identified in the fit-to-standard activities in the explore phase.
- **Custom code quality**
  This activity implements the required quality level for custom coding.
- **Cutover preparation**
  In this deliverable, the team creates the cutover plan.

Data Management

This workstream covers all aspects of the master data, transactional data, and data migration activities. It includes the following deliverables:

- **Data volume management configuration**
  This deliverable configures and tests the data volume based on the customer's requirements.
- **Data migration and verification**
  This deliverable is delivered by executing the perform load and verification runs (system conversion) tasks that are performed twice within the minimum downtime service.
- **Cutover preparation**
  In this deliverable, the team creates the cutover plan.

Integration

This workstream covers all aspects of the integration with other SAP or third-party systems, including the following deliverables:

- **Integration implementation**
  This deliverable ensures the implementation of a customer's specific integration requirements captured in the explore phase.
- **Cutover preparation**
  In this deliverable, the team creates the cutover plan and includes specifics about the integration.

Analytics

This workstream covers all aspects of the analytics and includes the following deliverables:

- **Analytics configuration**
  The team performs the analytics-related configurations based on the customer's requirements.
- **Cutover preparation**
  In this deliverable, the team creates the cutover plan and includes specifics about the analytics.

Operations and Support

This workstream covers all aspects of the operation and support post-hypercare. It includes the following deliverables:

- **Operation implementation**
  The team carried out the operation impact evaluation in the explore phase of the project and listed their findings. Based on the findings, the target support operations should be implemented and/or adjusted.
- **Cutover preparation**
  In this deliverable, the team creates the cutover plan.

Deploy Phase

In the deploy phase of the project, the business switches the operation to the new PROD environment. This is the final phase of the project in which the team will close all open issues, ensure organizational readiness, and execute the production cutover so that the business can realize the benefits of the newly implemented solution. Figure 9.12 shows the deliverables in the deploy phase of the project, which we'll discuss in the following sections.

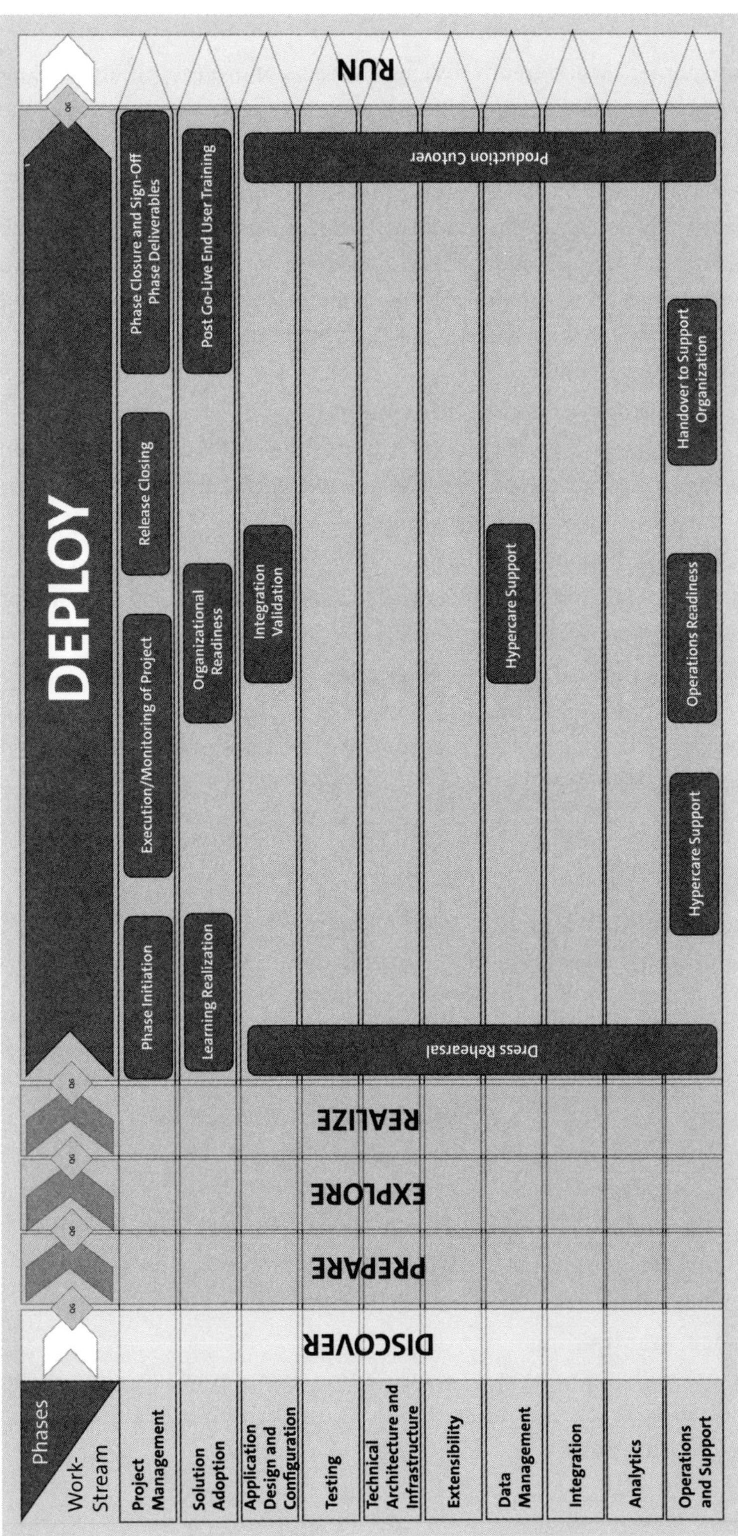

Figure 9.12 Deploy Phase Deliverables

Project Management

The project management workstream covers all aspects of project initiation, planning, execution, monitoring and controlling, and closure activities. It includes the following deliverables:

- **Phase initiation**
  The objective of this deliverable is to recognize formally the start of the deploy phase of the project. During this deliverable, the project manager will work with the client manager to review the upcoming deliverables during this phase and its timeline, as well as revisit the client's commitment (along with the RACI chart) to deliver the deliverables.
- **Execution, monitoring, and controlling results**
  This deliverable ensures the continuous monitoring of the project execution and controls the execution in case there's any deviation from the planned activities, schedule, costs, or any other constraints.
- **Release closing**
  The purpose of this deliverable is to formally close the release and prepare for the next release or sprint planning meeting.
- **Project closure and sign-off project deliverables**
  The purpose of the phase closure and sign-off is to close all the outstanding issues and ensure that all the agreed-upon deliverables are submitted and signed-off by the customer.

Solution Adoption

The solution adoption workstream ensures the high adoptability of the solution within the organization and includes the following deliverables:

- **Learning realization**
  The team created the learning design in the explore phase. In this phase, the team will implement the design to create the end-user training materials, such as business process documents, PowerPoint presentations, videos, and so on, and train the end users.
- **Organizational readiness**
  This deliverable checks the organizational readiness for the system go-live. There are many tools to check the readiness, such as surveys, closed-loop feedback, and so on.
- **Post go-live end-user training**
  The purpose of end-user training is to ensure that end users have adopted the solution, knowledge resources are maintained, and responses to the end-user acceptance survey are positive.

Application Design and Configuration

This workstream ensures seamless application design and configuration. It includes the following deliverables:

- **Integration validation**
  The key deliverable ensures that the project team completes the integration work per the requirements. The integration validation addresses the following aspects:
  - Data consistency
  - Business process monitoring and exception management
  - Performance and scalability
- **Dress rehearsal**
  Around two–four weeks prior to the go-live, the team executes the cutover plan on a test environment to ensure that the plan is complete and covers all aspects of the go-live. The prerequisites are as follows:
  - The detailed cutover plan with owners, dependencies, and durations fully documented
  - The involvement of all task owners
  - A test environment representative of the source and target platforms for production
  - The technical cookbook, which details all the required technical migration steps
- **Production cutover**
  The purpose of this deliverable is to perform the cutover to the production software and go-live. At this point, the organizational, business, functional, technical, and system aspects of the project are ready to be used in production.

Testing

This workstream covers all aspects of testing the solution and includes the following deliverables:

- **Dress rehearsal**
  Refer to the "Application Design and Configuration" section for the deploy phase.
- **Production cutover**
  Refer to the "Application Design and Configuration" section for the deploy phase.

Technical Architecture and Infrastructure

This workstream covers all aspects of the infrastructure requirements and the architecture. It includes the following deliverables:

- **Dress rehearsal**
  Refer to the "Application Design and Configuration" section for the deploy phase.
- **Production cutover**
  Refer to the "Application Design and Configuration" section for the deploy phase.

Extensibility

This workstream covers all aspects of the custom code requirement and extensibility features. It includes the dress rehearsal and production cutover deliverables, which don't differ from the application design and configuration workstream in the deploy phase.

Data Management

This workstream covers all aspects of the master data, transactional data, and data migration activities. It includes the following deliverables:

- **Dress rehearsal**
  Refer to the "Application Design and Configuration" section for the deploy phase.
- **Production cutover**
  Refer to the "Application Design and Configuration" section for the deploy phase.
- **Hypercare support**
  The team performs a specific task in the deploy phase where they delete obsolete data with the Obsolete Data Handling tool to offset the memory overhead from 5–10% of likely obsolete data. Refer to SAP Note 2661837 for more information.

Integration

This workstream covers all aspects of the integration with other SAP or third-party systems. It includes the dress rehearsal and production cutover deliverables, which don't differ from the application design and configuration workstream in the deploy phase.

Analytics

This workstream covers all aspects of the analytics. It includes the dress rehearsal and production cutover deliverables, which don't differ from the application design and configuration workstream in the deploy phase.

Operations and Support

This workstream covers all aspects of the operation and support post-hypercare. It includes the following deliverables:

- **Operational readiness**
  The purpose of this survey is to take the pulse of the organization, prior to go-live, to determine the general comfort level with the upcoming changes. If that comfort level isn't there, it's critical to determine where additional OCM work needs to be focused. In addition, the check of production support readiness is to ensure that the resources and processes are in place to support the solution after cutover.
- **Dress rehearsal**
  Refer to the "Application Design and Configuration" section of the deploy phase.
- **Production cutover**
  Refer to the "Application Design and Configuration" section of the deploy phase.
- **Hypercare support**
  This is the period just after go-live and before handing over the solution to the run organization. In this period, the team analyzes the following aspects and make changes to improve the system performance:
  - Workload analysis
  - Health check and scalability analysis
  - Sizing verification
  - Requirements and constraints
  - Security activities
- **Handover to support organization**
  The team, after completion of the hypercare period, hands over the solution to the operations team at the customer site. It includes the following:
  - Finalized system documentation
  - Finalized operational procedures as part of the operations handbook
  - Check of the customer support organization

Run Phase

This phase starts after the hypercare, during the previous phase of the project, to optimize the overall operation. During this phase, the support is provided by the customer IT team, and they continue to strive for optimization, automate the application processes, ensure system availability, and provide system performance. Figure 9.13 shows the deliverables in the run phase of the project, which we'll discuss in the following sections.

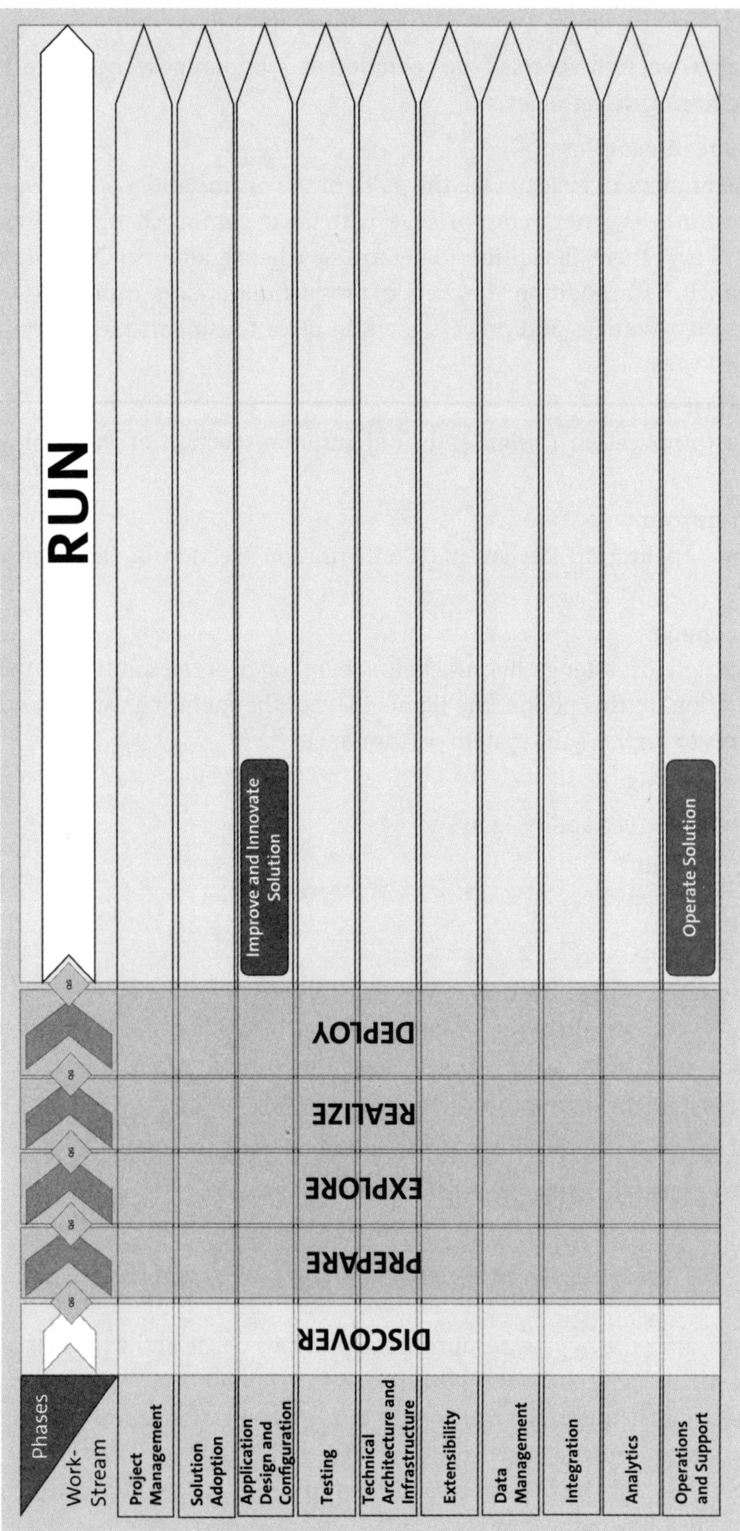

Figure 9.13 Run Phase Deliverables

Application Design and Configuration

This workstream ensures seamless application design and configuration. It includes the following deliverable:

- **Improve and innovate solution**
  The customer updates the SAP system periodically.

Operations and Support

This workstream covers all aspects of the operation and support post-hypercare. It includes the following deliverable:

- **Operate solution**
  With the end of the project, the project team hands over the solution to the operate organization who is responsible for operating the solution. It ensures efficient operations and continuous improvement.

Important Terminology

For this exam objective, you're expected to understand the following terms:

- **Readiness check**
  This assessment is carried out in the discover phase of the project to check for the relevant simplification item.
- **Simplification list**
  The simplification list is a document created by SAP for each SAP S/4HANA release listing the business functionality, its availability in the given version, and any changes in status, such as obsolete.
- **System conversion**
  System conversion is one of the transition paths to move to SAP S/4HANA from an existing SAP solution.

 Practice Questions

These practice questions will help you evaluate your understanding of the topics covered in this chapter. The questions shown are similar in nature to those found on the certification examination. Although none of these questions will be found on the exam itself, they will allow you to review your knowledge of the subject. Select the correct answers, and then check the completeness of your answers in the "Practice Question Answers and Explanations" section. Remember that on the exam, you must select all correct answers and only correct answers to receive credit for the question.

1. What are the scenarios to consider for the system conversion? (There are three correct answers.)

☐ **A.** The customer doesn't want to retain the existing customization.

☐ **B.** The project is IT driven.

☐ **C.** The customer wants to retain all their existing data.

☐ **D.** There are two interfaces.

☐ **E.** The customer has a limited budget but plans to invest in the transformation over a period of five years.

2. The current quality system is refreshed from the existing PROD environment in a system conversion project. True or false?

☐ **A.** True

☐ **B.** False

3. The team has created the sandbox environment and showcased the capabilities to the customer. Now, they are making the changes again in the DEV environment. What is wrong in this scenario?

☐ **A.** The team can transport the changes to the DEV environment.

☐ **B.** Nothing is wrong with the current scenario.

☐ **C.** The sandbox environment isn't for showcasing the SAP S/4HANA capabilities. They should have used the trial system.

☐ D. None of the above.

4. Strategic planning isn't part of which of the following workstreams? (There are three correct answers.)

☐ **A.** Project management

☐ **B.** Customer team enablement

☐ **C.** Solution adoption

☐ **D.** Data management

☐ **E.** Analytics

5. What are the phases where a team works on the prototype? (There are three correct answers.)

☐ **A.** Run

☐ **B.** Realize

☐ **C.** Deploy

☐ **D.** Discover

☐ **E.** Explore

☐ **F.** Prepare

6. What are the deliverables in the fit-to-standard process in the explore phase of the project? (There are two correct answers.)

☐ **A.** Workshop preparation

☐ **B.** Activate solution

☐ **C.** Sandbox conversion

☐ **D.** Workshop validation

☐ **E.** Analytics design

7. You're in the realize phase of a system conversion project. You've completed the data volume management configuration, data migration, and verification. What is the reason behind the deliverables?

☐ **A.** You *must* migrate all the data; it's one of the key considerations for the system conversion project.

☐ **B.** You captured the customer's requirement, so you had to deliver even though it was outside the scope of work.

☐ **C.** You explained data aging and archiving to the client.

☐ **D.** You're building the analytics solution for the client.

☐ **E.** None of the above.

8. What are three deliverables from the realize phase of a system conversion project? (There are three correct answers.)

☐ **A.** Fit-to-standard

☐ **B.** Configuration

☐ **C.** Analytics configuration

☐ **D.** Sprint closing

☐ **E.** Project kick-off

9. What are the deliverables from the deploy phase of the project? (There are two correct answers.)

☐ **A.** Dress rehearsal

☐ **B.** Learning realization

☐ **C.** Test planning

☐ **D.** Customer team self-enablement

☐ **E.** Organizational change management roadmap

10. What is a deliverable from the run phase of the project?

☐ **A.** Improve and innovate solution

☐ **B.** Hypercare support

☐ **C.** Continuous improvement

☐ **D.** Incident management

☐ **E.** All of the above

Practice Question Answers and Explanations

1. Correct answers: **B, C, E**
   An IT-driven transformation project (option B) where the customer wants to retain all of their data (option C) is a clear indication of a system conversion project. Additionally, the customer wants to slowly consume the innovations as stated in option E with long-term planning.
2. Correct answer: **A**
   True. In a system conversion project, the team refreshes the quality system from the existing PROD environment.
3. Correct answer: **B**
   A transport management system isn't available on the sandbox environment. Moreover, you can't make changes in the trial system, and the team correctly showcased the SAP S/4HANA capabilities in the sandbox environment. There is nothing wrong with the presented scenario.
4. Correct answers: **A, B, C**
   The question mentions strategic planning, which means you're in the discover phase of the project. It's part of all the workstreams except the project management workstream and the solution adoption workstream. If you look closely, customer team enablement isn't a workstream in the system conversion project.
5. Correct answers: **D, E, F**
   The prototype work starts in the discover phase where the customer and SAP agree to build a prototype. The work continues in the prepare and the explore phases of the project.
6. Correct answers: **A, D**
   Workshop preparation and workshop validation are the deliverables listed here, which are part of the fit-to-standard deliverable.
7. Correct answer: **C**
   Option A is to confuse you. Although it's one of the considerations, it isn't the reason you delivered data volume management configuration, data migration,

and verification. Even in the system conversion project, a customer can opt for data aging and data archiving. Option C is the right choice.

8. Correct answers: **B, C, D**
   In the realize phase, the team mainly works on the configuration, unit and string testing, solution walkthrough, bug fixing, and documentation. The project kick-off is a deliverable from the prepare phase, while the team carries out the fit-to-standard workshops in the explore phase of the project.
9. Correct answers: **A, B**
   Dress rehearsal and the learning realization are the only two deliverables listed from the deploy phase. Don't get confused with the name "learning realization."
10. Correct answer: **A**
    The team aims for continuous improvement, and incident management is a process set for support activities. Hypercare support is provided in the deploy phase of the project. Option A is the only correct choice.

Takeaway

In this chapter, we looked into the system conversion transition path and delved into the decision processes leading to the system conversion. Additionally, we reviewed the landscape lifecycle for the system conversion and concluded the overview session by understanding the benefits of the system conversion process.

We continued our course in the standard fashion by reviewing the deliverables and the corresponding tasks from the discover phase to the run phase of the project. During these deliverables explanations, we reviewed the transition plan, transition preparation, prototyping, and several other aspects of the system conversion. Finally, we concluded the chapter by answering the practice questions.

Summary

This chapter discussed the system conversion, one of the most widely used approaches to transition to SAP S/4HANA. We discussed the details and the scenarios in which you can choose to transition to SAP S/4HANA from an existing SAP system. In the next and final chapter, we'll review the last transition path—selective data transition.

Chapter 10
Selective Data Transition Path

Techniques You'll Master

- Understand selective data transition and the applicable scenarios
- Explain the differences between the system conversion and selective data transition
- Know the deliverables and activities during the conversion phases

In this last chapter, we'll focus on the last transition path, that is, the *selective data transition*. As the name suggests, this approach is useful when you need to migrate only a subset of data from the existing SAP ERP solution to the on-premise implementation of SAP S/4HANA. Additionally, we use this transition approach on top of the system conversion to standardize business functions.

We'll start our chapter by discussing the approach, reviewing the deliverables and activities—focusing only on the deliverables or activities that are different from the system conversion—and finally close the chapter by comparing the three transition approaches.

Real-World Scenario

As an SAP sales executive, you're looking forward to attending your second SAPPHIRE in Orlando, FL. You've prepped yourself on the different transition approaches, especially the selective data transition, which is a bit confusing.

At SAPPHIRE, you met Ms. Brown, who is the senior IT manager of a multimillion-dollar auto parts manufacturing organization. Ms. Brown, who previously led and has a sound technical understanding of SAP ERP 6.0 implementations, explained that the current finance system has an exceptionally higher level of customization as compared to the logistics modules. She also mentioned that the business initially liked the system (about 10 years ago), but, of late, especially after the change in business leadership, they are looking for the business transformation. However, the logistics teams distributed across the globe are very happy with the current functionalities and not willing to make changes and "rock the boat."

Luckily, you're thoroughly prepared to explain, in detail, how to transition to SAP S/4HANA in such a complex scenario when a part of the business is looking to innovate while another part of the business wants to maintain the same functionalities.

Objectives of This Portion of the Test

The certification examination will test your knowledge about the following topics:

- Considerations for the selective data transition path
- Deep understanding of the transition process
- Activities during the selective data transition
- Associated deliverables in this approach

In the subsequent sections, you'll learn these key concepts followed by some questions and answers.

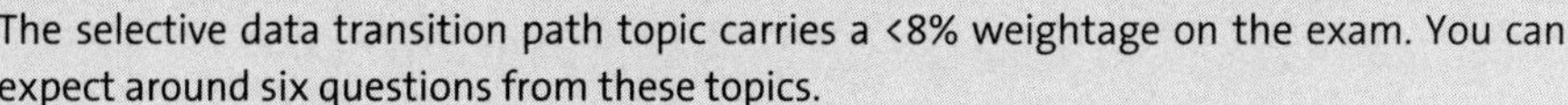

Note
The selective data transition path topic carries a <8% weightage on the exam. You can expect around six questions from these topics.

Key Concepts Refresher

This section will help you understand the selective data transition path and will advance your abilities to carry out given activities and deliver the desired deliverables. These concepts are critical for you to pass the exam.

Navigating the Roadmap Viewer

You can navigate to the deliverables and the activities for the selective data transition path in the Roadmap Viewer by following the steps shown in Figure 10.1:

❶ Go to the Roadmap Viewer, and click on **Solution Specific**.

❷ Navigate right and click on **SAP Activate Methodology for Transition to SAP S/4HANA** to go to the overview page.

❸ Click on the **Content** menu shown in the upper-left portion of the screen to go to the content page.

❹ Scroll down until you see **More** on the left pane of the window. Select the **Selective Data Transition** checkbox (see Figure 10.2) to include only the deliverables, tasks, and accelerators from the system conversion transition path.

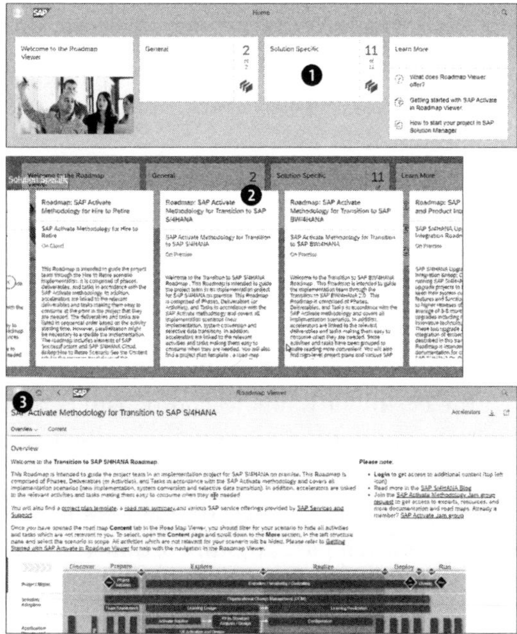

Figure 10.1 Navigating Roadmap Viewer for Selective Data Transition Path

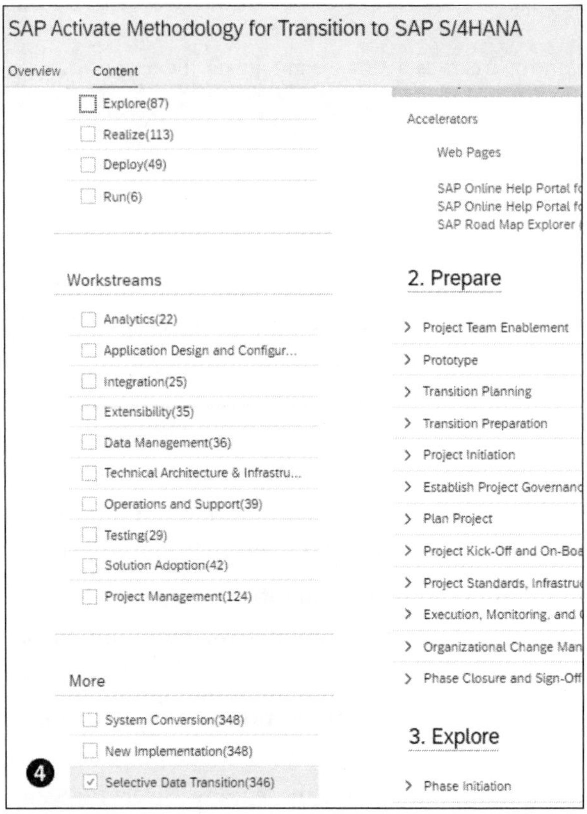

Figure 10.2 Selective Data Transition Option

What Is Selective Data Transition?

As the name suggests, it provides a "selective" approach to migrate the best of both worlds—data and processes—to the new SAP S/4HANA environment. In this alternative approach to the greenfield or brownfield implementations, a customer can choose to reuse the current processes as well as redesign some of the existing processes. For example, a customer may want to reuse the logistics processes while redesigning the finance processes or vice versa. Furthermore, the customer can choose to selectively—all or time chunk—migrate company code-specific data to the new environment.

Let's consider an example. Figure 10.3 shows an aspect of the selective data transition from a real-life project in which the customer wants to consolidate two of their instances and use selective data from both instances. In this case, the team created a shell copy of the first instance and carried out the system conversion of the copied instance. In the final step, the team uses the selective data transition approach to migrate the agreed-upon data, which is based on the customer's functional or regulatory requirements, from all the instances and merge the configurations and the development work.

After creation of the SAP S/4HANA enterprise, instance A and instance B should be decommissioned. Now, from here, the SAP S/4HANA innovation journey starts. Following are the scenarios for which you should consider selective data transition:

- Phased go-live approach (in our example, the organization went live for instance A first and then for instance B after the configuration and development merger)
- To de-risk the big-bang approach
- When there's no need for a large chunk of legacy data
- When merging or splitting the existing SAP ERP instances.

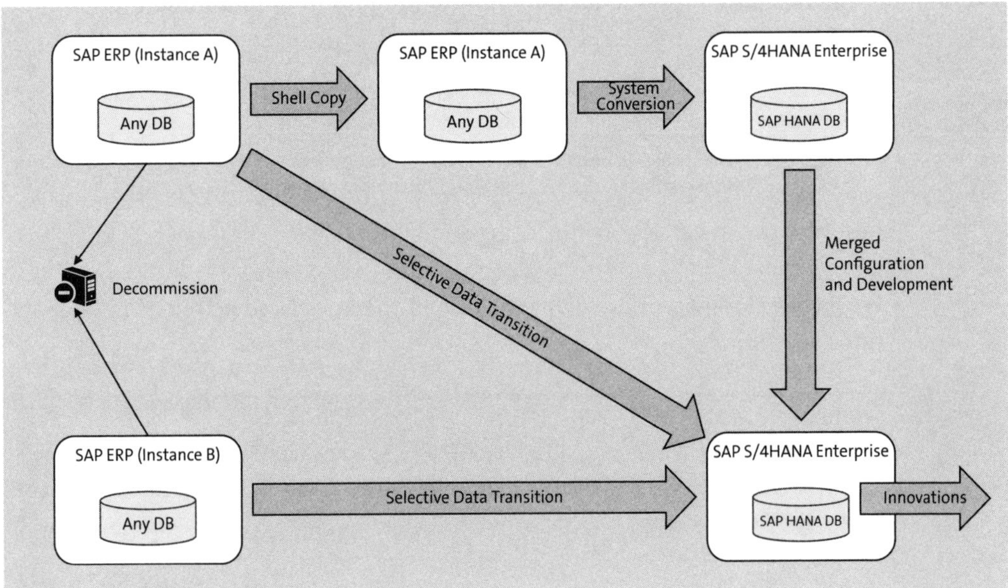

Figure 10.3 Selective Data Transition

Overview

Figure 10.4 summarizes the key activities carried out by the team in the selective data transition approach. In the discover phase of the project, the team accesses the trial system to understand the innovations and the functionalities of the SAP S/4HANA system. In the prepare phase, apart from project kick-off and other project management activities, the team completes the setup and enablement activities, performs custom code analysis to identify any changes, retires unused code, modifies incompatible code, and provides high-level estimates of the changes. In the explore phase, the team sets up the sandbox environment from the current production (PROD) environment, carries out the fit-gap analysis, and prepares the product backlog based on the delta design workshops. In the realize phase, the team completes the implementation, tests the converted solution and the data migration in the quality assurance (QA) environment, and migrates the selective data. During this phase, the team also creates the new PROD environment. Finally, in the deploy phase, the team rehearses the production conversion, and carries out the production conversion, data migration, go-live, and hypercare. At the end of the deploy phase, the build team hands over the solution to the operate team to commence the run phase of the project.

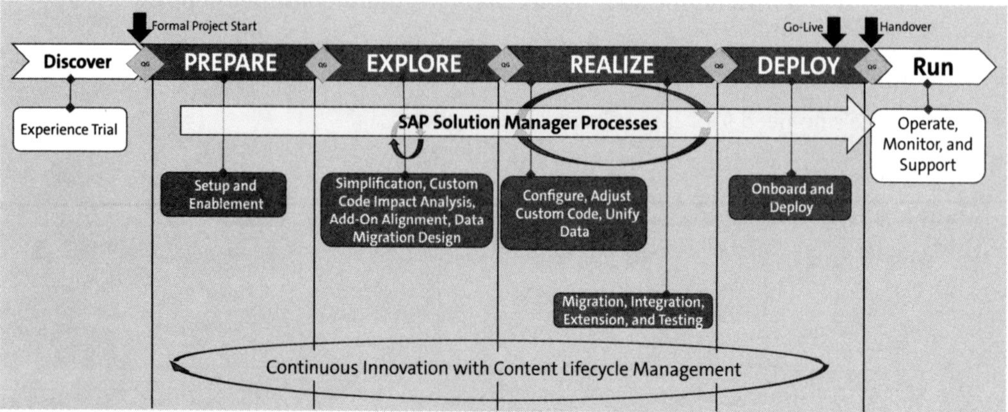

Figure 10.4 Overview of Selective Data Transition

We'll look closely at these deliverables and the associated activities in later sections.

Note

In the new implementation transition path for SAP S/4HANA, the team configures and tests, while in the system conversion and selective data transition, the team adjusts the custom code.

Approaches

Selective data transition uses Data Management and Landscape Transformation (DMLT) services to move "selective" data from the current SAP ERP system to the new SAP S/4HANA environment.

Tip

You may get a question asking about the tool that you can use in the selective data transition path. You can use Data Management and Landscape Transformation (DMLT)—formerly known as SAP Landscape Transformation—for either of the target platforms.

You can select the following data for the transition:

- **Shell conversion**
  In this approach, the team creates a copy of the existing PROD environment without master and transactional data but includes the ABAP Repository and configuration (Customizing.)

- **Client transfer**
  In this case, you select a client and the underlying master and transactional data with the configuration (Customizing) to transition to the target SAP S/4HANA environment.
- **Company code transfer**
  In this approach, you can select a company code from the current setup to create a single client on the new SAP S/4HANA system. You can select the master or transactional data from the client to transition to the new environment. Alternatively, you can select the configuration (Customizing) with or without the master data to move over to the target environment.
- **System merge**
  In the process of system merge, you can merge business data from two or more clients to create an empty instance of SAP S/4HANA. These clients can be from the same or multiple SAP ERP systems.

There are two approaches for the target system creation:

- **Mix-and-match approach**
  In this approach, the project team creates a new SAP S/4HANA installation and then transports or manually transfers the ABAP Repository and configurations (Customizing) to the target environment.
- **Shell conversion**
  In this approach, the team creates a shell copy of the current PROD environment that includes the ABAP Repository and the configuration (Customizing) without any master or transactional data. The project team, using system conversion, converts this shell copy to an SAP S/4HANA instance. In the absence of master and the transactional data, the conversion process is simpler and faster. Furthermore, the team can easily adjust the simplification list items without the business data.

Note
In the selective data transition path, you're doing the following:

- Migrating a selection of data
- Reusing some of the current functionalities and redesigning some of the functionalities

Landscape

Figure 10.5 shows the lifecycle of the existing environments in the selective data transition approach:

❶ The discover phase of the project starts with the trial system access to review the innovations and the fitment of current business requirements. The team then builds the sandbox environment by shell copying the existing PROD environment. The team will use the sandbox system to drive the delta design workshops in the explore phase of the project.

❷ In the second step, during the explore phase, you need to shell copy the sandbox environment to the SAP S/4HANA development (DEV) environment. The project team will continue the configuration work based on the product backlog.

❸ In the next step, the project team creates the QA environment by shell copying from the DEV environment.

❹ In the QA system, the team completes all the testing activities, including selective data migrations.

❺ The team should fix any bugs in the SAP S/4HANA DEV environment and transport the fixes to the QA system for further testing.

❻ After successful completion of user acceptance testing (UAT), the team will shell copy the solution from the QA system to the PROD system and then perform the selective data migration ❻a, as shown in Figure 10.5, from the existing PROD environment to the new PROD environment.

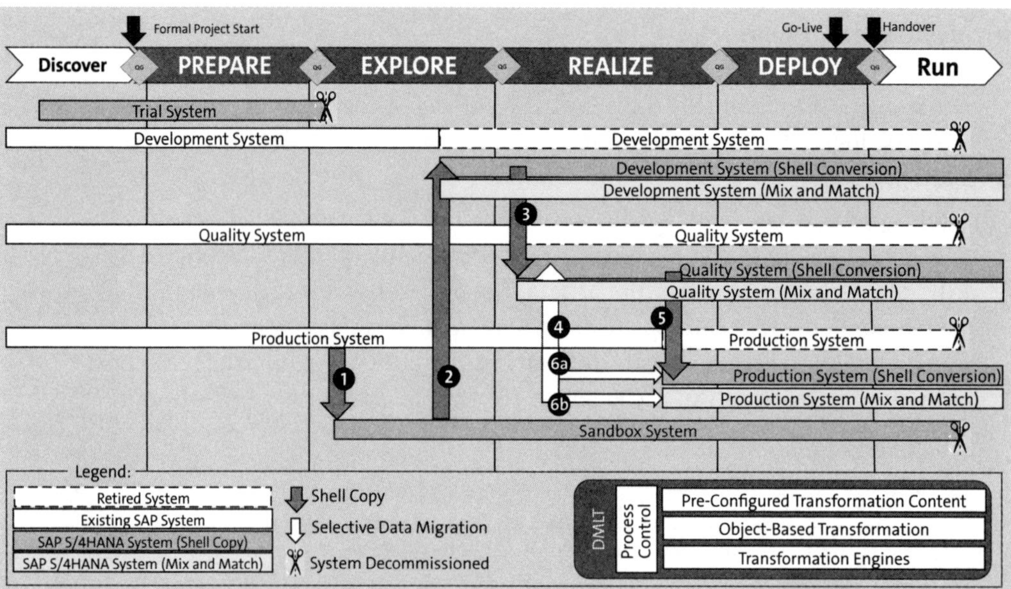

Figure 10.5 Landscape Overview

However, for the mix-and-match approach, the DEV, QA, and PROD environment are built using a fresh install. In the final step ❻b of the approach, the team completes the selective data migration from the existing PROD environment to the new PROD environment.

Benefits

Following are some of the benefits of the selective transition approach:

- Customers can consolidate multiple SAP ERP systems into one SAP S/4HANA system.
- Applications can be reused and redesigned.
- Phased go-live lowers the risks of the big-bang approach.

Comparison

Figure 10.6 shows the differences between system conversions and selective data transitions. The prime difference between the two approaches is the use of tools; while you use Software Update Manager (SUM) for the system conversion and convert the data, you use DMLT for selective data transition and migrate the data. The selective data transition approach requires data migration of limited master and transactional data due to the consolidation of several systems or splitting into several systems.

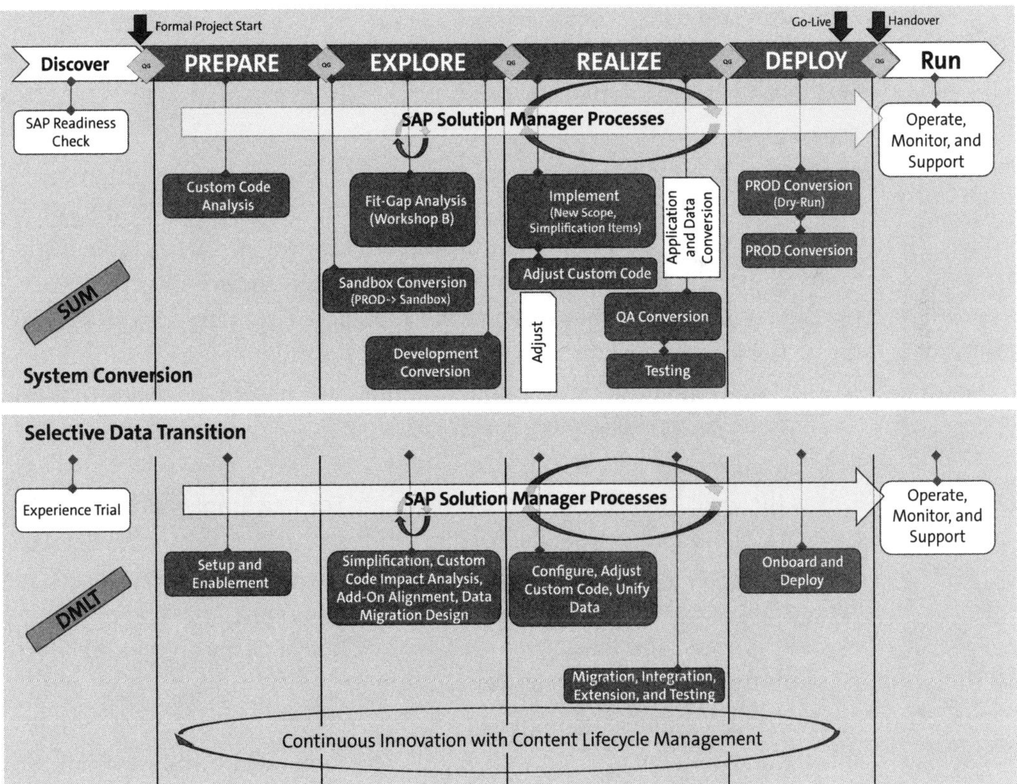

Figure 10.6 Differences between Selective Data Transition and System Conversion

Figure 10.7 shows the comparisons among the new implementation, selective data transition, and the system conversion approaches.

Greenfield ⟷ Brownfield

Criteria	New Implementation	Selective Data Transition		System Conversion
		Mix and Match	Shell Conversion	
Process Redesign	1	2	4	4
Process Reuse	5	4	2	1
Master/Transactional Data Migration	4	2	2	1
Data Transformation	1	2	2	3
Data Cleansing	1	2	2	4
Target SAP S/4HANA System	Any	On-Premise and Extended Edition	On-Premise and Extended Edition	On-Premise
Phased Go-Live	1	1	1	5
System Split/Consolidation	5	1	1	1

1 Fully possible · 2 Possible to a great extent · 3 Possible to a certain extent · 4 Limited possibility · 5 Not possible

Figure 10.7 Comparison of the Three Approaches

Let's review each characteristic in detail:

- **Process redesign**
  In the new implementations, you can redesign and reengineer all processes, including the change in the organizational structure, whereas in the system conversion, you can't redesign the processes. However, if you consume further innovations, you can redesign those processes after system conversion. Selective data transition is in between the two approaches whereby you can redesign the processes to a great extent, including the possibility of the organizational structural change in the mix-and-match approach while the shell conversion presents limited possibility of process redesign.
- **Process reuse**
  This is the exact opposite of process redesign. For new implementations, you can't (and should not) reuse the existing processes, whereas you can fully reuse the existing processes in the case of system conversion. The mix-and-match approach of the selective data transition presents a limited possibility to reuse existing processes, whereas the shell conversion presents the possibility to reuse the existing processes to a certain extent.
- **Master/transactional data migration**
  For the new implementations, it's highly recommended to migrate only the master data and limited transactional data to the new environment. In the selective data transition approach, you can migrate the data selectively, so the indicator is set at "possible to a great extent." On the other side of the spectrum, for system conversion, you can migrate all the data from the current environment to the target system.

- **Data transformation**
  In new implementations, with the new processes, the new data is transformed fully. In the system conversion, on the other hand, you use the same data with the change in data model. Both the options of selective data transition approaches present a great possibility of data transformation.
- **Data cleansing**
  In new implementations, with the new processes, you get cleaned data. However, in the system conversion, the team can archive and cleanse the data prior to the implementation project. The selective data transition also presents a great possibility of cleansed data.
- **Target SAP S/4HANA system**
  A customer can choose any platform—on-premise SAP S/4HANA; SAP S/4HANA Cloud, extended edition; or SAP S/4HANA Cloud, essentials edition—for the new implementations. However, in system conversion, SAP S/4HANA is the only target platform. You can select either SAP S/4HANA Cloud, extended edition, or SAP S/4HANA Cloud as the target platform for both the approaches of the selective data transition.

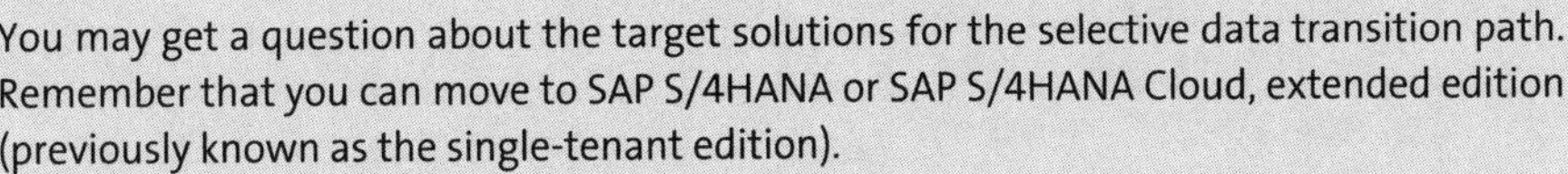

Tip

You may get a question about the target solutions for the selective data transition path. Remember that you can move to SAP S/4HANA or SAP S/4HANA Cloud, extended edition (previously known as the single-tenant edition).

- **Phased go-live**
  A new implementation for both approaches of a selective data transition can decide to go for a phased approach that isn't possible for the system conversion projects.
- **System split/consolidation**
  New implementations don't allow you to merge/spilt the existing instances, whereas the rest of the approaches do provide that flexibility.

In the following sections, we'll review the deliverables and the activities during each phase of the projects. Because the selective data transition is similar to the system conversion, we've referred many of the topics back to Chapter 9.

Discover Phase

The objective of this phase is for customers to understand the business functionality of SAP S/4HANA and the benefits they can reap by using this enterprise resource planning (ERP) system.

The deliverables of the discover phase are as follows:

- Strategic planning
- Application value and scoping
- Trial system provisioning

These deliverables are covered in the "Discover Phase" section in Chapter 6. Figure 10.8 shows the deliverables in the discover phase of the selective data transition approach.

Figure 10.8 Discover Phase Deliverables

However, there is one subtle difference in the activities of the three approaches, as shown in Table 10.1.

New Implementation	System Conversion	Selective Data
Identifies the impact of SAP S/4HANA on existing business processes	Performs additional activity to check the conversion readiness of SAP ERP	No need to identify the impact of SAP S/4HANA on existing business processes

Table 10.1 Differences in the Discover Phase

Prepare Phase

In the prepare phase, the project team will plan and prepare several planning documents from kick-off to phase closure. In this section, we'll review the prepare phase activities and the corresponding deliverables for the SAP S/4HANA selective data transition.

Before the start of this phase, the sponsor has approved the project, and the team is already assigned. During this phase of the project, the team will work closely with the customer's project manager to create several planning documents. Figure 10.9 shows the deliverables in the prepare phase of the project. There is no change in the deliverables as compared to that of the system conversion approach. Refer to the "Prepare Phase" section in Chapter 9 for a detailed understanding of these deliverables.

There are no significant differences in the prepare phase of the project except that the team may want to perform certain data clean-up and custom code clean-up work, as shown in Table 10.2.

Deliverable	New Implementation	System Conversion	Selective Data Transition
Transition preparation	No data clean-up or custom code assessment	Additional tasks: ▪ Cleaning up archive data ▪ Cleaning up unused code ▪ Improving custom code quality measure	Additional tasks: ▪ Cleaning up archive data ▪ Cleaning up unused code ▪ Improving custom code quality measure

Table 10.2 Differences in the Prepare Phase

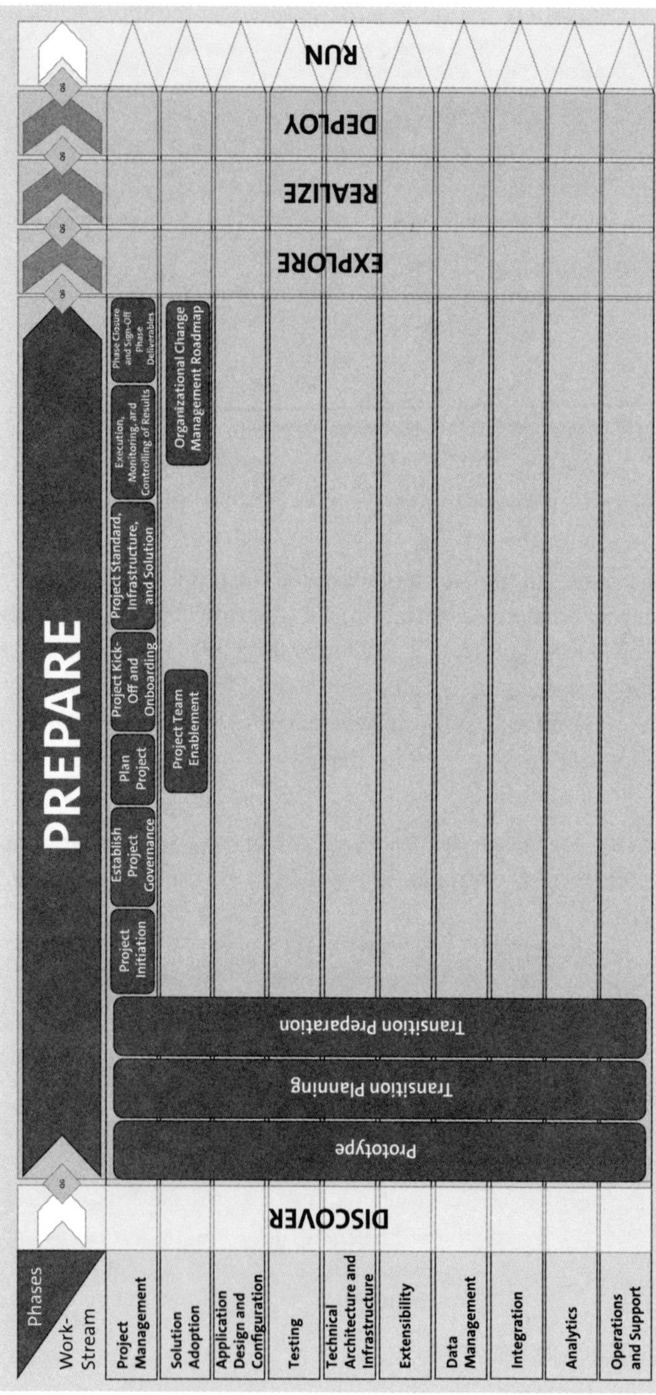

Figure 10.9 Prepare Phase Deliverables

Explore Phase

During this phase of the project, the team performs the fit-gap analysis and prepares the product backlog. All the planning is done during the prepare phase, and the customer has signed off the phase. In the explore phase, the team will focus on the requirements. Figure 10.10 shows the deliverables in the explore phase of the project.

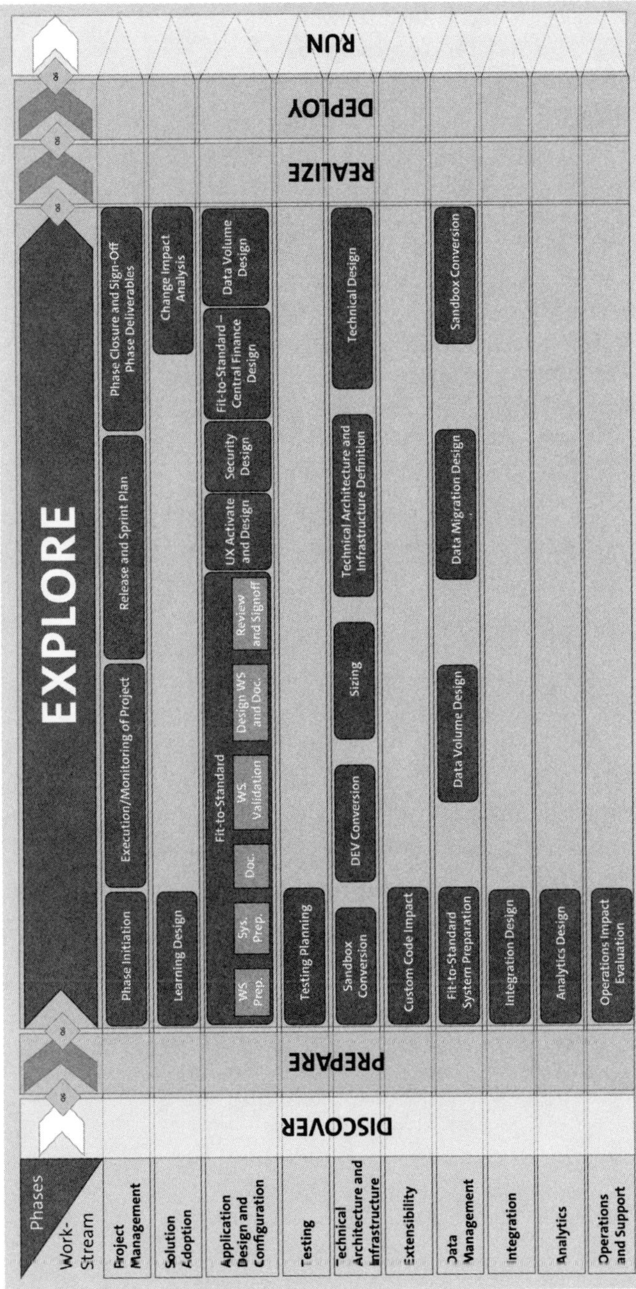

Figure 10.10 Explore Phase Deliverables

There are a few differences between the three approaches, as noted in Table 10.3.

Deliverable	New Implementation	System Conversion	Selective Data Transition
Activate solution	The team reconfirms the scope for activation, activates the best practices, and tests them. The team also sets up the integration with other test systems.	There's no need to reconfirm the scope, activate the best practices, and test them. However, the team prepares the system conversion activities and sets up the integration with other test systems.	Selective data transition doesn't have this deliverable.
Data migration design	The team should migrate only the master data and the essential transactional data. Based on that, the team should build the strategy and carry out the activities.	No data migration occurs in the system conversion approach.	Set up the DMLT software.
Custom code impact	No list is needed.	Create a list of impacted custom code.	Create a list of impacted custom code.

Table 10.3 Differences in the Explore Phase

Realize Phase

The purpose of this phase is to realize the build incrementally and iteratively based on the business requirements and scenarios identified during the previous phases of the project. The team is deep into system configuration based on the fit-gap analysis and the prioritized product backlog. In addition, during this phase, the legacy data load starts, solution adoption continues, and operation planning happens. Figure 10.11 shows the deliverables in the realize phase of the project.

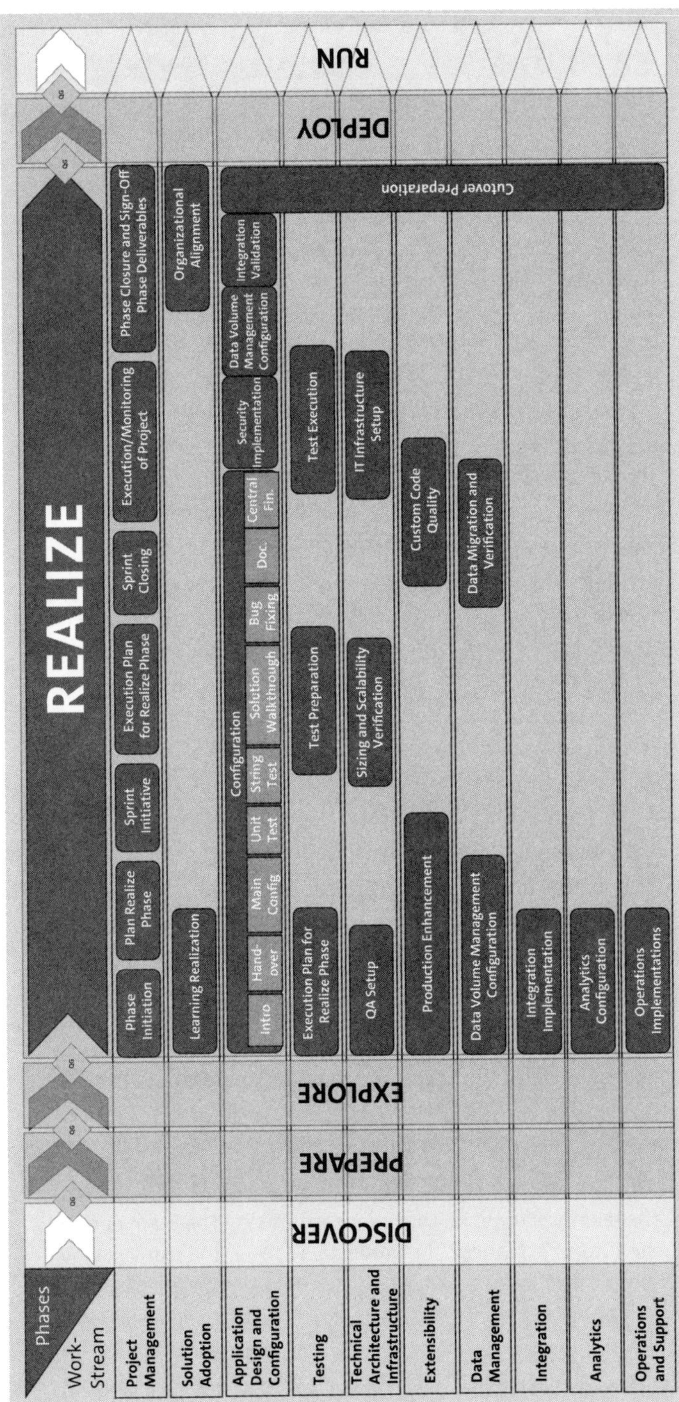

Figure 10.11 Realize Phase Deliverables

There are a few differences between the three approaches, as noted in Table 10.4.

Deliverables	New Implementation	System Conversion	Selective Data Transmission
Central Finance configuration	Not required.	Not required.	Additional activity in the configuration.
Clean up or archive data	No such activity.	Data clean up and archival needed.	No such activity.
Data migration and validation	The team does the legacy data migration.	The team performs the load and verification runs.	Depending on the scenario, the team performs the client transfer, system merge, or company code transfer.
QA system setup/ conversion	The team performs the QA system setup.	The team performs the system conversion for the QA environment.	The team performs both setup and conversion.
Cutover plan	Create the plan specific to the new implementation.	Create the plan specific to the system conversion.	Create the plan specific to the selective data transition.

Table 10.4 Differences in the Realize Phase

Deploy Phase

In the deploy phase of the project, the business switches the operation to the new PROD environment. This is the final phase of the project in which the team will close all the open issues, ensure the organizational readiness, and execute the production cutover so that the business can realize the benefits of the newly implemented solution. Figure 10.12 shows the deliverables in the deploy phase of the project.

There are a few differences between the three approaches, as noted in Table 10.5.

Deliverables	New Implementation	System Conversion	Selective Data Transmission
Production cutover	The team performs the cutover activities specifically for the new implementation.	The team performs the productive conversion.	The team performs the cutover activities specifically for the selective data transition.
Hypercare support	The team deletes the obsolete data using the Obsolete Data Handling tool.	The team deletes the obsolete data using the Obsolete Data Handling tool.	No such activity occurs in the selective data transition path.

Table 10.5 Differences in the Deploy Phase

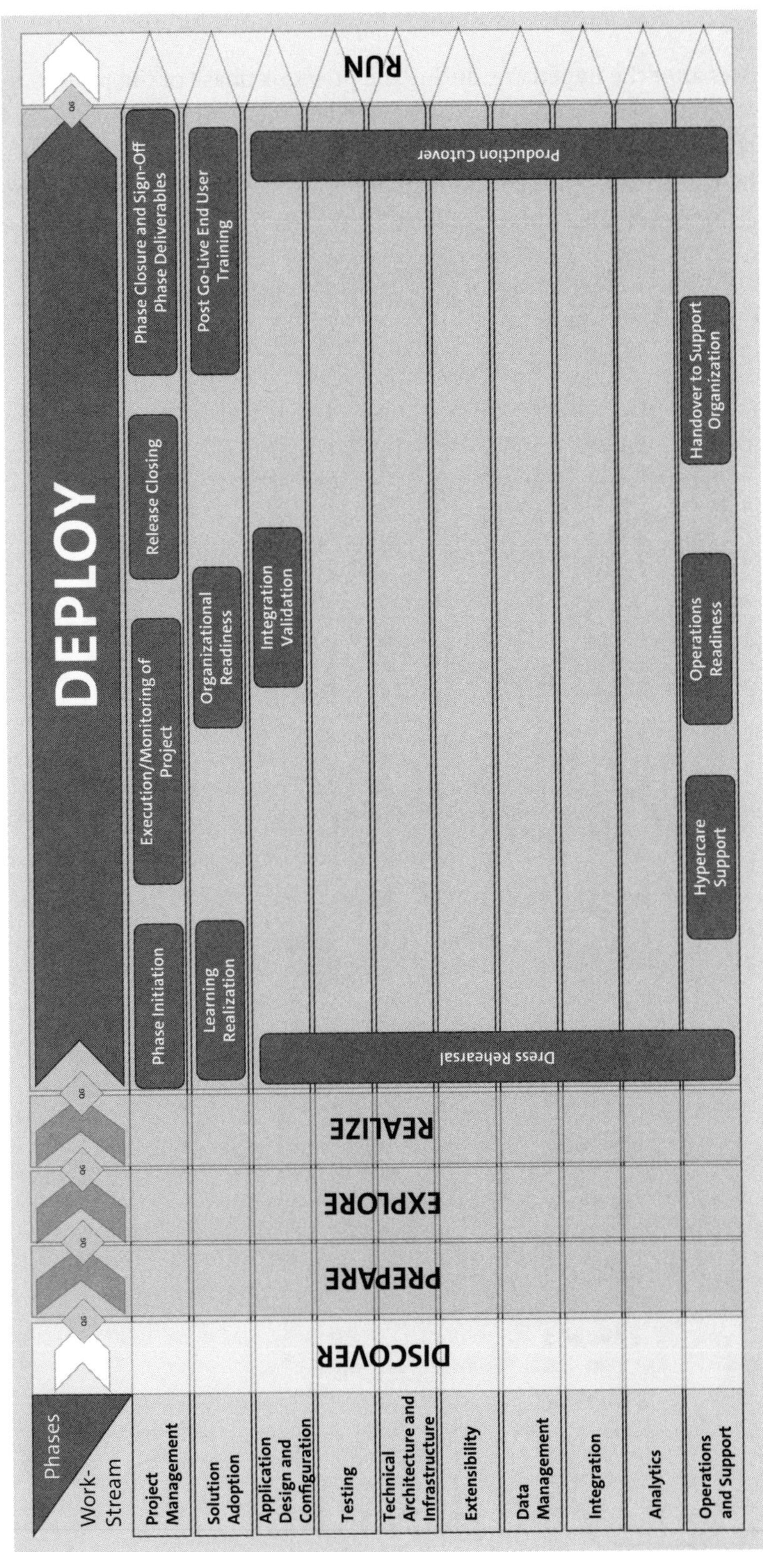

Figure 10.12 Deploy Phase Deliverables

Run Phase

This phase starts after the hypercare, during the previous phase of the project, to optimize the overall operation. Support is provided by the customer IT team, and they continue to strive for optimization, automate the application processes, ensure system availability, and provide system performance. Figure 10.13 shows the deliverable in the run phase of the project.

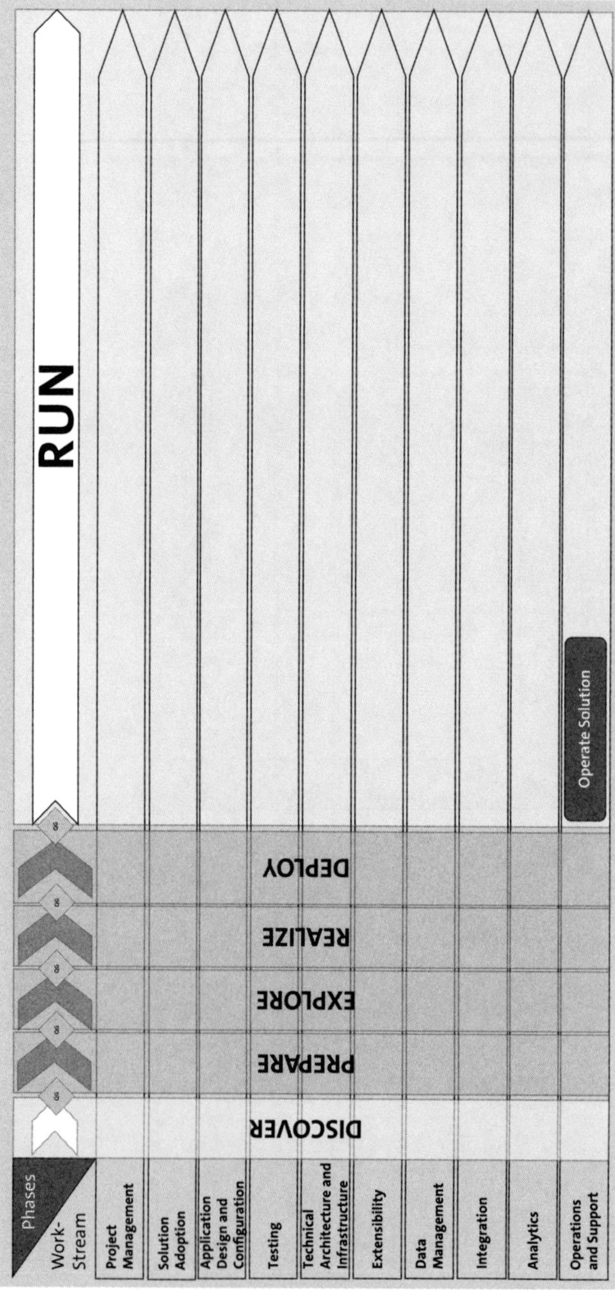

Figure 10.13 Run Phase Deliverables

There's one difference between the three approaches, as noted in Table 10.6.

Deliverables	New Implementation	System Conversion	Selective Data Transmission
Improve and innovate solution	Consume the periodical innovation releases from SAP.	Consume the periodical innovation releases from SAP.	You have limited options to consume innovations.

Table 10.6 Differences in the Run Phase

Shell Copy Example

Let's consider an example of a selective data transition project. This is a real-life project for a toy manufacturing company that wants to move to SAP S/4HANA without affecting the current functionalities and migrate only a subset of data. Their implementation phases would look as follows:

- **Discover phase**
  After initial discussions with the client, it was clear that they want to move cautiously, so the team proposes the selective data transition approach. In accordance with the selective data transition roadmap, the team builds the strategy and roadmap in partnership with SAP. The lean project team understood the criticality and the need of the legacy data that they wanted to migrate, decided to procure the DMLT services from SAP, and formally signed the contract.

  Since its inception, DMLT has provided excellent solutions and accelerators for many scenarios, including SAP landscape harmonization, organizational merger and acquisitions, and any other organizational changes. It helps migrate huge data sets using a robust yet flexible framework between SAP instances.
- **Prepare phase**
  In the prepare phase, the team carried out the following activities other than their normal work such as project planning, transition planning, project team enablement, and the organizational change management (OCM) roadmap:
  - Engaged with the DMLT service team who, after due diligence, advised them to use the shell conversion approach for the data migration
  - Used the DMLT to perform the source system analysis, identified the data to archive, and removed the unwanted data such as logs
- **Explore phase**
  The team carried out the following activities:
  - Copied the latest PROD environment to the sandbox system using the shell copy (for details of the landscape, refer to Figure 10.5)
  - Converted the shell copy to the SAP S/4HANA instance using system conversion

  - Carried out the fit-gap analysis activities, and then built and prioritized the product backlog
- **Realize phase**
  In the realize phase, the team carried out the following activities:
  - Created an SAP S/4HANA-based DEV environment using the shell copy from the sandbox environment
  - Set up the DMLT tool and tested the data migration cycles in the sandbox environment
  - Performed the implementation for such requirements based on the custom code impact analysis and the analysis of integration and analytics requirements
  - Created the QA system using the shell copy of the DEV environment without master and transactional data
  - Carried out testing on the selective data migration in the QA system
  - Built the PROD environment by shell copying the QA environment without any master and transactional data
  - Ran integration and UAT
- **Deploy phase**
  After the infrastructure was ready and the selective data migration testing was complete in the previous phase, the team carried out the following activities:
  - Rehearsed the production cutover three times
  - Migrated the production data and the historical transactional data
  - Performed the (limited) parallel run for a period of four weeks (this is an optional step)
  - Migrated the production, historical, and open transactional data, and performed go-live activities
  - Decommissioned the old infrastructure

The second phase of the project was to adopt the innovations. In this case, we revisited certain business processes and adopted the innovations. In the case described in the "Real-World Scenario" box at the beginning of the chapter, you would do the selective data transition for the procurement process because the business is happy with the current functionality. However, for the finance processes, you'll start adopting the innovations because the customer wants to enhance the system that was a decade old.

Important Terminology

For this exam objective, you're expected to understand the following terms:

- **Mix-and-match conversion**
  In the mix-and-match approach, another way to migrate data in the selective

data transition approach, the team manually transports the ABAP Repository and Customizing.

- **Selective data transition**
  This is one of the three transition paths of business transformation to SAP S/4HANA, and it's used when you only need to migrate a subset of data from the existing SAP ERP solution to SAP S/4HANA. It's one of the most complex processes.
- **Shell conversion**
  This is one of the approaches of the selective data transition where the team creates a skeleton copy of the source environment without any master or transactional data.

 Practice Questions

These practice questions will help you evaluate your understanding of the topics covered in this chapter. The questions shown are similar in nature to those found on the certification examination. Although none of these questions will be found on the exam itself, they will allow you to review your knowledge of the subject. Select the correct answers, and then check the completeness of your answers in the "Practice Question Answers and Explanations" section. Remember that on the exam, you must select all correct answers and only correct answers to receive credit for the question.

1. What are the scenarios to consider for the selective data transition? (There are three correct answers.)

☐ **A.** The customer wants a phased go-live approach.

☐ **B.** The customer wants to reduce risks.

☐ **C.** The customer has two SAP ERP instances to consolidate.

☐ **D.** The customer has a regulatory requirement to select all the data from the SAP ERP system and transition it to the new SAP S/4HANA environment.

☐ **E.** The customer can always enhance its business functionalities.

2. The project team has created a copy of the PROD environment by copying metadata, customization, and repository data, and now they have followed the system conversion transition path to move to SAP S/4HANA. The project team members are in discussion with the client to consolidate their two instances into one. What is the transition path discussed in the given scenario?

☐ **A.** System conversion

☐ **B.** New implementation

☐ **C.** Selective data transition

☐ **D.** Hybrid approach

3. What are the two benefits of selective data transition? (There are two correct choices.)

☐ **A.** It's the simplest transition path.

☐ **B.** It's the fastest transition path.

☐ **C.** It gives an option for phased go-live, de-risking project risks.

☐ **D.** It provides the ability to merge multiple SAP ERP instances.

☐ **E.** It reduces the total cost of operation.

4. Which one of the following options is the difference of approach between the selective data transition and system conversion?

☐ **A.** Custom code adjustment isn't needed in the selective data transition.

☐ **B.** Data migration is only possible in the selective data transition.

☐ **C.** While we use the DMLT tool in the selective data transition, we use SUM in the system conversion approach.

☐ **D.** The only difference is that in the selective data transition, we migrate only selective data; however, system conversion requires all data to be migrated.

5. What is the difference between the shell conversion and the mix-and-match approach of the selective data transition?

☐ **A.** You can use DMLT for shell conversion but not for mix and match.

☐ **B.** You can use DMLT for mix and match but not for shell conversion.

☐ **C.** Shell conversion can only migrate the company code data, whereas the mix-and-match approach can migrate the complete data.

☐ **D.** In shell conversion, the team creates a copy of the PROD environment without any master and transactional data, whereas in the mix-and-match approach, we use a new SAP S/4HANA installation.

6. Which of the following activities is *not* performed during the discover phase of the project? (There are two correct answers.)

☐ **A.** Provide a trial system

☐ **B.** Create a POV document.

☐ **C.** Identify the selective data transition approach—shell conversion versus mix-and-match approach.

☐ **D.** Discuss the implementation strategy and roadmap.

☐ **E.** Understand the impact of SAP S/4HANA on the existing business processes.

7. Which of the following deliverables is a part of the selective data transition but not the system conversion?

☐ **A.** Configure: Solution walkthrough

☐ **B.** Configure: Documentation

☐ **C.** Configure: Central Finance implementation

☐ **D.** Configure: Unit test

☐ **E.** None of the above

8. What are two deliverables from the explore phase of a selective data transition project? (There are two correct answers.)

☐ **A.** Custom code impact in the solution adoption workstream

☐ **B.** DEV system

☐ **C.** Project kick-off

☐ **D.** Data migration design

☐ **E.** Transition plan

9. What are the two tasks that a team executes to complete the transition plan in a selective data transition project? (There are two correct answers.)

☐ **A.** Define the cutover approach.

☐ **B.** Define the objective and goals.

☐ **C.** Create a test plan.

☐ **D.** Approve the project charter.

☐ **E.** Map the interface and integration.

10. In the deploy phase of a selective data transition project, which two of the following deliverables touches the application design and configuration, testing, and extensibility workstreams? (There are two correct answers.)

☐ **A.** Learning realization

☐ **B.** Cutover preparation

☐ **C.** Operation readiness

☐ **D.** Production cutover

☐ **E.** Dress rehearsal

Practice Question Answers and Explanations

1. Correct answers: **A, B, C**

   The selective data transition approach provides the flexibility of phased go-live, lower risks, and the ability to merge (or split) SAP instances. It doesn't, however, provide a capability to migrate "all" data nor an ability to "always" enhance business functionalities.

2. Correct answer: **C**

   The team is using the selective data transition approach, which is clear from the last sentence of the question, which is "consolidate two instances."

3. Correct answers: **C, D**

   The two benefits are the phased approach and the ability to merge SAP instances. It doesn't reduce the total cost of operation, nor is it the fastest or simplest transition path.

4. Correct answer: **C**

   Option C is the right choice. The team needs to analyze the custom code impact and adjust if needed in the selective data transition. Furthermore, historical data migration, using SUM, is a key functionality of system conversion. In the selective data transition approach, we use the DMLT tool.

5. Correct answer: **D**

   For data migration, you can use the DMLT tool in either of the selective data transition approaches; therefore, options A and B are incorrect.

6. Correct answers: **C, E**

   During the discover phase of the project, the team accesses the trial environment, creates point of value (POV) documentation, and discusses the implementation strategy and roadmap. However, they don't go into detail regarding the shell conversion versus mix-and-match approach. Furthermore, understanding the impact of SAP S/4HANA on the existing business processes is a key activity in the discover phase of a new implementation and system conversion.

7. Correct answer: **C**

   Central Finance implementation is the deliverable that we work on in a selective data transition approach.

8. Correct answers: **B, D**

   Custom code impact is a deliverable of the extensibility workstream and not solution adoption. The project kick-off and transition plan are the deliverables of the prepare phase of the project. The team creates the DEV environment and the data migration design in the explore phase of a selective data transition project.

9. Correct answers: **A, B**

   We start the transition planning by defining the objectives and goals of the plan. The transition plan includes the activity to create the cutover approach.

10. Correct answers: **D, E**
    Cutover preparation touches all the mentioned workstreams, but it's a part of the realize phase deliverable. The only correct answers are production cutover and dress rehearsal.

Takeaway

In this final chapter, we studied selective data transition, discussed the two approaches (shell conversion and mix and match), reviewed the landscape, and compared the three transition paths. Furthermore, we understood the high-level use of the DMLT tool from a selective data transition perspective and reviewed the deliverables related to Central Finance. Finally, we explained the differences in deliverables and activities in the selective data transition approach as compared to that of the other two approaches.

Summary

This final chapter concludes the three transition paths that we started reviewing from Chapter 6. You learned about the selective data transition approach and its differences compared with the other two approaches. Now you're ready for the first practice test.

Appendices

Appendix A
Practice Test 1

1. Which of these tools do you use in the data management workstream? (There are three correct answers.)

☐ **A.** SAP Data Services

☐ **B.** SAP S/4HANA migration cockpit

☐ **C.** SAP Landscape Transformation

☐ **D.** Roadmap Viewer

☐ **E.** SAP Best Practices

2. Which is the correct sequence of project lifecycle steps in a new implementation of SAP S/4HANA Cloud, essentials edition?

☐ **A.** 1) Experience trial, 2) fit-to-standard, 3) setup and enablement, 4) configure, 5) integrate, extend, and test, 6) onboard and deploy, 7) operate, monitor, and support

☐ **B.** 1) Experience trial, 2) fit-to-standard, 3) setup and enablement, 4) configure, 5) migrate, integrate, extend, and test, 6) onboard and deploy, 7) operate, monitor, and support

☐ **C.** 1) Experience trial, 2) setup and enablement, 3) fit-to-standard, 4) configure, 5) migrate, integrate, extend, and test, 6) onboard and deploy, 7) operate, monitor, and support

☐ **D.** 1) Experience trial, 2) fit-to-standard, 3) setup and enablement, 4) configure, 5) migrate, integrate, extend, and test, 6) operate, monitor, and support, 7) onboard and deploy

3. Which of the following are SAP Activate workstreams? (There are two correct answers.)

☐ **A.** Customer team enablement

☐ **B.** Data migration

☐ **C.** Organizational change management

☐ **D.** Realize

☐ **E.** Project management

4. Which of the following are the characteristics of SAP S/4HANA Cloud, extended edition? (There are two correct answers.)

☐ **A.** Full SAP S/4HANA extensibility

☐ **B.** Customization of SAP standard code

☐ **C.** On-premise edition scope

☐ **D.** No integration with third-party products

5. Which of the following is a major accelerator in the realize phase that you can use in the integration workstream?

☐ **A.** Business Process Modeling Language (BPML)

☐ **B.** Interface register template

☐ **C.** Technical specification – enhancement template

☐ **D.** SAP Solution Manager 7.2

6. Consultants can configure using the Self-Service Configuration User Interface (SSCUI) in a new implementation of SAP S/4HANA on-premise edition. True or false?

☐ **A.** True

☐ **B.** False

7. When does the product owner provide formal confirmation that user stories are completed to their satisfaction?

☐ **A.** During the sprint review.

☐ **B.** During the Scrum meeting.

☐ **C.** During the phase acceptance process.

☐ **D.** During the sprint retrospective.

8. Which of the following roles within the project management workstream will be fulfilled by the implementation partner? (There are two correct answers.)

☐ **A.** Project manager

☐ **B.** Quality manager

☐ **C.** Quality assurance (QA) tester

☐ **D.** Business manager

9. The SAP Activate project library content for SAP S/4HANA consists of which of the following? (There are two correct answers.)

☐ **A.** Project plan

☐ **B.** Ready-to-run systems

☐ **C.** SAP Best Practices

☐ **D.** Accelerators

☐ **E.** Organizational tools

10. The product backlog is a list of all items that should be done within the project. It replaces the traditional requirements specification document. True or false?

☐ **A.** True

☐ **B.** False

11. Which of the following tasks are included in the deploy phase of the system conversion transition path?

☐ **A.** Configuration

☐ **B.** Final testing

☐ **C.** Value discovery

☐ **D.** Finalizing the product backlog

12. SAP provides ready-to-run systems for SAP S/4HANA deployment using the SAP Cloud Appliance Library and Blue-ray. True or false?

☐ **A.** True

☐ **B.** False

13. What are the outputs of the SAP Transformation Navigator?

☐ **A.** Transformation guide, implementation guide, technical guide

☐ **B.** Transformation guide, business guide, technical guide

☐ **C.** Business guide, implementation guide, technical guide

☐ **D.** Transformation guide, business guide, technical guide

14. One agile delivery concept is frequent checkpoints with end users. How is this accomplished? (There are two correct answers.)

☐ **A.** Daily interaction using daily Scrum meetings.

☐ **B.** Sprint review meetings.

☐ **C.** Sprint planning meetings.

☐ **D.** User acceptance testing (UAT).

15. The team conducts only delta design workshops in a new implementation of SAP S/4HANA Cloud, essentials edition. True or false?

☐ **A.** True

☐ **B.** False

16. In a new implementation of SAP S/4HANA Cloud, essentials edition, the starter system shutdown is automatically initiated after requesting a production (PROD) system in the realize phase of the project. True or false?

☐ **A.** True

☐ **B.** False

17. Which of the following artifacts are from the requirement-to-deploy (R2D) value chain of SAP Solution Manager 7.2?

☐ **A.** Work package, incident

☐ **B.** Test case, problem

☐ **C.** Incident, problem

☐ **D.** Work package, test case

18. Which of the following does SAP mandate to its customers using the SAP S/4HANA Cloud, extended edition release cycle?

☐ **A.** They must consume quarterly releases.

☐ **B.** They must consume yearly releases.

☐ **C.** They must consume any two releases in a three-year period.

☐ **D.** SAP S/4HANA Cloud does not have any such constraints.

19. Which of the following approaches does selective data transition support? (There are two correct answers.)

☐ **A.** Selected business unit migration.

☐ **B.** Migration to SAP S/4HANA Cloud, essentials edition.

☐ **C.** Migration of specific SAP modules only, one at a time.

☐ **D.** System consolidation.

20. What are the IT responsibilities during release planning? (There are two correct answers.)

☐ **A.** Prioritize the sprint backlog.

☐ **B.** Analyze technical dependencies.

☐ **C.** Estimate user stories.

☐ **D.** Identify technical debt in the user stories.

21. What is the goal of the firm-up sprint?

☐ **A.** Finish the integration testing from the previous sprints.

☐ **B.** Plan for the subsequent sprints.

☐ **C.** Integrate the product increments delivered within previous build sprints.

☐ **D.** Set up initial configurations such as organization structure or chart of accounts.

22. Which of the following is an appropriate definition of the prepare phase?

☐ **A.** The team will start the project, plan the project (including all its component plans), onboard the resources, etc.

☐ **B.** The team builds the product backlog.

☐ **C.** The team spends most of their time ensuring that the go-live is successful.

☐ **D.** The consultants are busy configuring and unit testing the solution.

23. The team is performing a selective data transition. Which of the following can be the target platforms? (There are two correct answers.)

☐ **A.** SAP S/4HANA Cloud, essentials edition

☐ **B.** SAP S/4HANA Cloud, extended edition

☐ **C.** SAP S/4HANA (on-premise)

☐ **D.** SAP ERP 6.0 EHP 08, Unicode, single-stack implementation

☐ **E.** Any third-party ERP system

24. Product owners perform which of the following activities during release and sprint planning? (There are two correct answers.)

☐ **A.** Estimate user stories.

☐ **B.** Prioritize the product backlog.

☐ **C.** Identify technical dependencies.

☐ **D.** Identify out-of-scope items.

☐ **E.** Define the release objective.

25. Which of the following are part of the SAP quality principles? (There are two correct answers.)

☐ **A.** Plan ahead.

☐ **B.** Achieve production readiness.

☐ **C.** Exploit standard functionalities and deliver best practices.

☐ **D.** Ensure delayed delivery to increase project cost.

☐ **E.** Scope during the realize phase to reduce uncertainty.

26. The technical lead for an on-premise SAP S/4HANA deployment refused to complete the sizing exercise and stated that it's not necessary for on-premise implementations. Is their statement true or false?

☐ **A.** True

☐ **B.** False

27. What are the two differences between a new implementation of on-premise SAP S/4HANA and a new implementation of SAP S/4HANA Cloud? (There are two correct answers.)

☐ **A.** On-premise SAP S/4HANA uses the IMG while SAP S/4HANA Cloud uses the SSCUI.

☐ **B.** SAP S/4HANA Cloud uses the IMG while on-premise SAP S/4HANA uses the SSCUI.

☐ **C.** SAP manages upgrade cycles for SAP S/4HANA Cloud while the customer manages on-premise upgrades.

☐ **D.** The customer manages upgrade cycles for SAP S/4HANA Cloud, extended edition while SAP manages upgrade cycles for SAP S/4HANA Cloud, essentials edition.

☐ **E.** The customer manages upgrade cycles for SAP S/4HANA Cloud, essentials edition while SAP manages upgrade cycles for SAP S/4HANA Cloud, extended edition.

28. In the selective data transition path, which tool will you use?

☐ **A.** Software Update Manager (SUM)

☐ **B.** SAP S/4HANA migration cockpit

☐ **C.** Data Management and Landscape Transformation (DMLT)

☐ **D.** Roadmap Viewer

29. The product owner can add new user stories in the sprint backlog during the sprint execution. True or false?

☐ **A.** True

☐ **B.** False

30. Your team is ensuring that no additional defects are added to the solution due to new functionalities. What are they doing?

☐ **A.** Regression testing

☐ **B.** Preventing scope creep

☐ **C.** String testing

☐ **D.** Change management

31. What is an epic?

- ☐ **A.** A small user story that doesn't require more than a day of work.
- ☐ **B.** The description written from the user's perspective.
- ☐ **C.** A large user story that spans across multiple sprints.
- ☐ **D.** None of the above.

32. Which of the following are not the characteristics of the product backlog? (There are three correct answers.)

- ☐ **A.** Design documentation.
- ☐ **B.** List of activities for how to transform requirements into a product.
- ☐ **C.** Requirement specification document with a lot of details.
- ☐ **D.** A live document listing prioritized requirements.

33. From the security tasks and responsibilities perspective, which of the following are main categories? (There are four correct answers.)

- ☐ **A.** Secure operation
- ☐ **B.** Secure code
- ☐ **C.** Secure setup
- ☐ **D.** Security compliance
- ☐ **E.** Room security

34. Which of the following are analytics and reporting options? (There are four correct answers.)

- ☐ **A.** SAP Digital Boardroom
- ☐ **B.** SAP BW/HANA
- ☐ **C.** Embedded analytics
- ☐ **D.** SAP S/4HANA for advanced compliance reporting
- ☐ **E.** SAP FICO
- ☐ **F.** SAP governance, risk, and compliance solutions

35. The recommended landscape for a new implementation of on-premise SAP S/4HANA is three tiered (development [DEV], quality assurance (QA), production [PROD]). True or false?

- ☐ **A.** True
- ☐ **B.** False

36. What are the tasks for the Scrum master during project preparation? (There are three correct answers.)

☐ **A.** Perform project setup

☐ **B.** Perform DEV environment setup

☐ **C.** Ensure the availability of high-level requirements

☐ **D.** Project estimation

☐ **E.** Establish a timesheet system

37. Which of the following is true about the elements of the SAP Activate implementation framework? (There are two correct answers.)

☐ **A.** It combines core and supporting methodology elements (a sequence of actions based on methodological elements, SAP content, and SAP tools), a foundation for QA services, and a foundation for the SAP Certified Associate – SAP Activate Project Manager certification.

☐ **B.** Tools are part of the project infrastructure. They provide the team with an interface to access and manage information (migrate data, interact with global SAP communities, access ready-to-use content, configure the SAP S/4HANA system, and so on).

☐ **C.** SAP Best Practices provide a productive environment where the team can utilize a ready-to-run system supported by the SAP Activate framework.

☐ **D.** The SAP Activate framework provides accelerators that will help you complete the project without any hassle.

38. The team executes tasks in a time-boxed setup to complete the committed user stories. This is called project execution. True or false?

☐ **A.** True

☐ **B.** False

39. Which of the following are provided by the content element of the SAP Activate methodology? (There are two correct answers.)

☐ **A.** WRICEF objects

☐ **B.** Business process content

☐ **C.** Integration content

☐ **D.** End user guide

☐ **E.** Project plan

40. Which of the following is true for the Scrum of Scrums meeting? (There are three correct answers.)

☐ **A.** It is a problem-solving meeting.

☐ **B.** It can be time-boxed to 45 – 60 minutes.

☐ **C.** It is a daily meeting.

☐ **D.** It focuses on overlap and integration.

☐ **E.** At least two members of each Scrum team should participate.

41. On what basis does the product manager prioritize user stories?

☐ **A.** Business value

☐ **B.** Revenue

☐ **C.** Simplicity of the requirement

☐ **D.** The MoSCoW method

42. Which tool would you prefer to use for on-premise to on-premise integration?

☐ **A.** SAP Process Orchestration

☐ **B.** SAP Cloud Platform Integration

☐ **C.** Both A and B

☐ **D.** Depends on the customer

43. During which phase of a new implementation of on-premise SAP S/4HANA is the DEV system installed and technically configured and scope items activated based on results from fit-gap workshops?

☐ **A.** Realize

☐ **B.** Explore

☐ **C.** Discover

☐ **D.** Deploy

44. Which end-to-end, turn-key application lifecycle management (ALM) solution can support you in managing requirements and software development for large, agile projects?

☐ **A.** Traceability matrix

☐ **B.** RACI chart

☐ **C.** Focused Build for SAP Solution Manager

☐ **D.** Scrum board

45. Which are correct statements regarding the transition path selective data transition? (There are two correct answers.)

☐ **A.** You migrate a portion of data based on the customer's needs.

☐ **B.** It's a big-bang, global go-live.

☐ **C.** You can reuse some parts and redesign some parts.

☐ **D.** It does not use SAP Activate methodology.

☐ **E.** It does not use SAP Best Practices.

46. What is the first step in writing a user story?

☐ **A.** As a "user" ...

☐ **B.** As an "owner" ...

☐ **C.** As a "stakeholder" ...

☐ **D.** As a "consumer" ...

47. The fit-to-standard and solution definition workshops are part of the prepare phase. True or false?

☐ **A.** True

☐ **B.** False

48. What are the key measures of data volume management?

☐ **A.** Data archiving, data summarization, data deletion, and data cleansing

☐ **B.** Data archiving, data summarization, data deletion, and data avoidance

☐ **C.** Data cleansing, data summarization, data deletion, and data avoidance

☐ **D.** Data archiving, data cleansing, data deletion, and data avoidance

49. Which of the following statements is correct for the product owner?

☐ **A.** The product owner is the sponsor of the program.

☐ **B.** The product owner manages the development of the product.

☐ **C.** The product owner provides and prioritizes the user stories.

☐ **D.** In a small project, the product owner and Scrum master can be the same person.

50. What is the purpose of daily standup meetings? (There are two correct answers.)

☐ **A.** Problem solving.

☐ **B.** Prioritizing today's work.

- ☐ **C.** Answering questions (what was done, what is today's work, what are any issues).
- ☐ **D.** Demo the solution.

51. Which of these are SAP Solution Manager 7.2 value chains?

- ☐ **A.** Portfolio to project, requirement to deploy, detect to correct, hire to retire
- ☐ **B.** Procure to pay, requirement to deploy, detect to correct, request to fulfill
- ☐ **C.** Portfolio to project, requirement to resolution, detect to correct, request to fulfill
- ☐ **D.** Portfolio to project, requirement to deploy, detect to correct, request to fulfill

52. The product backlog represents the list of requirements that haven't been built during the baseline build but need to be delivered to the business. The Scrum team will prioritize the list once it is completed. It's important to capture all requirements before focusing on prioritization. True or false?

- ☐ **A.** True
- ☐ **B.** False

53. In a new implementation of SAP S/4HANA Cloud, essentials edition, during the explore phase, which type of workshop is conducted?

- ☐ **A.** Fit-to-standard.
- ☐ **B.** Fit-gap.
- ☐ **C.** Standard-to-retire.
- ☐ **D.** Premise-to-cloud.

54. What is the recommended duration of a build sprint?

- ☐ **A.** 1 week.
- ☐ **B.** 2 – 4 weeks.
- ☐ **C.** 5 – 6 weeks.
- ☐ **D.** 10 weeks.

55. Which of the following are key questions in the sprint retrospective meeting? (There are three correct answers.)

- ☐ **A.** What do we want to continue doing?
- ☐ **B.** What went wrong?
- ☐ **C.** What can we improve in the next sprint?

- ☐ **D.** What scope items did we miss?
- ☐ **E.** Why there is a scope creep?

56. Which of the following workstreams are part of the SAP Activate methodology? (There are five correct answers.)

- ☐ **A.** Customer team enablement
- ☐ **B.** Project management
- ☐ **C.** Extensibility
- ☐ **D.** Discover
- ☐ **E.** Integration
- ☐ **F.** Solution adoption

57. Which of the following tools/content is responsible for software product and content reuse across scenarios, in-application help, performance support, training simulation, and test script creation?

- ☐ **A.** KPI catalog
- ☐ **B.** SAP MaxAttention
- ☐ **C.** SAP Enable Now
- ☐ **D.** Guided configuration

58. The project manager organizes and facilitates the sprint review meeting. True or false?

- ☐ **A.** True
- ☐ **B.** False

59. Which of the following are DevOps tools? (There are three correct answers.)

- ☐ **A.** Trello
- ☐ **B.** Cross-system object lock (CSOL)
- ☐ **C.** SAP Test Data Migration Server
- ☐ **D.** Change request management (ChaRM)
- ☐ **E.** ABAP Workbench

60. The readiness quality gate verifies that project is well-prepared to start a new phase. True or false?

- ☐ **A.** True
- ☐ **B.** False

61. In which phase do you execute user acceptance testing (UAT)?

☐ **A.** Discover

☐ **B.** Prepare

☐ **C.** Explore

☐ **D.** Realize

62. Which of the following are benefits of using ready-to-use content? (There are two correct answers.)

☐ **A.** Faster time-to-value.

☐ **B.** No indirect costs.

☐ **C.** Predictable results.

☐ **D.** Minimized total cost of ownership (TCO).

☐ **E.** Build SAP like a factory.

63. What's the preferred integration option for SAP S/4HANA Cloud, extended edition?

☐ **A.** SAP Cloud Platform Integration

☐ **B.** SAP Process Orchestration

☐ **C.** SAP Integration Inspector

☐ **D.** Maintenance planner

64. What are the responsibilities and tasks of the Scrum master? (There are two correct answers.)

☐ **A.** Provide the requirements.

☐ **B.** Facilitate agile project execution.

☐ **C.** Help the team adhere to Scrum principles and values.

☐ **D.** Provide technical solutions to the team.

☐ **E.** Provide formal approval of the work done.

65. What's the preferred application lifecycle management (ALM) solution for SAP S/4HANA Cloud, extended edition?

☐ **A.** SAP Best Practices Explorer

☐ **B.** Roadmap Viewer

☐ **C.** Implementation portal for SAP S/4HANA Cloud

☐ **D.** SAP Solution Manager

66. Which of the following are content provisioning tools? (There are three correct answers.)

☐ **A.** SAP Best Practices Explorer

☐ **B.** Roadmap Viewer

☐ **C.** Implementation portal for SAP S/4HANA Cloud

☐ **D.** SAP Help Portal

☐ **E.** SAP Landscape Transformation

☐ **F.** SAP Fiori apps reference library

67. Which of the following are sprint types of the SAP Activate methodology?

☐ **A.** Foundation sprint, firm-up sprint, design sprint

☐ **B.** Test sprint, firm-up sprint, build sprint

☐ **C.** Foundation sprint, integration sprint, build sprint

☐ **D.** Foundation sprint, firm-up sprint, build sprint

68. What of the following activities and artifacts are part of the system conversion explore phase? (There are four correct answers.)

☐ **A.** Trial provisioning

☐ **B.** Application conversion

☐ **C.** Database migration

☐ **D.** Extensibility testing

☐ **E.** Data structure conversion

☐ **F.** Custom code worklist

69. The sprint duration may vary from sprint to sprint within a project. True or false?

☐ **A.** True

☐ **B.** False

70. What are the purposes of fit-to-standard/fit-gap activities in the explore phase? (There are three correct answers.)

☐ **A.** Challenge changes to SAP Best Practices.

☐ **B.** Identify additional scope items.

☐ **C.** Build the product backlog.

☐ **D.** Identify gaps.

☐ **E.** Prioritize the product backlog.

71. Focused Build for SAP Solution Manager is a powerful solution for service providers and larger customers who want to manage all their systems in a central, scalable, and automated environment. True or false?

☐ **A.** True

☐ **B.** False

72. During which phase of a new implementation of on-premise SAP S/4HANA is the solution documentation imported from the SAP Best Practices Explorer into SAP Solution Manager and updated with a description of gaps, WRICEF, custom developments, and more?

☐ **A.** Discover

☐ **B.** Prepare

☐ **C.** Explore

☐ **D.** Realize

73. Which is the correct description for the detect-to-correct value chain of SAP Solution Manager 7.2?

☐ **A.** Incident, monitor, fix, optimize

☐ **B.** Incident, monitor, problem, optimize

☐ **C.** Monitor, incident, problem, optimize

☐ **D.** Problem, incident, monitor, optimize

74. What are the business responsibilities during release planning? (There are two correct answers.)

☐ **A.** Define the product backlog.

☐ **B.** Prioritize the product backlog.

☐ **C.** Define the definition of done.

☐ **D.** Define the definition of ready.

☐ **E.** Estimate user stories.

75. What is SAP Activate?

☐ **A.** A methodology to deploy SAP S/4HANA Cloud and on-premise.

☐ **B.** A project management framework for any ERP system.

☐ **C.** A group of best practices bundled together to lower the implementation cost.

☐ **D.** A set of processes, documentation, and accelerators to enhance the TCO.

76. What's the default ALM solution for on-premise SAP S/4HANA?

☐ **A.** SAP Solution Manager 7.2

☐ **B.** SAP Solution Manager 7.1

☐ **C.** Implementation portal for SAP S/4HANA Cloud

☐ **D.** Any of the above

77. What are the substreams of the solution adoption workstream?

☐ **A.** End user training, organizational change management, value management

☐ **B.** Organizational training, organizational change management, value management

☐ **C.** End user training, organizational support, value management

☐ **D.** End user training, organizational change management, data volume management

78. Which is the correct description for workstream state preparation?

☐ **A.** Set up tools and establish the framework.

☐ **B.** Create results, deliverables, and articles.

☐ **C.** Use tools, procedures, and accelerators.

☐ **D.** Perform team building and develop the implementation strategy.

79. Which of the following are components of SAP Model Company?

☐ **A.** Pre-configured implementation strategy, accelerators, and business process content for SAP Solution Manager.

☐ **B.** Pre-configured solution, accelerators, and business process content for SAP Solution Manager.

☐ **C.** Pre-configured solution, completed project plan, and business process content for SAP Solution Manager.

☐ **D.** Pre-configured solution, accelerators, and the fully-loaded solution.

80. Which of the following is part of the SAP Activate integration content for SAP S/4HANA?

☐ **A.** System content

☐ **B.** Guidance

☐ **C.** Pre-configured solution

☐ **D.** SAP's integration strategy

The practice test answers are listed in Table C.1 in Appendix C.

Appendix B
Practice Test 2

1. Which of the following is the correct description for the realize phase?

☐ **A.** The team will focus on multiple workshops to build and prioritize the product backlog.

☐ **B.** The team will repeatedly build the software product through multiple sprints based on a document, named the product backlog.

☐ **C.** The team will iteratively build the project plan in partnership with the client organization.

☐ **D.** The team executes a set of action items iteratively that was built during the initial phase (or phases) of the project. The purpose of this document is to list the activities that team should do in a specific sequence to ensure that the solution is available to end users.

☐ **E.** The team, in partnership with SAP, checks for organizational readiness to "realize" whether SAP S/4HANA is the right fit for the organization.

2. For SAP S/4HANA Cloud, essentials edition, upgrades are generally scheduled in which time period?

☐ **A.** Monthly

☐ **B.** Quarterly

☐ **C.** When needed

☐ **D.** Every two years in a three-year period

3. Which of the following tools provides guidance on replacing custom code development for SAP ERP with SAP S/4HANA functionality for the system conversion transition path?

☐ **A.** Simplification item check

☐ **B.** Maintenance planner

☐ **C.** Software Update Manager (SUM)

☐ **D.** SAP Business Scenario Recommendations

4. Which of the following tools do you use for the new implementation transition path?

☐ **A.** SAP Business Scenario Recommendations

☐ **B.** Maintenance planner

☐ **C.** SUM

☐ **D.** SAP S/4HANA migration cockpit

5. Who determines the priority of user stories in the backlog of an agile project?

☐ **A.** Sponsor

☐ **B.** Sponsor in partnership with the product owner

☐ **C.** Product owner

☐ **D.** Product owner in partnership with the Scrum master

6. A definition of ready signifies that a user story has been completed. True or false?

☐ **A.** True

☐ **B.** False

7. The sprint review meeting's focus is on what the team has delivered during the sprint, identification and prioritization of any new requirements, and an update or review of the product backlog. True or false?

☐ **A.** True

☐ **B.** False

8. What are outputs relating to the business process workshop?

☐ **A.** Initial backlog, issue list, business process diagram

☐ **B.** Initial backlog, risk register, business requirements

☐ **C.** Initial backlog, issue list, business requirements

☐ **D.** Initial backlog, Scrum list, business requirements

9. Which of the following are examples of ready-to-run SAP S/4HANA systems?

☐ **A.** SAP Model Company and SAP S/4HANA fully activated appliances

☐ **B.** SAP Cloud Platform Integration Suite and SAP S/4HANA fully activated appliances

☐ **C.** SAP Model Company and SAP Best Practices

☐ **D.** SAP Best Practices and SAP S/4HANA fully activated appliances

10. Which of the following collaboration features can SAP Jam users access in the SAP methodologies SAP Jam group? (There are two correct answers.)

☐ **A.** Tweet questions and answers.

☐ **B.** Provide your comments.

☐ **C.** Ask questions.

☐ **D.** After Facebook integration, edit a list of deliverables.

☐ **E.** Integrate with LinkedIn in the upcoming version of SAP Jam.

11. In SAP Activate, which of the following governance bodies are recommended? (There are three correct answers.)

☐ **A.** Executive committee

☐ **B.** Operating committee

☐ **C.** Supervisor committee

☐ **D.** Steering committee

☐ **E.** Scrum committee

12. Simplification and custom code impact analysis with test conversion is part of the realize phase during a system conversion. True or false?

☐ **A.** True

☐ **B.** False

13. Which of the following tools provide sizing estimations for the system conversion transition path?

☐ **A.** Scope and Effort Analyzer (SEA)

☐ **B.** Roadmap Viewer

☐ **C.** SAP Readiness Check

☐ **D.** Quick Sizer tool

14. What is a user story in the product backlog?

☐ **A.** Desired functionality described from an end user perspective.

☐ **B.** Desired functionality described by the Scrum master.

☐ **C.** Desired functionality described from a sponsor perspective.

☐ **D.** Desired functionality described by the Scrum team.

15. Which of the following are the most important questions in the daily standup meeting?

☐ **A.** What did you do, are there any issues, what will you do?

☐ **B.** How is the team member wellbeing, are there any challenges, what will you do?

☐ **C.** What, when, and how? (About a show-stopper issue).

☐ **D.** Any three questions based on the Scrum master's needs.

16. In which phase should you create a data migration design during a selective data transition project?

☐ **A.** Realize

☐ **B.** Run

☐ **C.** Deploy

☐ **D.** Explore

17. What are the three substreams of the data management workstream?

☐ **A.** Data migration tools, data migration, master data management

☐ **B.** Data volume management, data migration, master data management

☐ **C.** Organizational change management, data migration, master data management

☐ **D.** Organizational change management, transaction data management, master data management

18. What is the purpose of the Scrum board?

☐ **A.** Visualize team progress.

☐ **B.** Visualize obstacles.

☐ **C.** Visualize resource utilization.

☐ **D.** Visualize team success stories.

19. What is the term used for workshops that are intended to set value targets, validate SAP standard functionality against customer requirements, and collect delta requirements in the new implementation transition path?

☐ **A.** Design workshop

☐ **B.** Design thinking

☐ **C.** Solution validation workshop

☐ **D.** Solution thinking

20. Which of the following activities help the project team add user stories to the product backlog?

☐ **A.** Conducting fit-to-standard or fit-gap analysis.

☐ **B.** Conducting blueprinting.

☐ **C.** Conducting a product grooming meeting.

☐ **D.** Conducting sprint planning.

21. Which of the following will help you avoid modification of standard functionality in SAP S/4HANA Cloud, extended edition? (There are two correct answers.)

☐ **A.** The five golden rules.

☐ **B.** Quality built-in (a key element of SAP Activate).

☐ **C.** Side-by-side and in-app extensibility.

☐ **D.** Extensibility and integration options.

☐ **E.** Contract restriction.

22. What's the recommended choice for cloud-to-cloud integration scenarios?

☐ **A.** SAP Cloud Platform Integration Suite

☐ **B.** SAP Process Orchestration

☐ **C.** Business application programming interfaces (BAPIs)

☐ **D.** SAP S/4HANA embedded tools

23. Which of the following artifacts belong to the detect-to-correct value chain of SAP Solution Manager 7.2? (There are two correct answers.)

☐ **A.** Problem

☐ **B.** Incident

☐ **C.** Request for change

☐ **D.** Defect

24. For S/4HANA Cloud, essentials edition, all customers are on the same release and hotfix package. True or false?

☐ **A.** True

☐ **B.** False

25. For SAP S/4HANA Cloud, extended edition, all customers are on the same release and hotfix package. True or false?

☐ **A.** True

☐ **B.** False

26. How do you set up Scrum teams? (There are two correct answers.)

☐ **A.** Scrum teams are cross-functional.

☐ **B.** Based on the customer's requirements.

☐ **C.** Based on end-to-end processes such as procure to pay, order to cash, etc.

☐ **D.** Based on SAP modules such as financial accounting, controlling, and materials management.

☐ **E.** Based on the suitability of the implementation partner.

27. The main activities during a foundation sprint are the definition of organizational structure and master data. True or false?

☐ **A.** True

☐ **B.** False

28. Working in an agile approach, what should your planning look like at the beginning of the realize phase?

☐ **A.** User stories are completely ready for at least the next ten sprints.

☐ **B.** User stories are completely ready for the project scope.

☐ **C.** User stories are ready based on the definition of ready for a couple of sprints to start the work.

☐ **D.** User stories are defined based on the definition of done.

29. What are Scrum master tasks during the sprint review? (There are two correct answers.)

☐ **A.** Facilitate discussion.

☐ **B.** Introduce the product backlog and sprint backlog.

☐ **C.** Ensure the development (DEV) environment readiness.

☐ **D.** Share the agenda of the sprint review with the participants.

☐ **E.** Congratulate the product owner on their success or conduct a sprint retrospective meeting in case of failure.

30. Fit-to-standard workshops are conducted during the explore phase of an on-premise SAP S/4HANA implementation. True or false?

☐ **A.** True

☐ **B.** False, fit-gap analysis is conducted

31. What is the purpose of sprint retrospective meetings?

☐ **A.** Identify the reason for failure.

☐ **B.** Identify areas of improvement.

☐ **C.** Discuss the build solution with the product owner based on the sprint backlog.

☐ **D.** Plan the sprint based on the sprint backlog.

32. What are Data Management and Landscape Transformation (DMLT)-enabled scenarios?

☐ **A.** Consolidation

☐ **B.** Migrate to SAP S/4HANA Cloud, essentials edition

☐ **C.** Both A and B

☐ **D.** None of the above

33. Which of the following tools is used for the software update and can also be used for migration, if needed, with the Database Migration Option (DMO) when converting the system from SAP ERP 6.0 to on premise SAP S/4HANA?

☐ **A.** Software Update Manager

☐ **B.** Business Process Change Analyzer

☐ **C.** Maintenance planner

☐ **D.** SAP Activate methodology

34. What is the primary purpose of the SAP Activate methodology?

☐ **A.** It provides accelerators.

☐ **B.** It aims to modernize the ASAP methodology.

☐ **C.** It provides a sequence of steps to transition to SAP S/4HANA.

☐ **D.** It provides a ready-to-run solution.

35. Which of the following is a method to work on a flat backlog (a list of all the known items that the Scrum team should deliver)?

☐ **A.** User story mapping

☐ **B.** The MoSCoW method

☐ **C.** Planning poker

☐ **D.** Story points

36. In the discover phase of a new implementation of SAP S/4HANA Cloud, essentials edition, the application lifecycle management (ALM) roadmap defines the ALM tool for the SAP S/4HANA Cloud implementation. For SAP S/4HANA Cloud, essentials edition installations, SAP Solution Manager is the default choice. True or false?

☐ **A.** True

☐ **B.** False

37. SAP Best Practice Explorer is the central location for SAP Activate methodology. It provides detailed information about project activities and project library accelerators. True or false?

☐ **A.** True

☐ **B.** False

38. Which of the following accelerators support fit-to-standard workshops? (There are two correct answers.)

☐ **A.** Business-driven configuration questionnaire

☐ **B.** SUM

☐ **C.** Product backlog template

☐ **D.** Test strategy

☐ **E.** Cutover checklist

39. In a new implementation of SAP S/4HANA Cloud, essentials edition, during the prepare phase, SAP's ALM training is replaced with onboarding for the implementation portal for SAP S/4HANA Cloud. The customer team uses a built-in web assistant in the starter system for SAP S/4HANA Cloud functionality discovery. True or false?

☐ **A.** True

☐ **B.** False

40. Which of the following are benefits that you may get by "running SAP like a factory"? (There are two correct answers.)

☐ **A.** Higher degree of automation.

☐ **B.** Better business performance.

☐ **C.** Enhanced throughput.

☐ **D.** Reduced efficiency.

☐ **E.** Improved business continuity.

41. Which of the following artifacts are part of the solution adoption workstream? (There are two correct answers.)

☐ **A.** Organizational change management checklist

☐ **B.** Point of view (POV) document

☐ **C.** Project plan

☐ **D.** RACI chart

☐ **E.** Risk register

42. What is the available target solution for the system conversion transition path?

- ☐ **A.** On-premise SAP S/4HANA
- ☐ **B.** SAP S/4HANA Cloud, extended edition
- ☐ **C.** SAP S/4HANA Cloud, essentials edition
- ☐ **D.** SAP Customer Experience
- ☐ **E.** SAP BW/4HANA

43. What is the minimum number of quality gates mandated by the SAP Activate methodology?

- ☐ **A.** 4
- ☐ **B.** 5
- ☐ **C.** 6
- ☐ **D.** 3

44. For SAP S/4HANA Cloud, essentials edition, content corrections are generally scheduled in what time period?

- ☐ **A.** Quarterly
- ☐ **B.** Biweekly
- ☐ **C.** Weekly
- ☐ **D.** Monthly

45. Which of the following are responsibilities and tasks of the product owner? (There are three correct answers.)

- ☐ **A.** Accept or reject work results.
- ☐ **B.** Prioritize the product backlog.
- ☐ **C.** Define the sprint objective.
- ☐ **D.** Provide high-level effort estimates for the user stories.
- ☐ **E.** Attend daily Scrum meetings to understand the progress.

46. SAP Best Practices Explorer is the central place for solution documentation. It hosts information on business process flows and SAP S/4HANA configuration guidelines. True or false?

- ☐ **A.** True
- ☐ **B.** False

47. In a new implementation of SAP S/4HANA Cloud, essentials edition, the starter system includes configuration and master data for selected cloud solutions for the targeted enablement of the project team on SAP standard processes and to be the host environment of the fit-to-standard workshops. True or false?

☐ **A.** True

☐ **B.** False

48. What does side-by-side extensibility mean?

☐ **A.** It is the same as classic extensions.

☐ **B.** End users can build extensions of their own.

☐ **C.** It is based on SAP Cloud Platform Integration Suite and application programming interfaces (APIs).

☐ **D.** It is the same as end-user extensions.

49. A user story map arranges user stories into a useful model to help understand the functionality of the system, identify holes and omissions in the backlog, and effectively plan holistic releases that deliver value to users and businesses with each release. True or false?

☐ **A.** True

☐ **B.** False

50. Which of the following do you use for a ready-to-run SAP S/4HANA system with prebuilt solution documentation that supports end-to-end processes for a specific industry so that the project team can focus on differentiation and innovation?

☐ **A.** SAP Best Practices

☐ **B.** SAP Activate methodology

☐ **C.** SAP Model Company

☐ **D.** SAP Cloud Appliance Library

51. What is the order of artifacts within the technical architecture and infrastructure workstream in the prepare phase?

☐ **A.** Parameter hardware sizing calculation, hardware sizing result, hardware specification from vendor, technical strategy

☐ **B.** Technical strategy, hardware specification from vendor, parameter hardware sizing calculation, hardware sizing result

☐ **C.** Technical strategy, parameter hardware sizing calculation, hardware sizing result, hardware specification from vendor

☐ **D.** Hardware specification from vendor, technical strategy, parameter hardware sizing calculation, hardware sizing result

52. Which of the following are workstream states in the SAP Activate methodology? (There are four correct answers.)

☐ **A.** Operation preparations

☐ **B.** Execution

☐ **C.** Preparation

☐ **D.** Delivery

☐ **E.** Realization

☐ **F.** Planning

53. Which new project roles are introduced with the SAP Activate methodology for the agile delivery approach?

☐ **A.** Product owner and product sponsor.

☐ **B.** Product owner and project master.

☐ **C.** Project manager and Scrum master.

☐ **D.** Product owner and Scrum master.

54. Who determines the tasks that are required to complete the committed backlog items in a sprint?

☐ **A.** Scrum team

☐ **B.** Scrum master

☐ **C.** Product owner

☐ **D.** Project manager

55. Which of the following artifacts in the testing workstream do you create during the realize phase for a new implementation of SAP S/4HANA Cloud, essentials edition? (There are two correct answers.)

☐ **A.** User acceptance plan

☐ **B.** Functional test scenarios

☐ **C.** Test strategy

☐ **D.** String test plan

☐ **E.** Performance test

56. The readiness quality gate verifies that the project meets acceptance criteria for phase closure. True or false?

☐ **A.** True

☐ **B.** False

57. Which of the following accelerators can help you document the configuration definition in the explore phase?

☐ **A.** Backlog template

☐ **B.** Cloud Integration Automation service user guide

☐ **C.** Phase sign-off template

☐ **D.** Checklist for the five golden rules

58. What can you find in the SAP solution implementation roadmaps?

☐ **A.** Accelerators, deliverables, and tasks

☐ **B.** Accelerators, deliverables, and value maps

☐ **C.** Accelerators, value maps, and tasks

☐ **D.** Value maps, deliverables, and tasks

59. Which of the following are key characteristics of implementation approaches in SAP Activate methodology? (There are two correct answers.)

☐ **A.** Cloud ready

☐ **B.** Validation based

☐ **C.** Premium capable

☐ **D.** Quality plug-in

☐ **E.** Based on ready-to-use content

60. The sprint retrospective meeting's purpose is to continuously improve the Scrum process using lessons learned from the sprint execution. True or false?

☐ **A.** True

☐ **B.** False

61. The project team sets up and tests the IT infrastructure in the technical architecture and infrastructure workstream during the realize phase of new implementations for both on-premise and cloud versions. True or false?

☐ **A.** True

☐ **B.** False

62. What criterion does the product owner use to sequence the product backlog?

☐ **A.** Business value

☐ **B.** Business risk

☐ **C.** Sunk cost

☐ **D.** Simplicity

63. In SAP Activate, what tool do you use in the agile delivery approach during the realize phase to make forecasts based on actual data?

☐ **A.** Increment

☐ **B.** Project plan

☐ **C.** Burndown chart

☐ **D.** Scrum board

64. SAP Activate uses concepts, ceremonies, and roles introduced by the agile framework and expands them with solution implementation specifics. True or false?

☐ **A.** True

☐ **B.** False

65. That you should stick to the security standards per the customer's organizational policy is one of the five golden rules for SAP S/4HANA Cloud, extended edition. True or false?

☐ **A.** True

☐ **B.** False

66. Which of the following is the correct description for the process step library?

☐ **A.** A step-by-step process to access the SAP content library.

☐ **B.** A building block for all processes.

☐ **C.** A guiding principle called the five golden rules.

☐ **D.** A framework for project management.

67. You can use SAP Jam to collaborate with other SAP Activate methodology practitioners. True or false?

☐ **A.** True

☐ **B.** False

68. Fit-to-standard is a part of the explore phase in the new implementation of SAP S/4HANA Cloud, essentials edition transition path. True or false?

☐ **A.** True

☐ **B.** False

69. What does SAP Activate recommend to keep team members informed and aligned about the work done, today's work, and any impediments?

☐ **A.** Daily Scrum meetings

☐ **B.** Daily emails

☐ **C.** Daily 30-minute meetings

☐ **D.** Sprint reviews

70. What is the basis for approving work results (signing act of acceptance) on a project phase level?

☐ **A.** Definition of done

☐ **B.** Quality gate

☐ **C.** Definition of ready

☐ **D.** Sprint review

71. What are the phases of the Activate methodology?

☐ **A.** Discover, prepare, explore, realize, deploy, run

☐ **B.** Initiation, planning, execution, monitoring and controlling, closure

☐ **C.** There are eleven phases, including as project management, extensibility, integration, and so on.

☐ **D.** There are ten phases, including project scope management, project integration management, project risk management, and so on.

72. With Focused Insights for SAP Solution Manager, you can build and distribute powerful customer-specific dashboards in minutes. True or false?

☐ **A.** True

☐ **B.** False

73. The product owner is one of the two new roles in SAP S/4HANA implementations. True or false?

☐ **A.** True

☐ **B.** False

74. What tool would you use for managing project tasks and solution documentation when implementing SAP S/4HANA Cloud?

- ☐ **A.** Implementation portal for SAP S/4HANA Cloud
- ☐ **B.** SAP Solution Manager
- ☐ **C.** SAP Activate methodology
- ☐ **D.** SAP Best Practices

75. You can use user story mapping techniques to identify any gaps in the end-to-end process. True or false?

- ☐ **A.** True
- ☐ **B.** False

76. "Build SAP like a factory" and "run SAP like a factory" are premium offerings from SAP. True or false?

- ☐ **A.** True
- ☐ **B.** False

77. Which of the following are the transition paths to SAP S/4HANA? (There are three correct answers.)

- ☐ **A.** New implementations
- ☐ **B.** System conversion
- ☐ **C.** Updates
- ☐ **D.** Database migration
- ☐ **E.** Selective data transition

78. Configure and adjust is the way to describe the realize phase of a new implementation of SAP S/4HANA Cloud, essentials edition. True or false?

- ☐ **A.** True
- ☐ **B.** False

79. In what phase do you create an ordered list of requirements that will define all the work to be done by the project team?

- ☐ **A.** Discover
- ☐ **B.** Prepare
- ☐ **C.** Explore
- ☐ **D.** Realize

80. Expert configuration allows the implementation of customer-specific requirements with restrictions. Expert configuration is implemented in the quality assurance (QA) system by the SAP service center. Expert configuration allows which of the following? (There are three correct answers.)

- ☐ **A.** Consideration of namespaces for customer-owned processes.
- ☐ **B.** Creation of new processes in customer-owned areas.
- ☐ **C.** Adaptation of editable fields within SAP Best Practices content.
- ☐ **D.** Change of security settings so that you can see your competitors' reports.
- ☐ **E.** Enhancement of the procure-to-pay process.

The practice test answers are listed in Table C.2 in Appendix C.

Appendix C
Practice Test Answers

The answers to Practice Test 1 from Appendix A are listed in Table C.1. Check your answers, and feel free to tally and score your percentage correct.

1. A, B, C	21. C	41. A	61. D
2. C	22. A	42. A	62. A, C
3. A, E	23. B, C	43. B	63. A
4. A, C	24. B, E	44. C	64. B, C
5. C	25. B, C	45. A, C	65. D
6. B	26. B	46. A	66. A, B, D
7. A	27. A, C	47. B	67. D
8. A, B	28. C	48. B	68. B, C, E, F
9. A, D	29. B	49. C	69. B
10. A	30. A	50. B, C	70. A, B, D
11. B	31. C	51. D	71. B
12. A	32. A, B, C	52. B	72. C
13. D	33. A, B, C, D	53. A	73. C
14. B, D	34. A, B, C, D	54. B	74. A, B
15. B	35. A	55. A, B, C	75. A
16. A	36. A, B, C	56. A, B, C, E, F	76. A
17. D	37. A, B	57. C	77. A
18. C	38. B	58. B	78. A
19. A, D	39. B, C	59. B, C, D	79. B
20. B, C	40. A, B, D	60. A	80. A

Table C.1 Answers to Practice Test 1

Total number of correct answers: _____

Percentage of correct answers: _____

The answers to Practice Test 2 from Appendix B are listed in Table C.2. Check your answers, and feel free to tally and score your percentage correct.

1. B	21. A, E	41. A, B	61. B
2. B	22. A	42. A	62. A
3. A	23. B, C	43. A	63. C
4. D	24. A	44. B	64. A
5. C	25. B	45. A, B, C	65. B
6. B	26. C, D	46. A	66. B
7. B	27. A	47. A	67. A
8. C	28. C	48. C	68. A
9. A	29. A, D	49. A	69. A
10. B, C	30. B	50. C	70. B
11. A, B, D	31. B	51. C	71. A
12. B	32. A	52. A, B, C, E	72. A
13. D	33. A	53. D	73. A
14. A	34. C	54. A	74. A
15. A	35. A	55. A, B	75. A
16. D	36. B	56. B	76. A
17. B	37. B	57. A	77. A, B, E
18. A	38. A, C	58. A	78. A
19. C	39. A	59. A, B	79. C
20. A	40. A, B	60. A	80. A, B, C

Table C.2 Answers to Practice Test 2

Total number of correct answers: ______

Percentage of correct answers: ______

Appendix D
The Author

Aditya Lal is an SAP program director with more than 24 years of experience in large and complex project management spanning across geographies, domains, and business units. He has extensive experience in managing global implementations of SAP ERP 6.0, and for last few years, he has focused on the implementation of SAP S/4HANA. He has worked on and managed several global business and digital transformation initiatives to SAP S/4HANA. Aditya has several certifications including the SAP Certified Associate – SAP Activate Project Manager, Six Sigma Green Belt, Project Management Professional (PMP), Program Management Professional (PgMP), Portfolio Management Professional (PfMP), Professional Scrum Master I and II, and SAFe 5.0 Agilist.

He holds a bachelor's degree in engineering from the Birla Institute of Technology, Mesra and is pursuing a master's degree in data analytics from the Georgia Institute of Technology.

Index

A

B

E

O

P

Q

R

S

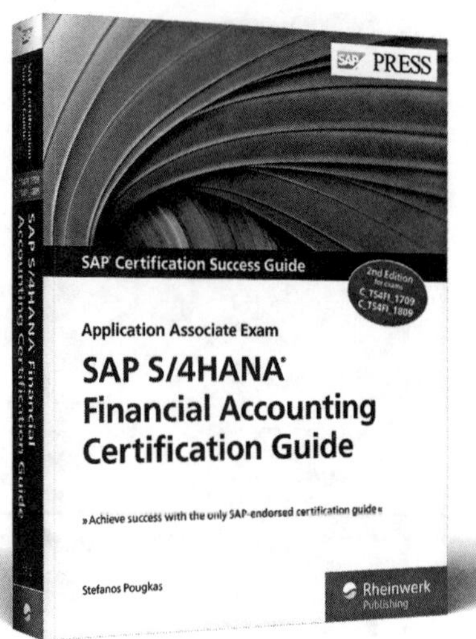

- Learn about the SAP S/4HANA Finance certification test structure and how to prepare
- Review the key topics covered in each portion of your exam
- Test your knowledge with practice questions and answers

Stefanos Pougkas

SAP S/4HANA Financial Accounting Certification Guide

Application Associate Exam

Preparing for your financial accounting exam? Make the grade with this SAP S/4HANA 1709 and 1809 certification study guide! From general ledger accounting to financial close, this guide will review the key technical and functional knowledge you need to get a high score. Explore test methodology, key concepts for each topic area, and practice questions and answers. Your path to financial accounting certification begins here!

507 pages, 2nd edition, pub. 05/2019
E-Book: $69.99 | **Print:** $79.95 | **Bundle:** $89.99

www.sap-press.com/4856

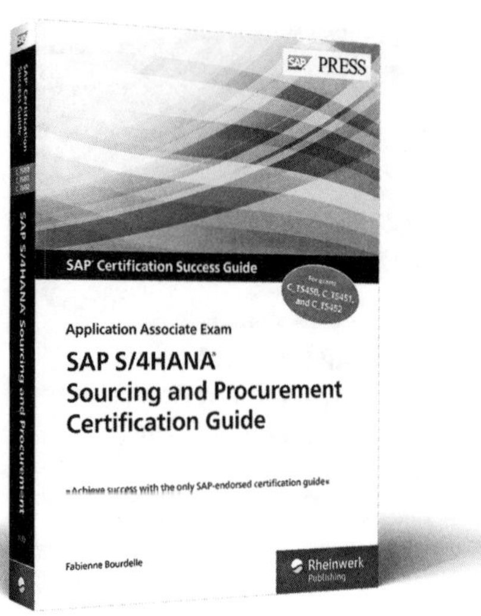

- Learn about the SAP S/4HANA certification test structure and how to prepare
- Review the key topics covered in each portion of your exam
- Test your knowledge with practice questions and answers

Fabienne Bourdelle

SAP S/4HANA Sourcing and Procurement Certification Guide

Application Associate Exam

Preparing for your sourcing and procurement exam? Make the grade with this SAP S/4HANA Sourcing and Procurement Application Associate Exam certification study guide! From stock material to purchasing, review the key technical and functional knowledge you need to pass with flying colors. Explore test methodology, key concepts for each topic area, and practice questions and answers. Your path to SAP S/4HANA Sourcing and Procurement certification begins here!

452 pages, pub. 12/2020
E-Book: $69.99 | **Print:** $79.95 | **Bundle:** $89.99

www.sap-press.com/5124